Classic Ideas and Current Issues in American Government

Classic Ideas and Current Issues in American Government

Meena Bose
United States Military Academy

John J. DiIulio, Jr.
University of Pennsylvania

Houghton Mifflin Company   *Boston   New York*

For our students, who instill faith in the future of Madisonian democracy.

Publisher: Charles Hartford
Sponsoring Editor: Katherine Meisenheimer
Senior Development Editor: Jeffrey Greene
Editorial Assistant: Kristen Craib
Associate Project Editor: Teresa Huang
Editorial Assistant: Katherine Leahey
Senior Art and Design Coordinator: Jill Haber Atkins
Composition Buyer: Chuck Dutton
Associate Manufacturing Buyer: Brian Pieragostini
Executive Marketing Manager: Nicola Poser
Marketing Associate: Kathleen Mellon

Cover image: © Guido Rossi/TIPS Images.

Printed in the U.S.A.

Library of Congress Control Number: 2005936794

Instructor's exam copy:
ISBN-13: 978-0-618-73136-7
ISBN-10: 0-618-73136-9

For orders, use student text ISBNs:
ISBN-13: 978-0-618-45644-4
ISBN-10: 0-618-45644-9

23456789-MP-10 09 08 07 06

CONTENTS

7

Elections and Campaigns

8

The Media

9
The Congress   353

10
The Presidency   405

11
The Bureaucracy   447

TOPIC CORRELATION CHART

Although the chapters of this book have been organized to mesh with the coverage of most American government textbooks, many subjects receive attention in more than one chapter. The following chart permits students and instructors to locate relevant readings for twenty-six subjects, ranging (in alphabetical order) from bureaucracy to the Washington establishment.

Topic:	Covered in:
Bureaucracy	Chapter 11
Bush Presidency	7.3; 8.3; 9.5; 10.3; 11.2
Campaigns and Elections	Chapter 7
Congress	Chapter 9
Constitution	Chapter 1
Domestic Policy	2.3; 3.3; 4.2; 5.4
Election 2004	6.1; 6.2; 7.3
Federalism	Chapter 2
The Founding	1.1; 1.2; 1.3; 1.4; 1.5; 1.6; 1.7; 2.1; 9.1; 9.2; 10.1; 12.1
Impeachment	1.8
Interest Groups	6.5; 6.6
Leadership	1.6; 1.7; 8.1; 9.3; 9.4; Chapter 10; 12.3; 12.4
Mass Media	Chapter 8
Money and Politics	6.1; 6.2; 7.3
Participation	Chapter 5
Policymaking Process	2.3; 3.3; 5.4; 7.3; 9.5; 11.2
Political Culture	Chapter 3
Political Parties	6.1; 6.2; 6.3; 6.4
Presidency	8.1; Chapter 10
Public Opinion	5.1; 5.2; 5.3

Reform	1.8; 5.4; 11.2
Representation	1.1; 1.2; 1.3; 1.4; 1.5; 1.6; 1.7; 4.2; 4.3; 5.3; 5.4; 6.5; 6.6; 9.1; 9.2; 9.3; 9.4
Separation of Powers	1.4; 1.5; 1.8; 2.1; 2.4; 10.4; 11.3; 11.4; 12.1
Supreme Court and the Judiciary	Chapters 12 and 13
Technology and Politics	8.4; 11.1; 11.2
Washington Establishment	8.2; 8.4; 9.5; 10.2; 11.1; 11.2; 12.3; 12.4

PREFACE

OUR CONVICTION: UNDERSTANDING AMERICAN GOVERNMENT MATTERS— *FOR REAL*

We composed this text and selected its readings for you, our college and advanced high school students; for you, our colleagues who teach American government or civics; and for you, the students we teach at our own schools.

We did it for you, but also for ourselves—two college professors who have been teaching American government for a combined three decades, but who have always wished for a text on the subject that provided solid but succinct overviews of key topics, such as the Constitution, federalism, political culture, Congress, political parties and interest groups, civil rights and civil liberties, and others. This text offers such overviews in addition to timely and timeless readings that bring classic ideas to bear on current issues.

Our fellow teachers who lead advanced American Government or high school civics classes will find that we have been careful to define key concepts and include excerpts from key historical documents and major court cases. Our college and university colleagues in political science will find that, with no pretense of including everything (or everyone), we have done due diligence in sampling and summarizing some of the best that our field has to offer, from David Mayhew and Richard F. Fenno on Congress, to Richard E. Neustadt and Fred I. Greenstein on the presidency. And we hope that our student readers, including our own students, will find our commentary useful and the reading selections interesting, despite the complexity of some of the texts.

We have taught at several different colleges and universities as faculty members or visitors, and done a little guest teaching at high schools. We love the subject, and we want others to love it, too. We believe that learning about politics and government is central to any solid secondary education and essential to any good college or university liberal arts education. And we believe that the subject is endlessly fascinating and even (if you will forgive us our passion) fun.

But we bring an even more important conviction to this text: American government matters—*for real*.

Today, many Americans are learning about American government, how it works, and what might be done to improve it—learning the hard way. One "lesson" began on September 11, 2001, with the terrorist attacks on the United States. Ever since, average citizens and elected officials have been asking and debating what government might have done to prevent those attacks, and what it might do to prevent future attacks. One big answer revolves around what seems like a tiresome academic subject: bureaucracy.

As we discuss in Chapter 9, just days after 9/11, some in Congress called for a new "Department of Homeland Defense." For months the White House rejected that call, but it later changed its view. In 2002 the new Department of Homeland Security was established. Overnight it became the third largest department of the federal government, encompassing twenty-two separate agencies, more than 170,000 employees, and an annual budget of roughly $40 billion. But in July 2004, before the department was two years old, out came *The 9/11 Commission Report: Final Report of the National Commission on Terrorist Attacks upon the United States.*

Our excerpt from that 567-page, single-spaced, mini-font document (yes, we read it all and selected the most essential parts so you don't have to) begins with its concluding chapter, which is headed "How to Do It? A Different Way of Organizing Government." The report recommends five far-reaching "changes in the organization of government," politely but pointedly calls on the Department of Homeland Security to get its act together ("go beyond pre-existing jobs of the agencies that have been brought together inside" it), and urges Congress to "create a single, principal point of oversight and review for homeland security."

Here is how sure we are that all of that will *not* happen before this text is in its second edition: we hereby pledge that we will donate all of our royalties on the book to the American Political Science Association if it does. Why are we so sure? Because, as we explain in Chapter 9 on Congress, the nation's legislature has become so ideologically polarized and partisan that concerted action of the type that would be necessary to implement the 9/11 Commission's recommendations anytime soon is impossible.

Indeed, as revealed by one of our reading selections—Helen Fessenden's story for *Congressional Quarterly Weekly*—Congress created the 9/11 Commission in the first place "because of distrust between the parties: Republicans worried that Democrats . . . would lead the inquiry into an indictment of Bush policies, while Democrats feared a Republican whitewash." The 9/11 Commission is not naïve about the likely political fate of its proposals. "Few things are more difficult to change in Washington," its report acknowledges, "than congressional committee jurisdiction and prerogatives." They can say that again.

But why is it so hard to change how Congress is organized, and why can't the president and Congress get on the same page, politically speaking, about even so significant a public priority as getting government better-positioned to protect people from terrorist attacks? Even when faced with pressing public policy challenges, domestic or international, American government cannot snap to attention, make a decision, implement it, and move on.

The reason lies in the value choices embodied in the Constitution and respected in court decisions concerning civil rights and civil liberties. As we explain in Chapter 1, the Framers of the Constitution valued many things, but they were especially committed to liberty, to limited government, and so to ensuring—as James Madison wrote in the Federalist No. 51—that government is "obliged to control itself." (Don't worry, we explain what a Federalist is, and even, in fact, what an Anti-Federalist is when the time comes.)

Control itself how? Mainly by putting legislative, executive, and judicial powers into three separate branches (Congress, the presidency, and the Supreme Court, respectively); by giving each branch both legal standing and political incentives to check and balance the others (or, in today's Washington, we might instead say "block and tackle" the others); and by further dividing power between national, state, and local governments. You may not understand why now, but a good essay topic for when you are through reading this text might be: "Why the first Department of Homeland Security Director, Tom Ridge, has James Madison to blame for his agency's troubles with Congress and the courts." Another might be: "Why the U.S. Conference of Mayors is as important to 'homeland security' as the U.S. Congress."

James L. Sundquist, whose writing on constitutional reform is excerpted in Chapter 1, has argued that the United States needs to weaken the separation of powers, strengthen the executive branch, limit local influences on national decision-making, and, in effect, make American government more like its (ostensibly more effective) cousins in parliamentary democracies like the United Kingdom. Does the rise of "homeland security" as a public concern make such reforms more necessary, or does it mean we should cling ever more tightly to our crazy-quilt, slow-moving, separation-of-powers, federal-state-local, small-d democratic decision-making system? (We think the latter, but you can read the text and decide for yourself.)

Another topic you might consider as you move through the text (especially if you are one of our younger readers) is "Why young Americans volunteer lots but vote less." Why? We do not know, but, in Chapter 3, we cover American political culture. We focus on concerns voiced by Harvard University's Robert D. Putnam and others about how Americans, once a nation of "joiners," seem to be joining clubs, churches, civic associations, and other groups less than they once did, and how religious affiliations and organizations may help to replenish "social capital." In Chapters 4 and 5, we review what is known about public opinion and political participation, including new (better?) ways of calculating voter turnout, and older (wiser?) thoughts about stimulating interest in politics among young adult citizens.

For anyone still trying to figure out what happened in the 2004 presidential election (and that includes us), Chapter 7 should raise two questions. First, campaign finance reform might be a good idea, but is it working? No, not if we measure its success by how much money gets spent by the parties, the candidates, and their supporters: tons and tons, with new records set with every election cycle. (Still, as you read about the 2002 campaign finance law, ask yourself, "what else might be done, or what might be done differently?") Second, why did most people vote as they did? Did they make a largely retrospective decision based on economic factors—that's where the Morris P. Fiorina reading would point—or did they respond mainly to symbols and rhetoric (or valence) appeals, as the material from the late Donald E. Stokes would bet? (We're with Stokes—not surprising since one of us co-authored the selection with him; but are we right?)

And don't just focus on national elections. Focus on Chapter 2 and federalism, too. Learn why state and local governments have a profound bearing on how, and how well, most Americans live. Ask yourself how, if at all, the "devolution revolution" discussed in those pages has affected you, your community, or your city.

Likewise, after or as you read Chapter 8 on the media, watch network and cable news programs and see if you detect a "spin cycle" (per the reading selection from Howard Kurtz's book) or "liberal bias" (per the reading selection from the Media Research Center).

Finally, as you pore through the court cases on civil rights and civil liberties in Chapter 13, decide for yourself how you would have decided these same cases, and according to what values or principles. Then ask yourself which, if any, of the issues raised by these cases is, or is likely to become, an issue in your own life or in the lives of people who you care about.

With more than fifty entries, each of us has our favorite (and least favorite!) readings. But, were we forced to choose just one reading that, by virtue of its historical importance and contemporary message, justifies our conviction that understanding American government matters, *for real*, we would—well, we would cheat and pick a pair: the Declaration of Independence and Martin Luther King, Jr.'s "I Have a Dream" speech.

The Declaration anticipated the public philosophy that shaped the Constitution (favored by the Federalists) and the Bill of Rights (the first ten amendments to the Constitution, favored by the Anti-Federalists). Dr. King's speech reiterated and reanimated the promises of the Declaration—its classic ideas about liberty and equality—and thereby changed how many Americans understood a current issue—full civil rights for black Americans.

Alas, where understanding American government is concerned, classic ideas and current issues can be an explosively good mix. So teach, be taught; read, reflect—explode! And thanks for permitting us to join your journey on the subject as student or teacher.

As an aid to your teaching, we offer an Instructor's Resource Manual with test questions. For each reading, there is an explanation of how each reading can be used in conjunction with *American Government* by James Q. Wilson and

John J. DiIulio, Jr. In addition, there are four multiple-choice questions for each reading and one short answer/essay question. These questions are designed to test whether or not students have read and understood the reading.

We thank our colleagues whose insightful comments helped us shape this reader: Jamie L. Carson, University of Georgia; Sherryl Eldred, Forest High School, Florida; Anthony Nownes, University of Tennessee at Knoxville; and Dennis Simon, Southern Methodist University.

M. B.
J. J. D.

Classic Ideas and Current Issues in American Government

CHAPTER 1

American Government and the Constitution

Whe n the Framers debated and drafted the Constitution in the long, hot Philadelphia summer of 1787, they faced a daunting task. Having only recently liberated the American colonies from England's King George III, a monarchy, of course, was unacceptable. They wanted a democratic government, one in which the people always had a say, but without letting popular majorities always have their way. They also recognized the defects of a national government that was far weaker than its constituent states. So they sought to create a limited but effective, energetic but not imperial, popular but not purely democratic national government for a new nation to be called "the United States of America." But how?

They started with the values that mattered most to them. Foremost in the Framers' hearts and minds was the importance of preserving and, in due course, advancing the value of liberty. The Declaration of Independence had delineated the offenses that King George III had committed, many of which violated individual rights. Consequently, the Framers were determined to ensure that the new government did not assume too much power, though it of course would require more authority than allowed by the government created under the Articles of Confederation. Under the articles, the national government could do virtually nothing without the consent of each and every state— and nothing is what it often did, even in the face of domestic insurrections, financial disasters, and foreign military threats. Still, the Framers did not want a national government that would address these problems and unite the country at the expense of threatening the cause of liberty and individual rights.

The Framers' ideas about liberty and individual rights were influenced by the English philosopher John Locke, who argued in the seventeenth century that humans possessed certain natural rights that government not only must respect but also must exist to protect. As the Declaration of Independence phrased it, these natural rights were "unalienable." Government did not create or grant these rights—people possess them simply by virtue of being human and so "endowed by their Creator"—and so no government may deprive its citizens of "life, liberty, or the pursuit of happiness" without just cause and by lawful means. In sum, these natural rights existed not because of government but prior to and independent of it; people created civil societies and formed governments to ensure that those rights would be honored and upheld. This belief in natural rights guided the debates over the Declaration and grounded the debates that produced the U.S. Constitution.

The readings in this section are mostly primary texts because these sources are open windows on the beliefs that the drafters of the Constitution held dear. We begin with texts that underwrite the Constitution, either by embodying the Framers' first principles, such as Locke's *The Second Treatise of Government* (1690), or by exemplifying alternatives they considered or experienced but rejected, as with the Articles of Confederation. We then turn to the Federalist and Anti-Federalist debates that marked the struggle over the ratification of the Constitution in 1787–1788. These debates raised critical questions about the role of elected representatives in a democracy, the need for separation of powers and checks and balances, and the rationale for a federal system of government.

The Framers designed a government that they expected to endure, but they also expected that it would evolve—indeed, they included the amendment process for that very reason. Among the most significant changes to the original Constitution is the expansion of rights to women and black Americans. Women were not mentioned at all in the Constitution, and slaves were counted as three-fifths of a person. Slavery was abolished with the Thirteenth Amendment in 1865, and the Fourteenth and Fifteenth Amendments granted black Americans due process, equal protection under the laws, and the right to vote, though these rights were not actually enforced as a matter of national law and policy until the civil rights revolution of the 1960s. Women were not granted the right to vote until passage of the Nineteenth Amendment in 1920. Elizabeth Cady Stanton's Declaration of Sentiments (1848) and Martin Luther King, Jr.'s speech, "I Have a Dream" (1963), are included in this opening chapter to illustrate some of the fundamental debates about government and liberty that the Framers left for future generations to decide.

Finally, we examine a contemporary critique of the American political system. James L. Sundquist questions whether the system that the Framers designed in the late 1780s can meet the needs of the United States today. In essence, the first critics of the Constitution, the Anti-Federalists, insisted that the document made the national government too strong and centralized. Today, however, argues Sundquist, the national government is too weak and decentralized. To make the national government better able to plan ahead, act quickly in response to crises, and enact and implement public policies, he proposes amending the Constitution to adopt several features that would create a quasi-parliamentary system of government by weakening the separation of powers and strengthening the executive branch.

While these proposals are highly unlikely to be embraced widely, let alone result in new amendments, they remind us that the Constitution embodies institutional features (such as the separation of powers and federalism) and value choices (such as the primacy of liberty and individual rights) that were not universally approved when the document was first debated, have been challenged throughout American history, and are being questioned in our own day.

1.1   The Second Treatise of Government (1690)

JOHN LOCKE

INTRODUCTION

Writing in the late seventeenth century, just two years after England's Glorious Revolution, British philosopher John Locke propounded the virtues of a political order that would protect individuals' natural rights. In advocating a limited government, Locke responded to the views of Thomas Hobbes, who maintained that an absolute sovereign was necessary to control the vices of human nature. Locke presented a more optimistic view of human nature, writing that humans possess certain natural rights, including the right to own property, but they choose to create a political order to resolve "these inconveniences of the state of Nature." The principles articulated in *The Second Treatise of Government* are echoed in the Declaration of Independence and the Constitution.

■

87. Man, being born, as has been proved, with a title to perfect freedom and uncontrolled enjoyment of all the rights and privileges of the law of nature equally with any other man or number of men in the world, has by nature a power not only to preserve his property—that is, his life, liberty, and estate—against the injuries and attempts of other men, but to judge of and punish the breaches of that law in others as he is persuaded the offense deserves, even with death itself in crimes where the heinousness of the fact in his opinion requires it. But because no political society can be, nor subsist, without having in itself the power to preserve the property and, in order thereunto, punish the offenses of all those of that society, there and there only is political society where every one of the members has quitted his natural power, resigned it up into the hands of the community in all cases that exclude him not from appealing for protection to the law established by it. And thus all private judgment of every particular member being excluded, the community comes to be umpire by settled standing rules, indifferent and the same to all parties, and by men having authority from the community for the execution of those rules decides all the differences that may happen between any members of that society concerning any matter of right, and punishes those offenses which any member has committed against the society with such penalties as the law has established; whereby it is easy to discern who are, and who are not, in political society together. Those who are united into one body and have a com-

John Locke, *The Second Treatise of Government*, 1st Edition, ed. Thomas P. Peardon (New York: Liberal Arts Press, 1952), 48–54. © 1952. Reprinted by permission of Pearson Education, Inc., Upper Saddle River, N.J.

mon established law and judicature to appeal to, with authority to decide controversies between them and punish offenders, are in civil society one with another; but those who have no such common appeal, I mean on earth, are still in the state of nature, each being, where there is no other, judge for himself and executioner, which is, as I have before shown it, the perfect state of nature.

88. And thus the commonwealth comes by a power to set down what punishment shall belong to the several transgressions which they think worthy of it committed amongst the members of that society—which is the power of making laws—as well as it has the power to punish any injury done unto any of its members by any one that is not of it—which is the power of war and peace—and all this for the preservation of the property of all the members of that society as far as is possible. But though every man who has entered into civil society and is become a member of any commonwealth has thereby quitted his power to punish offenses against the law of nature in prosecution of his own private judgment, yet, with the judgment of offenses which he has given up to the legislative in all cases where he can appeal to the magistrate, he has given a right to the commonwealth to employ his force for the execution of the judgments of the commonwealth, whenever he shall be called to it; which, indeed, are his own judgments, they being made by himself or his representative. And herein we have the original of the legislative and executive power of civil society, which is to judge by standing laws how far offenses are to be punished when committed within the commonweath, and also to determine, by occasional judgments founded on the present circumstances of the fact, how far injuries from without are to be vindicated; and in both these to employ all the force of all the members when there shall be need.

89. Whenever, therefore, any number of men are so united into one society as to quit every one his executive power of the law of nature and to resign it to the public, there and there only is a political or civil society. And this is done wherever any number of men, in the state of nature, enter into society to make one people, one body politic, under one supreme government, or else when any one joins himself to, and incorporates with, any government already made; for hereby he authorizes the society or, which is all one, the legislative thereof to make laws for him as the public good of the society shall require, to the execution whereof his own assistance, as to his own decrees, is due. And this puts men out of a state of nature into that of a commonwealth by setting up a judge on earth, with authority to determine all the controversies and redress the injuries that may happen to any member of the commonwealth; which judge is the legislative, or magistrates appointed by it. And wherever there are any number of men, however associated, that have no such decisive power to appeal to, there they are still in the state of nature.

90. Hence it is evident that absolute monarchy, which by some men is counted the only government in the world, is indeed inconsistent with civil society, and so can be no form of civil government at all; for the end of civil society being to avoid and remedy these inconveniences of the state of nature

which necessarily follow from every man being judge in his own case, by setting up a known authority to which everyone of that society may appeal upon any injury received or controversy that may arise, and which everyone of the society ought to obey. Wherever any persons are who have not such an authority to appeal to for the decision of any difference between them, there those persons are still in the state of nature; and so is every absolute prince, in respect of those who are under his dominion.

91. For he being supposed to have all, both legislative and executive, power in himself alone, there is no judge to be found, no appeal lies open to any one who may fairly and indifferently and with authority decide, and from whose decision relief and redress may be expected of any injury or inconvenience that may be suffered from the prince or by his order; so that such a man, however entitled, "czar," or "grand seignior," or how you please, is as much in the state of nature with all under his dominion as he is with the rest of mankind; for wherever any two men are who have no standing rule and common judge to appeal to on earth for the determination of controversies of right betwixt them, there they are still in the state of nature, and under all the inconveniences of it, with only this woeful difference to the subject, or rather slave, of an absolute prince: that, whereas in the ordinary state of nature he has a liberty to judge of his right and, according to the best of his power to maintain it; now, whenever his property is invaded by the will and order of his monarch, he has not only no appeal as those in society ought to have but, as if he were degraded from the common state of rational creatures, is denied a liberty to judge of or to defend his right; and so is exposed to all the misery and inconveniences that a man can fear from one who, being in the unrestrained state of nature, is yet corrupted with flattery and armed with power.

92. For he that thinks absolute power purifies men's blood and corrects the baseness of human nature need read but the history of this or any other age to be convinced of the contrary. He that would have been so insolent and injurious in the woods of America would not probably be much better in a throne, where perhaps learning and religion shall be found out to justify all that he shall do to his subjects, and the sword presently silence all those that dare question it; for what the protection of absolute monarchy is, what kind of fathers of their countries it makes princes to be, and to what a degree of happiness and security it carries civil society, where this sort of government is grown to perfection, he that will look into the late relation of Ceylon may easily see.

93. In absolute monarchies, indeed, as well as other governments of the world, the subjects have an appeal to the law and judges to decide any controversies and restrain any violence that may happen betwixt the subjects themselves, one amongst another. This everyone thinks necessary, and believes he deserves to be thought a declared enemy to society and mankind who should go about to take it away. But whether this be from a true love of mankind and society, and such a charity as we all owe one to another, there is reason to doubt;

for this is no more than what every man who loves his own power, profit, or greatness may and naturally must do—keep those animals from hurting or destroying one another who labor and drudge only for his pleasure and advantage; and so are taken care of, not out of any love the master has for them, but love of himself and the profit they bring him; for if it be asked, what security, what fence is there, in such a state, against the violence and oppression of this absolute ruler, the very question can scarce be borne. They are ready to tell you that it deserves death only to ask after safety. Betwixt subject and subject, they will grant, there must be measures, laws, and judges, for their mutual peace and security; but as for the ruler, he ought to be absolute and is above all such circumstances; because he has power to do more hurt and wrong, it is right when he does it. To ask how you may be guarded from harm or injury on that side where the strongest hand is to do it, is presently the voice of faction and rebellion, as if when men, quitting the state of nature, entered into society, they agreed that all of them but one should be under the restraint of laws, but that he should still retain all the liberty of the state of nature, increased with power and made licentious by impunity. This is to think that men are so foolish that they take care to avoid what mischiefs may be done them by polecats or foxes, but are content, nay, think it safety, to be devoured by lions.

94. But whatever flatterers may talk to amuse people's understandings, it hinders not men from feeling; and when they perceive that any man, in what station soever, is out of the bounds of the civil society which they are of, and that they have no appeal on earth against any harm they may receive from him, they are apt to think themselves in the state of nature in respect of him whom they find to be so, and to take care, as soon as they can, to have that safety and security in civil society for which it was instituted, and for which only they entered into it. And therefore, though perhaps at first (as shall be shown more at large hereafter in the following part of this discourse), some one good and excellent man, having got a pre-eminence amongst the rest, had this deference paid to his goodness and virtue as to a kind of natural authority, that the chief rule, with arbitration of their differences, by a tacit consent devolved into his hands, without any other caution but the assurance they had of his uprightness and wisdom; yet when time, giving authority and (as some men would persuade us) sacredness to customs which the negligent and unforeseeing innocence of the first ages began, had brought in successors of another stamp, the people, finding their properties not secure under the government as then it was—whereas government has no other end but the preservation of property—could never be safe nor at rest nor think themselves in civil society till the legislature was placed in collective bodies of men, call them "senate," "parliament," or what you please. By which means every single person became subject, equally with other the meanest men, to those laws which he himself, as part of the legislative, had established; nor could any one, by his own authority, avoid the force of the law when once made, nor by

any pretense of superiority plead exemption, thereby to license his own or the miscarriages of any of his dependents. No man in civil society can be exempted from the laws of it; for if any man may do what he thinks fit, and there be no appeal on earth for redress or security against any harm he shall do, I ask whether he be not perfectly still in the state of nature, and so can be no part or member of that civil society; unless any one will say the state of nature and civil society are one and the same thing, which I have never yet found any one so great a patron of anarchy as to affirm.

1.2　The Declaration of Independence (1776)

When, in the course of human events, it becomes necessary for one people to dissolve the political bands which have connected them with another, and to assume, among the powers of the earth, the separate and equal station to which the laws of nature and of nature's God entitle them, a decent respect to the opinions of mankind requires that they should declare the causes which impel them to the separation.

We hold these truths to be self-evident: That all men are created equal; that they are endowed by their Creator with certain unalienable rights; that among these are life, liberty, and the pursuit of happiness; that, to secure these rights, governments are instituted among men, deriving their just powers from the consent of the governed; that whenever any form of government becomes destructive of these ends, it is the right of the people to alter or to abolish it, and to institute new government, laying its foundation on such principles, and organizing its power in such form, as to them shall seem most likely to effect their safety and happiness. Prudence, indeed, will dictate that governments long established should not be changed for light and transient causes; and accordingly all experience hath shown that mankind are more disposed to suffer, while evils are sufferable, than to right themselves by abolishing the forms to which they are accustomed. But when a long train of abuses and usurpations, pursuing invariably the same object, evinces a design to reduce them under absolute despotism, it is their right, it is their duty, to throw off such government, and to provide new guards for their future security. Such has been the patient sufferance of these colonies; and such is now the necessity which constrains them to alter their former systems of government. The history of the present King of Great Britain is a history of repeated injuries and usurpations, all having in direct object the establishment of an absolute tyranny over these states. To prove this, let facts be submitted to a candid world.

He has refused to assent to laws, the most wholesome and necessary for the public good.

He has forbidden his governors to pass laws of immediate and pressing importance, unless suspended in their operation till his assent should be obtained; and, when so suspended, he has utterly neglected to attend to them.

He has refused to pass other laws for the accommodation of large districts of people, unless those people would relinquish the right of representation in the legislature, a right inestimable to them, and formidable to tyrants only.

He has called together legislative bodies at places unusual, uncomfortable, and distant from the depository of their public records, for the sole purpose of fatiguing them into compliance with his measures.

He has dissolved representative houses repeatedly, for opposing, with manly firmness, his invasions on the rights of the people.

He has refused for a long time, after such dissolutions, to cause others to be elected; whereby the legislative powers, incapable of annihilation, have returned to the people at large for their exercise; the state remaining, in the mean time, exposed to all dangers of invasions from without and convulsions within.

He has endeavored to prevent the population of these states; for that purpose obstructing the laws for naturalization of foreigners; refusing to pass others to encourage their migration hither, and raising the conditions of new appropriations of lands.

He has obstructed the administration of justice, by refusing his assent to laws for establishing judiciary powers.

He has made judges dependent on his will alone, for the tenure of their offices, and the amount and payment of their salaries.

He has erected a multitude of new offices, and sent hither swarms of officers to harass our people, and eat out their substance.

He has kept among us, in times of peace, standing armies, without the consent of our legislatures.

He has affected to render the military independent of, and superior to, the civil power.

He has combined with others to subject us to a jurisdiction foreign to our constitution, and unacknowledged by our laws, giving his assent to their acts of pretended legislation:

For quartering large bodies of armed troops among us:

For protecting them, by a mock trial, from punishment for any murders which they should commit on the inhabitants of these states;

For cutting off our trade with all parts of the world;

For imposing taxes on us without our consent;

For depriving us, in many cases, of the benefits of trial by jury;

For transporting us beyond seas, to be tried for pretended offenses;

For abolishing the free system of English laws in a neighboring province, establishing therein an arbitrary government, and enlarging its boundaries, so as to render it at once an example and fit instrument for introducing the same absolute rule into these colonies;

For taking away our charters, abolishing our most valuable laws, and altering fundamentally the forms of our governments;

For suspending our own legislatures, and declaring themselves invested with power to legislate for us in all cases whatsoever.

He has abdicated government here, by declaring us out of his protection and waging war against us.

He has plundered our seas, ravaged our coasts, burned our towns, and destroyed the lives of our people.

He is at this time transporting large armies of foreign mercenaries to complete the works of death, desolation, and tyranny already begun with circumstances of cruelty and perfidy scarcely paralleled in the most barbarous ages, and totally unworthy the head of a civilized nation.

He has constrained our fellow-citizens, taken captive on the high seas, to bear arms against their country, to become the executioners of their friends and brethren, or to fall themselves by their hands.

He has excited domestic insurrection among us, and has endeavored to bring on the inhabitants of our frontiers the merciless Indian savages, whose known rule of warfare is an undistinguished destruction of all ages, sexes, and conditions.

In every stage of these oppressions we have petitioned for redress in the most humble terms; our repeated petitions have been answered only by repeated injury. A prince, whose character is thus marked by every act which may define a tyrant, is unfit to be the ruler of a free people.

Nor have we been wanting in our attentions to our British brethren. We have warned them, from time to time, of attempts by their Legislature to extend an unwarrantable jurisdiction over us. We have reminded them of the circumstances of our emigration and settlement here. We have appealed to their native justice and magnanimity; and we have conjured them, by the ties of our common kindred, to disavow these usurpations, which would inevitably interrupt our connections and correspondence. They, too, have been deaf to the voice of justice and of consanguinity. We must, therefore, acquiesce in the necessity which denounces our separation, and hold them, as we hold the rest of mankind, enemies in war, in peace friends.

We, therefore, the representatives of the United States of America, in General Congress assembled, appealing to the Supreme Judge of the world for the rectitude of our intentions, do, in the name and by the authority of the good people of these colonies, solemnly publish and declare, that these United Colonies are, and of right ought to be, *free and independent states;* that they are absolved from all allegiance to the British crown, and that all political connection between them and the state of Great Britain is, and ought to be, totally dissolved; and that, as free and independent states, they have full power to levy war, conclude peace, contract alliances, establish commerce, and do all other acts and things which independent states may of right do. And for the support of this declaration, with a firm reliance on the protection of Divine Providence, we mutually pledge to each other our lives, our fortunes, and our sacred honor.

JOHN HANCOCK [*President*]
[*and fifty-five others*]

1.3 The Articles of Confederation (1781)

INTRODUCTION

When the thirteen states drafted the Articles on Confederation during the War of Independence, their goal was to create a national government that would provide basic necessary services that they could not accomplish individually. The national government's responsibilities lay primarily in the area of foreign policy, from diplomacy to treaty negotiations to declarations of war. But the national government's power derived from the states, as evidenced by the description in the articles of a "league of friendship" among the constituent states. For example, nine states were required to give their assent to any decisions by the Congress on matters of war and peace. All thirteen states would have to agree to any changes in the articles. The articles governed the United States for almost a decade, but within a few years their shortcomings in creating an effective national government became apparent. The Constitution called for "a more perfect Union" in place of the article's "league of friendship." Twenty-seven amendments later, debate continues about just how "perfect" the government established by the Constitution is, whether the Constitution ought to be amended further, and how American government should be reformed.

◼

To all to whom these Presents shall come, we the under signed Delegates of the States affixed to our Names, send greeting.

Whereas the Delegates of the United States of America, in Congress assembled, did, on the 15th day of November, in the Year of Our Lord One thousand Seven Hundred and Seventy seven, and in the Second Year of the Independence of America, agree to certain articles of Confederation and perpetual Union between the States of Newhampshire, Massachusetts-bay, Rhodeisland

Herbert J. Storing, ed., *The Complete Anti-Federalist*, vol. 1, *What the Anti-Federalists Were For* (Chicago: University of Chicago Press, 1981), 101–108.

and Providence Plantations, Connecticut, New York, New Jersey, Pennsylvania, Delaware, Maryland, Virginia, North-Carolina, South-Carolina, and Georgia in the words following, viz. "Articles of Confederation and perpetual Union between the states of Newhampshire, Massachusetts-bay, Rhodeisland and Providence Plantations, Connecticut, New-York, New-Jersey, Pennsylvania, Delaware, Maryland, Virginia, North-Carolina, South-Carolina and Georgia.

Article I. The Stile of this confederacy shall be "The United States of America."

Article II. Each state retains its sovereignty, freedom, and independence, and every Power, Jurisdiction and right, which is not by this confederation expressly delegated to the United States, in Congress assembled.

Article III. The said states hereby severally enter into a firm league of friendship with each other, for their common defence, the security of their Liberties, and their mutual and general welfare, binding themselves to assist each other, against all force offered to, or attacks made upon them, or any of them, on account of religion, sovereignty, trade, or any other pretence whatever.

Article IV. The better to secure and perpetuate mutual friendship and intercourse among the people of the different states in this union, the free inhabitants of each of these states, paupers, vagabonds and fugitives from justice excepted, shall be entitled to all privileges and immunities of free citizens in the several states; and the people of each state shall have free ingress and regress to and from any other state, and shall enjoy therein all the privileges of trade and commerce, subject to the same duties, impositions and restrictions as the inhabitants thereof respectively, provided that such restriction shall not extend so far as to prevent the removal of property imported into any state, to any other state, of which the Owner is an inhabitant; provided also that no imposition, duties or restrictions shall be laid by any state, on the property of the united states, or either of them.

If any Person guilty of, or charged with treason, felony, or other high misdemeanor in any state, shall flee from Justice, and be found in any of the united states, he shall, upon demand of the Governor or executive power, of the state from which he fled, be delivered up and removed to the state having jurisdiction of his offence.

Full faith and credit shall be given in each of these states to the records, acts and judicial proceedings of the courts and magistrates of every other state.

Article V. For the more convenient management of the general interests of the united states, delegates shall be annually appointed in such manner as the legislature of each state shall direct, to meet in Congress on the first Monday in November, in every year, with a power reserved to each state, to recal its delegates, or any of them, at any time within the year, and to send others in their stead, for the remainder of the Year.

No state shall be represented in Congress by less than two, nor by more than seven Members; and no person shall be capable of being a delegate for more than three years in any term of six years; nor shall any person, being a delegate, be capable of holding any office under the united states, for which he, or another for his benefit receives any salary, fees or emolument of any kind.

Each state shall maintain its own delegates in a meeting of the states, and while they act as members of the committee of the states.

In determining questions in the united states in Congress assembled, each state shall have one vote.

Freedom of speech and debate in Congress shall not be impeached or questioned in any Court, or place out of Congress, and the members of congress shall be protected in their persons from arrests and imprisonments, during the time of their going to and from, and attendance on congress, except for treason, felony, or breach of the peace.

Article VI. No state, without the Consent of the united states in congress assembled, shall send any embassy to, or receive any embassy from, or enter into any conference, agreement, alliance or treaty with any King, prince or state; nor shall any person holding any office of profit or trust under the united states, or any of them, accept of any present, emolument, office or title of any kind whatever from any king, prince or foreign state; nor shall the united states in congress assembled, or any of them, grant any title of nobility.

No two or more states shall enter into any treaty, confederation or alliance whatever between them, without the consent of the united states in congress assembled, specifying accurately the purposes for which the same is to be entered into, and how long it shall continue.

No state shall lay any imposts or duties, which may interfere with any stipulations in treaties, entered into by the united states in congress assembled, with any king, prince or state, in pursuance of any treaties already proposed by congress, to the courts of France and Spain.

No vessels of war shall be kept up in time of peace by any state, except such number only, as shall be deemed necessary by the united states in congress assembled, for the defence of such state, or its trade; nor shall any body of forces be kept up by any state, in time of peace, except such number only, as in the judgment of the united states, in congress assembled, shall be deemed requisite to garrison the forts necessary for the defence of such state; but every state shall always keep up a well regulated and disciplined militia, sufficiently armed and accoutred, and shall provide and constantly have ready for use, in public stores, a due number of field pieces and tents, and a proper quantity of arms, ammunition and camp equipage.

No state shall engage in any war without the consent of the united states in congress assembled, unless such state be actually invaded by enemies, or shall have received certain advice of a resolution being formed by some nation of Indians to invade such state, and the danger is so imminent as not to admit of a delay till the united states in congress assembled can be consulted: nor shall any state grant commissions to any ships or vessels of war, nor letters of marque or reprisal, except it be after a declaration of war by the united states in congress assembled, and then only against the kingdom or state and the subjects thereof, against which war has been so declared, and under such regulations as shall be established by the united states in congress assembled, unless such state be infested by pirates, in which case vessels of war may be fitted out for that occasion, and kept so long as the danger shall continue, or until the united states in congress assembled, shall determine otherwise.

Article VII. When land-forces are raised by any state for the common defence, all officers of or under the rank of colonel, shall be appointed by the legislature of each state respectively, by whom such forces shall be raised, or in such manner as such state shall direct, and all vacancies shall be filled up by the State which first made the appointment.

Article VIII. All charges of war, and all other expences that shall be incurred for the common defence or general welfare, and allowed by the united states in congress assembled, shall be defrayed out of a common treasury, which shall be supplied by the several states in proportion to the value of all land within each state, granted to or surveyed for any Person, as such land and the buildings and improvements thereon shall be estimated according to such mode as the united states in congress assembled, shall from time to time direct and appoint.

The taxes for paying that proportion shall be laid and levied by the authority and direction of the legislatures of the several states within the time agreed upon by the united states in congress assembled.

Article IX. The united states in congress assembled, shall have the sole and exclusive right and power of determining on peace and war, except in the cases mentioned in the sixth article—of sending and receiving ambassadors—entering into treaties and alliances, provided that no treaty of commerce shall be made whereby the legislative power of the respective states shall be restrained from imposing such imposts and duties on foreigners as their own people are subjected to, or from prohibiting the exportation or importation of any species of goods or commodities, whatsoever—of establishing rules for deciding in all cases, what captures on land or water shall be legal, and in what manner prizes taken by land or naval forces in the service of the united states shall be divided or appropriated—of granting letters of marque and reprisal in times of peace—appointing courts for the trial of piracies and felonies committed on the high seas and establishing courts for receiving and determining finally appeals in all cases of captures, provided that no member of congress shall be appointed a judge of any of the said courts.

The united states in congress assembled shall also be the last resort on appeal in all disputes and differences now subsisting or that hereafter may arise between two or more states concerning boundary, jurisdiction or any other cause whatever; which authority shall always be exercised in the manner following. Whenever the legislative or executive authority or lawful agent of any state in controversy with another shall present a petition to congress stating the matter in question and praying for a hearing, notice thereof shall be given by order of congress to the legislative or executive authority of the other state in controversy, and a day assigned for the appearance of the parties by their lawful agents, who shall then be directed to appoint by joint consent, commissioners or judges to constitute a court for hearing and determining the matter in question: but if they cannot agree, congress shall name three persons out of each of the united states, and from the list of such persons each party shall alternately strike out one, the petitioners beginning, until the number shall be reduced to thirteen; and from that number not less than seven, nor more than nine names as congress shall direct, shall in the presence of congress be drawn out by lot, and the persons whose names shall be so drawn or any five of them, shall be commissioners or judges, to hear and finally determine the controversy, so always as a major part of the judges who shall hear the cause shall agree in the determination: and if either party shall neglect to attend at the day appointed, without showing reasons, which congress shall judge sufficient, or being present shall refuse to strike, the congress shall proceed to nominate three persons out of each state, and the secretary of congress shall strike in behalf of such party absent or refusing; and the judgment and sentence of the court to be appointed, in the manner before prescribed, shall be final and conclusive; and if any of the parties shall refuse to submit to the authority of such court, or to appear or defend their claim or cause, the court shall nevertheless proceed to pronounce sentence, or judgment, which shall in like manner be final and decisive, the judgment or sentence and other proceedings being in either case transmitted to congress, and lodged among the acts of congress for the security of the parties concerned: provided that every commissioner, before he sits in judgment, shall take an oath to be administered by one of the judges of the supreme or superior court of the state, where the cause shall be tried, "well and truly to hear and determine the matter in question, according to the best of his judgment, without favour, affection or hope of reward:" provided also, that no state shall be deprived of territory for the benefit of the united states.

All controversies concerning the private right of soil claimed under different grants of two or more states, whose jurisdictions as they may respect such lands, and the states which passed such grants are adjusted, the said grants or either of them being at the same time claimed to have originated antecedent to such settlement of jurisdiction, shall on the petition of either party to the congress of the united states, be finally determined as near as may be in the same manner as is before prescribed for deciding disputes respecting territorial jurisdiction between different states.

The united states in congress assembled shall also have the sole and exclusive right and power of regulating the alloy and value of coin struck by their own authority, or by that of the respective states—fixing the standard of weights and measures throughout the united states—regulating the trade and managing all affairs with the Indians, not members of any of the states, provided that the legislative right of any state within its own limits be not infringed or violated—establishing or regulating post-offices from one state to another, throughout all the united states, and exacting such postage on the papers passing thro' the same as may be requisite to defray the expences of the said office—appointing all officers of the land forces, in the service of the united states, excepting regimental officers—appointing all the officers of the naval forces, and commissioning all officers whatever in the service of the united states—making rules for the government and regulation of the said land and naval forces, and directing their operations.

The united states in congress assembled shall have authority to appoint a committee, to sit in the recess of congress, to be denominated "A Committee of the States," and to consist of one delegate from each state; and to appoint such other committees and civil officers as may be necessary for managing the general affairs of the united states under their direction—to appoint one of the number to preside, provided that no person be allowed to serve in the office of president more than one year in any term of three years; to ascertain the necessary sums of money to be raised for the service of the united states, and to appropriate and apply the same for defraying the public expences—to borrow money, or emit bills on the credit of the united states, transmitting every half year to the respective states an account of the sums of money so borrowed or emitted,—to build and equip a navy—to agree upon the number of land forces, and to make requisitions from each state for its quota, in proportion to the number of white inhabitants in such state; which requisition shall be binding, and thereupon the legislature of each state shall appoint the regimental officers, raise the men and cloath, arm and equip them in a soldier like manner, at the expence of the united states; and the officers and men so cloathed, armed and equipped shall march to the place appointed, and within the time agreed on by the united states in congress assembled: But if the united states in congress assembled shall, on consideration of circumstances judge proper that any state should not raise men, or should raise a smaller number than its quota, and that any other state should raise a greater number of men than the quota thereof, such extra number shall be raised, officered, cloathed, armed and equipped in the same manner as the quota of such state, unless the legislature of such state shall judge that such extra number cannot be safely spared out of the same, in which case they shall raise officer, cloath, arm and equip as many of such extra number as they judge can be safely spared. And the officers and men so cloathed, armed and equipped, shall march to the place appointed, and within the time agreed on by the united states in congress assembled.

The united states in congress assembled shall never engage in a war, nor grant letters of marque and reprisal in time of peace, nor enter into any treaties or alliances, nor coin money, nor regulate the value thereof, nor ascertain the sums and expences necessary for the defence and welfare of the united states, or any of them, nor emit bills, nor borrow money on the credit of the united states, nor appropriate money, nor agree upon the number of vessels of war, to be built or purchased, or the number of land or sea forces to be raised, nor appoint a commander in chief of the army or navy, unless nine states assent to the same: nor shall a question on any other point, except for adjourning from day to day be determined, unless by the votes of a majority of the united states in congress assembled.

The congress of the united states shall have power to adjourn to any time within the year, and to any place within the united states, so that no period of adjournment be for a longer duration than the space of six Months, and shall publish the Journal of their proceedings monthly, except such parts thereof relating to treaties, alliances or military operations, as in their judgment require secrecy; and the yeas and nays of the delegates of each state on any question shall be entered on the Journal, when it is desired by any delegate; and the delegates of a state, or any of them, at his or their request shall be furnished with a transcript of the said Journal, except such parts as are above excepted, to lay before the legislatures of the several states.

Article X. The committee of the states, or any nine of them, shall be authorized to execute, in the recess of congress, such of the powers of congress as the united states in congress assembled, by the consent of nine states, shall from time to time think expedient to vest them with; provided that no power be delegated to the said committee, for the exercise of which, by the articles of confederation, the voice of nine states in the congress of the united states assembled is requisite.

Article XI. Canada acceding to this confederation, and joining in the measures of the united states, shall be admitted into, and entitled to all the advantages of this union: but no other colony shall be admitted into the same, unless such admission be agreed to by nine states.

Article XII. All bills of credit emitted, monies borrowed and debts contracted by, or under the authority of congress, before the assembling of the united states, in pursuance of the present confederation, shall be deemed and considered as a charge against the united states, for payment and satisfaction whereof the said united states, and the public faith are hereby solemnly pledged.

Article XIII. Every state shall abide by the determinations of the united states in congress assembled, on all questions which by this confederation are submitted to them. And the Articles of this confederation shall be inviolably observed by every state, and the union shall be perpetual; nor shall any alteration at any time hereafter be made in any of them; unless such alteration be agreed to in a congress of the united states, and be afterwards confirmed by the legislatures of every state.

And Whereas it hath pleased the Great Governor of the World to incline the hearts of the legislatures we respectively represent in congress, to approve of, and to authorize us to ratify the said articles of confederation and perpetual union. Know Ye that we the undersigned delegates, by virtue of the power and authority to us given for that purpose, do by these presents, in the name and in behalf of our respective constituents, fully and entirely ratify and confirm each and every of the said articles of confederation and perpetual union, and all and singular the matters and things therein contained: And we do further solemnly plight and engage the faith of our respective constituents, that they shall abide by the determinations of the united states in congress assembled, on all questions, which by the said confederation are submitted to them. And that the articles thereof shall be inviolably observed by the states we respectively represent, and that the union shall be perpetual. In Witness whereof we have hereunto set our hands in Congress. Done at Philadelphia in the state of Pennsylvania the ninth day of July, in the Year of our Lord one Thousand seven Hundred and Seventy-eight, and in the third year of the independence of America.

1.4 The Federalist No. 10 and No. 51 (1787–1788)

JAMES MADISON

INTRODUCTION

When the limitations of the national government under the Articles of Confederation became evident, the leading political figures of the day decided to hold a national convention to revise the articles. Convention delegates actually went beyond this charge to draft a new Constitution in the summer of 1787. Once the drafting was complete, the Constitution went before the thirteen states for ratification, and the assent of nine was required. To build support for the new government, three Framers—Alexander Hamilton, James Madison, and John Jay—published a series of opinion pieces in New York newspapers during the winter of 1787–1788. These eighty-five writings became known as the *Federalist Papers.*

The two most famous writings in the *Federalist Papers* are the Federalist No. 10 and the Federalist No. 51, both crafted by Madison. In the Federalist No. 10, Madison lays out the case for representative, or republican, democracy. He also makes the novel argument that a large nation can better protect

James Madison, "The Federalist No. 10" (1787; Yale Law School Avalon Project, 1996), http://www.yale.edu/lawweb/avalon/federal/fed10.htm.

James Madison, "The Federalist No. 51" (1788; Yale Law School Avalon Project, 1996), http://www.yale.edu/lawweb/avalon/federal/fed51.htm.

the rights of its citizens than a small one because in a large country, special interests, or "factions," will be less likely to impose their will on the nation unless they have strong popular support. In the Federalist No. 51, Madison justifies the system of separation of powers, checks and balances, and federalism in the Constitution. Together, these two documents articulate the basic principles of American constitutionalism.

■

THE FEDERALIST NO. 10

November 22, 1787

Among the numerous advantages promised by a well constructed Union, none deserves to be more accurately developed than its tendency to break and control the violence of faction. The friend of popular governments, never finds himself so much alarmed for their character and fate, as when he contemplates their propensity to this dangerous vice. He will not fail therefore to set a due value on any plan which, without violating the principles to which he is attached, provides a proper cure for it. The instability, injustice and confusion introduced into the public councils, have in truth been the mortal diseases under which popular governments have every where perished; as they continue to be the favorite and fruitful topics from which the adversaries to liberty derive their most specious declamations. The valuable improvements made by the American Constitutions on the popular models, both ancient and modern, cannot certainly be too much admired; but it would be an unwarrantable partiality, to contend that they have as effectually obviated the danger on this side as was wished and expected. Complaints are every where heard from our most considerate and virtuous citizens, equally the friends of public and private faith, and of public and personal liberty; that our governments are too unstable; that the public good is disregarded in the conflicts of rival parties; and that measures are too often decided, not according to the rules of justice, and the rights of the minor party; but by the superior force of an interested and over-bearing majority. However anxiously we may wish that these complaints had no foundation, the evidence of known facts will not permit us to deny that they are in some degree true. It will be found indeed, on a candid review of our situation, that some of the distresses under which we labor, have been erroneously charged on the operation of our governments; but it will be found, at the same time, that other causes will not alone account for many of our heaviest misfortunes; and particularly, for that prevailing and increasing distrust of public engagements, and alarm for private rights, which are echoed from one end of the continent to the other. These must be chiefly, if not wholly, effects of the unsteadiness and injustice, with which a factious spirit has tainted our public administrations.

By a faction I understand a number of citizens, whether amounting to a majority or minority of the whole, who are united and actuated by some common impulse of passion, or of interest, adverse to the rights of other citizens, or to the permanent and aggregate interests of the community.

There are two methods of curing the mischiefs of faction: the one, by removing its causes; the other, by controlling its effects.

There are again two methods of removing the causes of faction: the one by destroying the liberty which is essential to its existence; the other, by giving to every citizen the same opinions, the same passions, and the same interests.

It could never be more truly said than of the first remedy, that it is worse than the disease. Liberty is to faction, what air is to fire, an aliment without which it instantly expires. But it could not be a less folly to abolish liberty, which is essential to political life, because it nourishes faction, than it would be to wish the annihilation of air, which is essential to animal life, because it imparts to fire its destructive agency.

The second expedient is as impracticable, as the first would be unwise. As long as the reason of man continues fallible, and he is at liberty to exercise it, different opinions will be formed. As long as the connection subsists between his reason and his self-love, his opinions and his passions will have a reciprocal influence on each other; and the former will be objects to which the latter will attach themselves. The diversity in the faculties of men from which the rights of property originate, is not less an insuperable obstacle to a uniformity of interests. The protection of these faculties is the first object of Government. From the protection of different and unequal faculties of acquiring property, the possession of different degrees and kinds of property immediately results: and from the influence of these on the sentiments and views of the respective proprietors, ensues a division of the society into different interests and parties.

The latent causes of faction are thus sown in the nature of man; and we see them every where brought into different degrees of activity, according to the different circumstances of civil society. A zeal for different opinions concerning religion, concerning Government and many other points, as well of speculation as of practice: an attachment to different leaders ambitiously contending for pre-eminence and power; or to persons of other descriptions whose fortunes have been interesting to the human passions, have in turn divided mankind into parties, inflamed them with mutual animosity, and rendered them much more disposed to vex and oppress each other, than to cooperate for their common good. So strong is this propensity of mankind to fall into mutual animosities, that where no substantial occasion presents itself, the most frivolous and fanciful distinctions have been sufficient to kindle their unfriendly passions, and excite their most violent conflicts. But the most common and durable source of factions, has been the various and unequal distribution of property. Those who hold, and those who are without property, have ever formed distinct interests in society. Those who are creditors, and those who are debtors, fall under a like discrimination. A landed interest, a manufacturing interest, a mercantile interest, a monied interest, with many lesser interests, grow up of necessity in civilized nations, and divide them into different classes, actuated by different sentiments and views. The regulation of these various and interfering interests forms the principal task of modern Legislation, and involves the spirit of party and faction in the necessary and ordinary operations of Government.

No man is allowed to be judge in his own cause; because his interest would certainly bias his judgment, and, not improbably, corrupt his integrity. With equal, nay with greater reason, a body of men, are unfit to be judges and parties, at the same time; yet, what are many of the most important acts of legislation, but so many judicial determinations, not indeed concerning the rights of single persons, but concerning the rights of large bodies of citizens, and what are the different classes of legislators, but advocates and parties to the causes which they determine? Is a law proposed concerning private debts? It is a question to which the creditors are parties on one side, and the debtors on the other. Justice ought to hold the balance between them. Yet the parties are and must be themselves the judges; and the most numerous party, or, in other words, the most powerful faction must be expected to prevail. Shall domestic manufactures be encouraged, and in what degree, by restrictions on foreign manufactures? are questions which would be differently decided by the landed and the manufacturing classes; and probably by neither, with a sole regard to justice and the public good. The apportionment of taxes on the various descriptions of property, is an act which seems to require the most exact impartiality; yet, there is perhaps no legislative act in which greater opportunity and temptation are given to a predominant party, to trample on the rules of justice. Every shilling with which they over-burden the inferior number, is a shilling saved to their own pockets.

It is in vain to say, that enlightened statesmen will be able to adjust these clashing interests, and render them all subservient to the public good. Enlightened statesmen will not always be at the helm: Nor, in many cases, can such an adjustment be made at all, without taking into view indirect and remote considerations, which will rarely prevail over the immediate interest which one party may find in disregarding the rights of another, or the good of the whole.

The inference to which we are brought, is, that the *causes* of faction cannot be removed; and that relief is only to be sought in the means of controlling its *effects*.

If a faction consists of less than a majority, relief is supplied by the republican principle, which enables the majority to defeat its sinister views by regular vote: It may clog the administration, it may convulse the society; but it will be unable to execute and mask its violence under the forms of the Constitution. When a majority is included in a faction, the form of popular government on the other hand enables it to sacrifice to its ruling passion or interest, both the public good and the rights of other citizens. To secure the public good, and private rights, against the danger of such a faction, and at the same time to preserve the spirit and the form of popular government, is then the great object to which our inquiries are directed: Let me add that it is the great desideratum, by which alone this form of government can be rescued from the opprobrium under which it has so long labored, and be recommended to the esteem and adoption of mankind.

By what means is this object attainable? Evidently by one of two only. Either the existence of the same passion or interest in a majority at the same time, must be prevented; or the majority, having such co-existent passion or interest, must be rendered, by their number and local situation, unable to concert and carry into effect schemes of oppression. If the impulse and the opportunity be suffered to coincide, we well know that neither moral nor religious motives can be relied on as an adequate control. They are not found to be such on the injustice and violence of individuals, and lose their efficacy in proportion to the number combined together; that is, in proportion as their efficacy becomes needful.

From this view of the subject, it may be concluded, that a pure Democracy, by which I mean, a Society, consisting of a small number of citizens, who assemble and administer the Government in person, can admit of no cure for the mischiefs of faction. A common passion or interest will, in almost every case, be felt by a majority of the whole; a communication and concert results from the form of Government itself; and there is nothing to check the inducements to sacrifice the weaker party, or an obnoxious individual. Hence it is, that such Democracies have ever been spectacles of turbulence and contention; have ever been found incompatible with personal security, or the rights of property; and have in general been as short in their lives, as they have been violent in their deaths. Theoretic politicians, who have patronized this species of Government, have erroneously supposed, that by reducing mankind to a perfect equality in their political rights, they would, at the same time, be perfectly equalized and assimilated in their possessions, their opinions, and their passions.

A republic, by which I mean a government in which the scheme of representation takes place, opens a different prospect, and promises the cure for which we are seeking. Let us examine the points in which it varies from pure democracy, and we shall comprehend both the nature of the cure and the efficacy which it must derive from the union.

The two great points of difference, between a democracy and a republic, are, first, the delegation of the government, in the latter, to a small number of citizens, elected by the rest; secondly, the greater number of citizens, and greater sphere of country, over which the latter may be extended.

The effect of the first difference is, on the one hand, to refine and enlarge the public views, by passing them through the medium of a chosen body of citizens, whose wisdom may best discern the true interest of their country, and whose patriotism and love of justice, will be least likely to sacrifice it to temporary or partial considerations. Under such a regulation, it may well happen, that the public voice, pronounced by the representatives of the people, will be more consonant to the public good, than if pronounced by the people themselves, convened for the purpose. On the other hand the effect may be inverted. Men of factious tempers, of local prejudices, or of sinister designs, may by intrigue, by corruption, or by other means, first obtain the suffrages, and then betray the interest of the people. The question resulting is, whether small or extensive republics are most favorable to the election of proper guardians of the public weal, and it is clearly decided in favor of the latter by two obvious considerations.

In the first place, it is to be remarked that, however small the republic may be, the representatives must be raised to a certain number, in order to guard against the cabals of a few; and that however large it may be, they must be limited to a certain number, in order to guard against the confusion of a multitude. Hence, the number of representatives in the two cases not being in proportion to that of the constituents, and being proportionally greatest in the small republic, it follows, that if the proportion of fit characters be not less in the large than in the small republic, the former will present a greater option, and consequently a greater probability of a fit choice.

In the next place, as each Representative will be chosen by a greater number of citizens in the large than in the small Republic, it will be more difficult for unworthy candidates to practise with success the vicious arts, by which elections are too often carried; and the suffrages of the people being more free, will be more likely to center on men who possess the most attractive merit, and the most diffusive and established characters.

It must be confessed, that in this, as in most other cases, there is a mean, on both sides of which inconveniences will be found to lie. By enlarging too much the number of electors, you render the representatives too little acquainted with all their local circumstances and lesser interests; as by reducing it too much, you render him unduly attached to these, and too little fit to comprehend and pursue great and national objects. The Federal Constitution forms a happy combination in this respect; the great and aggregate interests being referred to the national, the local and particular, to the state legislatures.

The other point of difference is, the greater number of citizens and extent of territory which may be brought within the compass of Republican, than of Democratic Government; and it is this circumstance principally which renders factious combinations less to be dreaded in the former, than in the latter. The smaller the society, the fewer probably will be the distinct parties and interests composing it; the fewer the distinct parties and interests, the more frequently will a majority be found of the same party; and the smaller the number of individuals composing a majority, and the smaller the compass within which they are placed, the more easily they will concert and execute their plans of oppression. Extend the sphere, and you take in a greater variety of parties and interests; you make it less probable that a majority of the whole will have a common motive to invade the rights of other citizens; or if such a common motive exists, it will be more difficult for all who feel it to discover their own strength, and to act in unison with each other. Besides other impediments, it may be remarked, that where there is a consciousness of unjust or dishonorable purposes, communication is always checked by distrust, in proportion to the number whose concurrence is necessary.

Hence it clearly appears, that the same advantage, which a Republic has over a Democracy, in controlling the effects of factions, is enjoyed by a large over a small Republic—is enjoyed by the Union over the States composing it. Does this advantage consist in the substitution of Representatives, whose enlightened views and virtuous sentiments render them superior to local prejudices, and to schemes of injustice? It will not be denied, that the Representation of the Union will be most likely to possess these requisite endowments. Does it consist in the greater security afforded by a greater variety of parties, against the event of any one party being able to outnumber and oppress the rest? In an equal degree does the increase variety of parties, comprised within the Union, increase this security? Does it, in fine, consist in the greater obstacles opposed to the concert and accomplishment of the secret wishes of an unjust and interested majority? Here, again, the extent of the Union gives it the most palpable advantage.

The influence of factious leaders may kindle a flame within their particular States, but will be unable to spread a general conflagration through the other States; a religious sect, may degenerate into a political faction in a part of the Confederacy but the variety of sects dispersed over the entire face of it, must secure the national Councils against any danger from that source: a rage for paper money, for an abolition of debts, for an equal division of property, or for any other improper or wicked project, will be less apt to pervade the whole body of the Union, than a particular member of it; in the same proportion as such a malady is more likely to taint a particular county or district, than an entire State.

In the extent and proper structure of the Union, therefore, we behold a Republican remedy for the diseases most incident to Republican Government. And according to the degree of pleasure and pride, we feel in being Republicans, ought to be our zeal in cherishing the spirit, and supporting the character of Federalists.

PUBLIUS

THE FEDERALIST NO. 51

February 6, 1788

To what expedient then shall we finally resort for maintaining in practice the necessary partition of power among the several departments, as laid down in the constitution? The only answer that can be given is, that as all these exterior provisions are found to be inadequate, the defect must be supplied, by so contriving the interior structure of the government, as that its several constituent parts may, by their mutual relations, be the means of keeping each other in their proper places. Without presuming to undertake a full development of this important idea, I will hazard a few general observations, which may perhaps place it in a clearer light, and enable us to form a more correct judgment of the principles and structure of the government planned by the convention.

In order to lay a due foundation for that separate and distinct exercise of the different powers of government, which to a certain extent, is admitted on all hands to be essential to the preservation of liberty, it is evident that each department should have a will of its own; and consequently should be so constituted, that the members of each should have as little agency as possible in the appointment of the members of the others. Were this principle rigorously adhered to, it would require that all the appointments for the supreme executive, legislative, and judiciary magistracies, should be drawn from the same fountain of authority, the people, through channels, having no communication whatever with one another. Perhaps such a plan of constructing the several departments would be less difficult in practice than it may in contemplation appear. Some difficulties however, and some additional expense, would attend the execution of it. Some deviations therefore from the principle must be admitted. In the constitution of the judiciary department in particular, it might be inexpedient to insist rigorously on the principle; first, because peculiar qualifications being essential in the members, the primary consideration ought to be to select that mode of choice, which best secures these qualifications; secondly, because the permanent tenure by which the appointments are held in that department, must soon destroy all sense of dependence on the authority conferring them.

It is equally evident that the members of each department should be as little dependent as possible on those of the others, for the emoluments annexed to their offices. Were the executive magistrate, or the judges, not independent of the legislature in this particular, their independence in every other would be merely nominal.

But the great security against a gradual concentration of the several powers in the same department, consists in giving to those who administer each department, the necessary constitutional means, and personal motives, to resist encroachments of the others. The provision for defense must in this, as in all other cases, be made commensurate to the danger of attack. Ambition must be made to counter-act ambition. The interest of the man must be connected with the constitutional right of the place. It may be a reflection on human nature, that such devices should be necessary to control the abuses of government. But what is government itself but the greatest of all reflections on human nature? If men were angels, no government would be necessary. If angels were to govern men, neither external nor internal controls on government would be necessary. In framing a government which is to be administered by men over men, the great difficulty lies in this: You must first enable the government to control the governed; and in the next place, oblige it to control itself. A dependence on the people is no doubt the primary control on the government; but experience has taught mankind the necessity of auxiliary precautions.

This policy of supplying by opposite and rival interests, the defect of better motives, might be traced through the whole system of human affairs, private as well as public. We see it particularly displayed in all the subordinate distributions of power; where the constant aim is to divide and arrange the several offices in such a manner as that each may be a check on the other; that the private interest of every individual, may be a sentinel over the public rights. These inventions of prudence cannot be less requisite in the distribution of the supreme powers of the state.

But it is not possible to give each department an equal power of self defense. In republican government the legislative authority, necessarily, predominates. The remedy for this inconvenience is, to divide the legislative into different branches; and to render them by different modes of election, and different principles of action, as little connected with each other, as the nature of their common functions, and their common dependence on the society, will admit. It may even be necessary to guard against dangerous encroachments by still further precautions. As the weight of the legislative authority requires that it should be thus divided, the weakness of the executive may require, on the other hand, that it should be fortified. An absolute negative, on the legislature, appears at first view to be the natural defense with which the executive magistrate should be armed. But perhaps it would be neither altogether safe, nor alone sufficient. On ordinary occasions, it might not be exerted with the requisite firmness, and on extraordinary occasions, it might be prefidiously abused. May not this defect of an absolute negative be supplied, by some qualified connection between this weaker department, and the weaker branch of the stronger department, by which the latter may be led to support the constitutional rights of the former, without being too much detached from the rights of its own department?

If the principles on which these observations are founded be just, as I persuade myself they are, and they be applied as a criterion, to the several state constitutions, and to the federal constitution, it will be found, that if the latter does not perfectly correspond with them, the former are infinitely less able to bear such a test.

There are moreover two considerations particularly applicable to the federal system of America, which place the system in a very interesting point of view.

First. In a single republic, all the power surrendered by the people, is submitted to the administration of a single government; and usurpations are guarded against by a division of the government into distinct and separate departments. In the compound republic of America, the power surrendered by the people, is first divided between two distinct governments, and then the portion allotted to each, subdivided among distinct and separate departments. Hence a double security arises to the rights of the people. The different governments will control each other; at the same time that each will be controlled by itself.

Second. It is of great importance in a republic, not only to guard the society against the oppression of its rulers; but to guard one part of the society against the injustice of the other part. Different interests necessarily exist in different classes of citizens. If a majority be united by a common interest, the rights of the minority will be insecure. There are but two methods of providing against this evil: The one by creating a will in the community independent of the majority, that is, of the society itself, the other by comprehending in the society so many separate descriptions of citizens, as will render an unjust combination of a majority of the whole, very improbable, if not impracticable. The first method prevails in all governments possessing an hereditary or self appointed authority. This at best is but a precarious security; because a power independent of the society may as well espouse the unjust views of the major, as the rightful interests, of the minor party, and may possibly be turned against both parties. The second method will be exemplified in the federal republic of the United States. While all authority in it will be derived from and dependent on the society, the society itself will be broken into so many parts, interests and classes of citizens, that the rights of individuals or of the minority, will be in little danger from interested combinations of the majority. In a free government, the security for civil rights must be the same as for religious rights. It consists in the one case in the multiplicity of interests, and in the other, in the multiplicity of sects. The degree of security in both cases will depend on the number of interests and sects; and this may be presumed to depend on the extent of country and number of people comprehended under the same government. This view of the subject must particularly recommend a proper federal system to all the sincere and considerate friends of republican government: Since it shows that in exact proportion as the territory of the union may be formed into more circumscribed confederacies or states, oppressive combinations of a majority will be facilitated, the best security under the republican form, for the rights of every class of citizens, will be diminished; and consequently, the stability and independence of some member of the government, the only other security, must be proportionally increased. Justice is the end of government. It is the end of civil society. It ever has been, and ever will be pursued, until it be obtained, or until liberty be lost in the pursuit. In a society under the forms of which the stronger faction can readily unite and oppress the weaker, anarchy may as truly be said to reign, as in a state of nature where the weaker individual is not secured against the violence of the stronger: And as in the latter state even the stronger individuals are prompted by the uncertainty of their condition, to submit to a government which may protect the weak as well as themselves: So in the former state, will the more powerful factions or parties be gradually induced by a like motive, to wish for a government which will protect all parties, the weaker as well as the more powerful. It can be little doubted, that if the state of Rhode Island was separated from the confederacy, and left to itself, the insecurity of rights under the popular form of government within such narrow limits, would be displayed by such reiterated oppressions of factious majorities, that some power altogether independent of the people would soon be called for by the voice of the very factions whose misrule had proved the necessity of it. In the extended republic of the United States, and among the great variety of interests, parties and sects which it embraces, a coalition of a majority of the whole society could seldom take place on any other principles than those of justice and the general good; and there being thus less danger to a minor from the will of the major party, there must be less pretext also, to provide for the security of the former, by introducing into the government a will not dependent on the latter; or in other words, a will independent of the society itself. It is no less certain than it is important, notwithstanding the contrary opinions which have been entertained, that the larger the society, provided it lie within a practicable sphere, the more duly capable it will be of self government. And happily for the *republican cause*, the practicable sphere may be carried to a very great extent, by a judicious modification and mixture of the *federal principle*.

PUBLIUS

1.5 The Anti-Federalist, Cato No. 3 and Brutus No. 2 (1787)

INTRODUCTION

The drafting of the Constitution sparked spirited debate in the thirteen states, as many leaders feared that the proposed national government would wield

Herbert J. Storing, ed., *The Complete Anti-Federalist*, vol. 2, *Objections of Non-Signers of the Constitution* and *Major Series of Essays at the Outset* (Chicago: University of Chicago Press, 1981), 109–113, 372–377.

too much power, thus sacrificing the independence for which the states had fought. These arguments were articulated in a series of editorials that became known as the *Anti-Federalist Papers.* Although the Anti-Federalists did not succeed in preventing the ratification of the Constitution, their critiques continue to merit attention. In many respects, the Anti-Federalists identified the dangers that could result from the new government if the individual states did not guard their authority zealously.

The two Anti-Federalist writings included here focus on the most pressing concerns of the Constitution's opponents: that the new government would govern over too large a territory to protect people's democratic rights, and that the Constitution did not explicitly enumerate those individual rights. Cato No. 3, widely believed to have been written by New York Governor George Clinton, presents a counterargument to the points advanced by Madison in the Federalist No. 10. It contends that democracy is best guarded in small societies, and that the government created by the Constitution will be so large, and will govern such a vast territory, that special interests, or "factions," will hinder efforts to develop national policies. The second piece, Brutus No. 2, probably written by New York judge Robert Yates, identifies the failure of the Constitution to include a Bill of Rights. The influence of the Anti-Federalists on the American political system is perhaps best exemplified by the incorporation of a Bill of Rights into the Constitution through the first ten amendments in 1791.

■

CATO NO. 3

To the Citizens of the State of New-York.

In the close of my last introductory address, I told you, that my object in future would be to take up this new form of national government, to compare it with the experience and opinions of the most sensible and approved political authors, and to show you that its principles, and the exercise of them [,] will be dangerous to your liberty and happiness.

Although I am conscious that this is an arduous undertaking, yet I will perform it to the best of my ability.

The freedom, equality, and independence which you enjoyed by nature, induced you to consent to a political power. The same principles led you to examine the errors and vices of a British superintendence, to divest yourselves of it, and to reassume a new political shape. It is acknowledged that there are defects in this, and another is tendered to you for acceptance; the great question then, that arises on this new political principle, is, whether it will answer the ends for which it is said to be offered to you, and for which all men engage in political society, to wit, the mutual preservation of their lives, liberties, and estates.

The recital, or premises on which this new form of government is erected, declares a consolidation or union of all the thirteen parts, or states, into one great whole, under the firm [form?] of the United States, for all the various and important purposes therein set forth.—But whoever seriously considers the immense extent of territory comprehended within the limits of the United States, together with the variety of its climates, productions, and commerce, the difference of extent, and number of inhabitants in all; the dissimilitude of interest, morals, and policies, in almost every one, will receive it as an intuitive truth, that a consolidated republican form of government therein, can never *form a perfect union, establish justice, insure domestic tranquility, promote the general welfare, and secure the blessings of liberty to you and your posterity,* for to these objects it must be directed: this unkindred legislature therefore, composed of interests opposite and dissimilar in their nature, will in its exercise, emphatically be, like a house divided against itself.

The governments of Europe have taken their limits and form from adventitious circumstances, and nothing can be argued on the motive of agreement from them; but these adventitious political principles, have nevertheless produced effects that have attracted the attention of philosophy, which has established axioms in the science of politics therefrom, as irrefragable as any in Euclid. It is natural, says Montesquieu, *to a republic to have only a small territory, otherwise it cannot long subsist: in a large one, there are men of large fortunes, and consequently of less moderation; there are too great deposits to intrust in the hands of a single subject, an ambitious person soon becomes sensible that he may be happy, great, and glorious by oppressing his fellow citizens, and that he might raise himself to grandeur, on the ruins of his country. In large republics, the public good is sacrificed to a thousand views; in a small one the interest of the public is easily perceived, better understood, and more within the reach of every citizen; abuses have a less extent, and of course are less protected*—he also shews you, that the duration of the republic of Sparta, was owing to its having continued with the same extent of territory after all its wars; and that the ambition of Athens and Lacedemon to command and direct the union, lost them their liberties, and gave them a monarchy.

From this picture, what can you promise yourselves, on the score of consolidation of the United States, into one government—impracticability in the just exercise of it—your freedom insecure—even this form of government limited in its continuance—the employments of your country disposed of to the opulent, to whose contumely you will continually be an object—you must risque much, by indispensably placing trusts of the greatest magnitude, into the hands of individuals, whose ambition for power, and aggrandizement, will oppress and grind you—where, from the vast extent of your territory, and the complication of interests, the science of government will become intricate and perplexed, and too misterious for you to understand, and observe; and by which you are to be conducted into a monarchy, either limited or despotic; the latter, Mr. Locke remarks, *is a government derived from neither nature, nor compact.*

Political liberty, the great Montesquieu again observes, *consists in security, or at least in the opinion we have of security;* and this *security* therefore, or the *opinion,* is best obtained in moderate governments, where the mildness of the laws, and the equality of the manners, beget a confidence in the people, which produces this security, or the opinion. This moderation in governments, depends in a great measure on their limits, connected with their political distribution.

The extent of many of the states in the Union, is at this time, almost too great for the superintendence of a republican form of government, and must one day or other, revolve into more vigorous ones, or by separation be reduced into smaller, and more useful, as well as moderate ones. You have already observed the feeble efforts of Massachusetts against their insurgents; with what difficulty did they quell that insurrection; and is not the province of Main at this moment, on the eve of separation from her. The reason of these things is, that for the security of the *property* of the community, in which expressive term Mr. Lock makes life, liberty, and estate, to consist—the wheels of a free republic are necessarily slow in their operation; hence in large free republics, the evil sometimes is not only begun, but almost completed, before they are in a situation to turn the current into a contrary progression: the extremes are also too remote from the usual seat of government, and the laws therefore too feeble to afford protection to all its parts, and insure *domestic tranquility* without the aid of another principle. If, therefore, this state, and that of N. Carolina, had an army under their controul, they never would have lost Vermont, and Frankland, nor the state of Massachusetts suffer an insurrection, or the dismemberment of her fairest district, but the exercise of a principle which would have prevented these things, if we may believe the experience of ages, would have ended in the destruction of their liberties.

Will this consolidated republic, if established, in its exercise beget such confidence and compliance, among the citizens of these states, as to do without the aid of a standing army—I deny that it will.—The mal-contents in each state, who will not be a few, nor the least important, will be exciting factions against it—the fear of a dismemberment of some of its parts, and the necessity to enforce the execution of revenue laws (a fruitful source of oppression) on the extremes and in the other districts of the government, will incidentally, and necessarily require a permanent force, to be kept on foot—will not political security, and even the opinion of it, be extinguished? can mildness and moderation exist in a government, where the primary incident in its exercise must be force? will not violence destroy confidence, and can equality subsist, where the extent, policy, and practice of it, will naturally lead to make odious distinctions among citizens?

The people, who may compose this national legislature from the southern states, in which, from the mildness of the climate, the fertility of the soil, and the value of its productions, wealth is rapidly acquired, and where the same causes naturally lead to luxury, dissipation, and a passion for aristocratic distinctions; where slavery is encouraged, and liberty of course, less respected, and protected; who know not what it is to acquire property by their own toil, nor to oeconomise with the savings of industry—will these men therefore be as tenacious of the liberties and interests of the more northern states, where freedom, independence, industry, equality, and frugality, are natural to the climate and soil, as men who are your own citizens, legislating in your own state, under your inspection, and whose manners, and fortunes, bear a more equal resemblance to your own?

It may be suggested, in answer to this, that whoever is a citizen of one state, is a citizen of each, and that therefore he will be as interested in the happiness and interest of all, as the one he is delegated from; but the argument is fallacious, and, whoever has attended to the history of mankind, and the principles which bind them together as parents, citizens, or men, will readily perceive it. These principles are, in their exercise, like a pebble cast on the calm surface of a river, the circles begin in the center, and are small, active, and forcible, but as they depart from that point, they lose their force, and vanish into calmness.

The strongest principle of union resides within our domestic walls. The ties of the parent exceed that of any other; as we depart from home, the next general principle of union is amongst citizens of the same state, where acquaintance, habits, and fortunes, nourish affection, and attachment; enlarge the circle still further, and, as citizens of different states, though we acknowledge the same national denomination, we lose the ties of acquaintance, habits, and fortunes, and thus, by degrees, we lessen in our attachments, till, at length, we no more than acknowledge a sameness of species. Is it therefore, from certainty like this, reasonable to believe, that inhabitants of Georgia, or New-Hampshire, will have the same obligations towards you as your own, and preside over your lives, liberties, and property, with the same care and attachment? Intuitive reason, answers in the negative.

In the course of my examination of the principals of consolidation of the states into one general government, many other reasons against it have occurred, but I flatter myself, from those herein offered to your consideration, I have convinced you that it is both presumptuous and impracticable consistent with your safety. To detain you with further remarks, would be useless—I shall however, continue in my following numbers, to anilise this new government, pursuant to my promise.

CATO

BRUTUS NO. 2

To the Citizens of the State of New-York.

I flatter myself that my last address established this position, that to reduce the Thirteen States into one government, would prove the destruction of your liberties.

But lest this truth should be doubted by some, I will now proceed to consider its merits.

Thought it should be admitted, that the argument[s] against reducing all the states into one consolidated government, are not sufficient fully to establish this point; yet they will, at least, justify this conclusion, that in forming a constitution for such a country, great care should be taken to limit and [define] its powers, adjust its parts, and guard against an abuse of authority. How far attention has been paid to these objects, shall be the subject of future enquiry. When a building is to be erected which is intended to stand for ages, the foundation should be firmly laid. The constitution proposed to your acceptance, is designed not for yourselves alone, but to generations yet unborn. The principles, therefore, upon which the social compact is founded, ought to have been clearly and precisely stated, and the most express and full declaration of rights to have been made—But on this subject there is almost an entire silence.

If we may collect the sentiments of the people of America, from their own most solemn declarations, they hold this truth as self-evident, that all men are by nature free. No one man, therefore, or any class of men, have a right, by the law of nature, or of God, to assume or exercise authority over their fellows. The origin of society then is to be sought, not in any natural right which one man has to exercise authority over another, but in the united consent of those who associate. The mutual wants of men, at first dictated the propriety of forming societies; and when they were established, protection and defence pointed out the necessity of instituting government. In a state of nature every individual pursues his own interest; in this pursuit it frequently happened, that the possessions or enjoyments of one were sacrificed to the views and designs of another; thus the weak were a prey to the strong, the simple and unwary were subject to impositions from those who were more crafty and designing. In this state of things, every individual was insecure; common interest therefore directed, that government should be established, in which the force of the whole community should be collected, and under such directions, as to protect and defend every one who composed it. The common good, therefore, is the end of civil government, and common consent, the foundation on which it is established. To effect this end, it was necessary that a certain portion of natural liberty should be surrendered, in order, that what remained should be preserved: how great a proportion of natural freedom is necessary to be yielded by individuals, when they submit to government, I shall not now enquire. So much, however, must be given up, as will be sufficient to enable those, to whom the administration of the government is committed, to establish laws for the promoting the happiness of the community, and to carry those laws into effect. But it is not necessary, for this purpose, that individuals should relinquish all their natural rights. Some are of such a nature that they cannot be surrendered. Of this kind are the rights of conscience, the right of enjoying and defending life, etc. Others are not necessary to be resigned, in order to attain the end for which government is instituted, these therefore ought not to be given up. To surrender them, would counteract the very end of government, to wit, the common good. From these observations it appears, that in forming a government on its true principles, the foundation should be laid in the manner I before stated, by expressly reserving to the people such of their essential natural rights, as are not necessary to be parted with. The same reasons which at first induced mankind to associate and institute government, will operate to influence them to observe this precaution. If they had been disposed to conform themselves to the rule of immutable righteousness, government would not have been requisite. It was because one part exercised fraud, oppression, and violence on the other, that men came together, and agreed that certain rules should be formed, to regulate the conduct of all, and the power of the whole community lodged in the hands of rulers to enforce an obedience to them. But rulers have the same propensities as other men; they are as likely to use the power with which they are vested for private purposes, and to the injury and oppression of those over whom they are placed, as individuals in a state of nature are to injure and oppress one another. It is therefore as proper that bounds should be set to their authority, as that government should have at first been instituted to restrain private injuries.

This principle, which seems so evidently founded in the reason and nature of things, is confirmed by universal experience. Those who have governed, have been found in all ages ever active to enlarge their powers and abridge the public liberty. This has induced the people in all countries, where any sense of freedom remained, to fix barriers against the encroachments of their rulers. The country from which we have derived our origin, is an eminent example of this. Their magna charta and bill of rights have long been the boast, as well as the security, of that nation. I need say no more, I presume, to an American, than, that this principle is a fundamental one, in all the constitutions of our own states; there is not one of them but what is either founded on a declaration or bill of rights, or has certain express reservation of rights interwoven in the body of them. From this it appears, that at a time when the pulse of liberty beat high and when an appeal was made to the people to form constitutions for the government of themselves, it was their universal sense, that such declarations should make a part of their frames of government. It is therefore the more astonishing, that this grand security, to the rights of the people is not to be found in this constitution.

It has been said, in answer to this objection, that such declaration[s] of rights, however requisite they might be in the constitutions of the states, are not necessary in the general constitution, because, "in the former case, every thing which is not reserved is given, but in the latter the reverse of the proposition prevails, and every thing which is not given is reserved." It requires but little attention to discover, that this mode of reasoning is rather specious than solid. The powers, rights, and authority, granted to the general government by this constitution, are as complete, with respect to every object to which they extend, as that of any state government—It reaches to every thing which concerns human happiness—Life, liberty, and property, are under its controul. There is the same reason, therefore, that the exercise of power, in this case, should be restrained within proper limits, as in that of the state governments. To set this matter in a clear light, permit me to instance some of the articles of the bills of rights of the individual states, and apply them to the case in question.

For the security of life, in criminal prosecutions, the bills of rights of most of the states have declared, that no man shall be held to answer for a crime until he is made fully acquainted with the charge brought against him; he shall not be compelled to accuse, or furnish evidence against himself—The witnesses against him shall be brought face to face, and he shall be fully heard by himself or counsel. That it is essential to the security of life and liberty, that trial of facts be in the vicinity where they happen. Are not provisions of this kind as necessary in the general government, as in that of a particular state? The powers vested in the new Congress extend in many cases to life; they are authorised to provide for the punishment of a variety of capital crimes, and no restraint is laid upon them in its exercise, save only, that "the trial of all crimes, except in cases of impeachment, shall be by jury; and such trial shall be in the state where the said crimes shall have been committed." No man is secure of a trial in the county where he is charged to have committed a crime; he may be brought from Niagara to New-York, or carried from Kentucky to Richmond for trial for an offence, supposed to be committed. What security is there, that a man shall be furnished with a full and plain description of the charges against him? That he shall be allowed to produce all proof he can in his favor? That he shall see the witnesses against him face to face, or that he shall be fully heard in his own defence by himself or counsel?

For the security of liberty it has been declared, "that excessive bail should not be required, nor excessive fines imposed, nor cruel or unusual punishments inflicted—That all warrants, without oath or affirmation, to search suspected places, or seize any person, his papers or property, are grievous and oppressive."

These provisions are as necessary under the general government as under that of the individual states; for the power of the former is as complete to the purpose of requiring bail, imposing fines, inflicting punishments, granting search warrants, and seizing persons, papers, or property, in certain cases, as the other.

For the purpose of securing the property of the citizens, it is declared by all the states, "that in all controversies at law, respecting property, the ancient mode of trial by jury is one of the best securities of the rights of the people, and ought to remain sacred and inviolable."

Does not the same necessity exist of reserving this right, under this national compact, as in that of these states? Yet nothing is said respecting it. In the bills of rights of the states it is declared, that a well regulated militia is the proper and natural defence of a free government—That as standing armies in time of peace are dangerous, they are not to be kept up, and that the military should be kept under strict subordination to, and controuled by the civil power.

The same security is as necessary in this constitution, and much more so; for the general government will have the sole power to raise and to pay armies, and are under no controul in the exercise of it; yet nothing of this is to be found in this new system.

I might proceed to instance a number of other rights, which were as necessary to be reserved, such as, that elections should be free, that the liberty of the press should be held sacred; but the instances adduced, are sufficient to prove, that this argument is without foundation.—Besides, it is evident, that the reason here assigned was not the true one, why the framers of this constitution omitted a bill of rights; if it had been, they would not have made certain reservations, while they totally omitted others of more importance. We find they have, in the 9th section of the 1st article, declared, that the writ of habeas corpus shall not be suspended, unless in cases of rebellion—that no bill of attainder, or expost facto law, shall be passed—that no title of nobility shall be granted by the United States, &c. If everything which is not given is reserved, what propriety is there in these exceptions? Does this constitution any where grant the power of suspending the habeas corpus, to make expost facto laws, pass bills of attainder, or grant titles of nobility? It certainly does not in express terms. The only answer that can be given is, that these are implied in the general powers granted. With equal truth it may be said, that all the powers, which the bills of right guard against the abuse of, are contained or implied in the general ones granted by this constitution.

So far it is from being true, that a bill of rights is less necessary in the general constitution than in those of the states, the contrary is evidently the fact.—This system, if it is possible for the people of America to accede to it will be an original compact; and being the last, will, in the nature of things vacate every former agreement inconsistent with it. For it being a plan government received and ratified by the whole people, all other forms which are in existence at the time of its adoption, must yield to it. This is expressed in positive and unequivocal terms, in the 6th article. "That this constitution and the laws of the United States, which shall be made in pursuance thereof, and all treaties made, or which shall be made, under the authority of the United States, shall be the supreme law of the land; and the judges in every state shall be bound thereby, any thing in the *constitution,* or laws of any state, *to the contrary* notwithstanding.

"The senators and representatives before-mentioned, and the members of the several state legislatures, and all executive and judicial officers, both of the United States, and of the several states, shall be bound, by oath or affirmation, to support this constitution."

It is therefore not only necessarily implied thereby, but positively expressed, that the different state constitutions are repealed and entirely done away, so far as they are inconsistent with this, with the laws which shall be made in pursuance thereof, or with treaties made, or which shall be made under the authority of the United States; of what avail will the constitutions of the respective states be to preserve the rights of its citizens? should they be plead, the answer would be, the constitution of the United States, and the laws made in pursuance thereof, is the supreme law, and all legislatures and judicial officers, whether of the general or state governments, are bound by oath to support it. No priviledge, reserved by the bills of rights, or secured by the state government, can limit the power granted by this, or restrain any laws made in pursuance of it. It stands therefore on its own bottom, and must receive a construction by itself without any reference to any other—And hence it was of the highest importance, that the most precise and express declarations and reservations of rights should have been made.

This will appear the more necessary, when it is considered, that not only the constitution and laws made in pursuance thereof, but all treaties made, or which shall be made, under the authority of the United States, are the supreme law of the land, and supersede the constitutions of all the states. The power to make treaties, is vested in the president, by and with the advice and consent of two thirds of the senate. I do not find any limitation, or restriction, to the exercise of this power. The most important article in any constitution may therefore be repealed, even without a legislative act. Ought not a government, vested with such extensive and indefinite authority, to have been restricted by a declaration of rights? It certainly ought.

So clear a point is this, that I cannot help suspecting, that persons who attempt to persuade people, that such reservations were less necessary under this constitution than under those of the states, are wilfully endeavouring to deceive, and to lead you into an absolute state of vassalage.

BRUTUS

1.6 The Declaration of Sentiments (1848)

INTRODUCTION

The original Constitution did not mention women at all, neither granting nor denying them rights. But in the eighteenth century, American women possessed few of the legal or political rights granted to men. In the 1840s, Elizabeth Cady Stanton, an advocate of the abolitionist movement to outlaw slavery, raised similar questions about the denial of rights to women. She and other activists organized a conference in Seneca Falls, New York, in 1848, where they signed a Declaration of Sentiments modeled on the Declaration of Independence. This statement became the foundation of the women's movement for equal rights in the United States.

■

When, in the course of human events, it becomes necessary for one portion of the family of man to assume among the people of the earth a position different from that which they have hitherto occupied, but one to which the laws of nature and of nature's God entitle them, a decent respect to the opinions of mankind requires that they should declare the causes that impel them to such a course.

We hold these truths to be self-evident: that all men and women are created equal; that they are endowed by their Creator with certain inalienable rights; that among these are life, liberty, and the pursuit of happiness; that to secure these rights governments are instituted, deriving their just powers from the consent of the governed. Whenever any form of government becomes destructive of these ends, it is the right of those who suffer from it to refuse allegiance to it, and to insist upon the institution of a new government, laying its foundation on such principles, and organizing its powers in such form, as to them shall seem most likely to effect their safety and happiness. Prudence, indeed, will dictate that governments long established should not be changed for light and transient causes; and accordingly all experience hath shown that mankind are more disposed to suffer, while evils are sufferable, than to right themselves by abolishing the forms to which they are accustomed. But when a long train of abuses and usurpations, pursuing invariably the same object, evinces a design to reduce them under absolute despotism, it is their duty to throw off such government, and to provide new guards for their future security. Such has been the patient sufferance of the women under this govern-

Elizabeth Cady Stanton, *A History of Woman Suffrage*, vol. 1 (Rochester, N.Y.: Fowler and Wells, 1889), 70–71.

ment, and such is now the necessity which constrains them to demand the equal station to which they are entitled.

The history of mankind is a history of repeated injuries and usurpations on the part of man toward woman, having in direct object the establishment of an absolute tyranny over her. To prove this, let facts be submitted to a candid world.

He has never permitted her to exercise her inalienable right to the elective franchise.

He has compelled her to submit to laws, in the formation of which she had no voice.

He has withheld from her rights which are given to the most ignorant and degraded men—both natives and foreigners.

Having deprived her of this first right of a citizen, the elective franchise, thereby leaving her without representation in the halls of legislation, he has oppressed her on all sides.

He has made her, if married, in the eye of the law, civilly dead.

He has taken from her all right in property, even to the wages she earns.

He has made her, morally, an irresponsible being, as she can commit many crimes with impunity, provided they be done in the presence of her husband. In the covenant of marriage, she is compelled to promise obedience to her husband, he becoming, to all intents and purposes, her master—the law giving him power to deprive her of her liberty, and to administer chastisement.

He has so framed the laws of divorce, as to what shall be the proper causes, and in case of separation, to whom the guardianship of the children shall be given, as to be wholly regardless of the happiness of women—the law, in all cases, going upon a false supposition of the supremacy of man, and giving all power into his hands.

After depriving her of all rights as a married woman, if single, and the owner of property, he has taxed her to support a government which recognizes her only when her property can be made profitable to it.

He has monopolized nearly all the profitable employments, and from those she is permitted to follow, she receives but a scanty remuneration. He closes against her all the avenues to wealth and distinction which he considers most honorable to himself. As a teacher of theology, medicine, or law, she is not known.

He has denied her the facilities for obtaining a thorough education, all colleges being closed against her.

He allows her in church, as well as state, but a subordinate position, claiming apostolic authority for her exclusion from the ministry, and, with some exceptions, from any public participation in the affairs of the church.

He has created a false public sentiment by giving to the world a different code of morals for men and women, by which moral delinquencies which exclude women from society, are not only tolerated, but deemed of little account in man.

He has usurped the prerogative of Jehovah himself, claiming it as his right to assign for her a sphere of action, when that belongs to her conscience and to her God.

He has endeavored, in every way that he could, to destroy her confidence in her own powers, to lessen her self-respect, and to make her willing to lead a dependent and abject life.

Now, in view of this entire disfranchisement of one-half the people of this country, their social and religious degradation—in view of the unjust laws above mentioned, and because women do feel themselves aggrieved, oppressed, and fraudulently deprived of their most sacred rights, we insist that they have immediate admission to all the rights and privileges which belong to them as citizens of the United States.

1.7 I Have a Dream (1963)

MARTIN LUTHER KING, JR.

INTRODUCTION

When the Framers drafted the Constitution, they sidestepped the simmering debate among the states over slavery. The Constitution said the following about slavery: Slaves would count as three-fifths of a person for purposes of determining a state's delegation in the House of Representatives; the importation of slaves would not be prohibited before 1808; and slaves who escaped would have to be returned. The debate grew more heated in the nineteenth century, culminating in the Civil War, which resulted in the abolition of slavery. The Thirteenth, Fourteenth, and Fifteenth Amendments granted black Americans legal rights, but the actual application of many of those rights would take another century to achieve.

On August 28, 1963, one hundred years after President Abraham Lincoln signed the Emancipation Proclamation freeing slaves in the southern states, Reverend Martin Luther King, Jr., spoke in front of the Lincoln Memorial at the historic civil rights march in Washington, D.C. In his renowned "I Have a Dream" speech, King outlined the failures of the United States to extend the equality enshrined in the Declaration of Independence to black Americans and called for the full guarantee of their civil rights. King's soaring rhetoric would become the hallmark of the civil rights movement and forms part of the

U.S. constitutional framework through its ringing call for the protection of constitutional rights for all Americans.

■

I am happy to join with you today in what will go down in history as the greatest demonstration for freedom in the history of our nation.

Five score years ago, a great American, in whose symbolic shadow we stand today, signed the Emancipation Proclamation. This momentous decree came as a great beacon light of hope to millions of Negro slaves, who had been seared in the flames of withering injustice. It came as a joyous daybreak to end the long night of their captivity.

But one hundred years later, the Negro still is not free. One hundred years later, the life of the Negro is still sadly crippled by the manacles of segregation and the chains of discrimination. One hundred years later, the Negro lives on a lonely island of poverty in the midst of a vast ocean of material prosperity. One hundred years later, the Negro is still languished in the corners of American society and finds himself an exile in his own land. And so we've come here today to dramatize a shameful condition.

In a sense we have come to our nation's capital to cash a check. When the architects of our republic wrote the magnificent words of the Constitution and the Declaration of Independence, they were signing a promissory note to which every American was to fall heir. This note was a promise that all men, yes, black men as well as white men, would be guaranteed the unalienable rights of life, liberty, and the pursuit of happiness. It is obvious today that America has defaulted on this promissory note, insofar as her citizens of color are concerned. Instead of honoring this sacred obligation, America has given the Negro people a bad check, a check which has come back marked "insufficient funds."

But we refuse to believe that the bank of justice is bankrupt. We refuse to believe that there are insufficient funds in the great vaults of opportunity of this nation. And so we have come to cash this check, a check that will give us upon demand the riches of freedom and the security of justice.

We have also come to this hallowed spot to remind America of the fierce urgency of Now. This is no time to engage in the luxury of cooling off or to take the tranquilizing drug of gradualism. Now is the time to make real the promises of democracy. Now is the time to rise from the dark and desolate valley of segregation to the sunlit path of racial justice. Now is the time to lift our nation from the quicksands of racial injustice to the solid rock of brotherhood. Now is the time to make justice a reality for all of God's children.

It would be fatal for the nation to overlook the urgency of the moment. This sweltering summer of the Negro's legitimate discontent will not pass until there is an invigorating autumn of freedom and equality. Nineteen sixty-three is not an end but a beginning. Those who hope that the Negro needed to blow off steam and will now be content will have a rude awakening if the nation returns to business as usual. There will be neither rest nor tranquility in America until the Negro is granted his citizenship rights. The whirlwinds of revolt will continue to shake the foundations of our nation until the bright day of justice emerges.

But there is something that I must say to my people who stand on the warm threshold which leads into the palace of justice. In the process of gaining our rightful place we must not be guilty of wrongful deeds. Let us not seek to satisfy our thirst for freedom by drinking from the cup of bitterness and hatred. We must ever conduct our struggle on the high plane of dignity and discipline. We must not allow our creative protest to degenerate into physical violence. Again and again we must rise to the majestic heights of meeting physical force with soul force.

The marvelous new militancy which has engulfed the Negro community must not lead us to a distrust of all white people, for many of our white brothers, as evidenced by their presence here today, have come to realize that their destiny is tied up with our destiny. And they have come to realize that their freedom is inextricably bound to our freedom. We cannot walk alone.

And as we walk, we must make the pledge that we shall always march ahead. We cannot turn back. There are those who are asking the devotees of civil rights, "When will you be satisfied?" We can never be satisfied as long as the Negro is the victim of the unspeakable horrors of police brutality. We can never be satisfied as long as our bodies, heavy with the fatigue of travel, cannot gain lodging in the motels of the highways and the hotels of the cities. We cannot be satisfied as long as a Negro in Mississippi cannot vote and a Negro in New York believes he has nothing for which to vote. No, no, we are not satisfied and we will not be satisfied until justice rolls down like waters and righteousness like a mighty stream.

I am not unmindful that some of you have come here out of great trials and tribulations. Some of you have come fresh from narrow jail cells. Some of you have come from areas where your quest for freedom left you battered by the storms of persecutions and staggered by the winds of police brutality. You have been the veterans of creative suffering. Continue to work with the faith that unearned suffering is redemptive. Go back to Mississippi, go back to Alabama, go back to South Carolina, go back to Georgia, go back to Louisiana, go back to the slums and ghettos of our northern cities, knowing that somehow this situation can and will be changed. Let us not wallow in the valley of despair, I say to you today, my friends. And so even though we face the difficulties of today and tomorrow, I still have a dream. It is a dream deeply rooted in the American dream.

I have a dream that one day this nation will rise up and live out the true meaning of its creed: We hold these truths to be self-evident that all men are created equal.

I have a dream that one day on the red hills of Georgia the sons of former slaves and the sons of former slave owners will be able to sit down together at the table of brotherhood.

I have a dream that one day even the state of Mississippi, a state sweltering with the heat of injustice, sweltering with the heat of oppression, will be transformed into an oasis of freedom and justice.

I have a dream that my four little children will one day live in a nation where they will not be judged by the color of their skin but by the content of their character. I have a *dream* today!

I have a dream that one day, *down* in Alabama, with its vicious racists, with its governor having his lips dripping with the words of interposition and nullification; one day right down in Alabama little black boys and black girls will be able to join hands with little white boys and white girls as sisters and brothers. I have a *dream* today!

I have a dream that one day every valley shall be exalted, and every hill and mountain shall be made low, the rough places will be made plain, and the crooked places will be made straight, and the glory of the Lord shall be revealed and all flesh shall see it together.

This is our hope. This is the faith that I will go back to the South with. With this faith we will be able to hew out of the mountain of despair a stone of hope. With this faith we will be able to transform the jangling discords of our nation into a beautiful symphony of brotherhood. With this faith we will be able to work together, to pray together, to struggle together, to go to jail together, to stand up for freedom together, knowing that we will be free one day. And this will be the day, this will be the day when all of God's children will be able to sing with new meaning, "My country 'tis of thee, sweet land of liberty, of thee I sing. Land where my fathers died, land of the Pilgrim's pride, from every mountainside, let freedom ring!" And if America is to be a great nation, this must become true.

And so let freedom ring—from the prodigious hilltops of New Hampshire.
Let freedom ring—from the mighty mountains of New York.
Let freedom ring—from the heightening Alleghenies of Pennsylvania.
Let freedom ring—from the snow-capped Rockies of Colorado.
Let freedom ring—from the curvaceous slopes of California.
But not only that.
Let freedom ring—from Stone Mountain of Georgia.
Let freedom ring—from Lookout Mountain of Tennessee.
Let freedom ring—from every hill and molehill of Mississippi.
From every mountainside, let freedom ring!

And when this happens, when we allow freedom to ring, when we let it ring from every village and every hamlet, from every state and every city, we will be able to speed up that day when *all* of God's children, black men and white men, Jews and Gentiles, Protestants and Catholics, will be able to join hands and sing in the words of the old Negro spiritual,

"Free at last, free at last.
Thank *God* Almighty, we are free at last."

1.8 Constitutional Reform and Effective Government (1992)

JAMES L. SUNDQUIST

INTRODUCTION

This chapter thus far focuses on readings that address the principles of American constitutionalism, as defined by the Framers and modified to incorporate groups left out of the original constitutional framework. American democracy, as we have seen, is grounded in the rights of liberty and equality, and the American political system guarantees those rights through representative government, separation of powers, and checks and balances. The underlying assumption is that this system of Madisonian democracy (as outlined by Madison in the Federalist No. 10 and No. 51) is necessary to protect people's constitutional rights. Other democracies, however, protect those rights with a different governmental structure.

Whereas the Anti-Federalists warned that even with a separation of powers the national government under the Constitution would become too strong and centralized, some contemporary critics argue that largely because of the separation of powers the national government has become too weak and divided to take concerted action in response to domestic needs and global challenges. The most common alternative to the American political system is a parliamentary democracy, and in the reading that follows, James L. Sundquist proposes adopting some features of a parliamentary system in the United States. Because these reforms would require constitutional amendments, they are unlikely to be adopted in the foreseeable future. Nevertheless, Sundquist's proposals merit attention because they pose important questions about why the United States adopted its system of government, and about the relative strengths and limitations of that political system.

■

THE CONSTITUTIONAL DILEMMA

. . . The Constitution achieved two purposes. First, it created a structure of government for the new republic; it defined the unique American tripartite system of independent yet interdependent branches (executive, legislative, and judicial), prescribed how those holding national office should be chosen, and sought to draw a boundary between the powers of the national government and those of the states. Second, it provided a limited body of fundamental substantive law, relating to such subjects of controversy at the time as slavery, civil liberties, the public debt, taxation, regulation of commerce, and titles of nobility.

When Madison was writing, public dissatisfaction centered on the second of these elements of the Constitution, its substantive provisions—specifically on the absence of a bill of rights. That omission was corrected when the First Congress proposed the ten amendments that the states ratified by 1791. Since then, the Constitution has been amended only seventeen times in two centuries, and most of those amendments have pertained also to substantive matters. Two of them—the Eighteenth, which prohibited alcoholic beverages, and the Twenty-first, which repealed the prohibition—left the document substantively unchanged. Of the remaining fifteen, seven further expanded the guarantees of civil rights. The Thirteenth outlawed slavery, and the Fourteenth guaranteed the rights of blacks and other citizens as well; four extended the right to vote, to blacks (the Fifteenth), to women (the Nineteenth), to young people at the age of eighteen (the Twenty-sixth), and to residents of the District of Columbia in presidential elections (the Twenty-third); and the Twenty-fourth Amendment abolished the poll tax as a requirement for voting. Two of the remaining amendments concerned the powers of the federal government: the Eleventh imposed a minor limitation on the jurisdiction of the federal courts, and the Sixteenth removed the constitutional prohibition against a graduated income tax. And the Twenty-seventh Amendment, proposed by the Congress in 1789 as part of its bill-of-rights package but not ratified until its rediscovery two centuries later, in 1992, attended to an administrative detail; it requires the Congress, whenever it raises the pay of its members, to postpone the effective date until after the next congressional election.

Only five of the twenty-seven amendments, then, dealt with the structure of the government created by the Constitution—which is the concern of this book—as distinct from the scope of its authority and the rights and liberties of U.S. citizens. And of those five, three can be considered technical or peripheral; they corrected flaws in the design of the structure or adapted it to new circumstances without altering the nature or relationships of the institutions as the framers had conceived them. The Twelfth Amendment, ratified in 1804, separated the balloting for president and vice president in the electoral college and thus accommodated to the age of parties the rather anomalous—from a modern perspective—nonpartisan presidential selection system conceived by the founders. The Twentieth Amendment, adopted in 1933, established the present January dates for the inauguration of presidents and the convening of Congresses, thus belatedly adjusting the political calendar to the development of steam transportation. The Twenty-fifth Amendment, approved in 1967, finally filled two gaps in the constitutional system that the founders had neglected to close. One provision established a procedure for the vice president to become acting president when the president is disabled. The second set up a process for the selection of a new vice president when that office becomes vacant—the process that was promptly used twice, when Gerald R. Ford was chosen to succeed Spiro T. Agnew and when Nelson A. Rockefeller was approved to replace Ford on the latter's advancement to the presidency.

That leaves only two amendments that have affected in any way the character of the institutions that were bequeathed to the twentieth century by the eighteenth. One was the Seventeenth Amendment, ratified in 1913, which provided that senators would be directly elected by the people rather than appointed by state legislatures. That action not only altered the constitutional balance between the federal government and the states but changed the nature of the Senate by introducing into its membership men and women of new political styles. The other was the Twenty-second Amendment, ratified in 1951, which limited presidents to two four-year terms and so decreed that each reelected president would enter his second term as a "lame duck," with whatever consequences that status might have on his relations with the Congress.

Even these two amendments influenced the institutions only indirectly, by affecting the selection or retention of the occupants of offices, not by adding to or subtracting from the constellation of institutions established by the Constitution or altering the formal distribution of power among them. The country's governmental architecture has proved, then, to be amazingly durable in a world of change. While some nations have shifted from monarchies to democracies to dictatorships and back again, while some have adopted and discarded and redesigned entire constitutions, the structure that was designed for the United States government in one eighteenth century summer remains in force essentially unchanged.

Does this mean that this human document was, after all, perfect in its basic design, despite the modest disclaimer of Gouverneur Morris? Many have thought so. It was William Ewart Gladstone, the British prime minister, who described the Constitution in a moment of ecstasy as "the most wonderful work ever struck off at a given time by the brain and purpose of man." Surely the durability of the constitutional structure and the growth and prosperity of the country governed by it are a testament to the wisdom and inspiration of the framers. Had the system they designed verged at any time on outright failure, serious and sustained movements to alter its basic features would have been born. Yet in two centuries, the only two significant movements for structural change were those that produced the Seventeenth and Twenty-

second amendments, and even those alterations did not reach to the fundamentals of the institutional system. In all that time, no failed movement of
any consequence can be added to the short list of reform efforts.

The Current Constitutional Debate

If the constitutional structure has served the country so well for so long, the
question is appropriate: Why discuss reform at all? The cliché "If it ain't broke,
don't fix it" makes a valid point. Trying to improve something that is working reasonably well can sometimes make things worse.

Yet that counsel is too negative. Its message is that breakdown must be
awaited, not averted. Moreover, breakdown is not usually an absolute but a
matter of degree. Weaknesses in a governmental system can debilitate and
devitalize a government, short of outright collapse. Should a partial breakdown, reflected in simple inefficiency and ineffectiveness, be tolerated on the
supposition that the cure will be worse than the ailment? After all, most of
the world's great inventions, in technology and social affairs alike, have sprung
from somebody's urge to make better what, at the time, most people undoubtedly considered good.

Inefficiency: Both Safeguard and Danger   Few would deny that the American
governmental system, in its two centuries, has shown weaknesses and ineffi-
ciencies. Defenders of the status quo respond simply that this is as it was
meant to be and should be. Writing just before his retirement in 1984, Barber
Conable, the veteran Republican representative from New York, acknowledged "the well-known mess which at any given time clutters up the Washington landscape" and the "laggard" character of the American government,
but argued that the system was intended to work that way and "we are better for it." "The Founding Fathers," wrote Conable, "didn't want efficient, adventurous governments, fearing they would intrude on our individual
liberties. I think they were right, and I offer our freedom, stability, and prosperity as evidence."

The danger lies in the fact that a government has objectives that all will
agree are good and necessary—national security and economic prosperity, to
name but two—in addition to whatever objectives some may deem unworthy.
And the good and bad cannot be separated. A government too inefficient to
embark on adventurous efforts to change society is also liable to be, by necessity, too inefficient to meet its inescapable, imperative responsibilities. U.S.
history abounds with illustrations of governmental failures that, if they did not
destroy "freedom, stability, and prosperity," at least threatened and sometimes impaired them. What constitutes failure may, of course, be disputed,
but contemporary popular opinion as well as the retrospective judgment of
history may be called on to help in identifying some examples.

The most indisputable of all the instances of failure—secession and civil
war—perhaps could not have been averted by any American government,

however structured. Maybe the same can be said of the crash of 1929 that precipitated the Great Depression. But the paralysis of the government for more than three years after that crash, in the face of increasing and intolerable suffering, is harder to explain away as reflecting virtue in the system. The constitutional structure provided no mechanism by which the people, when it was clear they had lost confidence in their leaders, could place in office new ones, with a fresh mandate to use the powers of government vigorously to alleviate suffering and restore prosperity. They could replace only a part of the government, in 1930, and that only intensified the policy deadlock that prevailed until the presidential election two years later.

The country's foreign affairs, in this century, offer innumerable examples of ineffective policy, brought about by the inability of leaders to harmonize all of the institutional elements that, under the Constitution, must act in concert before any decisive policy can be carried out. The country could participate in the sacrifices of World War I, by the will of the majority, but it could not join in the League of Nations that its president helped to design to construct and maintain the peace—not because the majority did not similarly will it, but because the constitutional system that requires a two-thirds majority of the Senate to approve treaties empowered the minority to rule. In Vietnam, the United States lost its first war—surely a failure by any objective standard—because it could not muster sufficient unity either to do whatever was necessary for victory or to disengage and withdraw cleanly at an early stage. Since then, conflict between the president and the Congress has rendered American policy ineffective—most conspicuously, in the 1980s, in the case of Nicaragua, where neither the president's policy of assisting the contra forces to overthrow the Sandinista government nor the congressional opposition's policy to withdraw support altogether could be pursued with firmness and decision. One consequence of that executive-legislative conflict was the so-called Iran-contra scandal uncovered in 1987–88, in which high administrative officials were convicted of taking illegal action to circumvent congressional prohibitions against assistance to the contras. President George Bush's success in obtaining the support of a majority in Congress for his intervention to free Kuwait in 1990–91 is more atypical than typical of interbranch relationships during the past quarter century.

In retrospect, the country clearly approves of social security, unemployment compensation, medicare, civil rights, and federal efforts to alleviate poverty and raise standards of education, housing, and nutrition. During the Reagan administration, the national commitment to some programs in these areas was scaled back but few were eliminated; the structure of the welfare state that remains in place reflects a genuine national consensus. But the welfare state came late to the United States; most of its major elements were adopted here decades later than in the industrial democracies of Europe, and in some of the essential elements that make up the welfare state, the United States still lags. Health care is the most conspicuous example; despite the almost universal recognition that the roughly 35 million Americans unprotected by medical insurance represent an urgent national problem, the instruments of government have been immobilized to deal with it. They are equally ineffective in providing, or influencing the market to provide, housing within the reach of low-income families. And in instances where effective policies are now in place, the process of pushing legislation to enactment has often been excruciatingly slow and painful. Civil rights legislation was stalled for years, even decades, until the logjam was broken by the televised images of law enforcement officers using police dogs and fire hoses on peaceful demonstrators. The social legislation that is deemed necessary and useful now would have been equally useful earlier, and the national consensus in support of most of the measures—civil rights is a conspicuous example—had formed two or three decades before they were eventually enacted. Failure to translate consensus into policy with reasonable promptness can be attributed in considerable measure to the multiple veto points that exist in a system of separate and coequal branches, which enabled minority interests in these cases to thwart, in the name of individual liberty, the will of the majority. The consequences of America's constitutional structure became the nation's loss.

In 1973 and 1974, the country witnessed the collapse of an administration mired in crime, but lacked the means to place a new leader in the White House—until by lucky accident an Oval Office tape recording was finally discovered that implicated the president in criminal activity beyond a reasonable doubt. President Richard M. Nixon's resignation restored the government, but only partially. The deadlock between the Republican president and the Democratic Congress that had rendered the government immobile in the Nixon period continued under Gerald Ford, with incessant quarreling between the branches over the whole range of foreign and domestic policy. . . .

The Recurrent Questions   Whenever the people sense that their government is failing, their tendency is to blame the individuals who hold elective office. Sometimes the condemnation falls on politicians as a class, as shown in the anti-incumbent mood that seemed to sweep the country in the early 1990s. But usually it has come to center upon the most conspicuous and powerful of all officeholders, the one who occupies the White House. It was not the system that failed, in the public view, but Herbert Hoover, or Lyndon Johnson, or Richard Nixon, or whoever. The process by which leaders are selected is a crucial part of any governmental system, of course, and some selection methods may produce better results than others. But granting that none of them can assure that ideal leaders will be chosen, the American constitutional system places extraordinary obstacles in the path of any leader. A president is expected to lead the Congress, but its two houses are independent institutions, and, most of the time of late, one or both are controlled by the political opposition. And when a president fails as leader—whether because the Congress chooses not to follow or because of any of the many possible forms of personal inadequacy—the system has no safeguard. The government cannot be reconstituted until the calendar announces that the day of the next presidential election has arrived. Unless one contends that all of the historical episodes cited here as examples of governmental failure were in fact successes, one is impelled to ask whether the constitutional system inherited from the eighteenth century is indeed adequate for the twenty-first. Specifically, five questions recur.

Would an electoral system that encouraged unified party control of the three centers of decisionmaking—presidency, Senate, and House—make for more effective, responsible, and accountable government?

Would longer terms for the president or for legislators, and a longer span between elections, enable leaders to rise to a higher level of statesmanship in confronting crucial issues, permit the resolution of issues that now go unresolved because of the short two-year life of each successive Congress, and allow greater deliberation and care in the legislative process?

Can a better solution be devised to deal with the immobility of government brought about by leadership failure, or deadlock and quarreling between the president and the Congress, than simply waiting helplessly until the next presidential election comes around?

Can harmonious collaboration between the executive and legislative branches be induced through formal interlocking of the branches or through strengthening the political parties that are the web that binds administrators and legislators to a common purpose?

Should any of the constitutional checks and balances by which the executive and legislative branches are enabled to thwart each other be modified to permit one or the other branch to prevail more readily and thus facilitate decisions? . . .

The Barriers to Constitutional Reform

If the founders wanted those who came after them to "exercise prudently the power of amendment," as [Gouvernor] Morris suggested, they still erected enormous barriers to that exercise—obstacles that proved to be greater, undoubtedly, than they anticipated. Approval of each amendment by two-thirds of both houses of the Congress, followed by its ratification by three-fourths of the states, can on occasion be attained, as the twenty-seven successful efforts attest. But this is more easily accomplished on a substantive matter, such as prohibition of alcoholic beverages or the repeal thereof, when waves of popular enthusiasm can be aroused. Issues pertaining to the structure of government do not stir mass excitement in the absence of outright governmental collapse. Such questions are examined closely by few except officeholders and politicians, and they are apt to appraise each proposal from the standpoint of its direct and immediate consequences to themselves, the offices they hold, and the parties they belong to.

Within the political elite, for an amendment to clear the barriers to passage, its acceptance must come close to unanimity, because it can be killed by one-

third plus one of those voting in either the Senate or the House, or, if it survives those hurdles, one-fourth plus one of the states—today, thirteen of fifty.
Yet the approval level in the states must usually be even higher than that, for
with one exception the states have two-house legislatures. Thus as few as thirteen of ninety-nine state legislative bodies can defeat the ratification of a con-
gressionally approved amendment; stated in reverse, as many as eighty-six of
the ninety-nine—or 87 percent—may still be insufficient, which amounts to a
requirement for virtual national unanimity. The Constitution does provide a
unicameral alternative to ratification by bicameral state legislatures; the Congress may specify that the states shall act through conventions, as they did in
ratifying the Constitution itself. But only one of the twenty-seven amendments—repeal of Prohibition—was adopted through that procedure.

The requirement for such extraordinary majorities means that, in the case
of structural amendments, any significant political bloc possesses an effective
veto. To succeed, a proposed amendment either must have no measurable adverse effect on anybody—as, say, the amendment that rescheduled inauguration days and congressional sessions—or must distribute its adverse effects
so nearly neutrally that no substantial interest is offended. It must be neutral
in its impact on the president and Congress, for either one can probably block
it (while the president is not part of the approval process, his influence and that
of past presidents and former executive branch officials who defend presidential prerogatives would usually be sufficient to give supporters of the presidency an effective veto). It must be neutral in its impact on Republicans and
Democrats, on incumbent officeholders and challengers, on liberals and conservatives, on professional politicians and amateurs, or on any other of the
dichotomous groups between which the political world can be divided. And
structural amendments, by their very nature, are rarely neutral. Altering an institutional structure inevitably redistributes power, taking from some and giving to others. In the long run, the country as a whole, and both parties, may
be better off by a redistribution. But it is in the short run that politicians plan
their careers. In the absence of a manifest collapse of government, the power
losers can be counted on to exercise their veto. Those who worry about the
shortcomings of their government, then, have traditionally sought remedies
that do not involve the obstacle-strewn route of constitutional reform. Laws
can be changed more readily, with simple majorities in both houses; political
party rules and institutions can be altered; and politicians can be exhorted to
change their ways.

But if these remedies are exhausted and the deficiencies of government remain, then there is no recourse but to reexamine the constitutional structure
itself.

The Parliamentary Model—and Incrementalism
Those who have been frustrated with the stalemates of the American system
over the years have looked longingly across the Atlantic and northward

toward Canada and admired the streamlined unity of other democratic governments. In the parliamentary democracies, the legislative majority is sovereign, and a committee of that majority—the cabinet—both leads the legislature and directs the executive branch. Power is unified. Responsibility is clearly fixed. Strong party discipline assures prime ministers and their cabinets that they normally can act quickly and decisively without fear of being repudiated by their legislatures. Yet the leaders are held accountable by the requirement that, to remain in power, they must maintain the confidence of the parliamentary majority that chose them. In two-party parliamentary systems, of which Great Britain is the prototype, votes of nonconfidence are rare, but on occasion the majority has forced a prime minister in which it has lost confidence to resign—as when Neville Chamberlain was compelled to give way to Winston Churchill early in World War II and Margaret Thatcher to John Major in 1990. In the multiparty parliamentary systems of the European continent, governments are usually formed by coalitions, and they collapse when the parties making up a government fall into conflict. As long as they can resolve disagreements—or postpone or evade issues—within their cabinets, however, they are as certain of legislative support as are the governments of Britain. Under any of these parliamentary systems, governments can be formed, in Lloyd Cutler's phrase. They can act. They can speak to the world with a single, clear voice. . . .

THE PROSPECTS FOR CONSTITUTIONAL REFORM

That there has been no powerful popular, or even elitist, movement on behalf of fundamental alteration in the governmental structure at any time in two hundred years testifies that the government has, most of the time, lived up to the expectations of the people. When failures have occurred, they have proven to be temporary and correctable. Yet some of the experienced leaders who are advocating constitutional revision today are profoundly convinced that the United States has been lucky in the past and that, in the future, the deadlock and indecision built into the governmental structure will sooner or later place the nation in peril. Perhaps the country's luck, if that is what it has been, will continue. But there have been enough periods of governmental failure in the nation's past to suggest the imprudence of continuing to rely on providence if the weaknesses in the governmental system can be identified and timely remedies can be adopted.

In today's world, two dangers seem paramount. One is that the division of power among the president, the Senate, and the House—coupled with a partisan split between the branches—will render it impossible to bring the national budget deficit under control, and the accumulated weight of national debt will eventually produce a sudden, or a gradual, economic calamity. The other is that division of power will produce a paralysis in foreign policy at a time of crisis, leaving the president unable to conduct foreign relations in a coherent and effective manner with the harmonious assured participation and support of congressional majorities.

If one accepts the proposition that indecisive, stalemated government can place the nation in peril—and that those risks outweigh the danger that decisive government will make unwise decisions—the preceding chapters suggest a range of remedies. Without regard to the question of what may or may not be politically feasible, an ideal series of amendments to the U.S. Constitution would include these, roughly in order of importance. . . .

1.   *The team ticket.* The separation of powers is far more likely to lead to debilitating governmental deadlock when the organs of government are divided between the parties. Several measures give promise of discouraging the ticket splitting that produces divided government, but only one would prohibit it outright. That is the team ticket, which would combine each party's candidates for president, vice president, Senate, and House into a slate that would be voted for as a unit.

2.   *Four-year House terms and eight-year Senate terms.* Even a united government is constantly distracted by the imminence of the next election, which is never more than two years away. The two-year life of the Congress—shortest of any national legislature in the world—normally limits an incoming president to barely a year as his "window of opportunity" to lead his party in enacting the program for which it sought its victory. To eliminate the midterm election and thereby lengthen the period of relative freedom from election pressure would require four-year House terms and either four-year or eight-year Senate terms, with the latter more in accord with the staggered-term tradition of the Senate. Presidents and Congresses alike would be better able to undertake short-term measures that might be unpopular, in order to achieve a greater long-run good, and the legislative process would benefit from a more deliberate tempo.

3.   *A new or modified procedure for selecting the president.* The problem of the faithless elector, the danger of rejection by the electoral college of the popular vote winner, and the unfairness and disruptive nature of the contingency procedure for selection of the president by the House must all be dealt with. The national bonus plan proposed by a task force in 1978 appears to be the best approach to resolving all of these difficulties at the same time.

4.   *A method for special elections to reconstitute a failed government.* . . . . If the mechanism is to be suitable for use in all of the kinds of emergency circumstances that can produce governmental failure, the special election should be call able at any time, by the president or a majority of either house of Congress. All seats in both houses, as well as the presidency and vice presidency, should

be filled at the election. Those elected should serve full terms (except half the senators would serve for only four years); and the terms could be adjusted by a few months so that the next regular election would fall on the customary November date.

5. *Removal of the prohibition against dual officeholding.* Permitting members of Congress to serve in the executive branch might turn out not to be practical, but removing the prohibition would permit constructive experimentation with that means of linking the executive and legislative branches.

6. *A limited item veto.* An item veto that could be overridden by absolute majorities of the two houses would give the president a means to publicize egregious "pork barrel" appropriations—and get at least some of them eliminated—yet not upset the executive-legislative balance of power.

7. *Restoration of the legislative veto.* This, too, might be limited, permitting only two-house vetoes.

8. *A war powers amendment.* Writing the essential terms of the War Powers Resolution of 1973 into the Constitution would clear up the unsettled question as to whether that resolution is valid and presidents are required to conform to its provisions.

9. *Approval of treaties by a majority of the membership of both houses.* This would remove the power to dominate critical foreign policy decisions from a minority of the Senate and restore it, like other governmental powers, to the majority.

These constitutional amendments could be supplemented by statutes and changes in party rules that would serve the same objectives, such as increasing the proportion of members of Congress, candidates for Congress, and other party leaders as delegates to presidential nominating conventions and providing for partial financing of congressional campaigns with public funds administered by party committees. . . .

The question arises, then: Should the advocates of constitutional change in the interest of more effective government turn their attention first to modifying the amendment process itself—for instance, by providing that amendments be submitted for approval by a national popular vote rather than by three-fourths of the states? Probably not. A simplified amendment procedure would never be considered in the abstract, simply as a theoretical proposition in the interest of good government. To win any significant backing, it would have to be seen as making the course easier for one or more specific, popular amendments whose supporters could then be mobilized behind it. But arrayed against the change would be the opponents of not only those amendments but all the many other alterations in the Constitution that might be under public discussion at the time, including those that would modify the Bill of Rights. The proposal would be seen as a devious attempt to slip into the Constitution bad ideas that could not win approval otherwise, on their merits. It would simply carry too much baggage.

Variations in the Amendment Process

Reformers might find some slight promise, however, in two elements of the existing amendment process that have been little used. One is the option of state ratification by unicameral conventions rather than by bicameral legislatures, which would—in theory, at least—somewhat reduce the mathematical odds against approval of any proposition by three-fourths of the states. On the one occasion when that method was used—the Twenty-first Amendment repealing Prohibition—it was resoundingly successful. Ratification was completed in the course of barely nine months, between February 20 and December 5, 1933. As to why that expeditious procedure was not chosen by the Congress in any other instance, the historical record is blank; presumably the sponsors of the various amendments were confident that they could win approval by the legislatures readily enough, obviating the need for the expense and trouble of organizing state conventions. Or perhaps they feared that taking their case to the people, who would elect the convention delegates, would involve more risk than relying on the more experienced politicians who constitute the legislatures. If a proposed amendment is unpopular, the powerful lobbying organizations that support it are sometimes able to prevail on the legislators to approve it anyway, as the Senate debate of 1924 . . . brought out.

The second optional procedure is the initiation of amendments by constitutional convention rather than by Congress. A convention must be called, under the Constitution, on petition of the legislatures of two-thirds of the states. No such gathering has ever been held, but for any amendment that would be seen by a substantial bloc in the Congress as restricting in any way the powers of the legislative branch, the convention process would appear to be essential as the only way of bypassing the congressional opposition. Such was the case early in this century, when advocates of the direct election of senators began a drive for a convention in order to circumvent the Senate, which was stubbornly refusing to reform itself. When one legislature after another passed the necessary resolution and the move appeared headed for success, the Senate reluctantly yielded and joined the House in proposing the amendment to the states. Since then, the only significant attempt to call a convention has been the one that gathered force in the 1980s but seems to have lost momentum since, organized to support an amendment to require a balanced federal budget except in certain specified circumstances.

Constitutional lawyers dispute whether, if the Congress attempted to limit a convention to a single subject—such as a balanced budget amendment—the limitation would be binding. In the total absence of precedent, no one can be sure. It is unlikely that the delegates would choose to disregard any congressional limitation, because they would have been chosen to deal with only one subject and would not be prepared to cope with others. But if they did elect to broaden their agenda, it is clear that no one outside their body would have authority to prevent their doing so. The delegates of 1787, after all, had been assigned only to propose amendments to the Articles of Confederation but, once they met, they set their own agenda. Another such "runaway convention" is not beyond the realm of possibility, and the question would be what happened afterward. To the extent that the convention exceeded its mandate from the Congress, it would plunge itself into a public controversy that would create a negative presumption against all of its actions, and the accusation of illegality could be exploited in the state ratification process. But if, nevertheless, three-fourths of the states took cognizance of the challenged proposals and gave their approval, the amendments would no doubt ultimately become part of the Constitution—either because the Supreme Court validated the disputed amendments or because Congress took the initiative to resubmit them. Should the balanced budget movement succeed in compelling a convention, then, and that body decide to consider additional matters, critics of the governmental structure would have an opportunity to advance any proposals that, because of their effect on the Congress itself, would not be likely to be initiated by the legislators in the normal manner.

The Problem of Gainers and Losers

Still, ratification by three-fourths of the states would remain as formidable a barrier as ever. Institutional structure is not an issue likely to arouse popular fervor, in the absence of a patent breakdown in the functioning of government, and even then—as at the time of Watergate—most people would be inclined to place the blame on the failure of individual leaders rather than of institutions. Proposals for structural change may not arouse fervent opposition either, but in the absence of popular support any organized institutional opposition is likely to prevail. If either of the major parties sees its interests jeopardized by a proposal, or incumbent legislators discern a loss of power for their branch, or the president and defenders of presidential power foresee a weakening of the executive, the proposal is doomed. Any significant ideological bloc, also, would surely have enough strength in enough states to block an amendment; so no proposal has much chance of success if it arouses conservative concern that it hides a bias toward big government, or liberal concern that it fetters government, or elitist worry that it embodies an excess of democracy, or antiestablishment fear that it upsets the balance the other way.

But institutional changes are seldom neutral, and even if one (or a package of several) could be conceived that is truly neutral—and would be perceived that way—neutrality is not enough. Each of the elements of the institutional system, and each major ideological group as well, must see some benefit. Unless something is to be gained, why risk change at all? But gain for everyone is a logical impossibility. True, the government as a whole can accrue power, as it has been doing for most of two centuries, but the division among institutions and officeholders of the right to exercise any given aggregate of power becomes a zero-sum game. If one institution or one political party or one ideological group gains, another loses. That, at bottom, is why there has not been a single amendment in two hundred years that redistributed governmental power. The two amendments that can be classed as even affecting the institutional structure at all—the Seventeenth (direct election of senators) and the Twenty-second (the two-term limit on the presidency)—concerned only the selection of the individuals who would wield institutional power, not the scope of the institutional authority itself.

But the distribution of power among the elements of the governmental system is what all of the constitutional changes discussed in this book would, in one or another degree, affect. The scale of the benefit to governmental effectiveness to be derived from any measure or set of measures would depend on the magnitude of that effect. But so would the vigor of the opposition each measure would incite. It becomes an axiom of constitutional reform, then, that any structural amendment that would bring major benefits cannot be adopted—again, barring a governmental collapse that can be clearly attributed to the constitutional design—while any measure that stands a chance of passage is likely to be innocuous.

The strategy of reformers, in such a circumstance, must be to search for trade-offs, based on the possibility that institutions and groups affected may weigh gains and losses on different scales. If party A to a negotiation considers proposition X to be far more important than proposition Y, while party B perceives them in the opposite relation, then party A will gladly trade Y for X and party B will accept the trade. Constitutional amendments are, unfortunately, not easily combined in logical packages for trade-off purposes, nor can the parties involved be brought to a table for direct negotiations.

If one concludes, for instance, that much of the problem of governmental incapacity arises from divided government, . . . there appears to be no practicable remedy. The axiom applies: the only modifications that would come close to forestalling divided government—bonus seats and the team ticket—would encounter insurmountable opposition. Bonus seats would dilute the power and influence of every legislator elected through the normal process, thus solidifying the entire Congress as an opposition bloc. As for the team-ticket idea, only one of the two parties, at any given time, would see a possible gain, while the other would anticipate a certain loss. In the 1980s, the team ticket would have helped the Republicans. Ronald Reagan's strength in 1984 would surely have won GOP control of the House as well as the Senate. Even so, Republicans have not embraced or even discussed the idea, and were it to be seriously advanced it would no doubt be dismissed out of anticipation, among other reasons, that at some future date the situation might be reversed. Meanwhile, the Democrats would look at recent presidential elections and reflect on how many House and Senate seats they would have lost if their congressional candidates had been tied to George McGovern, Walter Mondale, and Michael Dukakis. All this would be opposition enough but, meanwhile ideological opponents would also appear. The right to split tickets would be touted as one of the inalienable rights of citizenship, not to be abridged for the politicians' gain.

The other two proposals . . . would arouse less opposition simply because they would be potentially less effective, but at least one of the parties, at any given time, would find any measure that tended to promote united government against its short-run electoral interest. In the current period, when Republicans succeed in presidential elections while Democrats win more congressional contests, why would any Democrat wish to increase the chance that every time the Republicans won the White House they would sweep the House and Senate also?

Of all the proposals considered in this book, lengthening of congressional terms would seem to come closest to making everyone concerned a gainer, and none a loser—at least at first glance. House members should be expected to prefer terms of four years instead of two, Senate members ought to like eight-year terms better than six, and presidents should see benefit in electing members of Congress only in presidential years. But the rejection of Lyndon Johnson's 1966 proposal for four-year House terms coincident with the president's is instructive. Republican representatives saw their party placed at a disadvantage vis-à-vis the Democrats, and Democrats came to fear a loss of congressional independence vis-à-vis the president. Perhaps the latter worry could be shown to be ill founded—representatives would not have to run on a presidential ticket any oftener than they do at present—but the former concern is surely real, for one party or the other. In recent midterm elections, one of the parties would have been the gainer, and that party would be loath to see its opportunity for future gains eliminated. Only if recent midterm elections had been close to a dead heat would it appear possible to persuade members of both parties to assess the personal convenience of a longer term as outweighing any potential partisan loss.

As for the public reaction, the Johnson proposal met with some approbation, much indifference, but no mass cry of outrage. Perhaps that was because the amendment made so little progress on Capitol Hill. If a new proposal were to win serious consideration, a principled opposition would undoubtedly arise to contend that popular control over elected officials was being lessened. The public, it would be argued, should have the right to "throw the rascals out" at less than four-year intervals. The argument would be persuasive, even though the midterm election does not fully serve that purpose now because the president and two-thirds of the Senate cannot be touched. . . . [T]he country has always needed a truly effective mechanism for reconstituting failed governments, and lengthened terms would make the need more evident.

The prospect for winning longer terms might be enhanced, then, if that proposal were accompanied by a companion scheme to provide the people a genuine opportunity, in times of need, to redirect the course of government between presidential elections. But the exploration . . . of the range of remedies that would permit a complete reconstitution of the government between presidential elections confirms that no conceivable remedy is apt to be perceived as making all gainers and no losers. Presidents and legislators alike are sure to suspect that any proposed scheme for special intraterm elections would remove whatever advantages might be conferred by the lengthened terms. If the public gains control, the politicians lose it, that, too, is a zero-sum game. Perhaps it is not beyond reason that a combination of longer terms and special elections could be so designed that presidents, senators, and representatives would all see more benefit than loss. But the task for institutional architects is a forbidding one.

Finally, an opportunity for a trade-off may arise if the movement for limiting the number of terms a House member may serve continues to gather force. If those who favor the four-year term also see merit in term limitation (or if they see the latter proposition as likely to be adopted in any case), they could propose that the two changes be combined. Members of Congress, and the public generally, might see more gain than loss if the choice were between both measures or neither.

The proposal . . . for removing the prohibition against dual officeholding might encounter minimal opposition, for both branches might be seen to be the gainers. The president would gain the right to appoint legislators to executive office, yet without compulsion to do so; and legislators would gain at least a chance for broader responsibilities. Moreover, the amendment would require each specific use of the new authority to be approved by the Senate, and perhaps by the House too, as provided by law. The issue of gainers and losers would simply be deferred, and each particular appointment would have to worked out in such a way that both branches at that time were perceived to gain. The difficulty of achieving that objective would probably be great enough that, when the practical obstacles to combining executive and legislative work loads were also considered, the amendment would turn out to be inconsequential.

The proposals for strengthening political parties . . . , which do not require constitutional amendment, are clearly more feasible for that reason, but they nevertheless encounter the same problem of winners and losers. Passing laws usually requires some degree of bipartisan support, and any fundamental redesign of party institutions would have to be backed by all the major factions within a party. But changes in election laws, including controls over campaign finance, inevitably favor one party against another, some factions against others, incumbents against challengers or vice versa. Modifications in the presidential nomination process may also run afoul of state laws and of popular sentiment in favor of the broadest possible public participation and control. Changes in party and electoral institutions have occurred in the past, however, and reforms that enjoy broad though not overwhelming popular support can—unlike constitutional amendments with the same degree of public approval—eventually win adoption.

The possibility that the item veto and the legislative veto might be combined in a trade-off. . . . The president might find the item veto so appealing that he would concede the legislative veto in exchange, in the knowledge that the Congress will find ways of imposing its veto anyway and that the executive branch has often gained, because of a veto provision, a delegation of power it would not otherwise have received. The trade might not be seen by the legislators as an even one, unless the president's item veto could be overridden by a majority of the membership of both houses, as in Illinois. In that case, of course, the president might lose his interest. But the issue does appear to be one that lends itself to more or less formal interbranch negotiation. The war power and the requirements for treaty approval might be included in the bargaining as well.

All of the seemingly insurmountable obstacles to constitutional change could be overcome, of course, if the government were indeed to fail, palpably and for a sustained period. But the necessity to experience governmental failure, in order to prepare for it, is not a happy prospect. This book must end, then, on a pessimistic note. Nothing is likely to happen short of crisis—which is, of course, the case with all fundamental constitutional reform, in every country of the world and throughout history.

Nevertheless, nothing can be lost if, as the Constitution enters its third century, the public can be brought to look hard at the weaknesses of the American governmental system and consider what, if the worst comes to pass, the remedies might be. Even among those who believe no constitutional crisis lies ahead, few argue that the workings of governmental institutions are beyond improvement. Whatever the future may hold, much is to be gained if politicians, statesmen, and scholars carry forward the kind of analysis this book has attempted to provide, trying to separate the workable modifications in the constitutional structure from the unworkable, the effective from the ineffective, the possibly feasible from the wholly infeasible, all in an uncharted area of institutional design where there are few precedents to be evaluated and no one can be sure.

CHAPTER 2

Federalism

*T*he Constitution gives certain powers exclusively to the national government. Among these *expressed, delegated,* or *enumerated* powers of the national government are printing money, making treaties, and declaring war. Under the Tenth Amendment to the Constitution, the states have *reserve powers,* defined broadly as any powers that the Constitution does not explicitly give to the national government or specifically deny to the states—such as establishing licensing requirements for certain professions, administering elections, and running public schools, to cite just three examples. Thus, for instance, the national government's enumerated powers include regulating interstate commerce (commerce between states), while the states' reserve powers include regulating intrastate commerce (commerce within a state).

In addition, there are some powers that the national government exercises in collaboration with state governments. Among these *concurrent powers* are laying and collecting taxes, building highways, and administering criminal justice agencies. Finally, there are some powers that neither the national government nor the states may constitutionally claim or exercise, such as granting titles of nobility and issuing bills of attainder (acts declaring a citizen guilty of a capital crime without a trial), among many others.

Under the *supremacy clause* contained in Article VI of the Constitution, most conflicts between national or federal laws, on the one side, and state laws, on the other, are to be resolved in favor of the national government. Likewise, the *necessary and proper clause,* also known as the *elastic clause,* of the Constitution (Article I, Section 8, Clause 18) gives the national government *implied powers* to implement its enumerated powers; for example, the Constitution does not explicitly provide for a cabinet in the executive branch, but appointing and maintaining a cabinet to implement the president's constitutional powers as specified in Article II is an implied power of the national government.

In the *Federalist Papers,* the Framers made the case for federalism, arguing that a system of mixed sovereignty would provide more protection of people's rights than the alternatives of a national system (one in which the national government has full sovereignty over constituent states) or a confederal government (one in which constituent states exercise sovereignty over their national government). The federal system envisioned by the Framers would be a new approach to democratic governance that would combine the best features of national and confederal systems. Although other countries, such as Canada, Germany, and India, also have a federal system of government today, the United States was the first to adopt one. As such, the United States in the eighteenth century faced the daunting task of putting federalism into practice. This complicated process continues to evolve today.

Perhaps the most contentious debates about federalism involve two questions: What powers may legitimately be considered implied powers, and what is the proper balance between the national government's powers and the powers of the states? During the Constitutional Convention in 1787, the Framers juggled the delicate task of balancing the interests of large and small states in redesigning the national government. Advocates of the Virginia Plan favored assigning seats in Congress based on a state's population, while supporters of the New Jersey Plan argued that every state should be represented equally in the national government regardless of size. The famous "Great Compromise" broke the deadlock by allocating seats in the House of Representatives based on a state's population and granting two seats in the Senate to every state.

In the first decades following the Constitution's ratification, the Supreme Court reviewed several cases about the authority of the national government and the division of power between it and the states. Two of the most famous cases are *McCulloch v. Maryland* (1819), which dealt with the national government's powers of banking, taxation, and commerce, and *Gibbons v. Ogden* (1824), which addressed interstate commerce. In both cases, the Supreme Court ruled in favor of interpreting the Constitution broadly to extend the powers of the national government. But the national government has not always prevailed in disputes over sovereignty with the states.

It would be a big mistake to assume that the Constitution's supremacy and elastic clauses, together with these early court decisions, settled matters. The nature and scope of the national government's powers, and the balance between its powers and those of the states, have been debated and litigated for two hundred years. The Civil War (1861–1865) marked the height of division in the nineteenth century between the national government and the states over federalism. In the battle over who had authority to make decisions about slavery, the national government ultimately prevailed. But, as you will see in Chapter 13, the national government did not require states to protect the civil rights of black Americans until well into the twentieth century. In this respect, states continued to exercise sovereignty in areas such as voting eligibility, and they still have primary responsibility in many vital areas, including public school education and the administration of criminal justice.

The New Deal era of the 1930s and the civil rights revolution of the 1960s both marked an expansion in the authority of the federal government. As part of President Franklin D. Roosevelt's New Deal, the federal government created economic programs for the elderly and the poor, Social Security and welfare, respectively. In the 1960s, President Lyndon B. Johnson's Great Society agenda extended access to health care to the elderly and the poor through Medicare and Medicaid, respectively. In each of these areas, the federal government assumed authority in areas that previously had been left up to the states.

The late twentieth century, however, witnessed a return of some authority to the states. Both President Richard M. Nixon and President Ronald Reagan advocated a "new federalism," in which states and individuals would regain some of the authority that the national government had accrued in previous decades. During the 1980 presidential campaign, for example, Reagan said he would seek to close the U.S. Department of Education in order to restore full authority over education to the individual states. As president, however, Reagan found that decreasing the size of the federal government presented numerous obstacles. Still, Reagan's statement in his first inaugural address that "government is not the solution to our problem; government is the problem" marked a new stage in federalism, one in which politicians across political parties would work to limit the federal government's authority in certain areas.

Generally speaking, the Supreme Court has gone back and forth in its post-1980 opinions concerning federal-state relations. For example, in *South Carolina v. Dole* (1987), the Court ruled that the national government could deny federal funds for highway construction to any state that failed to raise its legal drinking age to twenty-one. A decade later, in *Printz v. United States* (1997), the Court ruled that the national government could not require a state government to implement federal laws without supplying federal funds for the purpose.

Whatever the Court decides in given cases concerning federalism, debates continue over how the national government should relate to the states and local governments in such seemingly disparate areas as homeland security and social welfare programs. Many big-city mayors and public administration analysts have raised concerns about whether key parts of the national government's homeland security policies constitute an unfunded federal mandate on states and local governments. More broadly, the ongoing post-1980 *devolution* of federal power and authority to the states—policies that return policy-making responsibility in given areas mostly or entirely to the states or that give the states greater authority to make, administer, or finance given federal policies—has affected several major domestic programs.

One important example of devolution in motion is Temporary Assistance to Needy Families (TANF), which replaced the Aid to Families with Dependent Children (AFDC) program under the terms of the 1996 welfare reform package signed into law by President Bill Clinton. The Personal Responsibility and Work Opportunity Reconciliation Act of 1996 marked the first significant change in welfare since its creation in 1935. Poor families would no longer be guaranteed cash payments of assistance; instead, aid would be tied to work, either through jobs or education that would lead to employment. States would have more authority over the disbursement of welfare funds and would be able to design programs to encourage people to move from welfare into work. The change in the federal program's name signified the shift in focus.

Some analysts endorse devolution as a means of revitalizing federalism and its "laboratories of democracy," the states, which now are supposedly freer to experiment with ways of achieving given public policy goals, learn what works, and change course as necessary without undue oversight or interference from the national government. Other analysts denounce devolution for supposedly reducing overall government spending for social welfare and other programs, and for permitting greater interstate differences in "who gets what" depending on "who lives where." Richard P. Nathan, a public policy scholar who worked on federalism issues in the Nixon administration, offers an expert and largely dispassionate overview of the latest "new federalism" and the "devolution revolution."

The ongoing debates over devolution, however, are merely the latest chapter in the history of debates over federalism. As political scientist Martha Derthick reminds us in this chapter, federalism challenges Americans with the fundamental question of whether they are or ought to be one, two, or many different political communities—and on what terms.

2.1 The Federalist No. 39 (1788)
JAMES MADISON

INTRODUCTION

In the Federalist No. 39, James Madison justifies the "plan of government" under the Constitution, focusing on the division of power between the national government and the states. He identifies the new government as being both "national" and "federal" in character, defining "national" as "a *consolidation* of the states," and "federal" as "a *confederacy* of former states." The United States would be both national and federal because power would derive from the people as well as the states. By describing the various features of the new government, from the bicameral Congress to the amendment process, Madison illustrates its distinctive structure with "neither a national nor a federal Constitution, but a composition of both."

■

To the People of the State of New York:

The last paper having concluded the observations which were meant to introduce a candid survey of the plan of government reported by the convention, we now proceed to the execution of that part of our undertaking.

The first question that offers itself is, whether the general form and aspect of the government be strictly republican. It is evident that no other form would be reconcilable with the genius of the people of America; with the fundamental principles of the Revolution; or with that honorable determination

James Madison, "The Federalist No. 39" (1788; Yale Law School Avalon Project, 1996), http://www.yale.edu/lawweb/avalon/federal/fed39.htm.

which animates every votary of freedom, to rest all our political experiments on the capacity of mankind for self-government. If the plan of the convention, therefore, be found to depart from the republican character, its advocates must abandon it as no longer defensible.

What, then, are the distinctive characters of the republican form? Were an answer to this question to be sought, not by recurring to principles, but in the application of the term by political writers, to the constitution of different States, no satisfactory one would ever be found. Holland, in which no particle of the supreme authority is derived from the people, has passed almost universally under the denomination of a republic. The same title has been bestowed on Venice, where absolute power over the great body of the people is exercised, in the most absolute manner, by a small body of hereditary nobles. Poland, which is a mixture of aristocracy and of monarchy in their worst forms, has been dignified with the same appellation. The government of England, which has one republican branch only, combined with an hereditary aristocracy and monarchy, has, with equal impropriety, been frequently placed on the list of republics. These examples, which are nearly as dissimilar to each other as to a genuine republic, show the extreme inaccuracy with which the term has been used in political disquisitions.

If we resort for a criterion to the different principles on which different forms of government are established, we may define a republic to be, or at least may bestow that name on, a government which derives all its powers directly or indirectly from the great body of the people, and is administered by persons holding their offices during pleasure, for a limited period, or during good behavior. It is *essential* to such a government that it be derived from the great body of the society, not from an inconsiderable proportion, or a favored class of it; otherwise a handful of tyrannical nobles, exercising their oppressions by a delegation of their powers, might aspire to the rank of republicans, and claim for their government the honorable title of republic. It is *sufficient* for such a government that the persons administering it be appointed, either directly or indirectly, by the people; and that they hold their appointments by either of the tenures just specified; otherwise every government in the United States, as well as every other popular government that has been or can be well organized or well executed, would be degraded from the republican character. According to the constitution of every State in the Union, some or other of the officers of government are appointed indirectly only by the people. According to most of them, the chief magistrate himself is so appointed. And according to one, this mode of appointment is extended to one of the coordinate branches of the legislature. According to all the constitutions, also, the tenure of the highest offices is extended to a definite period, and in many instances, both within the legislative and executive departments, to a period of years. According to the provisions of most of the constitutions, again, as well as according to the most respectable and received opinions on the subject, the members of the judiciary department are to retain their offices by the firm tenure of good behavior.

On comparing the Constitution planned by the convention with the standard here fixed, we perceive at once that it is, in the most rigid sense, conformable to it. The House of Representatives, like that of one branch at least of all the State legislatures, is elected immediately by the great body of the people. The Senate, like the present Congress, and the Senate of Maryland, derives its appointment indirectly from the people. The President is indirectly derived from the choice of the people, according to the example in most of the States. Even the judges, with all other officers of the Union, will, as in the several States, be the choice, though a remote choice, of the people themselves, the duration of the appointments is equally conformable to the republican standard, and to the model of State constitutions. The House of Representatives is periodically elective, as in all the States; and for the period of two years, as in the State of South Carolina. The Senate is elective, for the period of six years; which is but one year more than the period of the Senate of Maryland, and but two more than that of the Senates of New York and Virginia. The President is to continue in office for the period of four years; as in New York and Delaware, the chief magistrate is elected for three years, and in South Carolina for two years. In the other States the election is annual. In several of the States, however, no constitutional provision is made for the impeachment of the chief magistrate. And in Delaware and Virginia he is not impeachable till out of office. The President of the United States is impeachable at any time during his continuance in office. The tenure by which the judges are to hold their places, is, as it unquestionably ought to be, that of good behavior. The tenure of the ministerial offices generally, will be a subject of legal regulation, conformably to the reason of the case and the example of the State constitutions.

Could any further proof be required of the republican complexion of this system, the most decisive one might be found in its absolute prohibition of titles of nobility, both under the federal and the State governments; and in its express guaranty of the republican form to each of the latter.

"But it was not sufficient," say the adversaries of the proposed Constitution, "for the convention to adhere to the republican form. They ought, with equal care, to have preserved the *federal* form, which regards the Union as a *confederacy* of sovereign states; instead of which, they have framed a *national* government, which regards the Union as a *consolidation* of the States." And it is asked by what authority this bold and radical innovation was undertaken? The handle which has been made of this objection requires that it should be examined with some precision.

Without inquiring into the accuracy of the distinction on which the objection is founded, it will be necessary to a just estimate of its force, first, to ascertain the real character of the government in question; secondly, to inquire how far the convention were authorized to propose such a government; and thirdly, how far the duty they owed to their country could supply any defect of regular authority.

First, in order to ascertain the real character of the government, it may be considered in relation to the foundation on which it is to be established; to the sources from which its ordinary powers are to be drawn; to the operation of those powers; to the extent of them; and to the authority by which future changes in the government are to be introduced.

On examining the first relation, it appears, on one hand, that the Constitution is to be founded on the assent and ratification of the people of America, given by deputies elected for the special purpose; but, on the other, that this assent and ratification is to be given by the people, not as individuals composing one entire nation, but as composing the distinct and independent States to which they respectively belong. It is to be the assent and ratification of the several States, derived from the supreme authority in each State, the authority of the people themselves. The act, therefore, establishing the Constitution, will not be a *national*, but a *federal* act.

That it will be a federal and not a national act, as these terms are understood by the objectors; the act of the people, as forming so many independent States, not as forming one aggregate nation, is obvious from this single consideration, that it is to result neither from the decision of a *majority* of the people of the Union, nor from that of a *majority* of the States. It must result from the *unanimous* assent of the several States that are parties to it, differing no otherwise from their ordinary assent than in its being expressed, not by the legislative authority, but by that of the people themselves. Were the people regarded in this transaction as forming one nation, the will of the majority of the whole people of the United States would bind the minority, in the same manner as the majority in each State must bind the minority; and the will of the majority must be determined either by a comparison of the individual votes, or by considering the will of the majority of the States as evidence of the will of a majority of the people of the United States. Neither of these rules have been adopted. Each State, in ratifying the Constitution, is considered as a sovereign body, independent of all others, and only to be bound by its own voluntary act. In this relation, then, the new Constitution will, if established, be a *federal*, and not a *national* constitution.

The next relation is, to the sources from which the ordinary powers of government are to be derived. The House of Representatives will derive its powers from the people of America; and the people will be represented in the same proportion, and on the same principle, as they are in the legislature of a particular State. So far the government is *national*, not *federal*. The Senate, on the other hand, will derive its powers from the States, as political and coequal societies; and these will be represented on the principle of equality in the Senate, as they now are in the existing Congress. So far the government is *federal*, not *national*. The executive power will be derived from a very compound source. The immediate election of the President is to be made by the States in their political characters. The votes allotted to them are in a compound ratio, which considers them partly as distinct and coequal societies, partly as unequal members of the same society. The eventual election, again, is to be made by that branch of the legislature which consists of the national representatives; but in this particular act they are to be thrown into the form of individual delegations, from so many distinct and coequal bodies politic. From this aspect of the government it appears to be of a mixed character, presenting at least as many *federal* as *national* features.

The difference between a federal and national government, as it relates to the *operation of the government,* is supposed to consist in this, that in the former the powers operate on the political bodies composing the Confederacy, in their political capacities; in the latter, on the individual citizens composing the nation, in their individual capacities. On trying the Constitution by this criterion, it falls under the *national,* not the *federal* character; though perhaps not so completely as has been understood. In several cases, and particularly in the trial of controversies to which States may be parties, they must be viewed and proceeded against in their collective and political capacities only. So far the national countenance of the government on this side seems to be disfigured by a few federal features. But this blemish is perhaps unavoidable in any plan; and the operation of the government on the people, in their individual capacities, in its ordinary and most essential proceedings, may, on the whole, designate it, in this relation, a *national* government.

But if the government be national with regard to the *operation* of its powers, it changes its aspect again when we contemplate it in relation to the *extent* of its powers. The idea of a national government involves in it, not only an authority over the individual citizens, but an indefinite supremacy over all persons and things, so far as they are objects of lawful government. Among a people consolidated into one nation, this supremacy is completely vested in the national legislature. Among communities united for particular purposes, it is vested partly in the general and partly in the municipal legislatures. In the former case, all local authorities are subordinate to the supreme; and may be controlled, directed, or abolished by it at pleasure. In the latter, the local or municipal authorities form distinct and independent portions of the supremacy, no more subject, within their respective spheres, to the general authority, than the general authority is subject to them, within its own sphere. In this relation, then, the proposed government cannot be deemed a *national* one; since its jurisdiction extends to certain enumerated objects only, and leaves to the several States a residuary and inviolable sovereignty over all other objects. It is true that in controversies relating to the boundary between the two jurisdictions, the tribunal which is ultimately to decide, is to be established under the general government. But this does not change the principle of the case. The decision is to be impartially made, according to the rules of the Constitution;

and all the usual and most effectual precautions are taken to secure this impartiality. Some such tribunal is clearly essential to prevent an appeal to the sword and a dissolution of the compact; and that it ought to be established under the general rather than under the local governments, or, to speak more properly, that it could be safely established under the first alone, is a position not likely to be combated.

If we try the Constitution by its last relation to the authority by which amendments are to be made, we find it neither wholly *national* nor wholly *federal*. Were it wholly national, the supreme and ultimate authority would reside in the *majority* of the people of the Union; and this authority would be competent at all times, like that of a majority of every national society, to alter or abolish its established government. Were it wholly federal, on the other hand, the concurrence of each State in the Union would be essential to every alteration that would be binding on all. The mode provided by the plan of the convention is not founded on either of these principles. In requiring more than a majority, and principles. In requiring more than a majority, and particularly in computing the proportion by *states*, not by *citizens*, it departs from the *national* and advances towards the *federal* character; in rendering the concurrence of less than the whole number of States sufficient, it loses again the *federal* and partakes of the *national* character.

The proposed Constitution, therefore, is, in strictness, neither a national nor a federal Constitution, but a composition of both. In its foundation it is federal, not national; in the sources from which the ordinary powers of the government are drawn, it is partly federal and partly national; in the operation of these powers, it is national, not federal; in the extent of them, again, it is federal, not national; and, finally, in the authoritative mode of introducing amendments, it is neither wholly federal nor wholly national.

PUBLIUS

2.2 *McCulloch v. State of Maryland* (1819)

INTRODUCTION

Although the Constitution established the powers of the national government, it left the extent of those powers open to interpretation. Such was the challenge of the Congress, president, and the courts in the early years of the republic. Several landmark Supreme Court cases in those years defined the national government's authority more broadly than a strict reading of

McCulloch v. State of Maryland, 17 U.S. 316 (1819).

the Constitution would suggest. Supreme Court Chief Justice John Marshall (1801–1835) wrote several of these rulings, including *McCulloch v. Maryland* (1819), which solidified the implied powers of Congress and the supremacy of the national government over the states.

The creation of a Bank of the United States in 1791 prompted much debate over Congress's authority to establish such an institution, as the Constitution does not explicitly provide for it to do so. Proponents of a strong national government, such as George Washington, supported the bank's creation, while supporters of more states' rights, such as Thomas Jefferson, opposed it. During Jefferson's presidency, the bank's charter was not renewed, but President James Madison supported the creation of a second Bank of the United States in 1816.

The state of Maryland opposed creation of a national bank and sought to close the Baltimore branch by levying an annual tax of $15,000 on it. When the bank cashier, James McCulloch, refused to pay the tax, Maryland sued. It declared that it had the power to tax entities within the state and, furthermore, that Congress did not have the power to charter a national bank in the first place.

After a state court convicted McCulloch, he appealed the decision, and the case eventually made its way to the Supreme Court. Writing for the majority, Chief Justice Marshall ruled in favor of the national bank. The decision was twofold, affirming the right of Congress to create a national bank and denying Maryland's effort to tax such an authority. Marshall established first that Article I, Section 8, of the Constitution gave Congress the power to charter a national bank. Although the clause does not discuss a national bank, it states Congress shall have power "To make all Laws which shall be *necessary and proper* [emphasis added] for carrying into Execution the foregoing Powers, and all other Powers vested by this Constitution in the Government of the United States, or in any Department or Officer thereof." The *implied power* in this clause provides sufficient authority for Congress to establish a national bank, as the bank is needed to assist Congress in regulating commerce and coining money, among other explicit provisions in the Constitution.

Marshall also wrote that Maryland did not have the power to tax the Bank of the United States. Article VI of the Constitution states that "This Constitution, and the laws of the United States which shall be made in Pursuance thereof . . . shall be the Supreme Law of the Land; and the Judges in every State shall be bound thereby, any Thing in the Constitution or Laws of any State to the Contrary notwithstanding." The *supremacy clause,* as this sentence is popularly known, affirms that states must abide by national laws, which means that they may not try to tax a federal entity out of existence. Thus, this Supreme Court case ensured a broad interpretation of congressional powers as well as the supremacy of the national government over the states.

■

Marshall, Ch. J., delivered the opinion of the court.

In the case now to be determined, the defendant, a sovereign state, denies the obligation of a law enacted by the legislature of the Union, and the plaintiff, on his part, contests the validity of an act which has been passed by the legislature of that state. The constitution of our country, in its most interesting and vital parts, is to be considered; the conflicting powers of the government of the Union and of its members, as marked in that constitution, are to be discussed; and an opinion given, which may essentially influence the great operations of the government. No tribunal can approach such a question without a deep sense of its importance, and of the awful responsibility involved in its decision. But it must be decided peacefully, or remain a source of hostile legislation, perhaps, of hostility of a still more serious nature; and if it is to be so decided, by this tribunal alone can the decision be made. On the supreme court of the United States has the constitution of our country devolved this important duty.

The first question made in the cause is—has congress power to incorporate a bank? . . .

This government is acknowledged by all, to be one of enumerated powers. The principle, that it can exercise only the powers granted to it, would seem too apparent, to have required to be enforced by all those arguments, which its enlightened friends, while it was depending before the people, found it necessary to urge; that principle is now universally admitted. But the question respecting the extent of the powers actually granted, is perpetually arising, and will probably continue to arise, so long as our system shall exist. In discussing these questions, the conflicting powers of the general and state governments must be brought into view, and the supremacy of their respective laws, when they are in opposition, must be settled.

If any one proposition could command the universal assent of mankind, we might expect it would be this—that the government of the Union, though limited in its powers, is supreme within its sphere of action. This would seem to result, necessarily, from its nature. It is the government of all; its powers are delegated by all; it represents all, and acts for all. Though any one state may be willing to control its operations, no state is willing to allow others to control them. The nation, on those subjects on which it can act, must necessarily bind its component parts. But this question is not left to mere reason: the people have, in express terms, decided it, by saying, "this constitution, and the laws of the United States, which shall be made in pursuance thereof," "shall be the supreme law of the land," and by requiring that the members of the state legislatures, and the officers of the executive and judicial departments of the states, shall take the oath of fidelity to it. The government of the United States, then, though limited in its powers, is supreme; and its laws, when made in pursuance of the constitution, form the supreme law of the land, "anything in the constitution or laws of any state to the contrary notwithstanding."

Among the enumerated powers, we do not find that of establishing a bank or creating a corporation. But there is no phrase in the instrument which, like the articles of confederation, excludes incidental or implied powers; and which requires that everything granted shall be expressly and minutely described. Even the 10th amendment, which was framed for the purpose of quieting the excessive jealousies which had been excited, omits the word "expressly," and declares only, that the powers "not delegated to the United States, nor prohibited to the states, are reserved to the states or to the people;" thus leaving the question, whether the particular power which may become the subject of contest, has been delegated to the one government, or prohibited to the other, to depend on a fair construction of the whole instrument. The men who drew and adopted this amendment had experienced the embarrassments resulting from the insertion of this word in the articles of confederation, and probably omitted it, to avoid those embarrassments. A constitution, to contain an accurate detail of all the subdivisions of which its great powers will admit, and of all the means by which they may be carried into execution, would partake of the prolixity of a legal code, and could scarcely be embraced by the human mind. It would, probably, never be understood by the public. Its nature, therefore, requires, that only its great outlines should be marked, its important objects designated, and the minor ingredients which compose those objects, be deduced from the nature of the objects themselves. That this idea was entertained by the framers of the American constitution, is not only to be inferred from the nature of the instrument, but from the language. Why else were some of the limitations, found in the 9th section of the 1st article, introduced? It is also, in some degree, warranted, by their having omitted to use any restrictive term which might prevent its receiving a fair and just interpretation. In considering this question, then, we must never forget that it is a *constitution* we are expounding.

Although, among the enumerated powers of government, we do not find the word "bank" or "incorporation," we find the great powers, to lay and collect taxes; to borrow money; to regulate commerce; to declare and conduct a war; and to raise and support armies and navies. The sword and the purse, all the external relations, and no inconsiderable portion of the industry of the nation, are intrusted to its government. It can never be pretended, that these vast powers draw after them others of inferior importance, merely because they are inferior. Such an idea can never be advanced. But it may with great reason be contended, that a government, intrusted with such ample powers, on the due execution of which the happiness and prosperity of the nation so vitally depends, must also be intrusted with ample means for their execution. The power being given, it is the interest of the nation to facilitate its execution. It can never be their interest, and cannot be presumed to have been their intention, to clog and embarrass its execution, by withholding the most appropriate means. Throughout this vast republic, from the St. Croix to the Gulf of Mexico, from the Atlantic to the Pacific, revenue is to be collected and expended, armies are to be marched and supported. The exigencies of the nation may require, that the treasure raised in the north should be transported to the south, that raised in the east, conveyed to the west, or that this order should be reversed. Is that construction of the constitution to be preferred, which would render these operations difficult, hazardous and expensive? Can we adopt that construction (unless the words imperiously require it), which would impute to the framers of that instrument, when granting these powers for the public good, the intention of impeding their exercise, by withholding a choice of means? If, indeed, such be the mandate of the constitution, we have only to obey; but that instrument does not profess to enumerate the means by which the powers it confers may be executed; nor does it prohibit the creation of a corporation, if the existence of such a being be essential, to the beneficial exercise of those powers. It is, then, the subject of fair inquiry, how far such means may be employed. . . .

But the constitution of the United States has not left the right of congress to employ the necessary means, for the execution of the powers conferred on the government, to general reasoning. To its enumeration of powers is added, that of making "all laws which shall be necessary and proper, for carrying into execution the foregoing powers, and all other powers vested by this constitution, in the government of the United States, or in any department thereof." The counsel for the state of Maryland have urged various arguments, to prove that this clause, though, in terms, a grant of power, is not so, in effect; but is really restrictive of the general right, which might otherwise be implied, of selecting means for executing the enumerated powers. In support of this proposition, they have found it necessary to contend, that this clause was inserted for the purpose of conferring on congress the power of making laws. That, without it, doubts might be entertained, whether congress could exercise its powers in the form of legislation.

But could this be the object for which it was inserted? A government is created by the people, having legislative, executive and judicial powers. Its legislative powers are vested in a congress, which is to consist of a senate and house of representatives. Each house may determine the rule of its proceedings; and it is declared, that every bill which shall have passed both houses, shall, before it becomes a law, be presented to the president of the United States. The 7th section describes the course of proceedings, by which a bill shall become a law; and, then, the 8th section enumerates the powers of congress. Could it be necessary to say, that a legislature should exercise legislative powers, in the shape of legislation? After allowing each house to prescribe its own course of proceeding, after describing the manner in which a bill should become a law, would it have entered into the mind of a single member of the convention, that an express power to make laws was necessary, to enable the legislature to make them? That a legislature, endowed with legislative powers, can legislate, is a proposition too self-evident to have been questioned. . . .

After the most deliberate consideration, it is the unanimous and decided opinion of this court, that the act to incorporate the Bank of the United States is a law made in pursuance of the constitution, and is a part of the supreme law of the land.

The branches, proceeding from the same stock, and being conducive to the complete accomplishment of the object, are equally constitutional. It would have been unwise, to locate them in the charter, and it would be unnecessarily inconvenient, to employ the legislative power in making those subordinate arrangements. The great duties of the bank are prescribed; those duties require branches; and the bank itself may, we think, be safely trusted with the selection of places where those branches shall be fixed; reserving always to the government the right to require that a branch shall be located where it may be deemed necessary.

It being the opinion of the court, that the act incorporating the bank is constitutional; and that the power of establishing a branch in the state of Maryland might be properly exercised by the bank itself, we proceed to inquire—

. . . Whether the state of Maryland may, without violating the constitution, tax that branch? That the power of taxation is one of vital importance; that it is retained by the states; that it is not abridged by the grant of a similar power to the government of the Union; that it is to be concurrently exercised by the two governments—are truths which have never been denied. But such is the paramount character of the constitution, that its capacity to withdraw any subject from the action of even this power, is admitted. The states are expressly forbidden to lay any duties on imports or exports, except what may be absolutely necessary for executing their inspection laws. If the obligation of this prohibition must be conceded—if it may restrain a state from the exercise of its taxing power on imports and exports—the same paramount character would seem to restrain, as it certainly may restrain, a state from such other exercise of this power, as is in its nature incompatible with, and repugnant to, the constitutional laws of the Union. A law, absolutely repugnant to another, as entirely repeals that other as if express terms of repeal were used.

On this ground, the counsel for the bank place its claim to be exempted from the power of a state to tax its operations. There is no express provision for the case, but the claim has been sustained on a principle which so entirely pervades the constitution, is so intermixed with the materials which compose it, so interwoven with its web, so blended with its texture, as to be incapable of being separated from it, without rending it into shreds. This great principle is, that the constitution and the laws made in pursuance thereof are supreme; that they control the constitution and laws of the respective states, and cannot be controlled by them. From this, which may be almost termed an axiom, other propositions are deduced as corollaries, on the truth or error of which, and on their application to this case, the cause has been supposed to depend. These are, 1st. That a power to create implies a power to preserve: 2d. That a power to destroy, if wielded by a different hand, is hostile to, and incompatible with these powers to create and to preserve: 3d. That where this repugnancy exists, that authority which is supreme must control, not yield to that over which it is supreme. . . .

If we apply the principle for which the state of Maryland contends, to the constitution, generally, we shall find it capable of changing totally the character of that instrument. We shall find it capable of arresting all the measures of the government, and of prostrating it at the foot of the states. The American people have declared their constitution and the laws made in pursuance thereof, to be supreme; but this principle would transfer the supremacy, in fact, to the states. If the states may tax one instrument, employed by the government in the execution of its powers, they may tax any and every other instrument. They may tax the mail; they may tax the mint; they may tax patent-rights; they may tax the papers of the custom-house; they may tax judicial process; they may tax all the means employed by the government, to an excess which would defeat all the ends of government. This was not intended by the American people. They did not design to make their government dependent on the states.

Gentlemen say, they do not claim the right to extend state taxation to these objects. They limit their pretensions to property. But on what principle, is this distinction made? Those who make it have furnished no reason for it, and the principle for which they contend denies it. They contend, that the power of taxation has no other limit than is found in the 10th section of the 1st article of the constitution; that, with respect to everything else, the power of the states is supreme, and admits of no control. If this be true, the distinction between property and other subjects to which the power of taxation is applicable, is merely arbitrary, and can never be sustained. This is not all. If the controlling power of the states be established; if their supremacy as to taxation be acknowledged; what is to restrain their exercising control in any shape they may please to give it? Their sovereignty is not confined to taxation; that is not the only mode in which it might be displayed. The question is, in truth, a question of supremacy; and if the right of the states to tax the means employed by the general government be conceded, the declaration that the constitution, and the laws made in pursuance thereof, shall be the supreme law of the land, is empty and unmeaning declamation. . . .

The court has bestowed on this subject its most deliberate consideration. The result is a conviction that the states have no power, by taxation or otherwise, to retard, impede, burden, or in any manner control, the operations of the constitutional laws enacted by congress to carry into execution the powers vested in the general government. This is, we think, the unavoidable consequence of that supremacy which the constitution has declared. We are unanimously of opinion, that the law passed by the legislature of Maryland, imposing a tax on the Bank of the United States, is unconstitutional and void.

This opinion does not deprive the states of any resources which they originally possessed. It does not extend to a tax paid by the real property of the bank, in common with the other real property within the state, nor to a tax imposed on the interest which the citizens of Maryland may hold in this institution, in common with other property of the same description throughout the state. But this is a tax on the operations of the bank, and is, consequently, a tax on the operation of an instrument employed by the government of the Union to carry its powers into execution. Such a tax must be unconstitutional.

2.3 Hard Road Ahead: Block Grants and the "Devolution Revolution" (1995)

RICHARD P. NATHAN

INTRODUCTION

When writing in the very midst of major changes in American politics and public policy, even the most astute government analysts can either be at a loss for perspective or make predictions that go awry. But writing a decade ago in the midst of the far-reaching changes to the nation's federal system, Richard P. Nathan got things right. His analysis of "Nixon's New Federalism" and "Reagan's New Federalism," and the "bumpy ride" that would accompany the shift to block grants, proved quite prescient.

■

In this essay, I synthesize reflections and research on block grants. I do so in relation to the contemporary debate in Congress and with due regard for our historical experiences with changes in federal-state relationships. Federalism, a subject considered boring by many, is now a hot topic, and I am both pleased and excited by that. No one who has been as close to these issues for as long as I have can honestly claim to enter the latest federalism fray in a totally disinterested way. But this essay, which I have prepared for the Brookings Center for Public Management, is as frank and balanced as I can make it. It begins with a brief review of certain fundamental facts about federal grants-in-aid. It ends on a cautionary note about what the devolution revolution now in the offing could mean.

Richard P. Nathan, "Hard Road Ahead: Block Grants and the 'Devolution Revolution' " (Discussion paper, Seminar for Journalists at The Brookings Institution, Albany, N.Y., October 27, 1995): 1–17 (excerpts), 24. Reprinted with permission from The Nelson A. Rockefeller Institute of Government, 411 State Street, Albany, NY 12203. www.rockinst.org.

1. BUILDING BLOCKS

Federal grants-in-aid from the federal government to states, localities, and non-profit groups are estimated at $238.5 billion for the fiscal year that began October 1 in President Clinton's FY '96 *Budget* submitted on February 6, 1995. This includes fifteen programs that are classified as block grants by the U.S. General Accounting Office and the U.S. Advisory Commission on Intergovernmental Relations.[1] These grants account for a relatively small share—15 percent—of total federal grant-in-aid spending (see Table 1). Block grants are broad fiscal subventions provided for a major functional area of government and distributed to states and localities on a formula allocation basis. Over half of total outlays for current block grant programs is for surface transportation, converted into flexible aid under the Interstate Surface Transportation Act of 1991.

The striking thing about block grants is that they are likely to make a huge leap upward this year. The new block grants now being considered in the 104th Congress are potentially a bigger deal for U.S. domestic policy than Lyndon Johnson's Great Society. They are a "big deal" because they represent a break with the past fifty years of steady accretion of entitlement-type federal grants-in-aid. Under entitlement programs, states receive payments on an open-ended basis equal to a fixed proportion of the income transfers they make to poor families and individuals. These grants are actually entitlements to states; the states in turn determine the benefits eligible individuals and families receive within the framework of federal laws and regulations. The two biggest grant-in-aid programs of this sort are medicaid and aid for families with dependent children (AFDC). Together they account for half of total federal grant-in-aid spending.

The purpose of medicaid is to provide health care services for the poor, including nursing home and other types of institutional care for the elderly and disabled. The AFDC program provides cash assistance to poor families with children. Under both programs the federal government pays states a share of the benefits provided to eligible families and individuals.

There are two ways to create block grants. One is the conventional way that has been used since the mid-1960s—bundling preexisting categorical grants and consolidating them into a lump sum payment. Some current proposals by leaders in the Congress follow this route. An example is the workforce development block grant, which would consolidate more than ninety employment and training programs into a three-part block grant. A second route for block granting is to convert open-ended grants to the states for income-transfer programs (for example, welfare and medicaid, as mentioned

---

[1]United States General Accounting Office, "Block Grants: Characteristics, Experience, and Lessons Learned," GAO/HEHS-95-74, February 1995. U.S. Advisory Commission on Intergovernmental Relations, "Characteristics of Federal Grant-in-Aid Programs to State and Local Governments: Grants Funded FY 1995," M-195, June 1995.

Table 1
1995 Block Grants

Block Grant	Estimated Expenditure (millions of dollars)
Surface transportation	$ 18,773
Community development	3,186
Social services	2,800
Federal transit capital and operating assistance	2,284
Community Devt. Block Grant states' program	1,346
Low income home and energy assistance program	1,319
Prevention and treatment of substance abuse	1,234
Job Training Partnership Act, Title II-A	1,055
Child care and development	935
Maternal and child health	684
Education (federal-state-local partnerships)	370
Community services	392
Community mental health services	275
Preventative health and health services	152
Assistance for transition from homelessness	29
Total	$ 34,834

Source: Budget of the U.S. Government, Fiscal Year 1996, Budget Information for the States (Washington: GPO, 1995).

above) into a lump sum payment. This involves closing the open end on spending and cutting the projected future growth of these programs, repealing restrictive requirements, and giving greater flexibility to the states. Creating block grants for AFDC and medicaid represents a profound change for both U.S. social policy and American federalism. Also under consideration by leaders in the 104th Congress as functional areas for new block grants are child welfare services, school feeding and other child nutrition programs, foster care and adoption programs, employment and training programs, and food stamps. If new block grants for medicaid, AFDC, workforce development, and welfare-related child care enacted, block grants as a class could account for 64.7 percent of total federal aid, a jump of 52 percentage points over their current share.

There are three main types of federal grants-in-aid: grants for operational purposes (education, child care); grants for capital purposes (surface transportation, wastewater treatment); and entitlement grants for income-transfer to families and individuals (medicaid and AFDC). . . .

Leaders in the Congress also seek to change federal grant-in-aid spending in other ways. They have proposed appreciable reductions in other grants-in-aid, that is, grants that are not currently block grants or recommended to be converted into block grants. It is estimated that this spending will be reduced by as much as 9 percent at the outset and by as much as 30 percent over time.

The 104th Congress is also cutting back on the regulatory requirements of these programs, that is, the conditions Congress has in the past placed on the receipt of federal grant funds. These conditions, often referred to as mandates, can involve requirements that are not intrinsic to the purposes of the provided funds. The mandates issue has created bad blood between national, state and local officials. As part of the "Contract With America," the Congress passed and the president signed a law to discourage future unfunded mandates on states and localities and to scrutinize existing major mandates. In addition, Congress this year has in some cases reduced conditions on some federal grants as part of its devolutionary purpose. In other cases, however, Congress has added or reinforced conditions related to federal grants. On the whole, the push to scrap mandates tied to grants is stronger, but the results are still unclear. . . .

Why a Devolution Revolution in 1995?

What explains this push for bigger block grants in 1995? There are two explanations: governors are demanding more authority; and budget pressures are acute. I do not see any way federal deficit-reduction targets can be met without striking a deal whereby governors get more power in exchange for going along with growth caps on open-ended grants-in-aid for medicaid and welfare. Once you put a growth cap on these programs, you have to give the states greatly added flexibility to meet them. Whether you call this a block grant or not does not matter. The result is programs that look and function like block grants.

The consequences of a devolution revolution in 1995 cannot be predicted, but the changes will be *large*. There may well be a race to the bottom—a turning away from the poor and minorities. Certainly, the financial incentives to run this race will be hard for some states to resist. As detailed in the recent Brookings report on welfare reform, under the new block grant regime, states will lose federal money when they increase benefits and gain it when they cut benefits.[2] At the same time, however, perhaps there will be real innovation on the part of states to create new integrated systems for social services.

2. BLOCK GRANTS—PAST AND PRESENT

During the period when the United States operated under the Articles of Confederation, the Continental Congress adopted the first grants-in-aid to the states—putting aside land for the support of public schools in territory west of the Ohio River.

---

[2]R. Kent Weaver and William T. Dickens, eds., *Looking Before We Leap: Social Science and Welfare Reform* (Brookings Institution, 1995).

However, cash grants-in-aid were not a big a part of the federal budget until the twentieth century. The Woodrow Wilson administration initiated a slow but steady rise in cash grants to the states for major and quite specific purposes that came to be known as *categorical* grants. Forty years ago, after Franklin Roosevelt's New Deal, these grants accounted for 10 percent of total state and local spending. Under President Johnson federal aid jumped to its current level. From the mid-1960s to the present, cash grants have represented 20 percent of total state and local spending. . . .

Block Grants under Johnson

Lyndon Johnson saw the writing on the wall in the form of growing state and local government resistance to the increasingly particularistic character of federal grants-in-aid. During Johnson's presidency the idea of broader and less conditional block grants began to take hold in response to what Walter Heller, chairman of Johnson's Council of Economic Advisors, called "the hardening of the categories."

Responding to pressures from governors and mayors, President Johnson in 1966 proposed that a block grant be created, consolidating several relatively small public health grants into a single comprehensive grant for a range of health services. In 1967, Johnson took a bigger leap into grant blocking (although not enthusiastically) when his administration, with Republican urging, backed the creation of the law enforcement assistance grant. LEAA funds were distributed on a formula basis to states with a requirement that 75 percent of the funds provided be passed on to localities.

The creation of most block grants in the modern era has involved the consolidation of preexisting categorical grants into broader grants allocated to states and localities on the basis of an automatic formula. President Nixon's new federalism successfully advocated the creation of several such block grants, notably for community development, employment and training, and social services. Nixon also won passage of a general revenue sharing program in 1972, which provided flexible aid on a formula basis to states and localities. But this was not called a block grant because the use of this aid was not limited to a particular function of government (such as law enforcement or community development).

Nixon's New Federalism

Federal grants comprise entitlement grants, operating grants, and capital grants. Nixon's new federalism called for blocking operating and capital grants but *not* entitlement grants. Nixon was a spender when it came to grants and domestic policies in general. His revenue sharing program involved distributing $5 billion per year in new funds to states and localities, and his block grants included funds known as "sweeteners." The term referred to extra funds provided on top of the money contained in the categorical grants bundled together in a new block. Nixon added these sweeteners as an inducement to state and local officials to support his initiatives.

Nixon did not, however, recommend blocking entitlement grants. In advocating the sorting out of functions in American federalism, Nixon was explicit. He argued that income transfers (cash, health care, foster care, school lunches, food stamps) should be made *more—not less*—national to ensure equal treatment of the needy and to share this fiscal burden on a national basis.

The three main block grants created under Nixon were for community development, employment and training, and social services. The consensus is that the community development block grant was the most successful of these three, moving away from huge renewal and slum clearance projects to more selective, targeted local development initiatives. Neither Nixon's family assistance plan (FAP) for welfare reform nor his family health insurance plan (FHIP), which was similar to Clinton's 1993 proposal, were enacted.

Reagan's New Federalism

President Reagan's brand of "new federalism" (a term the press used to describe Reagan's program) departed from Nixon's approach to blocking entitlements. Reagan was much less committed to the idea that entitlement-type grants, often referred to as "safety net" functions, should be dominated by or exclusively provided by the national government. In 1982 Reagan advanced a "swap and turn back" plan, which proposed that the national government take over medicaid. In exchange, the states would pick up the full responsibility for AFDC.

Reagan was on the fence intellectually on this federalism issue. He proposed centralizing one income transfer program (medicaid) and devolving another (AFDC). As it turned out, Reagan's swap and turn back plan was not even introduced in the Congress.

In the 1981 Omnibus Budget Reconciliation Act (OBRA), Ronald Reagan won enactment of nine new programs that his administration called block grants. They were, in the spirit of Nixon-era plans, for operating and capital functions, not for entitlement-type programs. Three were in the health field; they concerned mental health and the prevention and treatment of substance abuse, preventive public health services, and maternal and child health care. None of these programs was especially large, and four of the blocks contained only one preexisting categorical grant. In my view, Reagan as a grant blocker was overrated. His administration's new and revised block grants are shown in Table 2.

The block grants of the Reagan and Nixon administrations have one important point in common. Nine block grants were created in 1981 as part of the Reagan-Stockman new federalism. They fall into two categories:

- *Little if any increase.* Five block grants have decreased or remained about the same in terms of spending—those for social services, low-income en-

Table 2
Block Grants Enacted or Changed in 1981

Block Grant	Number of Programs Consolidated	Final Federal Fiscal Year 1982 Budget Authority (millions of dollars)
Social services	3	2,400
Low-income energy assistance	1	1,875
Small city community development	1	1,037
Elementary and secondary education	29	470
Alcohol, drug abuse, and mental health	3	432
Maternal and child health	7	348
Community services	1	348
Primary health care	1	248
Preventive health and health services	8	82
Total	**54**	**7,240**

Source: John W. Ellwood, ed., *Reductions in U.S. Domestic Spending* (New Brunswick, N.J.: Transaction Books, 1982), p. 341.

ergy assistance, community services, education (chapter 2), and the Job Training Partnership Act. (JPTA had a large increase in 1984 and no growth thereafter.) Since inflation was 44 percent between 1983 and 1984, the real size of these grants fell sharply.

- *Sporadic growth.* The other four block grants went through extended periods of little if any growth but had increased funding in the 1990s. The prevention/treatment of substance abuse block grant had a big funding increase from 1989 to 1991 but little growth otherwise. The preventive health and human services block grant did not start to grow rapidly until 1992. The maternal and child health block grant did not start to increase until 1987. The community development block grant did not significantly exceed its 1983 level until 1993.

Overall, these grants have *lost value,* both in nominal dollars and in real terms, that is, adjusted for inflation (as shown in Table 3). The cuts in real terms range from 53 percent for low-income energy assistance to 4 percent for the popular maternal and child health block grant. Funding for substance abuse rose by 64 percent and for preventive public health services by 17 percent.

The New(t) Federalism

Enter the new House Republican majority in 1995, decidedly *not* on the fence intellectually about block grants for welfare-type grant-in-aid programs. Early in the "100 Days," Speaker Gingrich and his House Republican colleagues set

Table 3

Reagan Block Grant Obligations, 1983–1993
Millions of dollars

	1983	1984	1985	1986	1987	1988	1989	1990	1991	1992	1993
Social services	2675	2700	2725	2584	2697	2700	2700	2762	2804	2800	2800
Low-income energy assistance	1975	2075	2100	2008	1822	1532	1383	1443	1610	1500	1346
Community services	373	348	368	352	368	363	319	322	436	360	372
Prevention/treatment of stubstance abuse[1]	468	462	490	469	509	487	806	1193	1269	1080	1108
Preventive health and human services	85	87	89	87	89	85	84	83	91	129	143
Maternal and child health	478	399	478	457	497	526	554	554	587	650	664
Chapter 2 (education)	462	451	500	477	501	478	400	519	449	446	440
Community development[2]	2380	2380	2388	2053	2059	1973	2053	1972	2203	2397	2790
Job training and partnership act[3]	1415	1886	1886	1783	1840	1809	1788	1745	1778	1773	1692

[1]. The prevention/treatment of substance abuse block grant included mental health until FY 1992.
[2]. Community development block grant data do not include undistributed allocations, or spending on the nonentitlement portion of the block grant.
[3]. The JPTA block grant is for the adult and youth training block grant portion of the JPTA program.

Source: Rockefeller Institute of Government, Center for the Study of the States, *State Fiscal Brief*, January 1995, No. 26.

about creating block grants for entitlement grant programs with a vengeance. *This is a distinction worth noting.* In effect, the new Republican majority in the Congress favors repealing the national safety net aspect of grants that provide aid (in cash and in kind) to poor families and individuals on an open-ended basis.

These devolutionary policies of the new majority in Congress do not stand alone. They are part of the strong conservative movement in the country toward limiting government, which is being played out in virtually every committee in Congress. Some see the new devolution as a tactic (even a cover) for shrinking government. This does not gainsay the point that the new devolution is distinctive historically and likely to cause powerful shifts in the balance of federalism.

The Politics of Printouts

One of the knottiest issues in converting entitlement grants to block grants is how to distribute funds to the states. Under the current system, the federal aid each state receives is determined by how much it asks for. States set benefit levels and determine who is eligible for aid. They then pay some percentage of the cost for each eligible case and bill Uncle Sam for the rest. The federal matching rate varies according to state per capita income, ranging from a ceiling of 80 percent to a floor of 50 percent, with thirteen states now at the 50 percent floor. Once the federal government closes the open end for the medicaid and AFDC programs, thereby giving each state a fixed amount of money each year, the obvious hot debate will be over what distribution formula should be used.

Formula writing is essentially political, reflecting different values. Before computers became widely available, distribution formulas were back-room decisions. Only a few gnarled veterans on congressional committee staffs knew who won and who lost. But in the electronic age, no self-respecting lawmaker would vote on a formula issue without having a printout showing the effect on every jurisdiction (state, city, county, school district) eligible to receive money under a grant-in-aid program.

Printouts have imparted several lessons about formula writing. One is that an old formula is a good formula. Formula changes that cause the least disruption to the status quo are those most likely to survive the political bargaining process. A second lesson is that formula options have to be tested, often in multiple iterations, to get the wrinkles out and develop a program that is both effective and politically feasible. A third lesson is that formulas should be simple—or at least they should sound simple so they can be explained and justified.

With this as background, we can consider the special case of closing the end on entitlement-type federal grant-in-aid programs like medicaid and AFDC. In both cases, if Congress just blocked the formula that is in place (give each state its current percentage share) high-user states would benefit most and states that expect population growth in future years might be the biggest losers. In the Senate, this issue became contentious for AFDC. Senator Kay Bailey Hutchinson (R-TX) and twenty-nine colleagues signed a letter complaining that high-growth states were getting short shrift in the planning for a welfare block grant formula that was based on current state allocations. As a result, the proposed formula was changed to include a supplemental fund that would be allocated to states with above-average population growth.

For medicaid, the issue appeared to be even more intractable because of the wide variations in state spending for the program—from $520 per recipient in Arizona to $5,975 in New York. Liberals advocated a "per-recipient" cap (although I find this approach incompatible with the goal of reducing federal spending on medicaid through block granting). Other proposed approaches for allocating medicaid block-grant funds mirror the compromises made in the AFDC debates.

Essential Questions

The essential questions raised by converting open-ended entitlement grants to block grants involve *basic program purposes*. Take the case of AFDC. Welfare today is hotly debated in ways that suggest that it is viewed by the public and most politicians as more than a check-writing (or pure income-transfer) program. Unlike the case of social security retirement benefits, for example, there has been an escalation of the rhetoric about transforming welfare policies from payment systems into service systems. The welfare debates of the past ten years have been mainly about social service interventions to change the behavior of welfare recipients. For example, this was the aim of the Family Support Act of 1988. Unlike that of the 1970s, the current welfare debate is not about minimum payment levels, benefit disregards, and marginal reduction rates. To a high degree, the debates today are about how to prevent children from being born out of wedlock to women—often very young women—and to fathers who are not willing to take responsibility for children in a traditional family setting. These debates have focused on social services that can prevent dependency on the part of poor parents through behavior-changing incentives and requirements and through the provision of job placement and counseling services, training, education, and child care.

Whether this social service/behavior modification function should be assigned primarily to the federal government or to the states is not an easy question to answer. Generally speaking, the literature on federalism suggests that income-transfer functions should be centralized, whereas social service functions should be decentralized. The point is often made that services (such as education, job training, child care) are not activities that can be orchestrated or managed by the central government in a nation as vast as ours. One benefit of federalism is that it allows for flexible state and local action to assess and deal with social service needs in ways that reflect different community conditions, attitudes, and aspirations. One can object to this argument in practice, but the main body of writing on federalism has treated decentralized social service provision as an advantage of our federal structure.

Other measures proposed by the 104th Congress concerned conversion of other entitlement-type programs—for example, foster care, school nutrition and welfare-related child care—into block grants; conversion of food stamps, now federal vouchers, into a block grant; creation of block grants through the consolidation of categorical grants (as in the case of workforce development, which combines nearly 90 existing programs into a three-part block grant); reduction of discretionary federal grant-in-aid programs by close to 10 percent this year; reduction of total projected federal aid by as much as 30 percent over seven years; and enhancement of state flexibility through the reduction of regulatory conditions attached to the receipt of federal grant-in-aid funds.

Taken together, this concerted push to decentralize presents a huge challenge to the states. The Center for Public Management, the Rockefeller Institute of Government, and the Taubman Center at Brown University are planning a longitudinal field network study of the new devolutionary changes in domestic policy. The study will broadly examine the effects of the devolution revolution on public finance, institutional structures, state and local politics and relationships, and social policies. In addition to the field data for a sample of ten state governments, national data will be collected.

Although it is not the aim of this paper to make an argument for a particular realignment of functions in American federalism, I want to make one point clear: *There is no magic formula for sorting out the functions of federalism.* Values and purposes change. In the 1970s, many viewed welfare and health care for the poor as income-transfer functions, indicating that they should be provided by the federal government. This is not the case today, however. There is no right or wrong answer to the basic questions posed by the devolution revolution of 1995.

Federalism and the Safety Net

James Madison is mischaracterized by conservatives who attribute to him the idea of devolving national programs to the states. Madison's constitutional purpose in 1787 was nation building and centralization. Indeed, his opening gambit at the Constitutional Convention was a plan that would have given the national government an absolute veto power over state laws. By the same token, classic public finance theory in the modern period assigns redistributional functions to the broadest population group to achieve equal (or close to equal) treatment for the needy and to share this fiscal burden widely. As a nation, we have done this—or at least moved in this direction strongly—since the 1930s. The United States is by no means first among the industrial democracies in centrally providing this safety-net function. But Americans have spent the past six decades building alliances, striking bargains, and forging political compromises that give the $1.6 trillion-per-year federal government a leading role in setting, administering, and financing a wide range of social policies. Nowhere has this process been more inexorable than in the steady increase in the federal role in social welfare policy. Thus block-granting income-transfer programs to the poor *represents a basic change in direction both for American federalism and for social policy.*

American federalism *is* a great experiment in historical terms. K. C. Wheare, a British political scientist and authority on federal systems of government, said that the American framers invented modern federalism in the sense that the citizen is a citizen of *both* the nation and the state, unlike the confederal form, where the states, in effect, are members of a league or club.[3] This is what Madison meant by his reference in *The Federalist Papers* (No. 39) to "the great composition," a system of government "that is neither wholly national, nor wholly federal." Madison in Philadelphia, along with his friend, Alexander Hamilton, wanted to centralize power. Appropriately, Madison and Hamilton used Madison Avenue techniques in writing *The Federalist Papers* to reassure the ratifying electorate of New York (which Library of Congress historian James Hudson called "the people out of doors,") that the states would still be very prominent. Madison the politician (never as good at that as Madison the political scientist) later shifted his ground on the very federalism bargain he crafted. But the original design was a centralizing design.[4]

Experts have argued since the founding that the clear trend has been to centralize, citing the Civil War, the New Deal, the strong role of the courts, and the advance of technology and economic interdependence as forces that fueled this centralization. Now there is a big push to decentralize and strengthen the role of the states. This is not out of character for Republicans or for conservatives generally. It is, however, distinctive in that the push to do so this year is much stronger than it has been at any time in the twentieth century.

Emerging Forces
While the picture is still unclear, devolutionary trophies for the nation's Republican governors, now thirty-strong, are likely. Only two of the ten most populous states (Florida and North Carolina) have Democratic governors. Governors John Engler of Michigan, Tommy G. Thompson of Wisconsin, and Jim Edgar of Illinois have led the charge for increased state power and deserve the greatest credit or blame—choose your descriptor—for the 1995-style New(t) federalism.

Beltway insiders can think of the great federalism debate of 1995 as one between the forces of Engler and the forces of Greenstein. Governor Engler, aided by an able staff, has been the strongest intellectual leader among politi-

---

[3]Richard P. Nathan, "The Role of the States in American Federalism," *The State of the States* (Washington, D.C.: Congressional Quarterly, 1992). Madison later shifted his ground in writing the Kentucky Resolution of 1798.

[4]Robert A. Goldwin and William A. Schambra, eds., *How Federal Is the Constitution?* (Washington, D.C.: American Enterprise Institute, 1987).

cians pushing the block grant strategy. From the outset, the Engler approach has been to abolish national entitlements, not raise Pandora's box formula issues, and remove state funding requirements. This approach clashed with that of liberals like Robert Greenstein of the Center on Budget and Policy Priorities. Greenstein and company have advanced proposals to meet the budget-reduction targets, but on a basis that preserves the entitlement status of existing programs (especially medicaid), retains state financing, and stirs up (and seeks to change policies on) formula distribution issues. Relatively few Democratic politicians have gone to the barricades on this issue. Senator Moynihan comes closest to a spokesperson against grant blocking and for keeping the open-ended character of safety net grant-in-aid programs. President Clinton's position on this issue can be described as muted and uncertain.

It is interesting to compare Nixon's, Reagan's, and Gingrich's brands of new federalism. Nixon, as noted, proposed increasing grant-in-aid spending on a basis that enhanced state flexibility—a "help 'em and bribe 'em" strategy grounded in revenue sharing and block grants to the states for operating and capital (but *not* entitlement) purposes. Reagan took a trade-off approach: We will give the states less money in exchange for more flexibility, while at the same time preserving a national safety net for the poor. Speaker Gingrich [went] further: less money, lots more state discretion, and devolution of the national safety net. . . .

4. CONCLUDING COMMENTS

I have tried in this paper to keep the focus on block grants and to avoid taking sides. On the one hand, there is ammunition to support critics who fear social program cuts and problems for the poor as a result of this shift, sometimes called a "shift and shaft" policy. On the other hand, there are likely to be large opportunities for state governments to reform and integrate delivery systems for domestic programs, in the process strengthening the ties people have to their state and local communities. The metaphor of converting problems into opportunities is as good as any to represent this choice. In truth, we do not know what effects will predominate and how they will play out. We can be pretty sure that state reactions will be *different;* they always have been. But beyond that it would be misleading to say with certainty what will happen if big block-grant changes are made, as seems likely.

In a larger context, one can portray this shift to the states as a reflection of the kinds of restructuring changes (including downsizing) that have occupied the corporate sector in recent years. Many observers see these institutional changes in the private sector as a function of growing international competitive pressures. It is not too big a stretch to apply the same point to the public sector. In the competitive global village, national economies are more connected; lower costs attract jobs and capital, and higher costs repel them.

Perhaps this phenomenon is the extension of international competitive pressure to the public sector. Our hyperpluralistic, wide-access political system always makes such adjustments difficult. It would be hard—I think wrong—to anticipate a smooth and graceful adjustment to these economic externalities in the whirling world of American government. *We are in for a bumpy ride.*

2.4 Keeping the Compound Republic: How Many Communities? (2001)

MARTHA DERTHICK

INTRODUCTION

No one has a keener grasp of how federalism has changed in the United States since the Constitution was ratified than Martha Derthick. Yet, for all the changes, she stresses that at each and every stage of federalism's evolution, certain fundamental questions have been asked, debated, and—in the 1860s, at least—literally warred over. The paramount question, as she captures it, has been "about how many communities to be." Americans' "original choices" favored localism, but American federalism "has steadily grown more centralized."

■

Everyone who knows anything about American government knows that it is federal. Asked what that means, most people say that functions are divided between one national government and many state governments. Politically sophisticated persons may add that the governments are constituted independently of one another. Their respective functions are constitutionally defined and thus cannot be altered by ordinary legislation.

This is, however, not the only and arguably not the most interesting way to conceive of federalism. In this essay I will borrow an idea from the late Martin Diamond and speak of federalism as an arrangement that is chosen by people who are unable to decide whether to be one community or many. To do justice to Diamond's subtlety, he put the point as follows:

> The distinguishing characteristic of federalism is the peculiar ambivalence of the ends men seek to make it serve. The ambivalence is quite literal: Federalism is al-

---

This essay first appeared as "How Many Communities? The Evolution of American Federalism," in Martha Derthick, ed., *Dilemmas of Scale in America's Federal Democracy* (Cambridge University Press, 1999), pp. 125–53.

Martha Derthick, "How Many Communities?" in *Keeping the Compound Republic: Essays on American Federalism* (Washington, D.C.: Brookings Institution, 2001), 9–24, 26–32 (excerpts). Copyright © 2001 Brookings Institution. Reprinted with permission.

ways an arrangement pointed in two contrary directions or aimed at securing two contrary ends. One end is always found in the reason why the member units do not simply consolidate themselves into one large unitary country; the other end is always found in the reason why the member units do not choose to remain simply small, wholly autonomous countries. The natural tendency of any political community, whether large or small, is to completeness, to the perfection of its autonomy. Federalism is the effort deliberately to modify that tendency. Hence any given federal structure is always the institutional expression of the contradiction or tension between the particular reasons the member units have for remaining small and autonomous but not wholly, and large and consolidated but not quite.[1]

Federalism involves, then, a choice about how many communities to be, which is not merely a matter of legal arrangements but one of the most fundamental of political questions. I am assuming that "communities" take the form of "polities." Polities have institutions through which people define the objectives of their collective life, whether through deliberation—the democratic ideal—or through a struggle among power holders, which is always in greater or lesser degree the reality. Polities make and enforce laws, raise taxes, and provide public goods and services.

I will argue that Americans chose originally—in the late eighteenth and early nineteenth centuries—to be both one great nation and many relatively quite small, local communities. Beginning with the states as a base, the core polities of their federation, Americans moved paradoxically both to centralize and decentralize. They opted for nationalism *and* localism.

For some time, national and local political development progressed simultaneously, without serious tension (even if national development was challenging the states). Indeed, the most eminent social commentators on the United States, from Tocqueville to David Potter, have argued that local mores helped to sustain national patriotism: in the nineteenth century, the two were mutually reinforcing.[2]

Eventually, however, tension was bound to develop. In the Progressive and New Deal Eras, and then more purposefully during the rights revolution of the 1950s and 1960s, national power was deliberately employed to reduce the place of the local polity in American life. In pursuing the choice to be one great nation, Americans steadily abandoned their historic localism—but not without reluctance and regret.

---

[1]Martin Diamond, "The Ends of Federalism," in William A. Schambra, ed., *As Far as Republican Principles Will Admit: Essays by Martin Diamond* (Washington: American Enterprise Institute, 1992), p. 145.

[2]Alexis de Tocqueville, *Democracy in America*, ed. J. P. Mayer (Anchor Books, 1969); and David M. Potter, "Social Cohesion and the Crisis of Law," in Lawrence M. Friedman and Harry N. Scheiber, eds., *American Law and the Constitutional Order: Historical Perspectives* (Harvard University Press, 1978), pp. 420–34.

ORIGINAL CHOICES

Americans' choice to be one great nation must be one of the best documented political decisions ever made. It is manifest principally in two events: the framing and ratification of the Constitution in 1787–89 and the Civil War, with associated constitutional amendments, in 1861–68. . . .

But if states were in principle the core polities, they did not for long enjoy as such the confidence of the people. Constitutional revisions occurring periodically in the nineteenth and early twentieth centuries curbed the powers of their legislatures and limited the frequency and duration of legislative sessions.[3] As of the mid-1930s, only five state legislatures met annually. All the rest met biennially except for that of Alabama, which met quadrennially.[4] While local governments enjoyed no legal independence, and in the case of big cities were frequently the object of intervention, they nonetheless benefited from these restrictions and the state governments' lethargy. They became the residual domestic governments of the American federal system. "Our local areas are not *governed*," Woodrow Wilson wrote in the late nineteenth century. "They act for themselves. . . . The large freedom of action and broad scope of function given to local authorities is the distinguishing characteristic of the American system of government."[5] County and municipal debt, at $800 million in 1880, was three and a half times the size of the states' debt.[6] . . .

Hand in hand with their becoming more democratic, counties also became much more numerous. The increase, between the time of the Revolution and the early twentieth century, was from 12 to 61 in New York, 12 to 67 in Pennsylvania, 34 to 97 in North Carolina, and 8 to 146 in Georgia. Americans had come to treat counties as institutions of local self-government, entitled as such to representation in state legislatures, rather than as administrative subdivisions of the state, serving the convenience of state governments.[7]

Over time, local governments and their electorates gained more power to tax, a third crucial element of the formal founding of local self-government. At least in New York, early municipal charters, following the precedents of

---

[3]On the elaboration of state constitutions as "the people's law," see Herbert Croly, *Progressive Democracy* (Macmillan, 1914), chap. 12, esp. p. 260.

[4]William Seal Carpenter and Paul Tutt Stafford, *State and Local Government in the United States* (F. S. Crofts, 1936), pp. 41–43.

[5]Woodrow Wilson, *The State,* rev. ed. (D. C. Heath, 1898), pp. 501, 506. Generally on the restriction of the powers of state legislatures, see Arthur N. Holcombe, *State Government in the United States* (Macmillan, 1926), chap. 5; and Howard Lee McBain, *The Law and Practice of Municipal Home Rule* (Columbia University Press, 1916).

[6]*American Almanac and Treasury of Facts, Statistical, Financial, and Political, for the Year 1886* (American News Company, 1886), p. 305.

[7]Alfred Zantzinger Reed, *The Territorial Basis of Government under the State Constitutions* (Columbia University, Studies in History, Economics, and Public Law, 1911), vol. 40, no. 3, p. 237.

English borough charters, did not confer on municipal corporations the power of taxation. When the colonial legislature authorized the cities to levy taxes, those authorizations were at first only for limited amounts necessary for specific purposes, and the tax laws had to be reenacted from year to year. Early in the nineteenth century, however, these special laws gave way to general authorizations, and new city charters allowed municipal corporations to levy taxes.[8] Having been lodged in local governments, decisions about taxing, spending, and borrowing then became susceptible to further decentralization to local electorates. State legislatures that had been made subject to constitutional limits on taxing and borrowing sometimes reacted by prescribing local referenda to check the powers of local governments.[9] Eventually it became common for state constitutions to limit the amount of tax that could be levied by local governments without popular approval in a referendum.

Resting on such foundations, local governments became for most Americans most of the time the most important domestic governments. As the twentieth century began, they administered and overwhelmingly financed schools, which as agents of socialization were the most important domestic public institutions. They predominated in the administration and finance of poor relief. They administered and overwhelmingly financed road construction. They financed and were responsible for police protection. They were raising more revenue and doing more spending than the federal and state governments combined. The bedrock of American domestic government was local.

To be sure, state governments retained a larger role than simple figures on revenue and expenditure might seem to indicate. Their courts created the framework of law within which American capitalism developed, family relations were structured, and the holding and transfer of real property took place. Their legislatures had promoted and subsidized economic development with measures for the construction of roads, canals, and reclamation works. They created penitentiaries, almshouses, orphan asylums, and reformatories in the early nineteenth century, in what one scholar has called "the discovery of the asylum."[10] Local governments were legally their creatures, and what local governments did was done under the authorization or command of state law. This gave local powers a contingent character. Whatever state constitutional conventions and legislatures gave, they could withdraw. On the other hand, the states' supervision of local governments' activity was initially minimal. As late as 1890, the median size of state departments of education was two

---

[8]John A. Fairlie, *The Centralization of Administration in New York State* (Columbia University Press, 1989; New York: AMS Press, 1969), p. 186.

[9]Holcombe, *State Government*, p. 134.

[10]David J. Rothman, *The Discovery of the Asylum: Social Order and Disorder in the New Republic* (Little, Brown, 1971).

persons, including the state superintendent.[11] Moreover, even where state governments had been most active—in regard to economic development—they tended over the course of the nineteenth century to become less so.[12]

In sum, the American choice—insofar as choice was made consciously through the medium of government—was for one large political community and many small ones.

THE EROSION OF LOCALISM

The bedrock of local government was deeper and firmer than the preceding discussion implies, because it was constituted of custom as well as consciously decentralizing choices. The bedrock functions—roads, poor relief, police, schools—developed at the local level originally. Before they were carried out by local governments, they were provided privately or not at all.

Although state laws mandating such functions were often filled with exhortation and command early in the nineteenth century, state governments lacked organizations and practical means with which to supervise local governments and enforce instructions. Thus Massachusetts law in the late 1820s prescribed in considerable detail the duty of towns to support schools, specifying the subjects to be taught, the number of teachers per household, the qualifications of teachers, and the moral content of instruction (they should teach "the principles of piety, justice, and a sacred regard to truth, love to their country, humanity and universal benevolence, sobriety, industry and frugality, chastity, moderation and temperance, and those other virtues which are the ornament of human society, and the basis upon which the republican Constitution is structured"). Towns were obliged to create school committees, which were enjoined to visit the schools and to report to the secretary of the commonwealth information about how many schools they maintained and what they spent. He was to furnish them with a blank form on which to report these returns.[13] That appears to have been the extent of state supervision.

As urbanization progressed later in the century, the states of the Northeast—Massachusetts and New York especially—began creating agencies with powers at least of information gathering and advice and sometimes more for-

---

[11]Michael W. Kirst, *Who Controls Our Schools? American Values in Conflict* (Stanford Alumni Association, 1984), p. 27.

[12]In a monograph on political development in New York between 1800 and 1860, L. Ray Gunn writes that beginning about 1840, public involvement in the economy began to contract. Mercantilist regulations disappeared from the statute books. Gunn also documents the shift of power from state to local governing institutions, arguing that delegation of authority to local governments invigorated them, county boards of supervisors especially. L. Ray Gunn, *The Decline of Authority: Public Economic Policy and Political Development in New York State, 1800–1860* (Cornell University Press, 1988), pp. 1, 199–200.

[13]*Town Officer: Or, Laws of Massachusetts Relative to the Duties of Municipal Officers*, 2d ed. (Worcester, Mass.: Dorr and Howland, 1829), pp. 177–85.

mal oversight. The professions were beginning to develop and find a toehold in state governments. The new agencies could take the form of individual offices or multimember boards of varying sizes, such as state commissioners or superintendents of instruction, boards of charities, or boards of public health. States to the west then followed the lead of Massachusetts and New York.[14]

One turn-of-the-century sign of the states' growing role was a change in spending ratios. Whereas local governments spent fourteen times as much on education as the states did in 1902 and forty-three times as much on roads, by 1913 these ratios had fallen to 9 to 1 and 15 to 1, respectively. State-level centralization proceeded, however, in halting fashion, affecting states and functions unevenly and not very deeply. State-level administrative centralization became penetrating and widespread only when national action caused it to.

In intergovernmental relations, national action during the Progressive Era took the form principally of grants-in-aid with conditions attached. The conditions suited both the administrative convenience of the federal government and the ideology of Progressive reform, one strand of which was marked by the pursuit of efficiency and expertise. Two bedrock functions in particular were affected: roads, for which federal aid began in 1916, following introduction of the automobile, and poor relief, for which federal aid was enacted in 1935, in response to the Great Depression.

Grant-in-aid conditions were above all delocalizing, quite deliberately so. The county, one eminent professional social worker declared, was the "dark continent" of American public administration.[15] State governments were to be prodded and helped in a modernizing, civilizing mission. They were required to match federal grants with state funds, secure statewide uniformity in program operations, create agencies that would be responsible to the federal administration for meeting statewide standards, and create merit systems of personnel administration. . . .

Similarly, when federal grants for public assistance were enacted in 1935, local responsibility for that function was still entrenched. Although most states had enacted laws for aid to mothers and the aged, these were not necessarily backed with state funds, and they were not always mandatory for local governments. Only half of the counties in the country that were authorized to give mothers' aid were actually doing so as of 1934. In only ten states were old age assistance laws in effect statewide. Administrative structures were likewise varied and haphazard, for state welfare agencies had developed unevenly.

---

[14]This development is documented in a series of studies done at Columbia University at the turn of the century: Fairlie, *Centralization of Administration;* Robert H. Whitten, *Public Administration in Massachusetts: The Relation of Central to Local Activity* (1898); Samuel P. Orth, *The Centralization of Administration in Ohio* (1903); Harold Martin Bowman, *The Administration of Iowa: A Study in Centralization* (1903); and William A. Rawles, *Centralizing Tendencies in the Administration of Indiana* (1903). All appeared in the series *Studies in History, Economics and Public Law,* edited by the political science faculty at Columbia, and were reprinted by AMS Press (New York) in 1968 and 1969.

[15]Cited in Martha Derthick, *The Influence of Federal Grants: Public Assistance in Massachusetts* (Harvard University Press, 1970), p. 20.

Responsibility for administration rested predominantly at the county level, with boards of commissioners or judges. Only twelve states had set up county welfare agencies.[16]

The Social Security Act required state financial participation and mandatory statewide operation, which the Social Security Board, as the federal administering agency, chose to interpret as a requirement of statewide uniformity. Beginning in 1946, it successfully pressured states to establish statewide standards of need and assistance, such that benefits would no longer vary among local places.[17] The ratio of local to state spending for assistance, which had been 5 to 1 in 1932, dropped to 1.3 to 1 in 1942. By 1952 state spending surpassed local spending.

The federal requirement that a single state agency administer assistance or supervise administration of it contributed to the formation and strengthening of state welfare departments. Federal law also fostered the professionalization of welfare agencies after amendments to the Social Security Act in 1939 authorized the Social Security Board to require the establishment of merit systems. As attachments of welfare workers to a profession grew with federal encouragement, attachments to place weakened: professionalization meant delocalization.

While merit system requirements did not extend to all federally aided agencies, a companion measure—the prohibition of partisan activity by state and local employees—did. This was enacted in 1940 as an amendment to the Hatch Act and upheld by the Supreme Court in *Oklahoma* v. *Civil Service Commission* (1947), a case involving the federal government's decision to withhold highway grant funds in order to secure removal of a state highway commissioner who was also chairman of the state Democratic Party. Breaking the ties of state and local employees to state and local parties was crucial to the Progressive Era project of rationalizing state and local administrative structures and making them responsive to national leadership.[18]

Scholarship on the New Deal has generally stressed the extent to which it honored the traditional prerogatives of the states, accommodating to the institutions of American federalism.[19] It is true that few purely national agencies were created, and those that were created often found that the price of

---

[16]*Social Security in America* (Washington: Social Security Board, 1937), chaps. 8, 13, 14, 19.

[17]Derthick, *Influence of Federal Grants*, pp. 72–73.

[18]For a detailed account of the federal effort in one state's welfare program, see ibid., esp. chaps. 5, 7. For a summary of the federal impact on state and local personnel systems generally, see Albert H. Aronson, "State and Local Personnel Administration," in U.S. Civil Service Commission, *Biography of an Ideal: A History of the Federal Civil Service* (Washington: n.d. [1973?]), pp. 127–59. When the Social Security Act was passed, only nine states had civil service systems. Federal requirements and advice contributed to their extension within and among the states. *Oklahoma* v. *Civil Service Commission* appears at 330 U.S. 127 (1947).

[19]For example, Philip Selznick, *TVA and the Grass Roots: A Study in the Sociology of Formal Organizations* (Harper and Row, 1966).

acceptance, if not survival, was to make adjustments at the grass roots. However, this interpretation overlooks the recasting that federal action achieved in state-local relations. Eroding slowly and steadily in any case, the bedrock of localism eroded much faster when federal grant programs came to bear.

Still, as the Progressive and New Deal Eras came to an end with World War II, much of the bedrock had barely been affected. Nothing that occurred before midcentury diminished the localism of police departments or, crucially, of schools. Neither function had been the beneficiary (or victim) of federal aid. The ratio of local to state spending for education, though tending to fall throughout the century, was 5 to 1 in 1942, at a time when state spending on roads had passed local spending. In one important respect the bedrock had actually been augmented. As urbanization progressed, state legislatures authorized zoning and land-use regulation, which became local functions. As such, they had considerable potential for defining the character of the local place, and hence sustaining a sense of community.

THE RIGHTS REVOLUTION

In the first half of the twentieth century, the national government's direct challenge to localism had been relatively confined. It concentrated on administrative structures in functions where grants-in-aid gave the federal government an entree and a stake. Also, it was spearheaded by professional administrators, and while they benefited from the strength of centralizing coalitions in regard to road construction and poor relief, their independent power was modest. Congress did not always give them the statutory authority that they sought for state-level reforms.

The rights revolution in the 1960s brought an attack of greater scope, depth, and legitimacy, officially led as it was by the nation's highest court. It also had far greater mobilizing power. As political goals, efficiency and expertise did not excite large numbers of people. Equality excited many more. Besides, egalitarianism is the greater enemy of federalism. It exalts the autonomous individual, whereas federalism, in honoring communities, implies acceptance of distinctions among and even within them. When the Warren court met the bedrock of localism, an epic contest occurred. . . .

The most fundamental of the Court's challenges to localism were its reapportionment decisions. These were the decisions of which Justice Earl Warren himself was most proud and the Court's critics most critical. "There is no better example of the Court's egalitarianism," Robert Bork observed, and "its disregard for the Constitution in whose name it spoke than the legislative reapportionment cases."[20]

---

[20]Robert Bork, *The Tempting of America: The Political Seduction of the Law* (Free Press, 1990), p. 84. On Warren's estimate of the importance of reapportionment, see Archibald Cox, *The Court and the Constitution* (Houghton Mifflin, 1987), p. 290.

The challenge to localism was twofold. It lay first in the Court's rejection of the local polity as an entity meriting representation in the state legislature and second in its indifference to claims that the people of the states were entitled to devise their own representative arrangements. The Court laid down a doctrinaire rule—one person, one (equally weighted) vote—for which there was no warrant in custom or the Constitution. In a dissent in *Baker* v. *Carr*, the Court's first step down this path, Justice Felix Frankfurter protested that this "was not the colonial system, it was not the system chosen for the national government by the Constitution, it was not the system exclusively or even predominantly practiced by the States at the time of adoption of the Fourteenth Amendment, it is not predominantly practiced by the States today."[21] . . .

It was not just what the Court did in these cases, but the grounds on which it chose to do it, that showed disdain for federalism and locality. That malapportionment was severe enough in some states to warrant a federal judicial remedy is conceded even by some of the Court's critics. But whereas the Court grounded its holding on the equal protection clause—equal numbers of people must have an equal number of legislative representatives—it might have supplied a remedy and honored federalism nonetheless by relying instead on the clause that guarantees each state a republican form of government. This dead letter, ignored since the mid-nineteenth century, might have been given life and logically applied to cases in which the state legislatures' failure to enact reapportionments violated their own state constitutions and thwarted government by majorities.[22] Such an approach would have been less likely to culminate in the Court's prescribing a "sixth-grade arithmetic" rule as a straitjacket on the states.[23]

In the wake of the reapportionment decisions, social entities defined by space—local communities—are often sacrificed. Legislative districting has been turned into an arcane exercise for computers, consultants, and constitutional lawyers, along with the usual array of incumbents trying to save their seats or party politicians trying to protect or gain majorities. District lines now cut arbitrarily through local places that once would have been respected as such and represented intact. . . .

In regard to schools, the Court laid down its constitutional principle in "*Brown* v. *Board of Education* in 1954—"separate educational facilities are "inherently unequal"—and then, in a rare burst of practicality, acknowledged a year later in *Brown II* that full implementation "may require solution of varied local school problems." School authorities had primary responsibility for

---

[21]369 U.S. 186, 301 (1962).

[22]This argument is made by Bork, *Tempting of America*, pp. 85–86.

[23]The phrase was used by Justices Clark and Stewart in dissent in the *Lucas* (Colorado) case, objecting to the majority's "uncritical, simplistic, and heavy-handed application of sixth-grade arithmetic."

solving these problems. Courts would have to consider whether their implementation was sufficient. Because of "their proximity to local conditions," district courts would bear this burden primarily. The Supreme Court said that in fashioning their decrees, lower courts should be guided by the principles of equity, a specialized legal term meaning that they would have a great deal of freedom. The lower courts might consider "problems related to administration, arising from the physical condition of the school plant, the school transportation system, personnel, revision of school districts and attendance areas . . . , and revision of local laws and regulations which may be necessary in solving the foregoing problems."[24] . . .

The Supreme Court gave leadership to the nation in this effort, and inspiration to the civil rights movement, but ultimately it needed the kind of help that only Congress could give. The Civil Rights Act of 1964 prohibited racial discrimination in the administration of federal grants-in-aid, and the Elementary and Secondary Education Act of 1965 authorized federal grants to elementary and secondary schools, giving the federal government enormous leverage over southern schools. They badly needed the federal money and stood to get a large part of it because it was designated for poor children. When the combined authority of all three branches of the federal government was brought to bear against the South after 1964, progress toward desegregation came swiftly.[25] . . .

THE STATES AS "WINNERS"

The Warren court made deep inroads on localism, but if local government was changed in the course of this conflict, so was the Court. The election in 1969 of Richard Nixon, who ran for the presidency in part by running against the Court, brought a change in its composition. Warren Burger replaced Earl Warren as chief justice in 1969. Of greater long-run importance for federalism, William H. Rehnquist and Lewis F. Powell were named in 1972. Powell was a former chairman of the Richmond school board, and Rehnquist had been active in Arizona politics. Both were judicial conservatives with ingrained respect for local custom. The reconstituted Court recoiled from the recasting of local institutions.[26]

As one sign of this change, the Court moderated its position on state legislative reapportionment to acknowledge the legitimacy of representation for

---

[24]347 U.S. 483 (1954); 349 U.S. 294 (1955).

[25]For an excellent account, see Gary Orfield, *The Reconstruction of Southern Education: The Schools and the 1964 Civil Rights Act* (Wiley-Interscience, 1969).

[26]On Rehnquist's commitment to federalism, see Sue Davis, *Justice Rehnquist and the Constitution* (Princeton University Press, 1989).

local communities. In *Mahan* v. *Howell* (1973), it held a 16.4 percent deviation from perfect proportionality in the lower house of the Virginia legislature to be justified by "the State's policy of maintaining the integrity of political subdivision lines." And, in *Brown* v. *Thomson* (1983), it upheld an apportionment plan of Wyoming's House of Representatives that allowed an average deviation from population equality of 16 percent and a maximum deviation of 89 percent, noting that "Wyoming's constitutional policy—followed since statehood—of using counties as representative districts and ensuring that each county has one representative is supported by substantial and legitimate state concerns."[27]

More telling signs came in cases dealing with school finance (*San Antonio* v. *Rodriguez*, 1973), school desegregation (*Milliken* v. *Bradley*, 1974), and exclusionary zoning (*Warth* v. *Seldin*, 1975). In each of these, the more conservative Court confronted the bedrock of localism and drew back. . . .

Seeking to build on the success of state-level constitutional cases in school finance, the National Association for the Advancement of Colored People in 1989 brought suit in a Connecticut court to compel racial desegregation of public schools in the city of Hartford and its suburban districts. A similar suit also developed in New Jersey. In 1996 the Connecticut Supreme Court ruled in *Sheff* v. *O'Neill* that racial segregation in Hartford's schools violated the state constitution and called on the state legislature to remedy the racial discrepancy between central-city and suburban schools.[28]

All of this action (and much more) has led numerous scholars to remark on the revival of state constitutional law, which is but one manifestation of the post-1960s renaissance of state governments generally.[29] At the heart of this renaissance is expansion of the states' role in education. Schools, the most durably local of the bedrock institutions, were very much changed by centralizing forces in the 1970s.

State spending for schools began to exceed local spending in the mid-1970s and continued to gain thereafter.[30] Federal aid, introduced on a large scale in the mid-1960s, may have given impetus to the change, but that is less clear in the case of education than it was for welfare and highways several decades earlier. If centralizing influences emanated from the national government above, some also rose from below, in the form of resistance from local prop-

---

[27]410 U.S. 315 (1973); 462 U.S. 835 (1983).

[28]Armor, *Forced Justice*, pp. 3, 60–61, 83; Elizabeth P. McCaughey, "Can Courts Order School Integration across Town Lines?" *Wall Street Journal*, October 28, 1992, p. A19; and "Hartford Court Bars Imbalance in the Schools," *New York Times*, July 10, 1996, pp. A1, B6.

[29]See, among many sources, G. Alan Tarr and Mary Cornelia Aldis Porter, *State Supreme Courts in State and Nation* (Yale University Press, 1988); and Advisory Commission on Intergovernmental Relations, *State Constitutional Law: Cases and Materials* (Washington, 1988).

[30]Kenneth K. Wong, "Fiscal Support for Education in American States: The 'Parity-to-Dominance' View Examined," *American Journal of Education*, vol. 97 (August 1989), pp. 329–57.

erty taxpayers to bearing the rising costs of education. Possibly the two forces were linked. Per-pupil spending more than doubled between 1960 and 1980, responding in part to national mandates such as that to provide a "free and appropriate education for all handicapped children." Taxpayer resistance to school spending measures rose in the late 1970s, and the passage of Proposition 13 in California in 1978 marked the start of a multistate property taxpayers' revolt. As states moved to assume a larger share of school costs, they did so with revenues from other sources: income and sales taxes. . . .

Grants-in-aid were just one means of national influence, and they did not grow very much, in contrast to the earlier pattern of federal spending for welfare and highways. Federal aid reached 10 percent of school spending in 1970 but began to fall in the early 1980s and stood at less than 7 percent in 1987. Ironically, in regard to schools, federal *retrenchment* may eventually have increased pressure on the states to spend, coming as it did after federal action had fostered organization and heightened expectations among a number of constituencies that were the beneficiaries of federal mandates.

Despite two centuries of national development, states remain the central polities of the United States in form. Under some conditions and for some functions, form becomes fact. The states are the "default setting" of the American federal system. To the extent that other levels of government lack the resources to act—authority, revenue, will power, political consensus, institutional capacity—the states have the job. They retain a vitality born of the limits of national institutions' capacity, limits that the Warren court's clash with the bedrock of localism helped to reveal. The national government did not seize control of the schools, nor did local governments maintain control of them. Neither possessed the resources that would have been required to do so. The states, possessors above all of clear constitutional authority, picked up the pieces and began to pay more of the costs. The result, as Kirst shrewdly observes, is not so much centralization as fragmentation. Everyone and no one is in charge of the schools.[31]

TODAY'S CHOICES

To borrow once again from Diamond, the history I have sketched is that of the national political community's struggle to attain "completeness . . . the perfection of its autonomy." Resistance came from a set of deeply rooted local institutions that were themselves not mere historical accidents. They were shielded by the original choice of federalism, embraced by nineteenth-century

---

[31]See also John Kincaid, "Is Education Too Intergovernmental?" *Intergovernmental Perspective* (Winter 1992), pp. 28–34.

America, and given up to central authority (both state and national) slowly and reluctantly.

To argue that communities have been shaped by deliberate choices is not to deny that other forces shape them as well. If localism lacks vitality in modern America, that is not because it was killed by the Warren court, still less by technicians crusading for civil service reform from within the Social Security Board in the 1930s. Both did their part, especially the Court, but the nation's numerous wars and rise to great-power status did more, both to enlarge the claim of the national government on public resources and to stimulate the geographic and social mobility of the populace. Economic development brought specialization and interdependence, creating national and international markets and exposing local economies to forces far beyond their power to control. Urbanization was followed by suburbanization and the separation of place of work and place of residence. Transportation and communication technologies changed in ways that helped integrate the national society while attenuating local ones. If World War II assaulted the local place metaphorically, in the abstract, the interstate highway system literally assaulted it with concrete, while federally sponsored urban renewal gutted its physical core, not always replacing what it destroyed. The many acts with which the national government directly attacked localism, such as *Reynolds* v. *Sims* and the later-model Voting Rights Act, were compounded by many more that did not have that purpose but produced that effect as an inescapable by-product of the exercise of national power.

As American federalism has steadily grown more centralized, it is tempting to attribute the change to the influence of such (presumably uncontrollable) forces and to overlook the extent to which choices steadily present themselves nonetheless. A leading example is the debates currently raging over the schools, localism's last bastion, only recently breached. Egalitarians attack what remains of local distinction with measures for equalization of per-pupil spending. They would erase the effects of interlocal differences in taxable wealth, denying people one of the most compelling reasons for attachment both to schools that excel and the places in which they excel. On the other hand, libertarians—the proponents of the more extreme forms of choice—would enable parents to select whatever schools they prefer, public or private, freeing them from an obligation to support the public schools in the place where they live. Policy choices about schools are choices as well about the nature and function of local communities, to which schools have been central, even defining.

There is also the question of whether the formation of private communities should be encouraged or discouraged. Private substitutes for public local governments have been proliferating since the 1960s. There were about 150,000 community associations in the United States as of the early 1990s, helping to administer the lives and property of 32 million people—one of every eight

Americans. In the fifty largest metropolitan areas, 50 percent or more of new home sales were in "common interest developments" or CIDs, as privately run communities have come to be called. In the metropolitan area of Washington, D.C., the figure was around 80 percent.[32]

The impetus for the formation of CIDs comes partly from developers, who, because of dwindling supplies of land, are under pressure to develop with greater density and who gain from putting playgrounds, pools, and tennis courts on commonly owned land. It also comes from financially pressed local governments that lack the capacity to supply services to large new developments and therefore welcome proposals that promise to relieve them of this burden.

While some CID associations are confined to responsibility for a single building, the vast majority administer territory as well as a building. They levy fees that are in effect taxes, and they provide a variety of services, such as roads, bus routes, television stations, security forces, parks, and swimming pools. Some of them are walled. Although most are associated with new developments, others have become established in older settings. St. Louis is laced with privately owned streets, complete with gatehouses.

Analysts of these quasi governments disagree about their implications for citizenship. They may be merely one more organized place in which Americans engage in "political" activity, arguing over how to define their shared interests. Even if most CID residents are apathetic, the figures on participation are impressive: 750,000 persons serve on the boards of directors. Dissident homeowners, chafing under restrictions about pets, alterations to their dwellings, and the like, resort to legal actions, counterorganization, and vocal assertions of their rights. All of this looks like normal American politics; people have merely invented a new setting in which to practice it. On the other hand, what is at issue here, even more precisely and narrowly than usual, are rights and responsibilities associated with the ownership of real property. These are thoroughly private-regarding places. Maintenance and protection of private property, to the exclusion of more encompassing purposes, unite (or divide) the members of the CID.

While exclusive, property-centered private community associations multiply, local public places continue to come under attack for not being inclusive enough. In the summer of 1991, President Bush's Advisory Commission on Regulatory Barriers to Affordable Housing (the Kemp commission)

---

[32]Mitchell Pacelle, "Not in Your Backyard, Say Community Panels in Suburban Enclaves," *Wall Street Journal,* September 21, 1994; Stephen E. Barton and Carol J. Silverman, eds., *Common Interest Communities: Private Governments and the Public Interest* (Berkeley: Institute of Governmental Studies, 1994); Evan McKenzie, *Privatopia: Homeowner Associations and the Rise of Residential Private Government* (Yale University Press, 1994); and Robert Jay Dilger, *Neighborhood Politics: Residential Community Associations in American Governance* (New York University Press, 1993).

recommended a series of federal actions that would compel local jurisdictions to relax restrictions on construction of low-cost housing. It proposed denial of federal housing assistance to state or local governments that failed to reduce regulatory barriers and denial of tax-exempt status to state and local bonds issued to finance housing construction in such jurisdictions.[33]

Such policy proposals and choices raise in turn a series of larger, underlying questions: How important is it to the well-being of society that spatially defined communities be sustained? Are they entitled to primacy, or may race under some circumstances supplant place, as it has come to do in the ideological framework of the Voting Rights Act? How important is it that spatial communities have a general-purpose public character? If they are to have a public character, to what extent, to what ends, and with what instruments should higher levels of government regulate their capacity to define themselves as communities? May federal judges impose taxes on states and localities (the issue raised in 1990 in the Kansas City school desegregation case, *Missouri* v. *Jenkins*)?[34] Should any autonomy remain to the local place in an America that increasingly searches for equality, including interjurisdictional equality? Should any autonomy be restored to the local place in an America that laments the loss of a sense of community, fears for personal safety, and worries about the alienation of citizens from politics?

Underpinning any answers to such questions are a series of value judgments and facts that political theory and behavioral social science ought to be able to help clarify. They ought to be able to illuminate the value and social function of the small-scale public place and weigh the differences in the citizen's relation to places of different scale. The starting point for any such effort remains today, as for 150 years, Tocqueville's argument for the importance of decentralization in democracies—not just of the execution of centrally framed laws, but of deliberation and lawmaking in matters of daily consequence to ordinary citizens.[35]

What Tocqueville sought to decentralize, according to Martin Diamond's interpretation, were "the daily things, the intra-regime things, that make up the vast bulk of a government's business—the little things, immensely interesting to most men . . . which may be done safely and salutarily by the local-

---

[33]Advisory Commission on Regulatory Barriers to Affordable Housing, *"Not In My Back Yard": Removing Barriers to Affordable Housing* (Washington, 1991); and Michael H. Schill, "The Federal Role in Reducing Regulatory Barriers to Affordable Housing in the Suburbs," *Journal of Law and Politics*, vol. 8 (Summer 1992), pp. 703–30; for a scholarly critique of exclusionary practices, see Michael N. Danielson, *The Politics of Exclusion* (Columbia University Press, 1976).

[34]495 U.S. 33 (1990).

[35]For recent empirical attempts by social scientists to come to grips with the contemporary value and meaning of small-scale communities, see, for example, Jane J. Mansbridge, *Beyond Adversary Democracy* (University of Chicago Press, 1983); and Harold A. McDougall, *Black Baltimore: A New Theory of Community* (Temple University Press, 1993).

ity in whatever way it chooses, because the doing of them affects the whole not at all or only insignificantly."[36] Yet in a society where a high school teacher's refusal to wear a tie can rise to the level of a constitutional question, it is hard to see what can be safeguarded to the local citizen who might have the time, taste, or temperament for participating in the labor of democratic governance.[37]

---

[36]Diamond, "The Ends of Federalism," p. 156.

[37]Richard S. Vacca and H. C. Hudgins Jr., *Liability of School Officials and Administrators for Civil Rights Torts* (Charlottesville: Michie Co., 1982), pp. 117–30. This source explains (p. 117) that "over the years the notion of people expressing themselves (speaking out) through their mode of dress and attire (including hair style) has developed . . . into an acceptable concept of constitutional law."

CHAPTER 3

American Political Culture

A merican democracy is distinctive in many ways. The structure of the U.S. political system contains some unique features—tens of thousands of local governments, an electoral college for the selection of the president, and many more. But what really makes the United States stand out from other democratic nations are its people's views on their political system. Unlike many other nations, the United States does not have a homogeneous population; its citizens come from numerous other countries, speak a variety of languages, and practice different religions. Nevertheless, this diverse population comes together in supporting—indeed, making possible—American democracy.

For all their great diversity, the vast majority of Americans share certain fundamental assumptions about how the political process should operate. For example, Americans assume that the candidate who loses an election should not try to prevent the winner from taking office. Likewise, Americans believe that nobody should automatically hold office or have a greater claim on political authority simply because he or she comes from a wealthy or an aristocratic family. In many societies, past and present, these are not widely shared assumptions about how politics and government ought to be carried out. But together with a widespread belief in such values as liberty, equality, individualism, and democracy itself, such bedrock civic sentiments define America's distinctive *political culture*.

In many respects, American political culture reflects American constitutionalism. The principles of American constitutionalism, as discussed in the two preceding chapters, include liberty, equality, individualism, majority rule, minority rights, limited government, separation of powers, checks and balances, and federalism. American political culture encompasses these principles and extends to public attitudes on American politics—specifically, public service (or civic virtue), public knowledge of governance and public policy, government responsiveness to public opinion, and so forth. While political culture is not easily analyzed or measured, most historians, political scientists, and other scholars seem to agree that it is central to American democracy.

Two widely noted features of American political culture that distinguish Americans from citizens of many other democracies, including Europe's, are Americans' tendency to join groups and form all manner of civic, community, and other associations—a nation of "joiners"—and Americans' propensity to describe themselves as "religious," attend worship services, and support community-serving religious charities. But as the readings in this chapter by Alexis de Tocqueville and Robert Putnam make clear, even these distinctive features of American political culture are dynamic, not static.

De Tocqueville visited the United States from France in the 1830s to study the American prison system, but he ultimately produced a sweeping survey of American political life in the nineteenth century. He was especially struck by how prone Americans were to come together and invent new private or community organizations to address public or social problems. Even today, many of his conclusions about the character of American democracy ring true.

Harvard University political scientist Robert D. Putnam's article, "Bowling Alone," is a more recent study of American civic life. Putnam finds that much has changed in levels of civic and community participation over the last fifty years. He reports that Americans are less involved in local associations, from education groups to sports teams, than they were after World War II, and he sees negative consequences for democracy from this decreased social interaction.

In the late 1990s, Putnam convened a group of several dozen policy-makers, journalists, clergy, academics, business leaders, community organizers, and others to study civic engagement in the United States. The group examined empirical evidence that fewer and fewer Americans were joining clubs, associations, churches, and other groups that promote civic trust and cooperation, held public hearings on the subject in several cities, and produced a report documenting the problem and what might be done to "replenish social capital."[1] Some of the evidence reviewed by the Putnam group was striking: Statically speaking, joining a group boosts your life expectancy as much as quitting smoking; cohesive low-income neighborhoods have lower rates of criminal victimization; people who like and socialize with co-workers are more productive on the job; young people who volunteer are more likely to vote than young people who do no community service; and much more.

The Putnam group stressed the "erosion of social capital" but also highlighted practical ways that it might be rebuilt in homes, workplaces, arts organizations, and elsewhere. One of the report's most striking sections concerns the civic role played by religious individuals and institutions in the United States today. Among other findings, it documents that houses of worship and so-called faith-based organizations are among the major suppliers of social welfare services to needy citizens and neighborhoods. America, the report concluded, still has vast "social capital resources."

This finding, and others like it, has influence on real-world politics, mixing old debates about "church and state" with new debates about "sacred places serving civic purposes." As part of the 1996 welfare reform law, the federal government made it possible for religious organizations to compete to administer various federally funded social service delivery programs on the same basis that all other nonprofit organizations compete to administer them. Section 104 of that law became known as *charitable choice*.

During the 2000 presidential campaign, both Democrat Al Gore and Republican George W. Bush endorsed "faith-based initiatives" and called for expanding the charitable choice provision of the 1996 welfare reform law. A 2001 survey by the Pew Forum on Religion and Public Life found that while most Americans want government to help support community-serving religious organizations that aid the poor, most also favor prohibiting the groups from using any public funds for proselytizing or other sectarian, rather than secular, purposes.

---

[1]Robert D. Putnam et al., *Better Together: The Report of the Saguaro Seminar* (Cambridge, Mass.: John F. Kennedy School of Government, 2001).

3.1 Democracy in America (1835–1840)

ALEXIS DE TOCQUEVILLE

INTRODUCTION

Alexis de Tocqueville's masterful analysis of the American political system and people aptly describes the American condition almost two centuries later. A French aristocrat, de Tocqueville studied law before visiting the United States at age twenty-five, sent by a French ministry to evaluate the American penal system and propose reforms for France's system. De Tocqueville and his colleague Gustave de Beaumont traveled throughout the United States for nine months, spending much of their time in Philadelphia, New York City, and Boston, but also going west to Michigan and south to New Orleans. They met with political and economic elites as well as with many average citizens from all walks of life.

In the first selection from *Democracy in America* that follows, de Tocqueville identifies a fundamental feature of American democracy: the tendency of people to join associations. He finds that people participate in groups for many reasons, ranging from social to political. Although de Tocqueville cautions that such groups can pose dangers to political stability, he argues that they provide a critical safeguard as well—namely, protection against "the tyranny of the majority."

In the second selection, de Tocqueville discusses why the United States is a democracy. He begins by discussing its special characteristics—for example, its geographic isolation renders it less susceptible to colonization. Furthermore, its vast territory provides abundant opportunity for individual prosperity. As de Tocqueville writes, "The physical causes, independent of the laws, which contribute to promote general prosperity, are more numerous in America than they have ever been in any other country in the world, at any other period of history."

Beyond its physical characteristics, de Tocqueville finds that the legal and constitutional underpinnings of the political system serve to protect democracy as well. In particular, he emphasizes the federal system of government, the authority of local institutions, and the judicial system. But de Tocqueville's primary case for the success of American democracy rests with the American people. He focuses on the "mores" of the people, which he defines broadly as their "whole moral and intellectual condition." Specifically, de Tocqueville shrewdly assesses the role of religion and education in shaping Americans' views about democracy. Together, de Tocqueville concludes, the physical

Alexis de Tocqueville, *Democracy in America*, vol. I, trans. Henry Reeve, with special introduction by John T. Morgan and John J. Ingalls (New York: The Colonial Press, 1900), 191–196, 292–295, 303–304, 328 (excerpts).

characteristics and legal structure of the United States, as well as public dedication to the political system and certain religious ideas and practices, create a vibrant democracy in America.

■

POLITICAL ASSOCIATIONS IN THE UNITED STATES

. . . In no country in the world has the principle of association been more successfully used, or more unsparingly applied to a multitude of different objects, than in America. Besides the permanent associations which are established by law under the names of townships, cities, and counties, a vast number of others are formed and maintained by the agency of private individuals.

The citizen of the United States is taught from his earliest infancy to rely upon his own exertions in order to resist the evils and the difficulties of life; he looks upon social authority with an eye of mistrust and anxiety, and he only claims its assistance when he is quite unable to shift without it. This habit may even be traced in the schools of the rising generation, where the children in their games are wont to submit to rules which they have themselves established, and to punish misdemeanors which they have themselves defined. The same spirit pervades every act of social life. If a stoppage occurs in the thoroughfare, and the circulation of the public is hindered, the neighbors immediately constitute deliberative body; and this extemporaneous assembly gives rise to an executive power which remedies the inconvenience before anybody has thought of recurring to an authority superior to the persons immediately concerned. If the public pleasures are concerned, an association is formed to provide for the splendor and the regularity of the entertainment. Societies are formed to resist enemies which are exclusively of a moral nature, and to diminish the vice of intemperance: in the United States associations are established to promote public order, commerce, industry, morality, and religion; for there is no end which the human will, seconded by the collective exertions of individuals, despairs of attaining.

I shall hereafter have occasion to show the effects of association upon the course of society, and I must confine myself for the present to the political world. When once the right of association is recognized, the citizens may employ it in several different ways.

An association consists simply in the public assent which a number of individuals give to certain doctrines, and in the engagement which they contract to promote the spread of those doctrines by their exertions. The right of association with these views is very analogous to the liberty of unlicensed writing; but societies thus formed possess more authority than the press. When an opinion is represented by a society, it necessarily assumes a more exact and explicit form. It numbers its partisans, and compromises their welfare in its cause: they, on the other hand, become acquainted with each other, and their zeal is increased by their number. An association unites the efforts of minds which have a tendency to diverge in one single channel, and urges them vigorously towards one single end which it points out.

The second degree in the right of association is the power of meeting. When an association is allowed to establish centres of action at certain important points in the country, its activity is increased and its influence extended. Men have the opportunity of seeing each other; means of execution are more readily combined, and opinions are maintained with a degree of warmth and energy which written language cannot approach.

Lastly, in the exercise of the right of political association, there is a third degree: the partisans of an opinion may unite in electoral bodies, and choose delegates to represent them in a central assembly. This is, properly speaking, the application of the representative system to a party.

Thus, in the first instance, a society is formed between individuals professing the same opinion, and the tie which keeps it together is of a purely intellectual nature; in the second case, small assemblies are formed which only represent a fraction of the party. Lastly, in the third case, they constitute a separate nation in the midst of the nation, a government within the Government. Their delegates, like the real delegates of the majority, represent the entire collective force of their party; and they enjoy a certain degree of that national dignity and great influence which belong to the chosen representatives of the people. It is true that they have not the right of making the laws, but they have the power of attacking those which are in being, and of drawing up beforehand those which they may afterwards cause to be adopted.

If, in a people which is imperfectly accustomed to the exercise of freedom, or which is exposed to violent political passions, a deliberating minority, which confines itself to the contemplation of future laws, be placed in juxtaposition to the legislative majority, I cannot but believe that public tranquillity incurs very great risks in that nation. There is doubtless a very wide difference between proving that one law is in itself better than another and proving that the former ought to be substituted for the latter. But the imagination of the populace is very apt to overlook this difference, which is so apparent to the minds of thinking men. It sometimes happens that a nation is divided into nearly equal parties, each of which affects to represent the majority. If, in immediate contiguity to the directing power, another power be established, which exercises almost as much moral authority as the former, it is not to be believed that it will long be content to speak without acting; or that it will always be restrained by the abstract consideration of the nature of associations which are meant to direct but not to enforce opinions, to suggest but not to make the laws.

The more we consider the independence of the press in its principal consequences, the more are we convinced that it is the chief and, so to speak, the constitutive element of freedom in the modern world. A nation which is determined to remain free is therefore right in demanding the unrestrained exercise of this independence. But the unrestrained liberty of political association cannot be entirely assimilated to the liberty of the press. The one is at the same time less necessary and more dangerous than the other. A nation may confine it within certain limits without forfeiting any part of its self-control; and it may sometimes be obliged to do so in order to maintain its own authority.

In America the liberty of association for political purposes is unbounded. . . .

It must be acknowledged that the unrestrained liberty of political association has not hitherto produced, in the United States, those fatal consequences which might perhaps be expected from it elsewhere. The right of association was imported from England, and it has always existed in America; so that the exercise of this privilege is now amalgamated with the manners and customs of the people. At the present time the liberty of association is become a necessary guarantee against the tyranny of the majority. In the United States, as soon as a party is become preponderant, all public authority passes under its control; its private supporters occupy all the places, and have all the force of the administration at their disposal. As the most distinguished partisans of the other side of the question are unable to surmount the obstacles which exclude them from power, they require some means of establishing themselves upon their own basis, and of opposing the moral authority of the minority to the physical power which domineers over it. Thus a dangerous expedient is used to obviate a still more formidable danger.

The omnipotence of the majority appears to me to present such extreme perils to the American Republics that the dangerous measure which is used to repress it seems to be more advantageous than prejudicial. And here I am about to advance a proposition which may remind the reader of what I said before in speaking of municipal freedom: There are no countries in which associations are more needed, to prevent the despotism of faction or the arbitrary power of a prince, than those which are democratically constituted. In aristocratic nations the body of the nobles and the more opulent part of the community are in themselves natural associations, which act as checks upon the abuses of power. In countries in which these associations do not exist, if private individuals are unable to create an artificial and a temporary substitute for them, I can imagine no permanent protection against the most galling tyranny; and a great people may be oppressed by a small faction, or by a single individual, with impunity. . . .

It cannot be denied that the unrestrained liberty of association for political purposes is the privilege which a people is longest in learning how to exercise. If it does not throw the nation into anarchy, it perpetually augments the chances of that calamity. On one point, however, this perilous liberty offers a security against dangers of another kind; in countries where associations are free, secret societies are unknown. In America there are numerous factions, but no conspiracies.

PRINCIPAL CAUSES WHICH TEND TO MAINTAIN THE DEMOCRATIC REPUBLIC IN THE UNITED STATES

A Democratic republic subsists in the United States, and the principal object of this book has been to account for the fact of its existence. Several of the causes which contribute to maintain the institutions of America have been involuntarily passed by or only hinted at as I was borne along by my subject. Others I have been unable to discuss, and those on which I have dwelt most are, as it were, buried in the details of the former parts of this work. I think, therefore, that before I proceed to speak of the future, I cannot do better than collect within a small compass the reasons which best explain the present. In this retrospective chapter I shall be succinct, for I shall take care to remind the reader very summarily of what he already knows; and I shall only select the most prominent of those facts which I have not yet pointed out.

All the causes which contribute to the maintenance of the democratic republic in the United States are reducible to three heads:—

I. The peculiar and accidental situation in which Providence has placed the Americans.

II. The laws.

III. The manners and customs of the people.

Accidental or Providential Causes Which Contribute to the Maintenance of the Democratic Republic in the United States.

. . . A thousand circumstances, independent of the will of man, concur to facilitate the maintenance of a democratic republic in the United States. Some of these peculiarities are known, the others many easily be pointed out; but I shall confine myself to the most prominent amongst them.

The Americans have no neighbors, and consequently they have no great wars, or financial crises, or conquest to dread; they require neither great taxes, nor great armies, nor great generals; and they have nothing to fear from a scourge which is more formidable to republics than all these evils combined, namely, military glory. It is impossible to deny the inconceivable influence which military glory exercises upon the spirit of a nation. General Jackson, whom the Americans have twice elected to the head of their Government, is a man of a violent temper and mediocre talents; no one circumstance in the whole course of his career ever proved that he is qualified to govern a free people, and indeed the majority of the enlightened classes of the Union has always been opposed to him. But he was raised to the Presidency, and has been maintained in that lofty station, solely by the recollection of a victory which he gained twenty years ago under the walls of New Orleans, a victory which was, however, a very ordinary achievement, and which could only be remembered in a country where battles are rare. Now the people which is thus carried away by the illusions of glory is unquestionably the most cold and calculating, the unmilitary (if I may use the expression), and the most prosaic of all the peoples of the earth.

America has no great capital city, whose influence is directly or indirectly felt over the whole extent of the country, which I hold to be one of the first causes of the maintenance of republican institutions in the United States. In cities men cannot be prevented from concerting together, and from awakening a mutual excitement which prompts sudden and passionate resolutions. Cities may be looked upon as large assemblies, of which all the inhabitants are members; their populace exercises a prodigious influence upon the magistrates, and frequently executes its own wished without their intervention.

To subject the provinces to the metropolis is therefore not only to place the destiny of the empire in the hands of a portion of the community, which may be reprobated as unjust, but to place it in the hands of a populace acting under its own impulses, which must be avoided as dangerous. The preponderance of capital cities is therefore a serious blow upon the representative system, and it exposes modern republics to the same defect as the republics of antiquity, which all perished from not having been acquainted with that form of government.

It would be easy for me to adduce a great number of secondary causes which have contributed to establish, and which concur to maintain, the democratic republic of the United States. But I discern two principal circumstances amongst these favorable elements, which I hasten to point out. I have already observed that the origin of the American settlements may be looked upon as the first and most efficacious cause to which the present prosperity of the United States may be attributed. The Americans had the chances of birth in their favor, and their forefathers imported that equality of conditions into the country whence the democratic republic has very naturally taken its rise. Nor was this all they did; for besides this republican condition of society, the early settlers bequeathed to their descendants those customs manners, and opinions which contribute most to the success of a republican form of government. When I reflect upon the consequences of this primary circumstance, methinks I see the destiny of America embodied in the first Puritan who landed on those shores, just as the human race was represented by the first man.

The chief circumstance which has favored the establishment and the maintenance of a democratic republic in the United States is the nature of the territory which the Americans inhabit. Their ancestors gave them the love of equality and of freedom, but God himself gave them the means of remaining equal and free, by placing them upon a boundless continent, which is open to their exertions. General prosperity is favorable to the stability of all governments, but more particularly of a democratic constitution, which depends upon the dispositions of the majority, and more particularly of that portion of the community which is most exposed to feel the pressure of want. When the people rules, it must be rendered happy, or it will overturn the State, and misery is apt to stimulate it to those excesses to which ambition rouses kings. The physical causes, independent of the laws, which contribute to promote general prosperity, are more numerous in America than they have ever been in any other country in the world, at any other period of history. In the United States not only is legislation democratic, but nature herself favors the cause of the people. . . .

Influence of the Laws upon the Maintenance of the Democratic Republic in the United States

. . . Three circumstances seem to me to contribute most powerfully to the maintenance of the democratic republic in the United States.

The first is that Federal form of Government which the Americans have adopted, and which enables the Union to combine the power of a great empire with the security of a small State.

The second consists in those municipal institutions which limit the despotism of the majority, and at the same time impart a taste for freedom and a knowledge of the art of being free to the people.

The third is to be met with in the constitution of the judicial power. I have shown in what manner the courts of justice serve to repress the excesses of democracy, and how they check and direct the impulses of the majority without stopping its activity.

Influence of Manners upon the Maintenance of the Democratic Republic in the United States

I have previously remarked that the manners of the people may be considered as one of the general causes to which the maintenance of a democratic republic in the United States is attributable. I here used the word *manners* with the meaning which the ancients attached to the word *mores*, for I apply it not only to manners in their proper sense of what constitutes the character of social intercourse, but I extend it to the various notions and opinions current among men, and to the mass of those ideas which constitute their character of mind. I comprise, therefore, under this term the whole moral and intellectual condition of a people. My intention is not to draw a picture of American manners, but simply to point out such features of them as are favorable to the maintenance of political institutions. . . .

The manners of the Americans of the United States are, then, the real cause which renders that people the only one of the American nations that is able to support a democratic government; and it is the influence of manners which produces the different degrees of order and of prosperity that may be distinguished in the several Anglo-American democracies. Thus the effect which the geographical position of a country may have upon the duration of democratic institutions is exaggerated in Europe. Too much importance is attributed to leg-islation, too little to manners. These three great causes serve, no doubt, to reg-ulate and direct the American democracy; but if they were to be classed in their proper order, I should say that the physical circumstances are less effi-cient than the laws, and the laws very subordinate to the manners of the peo-ple. I am convinced that the most advantageous situation and the best possible laws cannot maintain a constitution in spite of the manners of a country; whilst the latter may turn the most unfavorable positions and the worst laws to some advantage. The importance of manners is a common truth to which study and experience incessantly direct our attention. It may be regarded as a central point in the range of human observation, and the common termination of all inquiry. So seriously do I insist upon this head, that if I have hitherto failed in making the reader feel the important influence which I attribute to the prac-tical experience, the habits, the opinions, in short, to the manners of the Amer-icans, upon the maintenance of their institutions, I have failed in the principal object of my work.

3.2 Bowling Alone: America's Declining Social Capital (1995)

ROBERT D. PUTNAM

INTRODUCTION

In the mid-1990s, noted Harvard University political scientist Robert D. Put-nam reported evidence suggesting that fewer and fewer Americans were join-ing clubs, associations, churches, and other groups that promote civic trust and cooperation, or what he and other scholars term "social capital." As a metaphor for the broader decline of civic participation that concerned him, he highlighted the fact that since 1980 league bowling had dropped by 40 percent. Americans, once a nation of joiners, were now "bowling alone."

Both President Bill Clinton, a Democrat, and Republican leaders in Con-gress made public note of Putnam's findings. Some academic critics, however, found the evidence on civic decline to be more mixed than Putnam had ini-tially seemed to suggest it was. For example, the drop in league bowling oc-curred alongside a dozen-fold increase in softball leagues. More importantly, while church attendance had declined, other, less traditional forms of reli-gious association—community-serving ministries, bible study groups, and oth-

Robert D. Putnam, "Bowling Alone: America's Declining Social Capital," *Journal of Democracy* 6, no. 1 (January 1995): 65–78. Reprinted with permission.

ers—were stable or growing. Likewise, while voter turnout rates had declined among college-age citizens, young Americans were volunteering in their communities at historically high levels.

In his subsequent work, including a book by the same title as his famous article and the report that follows in this section, Putnam answers these and other criticisms and proposes practical ways that the decline in social capital could be halted or reversed.

■

Many students of the new democracies that have emerged over the past decade and a half have emphasized the importance of a strong and active civil society to the consolidation of democracy. Especially with regard to the postcommunist countries, scholars and democratic activists alike have lamented the absence or obliteration of traditions of independent civic engagement and a widespread tendency toward passive reliance on the state. To those concerned with the weakness of civil societies in the developing or postcommunist world, the advanced Western democracies and above all the United States have typically been taken as models to be emulated. There is striking evidence, however, that the vibrancy of American civil society has notably declined over the past several decades.

Ever since the publication of Alexis de Tocqueville's *Democracy in America,* the United States has played a central role in systematic studies of the links between democracy and civil society. Although this is in part because trends in American life are often regarded as harbingers of social modernization, it is also because America has traditionally been considered unusually "civic" (a reputation that, as we shall later see, has not been entirely unjustified).

When Tocqueville visited the United States in the 1830s, it was the Americans' propensity for civic association that most impressed him as the key to their unprecedented ability to make democracy work. "Americans of all ages, all stations in life, and all types of disposition," he observed, "are forever forming associations. There are not only commercial and industrial associations in which all take part, but others of a thousand different types—religious, moral, serious, futile, very general and very limited, immensely large and very minute. . . . Nothing, in my view, deserves more attention than the intellectual and moral associations in America."[1]

Recently, American social scientists of a neo-Tocquevillean bent have unearthed a wide range of empirical evidence that the quality of public life and the performance of social institutions (and not only in America) are indeed powerfully influenced by norms and networks of civic engagement. Researchers in such fields as education, urban poverty, unemployment, the control of crime and drug abuse, and even health have discovered that successful outcomes are more likely in civically engaged communities. Similarly, research

---

[1]Alexis de Tocqueville, *Democracy in America,* ed. J. P. Maier, trans. George Lawrence (Garden City, N.Y.: Anchor Books, 1969), 513–17.

on the varying economic attainments of different ethnic groups in the United States has demonstrated the importance of social bonds within each group. These results are consistent with research in a wide range of settings that demonstrates the vital importance of social networks for job placement and many other economic outcomes.

Meanwhile, a seemingly unrelated body of research on the sociology of economic development has also focused attention on the role of social networks. Some of this work is situated in the developing countries, and some of it elucidates the peculiarly successful "network capitalism" of East Asia.[2] Even in less exotic Western economies, however, researchers have discovered highly efficient, highly flexible "industrial districts" based on networks of collaboration among workers and small entrepreneurs. Far from being paleoindustrial anachronisms, these dense interpersonal and interorganizational networks undergird ultramodern industries, from the high tech of Silicon Valley to the high fashion of Benetton.

The norms and networks of civic engagement also powerfully affect the performance of representative government. That, at least, was the central conclusion of my own 20-year, quasi-experimental study of subnational governments in different regions of Italy.[3] Although all these regional governments seemed identical on paper, their levels of effectiveness varied dramatically. Systematic inquiry showed that the quality of governance was determined by longstanding traditions of civic engagement (or its absence). Voter turnout, newspaper readership, membership in choral societies and football clubs—these were the hallmarks of a successful region. In fact, historical analysis suggested that these networks of organized reciprocity and civic solidarity, far from being an epiphenomenon of socioeconomic modernization, were a precondition for it.

---

[2]On social networks and economic growth in the developing world, see Milton J. Esman and Norman Uphoff, *Local Organizations: Intermediaries in Rural Development* (Ithaca: Cornell University Press, 1984), esp. 15–42 and 99–180; and Albert O. Hirschman, *Getting Ahead Collectively: Grassroots Experiences in Latin America* (Elmsford, N.Y.: Pergamon Press, 1984), esp. 42–77. On East Asia, see Gustav Papanek, "The New Asian Capitalism: An Economic Portrait," in Peter L. Berger and Hsin-Huang Michael Hsiao, eds., *In Search of an East Asian Development Model* (New Brunswick, N.J.: Transaction, 1987), 27–80; Peter B. Evans, "The State as Problem and Solution: Predation, Embedded Autonomy and Structural Change," in Stephan Haggard and Robert R. Kaufman, eds., *The Politics of Economic Adjustment* (Princeton: Princeton University Press, 1992), 139–81; and Gary G. Hamilton, William Zeile, and Wan-Jin Kim, "Network Structure of East Asian Economies," in Stewart R. Clegg and S. Gordon Redding, eds., *Capitalism in Contrasting Cultures* (Hawthorne, N.Y.: De Gruyter, 1990), 105–29. See also Gary G. Hamilton and Nicole Woolsey Biggart, "Market, Culture, and Authority: A Comparative Analysis of Management and Organization in the Far East," *American Journal of Sociology* (Supplement) 94 (1988): S52–S94; and Susan Greenhalgh, "Families and Networks in Taiwan's Economic Development," in Edwin Winckler and Susan Greenhalgh, eds., *Contending Approaches to the Political Economy of Taiwan* (Armonk, N.Y.: M.E. Sharpe, 1987), 224–45.

[3]Robert D. Putnam, *Making Democracy Work: Civic Traditions in Modern Italy* (Princeton: Princeton University Press, 1993).

No doubt the mechanisms through which civic engagement and social connectedness produce such results—better schools, faster economic development, lower crime, and more effective government—are multiple and complex. While these briefly recounted findings require further confirmation and perhaps qualification, the parallels across hundreds of empirical studies in a dozen disparate disciplines and subfields are striking. Social scientists in several fields have recently suggested a common framework for understanding these phenomena, a framework that rests on the concept of *social capital.*[4] By analogy with notions of physical capital and human capital—tools and training that enhance individual productivity—"social capital" refers to features of social organization such as networks, norms, and social trust that facilitate coordination and cooperation for mutual benefit.

For a variety of reasons, life is easier in a community blessed with a substantial stock of social capital. In the first place, networks of civic engagement foster sturdy norms of generalized reciprocity and encourage the emergence of social trust. Such networks facilitate coordination and communication, amplify reputations, and thus allow dilemmas of collective action to be resolved. When economic and political negotiation is embedded in dense networks of social interaction, incentives for opportunism are reduced. At the same time, networks of civic engagement embody past success at collaboration, which can serve as a cultural template for future collaboration. Finally, dense networks of interaction probably broaden the participants' sense of self, developing the "I" into the "we," or (in the language of rational-choice theorists) enhancing the participants' "taste" for collective benefits.

I do not intend here to survey (much less contribute to) the development of the theory of social capital. Instead, I use the central premise of that rapidly growing body of work—that social connections and civic engagement pervasively influence our public life, as well as our private prospects—as the starting point for an empirical survey of trends in social capital in contemporary America. I concentrate here entirely on the American case, although the developments I portray may in some measure characterize many contemporary societies.

---

[4]James S. Coleman deserves primary credit for developing the "social capital" theoretical framework. See his "Social Capital in the Creation of Human Capital," *American Journal of Sociology* (Supplement) 94 (1988): S95–S120, as well as his *The Foundations of Social Theory* (Cambridge: Harvard University Press, 1990), 300–21. See also Mark Granovetter, "Economic Action and Social Structure: The Problem of Embeddedness," *American Journal of Sociology* 91 (1985): 481–510; Glenn C. Loury, "Why Should We Care About Group Inequality?" *Social Philosophy and Policy* 5 (1987): 249–71; and Robert D. Putnam, "The Prosperous Community: Social Capital and Public Life," *American Prospect* 13 (1993): 35–42. To my knowledge, the first scholar to use the term "social capital" in its current sense was Jane Jacobs, in *The Death and Life of Great American Cities* (New York: Random House, 1961), 138.

WHATEVER HAPPENED
TO CIVIC ENGAGEMENT?

We begin with familiar evidence on changing patterns of political participation, not least because it is immediately relevant to issues of democracy in the narrow sense. Consider the well-known decline in turnout in national elections over the last three decades. From a relative high point in the early 1960s, voter turnout had by 1990 declined by nearly a quarter; tens of millions of Americans had forsaken their parents' habitual readiness to engage in the simplest act of citizenship. Broadly similar trends also characterize participation in state and local elections.

It is not just the voting booth that has been increasingly deserted by Americans. A series of identical questions posed by the Roper Organization to national samples ten times each year over the last two decades reveals that since 1973 the number of Americans who report that "in the past year" they have "attended a public meeting on town or school affairs" has fallen by more than a third (from 22 percent in 1973 to 13 percent in 1993). Similar (or even greater) relative declines are evident in responses to questions about attending a political rally or speech, serving on a committee of some local organization, and working for a political party. By almost every measure, Americans' direct engagement in politics and government has fallen steadily and sharply over the last generation, despite the fact that average levels of education—the best individual-level predictor of political participation—have risen sharply throughout this period. Every year over the last decade or two, millions more have withdrawn from the affairs of their communities.

Not coincidentally, Americans have also disengaged psychologically from politics and government over this era. The proportion of Americans who reply that they "trust the government in Washington" only "some of the time" or "almost never" has risen steadily from 30 percent in 1966 to 75 percent in 1992.

These trends are well known, of course, and taken by themselves would seem amenable to a strictly political explanation. Perhaps the long litany of political tragedies and scandals since the 1960s (assassinations, Vietnam, Watergate, Irangate, and so on) has triggered an understandable disgust for politics and government among Americans, and that in turn has motivated their withdrawal. I do not doubt that this common interpretation has some merit, but its limitations become plain when we examine trends in civic engagement of a wider sort.

Our survey of organizational membership among Americans can usefully begin with a glance at the aggregate results of the General Social Survey, a scientifically conducted, national-sample survey that has been repeated 14 times over the last two decades. Church-related groups constitute the most common type of organization joined by Americans; they are especially popular with women. Other types of organizations frequently joined by women include school-service groups (mostly parent-teacher associations), sports groups, professional societies, and literary societies. Among men, sports clubs, labor unions, professional societies, fraternal groups, veterans' groups, and service clubs are all relatively popular.

Religious affiliation is by far the most common associational membership among Americans. Indeed, by many measures America continues to be (even more than in Tocqueville's time) an astonishingly "churched" society. For example, the United States has more houses of worship per capita than any other nation on Earth. Yet religious sentiment in America seems to be becoming somewhat less tied to institutions and more self-defined.

How have these complex crosscurrents played out over the last three or four decades in terms of Americans' engagement with organized religion? The general pattern is clear: The 1960s witnessed a significant drop in reported weekly churchgoing—from roughly 48 percent in the late 1950s to roughly 41 percent in the early 1970s. Since then, it has stagnated or (according to some surveys) declined still further. Meanwhile, data from the General Social Survey show a modest decline in membership in all "church-related groups" over the last 20 years. It would seem, then, that net participation by Americans, both in religious services and in church-related groups, has declined modestly (by perhaps a sixth) since the 1960s.

For many years, labor unions provided one of the most common organizational affiliations among American workers. Yet union membership has been falling for nearly four decades, with the steepest decline occurring between 1975 and 1985. Since the mid-1950s, when union membership peaked, the unionized portion of the nonagricultural work force in America has dropped by more than half, falling from 32.5 percent in 1953 to 15.8 percent in 1992. By now, virtually all of the explosive growth in union membership that was associated with the New Deal has been erased. The solidarity of union halls is now mostly a fading memory of aging men.[5]

The parent-teacher association (PTA) has been an especially important form of civic engagement in twentieth-century America because parental involvement in the educational process represents a particularly productive form of social capital. It is, therefore, dismaying to discover that participation in parent-teacher organizations has dropped drastically over the last generation, from more than 12 million in 1964 to barely 5 million in 1982 before recovering to approximately 7 million now.

Next, we turn to evidence on membership in (and volunteering for) civic and fraternal organizations. These data show some striking patterns. First, membership in traditional women's groups has declined more or less steadily since the mid-1960s. For example, membership in the national Federation of

---

[5]Any simplistically political interpretation of the collapse of American unionism would need to confront the fact that the steepest decline began more than six years before the Reagan administration's attack on PATCO. Data from the General Social Survey show a roughly 40-percent decline in reported union membership between 1975 and 1991.

Women's Clubs is down by more than half (59 percent) since 1964, while membership in the League of Women Voters (LWV) is off 42 percent since 1969.[6]

Similar reductions are apparent in the numbers of volunteers for mainline civic organizations, such as the Boy Scouts (off by 26 percent since 1970) and the Red Cross (off by 61 percent since 1970). But what about the possibility that volunteers have simply switched their loyalties to other organizations? Evidence on "regular" (as opposed to occasional or "drop-by") volunteering is available from the Labor Department's Current Population Surveys of 1974 and 1989. These estimates suggest that serious volunteering declined by roughly one-sixth over these 15 years, from 24 percent of adults in 1974 to 20 percent in 1989. The multitudes of Red Cross aides and Boy Scout troop leaders now missing in action have apparently not been offset by equal numbers of new recruits elsewhere.

Fraternal organizations have also witnessed a substantial drop in membership during the 1980s and 1990s. Membership is down significantly in such groups as the Lions (off 12 percent since 1983), the Elks (off 18 percent since 1979), the Shriners (off 27 percent since 1979), the Jaycees (off 44 percent since 1979), and the Masons (down 39 percent since 1959). In sum, after expanding steadily throughout most of this century, many major civic organizations have experienced a sudden, substantial, and nearly simultaneous decline in membership over the last decade or two.

The most whimsical yet discomfiting bit of evidence of social disengagement in contemporary America that I have discovered is this: more Americans are bowling today than ever before, but bowling in organized leagues has plummeted in the last decade or so. Between 1980 and 1993 the total number of bowlers in America increased by 10 percent, while league bowling decreased by 40 percent. (Lest this be thought a wholly trivial example, I should note that nearly 80 million Americans went bowling at least once during 1993, *nearly a third more than voted in the 1994 congressional elections* and roughly the same number as claim to attend church regularly. Even after the 1980s' plunge in league bowling, nearly 3 percent of American adults regularly bowl in leagues.) The rise of solo bowling threatens the livelihood of bowling-lane proprietors because those who bowl as members of leagues consume three times as much beer and pizza as solo bowlers, and the money in bowling is in the beer and pizza, not the balls and shoes. The broader social significance,

---

[6]Data for the LWV are available over a longer time span and show an interesting pattern: a sharp slump during the Depression, a strong and sustained rise after World War II that more than tripled membership between 1945 and 1969, and then the post-1969 decline, which has already erased virtually all the postwar gains and continues still. This same historical pattern applies to those men's fraternal organizations for which comparable data are available—steady increases for the first seven decades of the century, interrupted only by the Great Depression, followed by a collapse in the 1970s and 1980s that has already wiped out most of the postwar expansion and continues apace.

however, lies in the social interaction and even occasionally civic conversations over beer and pizza that solo bowlers forgo. Whether or not bowling beats balloting in the eyes of most Americans, bowling teams illustrate yet another vanishing form of social capital.

Countertrends

At this point, however, we must confront a serious counterargument. Perhaps the traditional forms of civic organization whose decay we have been tracing have been replaced by vibrant new organizations. For example, national environmental organizations (like the Sierra Club) and feminist groups (like the National Organization for Women) grew rapidly during the 1970s and 1980s and now count hundreds of thousands of dues-paying members. An even more dramatic example is the American Association of Retired Persons (AARP), which grew exponentially from 400,000 card-carrying members in 1960 to 33 million in 1993, becoming (after the Catholic Church) the largest private organization in the world. The national administrators of these organizations are among the most feared lobbyists in Washington, in large part because of their massive mailing lists of presumably loyal members.

These new mass-membership organizations are plainly of great political importance. From the point of view of social connectedness, however, they are sufficiently different from classic "secondary associations" that we need to invent a new label—perhaps "tertiary associations." For the vast majority of their members, the only act of membership consists in writing a check for dues or perhaps occasionally reading a newsletter. Few ever attend any meetings of such organizations, and most are unlikely ever (knowingly) to encounter any other member. The bond between any two members of the Sierra Club is less like the bond between any two members of a gardening club and more like the bond between any two Red Sox fans (or perhaps any two devoted Honda owners): they root for the same team and they share some of the same interests, but they are unaware of each other's existence. Their ties, in short, are to common symbols, common leaders, and perhaps common ideals, but not to one another. The theory of social capital argues that associational membership should, for example, increase social trust, but this prediction is much less straightforward with regard to membership in tertiary associations. From the point of view of social connectedness, the Environmental Defense Fund and a bowling league are just not in the same category.

If the growth of tertiary organizations represents one potential (but probably not real) counterexample to my thesis, a second countertrend is represented by the growing prominence of nonprofit organizations, especially nonprofit service agencies. This so-called third sector includes everything from Oxfam and the Metropolitan Museum of Art to the Ford Foundation and the Mayo Clinic. In other words, although most secondary associations are nonprofits, most nonprofit agencies are not secondary associations. To identify trends in the size of the nonprofit sector with trends in social connectedness would be another fundamental conceptual mistake.[7]

A third potential countertrend is much more relevant to an assessment of social capital and civic engagement. Some able researchers have argued that the last few decades have witnessed a rapid expansion in "support groups" of various sorts. Robert Wuthnow reports that fully 40 percent of all Americans claim to be "currently involved in [a] small group that meets regularly and provides support or caring for those who participate in it."[8] Many of these groups are religiously affiliated, but many others are not. For example, nearly 5 percent of Wuthnow's national sample claim to participate regularly in a "self-help" group, such as Alcoholics Anonymous, and nearly as many say they belong to book-discussion groups and hobby clubs.

The groups described by Wuthnow's respondents unquestionably represent an important form of social capital, and they need to be accounted for in any serious reckoning of trends in social connectedness. On the other hand, they do not typically play the same role as traditional civic associations. As Wuthnow emphasizes,

> Small groups may not be fostering community as effectively as many of their proponents would like. Some small groups merely provide occasions for individuals to focus on themselves in the presence of others. The social contract binding members together asserts only the weakest of obligations. Come if you have time. Talk if you feel like it. Respect everyone's opinion. Never criticize. Leave quietly if you become dissatisfied. . . . We can imagine that [these small groups] really substitute for families, neighborhoods, and broader community attachments that may demand lifelong commitments, when, in fact, they do not.[9]

All three of these potential countertrends—tertiary organizations, nonprofit organizations, and support groups—need somehow to be weighed against the erosion of conventional civic organizations. One way of doing so is to consult the General Social Survey.

Within all educational categories, total associational membership declined significantly between 1967 and 1993. Among the college-educated, the average number of group memberships per person fell from 2.8 to 2.0 (a 26-

---

[7]Cf. Lester M. Salamon, "The Rise of the Nonprofit Sector," *Foreign Affairs* 73 (July–August 1994): 109–22. See also Salamon, "Partners in Public Service: The Scope and Theory of Government-Nonprofit Relations," in Walter W. Powell, ed., *The Nonprofit Sector: A Research Handbook* (New Haven: Yale University Press, 1987), 99–117. Salamon's empirical evidence does not sustain his broad claims about a global "associational revolution" comparable in significance to the rise of the nation-state several centuries ago.

[8]Robert Wuthnow, *Sharing the Journey: Support Groups and America's New Quest for Community* (New York: The Free Press, 1994), 45.

[9]Ibid., 3–6.

percent decline); among high-school graduates, the number fell from 1.8 to 1.2 (32 percent); and among those with fewer than 12 years of education, the number fell from 1.4 to 1.1 (25 percent). In other words, at *all* educational (and hence social) levels of American society, and counting *all* sorts of group memberships, *the average number of associational memberships has fallen by about a fourth over the last quarter-century.* Without controls for educational levels, the trend is not nearly so clear, but the central point is this: *more Americans than ever before are in social circumstances that foster associational involvement (higher education, middle age, and so on), but nevertheless aggregate associational membership appears to be stagnant or declining.*

Broken down by type of group, the downward trend is most marked for church-related groups, for labor unions, for fraternal and veterans' organizations, and for school-service groups. Conversely, membership in professional associations has risen over these years, although less than might have been predicted, given sharply rising educational and occupational levels. Essentially the same trends are evident for both men and women in the sample. In short, the available survey evidence confirms our earlier conclusion: American social capital in the form of civic associations has significantly eroded over the last generation.

GOOD NEIGHBORLINESS AND SOCIAL TRUST

I noted earlier that most readily available quantitative evidence on trends in social connectedness involves formal settings, such as the voting booth, the union hall, or the PTA. One glaring exception is so widely discussed as to require little comment here: the most fundamental form of social capital is the family, and the massive evidence of the loosening of bonds within the family (both extended and nuclear) is well known. This trend, of course, is quite consistent with—and may help to explain—our theme of social decapitalization.

A second aspect of informal social capital on which we happen to have reasonably reliable time-series data involves neighborliness. In each General Social Survey since 1974 respondents have been asked, "How often do you spend a social evening with a neighbor?" The proportion of Americans who socialize with their neighbors more than once a year has slowly but steadily declined over the last two decades, from 72 percent in 1974 to 61 percent in 1993. (On the other hand, socializing with "friends who do not live in your neighborhood" appears to be on the increase, a trend that may reflect the growth of workplace-based social connections.)

Americans are also less trusting. The proportion of Americans saying that most people can be trusted fell by more than a third between 1960, when 58 percent chose that alternative, and 1993, when only 37 percent did. The same trend is apparent in all educational groups; indeed, because social trust is also correlated with education and because educational levels have risen sharply, the overall decrease in social trust is even more apparent if we control for education.

Our discussion of trends in social connectedness and civic engagement has tacitly assumed that all the forms of social capital that we have discussed are themselves coherently correlated across individuals. This is in fact true. Members of associations are much more likely than nonmembers to participate in politics, to spend time with neighbors, to express social trust, and so on.

The close correlation between social trust and associational membership is true not only across time and across individuals, but also across countries. Evidence from the 1991 World Values Survey demonstrates the following:[10]

1. Across the 35 countries in this survey, social trust and civic engagement are strongly correlated; the greater the density of associational membership in a society, the more trusting its citizens. Trust and engagement are two facets of the same underlying factor—social capital.
2. America still ranks relatively high by cross-national standards on both these dimensions of social capital. Even in the 1990s, after several decades' erosion, Americans are more trusting and more engaged than people in most other countries of the world.
3. The trends of the past quarter-century, however, have apparently moved the United States significantly lower in the international rankings of social capital. The recent deterioration in American social capital has been sufficiently great that (if no other country changed its position in the meantime) another quarter-century of change at the same rate would bring the United States, roughly speaking, to the midpoint among all these countries, roughly equivalent to South Korea, Belgium, or Estonia today. Two generations' decline at the same rate would leave the United States at the level of today's Chile, Portugal, and Slovenia.

WHY IS U.S. SOCIAL CAPITAL ERODING?

As we have seen, something has happened in America in the last two or three decades to diminish civic engagement and social connectedness. What could that "something" be? Here are several possible explanations, along with some initial evidence on each.

The movement of women into the labor force.   Over these same two or three decades, many millions of American women have moved out of the home into paid employment. This is the primary, though not the sole, reason why

---

[10]I am grateful to Ronald Inglehart, who directs this unique cross-national project, for sharing these highly useful data with me. See his "The Impact of Culture on Economic Development: Theory, Hypotheses, and Some Empirical Tests" (unpublished manuscript, University of Michigan, 1994).

the weekly working hours of the average American have increased significantly during these years. It seems highly plausible that this social revolution should have reduced the time and energy available for building social capital. For certain organizations, such as the PTA, the League of Women Voters, the Federation of Women's Clubs, and the Red Cross, this is almost certainly an important part of the story. The sharpest decline in women's civic participation seems to have come in the 1970s; membership in such "women's" organizations as these has been virtually halved since the late 1960s. By contrast, most of the decline in participation in men's organizations occurred about ten years later; the total decline to date has been approximately 25 percent for the typical organization. On the other hand, the survey data imply that the aggregate declines for men are virtually as great as those for women. It is logically possible, of course, that the male declines might represent the knock-on effect of women's liberation, as dishwashing crowded out the lodge, but time-budget studies suggest that most husbands of working wives have assumed only a minor part of the housework. In short, something besides the women's revolution seems to lie behind the erosion of social capital.

Mobility: The "re-potting" hypothesis.   Numerous studies of organizational involvement have shown that residential stability and such related phenomena as homeownership are clearly associated with greater civic engagement. Mobility, like frequent re-potting of plants, tends to disrupt root systems, and it takes time for an uprooted individual to put down new roots. It seems plausible that the automobile, suburbanization, and the movement to the Sun Belt have reduced the social rootedness of the average American, but one fundamental difficulty with this hypothesis is apparent: the best evidence shows that residential stability and homeownership in America have risen modestly since 1965, and are surely higher now than during the 1950s, when civic engagement and social connectedness by our measures was definitely higher.

Other demographic transformations.   A range of additional changes have transformed the American family since the 1960s—fewer marriages, more divorces, fewer children, lower real wages, and so on. Each of these changes might account for some of the slackening of civic engagement, since married, middle-class parents are generally more socially involved than other people. Moreover, the changes in scale that have swept over the American economy in these years—illustrated by the replacement of the corner grocery by the supermarket and now perhaps of the supermarket by electronic shopping at home, or the replacement of community-based enterprises by outposts of distant multinational firms—may perhaps have undermined the material and even physical basis for civic engagement.

The technological transformation of leisure.   There is reason to believe that deep-seated technological trends are radically "privatizing" or "individualizing" our use of leisure time and thus disrupting many opportunities for social-capital formation. The most obvious and probably the most powerful instrument of this revolution is television. Time-budget studies in the 1960s showed that the growth in time spent watching television dwarfed all other changes in the way Americans passed their days and nights. Television has made our communities (or, rather, what we experience as our communities) wider and shallower. In the language of economics, electronic technology enables individual tastes to be satisfied more fully, but at the cost of the positive social externalities associated with more primitive forms of entertainment. The same logic applies to the replacement of vaudeville by the movies and now of movies by the VCR. The new "virtual reality" helmets that we will soon don to be entertained in total isolation are merely the latest extension of this trend. Is technology thus driving a wedge between our individual interests and our collective interests? It is a question that seems worth exploring more systematically.

WHAT IS TO BE DONE?

The last refuge of a social-scientific scoundrel is to call for more research. Nevertheless, I cannot forbear from suggesting some further lines of inquiry.

- We must sort out the dimensions of social capital, which clearly is not a unidimensional concept, despite language (even in this essay) that implies the contrary. What types of organizations and networks most effectively embody—or generate—social capital, in the sense of mutual reciprocity, the resolution of dilemmas of collective action, and the broadening of social identities? In this essay I have emphasized the density of associational life. In earlier work I stressed the structure of networks, arguing that "horizontal" ties represented more productive social capital than vertical ties.[11]
- Another set of important issues involves macrosociological crosscurrents that might intersect with the trends described here. What will be the impact, for example, of electronic networks on social capital? My hunch is that meeting in an electronic forum is not the equivalent of meeting in a bowling alley—or even in a saloon—but hard empirical research is needed. What about the development of social capital in the workplace? Is it growing in counterpoint to the decline of civic engagement, reflecting some social analogue of the first law of thermodynamics—social capital is neither created nor destroyed, merely redistributed? Or do the trends described in this essay represent a deadweight loss?
- A rounded assessment of changes in American social capital over the last quarter-century needs to count the costs as well as the benefits of community engagement. We must not romanticize small-town, middle-class civic life in the America of the 1950s. In addition to the deleterious trends

---

[11]See my *Making Democracy Work,* esp. ch. 6.

emphasized in this essay, recent decades have witnessed a substantial decline in intolerance and probably also in overt discrimination, and those beneficent trends may be related in complex ways to the erosion of traditional social capital. Moreover, a balanced accounting of the social-capital books would need to reconcile the insights of this approach with the undoubted insights offered by Mancur Olson and others who stress that closely knit social, economic, and political organizations are prone to inefficient cartelization and to what political economists term "rent seeking" and ordinary men and women call corruption.[12]

- Finally, and perhaps most urgently, we need to explore creatively how public policy impinges on (or might impinge on) social-capital formation. In some well-known instances, public policy has destroyed highly effective social networks and norms. American slum-clearance policy of the 1950s and 1960s, for example, renovated physical capital, but at a very high cost to existing social capital. The consolidation of country post offices and small school districts has promised administrative and financial efficiencies, but full-cost accounting for the effects of these policies on social capital might produce a more negative verdict. On the other hand, such past initiatives as the county agricultural-agent system, community colleges, and tax deductions for charitable contributions illustrate that government can encourage social-capital formation. Even a recent proposal in San Luis Obispo, California, to require that all new houses have front porches illustrates the power of government to influence where and how networks are formed.

The concept of "civil society" has played a central role in the recent global debate about the preconditions for democracy and democratization. In the newer democracies this phrase has properly focused attention on the need to foster a vibrant civic life in soils traditionally inhospitable to self-government. In the established democracies, ironically, growing numbers of citizens are questioning the effectiveness of their public institutions at the very moment when liberal democracy has swept the battlefield, both ideologically and geopolitically. In America, at least, there is reason to suspect that this democratic disarray may be linked to a broad and continuing erosion of civic engagement that began a quarter-century ago. High on our scholarly agenda should be the question of whether a comparable erosion of social capital may be under way in other advanced democracies, perhaps in different institutional and behavioral guises. High on America's agenda should be the question of how to reverse these adverse trends in social connectedness, thus restoring civic engagement and civic trust.

---

[12]See Mancur Olson, *The Rise and Decline of Nations: Economic Growth, Stagflation, and Social Rigidities* (New Haven: Yale University Press, 1982), 2.

3.3   Lift Every Voice: A Report on Religion in American Public Life (2001)

THE PEW FORUM ON RELIGION AND PUBLIC LIFE

INTRODUCTION

In 1996, President Bill Clinton signed a sweeping welfare reform bill into law. One provision of that bill, Section 104, affirmed religious organizations' right to participate in the federal government's grant-making process on the same basis as all other nonprofit organizations. The bipartisan provision, known as charitable choice, reflected growing evidence suggesting that churches, synagogues, mosques, and independent faith-based organizations supplied numerous social services, especially in the nation's most distressed urban communities. It also reflected popular support for the idea that government should aid religious groups that serve the poor, provided that public funds are used only for secular purposes (such as offering after-school reading programs, treating drug addicts, sheltering the homeless, or finding welfare recipients decent jobs), and that no tax dollars support proselytizing, sectarian worship, or religious instruction.

During the 2000 presidential campaign, both Republican George W. Bush and Democrat Al Gore endorsed charitable choice and vowed to fully implement it if elected. In 2001, the Pew Forum convened leading experts and surveyed citizens concerning faith-based approaches to addressing social and urban challenges. After 2001, the consensus on charitable choice broke down as some supporters of President Bush's faith-based initiative insisted that charitable choice did not go far enough. They called for new laws and executive orders to permit religious groups to proselytize with public funds and hire only co-religionists—positions rejected by most policymakers and most voters alike.

■

LOOKING BACK FROM THE HILL TO THE MOUNTAINTOP

Religion in America, takes no direct part in the government of society, but it must be regarded as the first of their political institutions. . . . I do not know whether all Ameri-

The Pew Forum on Religion and Public Life, *Lift Every Voice: A Report on Religion in American Public Life* (Washington, D.C.: The Pew Forum on Religion and Public Life, 2001): 5–8, 18–20. Used with permission of the Pew Forum on Religion & Public Life, a project of the Pew Research Center.

cans have a sincere faith in their religion—for who can search the human heart?—but I am certain that they hold it to be indispensable to the maintenance of republican institutions. This opinion is not peculiar to a class of citizens or to a party, but it belongs to the whole nation and to every rank of society.

Alexis de Tocqueville

No self-respecting commentary on religion in America can refrain from citing Alexis de Tocqueville. And with good reason—170 years after his visit to our country, the Frenchman's observations still ring true in their astute analysis of the unique political and moral character of America. When Tocqueville noted that beliefs "about God and human nature are indispensable to the daily practice of men's lives," he identified the role religion has always played in shaping both American institutions and civil society. Tocqueville predicted that America would thrive as a model of democracy and equality precisely because of this pervasive religiosity and the cultural mores it helped form and popularize.

America's religiosity was self-evident to Tocqueville. And religion has remained a powerful influence in American public life throughout the intervening decades. Yet by 1976 when Jimmy Carter ran for the White House, personal religiosity had become an unusual phenomenon to some political and cultural observers. During the presidential campaign, NBC News anchorman John Chancellor showed a clip of Carter talking about the fact that he was "born again," and then felt obligated to inform the audience: "By the way, we've checked this out. Being 'born again' is not a bizarre, mountaintop experience. It's something common to many millions of Americans—particularly if you're Baptist."

Twenty-five years later, it seems unthinkable that any commentator would make such an aside. In the 2000 presidential election, the profession of being "born-again" seemed almost a requirement for candidates for the Republican nomination. Vice President Al Gore even commented on what the catchphrase "WWJD—What Would Jesus Do?" meant for his personal faith.

The acceptance of religion throughout the general culture and civil society has followed a similarly circuitous path. To understand our current situation, it is necessary to trace this development. The following is not an attempt to chronicle a definitive history of religion and public life in America, but is instead a description of some of the ways in which religious ideas and communities have been involved with American politics and public policy. America has always been home to a healthy variety of faiths, but different traditions have dominated public discourse during various eras in our history.

"The New Jerusalem"?

From the very beginning, religious pluralism and religious liberty have been vital to the American project. The centrality of religious freedom and of the sacredness of individual conscience in matters of religious belief did not necessarily translate into tolerance for other religious traditions, as many early Baptists, Catholics and Quakers discovered. But it did serve as an anchor for developing conceptions of America and the society it would foster.

When John Winthrop laid out the Puritan vision for the New World, referring to "a City upon a Hill" that he hoped the Massachusetts Bay Colony would become, he voiced the belief of many who viewed the land as the blessing of a divine promise, "the New Jerusalem," the promised land. "The eyes of all people are upon us," Winthrop reminded his fellow colonists, so it was incumbent upon them to model the faithful Christian life. The contrast between theocratic government and religious freedom was never more clear than when Roger Williams and others were banished from the Massachusetts Bay Colony. Williams, who founded Rhode Island on the principle of religious freedom, later wrote that "God requireth not a uniformity of religion to be enacted and enforced in any civil state."

The Flavor of Mainline Protestantism

A predominantly Protestant flavor of civic religion, while never officially established as the national religion, has always been pervasive in American public life. It has influenced general public policy, such as the way in which voluntary and charitable organizations have taken on many roles that the state plays in European countries. The current debate over cooperation between religious social service providers and the government can be seen as a clear continuation of these ideas in the public discourse. But the interplay of religion and politics has also resulted in the influence of democratic—and, later, capitalist—ideas on American religious communities. The notion of potential congregants acting as consumers choosing among a variety of denominations is quintessentially American.

The influence of Enlightenment thinkers like John Locke and Baron de Montesquieu on some of the founders of the republic and drafters of the Constitution has been covered elsewhere in significant detail and breadth. The same is true of the debate that led to the formation of the First Amendment guarantee of the free exercise of religion without the establishment of religion. The history of these subjects will not be reproduced here. It is important to note, however, that the free exercise of religion—and even the First Amendment provision for the freedom of speech—provided the foundation for an American society in which even the smallest of minority faiths could stake their claim for a voice in public discourse. Whether they chose to do so or not has often depended on an array of social and political factors.

In the 1800s, the robust interplay of religion (primarily mainline Protestantism) and politics influenced issues as various as the concept of manifest destiny, the abolition movement, women's suffrage and the Civil War. Interestingly, in most of these debates, people on both sides employed religious language and theological justifications. Discussions about public assistance to religious schools are hardly unique to today, but have their roots in the years before the

Civil War when immigrant Catholics began to develop a parochial school system in response to Protestant pervasiveness in public schools.

New Voices

Religious communities and traditions have developed their own understandings of what it means to be part of society. Discussion of these beliefs was reinvigorated by industrialization, which created concerns about labor, distribution of wealth, urbanization, care for the poor and other social issues. The Progressive Movement developed in response to this fundamental socio-economic change in American life and led to the collaboration of liberal mainline denominations and Catholics on a number of fronts. Catholics began increasingly to enter American public life during the Progressive Era. Under the leadership of such seminal thinkers as John Ryan, a progressive Catholic reform movement arose that combined the nascent Catholic social thought tradition with American progressive liberalism. For their part, many liberal Protestants were prompted by a post-millenialist belief in the ability to hasten the Kingdom of God on earth by pursuing social justice through the resources of society and the state.

By the mid-20th century, sociologist Will Herberg could note that America was a nation of Protestants, Catholics and Jews, but that the common characteristic was their American identity. And yet for most of American history, the public sphere was dominated by mainline Protestantism. Catholics and Jews were embattled religious minorities who often opted to coalesce into self-contained communities or quietly assimilate rather than openly challenge cultural practices. In the 1950s, however, some members of this mixed composition began to challenge the primacy of Protestant culture, particularly in public school systems where daily prayer and readings from the King James Bible were still the norm. The role of African-American religious leaders in the civil rights movement provided an opportunity for that community to enter the public square in a vocal and dynamic manner. And as the nation became more diverse—particularly in the wake of increased immigration from non-Western countries—American public life was altered by a series of U.S. Supreme Court decisions dealing with the free exercise of and establishment of religion. The Protestant hegemony dating back to the Puritans lessened and a greater degree of pluralism in the public sphere took its place.

Changing the Debate

Court decisions on school prayer and abortion polarized public opinion and created an environment in which the movement known as the "Religious Right"—characterized by the Moral Majority, Christian Coalition and other national organizations engaged in policy debates—rose to prominence. Religious conservatives had previously retreated from the public square for a number of reasons. The pre-millenialist belief that the moral condition of the world was degenerating compelled many to maintain a separation from public affairs. This interpretation led many conservative religious communities to focus their spiritual efforts on individuals and not the society as a whole. Some religious conservatives were also still stung from public reaction to their role in debates over evolution and the prohibition movement. Renewed concern about what they viewed as dangerous changes in social policy, however, spurred religious conservatives to involvement in public debate.

The rise of the religious conservative movement, in turn, created a strong reaction among religious liberals and progressives, and certainly among secular segments of society. The decades of the 1970s, 1980s and part of the 1990s were dominated by arguments for and against the "Religious Right." As public debate focused on social issues and debates about family values, some social observers commented that American society seemed to be polarized around two groups, with religious fundamentalists at one pole and secularists at the other. Although Catholics continued to gain influence—particularly with the American bishops' pastoral letters on the economy and on disarmament—other religious voices were often lost amid high-decibel debates over religious and political legitimacy. The movement known as the "Religious Right" began to lose its sway in the 1990s due to a number of factors. But a broad range of conservative religious leaders and communities continued to exert an important influence in public life.

The Harmonies of Liberty?

With the successive introduction of more and more religious voices to public life, Americans are in the midst of navigating the benefits and challenges presented by a diversity of views in public discourse. While different religious traditions have dominated various eras in American history, it seems fair to say that there are perhaps more religious communities actively engaged in public life now than ever before. Many agree with the perspective of University of Richmond law professor Azizah al-Hibri, who notes: "After decades of being coy and hesitant, people of faith have finally given themselves the permission to speak about God and religion in the public square."

The recent discussion of government aid to religious social service providers is an illustration of the way in which an increasingly diverse group of religious communities is participating in national policy discourse. Although Americans endorse the desire to help others, many are uneasy about the call for more engagement because of the fear that excessive entanglement with government will diminish the primary spiritual mission of churches, synagogues and mosques or that religion will have too much influence on public life. The issue has shaken up traditional discourse by bringing together unlikely partners and by prompting Americans to consider the ways in which religion directly impacts their communities.

Religious ideas and individuals—embraced most publicly in recent years primarily in Republican politics—are gaining acceptance in Democratic circles, giving religious voices a broader platform. After the emotional upheaval of the 2000 election, both presidential candidates gave speeches reflecting their personal religiosity and the degree to which expressions of piety have become an accepted—and some would say, expected—part of American politics. In his acceptance speech, George W. Bush asked for prayers for the nation and noted that the country would move forward "with God's help." For his part, Al Gore commented on the possible divine role in the election, referring to the outcome as "one of God's unforeseen paths." In addition, President Bush has made extensive efforts to reach out to Muslim, Catholic and African-American religious leaders, bringing some of the concerns and teachings of these communities to greater public attention.

The proliferation of religious voices in the public square does not mean that the issues of the day will suddenly be resolved. There will always be conflicts among religious perspectives. But the acceptance of diverse views and voices does allow communities to explore the civic possibilities of religious reflection. It should no longer come as a surprise to observers—be they visitors from other countries or television newscasters—that Americans of many backgrounds take religion seriously. . . .

FAITH-BASED LEGISLATION

The legislation that is at the heart of Bush's faith-based initiative—particularly the expansion of "charitable choice" provisions to a wealth of federal government programs—has been the focus of much public debate throughout 2001. Many political observers were surprised to hear conservatives such as Marvin Olasky and Pat Robertson express qualms about parts of the legislative proposal. Others did not expect the degree of enthusiasm that came from many African-American religious communities in response to Bush's announcement of his ideas about government and community partnerships. And as the public learned more about the details of the initiative, they expressed a complex variety of reactions.

While Americans tend to support the idea of faith-based groups receiving government funding to provide social services, many find the practical implications of this idea troubling. In particular, most Americans would not extend that right to non-Judeo-Christian groups such as Muslim Americans, Buddhist Americans, the Nation of Islam and the Church of Scientology. Beyond the questions of which religions are acceptable, the public expresses strong concern about both the influence of government on particular religious organizations and the impact of religious groups on the people they are trying to help. On the one hand, fully 68% worry that faith-based initiatives might lead to too much government involvement with religious organizations. On the other, six-in-ten express concerns that religious groups would proselytize among recipients of social services, and about the same percentage believe that groups that encourage religious conversion should not receive government funds. Americans have even greater apprehensions about government-funded organizations hiring only those who share their beliefs: 78% oppose the idea that religious groups receiving government funding should be allowed to hire only people who share their religious beliefs.

Still, many Americans find arguments in favor of faith-based funding to be compelling and a strong majority acknowledges the contributions churches, synagogues, mosques and other religious groups make to society. Nearly three-quarters (72%) cite the care and compassion of religious workers as an important reason for supporting the concept of faith-based groups receiving government funding. This reflects a public recognition of the strong connection between religious practice and social service. Three-quarters think that churches and other houses of worship contribute significantly to solving America's social problems.

Terms of the Debate
It is important to be clear about the terms used in the public discussion. Although the phrase "charitable choice" is often popularly used to refer to the general concept of government funding of faith-based social service programs, it is more accurately a term of art that refers to a precise legislative provision first enacted by Congress in the 1996 federal welfare reform law. Additional charitable choice provisions have since become law as part of other federal and state legislation.

Charitable choice does not represent the birth of involvement by faith communities in the social service arena—groups like Catholic Charities and Lutheran Social Services have a long history of receiving government funds to perform their work. But charitable choice does change previous practice through new federal law that specifically addresses the participation of religious social service providers. It permits all religious organizations to compete for government social service funding, regardless of their degree of religiosity. It does not set aside tax funds for religious organizations.

The phrase "faith-based initiative" has been broadly applied both to the White House Office of Faith-Based and Community Initiatives established by

Important Reasons for Backing Faith-Based Programs

	Important Reason %	Not an Important Reason %	Don't Know %
People should have a variety of options	77	20	3 = 100
Service providers more caring & compassionate	72	25	3 = 100
Power of religion can change people's lives	62	35	3 = 100
Faith-based programs more efficient	60	36	4 = 100

President Bush in January and to legislation proposed by his administration that would, among other things, expand charitable choice provisions to cover additional social services.

History

In 1996, Senator John Ashcroft (R-MO) developed a provision called charitable choice that denoted the new statutory conditions under which states may enter into funding relationships with any religious institution to provide social services using federal TANF (Temporary Assistance for Needy Families) funds. It was passed as part of the 1996 welfare reform law.

Congress has since passed additional legislation involving various charitable choice provisions, including the Welfare-to-Work program (1997); the Community Services Block Grant program funded by the Health and Human Services Reauthorization Act (1998); and drug treatment programs funded by the Substance Abuse and Mental Health Services Administration (SAMHSA) (2000). In addition, the Community Renewal and New Markets Act of 2000 included charitable choice language that referred to the same funds authorized in the SAMHSA legislation. Other legislative initiatives also popularly referred to as charitable choice have been introduced in a number of states. These apply variations of the original legislation to other program areas, such as drug rehabilitation or housing.

Religious Perspectives

The potential of charitable choice to significantly alter government financial collaboration with faith-based organizations has been applauded by some, but greeted with concern and skepticism by others. Organizations including the Center for Public Justice, the Christian Legal Society, the Free Congress Foundation, the National Association of Evangelicals, the National Center for Neighborhood Enterprise and the Union of Orthodox Jewish Congregations of America generally support the concept of charitable choice and believe that it is a necessary and belated correction to the exclusion of some religious

Important Concerns about Funding for Faith-Based Programs

	Important Concern %	Not an Important Concern %	Don't Know %
Gov't too involved with religious organizations	68	30	2 = 100
People forced to take part in religious practices	60	38	2 = 100
Would interfere with church-state separation	52	45	3 = 100
Might increase religious divisions	46	48	4 = 100

providers. These groups believe that charitable choice will have a beneficial effect on society by strengthening the ability of faith communities to solve social problems.

Groups like the American Civil Liberties Union, the American Jewish Committee, Americans United for the Separation of Church and State, the Baptist Joint Committee, the Coalition Against Religious Discrimination and the Interfaith Alliance generally oppose charitable choice. They are concerned that by allowing government funds to flow without adequate safeguards to pervasively religious institutions or to religiously affiliated programs, charitable choice unwisely and unconstitutionally permits government advancement of religion and risks a general weakening of religious autonomy and integrity.

Despite the wealth of differing opinions on this issue, there have been some notable areas of agreement. In February, a diverse group of religious and civic organizations issued a report, *In Good Faith: A Dialogue on Funding Faith-Based Social Services,* discussing ways in which the government and religious groups may work together to serve those in need. Although the group continued to disagree about some crucial issues, including the constitutionality and advisability of charitable choice provisions, they did agree that the government in some instances may fund religious groups' social service work and that religious organizations and the government may cooperate in a variety of ways to assist those in need.

Section 104 of the Personal Responsibility and Work Opportunity Reconciliation Act (1996)

SECTION 104. SERVICES PROVIDED BY CHARITABLE, RELIGIOUS, OR PRIVATE ORGANIZATIONS.

(a) In General—
　　(1) State Options—A State may—
　　　　(A) administer and provide services under the programs described in subparagraphs (A) and (B)(i) of paragraph (2) through contracts with charitable, religious, or private organizations; and

Personal Responsibility and Work Opportunity Reconciliation Act, Public Law 104-193, *U.S. Statutes at Large* 110 (1996).

(B) provide beneficiaries of assistance under the programs described in subparagraphs (A) and (B)(ii) of paragraph (2) with certificates, vouchers, or other forms of disbursement which are redeemable with such organizations.

(2) Programs Described—The programs described in this paragraph are the following programs:

(A) A State program funded under part A of title IV of the Social Security Act (as amended by section 103(a) of this Act).

(B) Any other program established or modified under title I or II of this Act, that—

(i) permits contracts with organizations; or

(ii) permits certificates, vouchers, or other forms of disbursement to be provided to beneficiaries, as a means of providing assistance.

(b) Religious Organizations—The purpose of this section is to allow States to contract with religious organizations, or to allow religious organizations to accept certificates, vouchers, or other forms of disbursement under any program described in subsection (a)(2), on the same basis as any other non-governmental provider without impairing the religious character of such organizations, and without diminishing the religious freedom of beneficiaries of assistance funded under such program.

(c) Nondiscrimination Against Religious Organizations—In the event a State exercises its authority under subsection (a), religious organizations are eligible, on the same basis as any other private organization, as contractors to provide assistance, or to accept certificates, vouchers, or other forms of disbursement, under any program described in subsection (a)(2) so long as the programs are implemented consistent with the Establishment Clause of the United States Constitution. Except as provided in subsection (k), neither the Federal Government nor a State receiving funds under such programs shall discriminate against an organization which is or applies to be a contractor to provide assistance, or which accepts certificates, vouchers, or other forms of disbursement, on the basis that the organization has a religious character.

(d) Religious Character and Freedom—

(1) Religious Organizations—A religious organization with a contract described in subsection (a)(1)(A), or which accepts certificates, vouchers, or other forms of disbursement under subsection (a)(1)(B), shall retain its independence from Federal, State, and local governments, including such organization's control over the definition, development, practice, and expression of its religious beliefs.

(2) Additional Safeguards—Neither the Federal Government nor a State shall require a religious organization to—

(A) alter its form of internal governance; or

(B) remove religious art, icons, scripture, or other symbols; in order to be eligible to contract to provide assistance, or to accept certificates, vouchers, or other forms of disbursement, funded under a program described in subsection (a)(2).

(e) Rights of Beneficiaries of Assistance—

(1) In General—If an individual described in paragraph (2) has an objection to the religious character of the organization or institution from which the individual receives, or would receive, assistance funded under any program described in subsection (a)(2), the State in which the individual resides shall provide such individual (if otherwise eligible for such assistance) within a reasonable period of time after the date of such objection with assistance from an alternative provider that is accessible to the individual and the value of which is not less than the value of the assistance which the individual would have received from such organization.

(2) Individual Described—An individual described in this paragraph is an individual who receives, applies for, or requests to apply for, assistance under a program described in subsection (a)(2).

(f) Employment Practices—A religious organization's exemption provided under section 702 of the Civil Rights Act of 1964 (42 U.S.C. 2000e-1a) regarding employment practices shall not be affected by its participation in, or receipt of funds from, programs described in subsection (a)(2).

(g) Nondiscrimination Against Beneficiaries—Except as otherwise provided in law, a religious organization shall not discriminate against an individual in regard to rendering assistance funded under any program described in subsection (a)(2) on the basis of religion, a religious belief, or refusal to actively participate in a religious practice.

(h) Fiscal Accountability—

(1) In General—Except as provided in paragraph (2), any religious organization contracting to provide assistance funded under any program described in subsection (a)(2) shall be subject to the same regulations as other contractors to account in accord with generally accepted auditing principles for the use of such funds provided under such programs.

(2) Limited Audit—If such organization segregates Federal funds provided under such programs into separate accounts, then only the financial assistance provided with such funds shall be subject to audit.

(i) Compliance—Any party which seeks to enforce its rights under this section may assert a civil action for injunctive relief exclusively in an appropriate State court against the entity or agency that allegedly commits such violation.

(j) Limitations on Use of Funds for Certain Purposes—No funds provided directly to institutions or organizations to provide services and administer programs under subsection (a)(1)(A) shall be expended for sectarian worship, instruction, or proselytization.

(k) Preemption—Nothing in this section shall be construed to preempt any provision of a State constitution or State statute that prohibits or restricts the expenditure of State funds in or by religious organizations.

CHAPTER 4

Public Opinion

*I*n a democracy, all citizens would participate in decision-making for the community, on matters both large and small. *Direct democracy* typically works best in small societies, when citizens have sufficient opportunity to engage in public debates and attempt to reach consensus on policy choices. The United States is a *republican,* or *representative, democracy,* as citizens elect representatives to exercise decision-making authority on their behalf. While Americans do engage in politics through many venues, from joining political organizations to running for office, for the most part they delegate policymaking to elected officials, who usually focus full-time on politics.

The framers of the Constitution designed a system of republican, or representative, democracy because they did not think direct governance would be feasible or desirable, especially at the national level. Public opinion would be gauged periodically at election time, and in between elections, people would tend to their daily matters and be involved in politics mostly at the local level. But the framers did not expect that elected officials would become professional politicians; rather, politicians would serve while the government was in session and then return to their primary occupations. In fact, Article I of the Constitution states that "The Congress shall assemble at least once in every Year," to ensure that the national government would meet annually. Article II gives the president the power "on extraordinary Occasions, [to] convene both Houses, or either of them," in case Congress is not in session during an emergency; President Abraham Lincoln exercised this power during the Civil War.

Today, the constitutional clauses quoted above almost seem unnecessary. Congress is in session virtually year-round, with short recesses for members to visit their home district or state. While elected officials in the nineteenth century considered Washington, D.C., a provincial city with few attractions, it has become a home for national politicians since the early twentieth century. The national government has become much larger than the framers likely ever anticipated.

At the same time, the role of the public in American politics continues to evolve. In the early years of the republic, the primary locus of governmental activity was at the state and local levels, which gave more people a chance to become involved with public life. But the expansion of the federal government in the early twentieth century, particularly during the New Deal era of the 1930s, made national politics a much more significant arena. With a population of more than 280 million today, the United States cannot realistically have each person voice their opinion on every issue facing the nation. Nevertheless, identifying public opinion on the pressing matters of the day remains a critical task.

Part of the challenge in the United States is maintaining public engagement with political affairs when the government often seems so far removed from people's daily lives. Commentator Walter Lippmann published a noted text in 1925, *The Phantom Public,* in which he questioned the very feasibility of democracy in the United States as it continued to advance and grow. But others see more possibilities for democracy to thrive in a large, technologically advanced society. After all, the public has many more venues for interacting with elected officials today, from Web sites to e-mail. Technology also permits more precise methods for public opinion surveys, which seek to identify popular views on a subject by questioning a small segment of the population.

By random sampling—polling randomly selected individuals by telephone surveys or other methods—pollsters can sometimes provide a fairly accurate measure of what nearly 300 million Americans think, or whether and how they are likely to vote, by hearing from a representative cross-section of the public consisting of as few as 1,500 people. But random polls are expensive and far from infallible. No poll is better than its wording, and even professional pollsters sometimes inadvertently "slant" questions. To gauge public opinion, politicians often rely instead on less scientific or nonscientific methods such as nonrandom polls, letters from constituents, newspaper reports, and their own political instincts.

Political scientists have struggled for many decades to figure out the conditions under which public opinion matters to everything from election outcomes to what gets on the public agenda to whether given bills become law. Likewise, they have studied closely why it is that on some issues elected politicians seem to follow the "will of the people"—what real or perceived popular majorities appear to want—while on others they do not. None of the answers that they have derived are either uncomplicated or uncontested. But a few points are clear: Some people care more about certain issues than other people do (*opinion saliency*); on some issues, public opinion is pretty steady, while on others it tends to be more volatile (*opinion consistency*); and, finally, on some issues elected officials and government itself seem largely in sync with popular views or majority sentiments, while on other issues they seem significantly out of sync (*opinion-policy congruence*). For example, most Americans have some opinion on U.S. military involvement in Iraq, but some feel more strongly about it than others do, and opinions on the war can change in response to news of positive or negative developments. In mid-2004, for instance, much news on the war in Iraq was negative, and public support for the war fell. So, too, did President Bush's approval ratings: Having hit post-September 11, 2001, highs in the 90s, by mid-2004 his approval ratings were in the 40s. Drawing on work by experts, John J. DiIulio, Jr., discusses how the president's post-9/11 popularity reflected "rally effects" rather than any lasting, massive shift in public support for Bush.

Identifying public opinion accurately also requires understanding which segments of the American population are most vocal in their policy views and why. Stanford University political scientist Morris P. Fiorina rejects the concept of a "culture war" in the United States, finding that the American public is not nearly as polarized as media commentators or political elites suggest. Instead, Fiorina argues, political activists have become more polarized, but their battles do not resonate with the population at large.

4.1 The Phantom Public (1925)

WALTER LIPPMANN

INTRODUCTION

Political commentator Walter Lippmann published several noted texts about public opinion in the early twentieth century. A progressive politician who helped create the Harvard Socialist Club as an undergraduate, Lippmann believed strongly in an active national government that would ensure the well-being of its citizenry. But in the aftermath of World War I, during which Lippmann both served in the U.S. Department of War and joined the American delegation to the Paris Peace Conference, he began to question the prospects for democracy in the large, industrialized United States. In this reading, Lippmann discusses the limits of public influence in policymaking.

■

WHAT THE PUBLIC DOES

. . . The rôle of public opinion is determined by the fact that its relation to a problem is external. The opinion affects an opinion, but does not itself control the executive act. A public opinion is expressed by a vote, a demonstration of praise or blame, a following or a boycotting. But these manifestations are in themselves nothing. They count only if they influence the course of affairs. They influence it, however, only if they influence an actor in the affair. And it is, I believe, precisely in this secondary, indirect relationship between public opinion and public affairs that we have the clue to the limits and the possibilities of public opinion. . . .

It may be objected at once that an election which turns one set of men out of office and installs another is an expression of public opinion which is neither secondary nor indirect. But what in fact is an election? We call it an expression of the popular will. But is it? We go into a polling booth and mark a cross on a piece of paper for one of two, or perhaps three or four names. Have we expressed our thoughts on the public policy of the United States? Presumably we have a number of thoughts on this and that with many buts and ifs and ors. Surely the cross on a piece of paper does not express them. It would take us hours to express our thoughts, and calling a vote the expression of our mind is an empty fiction.

Walter Lippmann, *The Phantom Public* (New York: Harcourt, Brace, and Co., 1925), 54–66, 69–74 (excerpts).

A vote is a promise of support. It is a way of saying: I am lined up with these men, on this side. I enlist with them. I will follow. I will buy. I will boycott. I will strike. I applaud. I jeer. The force I can exert is placed here, not there.

The public does not select the candidate, write the platform, outline the policy any more than it builds the automobile or acts the play. It aligns itself for or against somebody who has offered himself, has made a promise, has produced a play, is selling an automobile. The action of a group as a group is the mobilization of the force it possesses.

The attempt has been made to ascribe some intrinsic moral and intellectual virtue to majority rule. It was said often in the nineteenth century that there was a deep wisdom in majorities which was the voice of God. Sometimes this flattery was a sincere mysticism, sometimes it was the self-deception which always accompanies the idealization of power. In substance it was nothing but a transfer to the new sovereign of the divine attributes of kings. Yet the inherent absurdity of making virtue and wisdom dependent on 51 per cent of any collection of men has always been apparent. The practical realization that the claim was absurd has resulted in a whole code of civil rights to protect minorities and in all sorts of elaborate methods of subsidizing the arts and sciences and other human interests so they might be independent of the operation of majority rule.

The justification of majority rule in politics is not to be found in its ethical superiority. It is to be found in the sheer necessity of finding a place in civilized society for the force which resides in the weight of numbers. I have called voting an act of enlistment, an alignment for or against, a mobilization. These are military metaphors, and rightly so, I think, for an election based on the principle of majority rule is historically and practically a sublimated and denatured civil war, a paper mobilization without physical violence.

Constitutional democrats, in the intervals when they were not idealizing the majority, have acknowledged that a ballot was a civilized substitute for a bullet. . . .

But, while an election is in essence sublimated warfare, we must take care not to miss the importance of the sublimation. There have been pedantic theorists who wished to disqualify all who could not bear arms, and woman suffrage has been deplored as a falsification of the value of an election in uncovering the alignment of martial force in the community. One can safely ignore such theorizing. For, while the institution of an election is in its historical origins an alignment of the physical force, it has come to be an alignment of all kinds of force. It remains an alignment, though in advanced democracies it has lost most of its primitive association with military combat. It has not lost it in the South where the Negro population is disfranchised by force, and not permitted to make its weight felt in an election. It has not lost it in the unstable Latin American republics where every election is in some measure still an armed revolution. In fact, the United States has officially recognized this truth by proclaiming that the substitution of election for revolution in Central America is the test of political progress.

I do not wish to labor the argument any further than may be necessary to establish the theory that what the public does is not to express its opinions but to align itself for or against a proposal. If that theory is accepted, we must abandon the notion that democratic government can be the direct expression of the will of the people. We must abandon the notion that the people govern. Instead we must adopt the theory that, by their occasional mobilizations as a majority, people support or oppose the individuals who actually govern. We must say that the popular will does not direct continuously but that it intervenes occasionally.

THE NEUTRALIZATION OF ARBITRARY FORCE

1

If this is the nature of public action, what ideal can be formulated which shall conform to it?

We are bound, I think, to express the ideal in its lowest terms, to state it not as an ideal which might conceivably be realized by exceptional groups now and then or in some distant future but as an ideal which normally might be taught and attained. In estimating the burden which a public can carry, a sound political theory must insist upon the largest factor of safety. It must understate the possibilities of public action.

The action of a public, we had concluded, is principally confined to an occasional intervention in affairs by means of an alignment of the force which a dominant section of that public can wield. We must assume, then, that the members of a public will not possess an insider's knowledge of events or share his point of view. They cannot, therefore, construe intent, or appraise the exact circumstances, enter intimately into the minds of the actors or into the details of the argument. They can watch only for coarse signs indicating where their sympathies ought to turn.

We must assume that the members of a public will not anticipate a problem much before its crisis has become obvious, nor stay with the problem long after its crisis is past. They will not know the antecedent events, will not have seen the issue as it developed, will not have thought out or willed a program, and will not be able to predict the consequences of acting on that program. We must assume as a theoretically fixed premise of popular government that normally men as members of a public will not be well informed, continuously interested, nonpartisan, creative or executive. We must assume that a public is inexpert in its curiosity, intermittent, that it discerns only gross distinctions, is slow to be aroused and quickly diverted; that, since it acts by aligning itself, it personalizes whatever it considers, and is interested only when events have been melodramatized as a conflict.

The public will arrive in the middle of the third act and will leave before the last curtain, having stayed just long enough perhaps to decide who is the hero and who the villain of the piece. Yet usually that judgment will necessarily be made apart from the intrinsic merits, on the basis of a sample of behavior, an aspect of a situation, by very rough external evidence.

We cannot, then, think of public opinion as a conserving or creating force directing society to clearly conceived ends, making deliberately toward socialism or away from it, toward nationalism, an empire, a league of nations or any other doctrinal goal. For men do not agree as to their aims, and it is precisely the lack of agreement which creates the problems that excite public attention. It is idle, then, to argue that though men evidently have conflicting purposes, mankind has some all-embracing purpose of which you or I happen to be the authorized spokesman. We merely should have moved in a circle were we to conclude that the public is in some deep way a messianic force.

2

The work of the world goes on continually without conscious direction from public opinion. At certain junctures problems arise. It is only with the crises of some of these problems that public opinion is concerned. And its object in dealing with a crisis is to help allay that crisis. . . .

Public opinion, in this theory, is a reserve of force brought into action during a crisis in public affairs. Though it is itself an irrational force, under favorable institutions, sound leadership and decent training the power of public opinion might be placed at the disposal of those who stood for workable law as against brute assertion. In this theory, public opinion does not make the law. But by canceling lawless power it may establish the condition under which law can be made. It does not reason, investigate, invent, persuade, bargain or settle. But, by holding the aggressive party in check, it may liberate intelligence. Public opinion in its highest ideal will defend those who are prepared to act on their reason against the interrupting force of those who merely assert their will.

The action of public opinion at its best would not, let it be noted, be a continual crusade on behalf of reason. When power, however absolute and unaccountable, reigns without provoking a crisis, public opinion does not challenge it. Somebody must challenge arbitrary power first. The public can only come to his assistance.

3

That, I think, is the utmost that public opinion can effectively do. With the substance of the problem it can do nothing usually but meddle ignorantly or tyrannically. It has no need to meddle with it. Men in their active relation to affairs have to deal with the substance, but in that indirect relationship when they can act only through uttering praise or blame, making black crosses on white paper, they have done enough, they have done all they can do if they help to make it possible for the reason of other men to assert itself.

For when public opinion attempts to govern directly it is either a failure or a tyranny. It is not able to master the problem intellectually, nor to deal with it except by wholesale impact. The theory of democracy has not recognized this truth because it has identified the functioning of government with the will of the people. This is a fiction. The intricate business of framing laws and of administering them through several hundred thousand public officials is in no sense the act of the voters nor a translation of their will.

But although the acts of government are not a translation of public opinion, the principal function of government is to do specifically, in greater detail, and more continually what public opinion does crudely, by wholesale, and spasmodically. It enforces some of the working rules of society. It interprets them. It detects and punishes certain kinds of aggression. It presides over the framing of new rules. It has organized force which is used to counteract irregular force.

It is also subject to the same corruption as public opinion. For when government attempts to impose the will of its officials, instead of intervening so as to steady adjustments by consent among the parties directly interested, it becomes heavy-handed, stupid, imperious, even predatory. For the public official, though he is better placed to understand the problem than a reader of newspapers, and though he is much better able to act, is still fundamentally external to the real problems in which he intervenes. Being external, his point of view is indirect, and so his action is most appropriate when it is confined to rendering indirect assistance to those who are directly responsible.

Therefore, instead of describing government as an expression of the people's will, it would seem better to say that government consists of a body of officials, some elected, some appointed, who handle professionally, and in the first instance, problems which come to public opinion spasmodically and on appeal. Where the parties directly responsible do not work out an adjustment, public officials intervene. When the officials fail, public opinion is brought to bear on the issue.

4

This, then, is the ideal of public action which our inquiry suggests. Those who happen in any question to constitute the public should attempt only to create an equilibrium in which settlements can be reached directly and by consent. The burden of carrying on the work of the world, of inventing, creating, executing, of attempting justice, formulating laws and moral codes, of dealing with the technic and the substance, lies not upon public opinion and not upon government but on those who are responsibly concerned as agents in the affair. Where problems arise, the ideal is a settlement by the particular interests involved. They alone know what the trouble really is. No decision by public officials or by commuters reading headlines in the train can usually and in the long run be so good as settlement by consent among the parties at interest. No moral code, no political theory can usually and in the long run be imposed from the heights of public opinion, which will fit a case so well as direct agreement reached where arbitrary power has been disarmed.

It is the function of public opinion to check the use of force in a crisis, so that men, driven to make terms, may live and let live.

4.2 Election Results, Rally Effects, and Democratic Futures (2003)

JOHN J. DiIULIO, JR.

INTRODUCTION

Instant analyses of election results tend to be more provocative than they are profound. For example, in the 1994 midterm congressional election, when Republicans won control of the U.S. House of Representatives for the first time in forty years, many media commentators declared that the result reflected the rise of a new, powerful, and permanent voting bloc dubbed "angry white males." Two years later, in the 1996 presidential election that returned Democrat Bill Clinton to the White House for a second term, many of the same commentators made no mention of the "angry white males" but instead proclaimed the rise of a new, powerful, and permanent voting bloc dubbed "suburban soccer moms." Neither instant analysis stood up to subsequent academic scrutiny. The same is true for the media-manufactured impression that the razor-close 2000 presidential popular vote results were unprecedented; in fact, the popular vote in most modern presidential elections has been rather evenly divided.

Likewise, sudden shifts in public opinion, especially spikes or dips in presidential approval ratings, are often misinterpreted by the media. As this reading by John J. Dilulio, Jr., suggests, in the wake of national crises, Americans tend to rally around the incumbent president. Thus it was in the wake of the 9/11 terrorist attacks on the United States that President Bush's popularity ratings soared; but by 2003, the "rally effects" wrought by 9/11 had all but vanished.

■

John J. DiIulio, Jr., "Election Results, Rally Effects, and Democratic Futures," in *Crossroads: The Future of American Politics*, ed. Andrew Cuomo (New York: Random House, 2003), 94–100.

Many political observers believe that Republicans enjoy major electoral advantages over Democrats. Given the president's post–9/11 popularity and the huge role that the White House reportedly played in the 2002 midterm congressional elections,[1] some predict that a pro-GOP partisan realignment could occur as early as 2004, ushered in by a Bush-led Republican sweep that would make President Reagan's 1984 reelection landslide seem small by comparison.

In contemporary American politics, almost anything is possible. The relevant empirical evidence, however, paints a more complicated picture: Republicans are not yet dominant, but neither are Democrats at all poised to regain power.

INTERPRETING ELECTIONS

Nearly everything we hear in the immediate aftermath of an election about what the results mean proves, upon closer inspection, to be largely or totally false. For example, in 1992, after twelve straight years in which conservative Republicans called the White House home, many morning-after analysts asserted that Americans were suddenly open to progressive policy ideas. Two years later, the same consultants and commentators confidently proclaimed that the Republican "earthquake" victory in the midterm congressional elections reflected the rise of a new and powerful bloc of voters—"angry white males." Following the 1996 Clinton reelection, there was much media hype about Democratic "soccer moms"—married suburban white women with children.[2]

But as the Clinton administration learned during its first two years, most especially through the failure of its big-government health plan, in 1992 there was no emerging progressive majority. Likewise, in 1994, what felt like an electoral earthquake was really only small seismic shifts: Republicans gained fifty-four seats, but if fewer than a grand total of twenty thousand votes in just thirteen House districts had voted Democratic instead of Republican, Democrats and Tom Foley, not Republicans and Newt Gingrich, would have led the 104th Congress.

In every election from 1968 to 1992, the percentage of the popular vote for Republican candidates to the House was higher than the percentage of House seats that actually went to Republicans. For instance, in 1976 the Republicans won 42.1 percent of the vote but received only 32.9 percent of the seats. The

---

[1]Jim VandeHei and Dan Balz, "In GOP Win, a Lesson in Money, Muscle, Planning," *The Washington Post*, November 10, 2002, A01; Howard Fineman, "How Bush Did It," *Newsweek*, November 18, 2002, 29–34, 35–37.

[2]Parts of this section are adapted from my essay "Mandate Mongering," *The Weekly Standard*, November 18, 2002, 18–20.

gap is accounted for in part by the fact that Democrats tend to do very well in low-turnout districts such as minority-dominated inner cities, while Republicans tend to do better in suburban districts.

By 1992, for the first time, a majority of all House districts had suburban-majority populations. In 1994, the GOP vote-seat gap finally closed. Though only 19 percent of eligible voters cast a vote for a Republican, it was enough to best the Democrats, who won the votes of only 16.6 percent of eligible voters. Apparently, by 1996, the mythical Republican males had married the media-manufactured Democratic moms: married suburban white women with children supported Clinton over Dole, but they did so by almost exactly the same proportion as did the general electorate (49 to 42 percent); furthermore, they strongly favored congressional Republicans (55 to 45 percent).

Election myths can become gospel truths even among ostensibly data-savvy party gurus. Take, for example, the GOP orthodoxy that President George H. W. Bush lost to Clinton because he lost Republican voters by being too moderate (breaking his no-new-taxes pledge, failing to court religious conservatives, and so on). Actually, Bush 41's biggest losses were among independents and Democrats: after winning 55 percent of independents in 1988, he won only 32 percent of them in 1992; and having won 17 percent of Democrats in 1988, he won just 10 percent in 1992. Survey data suggest that, if anything, they defected because they perceived him as too far to the right on many issues.

Likewise, take the 2000 presidential election, the razor-close results of which supposedly revealed the country to be evenly divided into geographically concentrated red-Republican and blue-Democratic electoral zones. Nice and tidy maps, but there are many Democratic state and local leaders in the red zones, many Republican ones in the blue zones, and many states that voted Democratic or Republican in the 2000 national races that voted the other way twice or more since 1980. What *was* truly novel about the 2000 election results was *not* that the country was so evenly divided in popular vote terms, but that it was so evenly divided in terms of the electoral college.

The country has normally been *very* closely divided in presidential politics, and divided in ways that bunch partisan blocs by region (for example, the once Democratic but now largely Republican South). In 1980, Reagan won just 51 percent of the popular vote but 91 percent of the electoral college (EC) vote. Reagan thereby joined Truman (1948), Kennedy (1960), Nixon (1968), and Carter as a first-term president who won barely 50 percent of the popular vote. Clinton was twice a plurality-vote president. Bush 43's victory was exceptional only in that, rather than carrying 55 to 70 percent of the EC vote, he lost the popular vote and won the EC, *both* by razor-thin margins.

The 2002 midterm election results do represent a historic GOP win: "Not since 1934 has a president's party gained seats in both houses of Congress in a first-term midterm election, and not since 1882 has a midterm election transformed a divided party government into a unified one."[3]

But the GOP's 2002 victory was neither dramatic nor improbable. Republicans closed the aforementioned vote-seat gap in 1994, and have since had nearly a decade to exploit the considerable electoral advantages that, as numerous political science studies suggest, are afforded by incumbency. Since 1962, more than nine in ten House incumbents who ran for reelection won; only once since 1962 has the incumbent House party lost (1994). Likewise, in 2002, Republicans won the two closest Senate races, but a shift of just 12,000 votes in one (Missouri) and 9,500 in the other (New Hampshire) and the Democrats would have won.

RALLY EFFECTS

Still, the fact remains that Republicans now normally best Democrats at winning the close ones, and for reasons that are widely attributed to their fielding, funding, and focusing candidates (both incumbents and challengers) better, on average, than Democrats do. As one magazine phrased it, in 2002 "Bush was the driving force behind the Republican breeze that blew across the country."[4] How likely is it that in 2004 the "breeze" will become a whirlwind?

It is, of course, impossible to predict at this stage whether the president will be reelected, and if so, by how much, or with what, if any, partisan coattails. But this much is already known: while "Bush's personal popularity affected the voting for Republican congressional candidates," the president's post–9/11 popularity has not had any impact to date on party identification.[5] Following the terrorist attacks, "Republican identification actually held steady at 32 percent" and was still "in the low 30s by June 2002."[6]

Bush's approval rating soared from 51 percent on September 10, 2001, to 86 percent on September 15, 2001, and peaked at 90 percent on September 22, 2001, the highest presidential approval rating ever recorded. This was a classic "rally effect," defined as a "sudden and substantial increase in public approval . . . that occurs in response to certain kinds of dramatic international events involving the United States."[7] By "recruiting challengers to Democratic incumbents, raising funds ardently, and campaigning tirelessly," in 2002 Bush's post–9/11 popularity helped Republican congressional candidates.[8]

---

[3]Marc J. Hetherington and Michael Nelson, "Anatomy of a Rally Effect: George W. Bush and the War on Terrorism," *PS: Political Science and Politics* 36:1 (January 2003): 42.

[4]Fineman, "How Bush Did It," 36.

[5]Hetherington and Nelson, "Anatomy of a Rally Effect," 40, 42.

[6]Ibid., 40.

[7]Ibid., 37.

[8]Ibid., 42.

DEMOCRATIC FUTURES

In February 2003, the president's post–9/11 popularity was in the low 60s, about where Bush 41's was before the eighteen-point increase afforded by the 1991 Persian Gulf War's rally effect.

4.3 Culture War? The Myth of a Polarized America (2005)

MORRIS P. FIORINA

INTRODUCTION

In the aftermath of the 2000 and 2004 presidential elections, maps of Republican-red and Democratic-blue states were widely publicized, and political commentators declared that the maps portrayed a highly polarized electorate. Based on extensive data analysis, political scientist Morris P. Fiorina concludes that the dire warnings of a divided America miss the mark, and that in fact, Americans are much more centrist in their policy views, even on such controversial subjects as abortion and sexual orientation. In this selection, Fiorina discusses how American politics changed in the latter half of the twentieth century and the consequences of those changes for democracy. He finds "a disconnect between the world of contemporary Americans and the political order that purports to represent them."

■

Much has changed in American politics since the middle of the twentieth century. Looking back, the interaction of three major developments now seems to me to be of great importance for the state of politics today.[1]

THE ASCENDANCE OF THE PURISTS

In 1962 James Q. Wilson published *The Amateur Democrat*, discussing the rise of the "amateurs" (a term he was not altogether satisfied with), and contrast-

---

[1]The discussion that follows draws on and extends the discussion in two of my earlier articles, "Extreme Voices: A Dark Side of Civic Engagement," in Theda Skocpol and Morris Fiorina, eds., *Civic Engagement in American Democracy* (Washington, DC: Brookings, 1999): 395–425; "Parties, Participation, and Representation in America: Old Theories Face New Realities," in Ira Katznelson and Helen Milner, eds., *Political Science: The State of the Discipline* (New York: Norton, 2002): 511–41.

ing them with the "professionals" who had dominated American politics at least since the rise of mass parties in the 1830s.[2] A few years later, Aaron Wildavsky wrote about the "purists" who snatched the Republican Party away from the professionals in 1964 and nominated Barry Goldwater.[3] According to Wilson, the professional

> . . . is preoccupied with the outcome of politics in terms of winning or losing. Politics, to him, consists of concrete questions and specific persons who must be dealt with in a manner that will "keep everybody happy" and thus minimize the possibility of defeat at the next election. . . . Although he is not oblivious to the ends implied by political outcomes, he sees . . . the good of society as the by-product of efforts that are aimed, not at producing the good society, but at gaining power and place for one's self and one's party.[4]

Wildavsky's characterization of the professional is similar:

> The belief in compromise and bargaining; the sense that public policy is made in small steps rather than big leaps; the concern with conciliating the opposition and broadening public appeal; and the willingness to bend a little to capture public support. . . .[5]

In contrast, Wilson's amateur

> . . . is one who finds politics intrinsically interesting because it expresses a conception of the public interest. The amateur politician sees the political world more in terms of ideas and principles than in terms of persons. Politics is the determination of public policy, and public policy ought to be set deliberately rather than as the accidental by-product of a struggle for personal and party advantage.[6]

Similarly, the distinguishing characteristics of Wildavsky's "purists" are

> . . . their emphasis on internal criteria for decision, on what they believe "deep down inside"; their rejection of compromise; their lack of orientation toward winning; their stress on the style and purity of decision—integrity, consistency, adherence to internal norms.[7]

In these writings a generation ago Wilson and Wildavsky identified the wave of the future. In contrast to the 1950s, we no longer think of the Democrats as a cadre of political professionals leading a broad coalition of blue-collar working people, and Republicans as an opposing cadre leading a smaller but still broad coalition of white collar professionals and managers. True, unions, especially the public employee unions, continue to play an

---

[2]James Q. Wilson, *The Amateur Democrat* (Chicago: University of Chicago Press, 1962).

[3]Aaron Wildavsky, "The Goldwater Phenomenon: Purists, Politicians and the Two-Party System," *Review of Politics* 27 (1965): 386–413.

[4]Wilson, *The Amateur Democrat*: 4.

[5]Wildavsky, "The Goldwater Phenomenon": 396.

[6]Wilson, *The Amateur Democrat*: 3.

[7]Wildavsky, "The Goldwater Phenomenon": 399.

important role in the Democratic Party, as business does in the Republican, but today we are more likely to think of the Democrats as the party of the environmental, civil rights, pro-choice, gay-lesbian, and gun control groups, and the Republicans as the party of the pro-life, traditional values, antitax and pro-gun groups. Issue activists—Wildavsky's purists—largely define the party images today.

Why the change? . . . [T]o some extent it reflects the decline of material incentives for political participation. The implications of party control of government for employment opportunities greatly diminished as civil service protection and public sector unionization spread. Similarly, . . . conflict of interest laws, government in the sunshine laws, ethics codes, and investigative media made it harder to reward one's friends and punish one's enemies than a generation ago. As material incentives declined, fewer political activists were drawn from the ranks of people having a personal material stake in political participation.[8] More and more the field was left to those with policy or ideological motivations. To the former, compromise was a means to achieving their (material) goals; to the latter, compromise directly devalues their (ideological and programmatic) goals.

The increased importance of money in modern campaigns also contributed to the ascendence of the purists. Understandably, poor people don't contribute.[9] In order to raise money the Democrats had to move upscale and cultivate middle-class issue activists who had money to give. Thus, the economic liberalism of the 1950s Democrats evolved into the lifestyle liberalism of the 1980s. For the Republicans money was in less short supply than voters, so the Republicans allied with religious-right groups as a way of attacking the Democrats' majority status. The strategy succeeded, but by the 1990s the activist tail had come to wag the party dog. The economic conservatism of the 1950s Republicans has evolved into a social conservatism that dismayed Barry Goldwater before his death.

Finally, the media has made its contribution to the rise of the purists. People with deep issue commitments who express them in loud chants and strident rhetoric provide good copy and footage. The smallest demonstration will attract a camera crew and give a spokesperson or two the opportunity to provide a colorful quotation or sound bite. Seeing the success of fellow purists in getting recognition by the media, others no doubt were encouraged to follow a similar path. In a 1995 study Jeffrey Barry analyzed all evening news programs on the three major networks plus CNN, and reported that citizens'

---

[8]I emphasize the importance of the modifier "personal." Obviously the material consequences of government action are larger today than ever before. But whether you personally benefit from or suffer those consequences today has less to do with your political involvement than in the past. For example, in few cities today would a neighborhood lose its garbage collection for voting the "wrong way."

[9]Sidney Verba, Kay Schlozman, and Henry Brady, *Voice and Equality* (Cambridge, MA: Harvard, 1995): 361–66.

groups, composed largely of what we call purists, received a disproportionate share of coverage: "Although they were but a small part of the lobbying population, citizen groups constituted 45.6 percent of all the interviews with interest group representatives, mentions of specific lobbying organizations, and references to interest group sectors."[10]

THE EXPANSION OF GOVERNMENT

A second major development of the past half century is the expansion of government into spheres of life previously considered to be private. In the 1950s the idea that an apartment manager or bank loan officer should not be permitted to discriminate against members of a racial or ethnic minority was a highly contested notion. The idea that a developer could not fill in a swamp because of the presence of a salamander would have seemed ludicrous, let alone the notion that a citizen could petition government for a smoke-free environment.

The literature associates the expanded scope of government with a broad confluence of factors. An increasingly enlightened population demanded that long-festering racial injustices be redressed. An increasingly affluent population turned its attention to quality-of-life issues like the environment. What Mary Anne Glendon called the "rights revolution" enabled citizens to petition the courts for broad remedies to correct newly defined injustices.[11] Whereas rights battles once revolved around such weighty matters as voting, housing, and employment, aggrieved citizens now assert rights to exercise their dogs in public spaces, to be free of cigarette smoke out of doors, and to breast-feed in public.[12] Once a feminist rallying cry, "the personal is the political" spread far beyond its original context to become a general call for consistency between one's private behavior and public principles. But that consistency could be achieved not only by changing one's private behavior, but also by demanding that the public sector enforce one's personal principles.

Thus, education, affluence, and ideology supported demands for a vast increase in the sphere in which government could operate. The net result of these and other developments was a huge expansion in the jurisdiction of the public sector—the "new social regulation" of the 1960s and 1970s.[13] On the local

---

[10]Jeffrey Berry, "The Rise of Citizen Groups," in Theda Skocpol and Morris Fiorina, eds., *Civic Engagement in American Democracy* (Washington, DC: Brookings, 1999): 381.

[11]Mary Anne Glendon, *Rights Talk: The Impoverishment of Political Discourse* (New York: Free Press, 1991).

[12]I am not opposed to such demands; indeed, I am in favor of many of them, but elevating them to the level of rights exaggerates their importance as well as diminishes the importance of fundamental rights.

[13]William Lilly and James Miller, "The New Social Regulation," *Public Interest* 47 (1977): 49–62; David Vogel, "The 'New' Social Regulation in Historical and Comparative Perspective," in Thomas McGraw, ed., *Regulation in Perspective* (Cambridge, MA: Harvard University Press, 1981): 155–64.

level Nancy Burns reports a near-tripling in the number of "special districts" (local jurisdictions that deal with environmental, conservation, recreation, and other specific subjects) between mid-century and 1987, from a bit more than ten thousand to about thirty thousand.[14] No one can count the expansion of government as measured in total number of restrictions, regulations, and permits, or in the different areas of life in which government began to operate.

The expansion of the scope of government created myriad new opportunities for those with particular issue concerns to become active in politics. There have always been people who felt extraordinarily strongly about the height and color of neighbors' fences, the contents of children's textbooks, the serving of foie gras in restaurants, and so on, but in past times they were called cranks or busybodies and were generally ignored or left to settle their conflicts informally. Today they are called activists and they demand government action to enforce their views. A party that adopts the narrow agendas of such activists can enlist their energy and resources in support of its candidates.

THE RISE OF PARTICIPATORY DEMOCRACY

At about the same time that ideological and issue motivations for political participation were on the rise, and the scope of government was expanding, the United States experienced a significant participatory turn. Consider Table [1], which lists some of the important changes in politics between the elections of John Kennedy and Bill Clinton.

The most widely recognized of these changes is the transformation of the presidential nominating process. John Kennedy was nominated by Democratic Party professionals—cigar-chomping "bosses" who met in smoke-filled rooms, according to the popular image. Only four years later Goldwater was nominated by Wildavsky's purists, and eight years after that, opposing purists captured the Democratic party and nominated George McGovern, taking advantage of new rules changes that put the contemporary primary and caucus process in place.[15]

This transformation of the nomination process was only the most visible step in a move away from party-centered elections toward candidate-centered elections.[16] Soon political scientists noticed that a significant incumbency advantage had developed in elections for the House of Representatives: incumbents could win comfortable victories by emphasizing their personal

---

[14]Nancy Burns, *The Formation of American Local Governments: Private Values in Public Institutions* (New York: Oxford University Press, 1994): 6.

[15]Theodore White, *The Making of the President 1972* (New York: Bantam, 1973), especially Chapter 2.

[16]Martin Wattenberg, *The Decline of American Political Parties, 1952–1996* (Cambridge, MA: Harvard University Press, 1998).

Table [1]

Changes in American Politics Since 1960

Presidential nominating process
"Candidate-centered" politics
Open meetings
Recorded votes
Expanded rules of standing
Enhanced judicial review
Open bureaucracy
Intervenors
"Maximum feasible participation"
Proliferation of local bodies
Advocacy explosion
Propositions
Proliferation of polls
New technologies

characteristics, constituency service, and individual records even in areas seemingly more hospitable to the opposing party.[17] For their part voters seemed to be putting less weight on their party affiliations, and party cohesion in government broke down as individual office-holders sought to win the support of an increasingly volatile electorate.[18]

Government in the sunshine gained in popularity. Legislatures, boards, and councils around the country opened up their proceedings, allowing citizens to attend and to speak to a greater extent than previously considered advisable in a representative democracy. These same government bodies opened their heretofore closed deliberative proceedings to the public as well. And, increasingly, the actions of elected officials entered into the public record, as legislatures abandoned voice, standing, and other forms of anonymous voting in favor of recorded votes.

Both the courts themselves and Congress liberalized rules of standing so that citizens could use the courts to a much greater extent than previously.[19] A nature lover who had not suffered personal material damage from a new dam could not sue on behalf of salmon in 1960. Today such a right is taken for granted.[20] In associated developments courts that at one time had largely deferred to administrative rule-makers began to take an increasingly active and

---

[17]Gary Jacobson, *The Politics of Congressional Elections* (New York: Longman, 2001): 125–32.

[18]For a recent survey of these developments see Morris Fiorina, "Parties and Partisanship: A 40-Year Retrospective," *Political Behavior* 24 (2002): 93–115.

[19]Richard Stewart, "The Reformation of American Administrative Law." *Harvard Law Review* 88 (1975): 1169–1813.

[20]As a member of Trout Unlimited I certainly regard this as an advance in social welfare.

aggressive role in overseeing the administrative process.[21] Congress even subsidized intervenors in bureaucratic proceedings and allowed them to collect legal fees for challenging agency actions in the courts.

At the local level "maximum feasible participation" became the watchword of the time as the federal government used its sticks and carrots to open up local politics to new groups and subsidized the formation of such groups. And as we noted earlier, there was a huge increase in local government jurisdictions of various types.[22]

Meanwhile an advocacy explosion occurred as thousands of new groups organized and engaged in political activity.[23] Sometimes they circumvented uncooperative legislatures by sponsoring propositions—the use of propositions surged between 1960 and 2000.[24] Politicians became increasingly aware of popular reaction to their actions as polling became a pervasive feature of contemporary society, and new technologies that at first enabled politicians to better advertise to constituents soon got turned around as citizens' groups realized they could use the same technologies to pressure politicians.

In short, these changes and others stripped away the insulation that had long surrounded political institutions and processes, leaving them more exposed to popular scrutiny and far more open to popular participation. Seemingly American democracy became more democratic. Or did it?

THE HIJACKING OF AMERICAN DEMOCRACY

The three developments just discussed (along with others I have no doubt overlooked) have cumulated and interacted to produce the present disturbing state of American politics. How they have is not immediately obvious. For although government bodies make laws and issue regulations applying to a vastly larger range of economic and social activities, there are also vastly increased opportunities for Americans to participate in making those laws and applying those regulations. The problem is that relatively few people take advantage of those opportunities. Mostly, the purists do.

For most Americans, attending lengthy meetings of city councils, school boards, or planning commissions is not something high on the list of favorite

---

[21]R. Shep Melnick, *Regulation and the Courts* (Washington, DC: Brookings, 1983).

[22]According to the U.S. Census Bureau, there are now about 86,000 governmental jurisdictions in the United States, most of them at the local level.

[23]Kay Schlozman and John Tierney, *Organized Interests and American Democracy* (New York: Harper and Row, 1986); Jack Walker, *Mobilizing Interest Groups in America* (Ann Arbor, MI: University of Michigan Press, 1991); Jonathan Rauch, *Government's End: Why Washington Stopped Working* (New York: Public Affairs, 1999).

[24]A trend decried by some of our leading political commentators. See David Broder, *Democracy Derailed: Initiative Campaigns and the Power of Money* (New York: Harcourt Brace, 2000).

ways to spend an evening. Relaxing after a hard and stressful day's work, spending a little time with the kids, or enjoying a few hours of recreation generally come first. Similarly, when it comes to ways to spend a Saturday afternoon, attending a caucus comes in well below almost anything other than a dentist appointment. Whatever the literal meaning of the Greek, Aristotle is best translated as "Man is by nature a social animal," because the more common alternative "Man is by nature a political animal" is clearly wrong. Most people do not take inherent pleasure in political activity. For most of us, it is costly in time, energy, and resources that we would prefer to devote to other activities. Almost half of us do not even bother to vote in presidential elections. As the young Robert Putnam wrote,

> Most men are not political animals. The world of public affairs is not their world. It is alien to them—possibly benevolent, more probably threatening, but nearly always alien. Most men are not interested in politics. Most do not participate in politics.[25]

Who does participate? Who takes advantage of the multitudinous new opportunities to attend evening meetings, write checks, and work in campaigns? While there are a variety of reasons people participate, ranging from the social to the material, probably the most general is that the people who participate are for the most part those who care intensely about some issue or some complex of issues. They have deep policy, programmatic, or ideological commitments. That seems completely obvious—people who care expend their time, energy, and other resources to participate. People who do not care do not make the effort. One does not need a Ph.D. to point that out.

The problem is that people who care deeply also tend to have extreme views on the issues they care deeply about. The first observations to this effect were made by political scientists three-quarters of a century ago, and no doubt politicians have understood the association between intensity and extremity since the first chieftains heard the angry rumblings around the campfires eons ago.[26] Intensity and extremity go together as illustrated by the pairings of common political descriptors. We regularly read and hear about raging liberals but not raging moderates, rabid conservatives but not rabid middle-of-the-roaders, wishy-washy moderates but not wishy-washy liberals or conservatives, bitter partisans but not bitter independents.[27] To have an intensely held position generally is to hold an extreme position, and vice versa.

---

[25]Robert Putnam, *The Beliefs of Politicians* (New Haven, CT: Yale University Press, 1973): 1.

[26]Floyd Allport and D. A. Hartman. "The Measurement and Motivation of Atypical Opinion in a Certain Group," *American Political Science Review* 19 (1925): 735–60. See also Hadley Cantril, "The Intensity of an Attitude," *Journal of Abnormal and Social Psychology* 41 (1946): 129–35.

[27]In a column about the Middle East Thomas Friedman wishes for more "fanatical moderates," calling attention to the fact that such people are rare: "Wanted: Fanatical Moderates," *New York Times Op-ed*, November 16, 2003: 13.

Thus, not only is the desire to participate not very widely distributed in the general population, there is a strong bias in how it is distributed. The extremes are overrepresented in the political arena and the center underrepresented. The standard example is the party activists who dominate the presidential selection process. Activists are small minorities even within their own parties—the highest recorded turnout in the Iowa caucuses was 12 percent of the voting age population in 1988 when both parties had competitive nomination contests. Generally the turnout percentage is in single digits. In January of 2004, with no contest on the Republican side, some 120,000 of the most committed Democrats turned out to vote in the Iowa caucuses, about one-sixth as many as the 700,000 Iowans who voted for Al Gore in 2000. The situation is similar in the issue battles waged by the various cause groups. . . . [T]he terms of the abortion debate are set by the 10 percent or so of the population that occupy each tail of the distribution of abortion attitudes, while the three-quarters of the population of "pro-choice buts" goes largely unheard. Extremists march, work in campaigns, give money, and otherwise push their views more strongly than do moderates.

I emphasize that this pattern of biased participation is broad and pervasive. It extends well beyond partisanship and a few prominent issues like abortion, and it extends well below the national level as well. Indeed, the bias may be worst on the local level. Consider the following recent illustration from San Francisco.[28] Residents began complaining that someone was using axes and chain saws to girdle mature trees (eucalyptus, Monterey Pines, and cypress) on city property. Anti-environmentalists? Anti-social vandals? On investigation it turned out that it was citizen tax dollars at work. The city Recreation and Park Department contains a unit called the Natural Areas Program (NAP), which has both paid staff and volunteers. The trees were a casualty of a NAP master plan that among other things called for the eradication of "alien species." On further investigation it turned out that NAP volunteers had already begun restoring poison oak (a native species) to some city parks, and that future plans included replacing the turtles at a city lake with a more genetically correct species of tortoise.

San Francisco is an extremely liberal city and its residents yield to no one in their greenness, but even in San Francisco there is no majority in favor of poison oak. Having been made aware of what one of its tiny specialized agencies was up to, the Park Department appointed an advisory panel to oversee the NAP, "but then it was discovered that most of the organizations on the list [of advisory panel members] consisted of similar native plant supporters."[29] City supervisors then reconstituted the panel to include park users and elected officials.

---

[28]This vignette is drawn from Ken Garcia, "S.F. Residents Battling Plant Lovers—Little-Known Group Chopping Down Trees," *San Francisco Chronicle* April 23, 2002: A-13, and "Poison Oak Activists Restrained," *San Francisco Chronicle*, October 1, 2002: A-13.

[29]"Poison Oak Activists Restrained": A-13.

While this may seem like an extreme example, lesser examples at the local level are legion. A local official working in concert with a small constituency of committed issue activists formulates a proposal or plan that is far out of the mainstream of community sentiment (environmental and land use restrictions probably are the most common, but sex education in the schools provides some wild examples). At some point the proposal makes it onto the radar screens of normal people who do not participate in obscure government proceedings, a dust-up occurs, and the proposal is rejected or the program revised or terminated amidst acrimonious debate and popular disbelief.

In addition to pushing unrepresentative views on specific issues, two other characteristics of purists are worthy of note. The first is that the issues that motivate them often are different from those that are of most concern to the great mass of ordinary citizens. Most citizens want a secure country, a healthy economy, safe neighborhoods, good schools, affordable health care, and good roads, parks, and other infrastructure. Such issues do get discussed, of course, but a disproportionate amount of attention goes to issues like abortion, gun control, the pledge of allegiance, medical marijuana, and other narrow issues that simply do not motivate the great bulk of the American people. For example, despite the attention it receives in the political arena, abortion does not show up on lists of what citizens say are the most important issues facing the country.[30]

Gun control is a particularly illustrative issue.[31] A large majority of the country favors "common sense" gun control provisions—background checks, trigger locks, higher minimum age requirements, registration, prohibitions of high-capacity clips, and so on. But most Americans do not believe that additional restrictions will do much good. Perhaps for that reason few people feel very intensely about gun control—one national poll in the aftermath of Columbine had gun control twelfth in importance on a list of voting issues. Antigun and pro-gun activists are another story, of course, and they fight tooth and nail over what most Americans view as a relatively minor issue. Al Gore staked out a strong position on the issue in 2000, apparently to appeal to gun control activists in the Democratic primaries.[32] A more moderate position on gun control probably would not have cost him any blue states, but it might have kept enough hunters in the Democratic fold (or out of the electorate) to swing 2 percent of the vote in Ohio or Missouri or Tennessee, or 1 percent in

---

[30]Eight polls by five different polling organizations in 2002–2003 asked a version of the "most important problems facing the country" item. None received enough abortion responses to report them as a separate category. http://www.pollingreport.com/prioriti.htm, accessed January 5, 2004.

[31]The discussion in this paragraph draws on Morris Fiorina and Paul Peterson, *The New American Democracy*, 3rd ed. (New York: Longman, 2003): 150–152.

[32]In addition, Gore's strong antigun position may have been part of his attempt to appeal to women voters on child safety issues.

New Hampshire. Had Gore carried even one of these states, he would now be president—Florida would have been irrelevant.

Finally, because purists hold their views more intensely than ordinary people do, their operating style differs from that of most people. They are completely certain of their views: they are right and their opponents are wrong. Moreover, their opponents are not just misguided or misinformed, but corrupt, stupid, evil, or all three. There can be no compromise because truth does not compromise with error. Their issues are too serious to permit any levity to enter the discussion. Angry attacks substitute for reasoned discussion.

Most adult Americans spend their daily lives working in organizations where courtesy and civility are basic presumptions of how people should deal with each other. Moreover, discussion and negotiation underlie normal decision-making processes in the organizations and institutions of civil society and the economy. Americans contrast the environments in which they live their lives with a political order dominated by activists and elected officials who behave like squabbling children in a crowded sandbox. This is another reason why Americans dislike politics: they are put off by the people who specialize in politics.[33]

In sum, there is a disconnect between the world of contemporary Americans and the political order that purports to represent them. Citizens see a political order that characteristically debates policy proposals more extreme than necessary to address societal issues and community problems, a political order that spends inordinate amounts of time debating policy issues that most citizens do not view as among the more important issues facing the country, and a political order dominated by a political class whose behavior and operating style would be unacceptable outside of politics. Citizens hardly can be blamed if they increasingly regard government as something that tries to do things *to* them rather than *for* them.

---

[33]An Arizona state representative told me that he would look around the ballroom at his election night parties and think "these are the only parties these people ever get invited to."

CHAPTER 5

Political Participation

*T*he most readily observable way in which the American public expresses its views is through voting. When the Constitution was ratified, only white, male property owners could vote; since then, however, the United States has witnessed the steady expansion of the franchise. The property restriction largely disappeared in the 1820s, most notably with Andrew Jackson's campaign to grant working-class citizens the right to vote regardless of land ownership. The Fifteenth Amendment, ratified in 1870, declared that "The right of citizens of the United States to vote shall not be denied . . . on account of race, color, or previous condition of servitude," but the actual application of the right to vote regardless of race did not take place until the civil rights revolution of the 1960s. Women were granted the right to vote with the Nineteenth Amendment, ratified in 1920.

Surprisingly, as more people have gained the right to vote, turnout in the United States has begun to decline. Since the 1960s, the number of eligible voters participating in presidential elections typically has fallen between 50 and 60 percent. In nonpresidential election years, when congressional and state/local elections take place, turnout is even lower. Some scholars do not consider low voter turnout to be a problem, as they conclude that only informed voters will actually bother to participate. But political scientist V. O. Key, Jr., makes a persuasive case in *The Responsible Electorate* (1966) that even though most Americans do not follow politics closely on a daily basis, they still make rational calculations in deciding whom to support.

Rational or not, there is no question that much of the American electorate fails to vote even in hotly contested, once-every-four-years presidential elections. However, political scientists Michael P. McDonald and Samuel L. Popkin argue that the problem of "nonvoting" has been exaggerated by the imprecise way in which voter participation is generally measured—namely, against a baseline of all voting-age citizens rather than against one counting only all voting-eligible citizens (for example, excluding voting-age incarcerated persons, illegal immigrants, and others not eligible to vote).

At least with respect to college-age voters, however, nobody considers declining voter participation a myth. Youth voting has declined since eighteen-year-olds first won the right to vote with the Twenty-Sixth Amendment (1971). As nationally syndicated columnist Jane Eisner argues, there are many theories about why youth voting lags, including the view that today's young people consider volunteer activity (which today's college-age population does at record rates) virtuous and worthwhile but doubt whether voting, or "politics" more generally, is either.[1]

Working as a volunteer in an inner-city soup kitchen or after-school literacy program seems to catch the potential college-age voter's civic fancy; but voting in elections where candidates may have competing positions on policies

---

[1]See Jane Eisner, *Taking Back the Vote: Getting American Youth Involved in Our Democracy* (Boston: Beacon Press, 2004).

that could affect the need for soup kitchens and after-school programs, or competing approaches to government support for such programs, apparently does not. Kevin Mattson discusses a 2003 report on youth voting by the Century Foundation that proposes ways that more young voters might be motivated to exercise their most basic democratic right—and duty.

Given the fundamental importance of political participation in a democratic society, studying the voting practices in other democratic nations is valuable. Martin P. Wattenberg examines who votes in the United States, who doesn't, and why, and he considers how the voting process could be modified to encourage greater turnout. Underlying any such reforms is the question of how to balance voter responsibility with voting accessibility.

5.1   The Responsible Electorate (1966)
V. O. KEY, JR.

INTRODUCTION

The writings of political scientist Vladimir Orlando Key, Jr., serve as the foundation for studying political parties, interest groups, and public opinion in the United States. His book *The Responsible Electorate,* published posthumously in 1966, argued against the then-conventional wisdom that Americans were apathetic about politics. Instead, Key found that the American public was actually quite logical in its voting behavior. People might not follow the news closely on a daily basis, but they nevertheless were adept at evaluating governmental policies and performance in deciding for whom to vote. Key's astute analysis presents an optimistic perspective on American voting behavior and, consequently, on the health of American democracy.

■

In his reflective moments even the most experienced politician senses a nagging curiosity about why people vote as they do. His power and his position depend upon the outcome of the mysterious rites we perform as opposing candidates harangue the multitudes who finally march to the polls to prolong the rule of their champion, to thrust him, ungratefully, back into the void of private life, or to raise to eminence a new tribune of the people. What kinds of appeals enable a candidate to win the favor of the great god, The People?

V. O. Key, Jr., with the assistance of Milton C. Cummings, Jr., "The Voice of the People: An Echo," in *The Responsible Electorate: Rationality in Presidential Voting, 1936–1960* (Cambridge, Mass.: The Belknap Press of Harvard University Press, 1966), 1–8. Copyright © 1966 by the President and Fellows of Harvard College. Reprinted by permission of the publisher.

What circumstances move voters to shift their preferences in this direction or that? What clever propaganda tactic or slogan led to this result? What mannerism of oratory or style of rhetoric produced another outcome? What band of electors rallied to this candidate to save the day for him? What policy of state attracted the devotion of another bloc of voters? What action repelled a third sector of the electorate?

The victorious candidate may claim with assurance that he has the answers to all such questions. He may regard his success as vindication of his beliefs about why voters vote as they do. And he may regard the swing of the vote to him as indubitably a response to the campaign positions he took, as an indication of the acuteness of his intuitive estimates of the mood of the people, and as a ringing manifestation of the esteem in which he is held by a discriminating public. This narcissism assumes its most repulsive form among election winners who have championed intolerance, who have stirred the passions and hatreds of people, or who have advocated causes known by decent men to be outrageous or dangerous in their long-run consequences. No functionary is more repugnant or more arrogant than the unjust man who asserts, with a color of truth, that he speaks from a pedestal of popular approbation.

It thus can be a mischievous error to assume, because a candidate wins, that a majority of the electorate shares his views on public questions, approves his past actions, or has specific expectations about his future conduct. Nor does victory establish that the candidate's campaign strategy, his image, his television style, or his fearless stand against cancer and polio turned the trick. The election returns establish only that the winner attracted a majority of the votes—assuming the existence of a modicum of rectitude in election administration. They tell us precious little about why the plurality was his.

For a glaringly obvious reason, electoral victory cannot be regarded as necessarily a popular ratification of a candidate's outlook. The voice of the people is but an echo. The output of an echo chamber bears an inevitable and invariable relation to the input. As candidates and parties clamor for attention and vie for popular support, the people's verdict can be no more than a selective reflection from among the alternatives and outlooks presented to them. Even the most discriminating popular judgment can reflect only ambiguity, uncertainty, or even foolishness if those are the qualities of the input into the echo chamber. A candidate may win despite his tactics and appeals rather than because of them. If the people can choose only from among rascals, they are certain to choose a rascal.

Scholars, though they have less at stake than do politicians, also have an abiding curiosity about why voters act as they do. In the past quarter of a century they have vastly enlarged their capacity to check the hunches born of their curiosities. The invention of the sample survey—the most widely known example of which is the Gallup poll—enabled them to make fairly trustworthy estimates of the characteristics and behaviors of large human populations. This method of mass observation revolutionized the study of politics—as well as the management of political campaigns. The new technique permitted large-scale tests to check the validity of old psychological and sociological theories of human behavior. These tests led to new hunches and new theories about voting behavior, which could, in turn, be checked and which thereby contributed to the extraordinary ferment in the social sciences during recent decades.

The studies of electoral behavior by survey methods cumulate into an imposing body of knowledge which conveys a vivid impression of the variety and subtlety of factors that enter into individual voting decisions. In their first stages in the 1930's the new electoral studies chiefly lent precision and verification to the working maxims of practicing politicians and to some of the crude theories of political speculators. Thus, sample surveys established that people did, indeed, appear to vote their pocketbooks. Yet the demonstration created its embarrassments because it also established that exceptions to the rule were numerous. Not all factory workers, for example, voted alike. How was the behavior of the deviants from "group interest" to be explained? Refinement after refinement of theory and analysis added complexity to the original simple explanation. By introducing a bit of psychological theory it could be demonstrated that factory workers with optimistic expectations tended less to be governed by pocketbook considerations than did those whose outlook was gloomy. When a little social psychology was stirred into the analysis, it could be established that identifications formed early in life, such as attachments to political parties, also reinforced or resisted the pull of the interest of the moment. A sociologist, bringing to play the conceptual tools of his trade, then could show that those factory workers who associate intimately with like-minded persons on the average vote with greater solidarity than do social isolates. Inquiries conducted with great ingenuity along many such lines have enormously broadened our knowledge of the factors associated with the responses of people to the stimuli presented to them by political campaigns.

Yet, by and large, the picture of the voter that emerges from a combination of the folklore of practical politics and the findings of the new electoral studies is not a pretty one. It is not a portrait of citizens moving to considered decision as they play their solemn role of making and unmaking governments. The older tradition from practical politics may regard the voter as an erratic and irrational fellow susceptible to manipulation by skilled humbugs. One need not live through many campaigns to observe politicians, even successful politicians, who act as though they regarded the people as manageable fools. Nor does a heroic conception of the voter emerge from the new analyses of electoral behavior. They can be added up to a conception of voting not as a civic decision but as an almost purely deterministic act. Given knowledge of certain characteristics of a voter—his occupation, his residence, his religion, his national origin, and perhaps certain of his attitudes—one can predict with a high probability the direction of his vote. The actions of persons are made to appear to be only predictable and automatic responses to campaign stimuli.

Most findings of the analysts of voting never travel beyond the circle of the technicians; the popularizers, though, give wide currency to the most bizarre—and most dubious—theories of electoral behavior. Public-relations experts share in the process of dissemination as they sell their services to politicians (and succeed in establishing that politicians are sometimes as gullible as businessmen). Reporters pick up the latest psychological secret from campaign managers and spread it through a larger public. Thus, at one time a goodly proportion of the literate population must have placed some store in the theory that the electorate was a pushover for a candidate who projected an appropriate "father image." At another stage, the "sincere" candidate supposedly had an over-whelming advantage. And even so kindly a gentleman as General Eisenhower was said to have an especial attractiveness to those of authoritarian personality within the electorate.

Conceptions and theories of the way voters behave do not raise solely arcane problems to be disputed among the democratic and antidemocratic theorists or questions to be settled by the elegant techniques of the analysts of electoral behavior. Rather, they touch upon profound issues at the heart of the problem of the nature and work-ability of systems of popular government. Obviously the perceptions of the behavior of the electorate held by political leaders, agitators, and activists condition, if they do not fix, the types of appeals politicians employ as they seek popular support. These perceptions— or theories—affect the nature of the input to the echo chamber, if we may revert to our earlier figure, and thereby control its output. They may govern, too, the kinds of actions that governments take as they look forward to the next election. If politicians perceive the electorate as responsive to father images, they will give it father images. If they see voters as most certainly responsive to nonsense, they will give them nonsense. If they see voters as susceptible to delusion, they will delude them. If they see an electorate receptive to the cold, hard realities, they will give it the cold, hard realities.

In short, theories of how voters behave acquire importance not because of their effects on voters, who may proceed blithely unaware of them. They gain significance because of their effects, both potentially and in reality, on candidates and other political leaders. If leaders believe the route to victory is by projection of images and cultivation of styles rather than by advocacy of policies to cope with the problems of the country, they will project images and cultivate styles to the neglect of the substance of politics. They will abdicate their prime function in a democratic system, which amounts, in essence, to the assumption of the risk of trying to persuade us to lift ourselves by our bootstraps.

Among the literary experts on politics there are those who contend that, because of the development of tricks for the manipulation of the masses, practices of political leadership in the management of voters have moved far toward the conversion of election campaigns into obscene parodies of the models set up by democratic idealists. They point to the good old days when politicians were deep thinkers, eloquent orators, and farsighted statesmen. Such estimates of the course of change in social institutions must be regarded with reserve. They may be only manifestations of the inverted optimism of aged and melancholy men who, estopped from hope for the future, see in the past a satisfaction of their yearning for greatness in our political life.

Whatever the trends may have been, the perceptions that leadership elements of democracies hold of the modes of response of the electorate must always be a matter of fundamental significance. Those perceptions determine the nature of the voice of the people, for they determine the character of the input into the echo chamber. While the output may be governed by the nature of the input, over the longer run the properties of the echo chamber may themselves be altered. Fed a steady diet of buncombe, the people may come to expect and to respond with highest predictability to buncombe. And those leaders most skilled in the propagation of buncombe may gain lasting advantage in the recurring struggles for popular favor.

The perverse and unorthodox argument of this [reading] is that voters are not fools. To be sure, many individual voters act in odd ways indeed; yet in the large the electorate behaves about as rationally and responsibly as we should expect, given the clarity of the alternatives presented to it and the character of the information available to it. In American presidential campaigns of recent decades the portrait of the American electorate that develops from the data is not one of an electorate strait-jacketed by social determinants or moved by subconscious urges triggered by devilishly skillful propagandists. It is rather one of an electorate moved by concern about central and relevant questions of public policy, of governmental performance, and of executive personality. Propositions so uncompromisingly stated inevitably represent overstatements. Yet to the extent that they can be shown to resemble the reality, they are propositions of basic importance for both the theory and the practice of democracy.

To check the validity of this broad interpretation of the behavior of voters, attention will center on the movements of voters across party lines as they reacted to the issues, events, and candidates of presidential campaigns between 1936 and 1960. Some Democratic voters of one election turned Republican at the next; others stood pat. Some Republicans of one presidential season voted Democratic four years later; others remained loyal Republicans. What motivated these shifts, sometimes large and sometimes small, in voter affection? How did the standpatters differ from the switchers? What led them to stand firmly by their party preference of four years earlier? Were these actions governed by images, moods, and other irrelevancies; or were they expressions of judgments about the sorts of questions that, hopefully, voters will weigh as they responsibly cast their ballots? On these matters evidence is available that is impressive in volume, if not always so complete or so precisely relevant as hindsight would wish. If one perseveres through the analysis of this extensive body of information, the proposition that the voter is not so irrational a fellow after all may become credible.

5.2 The Myth of the Vanishing Voter (2001)

MICHAEL P. McDONALD AND SAMUEL L. POPKIN

INTRODUCTION

There can be no doubt that voter turnout rates in America have fallen in recent decades, especially among younger voters. Nor can there be any doubt that Americans go to the polls in national elections at rates far below those posted by citizens in many other democratic nations. Still, just how anemic is voter participation in the United States? In this reading selection, Michael P. McDonald and Samuel L. Popkin argue that the "apparent decline in voter participation in national elections since 1972 is an illusion created by using the Bureau of the Census estimate of the voting-age population (VAP) as the denominator of the turnout rate." In many states, convicted felons are not eligible to vote. Noncitizens, of course, are not eligible either. The authors document that it is the ineligible population, not the nonvoting-but-eligible population, that has been growing. To replace the VAP, they argue for a new measure, the voting-eligible population (VEP). Their essay also furnishes a fine example of contemporary political science scholarship on American politics and government as it appears in professional academic journals.

■

The decline in voter participation is "the most important, most familiar, most analyzed, and most conjectured trend in recent American political history" (Rosenstone and Hansen 1993, 57). Researchers, theorists, pundits, politicians, and reformers are searching for causes or cures. It is claimed that less expensive campaigns, loftier political rhetoric, weightier journalism, public financing, easier registration, online voting, or more distinctive party platforms will bring voters back to the polls.

Beginning with the work of Walter Dean Burnham (1965, 1982, 1985, 1987), an extensive literature seeks to explain the decline in turnout rates (e.g., Abramson and Aldrich 1982; Ansolabehere and Iyengar 1995; Cassel and Luskin 1988; Cavanagh 1981; Franklin and de Mino 1998; Miller and Shanks 1996; Putnam 1995, 2000; Rosenstone and Hansen 1993; Shaffer 1981; Teixeira 1992). The paradox is that while certain factors favor higher turnout, notably increased education levels, the removal of structural impediments such as poll taxes and Jim Crow laws, and less restrictive voter registration, turnout

Michael P. McDonald and Samuel L. Popkin, "The Myth of the Vanishing Voter," *American Political Science Review* 95, no. 5 (December 2001): 963–974. Copyright © 2001 Cambridge University Press. Reprinted with the permission of Cambridge University Press, Michael P. McDonald, and Samuel L. Popkin.

rates still dropped (Brody 1978). Echoing those who attempt to uncover biases in turnout (Leighly and Nagler 1992; Shields and Goidel 1997; Wolfinger and Rosenstone 1980), Rosenstone and Hansen (1993, 248) warn "the more recent decline of citizen involvement in government has yielded a politically engaged class that is not only growing smaller and smaller but is also less and less representative of the American polity."

Is electoral participation declining? Contrary to conventional wisdom, voters are not "disappearing" (Teixeira 1992). We show that although the turnout rate outside the South is lower than in the 1950s and early 1960s, there has been no downward trend during the last 30 years. The apparent decline since 1972 is an artifact of using the voting-age population (VAP) to calculate the turnout rate. As Bureau of the Census documentation clearly states, the VAP includes people who are ineligible to vote, such as noncitizens, felons, and the mentally incompetent, and fails to include those living overseas but otherwise eligible (Day 1998).

It is widely acknowledged that the VAP is substantively different from the eligible population (Andrews 1966; Bruce 1997; Burnham 1985; Gans 1997; Plissner and Mitofsky 1981; Wolfinger 1993; Wolfinger and Rosenstone 1980), but no one has collected the data necessary to estimate the turnout rate over time among eligible voters. We calculate an accurate estimate of the voting-eligible population (VEP) from the VAP and show that, since 1972, the ineligible population is growing faster than the eligible population, which gives rise to the perception that voter participation is decreasing.

CONSTRUCTING THE TURNOUT RATE

The turnout rate equals the total number of votes cast divided by the eligible electorate. As straightforward as this calculation may seem, a variety of measures for the numerator and denominator are used around the world (Lijphart 1997). In the United States, researchers primarily rely upon Census statistics of the VAP for the denominator. This is the most readily available number, but it does not constitute the eligible electorate by any but the most extreme definitions. More important, the errors that result are neither random nor constant over time.

We construct the turnout rate for post–World War II elections, 1948 to 2000, by carefully distinguishing the VEP from the VAP. We provide the numbers used in our adjustments so that anyone can redefine the VEP and recalculate the turnout rate to test whether a change in definitions or estimation procedures alters our conclusions.

Numerator: Total Votes Cast
Even a figure as apparently simple as the number of votes cast in an election must be constructed out of disparate data sources. Because the Constitution grants states the authority to regulate elections, there is no requirement of

uniform reporting of comparable election data, and there is no national election commission to collect these data. We use information provided by the Congressional Research Service, which in turn contracts Election Data Services to collect voting statistics from each state (see note 8 below).

The ideal numerator for the turnout rate is the total number of voters who cast any ballot for any office, but this measure is not available for all states. Only 17 states reported total turnout in 1948, and 13 still do not report this measure. Using this number where available would bias historical as well as interstate comparisons. Historical studies avoid this problem by using a number reported by all states for all years, the vote for highest office. In presidential election years, this is simply the total number of persons who voted for the presidential candidates. In other election years, this is the largest number of people who cast a vote in a statewide race, usually either for governor or U.S. senator. If there is no statewide race, the vote cast in all U.S. House elections in a state is combined (Crocker 1997, 6).

Using total turnout instead of the vote for highest office would, of course, increase the level of turnout. Our data and the historical analysis of Burnham (1985) suggest that total turnout is on average 2.3% greater than the vote for highest office in presidential elections and 2.6% greater for congressional elections. Nevertheless, if we compare elections or states using the vote for highest office, we are not distorting any comparisons between election years. Until total turnout is routinely reported by all states, researchers concerned with exact turnout figures, either for comparisons with other countries or because of the normative importance attached to a turnout rate of more than 50%, should multiply (not add) the reported turnout rate by 1.023 or 1.026.

Denominator: Voting-Age Population Versus Voting-Eligible Population

The turnout rate is highly sensitive to the specification of the total eligible population; seemingly insignificant changes in the denominator can reverse conclusions about the turnout rate. Nearly all reports are based on the VAP from the Bureau of the Census. Both the Congressional Research Service (Crocker 1996, 1997, 1999) and the widely cited Center for the Study of the American Electorate (Gans 1997) rely on the P-25 series of the bureau's Current Population Reports, entitled "Projections of the Voting-Age Population for States," for November of each election year. Although the VAP is commonly treated as the "true" error-free denominator, it is an estimate, albeit the best available, of the number of persons of voting age who reside in the 50 states. For non-Census years, the bureau estimates the VAP by adjusting the last full Census to account for deaths, the number of persons who reach voting age, immigration, and the number of people entering and leaving overseas military service. As defined by the bureau in 1998, "the voting-age population includes all U.S. residents 18 years and over. This consists of both people who are eligible to vote and those not eligible to vote, such as non-citizens, convicted felons, and prison inmates. These projections do not cover Americans living overseas who may vote" (Day 1998, 1).

Eligibility.   Who is an eligible voter? Who should be included in the denominator? Is an eligible voter a registered citizen, a citizen who could register, any citizen at all, or any person in the country who could be made eligible to vote? We do not believe that there is a good argument for including only the registered, but all other possibilities have proponents.

Although registration figures are widely used for the denominator in Europe, few in the United States defend studies of turnout based on registered voters. Turnout based on registration is used in Europe because registration is synonymous with eligibility: It is generally done by the government or required by law (Powell 1986, 21). There is widespread agreement that such a restricted definition of eligibility gives a misleading picture of the turnout rate. If registered voters were to be used as the denominator in the United States, comparisons between elections and among states would be confusing, because registration laws vary substantially. Besides, it is virtually impossible to gather accurate registration figures due to outdated registration rolls.

The inclusion of everyone of voting age in the denominator has proponents on both normative and practical grounds. Teixeira (1992, 6) argues for the VAP because each person in the country of voting age could be allowed to vote, should the already eligible so decide: "At the most basic level, the voting-age population is the eligible electorate. Although it is little known, citizenship is not a constitutional requirement for voting in the United States. Both the time it takes to become a citizen (national) and the actual restrictions of suffrage to citizens (states) are matters of legislation." Teixeira (1992, 6) also makes a pragmatic argument: Adjusting the VAP to remove ineligible voters is a "difficult and imprecise process." Gans (1997, 46) defends the VAP on scholarly grounds, because "consistency and comparability are the only way that students and scholars of voting research can do comparative research."

Nevertheless, consistency and comparability do not force scholars to use the VAP. Burnham's (1985, 1987) pioneering work, for example, is based on straightforward methods for estimating the number of eligible voters in the country for every election. To be sure, collecting the data necessary for correcting the VAP is a difficult and onerous task, but there is little justification for making policy and normative claims on the basis of a statistical measure that we shall show is confounded in some surprising ways.

Constructing the VEP.   The VAP both includes ineligible and excludes eligible voters. It includes noncitizens, disenfranchised felons, mental incompetents, and people who do not meet residency requirements. It excludes military personnel and civilians living outside the United States. Our more accurate VEP uses a variety of government statistical series to adjust the VAP. We remove noncitizens using estimates found in the Current Population Survey (CPS) and the full Census of Population. We remove persons who are ineligible due to criminality based on Department of Justice statistics on the correctional population. We add military and civilian personnel living overseas using statistics from the Bureau of the Census, Department of Defense, Office of Personnel Management, and the United States Consular Service.

We do not make two adjustments. We do not remove the number of people ineligible due to state residency requirements because the CPS question on mobility does not employ detailed response categories, so it is not possible to determine how various state residency requirements affect ineligibility. We believe that this number has remained approximately 1% of the VAP. We also do not remove the number of mentally incompetent persons because we lack a reliable source; we estimate that this number is approximately one-tenth of 1% of the VAP, or approximately 250,000 persons in 1995.[1]

The statistics we use are not fully reported for every year, and the various sources occasionally change their definitions. At times we must draw on different sources or impute missing data. The methods we employ are detailed in the Appendix. In every case we make a conservative adjustment to the VAP so that our corrections do not overstate the turnout rate.

Further Correction: The Census Undercount. The VAP estimate does not correct for the undercount of the population in the Census. The undercount is the net product of two errors: Some people are counted more than once (overcoverage), and others are not counted (undercoverage) (GAO 1997).[2] We do not correct for undercounting because we are not aware of a good way to determine how much this affects the VAP estimate generated between censuses. Correcting for undercoverage would actually strengthen the case that there is no ongoing decline in voter participation, as a more accurate count reduces the turnout rate, ceteris paribus. Therefore, by not making this correction we can be confident that we do not overstate trends.

The degree of undercoverage has declined since 1940. According to the U.S. General Accounting Office (GAO 1997), the estimated net undercoverage was 5.8% of the total population in 1940; 4.1% in 1950, 3.1% in 1960, 2.7% in 1970, 1.2% in 1980, and 1.8% in 1990. This decline would create the impression of declining turnout rates. For example, suppose that among a constant adult pop-

---

[1]Mentally incompetent persons can be found in high-level care nursing homes that address their special needs. Our estimate is drawn from the 1995 National Nursing Home Survey, the most recent of four surveys conducted in 1974, 1977, 1985, and 1995 by the National Center for Health Statistics. The exact number of mentally incompetent residents of voting age is unknown, since there is no breakdown of residents by type or age.

[2]Overcoverage and undercoverage are estimated by the Bureau of the Census in a postenumeration survey. A sample of persons in representative areas are interviewed following the Census to determine whether they were recorded once, twice, or not at all. The responses are extrapolated to the entire country to derive estimates of the net errors.

ulation of 100 million, 50 million voted in both 1940 and 1990. The 5.8% undercount in the 1940 Census would result in a reported turnout rate of 50/94.2 or 52.2%. The same turnout in 1990, with a smaller undercount of 1.8%, would result in a reported turnout rate of 50/98.2 or 50.9%. The increased accuracy of the more recent Census would result in a decline of 1.3% in the reported turnout rate.

The VAP and VEP Turnout Rates

In Table 1 we report the data necessary to construct the national turnout rate from 1948 to 2000 using the VAP and the VEP as the denominator. In addition, after 1971 we report an estimate of persons age 18–21 and the number who voted in order to account for the effects of the 26th Amendment. Below, we replicate our analysis within and outside the South to control for the dramatic rise in participation in that region.

In recent decades two major corrections to the VAP, noncitizens and ineligible felons, are segments that are increasing faster than the rate of population growth. The percentage of noncitizens among the voting-age population has risen steadily, from 2% in 1966 to 8.0% in 2000. As for ineligible felons, the historical average before 1982 was 0.5% of the voting-age population, and the figure rose to 1.4% in 2000. The number that needs to be added to the VAP—eligible voters living abroad—remained at nearly the same percentage throughout our analysis, about 1.5%, relative to the resident voting-age population; the percentage was higher during the Korean and Vietnam conflicts and at the peak of the Cold War in the 1980s. During the 1990s the overseas percentage slightly decreased as the U.S. military presence declined more than the number of civilians living abroad increased.

Figure 1 plots the VAP and VEP turnout rates for presidential elections since World War II. A glance at the VAP line shows why analysts who take the VAP turnout rate at face value are understandably worried about civic erosion, a possible dearth of social capital, and the decline of the public sphere in America. During the 1970s and 1980s there was a steady drop of nearly 10 percentage points from the high in 1960, and the lowest point in the postwar period—indeed, in the century—was reached in 1996. The post-1972 VEP turnout rate does not decline as much. Adjustments to the VAP do not simply move the VEP turnout rate upward a constant amount across time. The lines diverge after 1972, when the ineligible population began growing faster than the total population.

Although an informal view of the 1972–2000 figures in the figure may suggest continuing decline, a prudent and statistically sound assessment is that there is no post-1971 trend in the presidential turnout rate among those eligible to vote. Regressing the 1972–2000 VEP presidential turnout rate on a linear trend variable produces estimates of a miniscule decline of 0.007 percentage points per election, or a total drop of 0.05 percentage points for the period. Yet, the standard error is so large (0.40) relative to the estimated trend that we

Table 1
National Turnout Rates

Year	Vote for Highest Office (1000s)	Voting-Age Population (1000s)	Turnout Rate VAP (%)	Noncitizens (1000s)	Adj. (%)	Ineligible Felons (1000s)	Adj. (%)	Overseas VEP (1000s)	Adj. (%)	Turnout Rate VEP (%)	Citizens Age 18–20 (1000s)	Voters Age 18–20 (1000s)	Adj. (%)	Turnout Rate VEP Age 21+ (%)
1948	48833	95573	51.1	2198	+1.2	348	+0.2	440	−0.2	52.2				
1950	41984	98134	42.8	1880	+0.8	372	+0.2	391	−0.2	43.6				
1952	61552	99929	61.6	1899	+1.2	379	+0.2	1131	−0.7	62.3				
1954	43854	102075	43.0	1939	+0.8	411	+0.2	987	−0.4	43.5				
1956	62027	104515	59.3	1986	+1.1	428	+0.2	981	−0.6	60.2				
1958	47203	106447	44.3	2129	+0.9	464	+0.2	951	−0.4	45.0				
1960	68838	109672	62.8	2193	+1.3	481	+0.3	912	−0.5	63.8				
1962	53141	112952	47.0	2259	+1.0	491	+0.2	1113	−0.5	47.7				
1964	70645	114090	61.9	2282	+1.3	478	+0.3	1212	−0.7	62.8				
1966	56188	116638	48.2	2363	+1.0	448	+0.2	1621	−0.7	48.7				
1968	73213	120285	60.9	2766	+1.4	421	+0.2	1856	−0.9	61.5				
1970	58014	124498	46.6	3148	+1.2	443	+0.2	1765	−0.7	47.3	10725	4819	+1.0	57.2
1972	77719	140777	55.2	3640	+1.5	443	+0.2	1581	−0.6	56.2	11288	2126	+1.7	40.8
1974	55944	146338	38.2	4148	+1.1	496	+0.1	1510	−0.4	39.1	11706	4322	+1.6	56.4
1976	81556	152308	53.5	4558	+1.7	588	+0.2	1562	−0.5	54.8	11370	2062	+1.7	40.7
1978	58918	155609	37.9	5780	+1.5	629	+0.2	1753	−0.4	39.0	11538	4066	+1.5	56.2
1980	86515	163945	52.8	6827	+2.3	803	+0.3	1803	−0.6	54.7	10873	2028	+1.8	44.8
1982	67616	166724	40.6	10554	+2.7	932	+0.2	1982	−0.5	43.0	10302	3799	+1.4	58.6
1984	92653	173995	53.3	13252	+4.4	1153	+0.4	2361	−0.7	57.2	9839	1625	+1.4	40.4
1986	64991	177922	36.5	12223	+2.7	1308	+0.3	2216	−0.4	39.0	9732	3206	+1.3	55.5
1988	91595	181956	50.3	13942	+4.2	1533	+0.4	2527	−0.7	54.2	9644	1629	+1.4	41.2
1990	67859	185888	36.5	16297	+3.5	1845	+0.4	2659	−0.5	39.8	8546	3445	+1.1	61.7
1992	104405	189687	55.0	17826	+5.7	2117	+0.6	2418	−0.7	60.6				

1994	75106	193163	38.9	13205	+2.9	2365	+0.5	2229	−0.4	41.8	9464	1502	+1.4	43.2
1996	96263	196928	48.9	13948	+3.7	2545	+0.6	2499	−0.6	52.6	10021	3081	+1.3	53.9
1998	72537	200929	36.1	15070	+2.9	2822	+0.5	2937	−0.5	39.0	10416	1378	+1.5	40.5
2000	105326	205813	51.2	16500	+4.5	2851	+0.7	3008	−0.7	55.6	10786	3208	+1.5	57.1

Sources: Vote for Highest Office: Congressional Research Service "Voter Registration and Turnout: 1948–1994" and memorandum, "Voter Registration and Turnout: 1996." For 1998 provided by Royce Crocker at Congressional Research Service; 2000 provided by ABC News Polling Unit, compiled by Associated Press. Voting-Age Population: Bureau of the Census Current Population Report P25-1132, "Projections of the Voting-Age Population for States: November 1998" and previous issues of same series, 2000 projection from Census Bureau, http://www.census.gov/population/www/socdemo/voting.html, accessed 25 May 2001. Noncitizens: Current Population Survey, Voter Supplement File (various years), Bureau of the Census publication series P-20, "Voting and Registration in the Election of [various years]" and Census of the Population (various years). Ineligible Felons: *Correctional Populations of the United States* (various years), as of December 31), Department of Justice reports (Beck 2000, 2001; U.S. Department of Justice, Department of Justice Statistics 2000), and ICPSR Study #8912 "Historical Statistics on Prisoners in State and Federal Institutions, Yearend 1925–1986." Overseas VEP: *Statistical Abstract of the United States* (various years), unpublished reports from United States Consular Services (various years), Military Personnel Historical Reports (various years), and Office of Personnel Management Manpower Reports (various years). Persons Age 18–20 and turnout estimates: Current Population Survey Voter Supplement File (various years).

Note: VAP is the voting-age population, a Bureau of the Census estimate of people of voting age living within the United States. VEP is the voting-eligible population, our estimate of people eligible to vote in U.S. elections. Numbers are subject to rounding. Data include Washington, DC, in 1964, 1968, and 1972–2000 as well as Alaska and Hawaii as of 1960. Excluded is Louisiana 1978 and 1982 (no statewide November election).

Figure 1
National VAP and VEP Presidential Turnout Rates, 1948–2000

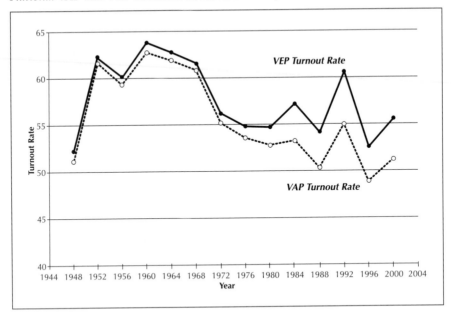

cannot reject the null hypothesis of no trend in the presidential VEP turnout rate from 1972 to 2000.

Recent rates are inconsistent and appear susceptible to short-term forces. The VEP in 1992 is no longer a minor deviation in a period of continual decline but is rather within the range of turnout rates in the 1950s and 1960s. Whatever else one may conclude about media, parties, campaigns, and civil society in the current era, turnout rates today can still attain their former level.

In 1996 the VAP rate reached its low since World War II, and the VEP rate dropped as well, to 52.7%, but that is slightly higher than the low of 52.2% in 1948. This is a small difference, but when the two VEP calculations are further corrected for the Census undercount, we find a difference of 2.5 percentage points.[3]

The low voter participation in 1948 is not given the attention it merits since the 1952 election is the starting point for most scholarly analyses. Although the decline from the 1950s and early 1960s buttresses the case for reform, the 1948 figure is not merely an aberration. Burnham (1987) adjusted turnout rates for the presence of noncitizens among the VAP before 1948, and his results show that voter participation from 1920 through 1948 is strikingly similar to the turnout rate after 1972. The highs in the 1950s and 1960s are actually quite

---

[3]After correcting for the undercount the 1948 turnout rate is 49.3% (52.2%/105.8) and the 1996 rate is 51.8% (52.7%/101.8), a difference of 2.5 percentage points.

unusual for the period after the weakening of political machines (Burnham 1987) and perhaps were more momentary than usually supposed.

The Twenty-Sixth Amendment.   The drop in turnout between 1968 and 1972 is usually attributed to expansion of the franchise from age 21 to age 18 (Rosenstone and Hansen 1993, 57).[4] This is a plausible assumption, since turnout rates for younger persons are lower than for older persons. Table 1 shows the turnout rate excluding persons under age 21. The numerator is derived by using the CPS figures to calculate the proportion of all votes reported by persons age 21 and older, and then multiplying that proportion by the total number of votes cast for highest office; the denominator is derived by removing the number of citizens age 18–20 from the VEP (see the Appendix). The average effect of removing this group since 1971 is an increase of 1.3 percentage points in presidential elections and 1.7 percentage points in congressional elections. That is slightly more than one-fourth the decrease of 4.7 percentage points for the VEP turnout rate between 1948–68 and 1972–2000. Because a large drop in voter participation occurred between 1968 and 1972, it is assumed that the new voters were a significant factor in the decline. Yet, the downward trend of the 1960s carries through to the 1972 election even though people age 18–20 are not included prior to 1972. And the turnout rate of voters under age 21 was 49.2% in 1972, according to the CPS, so their presence in that election only lowered the rate by a single percentage point.

Southern and Nonsouthern Turnout Rates.   We need to account for the dramatic rise in southern turnout rates during the 1960s to make comparisons of the aggregate turnout rate over time. The civil rights movement led to the Voting Rights Act, which effectively enfranchised blacks and poor whites in the South. Accordingly, voter participation rose dramatically in that region during the 1960s (Kousser 1999).

The increase in southern turnout masks some of the decline in the rest of the nation. The corrections performed in Table 1 are repeated in tables 2 and 3 for nonsouthern and southern states, respectively. Figure 2 plots the national, southern, and nonsouthern age 21+ VEP turnout rate for presidential elections since 1948, thereby controlling for the effects of the extended franchise and the elimination of Jim Crow laws. Turnout rates in the South rose precipitously as the electorate mobilized, but elsewhere the electorate contracted (DeNardo 1998).[5]

----

[4]Before 1971, four states allowed persons under age 21 to vote: Georgia since 1944 (18+), Kentucky since 1956 (19+), Alaska since 1960 (19+), and Hawaii since 1960 (20+) (GAO 1997).

[5]Southern states are Alabama, Arkansas, Florida, Georgia, Louisiana, Mississippi, North Carolina, South Carolina, Texas, and Virginia. The contribution of the southern turnout rate to the national figure increased over the last half of the twentieth century. In 1960, approximately one in four eligible voters resided in the South. As in-migration to that region increased, the number rose to almost one out of three in 1996. Thus, decline in nonsouthern voter participation is offset by the shift in distribution of eligible voters across regions.

Table 2
Nonsouthern Turnout Rates

Year	Vote for Highest Office (1000s)	Voting-Age Population (1000s)	Turnout Rate VAP (%)	Noncitizens (1000s)	Adj. (%)	Ineligible Felons (1000s)	Adj. (%)	Overseas VEP (1000s)	Adj. (%)	Turnout Rate VEP (%)	Citizens Age 18–20 (1000s)	Voters Age 18–20 (1000s)	Adj. (%)	Turnout Rate VEP Age 21+ (%)
1948	44129	76182	57.9	1752	+1.4	131	+0.1	356	−0.3	59.1				
1950	39393	77254	51.0	1468	+1.0	134	+0.1	313	−0.2	51.9				
1952	53890	77710	69.3	1476	+1.3	151	+0.1	899	−0.8	70.0				
1954	40386	79734	50.7	1515	+1.0	159	+0.1	785	−0.5	51.2				
1956	54343	81823	66.4	1555	+1.3	178	+0.1	781	−0.6	67.2				
1958	43750	82649	52.9	1653	+1.1	184	+0.1	751	−0.5	53.6				
1960	59618	86289	69.1	1726	+1.4	190	+0.2	717	−0.6	70.1				
1962	47431	88711	53.5	1774	+1.1	178	+0.1	874	−0.5	54.1				
1964	59476	89221	66.7	1784	+1.4	169	+0.1	948	−0.7	67.4				
1966	47803	91018	52.5	1820	+1.1	147	+0.1	1265	−0.7	52.9				
1968	59658	93594	63.7	2153	+1.5	180	+0.1	1444	−1.0	64.4				
1970	48488	96520	50.2	2413	+1.3	212	+0.1	1368	−0.7	50.9				
1972	63485	108494	58.5	3038	+1.7	242	+0.1	1219	−0.6	59.6	8621	4000	+1.2	60.8
1974	47171	111878	42.2	3244	+1.3	293	+0.1	1155	−0.4	43.1	9090	1840	+2.0	45.1
1976	64689	115823	55.9	3475	+1.7	326	+0.2	1188	−0.6	57.1	9284	3429	+1.8	58.9
1978	48490	119832	40.5	4673	+1.6	361	+0.1	1326	−0.4	41.8	9408	1746	+2.1	43.8
1980	67453	123573	54.6	5314	+2.5	473	+0.2	1354	−0.6	56.6	9659	3238	+2.0	58.7
1982	54595	126707	43.1	8869	+3.2	517	+0.2	1478	−0.5	46.0	8557	1638	+2.1	48.0
1984	71034	129436	54.9	10484	+4.8	632	+0.3	1752	−0.7	59.2	7931	2912	+1.6	60.7
1986	49490	131994	37.5	9636	+3.0	706	+0.2	1638	−0.5	40.1	7399	1237	+1.5	41.6
1988	69977	134951	51.9	11066	+4.6	847	+0.3	1866	−0.7	56.0	7372	2449	+1.4	57.5
1990	51326	136703	37.5	12850	+3.9	1020	+0.3	1957	−0.5	41.1	7117	1180	+1.5	42.6
1992	78842	138934	56.7	14171	+6.4	1187	+0.5	1772	−0.7	62.9	6268	2602	+1.1	64.0
1994	57023	141438	40.3	10042	+3.1	1307	+0.4	1628	−0.5	43.3	6847	1140	+1.5	44.8
1996	71871	142889	50.3	10161	+3.9	1419	+0.5	1784	−0.6	54.0	7055	2223	+1.4	55.3
1998	55123	145081	38.0	11461	+3.3	1567	+0.4	2121	−0.5	41.1	7356	1047	+1.6	42.6
2000	77995	148695	52.5	12289	+4.7	1520	+0.5	2174	−0.8	56.9	7703	2322	+1.6	58.5

Note: Nonsouthern is the District of Columbia plus all states except those listed in Table 3 as "southern."

Figure 2

Regional VEP Presidential Turnout Rate, Age 21+, 1948–2000

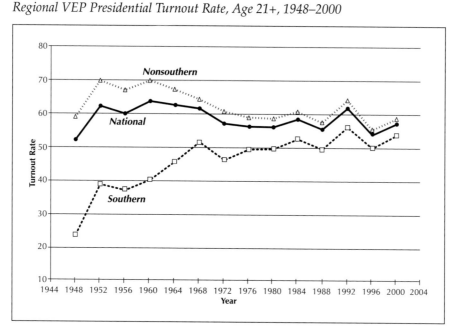

Nationally and regionally, using either VAP or VEP in the denominator of the turnout rate, there are two distinct eras of post–World War II turnout divided by 1971. The national VAP presidential turnout rate is an average 7.1 percentage points lower during 1972–2000 than during 1948–68. The VEP turnout rate is also on average lower, but by 4.7 percentage points. The gains in southern presidential turnout rates (an increase on average of 8.9 for VAP and 9.9 for VEP) are offset by losses outside the South (a decrease on average of 11.1 for VAP and 8.6 for VEP).

As shown in Table 2, the nonsouthern VAP turnout rate exhibits continued decline of greater magnitude than the national rate (Table 1), although both patterns are interrupted by the high turnout in the 1992 election.[6] The most noticeable disjunctures between the VAP and VEP nonsouthern turnout rates begin in 1972 (Table 2). For nonsouthern elections we estimate a small downward trend in VEP of 0.22 percentage points per election, with a standard error of 0.44, which implies no statistically significant trend. The southern presidential VEP turnout rate (Table 3) trends upward an estimated 0.87 percentage points per election, with a standard error of 0.37, which gives some confidence (90%) in the trend.[7]

---

[6]For nonsouthern states, we estimate a downward trend of 0.79 percentage point per election, with a standard error of 0.31.

[7]We estimate an upward trend for the southern VAP presidential turnout rate of 0.38 percentage point per election, but with a relatively large standard error of 0.30.

Table 3
Southern Turnout Rates

Year	Vote for Highest Office (1000s)	Voting-Age Population (1000s)	Turnout Rate VAP (%)	Noncitizens (1000s)	Adj. (%)	Ineligible Felons (1000s)	Adj. (%)	Overseas VEP (1000s)	Adj. (%)	Turnout Rate VEP (%)	Citizens Age 18–20 (1000s)	Voters Age 18–20 (1000s)	Adj. (%)	Turnout Rate VEP Age 21+ (%)
1948	4132	17888	23.1	411	+0.5	132	+0.2	84	−0.1	23.7				
1950	2590	19417	13.3	369	+0.3	137	+0.1	79	−0.1	13.6				
1952	7661	20016	38.3	380	+0.7	155	+0.3	232	−0.4	38.9				
1954	3469	20489	16.9	389	+0.3	163	+0.1	202	−0.2	17.2				
1956	7684	20919	36.7	397	+0.7	184	+0.3	200	−0.3	37.4				
1958	3453	21934	15.7	439	+0.3	191	+0.1	199	−0.1	16.1				
1960	9220	23383	39.4	468	+0.8	195	+0.3	194	−0.3	40.2				
1962	5710	24239	23.6	485	+0.5	182	+0.2	239	−0.2	24.0				
1964	11168	24869	44.9	497	+0.9	171	+0.3	264	−0.5	45.6				
1966	8385	25620	32.7	512	+0.7	147	+0.2	356	−0.4	33.1				
1968	13555	26734	50.7	615	+1.2	181	+0.3	412	−0.8	51.4				
1970	9526	27980	34.0	700	+0.9	215	+0.3	397	−0.5	34.7				
1972	14234	32282	44.1	613	+0.9	271	+0.4	363	−0.5	44.8	2668	797	+1.4	46.2
1974	8772	34458	25.5	896	+0.7	329	+0.2	356	−0.3	26.1	2822	307	+1.4	27.5
1976	16866	36486	46.2	1095	+1.4	364	+0.5	374	−0.5	47.6	3010	877	+1.8	49.4
1978	10427	35781	29.1	1048	+0.9	390	+0.3	427	−0.3	30.0	2927	334	+1.2	31.7
1980	19062	41024	46.5	1518	+1.8	329	+0.4	449	−0.5	48.1	3000	858	+1.6	49.7
1982	13020	40312	32.3	1896	+1.6	415	+0.3	504	−0.3	33.8	2714	352	+1.7	35.4
1984	21618	45030	48.0	2792	+3.2	521	+0.6	609	−0.6	51.1	2872	886	+1.5	52.5
1986	15501	46571	33.3	2655	+2.0	602	+0.4	578	−0.4	35.3	2764	403	+1.4	36.7
1988	21617	47827	45.2	2870	+2.9	686	+0.7	661	−0.6	48.1	2694	757	+1.3	49.4
1990	16533	49109	33.7	3438	+2.5	826	+0.6	703	−0.5	36.3	2821	446	+1.4	37.7
1992	25563	50595	50.5	3693	+4.0	930	+0.9	645	−0.6	54.8	2471	844	+1.2	56.0
1994	18082	52212	34.6	3237	+2.3	1058	+0.7	601	−0.4	37.3	2760	362	+1.5	38.7
1996	24392	53609	45.5	3109	+2.8	1126	+1.0	715	−0.6	48.7	2645	732	+1.2	49.9
1998	17414	55848	31.2	3518	+2.1	1255	+0.7	816	−0.4	33.6	3054	279	+1.5	35.1
2000	27331	57118	47.9	4209	+3.8	1330	+1.1	834	−0.7	52.1	3083	883	+1.5	53.6

Note: Southern states are Alabama, Arkansas, Florida, Georgia, Louisiana, Mississippi, North Carolina, South Carolina, Texas, and Virginia.

CONCLUSION

We attribute the apparent decline in turnout rate since 1972 to an increasing number of ineligible persons being counted among the VAP, which is the denominator for the calculations by the Bureau of the Census. We disagree with Abramson, Aldrich, and Rohde (1998, 68), who contend that correcting the denominator leads only to "relatively small differences in the overall estimate of turnout." Correcting the data changes the level of the turnout rate sufficiently to come to some different conclusions about the trends. Contrary to Teixeira (1992, 25), we agree with Wolfinger (1993, 7) that use of the VAP leads to errors that are unevenly distributed geographically and chronologically and produces "quite misleading distortions."

The great divide in the turnout rate is the 1972 election. Based on the VEP, with or without adjustments for the inclusion of younger voters, nationally and outside the South there are virtually no identifiable turnout trends from 1972 onward, and within the South there is a clear trend of increasing turnout rates. Our analysis points to a surge in nonsouthern voting in the 1950s, followed by a decline during the 1960s. Since then, turnout is lower, but there is no "downward trend." Absent further decline, divided government (Franklin and de Mino 1998), negative campaigning (Ansolabehere and Iyengar 1995), and declining civic engagement (Putnam 2000) have not depressed turnout. Whether due to the Cold War, a popular military hero as president, the emergence of national television news media not yet cynical and distrustful of power, or other factors, it was the 1950s that were unusual in being the high point of twentieth-century voter participation outside the Jim Crow South. Old theories will have to be transformed or new theories will have to be developed to explain the decline in the turnout rate during the 1960s.

An explanation for lower turnout in America than in most other industrial democracies, we suggest, must begin with the institutional structure of the political system, not the psychology of the voters or the tactics of the parties and candidates. Powell (1986) notes that in contrast to parliamentary systems, which foster strong national parties and clear lines of responsibility for government performance, responsibility is divided between state and national governments in the United States, and between two legislatures and an executive at each level. Federalism and the separation of powers increase the costs to voters to gather and process the information about which vote, for which candidate, for which office, on which date, matters for a given issue, and registration is neither done by the government nor compulsory. Furthermore, the frequent primary and general elections required to fill the many elected offices increase the burden of democracy for the voter. Indeed, the other two industrialized democracies with chronically low turnout rates are Switzerland and Japan, countries with diffused lines of authority and responsibility.

APPENDIX

The data and methods we used to construct our measure of the turnout rate among eligible voters are described below. Our sources do not report all the data we needed to construct fully each component measure for every year. When possible, we developed procedures for imputing the missing data, as detailed below.

When we analyze the effect of the 26th Amendment in 1971, we further adjust the VAP using estimates of the age distribution of the total population from the P-25 Current Population Reports. We use the Current Population Survey Voter Supplement File to determine the proportion of persons age 18–20 among eligible voters and remove this proportion from the vote for highest office.

Turnout
The numerator of the turnout rate is the number of persons who vote in a given election. Our national and state data are drawn from a 1996 Congressional Research Service (CRS) report on turnout in the 1948–94 elections, a 1997 memorandum on 1996, and a 1999 memorandum on the 1998 election (Crocker 1996, 1997).[8] As described in the text, two numbers found in these reports are commonly used as the numerator in studies of turnout, vote for highest office and total vote. We use the vote for highest office in our analysis.

Voting-Age Population
The base number for the denominator of the turnout rate is the national and state VAP estimates drawn from the P-25 series Current Population Reports.[9] The Bureau of the Census compiles these adjustments to the Census from various sources that report preliminary numbers. The bureau then releases final estimates. The 1994, 1996, 1998, and 2000 VAP estimates we use are preliminary figures still subject to minor changes.

Noncitizens
We use two methods to estimate the number of noncitizens among the VAP. From 1948 through 1966, we use a technique proposed by Burnham (1985) in

---

[8]Royce Crocker of the CRS provided the 1998 numbers to us as an Excel spreadsheet. Since 1986 the CRS has contracted with an outside vendor, Election Data Systems, to collect turnout and registration information from the states. Election Data Systems, in consultation with the CRS, compiled data from the CRS records, *America Votes,* and information supplied by Curtis Gans to construct turnout figures dating back to 1948 (personal correspondence with Royce Crocker, April 22, 1999).

[9]There is a slight discrepancy between the modern published reports of the 1948 presidential vote totals and historical reports, such as in P25–185. We use the slightly larger P25–185 number.

his study of turnout rates in the nineteenth century to interpolate the number of noncitizens for inter-Census years. We interpolate the percentage of noncitizens reported in the 1940 and 1950 Census and between the 1950 Census and the 1966 Current Population Survey (the 1960 Census did not include a citizenship question). Between 1950 and 1966 the number of noncitizens in the VAP was virtually unchanged, rising from 1.9% in 1950 to 2% in 1966. We are confident that this simple procedure does not miss an intervening wave of immigration, since legal inflows reported by the U.S. Immigration and Naturalization Service (1997) were small and stable from 1950 to 1966.

Beginning in 1966, we estimate the number of noncitizens in the VAP from the Current Population Survey Voter Supplement Files.[10] The CPS allows us to avoid the problems of interpolation during the wave of immigration that began in the 1970s and peaked in 1991.[11] Yet, use of the CPS introduces the sampling and measurement errors associated with surveys. In particular, there is a reported decline of 4.6 million noncitizens between the 1992 estimate of 17.8 million and the 1994 estimate of 13.2 million that is puzzling.[12] We believe the change in CPS methodologies is primarily responsible for the difference.

The CPS has used three different sets of citizenship questions. From 1966 to 1976, respondents were not directly asked if they were citizens but whether they were registered to vote. If not, they were asked why, and "not a citizen" was one of the options. From 1978 to 1992, respondents were queried directly about their citizenship status, and their "yes" or "no" answers were recorded. Between 1976 and 1978 the CPS revealed an increase in the number of noncitizens, from 4.5 million to 5.8 million. This is probably a true increase and not an artifact of changing survey methods. Although the increase is slightly larger than the 1970s trend, the U.S. Immigration and Naturalization Service (1997) reports a rise in legal immigration in 1978.

In 1994, the CPS citizenship item was changed again to determine possible types of status. Respondents were given five options: "Native, Born in the United States"; "Native, Born in Puerto Rico or U.S. Outlying Area"; "Native, Born Abroad of American Parent or Parents"; "Foreign Born, U.S. Citizen By Naturalization"; and "Foreign Born, Not a Citizen of the United States." Moreover, there were significant methodological changes that may affect the CPS estimates. The 1994 CPS was the first in our analysis to use the 1990 Census

---

[10]The first CPS Voter Supplement File questionnaire, in 1964, did not include a citizenship question.

[11]In 1991, the U.S. Immigration and Naturalization Service (1997) reports 1.8 million legal immigrants entered the country, the highest number in American history. Immigration has since declined slightly but still remains at historical highs.

[12]There is a spike in noncitizens between 1980 and 1982. Some of this is due to a flood of immigrants from Cuba who participated in the Mariel boatlift, as well as to new asylum laws that were introduced in late 1980.

as a baseline to construct weights and the first to use computer-aided interviews.[13]

Is it possible that the number of noncitizens declined between 1992 and 1994? We think not. In 1991 and 1992, there were 3.4 million legal immigrants who entered the country and 550,000 naturalizations. In 1993 and 1994, there were 1.9 million legal immigrants and 750,000 naturalizations (U.S. Immigration and Naturalization Service 1997). Since the net changes in legal immigration and naturalization cannot account for the decline, could a decrease this large occur solely due to large changes in the rates of out-migration and illegal immigration? There was heightened emphasis on controlling illegal entry under the Clinton administration, as well as more anti-immigration legislation. There could have been a true decline in illegal entry or greater reluctance of noncitizens to acknowledge their status, but we cannot say whether the 1994 number is more or less accurate than previous numbers. We do know, however, that legal immigration statistics clearly reveal a rise in the number of legal entrants that began in the 1970s, peaked in 1991, and declined slightly thereafter, consistent with the overall CPS trend. The numbers are consistent with two possibilities: less overreporting of citizenship in 1994 than in 1992, or more underreporting in 1994 than in 1992. Thus, while our calculation of the VEP for any one election is susceptible to errors in the CPS survey methodology, we are confident that the overall character of the trends in noncitizens we discuss is correct.

Ineligible Felons

Depending upon state law, felons may not vote if in prison, on probation, or on parole, and they may even be permanently disfranchised.[14] Four states, Maine, Massachusetts, Utah, and Vermont (now three, following the 2000 adoption of a restrictive constitutional amendment in Massachusetts), did not disfranchise even prisoners during the period of study. The first three categories of disfranchised felons (in prison, on parole, or on probation) are compiled for 1986–96 from the U.S. Department of Justice, Bureau of Justice Statistics, annual *Correctional Populations of the United States.*[15] Nearly all prisoners and parolees and half of all probationers have been convicted of a felony (U.S. Department of Justice, Bureau of Justice Statistics 2000, 2). We assume that all prisoners, all parolees, and half of all probationers are felons. For pre-

---

[13]Personal communication with Jennifer Day, May 8, 1999.

[14]See the Department of Justice report, "Civil Disabilities of Convicted Felons: A State-by-State Survey" (Love and Kuzma 1996).

[15]Footnotes in *Correctional Populations* detail that state agencies report their information with varying levels of accuracy, particularly the number of felons on parole and probation. States that do not report these data tend to be the same states that grant felons on probation or parole the right to vote. Additional error arises from the practice by some states of combining their prison and jail populations into one reported number. These five states (Alaska, Connecticut, Delaware, Hawaii, and Rhode Island), plus the District of Columbia, tend to have small prison populations.

1986 data, we used ICSPR Study #8912, "Historical Statistics on Prisoners in State and Federal Institutions, Year End 1925–1986" (U.S. Department of Justice, Bureau of Justice Statistics, 1997).[16] Some felony prisoners are noncitizens, although the exact number over time is unknown, so an adjustment is not made.[17]

We do not have a source for the number of felons on probation or parole before 1986, so we had to estimate this number. We calculate national and regional estimates for the number of ineligible felons using the ratio between the number of prisoners and the number on probation and parole for 1986 to 1996, for which all data are available. With the year as the unit of analysis, from 1986 to 1996 a regression estimates that nationally there were 1.50 ineligible felons on parole or probation for every ineligible felon in prison. The southern states had 2.18 ineligible probationers and parolees for every ineligible prisoner, and nonsouthern states had 1.13.[18]

Before 1972, we make one further adjustment to the estimate of the number of ineligible felons. We must calculate the percentage of felons age 18–20; otherwise, when we subtract felons from the VEP, we will overcorrect the denominator and overstate the true rate of turnout. We must estimate the unreported age distribution of felons. We begin by assuming that felons on probation and parole are older than 20. We then assume that 18-to-20-year-olds are 15% of the prison population.

It is more difficult to determine the numbers of felons permanently disenfranchised despite having completed probation or parole, and we have not included this group in our measure of ineligible felons.

The Sentencing Project and Human Rights Watch (Fellner and Mauer 1998) conducted an exhaustive study of state data and estimated that in 1996 there were approximately 1.39 million permanently disfranchised felons. They compiled the number of felons released since 1970 within states that have such laws and adjusted for recidivism. The study does not account for felons who vote despite being ineligible, moved or died.[19] Our measure of ineligible felons is most certainly an underestimate that probably is correlated with the actual number of disfranchised felons, since a felon must first go through the correctional system before becoming permanently disfranchised. If these 1996 reports are accurate, the permanently disfranchised number slightly more

---

[16]No breakdown of federal prisoners among the states is available. We divide federal prisoners among states by assuming that states have the same share of federal prisoners that they have of state prisoners.

[17]In 1994, about 30,000, or 1.2%, of the felony prisoners were identified as noncitizens (U.S. Department of Justice, Bureau of Justice Statistics, 1996).

[18]The regression estimate of this ratio is very consistent, with a standard error of less than .01. Unless major changes in incarceration patterns occurred in the past, we believe this imputation method is sound.

[19]A small number of permanently disfranchised felons have been granted the right to vote through pardons.

than one half of the 2.85 million disfranchised felons in prison, on probation, or on parole.

Eligible Overseas Voters

Eligible voters living overseas are comprised of military personnel and their dependents, nonmilitary government personnel, and nongovernment civilians. Our primary sources for these figures are the *Statistical Abstract of the United States* and the Census. Because the *Statistical Abstract* does not regularly report the total overseas population, let alone its age distribution, we must turn to other sources and make a number of assumptions. We supplement the *Statistical Abstract* and the Census with Department of Defense records, various Office of Personnel Management reports, and estimates provided by the U.S. Consular Services of the total number of civilians abroad (which includes those working for private companies).

The estimation procedures differ for the periods 1948–66, 1968–82, 1984–92, and 1994–96 because of changes in reporting. For some time periods there are separate numbers for military dependents, nonmilitary government personnel, and "other civilians," while for other years all nonmilitary categories are combined. For all years, we have accurate numbers on overseas military personnel, available on-line from the Department of Defense web site.[20] The post-Vietnam high was 609,000 overseas personnel in 1988, while today there are 240,000. We assume the age distribution of soldiers overseas is the same as the domestic population. We must use different techniques, however, for the number of overseas civilians.

1948–66.   To arrive at the number of eligible voters living overseas from 1948 to 1966, we estimate the nonmilitary number for the three years for which we have data: 1950, 1960, and 1968. We then interpolate that number for the years with missing data and add the number of eligible military personnel overseas (these data are available throughout the series).[21]

The 1950 Census reports the number of military personnel and their dependents living overseas. We do not know the age distribution of these groups, so we assume the relative proportions younger and older than 21 are the same as in the domestic population and that military personnel are at least 18 years old. We use the P-25 series report, which summarizes yearly estimates of the age distribution of the domestic population, to adjust the overseas population by removing the estimated number of persons under age 21.

The 1960 Census reports similar data and an additional category, the number of civilians living overseas. We make the same assumptions and adjustments as before for military personnel and their dependents. We assume that

---

[20]See http://web1.whs.osd.mil/mmid/mmidhome.htm (accessed 3 October 2001).

[21]For 1948, we use our estimate of the 1950 number of overseas civilians.

the age distribution of civilians living overseas is the same as the domestic population and remove persons under age 21.

1968–82.   The overseas eligible voters from 1968 to 1982 are estimated from the 1984 *Statistical Abstract,* Table 4, "U.S. Population Living Abroad: 1968 to 1981." Data are missing for some election years, so we use the closest year to fill in. Since there is little year-to-year variation in the numbers, we believe this is a good approximation. The *Statistical Abstract* provides the same categories as the 1960 Census, and we follow the same procedures to estimate the overseas civilian population, then use Department of Defense statistics to add the military personnel. For all adjustments, after 1971 we only remove an estimate of the number of persons under age 18.

1984–92.   From 1984 to 1992, the *Statistical Abstract* reports Department of State statistics on the number of nonmilitary persons who would need to be evacuated in the event of a crisis. We use this as the total of overseas civilians. Again, we make the same assumptions and adjustments for the age distribution of this group as before, and we use similar military statistics. We deflate these figures by an estimate of the number of persons under age 18.

1994–98.   We estimate the number of eligible voters overseas for 1994 and 1996 using unpublished reports of the overseas civilian population provided by the U.S. Consular Service. We again deflate this number by the proportion of the domestic population under age 18. We then add the number of military personnel abroad, provided by the Department of Defense, and the number of nonmilitary government personnel, from Office of Personnel Management reports (we assume these employees are at least 18 years old) to arrive at an estimate of the eligible voters overseas.

2000.   For 2000 we used the 1998 proportion of overseas citizens multiplied by the 2000 voting age population since the 2000 numbers were not available as of this writing.

The number of military and nonmilitary government employees living abroad is likely to be accurate, since these data are compiled and reported by the government. The estimates of civilians abroad is based on reports by consulates, which vary in the accuracy of their reporting. The total number of overseas civilians reported in 1998 was 3.1 million, a high since World War II. Footnotes that accompany data originating from the U.S. Consular Service (for 1968–81 in the 1984 *Statistical Abstract,* and unpublished data from 1987 through the present provided by the Consular Service) warn that the civilian population overseas is almost certainly underestimated.[22] A similar warning

---

[22]Based on information provided to us by the U.S. Department of State, consulates that serve a smaller number of people are less likely to report data, and this bias increases backward in time.

accompanies the 1960 Census, which stresses that participation in counting was voluntary. We are highly confident of the overseas military and government employee figures, but we are less confident about our estimates of overseas civilians.

Persons Age 18–20

In order to control for the effect of the 26th Amendment, we calculate a turnout rate for persons at least 21 years old. From the CPS we calculate the proportion of voters age 18–20 and the proportion age 21 and older. We use this latter figure and the total votes for highest office to calculate the number of votes cast by persons older than 20. We remove the number of citizens age 18–20 from our measure of the VEP. We similarly remove estimates of persons in that age group among felons and the overseas population, where appropriate, in order to avoid double counting. We then calculate a new turnout rate using the adjusted numerator and denominator.

Regional Analysis

In order to control for the effect of the civil rights movement on voter participation in the South, we estimate turnout rates for both southern and nonsouthern states. We have turnout statistics and VAP estimates for all states. We have the same information for ineligible felons, as described above, and make the same assumptions to arrive at regional numbers. The CPS is a survey of approximately 100,000 individuals and covers the entire country. We exploited the large regional subsamples of the CPS to make all the same adjustments using the CPS from 1966 onward, as detailed above.

For the remainder of our adjustments, data are missing, and we must make some assumptions. Before 1966, we use the national estimate of the proportion of noncitizens among the VAP as the regional estimate. In 1966, when regional numbers became available, both the southern and nonsouthern proportions of noncitizens were 2% of the regional VAP, so we believe this is a reasonable assumption. Because we do not know the home state of eligible voters living abroad, we allocate the overseas population between the two regions in proportion to the VAP of each region.

REFERENCES

Abramson, Paul R., and John H. Aldrich. 1982. "The Decline of Electoral Participation in American Politics." *American Political Science Review* 76 (September): 502–21.

Abramson, Paul R., John H. Aldrich, and David W. Rohde. 1998. *Change and Continuity in the 1996 Elections.* Washington, DC: Congressional Quarterly Press.

Abramson, Paul R., John H. Aldrich, and David W. Rohde. 1991. *Change and Continuity in the 1988 Elections*, rev. ed. Washington, DC: Congressional Quarterly Press.

Andrews, William. 1966. "American Voting Participation." *Western Political Quarterly* 19 (December): 636–52.

Ansolabehere, Steven, and Shanto Iyengar. 1995. *Going Negative: How Attack Ads Shrink and Polarize the Electorate.* New York: Free Press.

Beck, Allen J. 2000. "Prisoners in 1999." Washington, DC: U.S. Department of Justice, Bureau of Justice Programs.

Beck, Allen J. 2001. "Prisoners in 2000." Washington, DC: U.S. Department of Justice, Bureau of Justice Programs.

Brody, Richard A. 1978. "The Puzzle of Political Participation in America." In *The New American Political System,* ed. Anthony King. Washington, DC: American Enterprise Institute. Pp. 287–324.

Bruce, Peter. 1997. "Measuring Things: How the Experts Got Voter Turnout Wrong Last Year." *The Public Perspective* 8 (October): 39–43. New Haven, CT: The Roper Center for Public Opinion Research.

Burnham, Walter Dean. 1965. "The Changing Shape of the American Political Universe." *American Political Science Review* 59 (March): 7–28.

Burnham, Walter Dean. 1982. *The Current Crisis in American Politics.* New York: Oxford University Press.

Burnham, Walter Dean. 1985. "Those High Nineteenth-Century American Voting Turnouts: Fact or Fiction?" *The Journal of Interdisciplinary History* 26(4): 613–44.

Burnham, Walter Dean. 1987. "The Turnout Problem." In *Elections American Style,* ed. A. James Reichley. Washington, DC: Brookings Institution. Pp. 97–133.

Cassel, Carol A., and Robert C. Luskin. 1988. "Simple Explanations of Turnout Decline." *American Political Science Review* 82 (December): 1321–30.

Cavanagh, Thomas E. 1981. "Changes in American Voter Turnout, 1964–1976" *Political Science Quarterly* 96 (Spring): 53–65.

Crocker, Royce. 1996. "Voter Registration and Turnout: 1948–1994." CRS Report for Congress: CRS-122. Washington, DC: Congressional Research Service.

Crocker, Royce. 1997. "Voter Registration and Turnout: 1996." Memorandum. Washington, DC: Congressional Research Service.

Crocker, Royce. 1999. "Voter Registration and Turnout: 1998." Memorandum. Washington, DC: Congressional Research Service.

Day, Jennifer C. 1998. "Projections of the Voting-Age Population for States: November 1998." Current Population Reports, P25-1132. Washington, DC: U.S. Department of Commerce, Bureau of the Census.

DeNardo, James. 1998. "The Turnout Crash of 1972: Hard-Won Lessons in Electoral Participation." In *Politicians and Party Politics,* ed. John G. Geer. Baltimore, MD: Johns Hopkins University Press. Pp. 80–101.

Fellner, Jamie, and Marc Mauer. 1998. "Losing the Vote: The Impact of Felony Disenfranchisement Laws in the United States." Washington, DC: The Sentencing Project and Human Rights Watch.

Franklin, Mark N., and Wolfgang P. Hirczy de Mino. 1998. "Separated Powers, Divided Government, and Turnout in U.S. Presidential Elections" *American Journal of Political Science* 42 (January): 316–26.

Gans, Curtis. 1997. "Measuring Things: How the Experts Got Voter Turnout Wrong Last Year." *The Public Perspective* 8 (October): 44–8. New Haven, CT: The Roper Center for Public Opinion Research.

Kousser, Morgan J. 1999. *Colorblind Injustice: Minority Voting Rights and the Undoing of the Second Reconstruction.* Chapel Hill: University of North Carolina Press.

Leighley, Jan E., and Jonathan Nagler. 1992. "Individual and Systemic Influences on Turnout: Who Votes? 1984." *Journal of Politics* 54 (August): 718–40.

Lijphart, Arend. 1997. "Unequal Participation: Democracy's Unresolved Dilemma." *American Political Science Review* 91 (March): 1–14.

Love, Margaret C., and Susan M. Kuzma. 1996. "Civil Disabilities of Felons: A State-by-State Survey." Washington, DC: U.S. Department of Justice, Office of the Pardon Attorney.

Miller, Warren E., and J. Merrill Shanks. 1996. *The New American Voter.* Cambridge, MA: Harvard University Press.

Plissner, Martin, and Warren Mitofsky. 1981. "What If They Held an Election and Nobody Came?" *Public Opinion* (February/March): 50–1.

Powell, G. Bingham, Jr. 1986. "American Voter Turnout in Comparative Perspective." *American Political Science Review* 80 (March): 17–44.

Putnam, Robert D. 1995. "Bowling Alone: America's Declining Social Capital." *Journal of Democracy* 6 (January): 65–78.

Putnam, Robert D. 2000. *Bowling Alone: The Collapse and Revival of American Community.* New York: Simon and Schuster.

Rosenstone, Steven J., and John Mark Hansen. 1993. *Mobilization, Participation, and Democracy in America.* New York: Macmillian.

Shaffer, Stephan D. 1981. "A Multivariate Explanation of Decreasing Turnout in Presidential Elections, 1960–1976." *American Journal of Political Science* 25 (February): 68–95.

Shields, Todd G., and Robert K. Goidel. 1997. "Participation Rates, Socioeconomic Class Biases, and Congressional Elections: A Crossvalidation." *American Journal of Political Science* 41 (April): 683–91.

Teixeira, Ruy. 1992. *The Disappearing American Voter.* Washington, DC: Brookings Institution.

U.S. Department of Commerce, Bureau of the Census. Various years a. *Current Population Survey: Voter Supplement File* [computer files]. ICPSR version. Washington, DC: U.S. Department of Commerce, Bureau of the Census [producer], various years. Ann Arbor, MI: Inter-university Consortium for Political and Social Research [distributor], various years.

U.S. Department of Commerce, Bureau of the Census. Various years b. *Statistical Abstract of the United States.* Washington, DC: Government Printing Office.

U.S. Department of Commerce, Bureau of the Census. Various years c. "Projections of the Voting-Age Population for States: November." Current Population Reports, Series P25-[various]. Washington, DC: Government Printing Office.

U.S. Department of Justice, Bureau of Justice Statistics. 1996. "Non-Citizens in the Federal Criminal Justice System, 1984–1994." NCJ-160934. Washington, DC: Department of Justice.

U.S. Department of Justice, Bureau of Justice Statistics. 1997. *Historical Statistics on Prisoners in State and Federal Institutions, Yearend 1925–1986: United States* [computer file] (Study #8912). ICPSR ed. Ann Arbor, MI: Inter-university Consortium for Political and Social Research [producer and distributor].

U.S. Department of Justice, Bureau of Justice Statistics. 2000. "U.S. Correctional Population Reaches 6.3 Million Men and Women, Represents 3.1 Percent of the Adult U.S. Population." Washington, DC: U.S. Department of Justice.

U.S. Department of Justice, Bureau of Justice Statistics. Various years. *Correctional Populations in the United States.* Washington, DC: U.S. Government Printing Office.

U.S. General Accounting Office (GAO). 1997. "2000 Census: Progress Made on Design but Risks Remain." Washington, DC: U.S. Government Printing Office.

U.S. Immigration and Naturalization Service. 1997. *Statistical Yearbook of the Immigration and Naturalization Service, 1996*. Washington, DC: U.S. Government Printing Office.

Wolfinger, Raymond E. 1993. "Building a Coalition to Ease Voter Registration." Paper presented at the 1993 annual meeting of the American Political Science Association, Washington, DC.

Wolfinger, Raymond E., and Stephen J. Rosenstone. 1980. *Who Votes?* New Haven, CT: Yale University Press.

5.3   Engaging Youth: Combating the Apathy of Young Americans Toward Politics (2003)

KEVIN MATTSON

INTRODUCTION

When, following a forty-year struggle, the Twenty-Sixth Amendment passed in 1971, some hoped, while others feared, that newly enfranchised eighteen-year-olds would vote in vast numbers and begin to transform American politics. In fact, youth voting—voting by persons aged eighteen to twenty-four—has had remarkably little impact on elections or on the political system more generally, and for a rather obvious reason: Most young citizens old enough to vote simply don't.

More generally, college-aged citizens read relatively little political news, even on the Internet. As a group, they are apathetic or cynical, not activist or ideal-minded, about politics and toward politicians. There is, however, a seeming paradox here: The same young generation that votes little volunteers lots; the same college-aged Americans who eschew political participation embrace community service. What is more, many young citizens sense no civic connections between voting and volunteering, between political campaigns and community affairs. In this reading selection, a report by the nonpartisan Century Foundation, Kevin Mattson offers a pointed summary and critique of youth nonvoting and suggests steps for "moving beyond the disconnect" by "reconnecting voluntary service and political education."

Kevin Mattson, *Engaging Youth: Combating the Apathy of Young Americans Toward Politics* (New York: Century Foundation Press, 2003), 1–6, 37–44. Reprinted with permission.

INTRODUCTION: A NEW
LOST GENERATION?

Ever since the baby boom generation—those who were born in the wake of
World War II and came of age during the 1960s—won its label, pundits and
marketers have been searching for a new tag line for the next generation, those
born during and after the 1960s. For a while, members of this generation were
thought to be spoiled and withdrawn and were thus labeled "slackers." Then
came the blasé but less offensive "twentysomethings"; then the term that
stuck, "Generation X" (coined in Douglas Coupland's novel about young
adults frightened of commitment and working low-paying, service sector
"McJobs"). Then we heard that this Generation X (and those a bit younger
now known as Generation Y) was actually hardworking, pragmatic, even entrepreneurial, certainly ready for a "new economy." Young people were the
computer-savvy "netizens" who would lead us into the utopia of the 1990s
economic bubble. In all of this generational labeling—much of it invented by
corporate marketers interested in niche advertising—one characteristic has
seemed to stick: political apathy. If we take traditional forms of political participation—especially voting but also informing oneself about public affairs—
Generation X and Y come up short.

In 1971, the Twenty-sixth Amendment lowered the voting age to eighteen.
The first generation to benefit from this change votes in record low numbers.
Elizabeth Hubbard of the Pew Foundation recently noted, "Over the last twenty
years, the decline in voter turnout has been most apparent among young
adults."[1] In 1994, for instance, one in five eligible young voters (meaning those
registered, hence not all young people) showed up for midterm elections.[2] Recent estimates put the youth vote (eighteen- to twenty-nine-year-olds) in the
2000 presidential election at about 38 percent.[3] When asked about their political knowledge, young adults seem out of the loop. In a poll of college freshmen, only 26 percent said "keeping up to date with political affairs" was
important.[4] As political scientist Robert Putnam recently summed it up, members of Generation X, in comparison with those who came of age during World
War II (the "civic generation") and baby boomers, are "less interested in politics, less informed about current events (except for scandal, personality, and
sports), less likely to attend a public meeting, less likely to contact public offi-

---

[1]Elizabeth Hubbard, "Defy Convention: Court Young Voters," *Philadelphia Inquirer* (November 1,
1998), available at the Pew Charitable Trusts Website, www.pewtrusts.com.

[2]See Ted Halstead, "A Politics for Generation X," *The Atlantic Monthly*, August 1, 1999, pp. 33–42,
and Stephen Craig and Stephen Bennett, *After the Boom: The Politics of Generation X* (Lanham, Md.:
Rowman and Littlefield, 1997).

[3]See www.youthvote2000.org for recent figures.

[4]Sheilah Mann, "What the Survey of American College Freshmen Tells Us about Their Interest in
Politics and Political Science," *PS: Political Science and Politics*, June 1999, p. 263.

cials, less likely to attend church, less likely to work with others on some community project, and less likely to contribute financially to a church or charity or political cause."[5] Generation X now seems better labeled Generation Apathetic.

Some political, academic, and philanthropic leaders rank this youthful apathy as a fundamental problem. John McCain, for instance, took note of young people's cynicism about government. He warned during his primary campaign that "we must reform the way the campaigns are financed in America today to restore the confidence of these young people in the institutions of government."[6] Major foundations—including the Carnegie Corporation of New York, the Pew Charitable Trusts, the Ford Foundation, the Kellogg Foundation, and The Century Foundation—have programs directed at reengaging young people in political activity. Numerous colleges are experimenting with community service programs that educate young people in civic responsibility. Young people's political disaffection now appears to constitute a major American problem—and for obvious reasons.

Although saying so seems like a cliché, young people are America's future. If they are increasingly apathetic about public life, public life will continue to deplete itself. Indeed, in a recent national poll more than two out of three eighteen- to thirty-four-year-olds expressed detachment from their government.[7] This correlates with what Ruy Teixeira calls "an astonishing increase in political cynicism over the last several decades."[8] It is hard to imagine democracy operating in a healthy fashion with the levels of public mistrust among young people today. Government will increasingly find it difficult to justify its role in society. Youth apathy—especially if it continues to grow or even just holds steady—should trouble us.

With this in mind, though, it is important not to work ourselves into a collective lather or fall prey to hand-wringing laments about apathetic youth. I am wary of those from the right or left who claim that youth apathy about politics should lead us to overthrow our present political institutions. Rather, we should try to understand what youth apathy tells us about contemporary politics. Take the act of voting, for instance. Certainly, younger adults have shown higher levels of disengagement than other adults, and since World War II, young people have *always* been less likely to vote than other groups of citizens.[9] And even though voter decline is still happening across the board in America, the decline among young people is greater than that of all voters.

---

[5]Robert Putnam, *Bowling Alone: The Collapse and Revival of American Community* (New York: Simon and Schuster, 2000), p. 261.

[6]Lisa Rathke, "U.S. Senator John McCain Addresses Vermont State Republican Convention," Associated Press, May 20, 2000.

[7]Hart Research Associates, "America Unplugged: Citizens and Their Government." Poll conducted for the Council for Excellence in Government, available at www.excelgov.org.

[8]Ruy Teixeira, *The Disappearing American Voter* (Washington, D.C.: Brookings Institution, 1992), p. 31.

[9]Putnam, *Bowling Alone*, p. 247.

As two leading political scientists point out, "In general, as people grow older, their involvement in politics deepens."[10] Young people are in a phase of life less conducive to political and civic participation; they are busy moving around and finding work, not yet settled down. Thus, many political scientists counsel relaxation about Generation X's civic disaffection. After an in-depth exploration of research on Generation X and politics (much of it quite gloomy), two political scientists stated, "It is likely that X'ers will eventually find their political voice(s) and take their place, naturally enough, at the table of power."[11] As can be seen in Figure 1.1 . . . , Generation X'ers seemed to turn out in fairly larger numbers during Bill Clinton's first election—perhaps drawn to some of the more idealistic sentiments expressed in 1992 (plus concern about a sinking economy). The recent upswing in youth activism, witnessed in the anti-sweatshop movement on America's college campuses, should alleviate some of our concerns about Generation X's and Generation Y's apathy. And who knows what the recent terrorist attacks on America will bring in terms of changed perceptions among young people of government and public life?[12]

With all of this said, though, there does seem something quite different about Generation X. If anything, this generation seems to be *leading* other Americans in terms of an overall civic decline. Robert Putnam has gained much fame recently for warning that Americans are too often "bowling alone" and not joining local civic groups as they did in the past. Putnam's work is a provocative mix of social science and moral jeremiad. He worries quite a bit about Generation X but then celebrates the increasing hours of Generation X's voluntary and public service. He expresses exuberance about the "commitment to volunteerism" that he sees among young people today. In fact, he goes on to say, "This development is the most promising sign that America might be on the cusp of a new period of civic renewal, especially if this youthful volunteerism persists into adulthood and begins to expand beyond individual caregiving to broader engagement with social and political issues."[13] Here we come to the crux of the matter and to one of the central arguments of this report. In fact, volunteerism is *not* increasing more traditional forms of political engagement—voting, educating oneself about political issues, helping out on a campaign, contributing time and money to a political organization.[14] Indeed, young people's rising levels of volunteerism are accompanied

---

[10]Steven Rosenstone and John Hansen, *Mobilization, Participation, and Democracy in America* (New York: MacMillan, 1993), pp. 136–37.

[11]Craig and Bennett, *After the Boom*, p. 104.

[12]Liza Featherstone, "The Student Movement Comes of Age," *The Nation*, October 16, 2000, pp. 23–26.

[13]Putnam, *Bowling Alone*, p. 133.

[14]See the National Association of Secretaries of State, "New Millenium Project—Phase I: A Nationwide Study of 15–24 Year Old Youth," available at NASS Website, www.nass.org, 1999, pp. 17–18.

Figure 1.1

Voter Turnout in Presidential Years

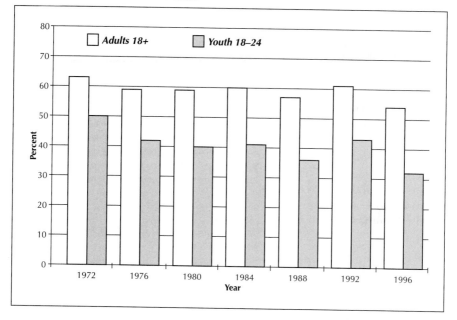

Source: Calculated from Federal Election Commission data, available at http://www.fec.gov/pages/agedemog.htm.

by continued political apathy. The idea that the public sector should play any role in our collective lives seems to be coming to an end.

Generation X is not composed only of libertarian conservatives (those who reject government out and out), for there are certainly younger progressives active today. This generation *has* been deeply influenced, however, by a rightward shift in American politics, captured in Ronald Reagan's famous quip that "government is not the solution but the problem." Even those who might be expected to have more idealistic views of government than Reagan did— especially those engaged in public and voluntary service—wind up showing distrust of government and the public sector. They characterize their personal acts of "doing good" as something above politics. At the same time, Generation X has witnessed the growing power of money in politics, an influence that further diminishes any idealism about political activism or hope in government (and one reason why McCain has been right to target youth disaffection as a major impetus to reforming campaign finance). We need to do something about campaign financing before we chastise young people for staying away from traditional politics. The renewal of progressivism and the cleaning up of American politics are inherently tied, in my opinion, to a need to reengage a generation that appears increasingly apathetic.

The emphasis on the progressive response to this problem is critical to my argument. While many bemoan a *general* civic crisis in America, I see a much greater crisis for progressive and liberal ideals. Since the rise of Barry Goldwater, conservative political philosophy has articulated distrust if not contempt of government. Today's distrust of government and the public sector is thus more damaging to progressives, who put much more faith in that sector. In keeping with Reagan's quip about government being the problem, numerous political leaders such as Phil Gramm and Dick Armey have attacked the federal government. Even a supposedly more centrist Republican such as George W. Bush complains that tax dollars are not the government's money—arguing against the whole premise of collective and public goods. In fact, many conservative organizations and pundits have done much to inflame youth dissatisfaction with government and public life. Conservatives might well bemoan the fact that young people do not vote, but they are probably less concerned with expressions of distrust in public life more generally. I suspect that political scientists, such as Robert Putnam, who have discovered a general civic crisis have not paid enough attention to the *political* dimensions of the problem.

This report begins by explaining how youth political disengagement fits into American history and political culture. The political beliefs of Generation X may not be easy to label (after all, class, race, and gender often determine beliefs more than age), but we can at least get a better handle on the *political world* within which many of its members (this author included) grew up. As with so much else, we need to go back to the 1960s to find some explanations of why young people might not be as active today as were their predecessors in the 1960s. Then we can analyze how pundits and other spokespeople have tried to interpret Generation X's existing political attitudes to support certain political conclusions and agendas that have an increasingly anti-government and right-wing leaning. Based on certain reported activities (including declines in voter participation and increases in voluntary service, for instance), conflicting conceptions of young people and politics have emerged. Much of this debate about Generation X's political beliefs seems shoddy. I offer here some of my own, albeit limited, proposals for counteracting young people's political apathy and rebuilding a more public-minded vision of politics. . . .

WHAT CAN BE DONE?

One thing is clear: Generation X's beliefs and behavior are diffuse. This generation holds a broad range of political beliefs—everything from conservatism (more often libertarian in nature than cultural) to anti-corporate leftist sentiments for social justice. It is therefore unfair to draw sweeping generalizations about young people and politics today. Nonetheless, there are some concerns that cut across all political beliefs: Young people as a whole are turning away from traditional political participation, partly because of an assault on traditional politics that has come mostly from the right. This is most clearly reflected in a lack of partisanship and knowledge about political issues. Even those we would normally expect to be politically engaged are not. For instance, both young people who perform service and young, progressive activists are prone to inactivity in the realm of more conventional politics. Activists express hostility and suspicion about electoral politics, despite the fact that their work assumes the need for responsiveness on the part of elected officials. (One young environmentalist working on the Alaska Wildlife Refuge issue told me he was not concerned with the outcome of the presidential election of 2000.) The few activists I spoke with who *did* care about electoral politics expressed exasperation about the lack of political commitment on the part of other activists.

The process of attracting young people to public life is one means to revive progressive politics. This is not because youthful idealism always tends leftward (as young people made clear when they voted for Reagan during the 1980s) but because the present-day distrust of government by youth makes progressive politics more difficult. To correct for the injustices of the day—lack of health care, unfair labor practices, environmental degradation—we need a stronger government and a sense that the government works for the public good. We should develop a twofold strategy that will reconnect young people to public life and democratic action while pointing out that there is a progressive alternative to the right's dominant political vision.

Much of what I discuss here draws from my own activity as research and associate director of the Walt Whitman Center for the Culture and Politics of Democracy at Rutgers University from 1995 to 2001. In my work at the center, I was constantly approached by progressive organizations that were trying to involve young people in public and civic life. As a result, I have developed a number of ideas—discussed here in no particular order and with varying amounts of attention. These ideas are not, of course, the last word on the subject; rather, I hope they will provoke further research and experimentation.

Traditional Civic Education—and Beyond

One of the easiest places to introduce young people to politics is in school. During the nineteenth century, civic education was pursued through the study of history—that is, the memorization of certain historical facts taken as essential for citizenship in a republic (often facts about previous republics and the founding of America). By the early twentieth century, the social sciences began to displace history in academia. This change filtered down to high schools. From the 1930s to 1950s, civic education became equated with "social studies," an amalgamation of different social science disciplines. The idea that social studies provided the best source for civic education came under criticism in the 1980s, however, and has never truly recovered.

In 1988, the Center for Civic Education and the Council for the Advancement of Citizenship released a report that assessed civic education at the high school level. The report was gloomy: "The question of what citizenship means was seldom addressed. Little was said about the aims of citizenship education. Descriptions of civic education as a subject tend toward conceptual fuzziness and diffusion. In only a few instances could a specific rationale for civic education be found." [15] The Center for Civic Education then went on to put forth a proposed set of national standards, published in *Civitas: A Framework for Civic Education*. In 1992, the federal government followed suit by creating its own set of standards through the passage of Goals 2000, otherwise known as the Educate America Act. It is debatable how effective either of these two initiatives has been.

There are numerous reasons why civic education has fallen into disarray and why some are pessimistic about any renewed call to standards to guide its renewal. First, standards in education—though much more popular today than in the 1960s—have always made many educators suspicious. Teachers complain about "teaching to the test" and turning learning into rote memorization. Besides, piling up a new set of demands on already overcommitted teachers creates understandable tension. Many critics also worry that, in a pluralistic society, common civic standards are difficult to define. (For instance, should we teach patriotism or civil disobedience?) Although others believe there are core civic standards, this debate makes clear how difficult it is to achieve consensus. In addition, there are so many different ways of approaching civic education—public service, experiential education, internships, formal lessons about how government works, and more—that it is difficult to get agreement among educators on the best method. Because of these conflicts, grounds for optimism about a renewal of civic education at the K–12 levels seem faint at best.

Opinions differ on whether the traditional civic education of yesteryear helped raise levels of political connectedness. [16] Perhaps the best way to move beyond this debate is to combine traditional civic education—some basic factual knowledge about the way American government works—and experiential education—allowing young people the opportunity to learn from community engagement. On this front, there seems to be some reason for hope. For instance, there is Kids Voting, a program that encourages young people to get their parents to take them voting. Teachers work with students

---

[15]Mary Jane Turner and Scott Richardson, "Civic/Citizenship Education and the Social Studies in the United States," Paper for the Close Up Foundation, no date, Circulated via the New Jersey Civic Education Consortium (Eagleton Institute, Rutgers University). This study covers more than forty state curricula.

[16]For a negative take on this, see Richard Rothstein, "What Produces a Voter? Seemingly Not Civics Class," *New York Times*, July 11, 2001, p. B10; William Galston argued at the American Political Science Association's 2000 roundtable on civic education that there is proof that basic knowledge about the way government works does enhance democratic participation.

on the project and give them general civic lessons along the way. This program has effectively involved young people in political education through family and community life and then merged this with more formal knowledge conveyed by teachers.[17] Another organization, Youth Vote 2000, has raised levels of voting by doing something as simple as making one-on-one phone calls to young people eligible to vote—prompting them to think about issues they care about and how those issues related to political choices in the voting booth. This was "estimated to have caused a 13.3 percentage point jump in the probability of voting."[18] Clearly, simple political discussion (with peers or parents) can enhance young people's interest in politics.

Unfortunately, some civic education programs outside of the world of schools take on the worst features of youth culture. Rock the Vote probably best exemplifies this. This organization, founded in 1990, received most of its funding from Warner Brothers and Capitol Records (as well as other corporations with an interest in the youth market). Its cofounder explained in 1992 that the group intended "to raise the political consciousness of kids and to make voting hip."[19] The first problem occurred when its major spokespeople—figures such as Madonna, who went on television draped in a flag to tell young people to vote—were discovered not to be registered to vote themselves.[20] This did little to overcome political cynicism. Even worse, however, is the slippery line between the noble act of increasing the vote and the corporate sponsors' self-interest. A spokesperson for Coors, another funder of Rock the Vote, explained, "I'm not going to sit here and try to tell you this is about voting. We're talking about selling beer and decided we could kill two birds with one stone."[21] In this day and age, it is probably safe to assume that young people receive the message to buy things even when it is latched onto the message to vote; it is easy to imagine them failing to hear Madonna begging them to vote and rather thinking about buying her next CD. Programs that move outside the walls of the traditional school need to be aware of the pernicious qualities of our consumer culture (something that Clinton's presidential summit ignored). It is doubtful how successful Rock the Vote has been in increasing young people's connection to politics.[22]

---

[17]See, for instance, Syd Golston, "Kids Voting USA," *Social Education*, October 1996, pp. 344–48.

[18]"First Ever Study of Youth Voter Mobilization Shows Success," posted at http://www.youthvote2000.org/events/viewnewsarticle.cfm?newsid=25.

[19]Quoted in "Rock the Vote," *Time*, June 15, 1992, p. 24.

[20]Michael Lewis, "The Herd of Independent Minds," *The New Republic*, June 3, 1996, p. 20.

[21]Quoted in Cyndee Miller, "Promoting Voting: It's Goodwill—and Good Business Too," *Marketing News*, October 26, 1992, p. 1.

[22]Rock the Vote has recently moved beyond simply getting out the vote. It mounted a new campaign with the title "I'm a Politician," a campaign that highlighted youth activists around the country. Though interesting, it is not clear what it has accomplished. It should also be noted that some experiential educators have experimented with "media education" whereby young people analyze advertising and popular culture for its pernicious qualities. This seems a healthy development in this context.

Moving Beyond the Disconnect: Reconnecting Voluntary Service and Political Education

With this danger in mind, it still seems best to approach young people about politics both within and outside the formal setting of schools. And today one of the best places to do this is whenever they perform public service. If participants in service programs can see the connections between their service and the wider world of public policy, then these programs will cultivate more engaged and thoughtful citizens. This requires more attention to the educational aspects of service.

There is some reason for hope here. Many colleges and universities have instituted what are called "service-learning programs." Students enrolled in these programs perform service but also discuss what they are doing in the classroom. They might, for instance, take a class on housing policy while working at a homeless shelter. Students then connect what they are doing at their service site with the bigger policy changes that shape or should shape their efforts. In studying these programs, researchers have found that students walk away with a deeper understanding of social issues and their political implications. Researchers (including myself) have found that programs with poor-quality classroom components increased students' levels of cynicism or detachment. But when the connections are made well, students do in fact increase their civic and political knowledge.[23]

This should provide us with hope for injecting an educational component into the many public service programs sprouting up in America today. During the past six years, I have worked with public service organizations to do precisely this. Margo Shea and I discovered that by simply discussing public service and its consequences, participants almost always made connections to wider political issues.[24] For instance, in 1997 I worked with participants in Public Allies in Wilmington, Delaware. This group was at first hostile to political discussion. One woman told me in our first meeting that she thought the term politics came from the combination of two different words: polis, which meant public (a correct definition) and ticks, those who leech off the public good. (Whether that part of her definition is correct depends, of course, on your outlook.) Most of the participants, almost all of whom had college educations, told me that they never voted—which should not surprise us. But they were eager, as were other members of their generation, to perform public service.

I met with this group for a year, and by the end of it, many of their attitudes had changed. First, they started making connections between their service

---

[23]See, here, The Walt Whitman Center for the Culture and Politics of Democracy, "Measuring Citizenship Final Report," 1997.

[24]Kevin Mattson and Margo Shea, "Building Citizens" (booklet funded by the Haas Foundation, published by the Walt Whitman Center, 1998); see also, Kevin Mattson, "Think About It," *Who Cares: A Toolkit for Social Change*, March/April 1998.

and local and national politics. One woman who worked in a transitional housing program discovered that there had been a whole host of reforms, both local and national, that made it more difficult for her to do her work. She decided to continue her service work while also scanning the horizon for political changes. At the conclusion of her one-year assignment, she believed that at some point she would need to go into advocacy work in order to protect the programs she had helped out with during her service. The woman who coined the term *poli-ticks* went through a similar experience. It would be presumptuous of me to claim that discussing issues during the course of the year was the sole reason for these young people's changed attitudes. But I am quite certain that without this opportunity many more of the participants would have remained locked in the cynical stage in which they began.

There are certainly some service programs that do a better job than others at making connections between service and political change. As two researchers, Joel Westheimer and Joseph Kahne, have pointed out, different organizations have very different ways of conceptualizing the goal of service. Drawing on a number of years of study for the Surdna Foundation, these researchers differentiate between those who conceive of service producing a "personally responsible citizen," a "participatory citizen," or a "justice-oriented citizen." The first "works and pays taxes, obeys laws, and helps those in need during crises such as snowstorms and floods." The second "actively participates in the civic affairs and the social life of the community at local, state, and national levels." The third "critically assesses social, political, and economic structures and explores collective strategies for change that challenge injustice and, when possible, addresses root causes of problems." As Westheimer and Kahne see it, these very different conceptions of citizenship help shape the outcomes of service programs.[25]

Westheimer and Kahne have found, perhaps not surprisingly, that programs with a justice-oriented model connect service participation to wider political engagement more effectively than others. By asking participants to think about how their service relates to wider issues (done through discussion, often moderated by a teacher), these programs show both the power and limitations of service. Young people understand what their service can and cannot accomplish. These programs also make sure that young people—even if they do not necessarily act on this knowledge immediately—at least think about what could be done at the larger level of policy to tackle problems they have encountered in service.

Even with all of this in mind, those voluntary programs that emphasize the connection between service and politics still draw from the "self-selecting" population. That is, they entice young people already committed to the ideals

---

[25]Joel Westheimer and Joseph Kahne, "What Kind of Citizen? The Politics of Educating for Democracy," forthcoming, *Harvard Education Review*.

of service. Young middle-class participants remain "do-gooders" and view those being served as "clients" at best. Those who are disaffected and perhaps most in need of such experiences do not join.

Fortunately, there are now programs in place that attempt to overcome this problem. From 1998 to 2000, I observed a program in Philadelphia that deserves attention precisely because it challenges growing inequalities and civic disaffection while also drawing out the political implications of service. The Center for Greater Philadelphia, housed at the University of Pennsylvania, has recently created what it calls a High School Partnership Project. This program brings students from inner-city schools (typically underfunded and thus poor) and students from suburban schools (typically quite well off) together to work on public service projects, such as cleaning up a public park or helping out a nonprofit organization. The program teaches important lessons to young people about the relation between socioeconomic inequality and the decline of American civic life. It also cuts against the tendency of middle-class do-gooders to see themselves as superior to those being served.

Young people in this program were forced to confront the disparities in their lives. During one group meeting, for instance, private school students assumed that everyone owned a computer and that the group could therefore create a website as a part of their project. The public school students admitted to not owning computers, which created an embarrassing situation that once again made it difficult for these students to work together but also forced them to think about inequality in a constructive manner.

In another case, students started to discuss what sort of projects they wanted to work on. Students from a wealthy suburban school wanted to focus on youth violence. Immediately, students from the inner-city school hedged on the project, arguing that youth violence is often puffed up by the mass media. They started giving examples of how news media trucks would zoom into their neighborhood any time an act of violence took place. The inner-city students were tired of focusing on violence, not because they denied its existence but because of how it fit into a stereotype of their neighborhoods and fellow citizens. In trying to come together in their public work, the students were left looking at a widening chasm—and at all of the ramifications of this divide.

In one group, students were exposed to the problems of pollution in their communities. These students started to recognize a link between their service and questions concerning public policy and saw the role that local citizen action could (and could not) play in problem solving. Of course, the service itself did not promise to be anything more than a temporary intervention; it was in discussion that students identified potential, long-term citizen action solutions and associated their work with wider civic possibilities. In another group meeting, the Partnership staff asked a group to discuss a social issue discovered in the process of service. The group, which worked on a variety of projects throughout Philadelphia, focused on "people moving out of the city into the suburbs." An exceptionally bright student from a suburban school argued that during the 1930s and 1940s "homes were segregated by street, but not by neighborhood." This initiated a debate about earlier segregation that became a general conversation about redlining and suburban sprawl. The discussion was quite sophisticated, with allusions to public policy and urban patterns and, eventually, taxation. Yet it never became too abstract because a teacher asked the students to think about their parents' attitudes toward taxation. All in all, it was a productive conversation on some major questions about socioeconomic inequality, and it showed that students from different backgrounds could work together to connect service to public policy.[26]

Nonetheless, this program in Philadelphia and the ones that Westheimer and Kahne discussed are exceptions. Most service programs are pressed for time and barely succeed in getting their participants to perform the necessary number of service hours, let alone talk and think about their work. Making wider connections seems like too much work (as many of those I worked with over the past few years have complained). Programs like AmeriCorps try to cut young people off from politics entirely. Those that try to tie service to wider political issues may be accused of being *too political*—of being indoctrination camps into left-wing causes. This is certainly a problem, but the alternative—allowing young people to see service as isolated from politics—seems too steep a price to pay. Service program leaders need to think critically and thoughtfully about how they can relate experiences in public service to politics. The fact that it can and has been done should provide some hope.

5.4   Where Have All the Voters Gone? (2002)

MARTIN P. WATTENBERG

INTRODUCTION

The practices of other democratic nations may provide useful models for increasing voter turnout in the United States. In the following selection, Martin P. Wattenberg discusses several possibilities for voting reform. These include mandatory participation, weekend elections, and voting holidays, among other options. While questions of liberty and cost are important to consider in

---

[26]I have reported these findings directly to the William Penn Foundation and published them in briefer form in "Can Americans Achieve Civic Equality?" *PEGS* 10, no. 1 (2001).

evaluating these proposals, their adoption in other democracies is also significant. Balancing the freedoms and traditions of American politics with the fundamental role of political participation in a democracy is a challenge that policymakers and voters alike must address.

■

HOW TO IMPROVE U.S. TURNOUT RATES: LESSONS FROM ABROAD

Americans need not be chastised for their low turnout rates, though any increase in voting participation would of course be desirable. Indeed, it is impressive how many Americans vote at present, considering the complex and non-user-friendly electoral process they are faced with. Political parties once played a much larger role in helping voters surmount the heavy demands upon them. As local party organizations and party identification have declined, both in the United States and throughout the other established democracies, turnout has fallen. The U.S. states that have seen the greatest turnout decline are those that once had strong traditional party organizations, which placed a high priority on getting out the vote and devoted substantial human resources to doing so. At the individual level, American turnout decline has been centered on the people who most need to have the electoral decision simplified for them through a strong party system—those with the least education, political interest, and life experience. The abysmal turnout rates of young Americans, who have never experienced anything other than candidate-centered politics, are particularly alarming as one looks toward the future.

Academics have often claimed that low turnout in the United States does not produce any important political bias. But such a position is hard to maintain in light of evidence that young people are being ignored by political campaigns (who naturally assume that most of them won't vote) and that their opinions differ dramatically from those of politically powerful senior citizens on many policies. A close analysis of turnout bias in the 2000 presidential election and 1994 House contests also reveals that who votes does make a difference. Furthermore, as the world learned during the controversy over the Florida presidential vote in 2000, turnout bias in the United States involves not just who votes but also which voters get a choice recorded. Many voters apparently approach lengthy and complex American ballots as they do standardized tests, and all too often they fail to complete much of their ballot. If the complexity of the ballot foils many who manage to go to the polls, it seems logical to infer that a fair number of those who do not vote are discouraged by the sheer difficulty of the voting task.

The key to improving U.S. turnout rates, therefore, is to make the electoral process more user friendly. Given that other established democracies have

more voter-friendly systems, there is much that can be learned from their experiences. As President Clinton was said to have occasionally remarked,
solutions to most public policy problems have already been found some-
where—we just have to scan the horizon for them. This is certainly the case
for increasing turnout. Gleaned from the track records of other countries, a
number of possible changes stand out as particularly apt to get Americans to
the polls. (. . . [N]o policies at the U.S. state level . . . have proved to be a clear
success in increasing turnout levels.) They will be addressed in order of their
likely effectiveness, which unfortunately is inversely related to the plausibil-
ity of their enactment in the United States.

Possible Measures to Improve U.S. Turnout

If in an ideal democracy everyone votes, a simple way to realize this goal is
to require people to participate. This is how Australians reasoned when they
instituted compulsory voting after their turnout rate fell to 58 percent in 1922.
Amazingly, there was overwhelming political consensus for this measure; the
Australian parliament adopted it following debates that lasted only 3 hours
and 26 minutes in the Senate and a scant 52 minutes in the House of Representatives.[1] Since then, Australia has consistently had one of the highest
turnout rates in the world, even though the maximum fine for nonvoting is
only about $35 and judges readily accept any reasonable excuse. In his 1997
presidential address to the American Political Science Association, Arend
Lijphart proposed mandatory election attendance as the most appropriate solution for inequalities in turnout rates.[2] He argued that besides increasing
turnout, mandatory voting would also stimulate interest and participation in
other political activities and decrease the role of money in politics.

   In the United States, the first question regarding mandatory turnout would
have to be whether it is constitutional. It seems inevitable that such a law
would be challenged in the courts. A case of such magnitude would almost certainly reach the Supreme Court, and how the Court would rule is by no means
certain. Yet there is good reason to believe that mandatory attendance at elections would pass constitutional muster. Opponents would no doubt object
that such a law violates First Amendment rights. Still, a compulsory attendance law requires one not to actually vote, but rather merely to show up at
the polls. An individual's right to abstain would thus not be infringed, because there would be no sanction against casting a blank ballot.

   Another constitutional question would be whether or not Congress has the
power to compel election attendance. Article I, Section IV, of the Constitution

---

[1] Malcolm Mackerras and Ian McAllister, "Compulsory Voting, Party Stability, and Electoral Advantage in Australia," *Electoral Studies* 18 (1999): 220.

[2] Arend Lijphart, "Unequal Participation: Democracy's Unresolved Dilemma," *American Political
Science Review* 91 (1997): 1–14.

states that "the Times, Places and Manner of holding Elections for Senators and Representatives, shall be prescribed in each State by the Legislature thereof; but the Congress may at any time by Law make or alter such Regulations." This broad power to make regulations concerning the manner of holding elections could well be stretched by the necessary and proper clause to give Congress the right to compel attendance at elections. This extension would be similar to Congress's assertion of its right to draft people as essential in order to carry out its mandate to raise military forces.

The biggest obstacle to imposing compulsory election attendance, however, stems from the country's political culture. American political culture, based on John Locke's views of individual rights, differs from Jeremy Bentham's concept of the greatest good for the greatest number, which has shaped Australian culture. Regardless of the legal considerations, most Americans—including elected officials—would probably assert that they have an inviolable right *not* to show up at the polls. As the former U.S. attorney general Griffin Bell remarked during a brief discussion of compulsory voting at a 2001 hearing of the National Commission on Federal Election Reform, "that is not a free country when you are doing things like that."[3] With such a prevailing attitude, it is hard to imagine the proposal ever getting off the ground in the United States, even if other OECD countries start to adopt this procedure.

Beyond that, it is debatable whether we really want to force turnout rates in America up to Australian levels. People with limited political knowledge might deal with a compulsory situation by making dozens of decisions the same way they choose lottery numbers. In Australia, this is known as the "donkey vote," for people who approach voting like the game of "Pin the Tail on the Donkey." Given Australia's relatively simple electoral process, this proportion of the voters is small; in America it would likely be greater.

Of course, just simplifying the electoral process itself would be another way to increase U.S. turnout. In 1930 Harold Gosnell wrote in *Why Europe Votes* that one of the reasons for America's low turnout is the fact that its voters are "given an impossible task to perform on election day."[4] Voters in most countries are faced with only one or two choices every time they go to the polls, whereas Americans typically are presented with dozens of decisions to make. Furthermore, they are called to go to the polls with mind-numbing frequency compared with Europeans, who typically vote once every other year. For example, when Vice President Dick Cheney was registered to vote in Dallas from 1996 through the summer of 2000, he was called to the polls for sixteen elections (only two of which he voted in).[5] Notably, Switzerland has

---

[3]Judge Griffin Bell, National Commission on Federal Election Reform, Public Hearing 1, Panel IV, transcript, p. 13.

[4]Quoted in Lijphart, "Unequal Participation," p. 8.

[5]See Megan Garvey and Mark Z. Barbak, "Cheney Admits to Sparse Texas Voting Record," *Los Angeles Times*, September 9, 2000, for the list of these sixteen elections.

also overwhelmed its citizens with voting opportunities, and it is probably not coincidental that they too have very low turnout rates along with major biases in participation by age and education. It is thus worrisome that the trend in recent years has been for many democracies to move toward the U.S.-Swiss model of democracy rather than the other way around. In Great Britain, for example, the Blair government has promised referenda on various issues and created more locally elected offices, such as a mayor for London (an election that not surprisingly drew a very poor turnout the first time it was held). In the face of growing worldwide acceptance of the principle that the cure for the problems of democracy is more democracy, it appears unlikely that America will soon reverse course, recognizing that there can indeed be too much democracy.

Yet another unlikely possibility is that America might join the worldwide democratizing trend by adopting a more proportional electoral system. . . . [E]vidence from around the world indicates that our turnout rates could also be increased if we adopted some form of proportional representation. In our winner-take-all system, many Americans rightly perceive that their vote is unlikely to affect election outcomes. Proportional representation changes this perception by awarding seats to smaller voting blocs. The threshold for representation varies by country, but typically any party that receives over 5 percent of the national vote earns seats in the legislature. With a number of viable parties to choose from rather than only two, people tend to feel that their party truly embodies their specific interests, and hence they are more likely to vote.

If Americans were to adopt proportional representation, new parties would probably be organized to directly represent the interests of groups such as African Americans, Latinos, and supporters of the new Christian Right. Although new parties would provide more incentives for people to vote, and particularly raise the low turnout rates of minority groups, there would be a substantial price to be paid. The current system brings diverse groups together under the umbrellas of two heterogeneous parties; a multiparty system would set America's social groups apart from one another. Proportional representation therefore hardly seems practical on the American scene and has never received serious consideration at the federal or state level.

What has received much attention is the goal of strengthening the American party system. Over fifty years ago, a committee of distinguished political scientists concluded that America's party system was functioning poorly in sustaining well-considered programs and mobilizing public support for them.[6] Numerous recommendations were compiled, all of which the scholars believed would facilitate a more responsible and more effective party system—

---

[6]American Political Science Association, "Toward a More Responsible Two-Party System: A Report of the Committee on Political Parties," *American Political Science Review* 44 (1950), supplement, number 3, part 2.

one that would be accountable to the public and able to deal with the problems of modern government. The APSA report argued that among the many tangible benefits of a strengthened party system would be an increase in voter interest and participation.[7] In line with this theory, as the party systems of the major industrial powers have withered in recent years turnout rates have fallen. . . .

The American case presents particular problems when it comes to reinvigorating the parties, however, because unlike parliamentary democracies the governmental structure is not organized around partisan politics. Even as the American parties have become more ideologically distinct, as the authors of the 1950 APSA report desired, their political role has been diminished. The rise of television broadcasting dramatically altered how politicians presented themselves as well as how the public received political information. Many politicians have come to realize that they do not need the parties to get their message across, and voters who are no longer exposed to a partisan environment have became accustomed to focusing on the candidates.[8]

The current narrowcasting revolution, epitomized by developments in cable television and the Internet, is likely to have a major impact as well. The much-anticipated proliferation of television channels and Web sites will offer more information than ever before in a wide array of formats. Some observers see these developments as offering "the prospect of a revitalized democracy characterized by a more active and informed citizenry."[9] The problem with such a rosy scenario, however, is that it is questionable whether many citizens will take advantage of this new wealth of information. With countless available information sources for a variety of specific interests, it will be easy for those who are not much interested in party politics to avoid the subject altogether. The result could well be a growing inequality of political information, with a small group of committed partisans becoming more knowledgeable while the rest of the public slips further into apathy concerning the parties. This scenario is especially likely to affect the next generation of citizens entering the electorate, who will be the first to be socialized in the Internet age. The generation gap in electoral participation—already wider than it probably has ever been—may well become even greater in the near future.

Lest one despair of any means for improving turnout in America, a simple yet effective change could be made in election timing. . . . [C]ountries that hold elections on leisure days have higher turnouts than would otherwise be expected. Learning from this lesson, the vast majority of new democracies have adopted this practice in recent years. It is doubtful that any American

---

[7]Ibid., p. 76.

[8]See Martin P. Wattenberg, *The Decline of American Political Parties, 1952–1996* (Cambridge: Harvard University Press, 1998).

[9]Anthony Corrado, "Elections in Cyberspace: Prospects and Problems," in *Elections in Cyberspace: Toward a New Era in American Politics,* ed. Anthony Corrado and Charles M. Firestone (Washington, D.C.: Aspen Institute, 1996), p. 29.

elections expert would recommend that a new democracy emulate the American example and vote instead on a Tuesday. So if Americans wouldn't recommend Tuesday elections to other countries, why should the United States continue this practice? By joining the modern world and voting on a leisure day, it is likely that American turnout would increase.

Many people assume that federal elections are held on Tuesdays because this was established in the U.S. Constitution. But this is not the case. Like many other aspects of the political process, the framers left it up to the Congress to establish procedures. During the first half of the nineteenth century, the timing of election day was shaped by the mores of American agrarian and religious life. Early November was seen as an ideal time of year for an election, as the fall harvest was over and in most places the weather was still mild enough to allow unimpeded travel over the primitive roads of the time. Holding an election on Sunday—the most common choice in Europe today—was out of the question at a time when Sundays were strictly reserved for rest. Furthermore, with nineteenth-century elections being occasions for drinking and gambling, Sunday would have been most inappropriate for a very religious country like the United States at that time. Because many people would not be able to travel to the county seat in a single day, Saturday and Monday were also ruled out, since choosing either one would make it difficult for these people to attend Sunday church services back home. Why Tuesday was chosen from the four remaining possible days remains unknown. But it seems clear that the law was written so as to rule out November 1st, because it is All Saints Day, a holy day of obligation for Catholics.

In the 1840s, a simple act of Congress established the first Tuesday after the first Monday in November as the date for presidential elections; this was extended to House elections in the 1870s, and then to Senate elections shortly after senators became directly elected. Americans have become quite accustomed to Tuesday elections, just as they have to other outdated practices such as the nonmetric system for weights and measures. State after state continues to set primary election dates on Tuesdays. In fact, forty-six out of the fifty states chose to hold their primaries on a Tuesday in 1998.[10] With such a well-accepted tradition, it will be difficult to change this custom. Furthermore, religious considerations still make weekend elections problematic. Although blue laws have largely been eliminated, there would probably be resistance from some Christians to holding elections on Sunday; Orthodox Jews would no doubt object to changing election day to Saturday.[11]

---

[10]The exceptions were Delaware, Hawaii, and Louisiana, which held their primaries on Saturday, and Tennessee, which held its primary on Thursday.

[11]Because the Jewish Sabbath ends at sundown, which would be fairly early in November, there would still be time for these people to vote. But clearly this would raise questions of fairness, and could lead to legal challenges.

As an alternative to weekend elections, another possibility would be to declare election day a national holiday. This was suggested just prior to the 1998 elections, and though the idea did not seem to grab the attention of anyone in government then, after the 2000 election controversy some major political figures at least began to talk about it.[12] About a week after the 2000 election, the House Democratic leader Richard Gephardt stated that he favored some change in election timing, saying, "I think having this on a Tuesday is unacceptable."[13] President Clinton also offered his endorsement for changing election day. In his last official message to Congress he wrote that "we should declare election day a national holiday so that no one has to choose between their responsibilities at work and their responsibilities as a citizen. In other countries that do this, voter participation dwarfs ours, and the most fundamental act of democracy gets the attention it deserves."[14] The National Commission on Federal Election Reform then offered a bipartisan endorsement of an election-day holiday in its report presented to President Bush at a White House ceremony in 2001. Commission members noted that besides the added time to vote on a holiday, other advantages would be that more public buildings could be used for polling places and more people (especially students) would be available for service as poll workers.

One possible objection to this proposal would involve the financial costs of yet another federally imposed holiday. An ideal solution would be to move election day to the second Tuesday of November and also designate it as Veterans' Day, which has traditionally been celebrated on November 11th.[15] Combining the two days into one holiday would send a strong signal to everyone about the importance that the country attaches to voting. And what better way could there be to honor those who fought for democratic rights than for Americans to vote on what could become known as "Veterans' Democracy Day"? As former president Jimmy Carter said in 2001, "Veterans, including myself, would be very proud to have us choose a president and U.S. Senators and congressmen and other state officials on our holiday."[16] In offering bipartisan endorsement for this proposal, the members of the National Commission on Federal Election Reform stated: "We reflected on the notion of holding the supreme national exercise of our freedom on the day we honor

---

[12]Martin P. Wattenberg, "Should Election Day Be a Holiday?" *Atlantic Monthly*, October 1998, pp. 42–46.

[13]Eric Lipton, "Problems Stir Calls to End '19th Century' Voting Process," *New York Times*, November 13, 2000.

[14]President William Jefferson Clinton, "The Unfinished Work of Building One America," message to Congress, January 15, 2001.

[15]In 2000, it was sadly ironic that on Tuesday, November 7th, many people did not have time in their busy day to vote, and less than a week later some of these same people were spending their Veterans' Day holiday at home glued to the continuous television coverage of the Florida recount.

[16]CNN, "Carter: U.S. Voting Systems Unacceptable," posted at www.cnn.com on March 27, 2001.

those who preserved it. On reflection, we found something very fitting about that too."[17]

As with any proposed change in public policy, there will be skepticism about whether it will work. Electoral reforms have often been known to have unintended and undesirable consequences. Ruy Teixeria expresses doubts about an election-day holiday, noting that it is "possible that the gain in turnout from hard workers who could not vote may be canceled out by the loss in turnout from citizens who decide to engage in holiday activities not conducive to voting."[18] R. Doug Lewis of the Election Center is even more direct on this score, writing in the *Washington Post* that "most people would use the day to play golf, go shopping or do chores."[19]

Although no one can know for sure until an election-day holiday is tried in the United States, there are nevertheless good reasons to think that such criticisms are not warranted. If voting is indeed a habit, it is hard to imagine that many of the people who are already into the routine will skip voting just because they have more free time on election day. And the people who currently mention lack of time as a reason for not voting are disproportionately younger, and hence probably are truly busy on a typical workday; a holiday creates more time in their schedules to vote.

A recent electoral reform in Japan provides evidence that extra time to vote facilitates turnout, especially among young people. Following record low turnouts in Japan in 1995 and 1996, political leaders decided that something had to be done to try to improve turnout. Although Japanese elections have long been held on Sunday, there were complaints that closing the polls at 6 P.M. was too early for people who had plans during the day. Thus it was decided to keep the polls open for an extra two hours in order to promote more participation. Not only did turnout go up overall in the next two elections, but there is evidence that the extra time to vote made a contribution to this phenomenon. An *Asahi Shimbun* poll in 1998 found that when people were asked why turnout had increased, 27 percent mentioned the extended poll hours— a response that was especially prevalent among young voters.[20] And in 2000, the same newspaper conducted an analysis of voting turnout hour by hour, by age. They found that people in their twenties and thirties made up a mere 14 percent of the voters in the first hour of voting but 40 percent in the last hour (which would have been unavailable to them under the old law).[21]

---

[17]National Commission on Federal Election Reform, "To Assure Price and Confidence in the Electoral Process," August 2001, p. 42.

[18]Ruy A. Teixeira, *The Disappearing American Voter* (Washington, D.C.: Brookings Institution, 1992), p. 143.

[19]R. Doug Lewis, "Fix the Vote, but Skip the Uniformity," *Washington Post,* December 24, 2000, p. B1.

[20]"Wide Public Support Eludes LDP Candidates," *Asahi Shimbun,* July 15, 1998.

[21]"Minshuto, Backed By Unaligned Voters, Rallied Late," *Asahi Shimbun,* July 1, 2000.

Making election day a holiday in the United States is probably not the reform that would improve turnout rates the most, but it does seem to be the easiest to accomplish—requiring only an act of Congress. The change could be made on a trial basis, to see how it works. If making voting more user friendly by giving people more time to accomplish the task doesn't produce the desired results, Congress can always change the law back to the traditional date. At the very least, such a visible national experiment would send a clear message to those who don't vote that politicians do care about them, and that everyone's participation at the polls is needed for democracy to work well. As an editorial in the *New York Times* stated, the holiday might "add a sense of importance and specialness to the day on which we go to the polls."[22]

In a review of Australian voting procedures, Malcolm Mackerras and Ian McAllister observe that "politicians and electoral officials have gone to considerable lengths to make the system voter friendly."[23] Indeed, they proudly proclaim that "Australia probably is the most voter-friendly country in the world." One can only hope that observers of American politics may soon be able to write that the U.S. electoral process is at least moving in the direction of being more user friendly. Such a development could only help promote the goal of higher voter turnout.

---

[22]"A Halfhearted Push for Reform," *New York Times*, August 6, 2001.
[23]Mackerras and McAllister, "Compulsory Voting," p. 233.

CHAPTER **6**

Political Parties and Interest Groups

READINGS IN THIS CHAPTER

*T*he Constitution does not discuss political parties or interest groups. The Framers were suspicious of groups that might advocate special interests at the expense of the common good. James Madison cautioned in the Federalist No. 10 that "factions" would threaten "the permanent and aggregate interests of the community" and enforce laws "adverse to the rights of other citizens." George Washington's Farewell Address of 1796 warned of "the baneful effects of the spirit of party generally."

Today, of course, both interest groups and political parties are central to policymaking in the United States. While the number of independent voters is growing, the majority of Americans still identify themselves as either Republicans or Democrats. Political parties date back to the early years of the republic: Although the Federalists and Anti-Federalists were more organized interests than actual parties, by 1800, presidential candidates were running under the banner of Federalists or Democratic-Republicans. The Democratic-Republican Party had evolved into the Democratic Party by Andrew Jackson's election to the presidency in 1828. The Republican Party originally was created as a third party, but it evolved into a major party with Abraham Lincoln's election to the presidency in 1860. Since 1860, the voting blocs that have supported either party—urban versus rural voters, agricultural versus manufacturing interests, and so on—have shifted, but the two political parties continue to dominate American elections.

Interest groups also have a long history in the United States. In a Chapter 3 reading selection, Alexis de Tocqueville describes the proliferation of interest groups in the United States in the early nineteenth century, stating that, "In no country in the world has the principle of association been more successfully used, or more unsparingly applied to a multitude of different objects, than in America." Today, interest groups press for policy change in areas ranging from education to the environment, health care to homeland security, the death penalty to tax reform. Engagement with interest groups can be as limited as writing a check or as extensive as leading letter-writing campaigns, organizing rallies, and meeting with public officials. While political parties focus on electing people to office, interest groups concentrate on influencing elected officials' policy positions.

The readings in this chapter examine how political parties and interest groups participate in the policymaking process. A common critique of the American political system is that the two major political parties control virtually all elected offices at the national, state, and even local levels. Only a handful of independent officials have held a seat in Congress, and even their votes have been closely aligned with one of the two major parties. No independent candidate has come close to winning the presidency; although Ross Perot won 19 percent of the popular vote in 1992, he did not garner a single electoral college vote. The winner-take-all system of elections in the United

States favors the two-party system, as the candidate who wins the most votes takes office, even if he or she wins by a plurality rather than a majority. Thus, smaller-party candidates have no opportunity for governing even if they win a significant percentage of the popular vote.

Critics of the two-party system also question whether Republicans and Democrats really offer voters a significant choice in elections. On many issues, the two parties differ only in degree on their positions. In 2003, for example, Democrats largely supported the October 2002 resolution authorizing the use of force in Iraq, but they criticized the timing of the war, stating that the Bush administration should have first permitted the completion of United Nations inspections. The relevant section of the 2004 Democratic Party platform was worded so that officials who backed President George W. Bush's position on Iraq, and those who opposed it, could agree to disagree. Similarly, in the early 1990s, both Democrats and Republicans advocated welfare reform, disagreeing only on details about time limits, work training requirements, and how much discretion states would have in operating the programs.

Thus, some observers suggest that the two-party system, despite much evidence of increased partisanship and party-line voting in the post-1980 Congress, may nonetheless limit opportunities for policy change, given how closely partisan political agendas often align. That was the crux of the critique of the two-party system made by Ralph Nader during his 2000 and 2004 presidential bids. Both parties, argued Nader, have become unduly influenced by large corporations and other moneyed interests, many of which fund both parties. As the two reading selections (by William Schneider and Scott Shane) on Nader's 2004 campaign make clear, this a-pox-on-both-parties message resonates with many Americans, though not with enough to make any major electoral difference.

However, other observers argue that the two-party system has the virtues of its vices: It brings important advantages to American politics, most notably stability and incremental policymaking. The winner-take-all system of elections means that extremist or fringe interests have virtually no opportunity to gain power, to initiate radical or reactionary changes, or to block important policy decisions on which most citizens agree. In countries where several political parties may share power in a coalition government, such as India or Israel, a small group of elected officials can pose daunting obstacles to legislation. Furthermore, the rise in *divided government*—a term that refers to one political party controlling Congress while the other controls the presidency— sometimes results in policy stalemates or "gridlock," but as often forces the two political parties to work together to pass legislation, thus prompting compromise and moderation in decision-making.

For several decades, academics have debated whether the two-party system is in decline. The answer depends on what aspect of the system is at issue and how one weighs competing evidence. For example, ever-more voters now register as independents, but most registered voters are affiliated with a party. And ever-more voters split their votes between Republicans and Democrats, but registered Democrats still vote mainly for Democrats, and registered Republicans still vote mainly for Republicans. Likewise, the local party organizations that once dominated urban America—the infamous political machines in cities like Boston, Detroit, New York, and Philadelphia—are long gone, but state party organizations vary in strength and significance, and each party's national committee plays a nontrivial role in funding, publicizing, and campaigning for its respective national standard-bearers.

Finally, by some measures, party has never been more important as a determinant of what positions state and federal legislators take and how they cast their votes. In Congress, conservative Republicans now routinely fight pitched legislative battles with liberal and moderate Democrats. Not a single Republican in Congress, for example, voted for Democratic President Bill Clinton's first budget plan in 1993, and only fifteen Democrats voted for President Bush's faith-based proposal in 2001—even though over a hundred had voted four times in favor of similar plans when Clinton was in office. As indicated above, this partisanship pleases some and frustrates others, but it is a reality.

Whether, increased legislative partisanship contributes to party vitality, however, and whether legislators have led or followed their constituents in becoming more ideological and partisan, are questions that scholars are only beginning to study. Astute scholars have finally begun to get a good handle on another vexing question related to political parties, their functions, and their future: What types of old or new political coalitions will form the basis of tomorrow's two-party system?

Political scientist V. O. Key, Jr., introduces the concept of *critical elections,* which he defines as "a sharp and durable electoral realignment between parties." Examples include the elections of 1860, 1896, and 1932. James L. Sundquist discusses the characteristics of party realignments and explains how they often extend far beyond an electoral cycle. In evaluating the prospects for a party realignment today, Georgetown University political scientist Stephen J. Wayne expertly sifts through the evidence on the "social bases" of contemporary American politics and suggests that, at least in "presidential electoral politics," we are witnessing a new era of "partisan parity."

Although interest groups do not have quite the same status as political parties in elections and governance, they nevertheless play a key role in American politics. The resources that interest groups provide to elected officials include *information* about their area of interest and *money* to finance political campaigns. Interest groups are best known for *lobbying* officials to pursue policies consistent with the group's agenda. For elected officials, an interest group is more likely to exercise influence if a significant proportion of an official's constituency belongs to or otherwise supports the group.

In the past, some analysts identified an *iron triangle* in American politics, wherein interest groups influence congressional committees, which, in turn, influence the departments or agencies overseeing the policy area affecting the relevant groups. The iron triangle concept suggests that interest groups wield too much power over the policy process, with well-funded organizations having more access to elected officials than groups with fewer resources. But the plethora of ways in which individuals and groups can reach elected officials or otherwise influence the policy process leads some observers to conclude that iron triangles, however prevalent they once were, are less significant today.

Political scientist E. E. Schattschneider's classic 1960 work, *The Semisovereign People,* maintains that the American public only partially governs, as organized interests exercise far more influence on elected officials than individual voters. Schattschneider's view of American politics presents a *pluralist theory* of governance, one in which diverse interests compete to set public agendas, develop policy, and drive legislation.

Journalists Jeffrey H. Birnbaum and Alan S. Murray's *Showdown at Gucci Gulch* (1987) provides a case study of pluralism at work, showing how interest groups shaped the sweeping Tax Reform Act of 1986. While many groups lobbied hard, they also often lobbied at cross-purposes with one another. In the end, the groups made a difference, but so did the ideas and convictions on the issue held by key elected officials in both parties and at both ends of Pennsylvania Avenue. While it goes too far to say that the case shows how "factions" were delimited, if not defeated, the "unlikely triumph of tax reform," as the authors term it, probably would make both Madison and Washington smile.

6.1 The Nader Calculation (2004)

WILLIAM SCHNEIDER

INTRODUCTION

Not long after graduating from Princeton University in 1955, Ralph Nader launched his career as a consumer advocate on auto safety, environmental protection, and other issues. He ran for president in 2000 as the candidate of the Green Party, and he ran in 2004 as an independent candidate in every state where he could get his name on the ballot. As the following two articles indicate, his message, including his attack on both political parties, was much the same in both campaigns. Although he won no state and got only a small percentage of votes, some debate whether he siphoned votes from the Democratic candidate (Al Gore in 2000, and John Kerry in 2004). Whatever the

William Schneider, "The Nader Calculation," *National Journal* (March 6, 2004): 760. Reprinted with permission from *National Journal*, March 6, 2004. Copyright 2004 *National Journal.* All rights reserved.

truth in that regard, one thing seems clear: Though Nader made little electoral headway, there are millions of Americans who mistrust government, blame both parties for the country's problems, and prefer candidates who distance themselves from traditional party politics.

■

Democrats have good reason to be freaked out that Ralph Nader is running for president. Look at what he did to Al Gore in 2000.

The TV networks' exit poll in 2000 asked Nader voters what they would have done had Nader not been on the ballot. Thirty percent of his supporters said they would not have voted at all. The rest said they would have voted for Gore over George W. Bush, by a ratio of better than 2-to-1 (48 percent to 22 percent).

Remember the agony of Florida? Nader got nearly 97,500 votes there. And Bush carried Florida by just 537. Democrats certainly haven't forgotten. "Every major liberal and progressive group who has supported the causes that [Nader] has worked on told him not to run," Democratic National Committee Chairman Terry McAuliffe said after Nader announced his bid.

It makes sense to vote for Nader only if you honestly think it makes no difference whether Bush is re-elected or the Democrats win. Does Nader think it makes no difference? "It's a question between both parties flunking; one with a D-minus—the Republicans; one with a D-plus—the Democrats," Nader said on *Meet the Press*.

Nader calls his campaign a "national liberation movement for the Democratic Party," aimed at keeping the Democrats from drifting too close to the center. *The Nation*, which shares that mission, published an editorial telling Nader, "The overwhelming mass of voters with progressive values . . . have only one focus this year: to beat Bush. Any candidacy seen as distracting from that goal will be excoriated by the entire spectrum of potentially progressive voters. If you run, you will separate yourself, probably irrevocably, from any ongoing relationship with this energized mass of activists."

Nader's response on *Meet the Press*? "We can't just sit back like *The Nation* magazine and betray its own traditions and the liberal intelligentsia, and once again settle for the least worst." Nader's real beef is with the two-party system. Of course, people have to vote for the lesser of two evils. That's how a two-party system works.

Nader seems to think legions of unhappy conservatives are ready to vote for him. "We hope to show that, increasingly, corporations are trampling conservative values," he said at the National Press Club. "Conservatives and independents who are very upset with the Bush administration's policies are left with two options: vote for the Democrats, which is unlikely, or vote for an independent ticket." Even though conservatives do have complaints about Bush (his immigration proposal, for example, and the massive budget deficit), no evidence suggests they are ready to abandon the president in large numbers, and certainly not for Nader.

In 2000, Nader was on the ballot in 43 states and the District of Columbia. Running as an independent in 2004 will make it harder for him to get on the ballot. He could still run as a minor-party candidate in states where those parties have a ballot line and accept him as their nominee. With the aid of minor parties, Nader could gain access to ballots in 50 states and D.C. by collecting approximately 620,000 signatures nationwide. He received five times that many votes in 2000.

Nader could be in a position to help Democrats make their case against Bush. "I'd like to make a personal statement to Terry McAuliffe, John Kerry, John Edwards, and ex-Governor Dean," Nader said: "Relax. Rejoice that you have another front carrying the ancient but unfulfilled pretensions and aspirations of the Democratic Party."

Moreover, Nader says the voters he will bring out could help Democrats running for Congress. "I would help deserving congressional candidates in key swing districts, because I want the Democrats to recover the House or the Senate, or both," he said at the Press Club.

Most of Nader's supporters from 2000 will probably not vote for him a second time, for one simple reason: They know what happened last time. In 2000, a vote for Nader was a vote for Bush. They might not have realized it then. They know it now.

What about the Deaniacs? Some fans of former Vermont Gov. Howard Dean are so unhappy that their guy was spurned by the Democrats that they are toying with the idea of supporting Nader. They might be even more likely to do so if Sen. John Kerry of Massachusetts is the Democratic nominee. There is no love lost between Dean and Kerry, and Dean supporters in several states rushed to endorse Sen. John Edwards of North Carolina in a move to stop Kerry, whom they regard as the ultimate Washington insider.

Dean's message to his supporters? Get over it. "I will support the nominee of our party," Dean said in his withdrawal statement on February 18. "I will do everything I can to beat George W. Bush. I urge you to do the same."

On February 23, Dean elaborated in a statement aimed at supporters tempted to vote for Nader: "If George W. Bush is re-elected, the health, safety, consumer, environmental, and open-government provisions Ralph Nader has fought for will be undermined. . . . It will be government by, of, and for the corporations—exactly what Ralph Nader has struggled against."

Why is Nader running? He draws a different lesson from 2000 than most others do. He seems to think the 2000 election gave him clout. After all, he determined the outcome. So this time, he feels that Democrats have to pay attention to what he says.

Nader Is Left with Fewer Votes, and Friends, After '04 Race (2004)

SCOTT SHANE

This time around, no one can blame Ralph Nader's presidential candidacy for derailing the Democrats. At fewer than 400,000 votes—less than one-sixth of his 2000 vote total—Mr. Nader's dismal showing at the polls Tuesday probably put more of a dent in his own reputation than in John Kerry's vote.

Support for Mr. Nader, 70, suffered a "late collapse," as many of his sympathizers decided that defeating President Bush was more important than casting a symbolic vote for Mr. Nader's progressive agenda, said Cal Jillson, a political scientist at Southern Methodist University.

But the collapse was on a Lilliputian scale, from roughly 1 percent in the pre-election polls to just a third of a percent of the popular vote.

"Those who chose Nader over Al Gore in 2000 realized what they'd done and bolted for Kerry," said Sandy Maisel of the Goldfarb Center for Public Policy at Colby College.

Evidently unembarrassed by his vote total or by his election-eve prediction of a big Kerry win, Mr. Nader hit the airwaves after the election in fine fettle. If voters' concern about moral values re-elected President Bush, he asked on CNN, "What about the morality of corporate crime, the morality of dangerous workplaces and deaths from air pollution and bad hospital practices?"

The returns seemed to repudiate Mr. Nader's argument that many Americans are looking for a progressive alternative to the two major parties, which he describes as "indentured to corporate power."

He had proposed radical prescriptions for the United States' future, including a "responsible withdrawal" of troops from Iraq within six months; Canadian-style government health insurance; and a guaranteed "living wage" for workers. But his platform never drew much attention, in part because of the distraction of some Democrats' fight to keep Mr. Nader off the ballot in key states.

"Nader is saying the corporations are dangerous to American democracy and we need to stomp them into submission," Mr. Jillson said. "But Americans say, 'Hey, that's the economy you're trying to stomp on.' His message just doesn't resonate."

Longtime allies had tried to talk Mr. Nader out of running for president this year, blaming him for stealing votes from Mr. Gore and sending Mr. Bush to the White House in 2000. They were relieved that he did not have such an impact this time, but they watched the denouement of his campaign with dismay.

"It never made sense for Ralph to be a candidate," said Michael Pertschuk, a former chairman of the Federal Trade Commission and a colleague of Mr. Nader. "So many people are full of rage at Ralph. I can't quite get there. But I feel an awful lot of frustration and sadness."

As a young Senate staff member 40 years ago, Mr. Pertschuk first met Mr. Nader, who rose to fame when his 1965 book on auto safety, *Unsafe At Any Speed,* prompted General Motors to hire a private detective to try to dig up dirt on him.

"He helped us to be much more ambitious in shaping the auto safety legislation," Mr. Pertschuk said. But when a compromise bill emerged, Mr. Nader backed it, he said.

Today, there is no note of negotiation or compromise in Mr. Nader's politics. His increasingly lonely, almost quixotic stance brings to Mr. Pertschuk's mind the image of the Old Testament prophets. "The prophets visualized a radically changed society," he said. "But they weren't looking at the next election."

It seemed a measure of Mr. Nader's diminishing relevance that late in his campaign he seemed to be just as exercised about the Democrats working against him as about his old adversaries, the giant corporations.

In an election night interview, Mr. Nader seemed particularly animated when he denounced the Democrats' "massive dirty tricks."

"Sure, they can compete and argue and debate," he said. "But they wanted to engage in an authoritarian slam by denying our voters the opportunity to vote for us."

One of the Democrats who worked against Mr. Nader, Toby Moffett, defended their efforts to challenge signatures on Nader ballot petitions and picket at his rallies.

"Ralph's the only one who's calling it unseemly," said Mr. Moffett, a Washington lobbyist and former Connecticut congressman. "We didn't do anything outside the law."

Mr. Moffett said bitterly of Mr. Nader, with whom he worked decades ago, "The guy hasn't done anything constructive in 25 years. He won't build coalitions. He won't work for compromise."

Howard Zinn, a historian retired from Boston University and a longtime Nader friend, said history's judgment was likely to be far kinder.

"Nader has been a heroic figure," Mr. Zinn said. "Presidents come and go, but Nader for decades has been a tireless advocate for the environment, for social justice and citizens' rights. The problem comes when he moves from that lofty place to the mean streets of politics. Some of the tarnish rubs off on him, whether he likes it or not."

6.2 Dynamics of the Party System: Alignment and Realignment of Political Parties in the United States (1983)

JAMES L. SUNDQUIST

INTRODUCTION

Although the Democratic and Republican parties have dominated American politics since the Civil War, membership in each organization has undergone significant transformation in that time. The following reading by James L. Sundquist examines *party realignment* in the United States, or "lasting change" in coalitions of voters who identify with a political party. Sundquist identifies party realignments in American history and discusses the difficulty of determining when a realignment has occurred. The very definition— "*lasting* change"—indicates that the expected alterations in voting patterns that take place in any election cannot be identified as a party realignment until enough time has passed to determine whether those changes are lasting. Still, the aftermath of a national election routinely sparks reassessments of the relative strength and appeal of the two political parties as well as questions about their future prospects.

■

THE MUDDIED CONCEPT OF PARTY REALIGNMENT

Systematic thinking about the nature and origin of fundamental changes in the party system had its beginning in 1955, in a pioneering article by V. O. Key, Jr. He called attention to the significance in party history of what he termed *critical elections:* "a type of election in which there occurs a sharp and durable electoral realignment between parties."[1] Key himself wrote further on the subject, and a generation of scholars has continued to probe the phenomenon of electoral realignment, using ever more sophisticated statistical techniques to determine which of the many elections in U.S. history should be classed as critical and to examine the shifts in party support that have occurred in the intervals between those votes. Yet, after a quarter century of study, the concept

---

[1] "A Theory of Critical Elections," *Journal of Politics,* vol. 17 (February 1955), pp. 3–18.

James L. Sundquist, *Dynamics of the Party System: Alignment and Realignment of Political Parties in the United States,* rev. ed. (Washington, D.C.: Brookings Institution, 1983), 3–12, 15–17. Copyright © 1983 by Brookings Institution. Reprinted with permission.

of party realignment is still far from clear. The writers all employ the same term—realignment—but it is difficult to find any two works that give it the same definition.

A distinguishing feature of a realignment is, of course, one identified by Key at the outset—durability. On this much there is no disagreement; without the notion of durability the concept would disappear altogether. Those who analyze alignment and realignment are probing beneath the immediate and transitory ups and downs of daily politics and periodic elections to discover fundamental shifts in the structure of the party system.

Every election sees some change in the distribution of the vote between the parties. A Democrat who dislikes his party's candidate or is attracted by the Republican nominee may vote Republican, or vice versa. A party's record in office, or its stand on particular issues, will attract or repel at least some voters, in every contest. But a voter who crosses the line to vote against the party he normally supports is not realigning unless he makes a lasting shift of party loyalty and attachment. If the shift is temporary, he is merely *deviating*. Sometimes the number of deviants in a particular election is so great that the whole election can be classed as a deviation from the political norm. Angus Campbell so identifies the presidential contest of 1916, when Democrat Woodrow Wilson was reelected in a period when the majority of the country's voters were, and remained, Republican, and the elections of 1952 and 1956, when Republican Dwight D. Eisenhower was victorious in a period when most voters were, and remained, Democrats.[2] To these the landslides of 1964 and 1972 can be added; most of the millions of Republicans who voted for Lyndon Johnson in his year of triumph did not thereupon become converts to the Democratic party, nor did most of the Democrats who voted for Richard Nixon's reelection become by that act Republicans.

It is when the political norm itself changes that realignment occurs. The concept applies, then, not to voting behavior as such, but to what underlies voting behavior—to the basic party attachments of the voting citizens. "Most members of the electorate feel some degree of psychological attachment to one of the major parties," Campbell wrote. "This partisan identification is remarkably resistant to passing political events and typically remains constant through the life of the individual." The voter's behavior at a particular election "derives from the interaction of his political predispositions and the short-term forces generated by the current political situation."[3] It is the pattern of those predispositions, of party identification within the electorate, that defines the alignment of the party system. Since a realignment is defined as a lasting change, it follows that whether a system is realigning cannot be known for certain until after the process is complete—until enough time has passed to

---

[2]Angus Campbell, "A Classification of the Presidential Elections," in Angus Campbell and others, *Elections and the Political Order* (Wiley, 1966), pp. 69–74.

[3]Angus Campbell, "Voters and Elections: Past and Present," *Journal of Politics*, vol. 26 (November 1964), p. 747. . . .

permit a judgment as to whether significant shifts in party support that may be observed have, or have not, endured beyond the life of the short-term forces that may have been at work. Indeed, as David H. Nexon well argues, it may never be known, for a realignment that otherwise would prove to be durable might be obliterated by a powerful set of forces that redrew the political map anew before the realignment had a chance to settle in.[4] The notion of durability itself has to be qualified, then, to include the *would have been* category (for which the election of 1928 is probably the leading candidate).

This one basic proposition—that a realignment is a shift in the distribution of basic party attachments, as distinct from a temporary alteration of voter behavior—leaves open the question of whether the label should be applied to *all* such shifts. If the answer is affirmative, the conceptual problem moves to the next level—to the identification and classification of types of realignments. If the answer is negative, then which of the shifts are realignments and which are not? What are the distinguishing attributes—besides durability—of the realignment phenomenon? And what are the other shifts in party attachment to be called?

The Question of Magnitude

Much of the writing on the subject of realignment introduces, explicitly or implicitly, a second criterion—one of magnitude. Thus a treatise entitled *Partisan Realignment* published in 1980, while essaying no formal definition, appears to confine the term to what are characterized as "major" or "historical" realignments. The "lasting electoral change" that occurs between realignments is variously referred to as "adjustments" or "realigning change of small or moderate magnitude."[5] Another 1980 study, which draws on earlier studies of the subject, defines realignment as "a durable *and significant* redistribution of party support."[6] Yet, one of the editors of the symposium in which that definition appears takes an opposing view; to him, realignment is "*any* shift in the partisan identification of the electorate."[7] Adding to the confusion, a 1981 book refers to a particular period of party change as a "major realignment," which seems to admit the possibility that realignments can be minor as well, but in the same paragraph terms the change "a party transformation major enough to merit

---

[4]"Methodological Issues in the Study of Realignment," in Bruce A. Campbell and Richard J. Trilling, eds., *Realignment in American Politics: Toward a Theory* (University of Texas Press, 1980), pp. 54–55.

[5]Jerome M. Clubb, William H. Flanigan, and Nancy H. Zingale, *Partisan Realignment: Voters, Parties, and Government in American History* (Sage, 1980), esp. pp. 26, 30, 31, 53–54, 105–06. Yet, since they use the phrase "major realignments," they suggest that realignments can be of minor scale as well.

[6]Lawrence G. McMichael and Richard J. Trilling, "The Structure and Meaning of Critical Realignment: The Case of Pennsylvania, 1928–1932," in Campbell and Trilling, *Realignment in American Politics*, p. 29; emphasis added.

[7]Campbell, "Realignment, Party Decomposition, and Issue Voting," in Campbell and Trilling, *Realignment in American Politics*, p. 83; emphasis in original.

the term 'realignment,'" which excludes minor changes from the definition.[8]

Applying a criterion of significance or scale, however, leaves the original definition with quite uncertain boundaries. Redistributions of party support, presumably, can be of any magnitude. If major political forces produce major upheavals, minor forces may produce, through the same process but within only some population groups, minor alterations in the patterns of party attachment. Some of the shifts that are registered in every election turn out, no doubt, to be durable. So how much shifting must there be before what has happened can be called a realignment? How significant is significant enough?

There is no disagreement at the upper end of the scale of magnitude. Two historic upheavals in the party system are designated as realignments in the definition of every analyst. One was in the period preceding and during the Civil War, when the Whig party died and the Republican party was born and came to power. The second was during the Great Depression of the 1930s, when the Republican party was discredited and the Democrats replaced it as the country's majority party—a position the Democrats still hold, although precariously, after half a century. The consensus is almost as complete that the events of the 1890s—when the Democratic party was radicalized and the Republicans made significant and lasting gains—fall within the appropriate definition of realignment. In each of these realignments, the composition of the parties (in the first case, even the identity of one) and the character of the political struggle between them were altered fundamentally, so that the country passed from one distinct "national party system" to another.[9]

Much of the analysis of the realignment process has concentrated on these three periods and, by so doing, has simply avoided the question of what to call the less drastic changes in the party system that appear to have taken place between those periods or in the half century since the last of them. Was there a realignment, for instance, in the 1870s or 1940s or 1960s? Those who use the 1890s and the 1930s as the measuring scale say no. Burnham, however, refers to the lesser shifts in party support between the great upheavals as realignments or as "subrealigning."[10] The authors of *Partisan Realignment* prefer to call

---

[8]John R. Petrocik, *Party Coalitions: Realignments and the Decline of the New Deal Party System* (University of Chicago Press, 1981), p. 11. In his formal definition, Petrocik holds only that the redistribution of party support among population groups must be "measurable": "A realignment occurs when the measurable party bias of identifiable segments of the population changes in such a way that the social group profile of the parties—the party coalitions—is altered."

[9]William N. Chambers, "Party Development and the American Mainstream," and Walter Dean Burnham, "Party Systems and the Political Process," in William N. Chambers and Walter Dean Burnham, eds., *The American Party System: Stages of Political Development* (Oxford University Press, 1967), pp. 3, 289–304. They identify five successive "national party systems" since the beginning of the republic: the two-party competition that ended with the collapse of the Federalists about 1820, the Whig-Democratic competition before the realignment of the 1850s, and the systems that followed the realignments of the 1850s, the 1890s, and the 1930s.

[10]*Critical Elections and the Mainsprings of American Politics* (Norton, 1970), pp. 17, 67.

them "adjustments." Nexon refers to 1964 flatly as a realignment[11] while other writers withhold the label. But the confusion surrounding the extensive discussion of whether 1964—or any other year outside the accepted three periods—was a realigning year grows out of an all-or-nothing fallacy: the conception that a redistribution of party support on a scale beyond some undefined boundary constitutes a realignment while anything less does not.

If two events share all essential characteristics except that of magnitude—if they are analogous in causation, process, and consequence—they are, presumably, the same phenomenon. Preferably, then, they should carry the same identifying label. And gradations in size can be indicated by adjectives or prefixes. *Major* realignments can be distinguished from *minor* (as in the first edition of this book), or a term such as Burnham's *subrealignments* can be used. This does not solve the boundary problem, of course, for a line must be drawn between any pair of modifiers denoting size. But it has the advantage of suggesting that large and small redistributions of party support are variations of the same phenomenon, different in degree but not in kind.

Questions of Antecedents and Consequences

Some writers have limited use of the term *realignment* by making it dependent on specified antecedents or consequences. Thus Gerald Pomper, in his classification of presidential elections, designates as "realigning" only those elections in which one party displaces the other as the majority party. An election that registers a "basic change in party support" but with the same party in the majority—1896, for instance—he calls "converting" rather than realigning.[12]

Similarly, the authors of *Partisan Realignment* contend that "shifts in partisan control of government and policy action . . . are integral and necessary elements of the process of partisan realignment." Discussing the major historical realignments, they observe that those occasions were marked by a national crisis, a consequent change in party control of the government, "effective policy action" by the winning party in coping with the crisis, and a consequent "new distribution of party loyalties in the electorate." The realignment, therefore, does not take place during a critical election but only afterward; it occurs "not as an instantaneous response to crisis, but as a more gradual process coming in response to policy action that can be seen as effectively addressing national problems."[13] Yet, while some of the major redistributions of party support that have marked U.S. history surely did take place in this manner, it is by no means proven that all did. As can be seen in the chapter reviewing events of

---

[11]"Methodological Issues," p. 55.

[12]Gerald M. Pomper, *Elections in America: Control and Influence in Democratic Politics* (Dodd, Mead, 1968), p. 104.

[13]Clubb, Flanigan, and Zingale, *Partisan Realignment*, pp. 12, 31, 268. Unlike Pomper, they apply the term realignment to the events of the 1890s (pp. 98–114).

the 1850s, the Republican party had replaced the Whig party as the principal competitor of the Democrats in many states in that decade—before the GOP had had its first chance to take any policy actions to address national problems. It was the shift in party support that had already taken place that made possible the Republican party's first victory, in 1860.

While in this case a shift in partisan control did follow the shift in party support, suppose it had not occurred. A sound theoretical classification system has to make room not only for what *does* happen but for what *can* happen or *could* have happened. Reviewing the Civil War period, one has to ask what might have happened if the Democrats had won the elections of 1860 and 1864 but the Republicans—solidly organized by then in most of the northern states—had survived as a powerful minority party, replacing the Whigs but with a significantly different composition. Would such an outcome have been a realignment? If not, what would it have been? *Partisan Realignment* makes its definition dependent not on what happened to the party system—the "new distribution of party loyalties"—but on the sequence of events that led up to it. And Pomper makes it dependent on what happened afterward. By its structure, the word *realignment* denotes the replacement of one alignment by another; it should not be limited to those that occurred in any specified manner or had only certain consequences.[14] Those distinctions can be better made, as in the case of magnitude, by modifiers.[15]

The Question of Geographic Scope

Analysts of party realignments have usually treated them as national phenomena, as changes in the national party system. Accordingly, some have sought to identify critical elections, or realigning periods, by analysis of returns in presidential and congressional elections for the nation as a whole. Yet parties in the United States have been uniquely decentralized; the patterns of political organization and competition have been profoundly different in the South and the North, during most of the nation's history. When one statistical technique places the critical election of the Civil War period in 1856 and another in 1864, the explanation may well be that neither date, or any other, was

---

[14]Richard J. Trilling and Bruce A. Campbell, "Toward A Theory of Realignment: An Introduction," in Campbell and Trilling, *Realignment in American Politics*, p. 6, agree that a realignment can occur "without the emergence of a new majority party . . . as in the case where a noncompetitive minority party becomes a competitive minority party." Petrocik, *Party Coalitions*, pp. 21–22, holds that a realignment may not alter the relative strength of the parties; he distinguishes such realignments with the adjective "noncritical."

[15]Clubb, Flanigan, and Zingale, *Partisan Realignment*, pp. 83–84, divide realigning elections still further, into "realigning surges" across-the-board in favor of one party, or "realigning interactions" that involve compensating shifts in both directions. Since some shifting in both directions must surely occur in every realignment, this distinction would require answering the question, how much compensation is compensation enough? In any case, I have not found it necessary to distinguish between these two types of realignment.

the critical election in the nation but that both of them, as well as some others of the period, marked critical shifts in party support *in different places.*

The assumption that critical elections, or realignments, occur across the whole nation at the same time can severely distort reality. Understanding the realignment process requires that national data be disaggregated; that events in individual states, their constituent counties and cities, and even, to the extent that data and time permit, their separate wards and precincts, be examined; and then that the data be reassembled according to whatever geographic and demographic patterns present themselves.

The Question of Pace of Change

Analysts of realignments have distinguished between transformations of the party system that appear to have occurred sharply and decisively during or in the wake of certain "critical elections"—notably those of 1860, 1896, and 1932—and redistributions of party strength that have occurred gradually over a period of time. It was the drastic upheavals, naturally enough, that first attracted attention to party realignment as a field for scholarly research, beginning with Key's theory of critical elections in 1955. Yet Key recognized that his theory did not explain all aspects of the realignment phenomenon. Four years later, he presented a concept of "secular realignment," a long-term, rather than a sharp and sudden, redistribution of party strength—the result of processes that "operate inexorably, and almost imperceptibly, election after election, to form new party alignments and to build new party groupings." He cited examples, such as the long-term drift to the Republican party of German-Americans in a rural Ohio county and the gradual movement of Jewish voters in a Boston ward toward the Democrats.[16] Burnham, simplifying Key's terminology, speaks of "critical realignment" and "secular realignment."[17]

The difficulty, however, is that the two are not as distinguishable as they at first appeared to be. Elections only register decisions about party support that individual voters have made at some time before the act of voting—presumably, if presidential voting alone is analyzed, at any point in the preceding four years. Yet, the judgment registered by an individual voter in even an election that appears to be critical may be no more than an act of protest, reflecting no shift in basic support on the part of the protesting voter—a deviating vote. Or it may be a tentative transfer of allegiance. Whether it is a lasting decision—a realignment decision—cannot be known until time has passed. In many cases, no doubt, the individual voter does not himself know when he first casts loose from his accustomed political moorings whether he intends to cross the party line for good; as the authors of *Partisan Realignment* contend,

---

[16]V. O. Key, Jr., "Secular Realignment and the Party System," *Journal of Politics*, 21 (May 1959), pp. 198–210; quotation from pp. 198–99.

[17]*Critical Elections*, chap. 1.

he may be waiting for satisfactory performance by the party to which he gave conditional approval by his vote.

In short, if realigning forces are at work, they necessarily have their effect on individual voters at different times—not simultaneously in any single election. For this reason, most analysts of realignment now talk of realigning periods or eras. To some degree, in other words, all realignments are long-term—that is, secular—and it confuses more than it clarifies to treat the critical and the secular as separate types of realignment rather than as phases of a single process. . . . [M]uch of the political change that has occurred since World War II has been a delayed, secular phase of the realignment that reached its climax in the critical elections of the 1930s—the aftershocks, so to speak, as the fault line created by the initial political earthquake settled into place.

Like magnitude, pace of change is a less than satisfactory criterion for classifying realignments. A single realignment may have both abrupt and slower paced phases, but it is still one phenomenon, one process of change. Critical elections, in sum, are episodes in most realignments; they do not define a type. . . .

CAUSATION, PROCESS, AND DATA

The modern study of realignment as a political phenomenon has been based primarily on the quantitative analysis of election returns, which for all of the last century and the early decades of this one is virtually the exclusive source of data on the political attitudes and party attachments of the electorate.

Election data have, however, the severe limitation of revealing only *what* happened, nothing about *why* or *how*. They have led to sterile debates about the dates of critical elections—with different statistical methods identifying different dates—but they tell nothing about the historical forces that converged upon those dates and gave them their significance.[18]

If there are many realigning forces at work simultaneously, moreover, the analysis of election data alone does little to help untangle them. Since a realignment is a chain of events proceeding from a causative factor through a sequence of responses, there must be as many realignments as there are separable identifiable causes, and more than one can be going on simultaneously. If it is accepted that even a critical realignment may take place over several elections, a new realignment can be set in motion by a new cause before an old one has worked its way through the party system. Election data, by compressing into a single set of figures the consequences of all the causative factors that may be in operation on a given November Tuesday, can be positively misleading, for the single correlation coefficient that measures the scale of

---

[18]The problems of identifying realigning elections through statistical analysis alone set out in Nexon, "Methodological Issues," pp. 56–62.

realignment between two elections tends to suggest that what is being measured is a singular phenomenon.

To analyze the whole process of any of the realignments that have taken place in U.S. history, the election returns are a starting point—but only that. In order to relate the outcomes they measure to the causes that produced them, the voting data have to be examined in the context of the historical events that influenced the political attitudes and behavior of the time. Quantitative methods have to be combined with traditional nonquantitative approaches. The content of the partisan conflict from year to year, and the behavior of party leaders, conventions, caucuses, and candidates and their organizations and supporters, are the sources of inferences as to the how and the why of the realignment process.

Since the second decade of this century, a second source of quantitative data has been available for some states—registration (or enrollment) of voters by party. Registration is a positive act by a voter to identify with a party as such, as distinct from giving his support to the party's candidate in a particular election. Registration data, then, have the advantage of ignoring the deviant voting behavior that so frequently confuses the interpretation of election returns: a deviant, by definition, does not change his party affiliation. Nevertheless, students of party alignment and realignment have paid virtually no attention to registration trends, perhaps because of certain weaknesses inherent in the data. Since registration is a public act, it is subject to coercive influences. In any local jurisdiction the majority party will always be overregistered. Some voters who oppose that party in November in the secrecy of the voting booth may register with it because it holds the more significant primaries. Or they may find it prudent to affiliate publicly with the party that controls local patronage as well as the police, the courts, and property tax assessment.[19] And since to change registration requires time and effort—perhaps a visit to the courthouse—registration shifts may lag behind permanent shifts in voting behavior. Registrars may also be slow in purging the voting lists of persons who have died or moved away. Party registration data, moreover, are not universally and readily available. In some states, voters are not required to register by party, and in others the figures are not centrally compiled and published. Despite these weaknesses, I have found registration data to be quite revealing when analyzed in combination with other data, and I use them in the chapters dealing with events since voter registration was introduced in the Progressive Era.

Finally, since the late 1930s, and especially since the mid-1950s, public opinion polls have provided a rich source of quantitative data to supplement what can be learned from election returns and registration figures. Polling data have, indeed, three great advantages over voting and registration statistics for our purposes. First, while election returns tell only of voting behavior,

---

[19]In one county in New York State in the 1950s, the local political folklore held that a property owner who changed his party enrollment would suffer an automatic $500 increase, or enjoy a $500 decrease, in the assessed value of his real estate, depending on the direction of the change.

from which shifts in underlying party attachments have to be inferred, pollsters have regularly asked direct questions about attachment. Second, while neither election results nor party registration data present any direct evidence about causation, pollsters can establish hypotheses about what may be influencing political behavior and attitudes and ask questions designed to test directly those hypotheses. Third, while election and registration data subdivide voters only by geography—which requires laborious analysis, based usually on scanty data, to determine how particular population groups may have behaved—polls can divide their samples into any system of categories that may seem relevant, so that one can ascertain the distribution of party support not only by geographical subdivision but also by race, religion, sex, age, income class, ideology or any other attribute, and determine how support may have shifted from time to time within the various groups. Sophisticated polling techniques therefore make it possible to discern and trace realignments while they are occurring and probe deeply into causes—the only limitation being the high cost of getting large enough samples from the sometimes small subsegments of the electorate that may be changing their political attachments.

THE INFINITE COMPLEXITY OF POLITICAL ALIGNMENTS

In any of the historic realignments of the American party system—even the most drastic—only a portion of the electorate was involved in the shuffle. The existing pattern of party attachments was not erased and a new one drawn, even during a realignment as traumatic and violent as that of the Civil War period. This must inevitably be the case in any democratic society with a mature party system. It is hardly conceivable that any political force could arise that would be sufficiently powerful to obliterate all the reasons for attachment by members of the electorate to the existing parties. Indeed, some writers find the continuity of voting patterns between the periods before and after a realignment to be more impressive than the change.[20]

In every new alignment of the party system, then, there will be large, perhaps dominant, elements carried over from the old. Successive realignments can best be understood as new patterns drawn on transparent overlays. Each overlay defines a new line of party cleavage within the electorate (or redelineates an old line) and so distributes some elements of the voting population on either side of that line in new arrangements. But beneath the latest overlay can be discerned all the lines of cleavage of the past, some more distinct than others by virtue of their recency or the strength of the color in which they were originally drawn.

---

[20]Clubb, Flanigan, and Zingale, *Partisan Realignment,* pp. 68–69, 114–15, 119, 214.

6.3 The Social Basis of Politics (2004)

STEPHEN J. WAYNE

INTRODUCTION

Every so often in American politics, there has been a massive and lasting shift in partisan loyalties or a mobilization of new voters—or both in tandem—resulting in new but stable political coalitions and new eras of party dominance. This was the case, many scholars contend, with the Great Depression and Democrat Franklin Delano Roosevelt's rise to the presidency. In effect, Roosevelt's New Deal coalition made the Democrats the nation's dominant party. For a variety of reasons, however, it is unlikely that the United States will see any such party realignment anytime soon. Rather, as Stephen J. Wayne argues in this reading selection, we are witnessing changes both in "the social basis of politics" and in the formation of new political coalitions in which "voters exercise a more independent judgment on election day" and "the major parties remain at rough parity with one another."

■

THE SOCIAL BASIS OF POLITICS

The New Deal Realignment

Political coalitions form during periods of partisan realignment. The last time a classic realignment occurred was in the 1930s. Largely as a consequence of the Great Depression, the Democrats emerged as the dominant party.[1] Their coalition, held together by a common economic belief that the government should play a more active role in dealing with the nation's economic problems, supported Franklin Roosevelt's New Deal program. Those who saw government involvement as a threat to the free enterprise system opposed much of Roosevelt's domestic legislation. They remained Republican in attitude and voting behavior.

The Democrats became the majority party during this period by expanding their base. Since the Civil War, the Democrats had enjoyed support in the

---

[1]This description of the New Deal realignment is based primarily on the discussion in Everett Carll Ladd Jr., with Charles D. Hadley, *Transformations of the American Party System* (New York: Norton, 1975), 31–87.

Stephen J. Wayne, *The Road to the White House, 2004: The Politics of Presidential Elections* (with InfoTrac), 7th edition (Belmont, Calif.: Wadsworth, 2004), 83–94. © 2004. Reprinted with permission of Wadsworth, a division of Thomson Learning: www.thomsonrights.com. Fax 800 730-2215.

South. White Protestants living in rural areas dominated the southern electorate; African Americans were largely excluded from it. Only in the election of 1928, when Al Smith, the Catholic governor of New York, ran as the Democratic candidate, was there a sizable southern popular and electoral vote for a Republican candidate at the presidential level. Being a Catholic and an opponent of prohibition made Smith unacceptable to many white Protestant fundamentalists who lived in the South.

As a group, Catholics also voted Democratic before the 1930s. Living primarily in the urban centers of the North, they became increasingly important to the Democrats as their numbers grew in the population. Poor economic and social conditions, combined with the immigrant status of many Catholics, made them dependent on big-city bosses, who were able to deliver a sizable Democratic vote. In 1928, for the first time, a majority of the cities in the country voted Democratic. Catholic support for Smith and the Democratic Party figured prominently in this vote.

The harsh economic realities of the Great Depression enabled Roosevelt to expand Democratic support in urban areas still further, especially among those in the lower socioeconomic strata. Outside the South, Roosevelt's political coalition was differentiated along class lines. It attracted people with less education and income and those with lower-status jobs. Organized labor, in particular, threw its support to Roosevelt. Union members became a core group in the Democratic Party's electoral coalition.

In addition to establishing a broad-based, blue-collar, working-class coalition, Roosevelt also lured specific racial and ethnic groups, such as African Americans and Jewish Americans, from their Republican roots. African Americans, who lived outside of the South, voted Democratic primarily for economic reasons, and Jewish Americans supported Roosevelt's liberal domestic programs and his anti-Nazi foreign policy. Neither of these groups provided the Democratic Party of the 1930s with a large number of votes, but their loyalty to it and long-term impact on it have been considerable.

In contrast, during the same period the Republican Party shrank. Not only were Republicans unable to attract new groups to their coalition, they were unable to prevent the defection of some supporters whose economic situation affected their partisan loyalties and influenced their vote. Although the Republicans did retain the backing of many business and professional people, they lost the support of much of the white Protestant working class. Republican strength remained concentrated in the Northeast, particularly in the rural areas.

Evolving Political Coalitions

The coalition that formed during the New Deal held together, for the most part, until the 1960s. During this period, African Americans and Jewish Americans increased their identification with and support of the Democratic Party and its candidates. Catholics tended to remain Democratic, although they fluctuated more in their voting behavior at the presidential level. Nonsouthern white Protestants continued to support the Republicans.

Some changes did take place, however, mainly along socioeconomic lines. Domestic prosperity contributed to the growth of a larger middle class. Had such a class identified with the Republicans for economic reasons, the Democratic majority would have been threatened. This identification did not occur, however. Those who gained in economic and social status did not, as a general rule, discard their partisan loyalties. The Democrats were able to hold on to the allegiance of a majority of this group and improve their position with the professional and managerial classes, which had grown substantially during this period. The Republicans continued to maintain their advantage with those in the upper socioeconomic strata. The economic improvement in the country had the effect of blurring class distinctions that were evident during the 1930s and 1940s.[2]

Partisan attitudes, however, were shifting in the South. White southerners, particularly those who first voted after 1940, began to desert their party at the presidential level, largely over civil rights issues. In 1948, Harry Truman won 52 percent of the southern vote, compared with Roosevelt's 69 percent four years earlier. Although Adlai Stevenson and John Kennedy carried the South by reduced margins, the southern white Protestant vote for president went Republican for the first time in 1960.

Major shifts in the national electorate began to be evident in the mid-1960s and continued through the 1990s. (See Table 1.) The continued defection of southern white Protestants to Republican candidates, not only at the presidential level but at the other levels as well, has been the most significant and enduring of these changes.

Since 1952, the decline in the partisan loyalty of southern whites has been substantial. Then, 85 percent of them identified with the Democratic Party; forty years later, that proportion had shrunk to less than 40 percent with the ratio of Democrats to Republicans in the South declining from approximately six to one to less than two to one.[3] Moreover, in the 1994 midterm elections, Republican congressional candidates won a majority of the southern vote, the first time that has happened since Reconstruction.[4] In subsequent elections, the Republicans maintained their southern majority in the House. The South was also the region of the country that voted most heavily for Robert Dole and George W. Bush.

Despite Republican gains in the South, it is still not as solidly Republican today as it was solidly Democratic from 1876 through 1944. According to political scientists Earl and Merle Black, Franklin Delano Roosevelt averaged 78 percent of the southern vote during his four presidential elections compared with 57 percent for Republican presidential candidates from 1972 to 1988.[5]

---

[2]Ibid., 93–104.

[3]Earl Black and Merle Black, *The Vital South: How Presidents are Elected* (Cambridge, Mass.: Harvard University Press, 1992), 27.

[4]Thomas B. Edsall, "Huge Gains in South Fueled GOP Vote in '94," *Washington Post*, June 27, 1995, A8.

Beginning in 1988, southern whites have been less apt to vote for the Democratic presidential candidate than have whites in any other region of the country. Arkansas Democrat, Bill Clinton, managed to split the southern vote with Robert Dole in 1996, with each receiving approximately 46 percent, but Tennessean Al Gore received only 36 percent. Had it not been for the growth of the African American electorate in the South and its overwhelming support for Democratic candidates, the defection of the southern states from the Democratic camp would have been even more dramatic.

Another potentially important shift has been occurring among new voters, particularly younger ones. During the 1980s, a plurality of this group turned to the Republican Party after being more Democratic than their elders since the 1950s. In 1984, eighteen- to twenty-nine-year-olds supported Ronald Reagan in his reelection bid just as strongly as did those over thirty. (See Table [1].) Their support of George Bush in 1988 was even greater. In 1992, however, the vote of younger Americans more closely reflected national voting trends, and in 1996, they provided Bill Clinton with more support than any other age cohort in the population. In 2000, voters under thirty leaned slightly toward Bush.

While Democrats have lost the allegiance of southern whites at the presidential level and have lost support from southern voters generally, they also saw electoral support dwindle from several of their key coalitions. Organized labor is a good example. In six of the eight presidential elections between 1952 and 1976, this group favored the Democratic candidate by an average of nearly 30 percentage points. In the 1980s, the results were closer although the Democrats still enjoyed an advantage. Labor support for the Democrats increased in recent presidential elections. Clinton received 55 percent of the vote from people who lived in union households in 1992 and 59 percent in 1996, while Gore also got 58 percent in 2000. However, as a group, organized labor has declined as a proportion of the total population. Members of union households made up 25 percent of the electorate in 1952; today they constitute only about 13 percent.[6] Although the proportion of the total vote the Democrats receive from labor has declined, the party's support among middle-class voters has increased.

Catholic allegiance to the Democratic Party has also weakened, declining from its high of 78 percent in 1960 to a low of 39 percent in 1984. Since then, Democratic candidates have recovered some of these losses. Clinton won 53 percent of the Catholic vote in 1996; Gore won 50 percent in 2000. They were both helped by the considerable support they received from the Hispanic community. In general, Catholics as a group now seem more susceptible to candidate-centered and issue-specific appeals than they were when their partisan identification had a stronger impact on them.[7]

---

[6]Paul R. Abramson, John H. Aldrich, and David W. Rohde, *Change and Continuity in the 2000 Elections* (Washington, D.C.: Congressional Quarterly, 2002), 112.

[7]Lyman A. Kellstedt, John C. Green, James L. Guth, and Corwin E. Schmidt, "Religious Voting Blocs in the 1992 Election: Year of the Evangelical?" *Sociology of Religion* 55 (1994): 307–326; Robert B. Fowler and Allen D. Hertzke, *Religion and Politics in America: Faith, Culture, and Strategic Choice* (Boulder, Colo.: Westview Press, 1995).

Age											
Under 30	47	38	15	48	52	53	45	1	47	41	11
30–49 years	44	41	15	33	67	48	49	2	38	52	8
50 years and older	41	47	12	36	64	52	48	—	41	54	4
Religion											
Protestants	35	49	16	30	70	46	53	—	39	54	6
Catholics	59	33	8	48	52	57	41	1	46	47	6
Politics											
Republicans	9	86	5	5	95	9	91	—	8	86	5
Democrats	74	12	14	67	33	82	18	—	69	26	4
Independents	31	44	25	31	69	38	57	4	29	55	14
Region											
East	50	43	7	42	58	51	47	1	43	47	9
Midwest	44	47	9	40	60	48	50	1	41	51	7
South	31	36	33	29	71	54	45	—	44	52	3
West	44	49	7	41	59	46	51	1	35	54	9
Labor Union											
Union families	56	29	15	46	54	63	36	1	50	43	5

(cont. on next page)

Table [1] (continued)

Vote by Groups in Presidential Elections, 1968–2000 (in Percentages)

	1984		1988		1992			1996			2000*		
	Mondale	Reagan	Dukakis	Bush	Clinton	Bush	Perot	Clinton	Dole	Perot	Gore	Bush	Nader
NATIONAL	41.0	59.0	46.0	54.0	43.2	37.8	19.0	50.0	41.0	9.0	48.0	48.0	3.0
Sex													
Men	36	64	44	56	41	37	22	45	44	11	42	51	4
Women	45	55	48	52	46	38	16	54	39	7	49	43	3
Race													
White	34	66	41	59	39	41	20	46	45	9	39	59	4
Nonwhite	87	13	82	18	77	11	12	82	12	6	81	9	5
Education†													
College	39	61	42	58	43	40	17	47	45	8	46	48	4
High School	43	57	46	54	40	38	22	52	34	14	41	51	5
Grade School	51	49	55	45	56	28	16	58	27	15	48	42	4
Age													
Under 30	40	60	37	63	40	37	23	54	30	16	43	46	8
30–49 years	40	60	45	55	42	37	21	49	41	10	43	51	3
50 years and older	41	59	49	51	46	39	15	50	45	5	48	43	3
Religion													
Protestants	39	61	42	58	41	41	18	44	50	6	—	—	—
Catholics	39	61	51	49	47	35	18	55	35	10	—	—	—

Politics													
Republicans	4	96	7	93	7	77	16	10	85	5	7	91	9
Democrats	79	21	85	15	82	8	10	90	6	4	85	10	9
Independents	33	67	43	57	39	30	31	48	33	19	37	42	3
Region													
East	46	54	51	49	47	35	18	60	31	9	52	38	6
Midwest	42	58	47	53	44	34	22	46	45	9	43	47	4
South	37	63	40	60	38	45	17	44	46	10	36	56	3
West	40	60	46	54	45	35	20	51	43	6	43	47	6
Labor Union													
Union families	52	48	63	37	—	—	—	—	—	—	58	31	6

* Gallup data in 2000 underestimated Gore's vote in most demographic categories. . . .

† In 2000, categories comprised College, Some college, and No college.

Notes: National figures are based on actual election outcomes, repercentaged to exclude minor third-party candidates. Demographic data are based on Gallup poll final preelection surveys, repercentaged to exclude "no opinions"; for 2000, data are based on Gallup six-day average, October 31–November 5, 2000, except Region.

Source: Gallup Organization, *"Vote By Groups,"* <http://www.gallup.com/poll/trends>, November 6, 2000; "Final Preelection Poll," November 7, 2000. Reprinted by permission.

Jewish voters have evidenced a much smaller decrease in their Democratic partisan sympathies and voting behavior, although as a group Jews have declined as a proportion of the population. They have remained loyal to the Democratic Party; approximately two-thirds of this group identify with the Democratic Party, and three-fourths have voted for its presidential candidates since 1928. The only election since World War II in which a majority of Jews did not vote Democratic occurred in 1980 when only 47 percent cast ballots for President Carter. Independent candidate John Anderson was the principal beneficiary of this defection, winning 14 percent of the Jewish vote. As a group, Jewish Americans returned to their traditional voting patterns after that election. Contributing to their support for the Democratic candidates has been the party's liberal position on social issues and, in 2000, the nomination of the first Jewish vice presidential candidate, Democrat Joseph Lieberman.

The Democratic electoral coalition has also retained and even increased its support among other key groups, notably African Americans and Hispanics. Today, more than 75 percent of African Americans consider themselves Democrats, with less than 10 percent considering themselves Republicans compared to the late 1950s when almost 25 percent considered themselves Republican.[8] While other groups have weakened their loyalty to the Democrats, African Americans have increased theirs; in fact, the smaller the Democratic vote, the larger the African American proportion of it. In 1996, one out of six Clinton voters was African American; and in 2000, one out of five of Gore's votes came from an African American voter.

But there has been a flip side to this African American support. Democratic positions on social issues, particularly civil rights, that appeal to African Americans have alienated some white working-class voters whose support for the Democrats has declined over the last three decades.[9]

Hispanic voters have also become an important component of the Democrats' electoral coalition, particularly as that group expands within the population. With the exception of Cuban Americans concentrated in south Florida, a majority of Hispanic voters identify with the Democratic Party, and two-thirds of them tend to vote for its candidates on a regular basis. Clinton received the support of almost three out of four Hispanic voters in 1996, and Gore, almost two out of three in 2000.

Since 1980, there have been discernible differences in the partisan identities and electoral voting patterns of men and women. This differential has produced a "gender gap," with women more likely to identify with and vote

[8]Everett Carll Ladd, "The 1992 Vote for President Clinton: Another Brittle Mandate?" *Political Science Quarterly* 108 (Spring 1993): 4. For a discussion of turnout among African Americans in 1984 and 1988, see Katherine Tate, "Black Political Participation in the 1984 and 1988 Presidential Elections," *American Political Science Review* 85 (December 1991): 1159–1176.

[9]For an extended discussion of the impact of race on the Democratic Party, see Robert Huckfeldt and Carol Weitzel Kohfeld, *Race and the Decline of Class in American Politics* (Urbana: University of Illinois Press, 1989).

Democratic and men more likely to prefer the Republican Party and its candidates.[10] The gap had been in the range of 4 to 8 percent until 1996, when it rose to 11 percent and remained at about that level in 2000. It is larger among whites than nonwhites, larger among those in the higher socioeconomic brackets than in lower groups, and larger among those with more formal education than less.[11] It is also greater among those who are unmarried than those who are married and those without children than those with them.[12]

In the light of these shifts, how can the composition of the major political parties be described today? The Democrats have become a diverse party in which ethnic and racial minorities and, increasingly, women constitute core constituencies. They still receive overwhelming support from those with the lowest incomes and those who live in the cities. However, the relatively small size of the latter two groups within the electorate today make them less important than they were in the past. The same can be said for organized labor which continues to vote Democratic but now accounts for a smaller percentage of the total electorate. Southern whites have exited in the largest proportions, but the Democrats have picked up support in the Northeast and the Pacific coast. Additionally, those voters who came of age during the Roosevelt presidency remain the party's most loyal age group but their children and grandchildren do not share the same strong Democratic allegiances.

Although the Democrats' New Deal coalition has eroded, the groups within that coalition, with the exception of southern whites, have not become Republican. They have simply provided less support for the Democrats. Although the Republican Party has gained adherents, it has not done so by virtue of a major exodus of groups from one party to the other, except in the South.

As a party, the Republicans have become more white, more middle class, more suburban, and more male. They have gained support in the South and Southwest, the so-called Sunbelt. Additionally, Republicans have gained adherents from white evangelical Christian groups that had supported the Democratic Party and voted for its candidates through 1976. By the end of the 1980s, a plurality of this group thought of themselves as Republican, with 80 percent voting for George Bush in 1988 and a similar percentage for his son in 2000. In 1992 and 1996, the Republican evangelic vote declined slightly. White evangelicals now constitute a core bloc within the Republican Party's

---

[10]There is also a gender gap within the parties. In an analysis of voting behavior in presidential primaries from 1980 to 2000, Professor Barbara Norrander found women more likely to consider themselves partisans than men. The differences were greater among Democratic voters than Republicans. Barbara Norrander, "The Intraparty Gender Gap: Differences between Male and Female Voters in the 1980–2000 Presidential Primaries," *PS: Political Science and Politics* 36 (April 2003): 181–186.

[11]Abramson, Aldrich, and Rohde, *Change and Continuity in 2000*, 100–102.

[12]Partisan voting trends are also evident on the basis of sexual orientation. According to the VNS exit polls in 2000, 70 percent of those who indicated that they were gay or lesbian voted for Gore.

electoral coalition almost as important to the GOP as African Americans are to the Democrats.[13]

The shift of white evangelical Christians, who constitute approximately one-fourth of the population, to the Republican Party has offset some of the reduction in that party's support from mainline Protestants, particularly those with liberal social views. The presidential votes of members of the latter group declined in the 1990s, as did their identification with the Republican Party. In general, regular churchgoers within both evangelical and mainline Protestant groups are more Republican in their party identification and voting behavior than those who do not attend church regularly. Nonchurchgoers, those who think of themselves as secular and rarely attend religious services, have become the least Republican group of all.[14] The contemporary Republican Party thus consists of racial and religious majorities, those in the higher socioeconomic brackets, and those in the professional and managerial ranks.

What conclusions can we draw about the social basis of politics today? It is clear that the old party coalitions have evolved and, in the Democrats' case, weakened. Today, voters exercise a more independent judgment on election day, a judgment that is likely to be influenced by factors that condition the environment in which the election occurs and by the campaign itself.

THE FUTURE OF THE PARTIES

Will there be a new partisan realignment? Will the GOP emerge as the new majority? The answer is still unclear, but three basic trends stand out.

1. The gap between the major party identifiers has narrowed, and when turnout is considered, may have been eliminated entirely.
2. The attachments people feel toward political parties have weakened over the years although partisan loyalties have held relatively constant since the late 1980s. Split-ticket voting, which had been rising, has also stabilized today.
3. There has been some partisan realignment. White southerners have switched their allegiances to the GOP while northeasterners have become less Republican. Group coalitions within the parties have also shifted. On balance, these changes have benefited the Republicans, but not to the extent of making them a plurality, much less majority party.

The major parties continue to be highly competitive at the national level. Within the states, however, the crafting of legislative districts to create as many

---

[13]The conservative policy orientation of this group has also colored the Republicans' position on some important and divisive social issues. For an excellent discussion of the religious right and its impact on the 1992 election see Lyman A. Kellstedt, John C. Green, James L. Guth, and Corwin E. Schmidt, "Religious Voting Blocs in the 1992 Election: Year of the Evangelical?" *Sociology of Religion* 55 (1994): 307–326.

[14]Ibid.

safe seats as possible for the parties has reduced that competitiveness, particularly in elections for members of the House of Representatives. Today, the major parties remain at rough parity with one another, the presidential election one that either party can win.

SUMMARY

The electorate is not neutral. People do not come to campaigns with completely open minds. Rather, their preexisting attitudes and accumulated experiences color their perceptions and affect their judgments, much as stimuli from the campaign affect those attitudes and experiences.

Of the political beliefs people possess, partisanship has the strongest impact on voting. It provides a perspective for evaluating the campaign and for deciding whether and how to vote. It is also a motive for being informed, for getting involved, and for turning out to vote.

Since 1960, there has been a decline in the proportion of the population who voted. This decline can be partially attributed to the weakening of party ties, to the increasing proportion of younger voters, and to the cynicism and apathy of the population as a whole.

Partisan attitudes have also eroded, particularly in the period from 1964 to the end of the 1980s. The percentage of people identifying with a party has declined. One consequence has been the increasing importance of short-term factors on voting. A second related one has been more split-ticket ballots. The relative parity of the major parties today has resulted in national elections that either party can win. It has produced a presidential vote that has less carryover to congressional and state elections. Presidential coattails have not been evident since 1980.

Group ties to the parties have also loosened. Partisan coalitions have shifted. The Democratic Party, which became dominant during the New Deal period, has lost the support of a majority of southern whites in presidential and congressional elections and has suffered defections from other groups such as non-Hispanic Catholics and Protestant fundamentalists. That some of these groups have also declined as a proportion of the population or have lower-than-average turnout has further aggravated the Democrats' problem. Racial minorities, such as African Americans and Hispanics, however, have retained their loyalty to the Democrats as have Jewish Americans. Women have become much more supportive of Democratic candidates and men more supportive of Republicans. Those with secular views have become more Democratic and those with sectarian views more Republican.

The Republicans have benefited from the fraying of the Democrats' partisan majority. The Republicans have gained in the South, benefited from the increased social and economic conservatism of a growing middle and upper-middle class, and made strides among younger voters. Although they won eight of the thirteen presidential elections beginning with the election of 1952, thus far they have not been able to expand their electoral coalition into a partisan plurality much less majority.

These changes within the political environment have important implications for presidential politics. The weakening of partisan attitudes and the splintering of the New Deal coalitions have augured in a new era in presidential electoral politics, one that is highly competitive. Partisan parity has increased the importance of short-term factors including political campaigns on election outcomes.

6.4 The Semisovereign People: A Realist's View of Democracy in America (1960)

E. E. SCHATTSCHNEIDER

INTRODUCTION

Political scientist E. E. Schattschneider famously analyzed political conflict in the United States. Government itself, Schattschneider suggested, must compete with business for political power and influence. Where government is concerned, interest groups, including business interests, employ pressure on elected officials to influence, if not dictate, their policy agendas and decisions. In the "realist's view of democracy in America," politics is defined by competition among such groups. But how can average citizens and the public at large meaningfully join the competition? "The problem," he argued, "is how to organize the political system so as to make the best possible use of the power of the public in view of its limitations." His essential two-word answer was "political parties"; but he acknowledged that ever-more Americans were becoming nonvoters, and he did not believe that the parties alone could save the "semisovereign people" or revitalize American democracy. Political parties can overcome the pressures of special interests, he reasoned, but only if they can provide benefits to their members (that is, elected officials) that rival the benefits supplied to them by interest groups.

■

Every regime lives on a body of dogma, self-justification, glorification and propaganda about itself. In the United States, this body of dogma and tradition centers about democracy. The hero of the system is the voter who is commonly described as the ultimate source of all authority. The fact that something like forty million adult Americans are so unresponsive to the regime that they do not trouble to vote is the single most truly remarkable fact about it. In the past seven presidential elections the average difference in the vote cast for the winning and the losing candidates was about one-fifth as large as the total number of nonvoters. The unused political potential is sufficient to blow the United States off the face of the earth.

Why should anyone worry about twenty or thirty or forty million American adults who seem to be willing to remain on the outside looking in? What difference do they make? Several things may be said. First, anything that looks like a rejection of the political system by so large a fraction of the population is a matter of great importance. Second, anything that looks like a limitation of the expanding universe of politics is certain to have great practical consequences. Does nonvoting shed light on the bias and the limitations of the political system?

In American history, every change in the scope of the political system has had an impact on the meaning and operation of the system. Broadly speaking, the expansion of the political community has been one of the principal means of producing change in public policy; expansion has been the grand strategy of American politics. Every major change in public policy (the Jefferson, Jackson, Lincoln and Roosevelt revolutions) have been associated with an enlargement of the electorate. Has something gone wrong with the basic pattern of American politics? Has the political system run out of gas? Have we lost the capacity to use the growth of the electorate to provide a new base for public policy? If we have lost the capacity to involve an expanding public in the political system, it is obvious that American democracy has arrived at a turning point.

What kind of system is this in which only a little more than half of us participate? Is the system actually what we have been brought up to think it is?

One of the easiest victories of the democratic cause in American history has been the struggle for the extension of the suffrage. After a few skirmishes in the first decades of the nineteenth century, the barriers against male suffrage gave way all along the line. A generation ago one distinguished United States senator was in the habit of saying that rivers of blood have been shed for the right to vote. No greater inversion of the truth is conceivable. The struggle for the ballot was almost bloodless, almost completely peaceful and astonishingly easy. . . .

The expansion of the electorate was largely a by-product of the system of party conflict. The rise of the party system led to a competitive expansion of the market for politics. The newly enfranchised had about as much to do with the extension of the suffrage as the consuming public has had to do with the expanding market for toothpaste. The parties, assisted by some excited minorities, were the entrepreneurs, took the initiative and got the law of the franchise liberalized. It has always been true that one of the best ways to win a fight is to widen the scope of the conflict, and the effort to widen the involvement of the more or less innocent bystanders produced universal suffrage. Our understanding of this development has been greatly confused by the compulsion to interpret our past in terms of the classical definition of democracy which inevitably assigns a dramatic place in history to the seizure of power by the people. . . .

The socialization of politics as far as the right to vote is concerned has now been nearly complete for a generation, but the *use* of the ballot as an effective instrument of democratic politics is something else altogether. This is the point at which the breach between theory and practice of American democracy appears to be widest. If we do not understand what this breach is about we simply do not understand American politics. The question is: If the conflict system is responsible for the extension of the legal right to vote, is it also responsible for limiting the practice of voting?

It is reasonable to look for some of the causes of massive self-disfranchisement in the operation of the political system. What is there about the system that depresses participation? Obviously, the relation of the electorate to the government is not as simple as it is commonly supposed to be.

The American political system is less able to use the democratic device of majority rule than almost any other modern democracy. Nearly everyone makes obeisance to the majority, but the idea of majority rule has not been well institutionalized and has never been fully legitimatized. The explanation of the ambivalence of the system is historical.

Democracy as we now understand it has been superimposed on an old governmental structure which was inhospitable to the idea. The result is a remarkable makeshift. Resistance to the growth of the political community has taken the form of attacks on all efforts to organize the majority, attacks on politics, politicians and political parties. The offspring of this mixed parentage is a kind of monstrosity, a nonpolitical antimajoritarian democracy.

Massive nonvoting in the United States makes sense if we think of American government as a political system in which the struggle for democracy is still going on. The struggle is no longer about the *right to vote* but about the *organization of politics*. Nowadays the fight for democracy takes the form of a struggle over theories of organization, over the right to organize and the rights of political organizations, i.e., about the kinds of things that make the vote valuable.

Another way of saying the same thing is to say that the vote can be vitiated as effectively by placing obstacles in the way of organizing the electorate as it can be a denial of the right to vote. Nonvoting is related to the contradiction, imbedded in the political system, between (1) the movement to universalize suffrage and (2) the attempt to make the vote meaningless. We get confused because we assume that the fight for democracy was won a long time ago.

We would find it easier to understand what is going on if we assumed that the battle for democracy is still going on but has now assumed a new form.

The success or failure of the political system in involving a substantial fraction of the tens of millions of nonvoters is likely to determine the future of the country. This proposition goes to the heart of the struggle of the American people for democratic self-realization.

In spite of the fact that there have been a number of get-out-the-vote movements, it is obvious that no serious measures have been taken to bring the forty million into the political system, nothing half as serious as the enactment of a uniform national elections law, for example.

Why has so little been done? Perhaps we shall be near to the truth if we say that little has been done because the question is too important, too hot to be handled. It is by a wide margin the most important feature of the whole system, the key to understanding the composition of American politics. Anyone who finds out how to involve the forty million in American politics will run the country for a generation.

Unquestionably, the addition of forty million voters (or any major fraction of them) would make a tremendous difference. The least that the forty million might do to the political system would be to enhance tremendously the authority of the majority. . . .

We might make greater progress toward an understanding of the dynamics of American politics if we ignored the complexities of the governmental structure and began to examine the struggle for power in a new dimension. Is it not likely that the separation of powers reflects obsolete conflicts that have little relevance to the contemporary struggle? The whole of the ancient British social structure around which the separation of powers was built originally has long since passed into the limbo. The deepest cleavages in the modern world are no longer those that turn the President against Congress or the courts. We get confused because we cling to the ancient battlements long after the armies have abandoned them and the conflict has moved to new battlefields. The scene of conflict has shifted so greatly that the government itself is now involved in a wholly new dimension of conflict. The unresolvable conflicts are no longer carried on *within* the old governmental structure; the new conflicts characteristically involve the whole government in struggles with powers wholly *outside* of the government. Today the government itself competes for power.

It may be useful to examine two of the greatest of modern built-in, unresolvable conflicts to see what light they shed on this discussion.

The conflict of government and business illustrates the new dimensions of the dominant tensions. It requires no demonstration to support the proposition that the relation between government and business has given rise to some of the greatest tensions in modern life and that these tensions tend to dominate the political system.

Business so dominates the nongovernmental world that it looks very much like a power system able to compete with the government itself. Once upon a time the church was the principal nongovernmental institution; today it is business. Nowadays business plays so great a role in the community, it has developed so great an organization, has such vast resources that it is inevitably the principal focus of power outside of the government, a focus of power that challenges the supremacy of government in the modern community. As a matter of fact, the relations of government and business largely determine the character of the regime. Seen this way the struggle for power is largely a confrontation of two major power systems, government and business. . . .

The mixture of capitalism and democracy in the American regime presupposes tension. Tension is increased by the fact that power in the two systems is aggregated on radically different principles. The political system is broadly equalitarian, *numbers* are important in politics. The whole emphasis of the law and tradition of the political system is designed to invite the widest possible participation in the process.

On the other hand, the economic system is exclusive; it fosters a high degree of inequality and invites concentration of power. There is, moreover, a strong dogmatic base for the assumption that the *public* responsibilities of business are limited. The bias of the two systems is profoundly different. . . .

The beginning of wisdom in democratic theory is to distinguish between the things the people can do and the things the people cannot do. The worst possible disservice that can be done to the democratic cause is to attribute to the people a mystical, magical omnipotence which takes no cognizance of what very large numbers of people cannot do by the sheer weight of numbers. At this point the common definition of democracy has invited us to make fools of ourselves.

What 180 million people can do spontaneously, on their own initiative, is not much more than a locomotive can do without rails. The public is like a very rich man who is unable to supervise closely all of his enterprise. His problem is to learn how to compel his agents to define his options.

What we are saying is that conflict, competition, leadership, and organization are the essence of democratic politics. Inherent in the operations of a democracy are special conditions which permit large numbers of people to function.

The problem is how to organize the political system so as to make the best possible use of the power of the public in view of its limitations. A popular decision bringing into focus the force of public support requires a tremendous effort to define the alternatives, to organize the discussion and mobilize opinion. The government and the political organizations are in the business of manufacturing this kind of alternatives.

What has been said here has not been said to belittle the power of the people but to shed some light on what it is. The power of the people is not made less by the fact that it cannot be used for trivial matters. The whole world can be run on the basis of a remarkably small number of decisions. The power of the people in a democracy depends on the *importance* of the decisions made by the electorate, not on the *number* of decisions they make. Since the adoption of the Constitution the party in power has been turned out by the opposition party fourteen times, and in about six of these instances the consequences have been so great that we could not understand American history without taking account of them.

The most important thing about any democratic regime is the *way* in which it *uses* and exploits popular sovereignty, what questions it refers to the public for decision or guidance, how it refers them to the public, how the alternatives are defined and how it respects the limitations of the public. A good democratic system protects the public against the demand that it do impossible things. The unforgivable sin of democratic politics is to dissipate the power of the public by putting it to trivial uses. What we need is a movement for the conservation of the political resources of the American people.

Above everything, *the people are powerless if the political enterprise is not competitive.* It is the competition of political organizations that provides the people with the opportunity to make a choice. Without this opportunity popular sovereignty amounts to nothing.

6.5 Showdown at Gucci Gulch: Lawmakers, Lobbyists, and the Unlikely Triumph of Tax Reform (1987)

JEFFREY H. BIRNBAUM AND ALAN S. MURRAY

INTRODUCTION

"Gucci Gulch" refers to the hallways in Congress where lobbyists gather, seeking to speak to members or their staff aides about pending legislation. The common view is that lobbyists for well-resourced interest groups, especially corporate or business interests, typically succeed in promoting their policy agendas because they have ample opportunity to gain access to elected officials through meetings and fundraisers. Journalists Jeffrey H. Birnbaum and Alan S. Murray skillfully demonstrate, however, that in the case of tax reform, public officials succeeded in lowering tax rates and closing many loopholes in the tax code. This "unlikely triumph" occurred despite the efforts of opposing lobbyists and the lack of a strong public voice on the matter. Leaders in both parties and at both ends of Pennsylvania Avenue forged alliances, made bargains, and effected compromises that left the lobbyists wondering what happened. Their epilogue summarizes the factors contributing to the bill's success, and the consequences, both positive and negative, for relevant interests.

■

The final version of the Tax Reform Act of 1986 sailed through both chambers of Congress with little fuss. The House affirmed the conference report 292–136 on Thursday, September 25. Two days later, in an unusual Saturday session, the Senate gave its approval by a vote of 74–23. It was then sent to the White House for the president's signature.

President Reagan signed the bill on the South Lawn of the White House on Wednesday, October 22. It was a gloriously sunny autumn day, and the Truman Balcony behind him was decorated with rows of bright yellow chrysanthemums. More than fifteen hundred people gathered for the occasion—the largest audience for a bill signing during the Reagan administration. Seated on the podium with the president were many of the key players in the tax-reform drama, including Rostenkowski, Baker, Regan, Long, Dole, and Kemp. Packwood was not there; he decided his time was better spent campaigning for his reelection in Oregon. Bradley, ironically, was also in Oregon, campaigning for Democratic political candidates, and was prevented by fog from flying back to Washington.

For President Reagan, the signing marked a great victory. He had managed to win the most sweeping overhaul of the tax code in the nation's history. He stood before the signing-ceremony audience proud and triumphant:

> The journey has been long and many said we'd never make it to the end, but as usual the pessimists left one thing out of their calculations—the American people. They haven't made this the freest country and mightiest economic force on this planet by shrinking from challenges. They never gave up, and after almost three years of commitment and hard work, one headline in *The Washington Post* told the whole story: THE IMPOSSIBLE BECAME THE INEVITABLE and the dream of America's fair share tax plan became a reality.

How did it happen? What created this legislative miracle that defied all the lessons of political science, logic, and history? How could Congress—an essentially conservative institution that most experts thought could only enact major changes at a slow, incremental pace—accomplish such a large, complex, and far-reaching tax overhaul? Why were lawmakers, more beholden than ever before to campaign contributors, willing to vote against such a multitude of special interests? What motivated the bill's unlikely heroes to work together, buck the conventional wisdom, and achieve one of the most impressive legislative victories of recent times?

. . . [T]he answer is not a simple one. In part, the deterioriation of the tax code had gone so far that something had to be done. The American people were disgusted with the system, and that disgust represented a latent political force waiting to be tapped. Tax revolts, such as the Proposition Thirteen campaign in the 1970s to slash California property taxes, attempted to draw from this reservoir of disenchantment. President Reagan's tax cuts in 1981 also were intended to ease the problem, although the bevy of new tax breaks in that year's bill worked instead to fuel public disillusionment. By the mid-1980s, the loophole-ridden tax system cried out for a fix.

To be sure, public support for the reform proposals debated within the administration and in Congress was never particularly strong. The president's occasional efforts to rouse audiences to the cause almost always fell flat. Opinion polls showed that the public was outraged with the existing system, but had little trust in the government's ability to fashion something better. There was a deep public cynicism, fed by the government's long history of bungled or misguided attempts to fulfill the promise of reform. People doubted that their elected leaders could really achieve such a bold break with the past, and that doubt dampened their interest in the Washington debate.

Smart politicians knew that beneath the apparent public indifference, however, boiled a potential gusher of discontent that could prove to be a fearsome force. Few members of Congress cherished the thought of ending up on the wrong side of the popular president's battle against the special interests. They may not have wanted reform, but they were not about to be seen standing in its way either. As a result, tax reform acquired an extraordinary momentum once it got rolling. "It breathes its own air," said an amazed Illinois Senator Alan Dixon as the bill made its way through the Senate.

Reform was also achieved because it combined goals that were important to both political parties. Ending loopholes for the privileged had long been the desire of some Democrats. But the 1980s also saw the emergence of a new wing of the Republican party that was crucial to tax reform's success—the supply-siders, whose influence grew dramatically after President Reagan's election and who were passionately committed to lowering tax rates. These activist-conservatives had no deep interest in closing loopholes, but if that was the only way to pay for lower rates, they were willing to go along. By combining with the older Democratic reformers, they created an impressive bipartisan coalition.

To be sure, the opponents of reform in both parties initially outnumbered the proponents. Traditional Republican legislators were hesitant to back an effort that would offend so many of their business constituents; many Democrats, as well, had special interests to protect. Some liberal Democrats also disliked the sharp cut in the top individual tax rate, which seemed to help only high-income Americans.

Nevertheless, a pro-reform coalition emerged that was at once strange and impressive. It linked Ronald Reagan, the most conservative president in modern history, with George McGovern, the Democrat's most liberal candidate in decades. It paired Kemp, the conservative darling of the supply-side movement and a driving force behind the 1981 tax bill, with Bradley, a liberal Democrat and a fervent opponent of the 1981 bill. It even united General Motors's chairman, Roger Smith, with his company's long-standing nemesis, consumer activist Ralph Nader.

The most important player in tax reform was Ronald Reagan himself. The president seldom took an active role in the two-year tax debate; when the Finance Committee held its critical vote to approve the bill, for example, he was seven thousand miles away at the summit of industrialized nations in Tokyo. Nevertheless, the conservative president's support for an effort once considered the bastion of liberals carried tremendous symbolic significance. Without his backing, tax reform could never have happened. With it, it became a powerful political juggernaut. Reagan wanted to go down in history as the president who cut the top tax rate at least in half, from 70 percent to 35 percent or lower. If abandoning business tax breaks and raising corporate taxes was the price he had to pay to achieve that goal, so be it. Reagan had been reelected in 1984 in a forty-nine-state landslide and, at that point, was one of the most popular presidents of this century. When he put his full weight and power behind an idea that tapped such a fundamental frustration of the American people, others in Washington could hardly ignore it.

The other major players had their own odd assortment of reasons for backing reform. Don Regan became a reformer in part because he sensed the president's passion for lower rates and was eager to win a prominent place for himself on the president's agenda. James Baker became a reformer because he was a loyal soldier and because his success as Treasury Secretary depended on his ability to achieve the president's top domestic policy goal. Dan Rostenkowski became a reformer because the president's endorsement of reform represented a challenge and a threat to both him and his party: The Republican president was trying to steal the Democratic mantle of "tax fairness," and Rostenkowski vowed not to let that happen. Bob Packwood became a reformer out of desperation: With Reagan and Rostenkowski moving together, he had no choice but to produce a bill or be branded a sellout to special interests; he was sucked into the great maw of reform.

One of the most intriguing questions raised by the two-year tax debate in Congress was why the many powerful interest groups lined up in opposition to reform never joined forces to defeat it. The total firepower of these special interests was potentially fatal to any piece of legislation, yet they never managed to form an effective "killer" coalition. Darman marveled at their fractiousness. "I couldn't help thinking that if I were a lobbyist, I would stand in the hallway with a big sign saying: EVERYONE INTERESTED IN KILLING THIS BILL, PLEASE MEET IN THE NEXT CORRIDOR," he said at one point during the debate.

"There would have been an enormous rush, and they would have seen the power of their collective action."

The lobbyists never did that. In part, they, like the politicians they worked with, were afraid to be pinned as opponents of reform. Indeed, most of the groups opposing reform insisted in public that they were for it—they just wanted to make certain it did not hurt them. "They were brought down by the narrowness of their vision," Darman said. "Precisely because they defined themselves as representatives of single special interests, they failed to notice their collective power."

The lobbyists' failure also reflected the difficulty interest groups face in combating "populist" legislation. Even though they had made enormous campaign contributions and had much-vaunted access to important legislators, the anti-reform lobbyists remained outsiders throughout the tax-reform debate. They could find few allies in the highest councils of power. At each step President Reagan threatened to label lobbyists' friends in Congress as toadies to the special interests and enemies of rate cuts for the people, and that was a threat that could not be taken lightly.

Of course, special-interest politics remained strong throughout the tax-reform debate. Some lobbyists, whose clients had only a handful of tax breaks to protect, promoted reform from the beginning, and helped to pass the legislation. Others battled vigorously to retain as many of their tax benefits as possible. Although they failed to halt the bill, anti-reform lobbyists won significant battles: A coalition of labor groups and insurance companies staved off the effort to tax fringe benefits; life insurers succeeded in preserving the tax-favored status of their most lucrative product, cash-value insurance; oil and gas interests kept their pain to a minimum; and hundreds of individual companies won special transition rules.

The special-interest victories, however, were far outweighed by the special-interest defeats. The bill closed loopholes worth roughly $300 billion over five years and replaced them with lower tax rates. It also raised corporate taxes by $120 billion over five years, the largest corporate tax increase in history. Congress was acting in response to larger, broader forces, which, in the end, prevailed.

Tax reform was a uniquely American idea—that somehow the nation could start over and rebuild its entire tax system. "No other country would try anything like this, to go back to the beginning, to be born again," said Aaron Wildavsky, a political scientist at the University of California at Berkeley. "It was quite a radical proposal."

Yet even before President Reagan signed the historic measure, pundits began raising serious questions about its economic and political value. In the long run, few experts doubted that lower tax rates would improve the efficiency of the economy and boost the chances for economic growth, but in the short term, many felt the abrupt repeal of investment incentives would cause some serious dislocations. The economy had become addicted to tax stimulants, and a cold-turkey repeal was certain to cause pain: Investment would probably suffer, real estate construction would decline, and charitable giving stood to take a hit. Such radical tax change, whatever its long-term value, would undoubtedly have some unpleasant side effects.

Likewise, the political value of the effort also came under doubt. To be sure, tax reform helped the careers of a few legislators like Rostenkowski, Bradley, and Packwood, but it clearly did not create the grand national "realignment" of party loyalties that some members of both parties had hoped for. Indeed, in the congressional election campaigns that were underway when the president signed the bill in 1986, it was difficult to find any candidate—other than Packwood—who spent much time talking about tax reform or who was either helped or hurt by it. One reason for this might have been Rostenkowski's ability to make the 1986 tax bill as much a Democratic as a Republican document. Since the legislation was bipartisan, neither side could get credit—or blame.

Whatever its economic and political consequences, tax reform was, without doubt, a landmark piece of social legislation. It took more than four million impoverished working people off the income tax rolls. It also launched a no-holds-barred attack on tax shelters, a growing blight on the American economic landscape. In addition, it ended the ability of large and profitable corporations to escape paying taxes, which, whatever its economic merits or demerits, had become a galling spectacle to the American public. Most important, reform narrowed the enormous inequities that permeated the existing tax system. Although it made no fundamental changes in the distribution of the tax burden among income groups, it did make it more likely that individuals and corporations with similar incomes would pay similar taxes. In that way, it made the tax system more fair.

The legislation also offered the hope of beginning to mend people's faith in government. Over the previous two decades, Americans had lost their confidence in their country's capacity to accomplish great things. The triumph of tax reform was a sign that the tide might be turning. As President Reagan said: "America didn't become great being pessimistic and cynical. America is built on a can-do spirit that sees every obstacle as a challenge, every problem as an opportunity." Tax reform was that challenge and opportunity.

In terms of its substance, the tax bill was an awkward, hodgepodge attempt at reform, not at all like the pure proposals that so frequently came out of academia or Washington think tanks. It attacked tax breaks with an uneven hand—severely paring preferences for real estate developers, for instance, while preserving most of the generous loopholes enjoyed by the oil industry. It had elements of deceit—the advertised top rate of 28 percent belied hidden surtaxes that raised the top marginal tax rate to 33 percent, and in some cases even higher. It certainly was not simple; but then, it probably never could be. Former IRS Commissioner Sheldon Cohen explained it this way:

People think taxation is a terribly mundane subject. But what makes it fascinating is that taxation, in reality, is life. If you know the position a person takes on taxes, you can tell their whole philosophy. The tax code, once you get to know it, embodies all the essence of life: greed, politics, power, goodness, charity. Everything's in there. That's why it's so hard to get a simplified tax code. Life just isn't simple.

Despite its warts and wrinkles, the bill succeeded at the fundamental purpose of reform. To those who had grown accustomed to abusing the tax system and its many chinks and loopholes, it dealt a heavy blow, but to those who paid their taxes each year without taking advantage of the long lists of deductions, exclusions, and credits, the tax plan offered a hefty bonus. It was a heroic effort to address a profound and pervasive social and cultural problem that had been ignored for too long. For all its faults, the Tax Reform Act of 1986 was the rough-hewn triumph of the American democratic system.

Rostenkowski frequently joked during 1985 and 1986 that when the tax bill was completed, he planned to hang a sign on his door that read: GONE FISHIN'. But everyone in Washington knew that the battle was by no means over. Congress had passed a major tax bill roughly every year and a half since the income tax was enacted, and there was no reason to expect that to change. Older legislators remembered that Congress had made a less ambitious attempt at reforming the tax code in 1969, only to find much of its work reversed in the next few years. The investment tax credit, in particular, had been through several deaths and reincarnations. Even before the 1986 tax law was signed, defeated lobbyists were already preparing to launch a campaign to restore their favorite tax breaks as part of the "technical corrections" bill of 1987. Charls Walker noted philosophically that tax sentiment is "cyclical," and he expressed little doubt that the push for investment tax breaks would soon be resumed.

Regardless of the tax changes to come, tax writers realized that it would be a long time before they were back in this sort of spotlight. "We'll never be center stage like we were with tax reform," Rostenkowski said.

The elections in November 1986 brought about some important political changes that raised more questions about the future of reform. The Democrats took majority control of the Senate, forcing Packwood out of his chairmanship of the Finance Committee. The new chairman for the 100th Congress, which convened in January 1987, was Democratic Senator Lloyd Bentsen of Texas, one of the most reluctant reformers on the Finance Committee. Bentsen promised to emphasize trade legislation over taxes, but the lobbyists still had hope. After steering the Senate to triumph on the landmark tax-reform bill and easily winning reelection, Packwood was relegated to head the minority portion of the committee.

Every Finance Committee member who sought reelection in 1986 won, but only one of the three Ways and Means members who wanted to move up to the Senate was elected: Wyche Fowler of Georgia. Henson Moore of Louisiana and James Jones of Oklahoma were defeated in their bids.

Rostenkowski remained in the chair at the Ways and Means Committee, but he served in the 100th Congress under a new speaker, Jim Wright of Texas, who was at times a Rostenkowski rival. Before the tax-reform debate, Rostenkowski had created friction with Wright by expressing interest in usurping Wright's claim to the speakership. Later, Wright angered the Ways and Means chairman by publicly opposing tax reform. After being selected as their speaker by the House Democrats, Wright signaled an attack at the heart of the new law: He proposed freezing the top individual tax rate at the 38.5-percent level the legislation had set as an interim rate for 1987. Though the proposal was roundly criticized, more run-ins between the two leaders seemed inevitable.

Russell Long retired to become a Washington lawyer and elder statesman, but he did not leave Congress without first making his mark on the new tax law. He got the better of Rostenkowski by securing for a Louisiana-based utility company the same kind of favored treatment in the minimum tax that Rostenkowski won for an Illinois utility. The Ways and Means chairman tried to camouflage the recipient of his break by describing the size of the utility's power generator rather than using its name. What Long knew—and what Rostenkowski found out—was that the Louisiana utility had the same size machine and was also eligible for the break. By waiting patiently in the wings until it was too late to turn back, Long secured a $140 million benefit for Middle South Utilities.

In a more far-reaching development, a Russell Long provision in the bill was belatedly discovered to, effectively, all but repeal the estate tax. The senator was trying to bolster tax benefits for employee stock-ownership plans, a cause he had long championed. Instead, he created a $20 billion loophole that would allow wealthy people to convert their bequests into stock, sell them to an employee stock-ownership plan, and in the process, escape estate taxation. Senator Bentsen, in his new role as Finance Committee chairman, promised to close the loophole as soon as he was able.

Only two weeks after the signing of the reform bill, President Reagan became embroiled in the biggest crisis of his two terms in office. Newspaper reports revealed that the administration had shipped arms to the revolutionaries in Iran, bitter enemies of the American people since their seizure of American hostages during the Carter administration. Moreover, some of the proceeds of the secret sale were reportedly diverted to help fund the contras' fight against the Nicaraguan government. The public perception of the president plummeted in opinion polls, and new revelations threatened to prolong the crisis, leaving the White House sinking in a quagmire of scandal and doubt.

The Iranian crisis dragged on for months. The president's inattention to even the most important details of government, which had been evident throughout the tax-reform effort, became the subject of increasing national debate. Chief of Staff Regan was drummed out of office by a torrent of criticism, coming most importantly from the president's wife, Nancy, who had been skeptical of his appointment from the beginning. And in early April, Deputy Treasury Secretary Darman, discouraged by the administration's inability to move on any major policy issues, left to become a managing director at an investment banking firm. Tax reform seemed destined to become the last highpoint of the Reagan presidency.

Elections and Campaigns

*I*n a representative democracy, political leaders are authorized to make decisions by winning a competitive contest for the popular vote. The Framers expected that elected officials would make all major governmental or public policy decisions; hence, Article I of the Constitution discusses the responsibilities and powers of Congress, and Article II discusses those of the presidency. But the Constitution says little about elections beyond eligibility for office, selection process, and term length for members of Congress and the president. The Constitution makes no mention of political parties, interest groups, or campaign finance. The Framers did not anticipate that most of the nation's elected officials would be full-time politicians. Thus, today's elections and campaigns involve myriad activities—from constant fundraising and regular public opinion polling to continuous media coverage—that would have surprised, and might well have dismayed, the Framers.

Running for office in the twenty-first century is a full-time occupation that requires vast financial and staffing resources. In 1996, for example, Bob Dole resigned from the U.S. Senate and gave up his post as Republican majority leader so that he could concentrate fully on the task of running for president against incumbent Bill Clinton. George W. Bush became a likely presidential contender in Republican circles soon after his reelection as governor of Texas in 1998, two years before the presidential race. To challenge Bush in 2004, U.S. Senator John Kerry, a Democrat, had to campaign for nearly two years, first to win his party's nomination through a long presidential primary season, and then to compete against Bush in the general election.

Any credible political candidate today needs time to develop an effective campaign organization that will have sufficient opportunity to raise funds, build name recognition, introduce the candidate to voters, and so forth. A presidential campaign staff will include, at a minimum, a campaign manager, press secretary, pollster, policy advisers (specializing in both domestic and foreign issues), fundraising coordinators, liaisons to constituent groups, as well as organizations in every state. Some observers refer to contemporary presidential politics as "the permanent campaign."

Likewise, members of Congress are "always" running for reelection. House members return home most weekends not only to do constituency service but to court local financial contributors and secure their electoral base. Even U.S. senators, who run but once every six years, have begun behaving more like their colleagues in the House with respect to near-constant campaigning, constituency service, fundraising, self-advertising, and other activities intended to help ensure that they can defeat or "scare off" likely primary and general election challengers.

Although a great deal of research has been done on the issue of just how much a financial advantage matters in determining election outcomes, there is as yet no firm scholarly consensus on the subject. However, most politicians and many journalists believe that money is perhaps the single most critical variable in elections today. A candidate for the U.S. House of Representatives typically will spend more than $500,000 for a campaign, while a U.S. Senate candidate may well spend upwards of $5 million. Campaign ads account for a large portion of costs, but candidates also must pay for staff salaries, travel, mailings, and all other election-related expenses. The United States does not provide public funding for congressional campaigns, so candidates either must spend their own money to run for office or follow federal fundraising guidelines in raising money from individuals and interest groups.

Until the 1970s, the federal government did not exercise a large role in campaign finance. Laws passed in the early twentieth century prohibited direct campaign donations from unions and corporations, though for the most part candidates were legally unfettered in their efforts to raise money in seeking public office. Concerns about corruption in mixing money with politics, however, spurred calls for reform, especially in the aftermath of the Watergate scandal that led to President Richard Nixon's resignation in 1974. The Federal Election Campaign Act of 1970 and subsequent amendments passed in 1974 established regulations to govern fundraising in federal races and created the Federal Election Commission (FEC) to oversee implementation of those rules. Candidates were limited in the amounts of money they could raise per election from individuals, interest groups, and political parties (though not in the total amount of money they could raise), and groups that made campaign donations would do so through legally regulated political action committees (PACs).

Although the law did not provide public funds for congressional races, it did do so for presidential contenders. Presidential candidates whose political party had garnered a certain percentage of the popular vote in the previous presidential election would be eligible for matching funds in primary races and full funding for the general election. The law initially limited the amount of money that an individual could spend from personal resources, but the Supreme Court ruled in *Buckley v. Valeo* (1976) that candidates could spend as much of their own money as they liked *if* they did not accept public funds. A candidate's political party also would receive funding for organizing the national nominating convention before the general election.

The structure of the American political system makes campaigning and fundraising difficult for candidates who do not belong to the two major political parties. The winner-take-all feature of congressional elections means that minor-party candidates are not represented unless they win a seat. A congressional candidate needs to win only a plurality, or the most votes, in the election, not an absolute majority. Losing candidates have no share of representation in Congress, regardless of how tiny the margin of difference may be. In contrast, democracies with a system of *proportional representation* allocate seats based on the percentage of votes that a political party wins. U.S. elections focus on individuals, not political parties, and candidates representing the major political parties are far more likely to have the resources necessary to win office. Hence it is hardly surprising that in 2005, of the 535 members of Congress, only one was a registered Independent, Representative Bernie Sanders of Vermont.

The winner-take-all feature also exists in presidential races. The Framers designed a unique system for electing the president. A candidate wins only by having an absolute majority of votes in the electoral college. In 1992, Ross Perot won 19 percent of the popular vote, but he did not win a single electoral college vote. A parliamentary system would create a coalition government if no candidate or party polled a majority, but in the United States a majority is required only in the electoral college, not in the popular vote. Typically, the candidate who wins the electoral college vote also wins the popular vote, but this does not always happen. Most recently, in the 2000 presidential race, George W. Bush received fewer popular votes nationally than Al Gore, but Bush, following a controversy over the vote-counting in Florida, secured the electoral college majority and became president.

The four readings in this chapter examine U.S. elections from the perspective of both voters and candidates. One critical question is *how* voters decide who to support. Political scientist Morris P. Fiorina observes that, while most voters do not follow politics closely on a regular basis or possess detailed knowledge about policy issues, they nevertheless are capable of figuring out their basic interests in relation to politics. When it comes to presidential elections, most average voters, argues Fiorina, vote "retrospectively," looking at how things have gone in the recent past and then voting for the party that controls the White House if they like what has happened or voting against that party if they don't like what has happened. Retrospective voting, he suggests, is rational for voters who do not have a lot of information; all they need to know are some basic facts about each candidate's background and positions, and then ask themselves whether things have, in their view, gotten better or worse for themselves, for the country, or both.

During the 2004 presidential campaign, challenger John Kerry and the Democratic Party used certain words and images to project a positive public image. The key word was *strong,* used over a hundred times in the official 2004 Democratic Party platform statement and used repeatedly by Kerry in speeches and "town meetings." The incumbent George W. Bush and the Republican Party used that word a lot, too, but they also stressed *opportunity* and *culture of ownership.* In ads, speeches, Internet postings, and press briefings, Kerry and the Democrats tried to project a negative public image of Bush and the Republicans as untruthful, unintelligent extremists closely associated with far-right religious leaders and corrupt corporations. Bush and the Republicans did the same vis-à-vis Kerry and the Democrats, depicting them as vacillating ("flip-flopper"), elitist liberals closely associated with far-left Hollywood idols and selfish trial lawyers.

Neither side issued much in the way of highly detailed or specific public policy papers, not even on such high-profile issues as how to handle subsequent phases of the war and occupation in Iraq, what changes in intergovernmental relations were needed to make federal homeland security efforts effective, or how to boost the economy. Does the policy-light, symbol-heavy presidential campaign of 2004 fit a general or preexisting pattern?

In a word, yes. As Donald E. Stokes and John J. DiIulio, Jr., explain in this chapter, in contemporary elections and campaigns there are two different kinds of issues: position and valence issues. A *position issue* is both an issue on which the rival candidates have opposing views and one that divides voters. Stem-cell research is a recent example. In 2004, Kerry favored full federal funding for embryonic stem-cell research, whereas Bush supported limited federal funding for the same. Similarly, Kerry opposed any effort to privatize Social Security, whereas Bush advocated certain steps to do just that. But often voters are not divided on important issues. Instead, the question is whether a candidate or party fully supports the public's view on a matter about which nearly everyone agrees. These are called *valence issues.* For instance, nearly all Americans want a strong national defense, truthful leaders, a better economy, and a tough stand against terrorism. No candidate or party would advocate increased unemployment or come out for irresolute leadership, political corruption, bad economic times, or toleration of terrorists. What voters look for on valence issues is the candidate or party that seems most closely linked to a universally shared view.

As Stokes and DiIulio's analysis suggests, the 2004 presidential race was like most modern presidential contests. The campaign involved a mix of position and valence issues, but it was dominated by valence issues—that is, issues on which voters distinguish parties and candidates less by their actual differences on position issues than by the degree to which the parties and candidates are linked in voters' minds with conditions, symbols, or goals that are almost universally approved or disapproved by the electorate (such as prosperity, honesty, and resolute leadership). Each campaign invested most of its money, manpower, and media (both positive and negative ads) in courting voters on valence terms.

The expenses required to mount a successful campaign for Congress or the presidency as well as the political structure that benefits major-party candidates illustrate the advantages that accrue to incumbents running for reelection. Incumbents benefit from media coverage that comes with their job; they do not have to build name recognition as many of their competitors do. In fulfilling their professional responsibilities, incumbents also have the opportunity to advertise their accomplishments to constituents via direct mailings, speeches, and meetings. Challengers typically need to cultivate a constituency and develop fundraising and personnel resources to wage an effective campaign.

The spiraling cost of political campaigns in the United States has sparked many calls for reform in recent years. Proposals for full public funding of campaigns typically prompt debate, but they gain little traction and seem unlikely to be adopted in the near future. (After all, a decreasing number of taxpayers are checking the box on their annual income tax return that would donate a few dollars of their taxes to the federal election fund but not increase their total tax bill in any way.) More moderate reforms include the Bipartisan Campaign Reform Act of 2002 (popularly known as the McCain-Feingold law), which bans soft money contributions, or money donated to political parties without the contribution limits attached to donations to individuals or PACs (limits that the law also raised). The law also limits "advocacy" advertisements in the thirty days preceding an election. The Supreme Court has upheld the basic provisions of the McCain-Feingold law, but as the article by Glenn Justice shows, debate continues about whether regulations on campaign fundraising amount to restrictions on free speech.

The contested 2000 presidential election, ultimately decided by a 5–4 Supreme Court decision, prompted many calls for changing the presidential selection process. Many observers criticized the electoral college system because winning a majority of the popular vote does not equate to winning a majority of electoral college votes and, consequently, the election. In fact, the president has won the electoral college vote but not the popular vote only three times in U.S history: 1876, 1888, and 2000. But calls for reform dissipated quickly after the 2000 contest, and the electoral college seems secure for the foreseeable future. In this chapter's final reading selection, presidential scholar Stephen J. Wayne discusses alternatives to the current system and explains why the Framers' design remains intact.

7.1 Theories of Retrospective Voting (1981)

MORRIS P. FIORINA

INTRODUCTION

In 1980, Republican Ronald Reagan challenged incumbent Democratic President Jimmy Carter. In one of their debates, Reagan looked wistfully into the camera and asked Americans to ask themselves whether they were better off than they were four years earlier. At that moment, the country's economy was in tatters, street crime was on the rise, and Americans were held hostage by the Iranian government. Whether Carter's administration was responsible, in whole or in part, for these and other negative conditions was not what Reagan asked. Nor did he ask voters to read his detailed tax-cut plan and compare it to the new economic policy white papers offered by the incumbent. Rather, at a time of economic uncertainty, domestic unrest, and international turmoil, he simply asked voters to ask themselves, "Are you better off?"

Reagan had not read Morris P. Fiorina's classic text on voting (it had not yet been published), but his memorable question squares with the book's main message: Most people who vote in national elections tend to vote retrospectively. They loosely evaluate an incumbent's performance in office. If they are pleased, then they will likely vote to keep the person and his or her party in office. If they are displeased, then they will vote against the incumbent and his or her party, but this does not necessarily mean that they support the challenger's partisan views or policy agenda (or even that they know much about those views and that agenda). To typical retrospective voters, suggests Fiorina, economic conditions matter most. Distant though it is from democratic ideals of informed citizenship, he argues, retrospective voting is "rational."

∎

Let us step back for a moment and consider a deceptively simple question. What is an election? In principle, two or more groups of like-minded people put forth alternative visions of future societies. After carefully weighing the alternatives, the citizenry entrusts one of the competing parties with the mantle of leadership. In practice, however, an incumbent party attempts to convince an appropriate proportion of the electorate that it lives in the best of all possible worlds, while an opposition rails at the incumbents and advances a collection of unrealistic promises.

Citizens are not fools. Having often observed political equivocation, if not outright lying, should they listen carefully to campaign promises? Having heard the economic, educational, sociological, defense, and foreign policy expert advisors disagree on both the effects of past policies and the prospects of future ones, should they pay close attention to policy debates? Even if concerned and competent, citizens appear to have little solid basis on which to cast their votes, save on those rare occasions when candidates take clear and differing positions on salient specific issues (e.g., busing, abortion, the Equal Rights Amendment).

But are the citizens' choices actually so unclear? After all, they typically have one comparatively hard bit of data: they know what life has been like during the incumbent's administration. They need *not* know the precise economic or foreign policies of the incumbent administration in order to see or feel the *results* of those policies. And is it not reasonable to base voting decisions on results as well as on intentions? In order to ascertain whether the incumbents have performed poorly or well, citizens need only calculate the changes in their own welfare. If jobs have been lost in a recession, something is wrong. If sons have died in foreign rice paddies, something is wrong. If thugs make neighborhoods unsafe, something is wrong. If polluters foul food, water, or air, something is wrong. And to the extent that citizens vote on the basis of such judgments, elections do not signal the direction in which society should move so much as they convey an evaluation of where society has been. Rather than a prospective decision, the voting decision can be more of a retrospective decision. In 1972, for example, some voters may have based their voting decision on an explicit comparison of the Vietnam policies of Richard Nixon and George McGovern. But perhaps more common was comparison of the Vietnam situation in 1968 with the Vietnam situation in 1972. A voting decision based on the latter comparison might well differ from one based on the former.

The foregoing argument is not original. Anyone familiar with the works of V. O. Key, Jr., will recognize it as the traditional reward-punishment theory of elections, a theory based on the assumption that citizens vote *retrospectively*. But despite the theory's familiarity, we know almost nothing specific about retrospective voting, about its prevalence, variability, origins, and consequences. Ironically, our failure to address the question of retrospective voting in any depth probably stems from our implicit acceptance of a particular civics-book notion—that of an election as a purely prospective decision. . . .

THE NATURE AND SIGNIFICANCE OF TRADITIONAL RETROSPECTIVE VOTING

What intellectual gains might result from maintenance of the conceptual distinction between retrospective and prospective voting? The prefatory discussion of the reward-punishment theory suggests three possibilities.

First, electoral outcomes may signify quite different things, depending on whether citizens are in a primarily retrospective or prospective frame of mind. Late every election night we sit before our TVs watching Cronkite, Brinkley, Reasoner, and their supporting casts struggle to make sense of the outcomes. In succeeding days, Broder, Kraft, Kilpatrick, and untold others advance their divinations in the columns of the print media. Party officials woefully or joyfully pore over the returns, trying to confirm their notions of what it all means. This concentrated attention of so many capable people does not stem solely from idle curiosity or a commercial desire to entertain the population. Elections are the ultimate tie between the governed and the governors in a democratic society. Polls may inform the governing elites about the views of the citizenry, but only elections can enforce those views. And therein lies the rub. Just what views are being enforced? Let us consider some cases that are clear, at least from the standpoint of many popular commentators and relative to many cases that are less so.

In 1964 there was a great clash between liberalism and conservatism, between visions of a Great Society and views of a stingy, chip-on-the-shoulder society. According to liberal commentators, progressive ideas won a clear victory, and Lyndon Johnson received a mandate to lead the country forward.

Alas, mandates are short-lived. In 1972 there was another great clash between liberalism and conservatism, between a subculture that upheld traditional American values and one that incorporated wild-eyed radical schemes destructive of those values. According to conservative commentators, Americanism won, and Richard Nixon received a mandate to lead the new majority out of the wilderness of the New Deal Democracy. (Moderate commentators, reading such interpretations, could only wonder at the fickle electorate. Cynical commentators, along with poor losers, could juxtapose the two electoral outcomes to indicate the true magnitude of the advantages of incumbency.)

But there are other plausible interpretations of 1964 and 1972. In 1964 Democratic identifiers were monolithic in their support of a Democratic president, while Republicans defected to him in greater than usual numbers. The mirror-image situation occurred in 1972. A look at the data might call to mind Key's argument:

> The patterns of flow of the major streams of shifting voters graphically reflect the electorate in its great, and perhaps principal, role as an appraiser of past events, past performance, and past actions. It judges retrospectively; it commands prospectively only insofar as it expresses either approval or disapproval of that which has happened before.[1]

The student of Key might propose a far less dramatic interpretation of the 1964 and 1972 outcomes than the liberal and conservative interpretations caricatured above. Lyndon Johnson took office at a time of national trauma and presided over a year of relative calm and prosperity. Many Americans did not feel that there were sufficient grounds to support a change to a third presidential administration within a two-year period. And many of them would have felt the same way had they been presented with a Scranton or a Rockefeller instead of a Goldwater.

In 1972 the situation was even clearer. When Nixon took office in 1968, more than five hundred thousand American soldiers were in Vietnam, cities were literally aflame, and college campuses were engulfed in protest. Each of these highly visible irritants on the body politic had gone into dramatic remission by 1972. And such recoveries were independent of whether McGovern or Humphrey headed the Democratic ticket.

The proponent of the retrospective voting interpretation need not deny that prospective voting takes place; Scranton in 1964 and Muskie in 1972 no doubt

---

[1] V. O. Key, Jr., *The Responsible Electorate* (New York: Vintage, 1966).

would have received more votes than the actual nominees of their respective parties. But the proponent of retrospective voting is less likely to wax eloquent about "electoral mandates," and other exaggerations by the media and personally involved political actors. In 1972, for example, he would not have advised the Democratic party to bury the guaranteed annual income, national health insurance, and other "radical" schemes. He would have advised the Democrats to bide their time and wait for the Republicans to mess things up.

In sum, the interpretations placed on electoral outcomes may differ considerably, depending on whether the contest is viewed by the electorate in prospective or retrospective terms. If we grant that it is important to interpret electoral outcomes as accurately as possible, then we perforce grant the theoretical significance of the retrospective-prospective distinction.

A second justification for maintaining the retrospective-prospective distinction stems from the differing presumptions of the two notions about the primary concerns of the citizen. The traditional theory of retrospective voting implicitly assumes that citizens are more concerned about actual outcomes than about the particular means of achieving those outcomes, that citizens care about *results* rather than the *policies* that produce those results—for example: "End the war. Whether you bomb them back to the Stone Age or withdraw and claim victory, just end the war."

The presumption that citizens are generally more concerned with policy outcomes than with policy instruments leads to further implications. First, it suggests that citizens pay scant attention to the esoteric policy debates of the party brain trusts. Instead, they simply sit back and see what works. This behavior demands far less of voters than the presumption that they examine specific policy positions, judge their likely efficacy, and then choose the candidate associated with the seemingly more efficacious platform. The more modest view of the citizen implicit in the traditional theory of retrospective voting produces, in turn, an additional consequence: parties and candidates are not tightly constrained by the policy promises they make. Key writes:

> Voters may reject what they have known; or they may approve what they have known. They are not likely to be attracted in great numbers by promises of the novel or unknown. Once innovation has occurred they may embrace it, even though they would have, earlier, hesitated to venture forth to welcome it.[2]
>
> Only infrequently is a new program or a new course of action advocated with such force and the attention it receives so widespread that the polling may be regarded as advance approval of a proposed course of action. Those governments that regard elections as clear mandates for new policy actions probably often mirror the beliefs of the political elite rather than reflect an understanding of the vote widely shared in the population.[3]

---

[2]Key, *The Responsible Electorate*, p. 61.

[3]V. O. Key, Jr., *Public Opinion and American Democracy* (New York: Knopf, 1961), p. 474.

In sum, prospective voting presumes a policy orientation in the electorate, whereas Key's notion of retrospective voting presumes a result orientation. As a consequence, prospective voting demands more of the citizen than does retrospective voting, and prospective voting invests elections with more policy significance than does retrospective voting. These considerations lead directly to a third argument for the conceptual distinction between retrospective and prospective voting, an argument infused with normative considerations.

The third reason for maintaining the prospective-retrospective distinction inheres in its implications for the responsible electorate debate. As mentioned earlier, the view prevailing in the 1960s emphasized those survey findings that cast the electorate in an irresponsible and/or incompetent light. In *The American Voter*, for example, we find a "test" that citizens must pass in order to qualify as issue-oriented (i.e., rational, responsible) voters. Campbell, Converse, Miller, and Stokes argue that the following conditions are *necessary* conditions for issue-based voting:

1. the citizen must express an opinion on an issue ("cognize" the issue);
2. the citizen must have knowledge of current government policy on the issue;
3. the citizen must have knowledge of the policy alternatives offered by the competing parties;
4. the citizen must feel sufficiently strongly about the issue to make use of the aforementioned knowledge in casting his vote.[4]

Campbell and his associates "tested" the American electorate (i.e., the 1956 pool of potential voters) and found that across sixteen public policy domains, only a fifth to a third of the potential electorate satisfied the necessary conditions for issue-based voting behavior. Although the Michigan team was reasonably cautious in interpreting such findings, many others drew the conclusion that the typical American citizen was an irresponsible political actor caught in the coils of such arational influences as party identification and interpersonal relations. This was the prevailing view for approximately a decade.

In recent years revisionist scholars have carried out a partial rehabilitation of the American voter. Data from more recent elections, changes in the survey instrument, and methodological advances, singly and in combination, have upgraded the image of the citizen. Nevertheless, the revisionist findings are subject to overstatement. Despite the recent attention given to issues and ideology, party identification remains the variable most closely associated with the vote (although interpretation of that variable is itself undergoing revision). . . .

But as Schattschneider asks, who are we to "test" the electorate?[5] Who appointed us the ultimate arbiters of voter rationality and/or responsibility?

---

[4] Angus Campbell, Philip Converse, Warren Miller, and Donald Stokes, *The American Voter* (New York: Wiley, 1960), chapter 8.

[5] E. E. Schattschneider, *The Semi-Sovereign People* (New York: Holt, Rinehart and Winston, 1960), p. 135.

Perhaps we find the electorate wanting because our tests are wanting. If so, we are the irresponsible ones for pronouncing others irresponsible on the basis of such tests.

. . . [R]etrospective voting requires far less of the voter than prospective voting. The retrospective voter need not spend his life watching *Meet the Press* and reading the *New York Times*. He can look at the evening news and observe the coffins being unloaded from Air Force transports, the increasing price of a basket of groceries between this month and last, and the police arresting demonstrators of one stripe or another. What does it matter if this voter is not familiar with the nuances of current government policies or is not aware of the precise alternatives offered by the opposition? He is not the professional policy formulator. He has not devoted a career to pursuit of public office nor sought such office on the basis of his competency to govern. Perhaps he can't "cognize the issue in some form," but he can go to the polls and indicate whether or not he likes the way those who can "cognize the issue" are in fact doing so. He passes judgment on leaders, not policies.[6]

I suspect that the preceding view of the citizen is common among professional politicians, especially those who are relatively successful at their profession. In formulating policies they do not feel tightly bound by citizen preferences (except on occasional highly salient issues). Rather, they feel constrained to have those policies appear successful by the time of the next election. Politicians need not discern the precise policy preferences of their constituents. They need only *anticipate* the *reactions* of their constituents to the conditions brought about by the policy instruments they adopt.[7] And the latter is not so difficult. I feel safe in claiming that large majorities prefer peace to war, high employment and stable prices to unemployment and inflation, social harmony to social tension, energy self-sufficiency to dependence on imported oil, and so forth. Knowing this, it is (and should be) the responsibility of those who make their livelihood from policymaking positions to ascertain which policy instruments lead to the desired outcomes. To await guidance from a prospective voting electorate is to abdicate that responsibility. Perhaps contemporary political science dwells excessively on the irresponsibility of our electorate and insufficiently on the irresponsibility of our leaders.

In sum, the third argument for maintaining the retrospective-prospective distinction is largely a normative argument that builds on the previously discussed positive arguments concerning the interpretation of elections and citizen concern over policy instruments vis-à-vis policy outcomes. A retrospective voting electorate does not constrain the formation of public policy to the degree that a prospective voting electorate does. But that is not to say that a retrospective voting electorate is irresponsible. Given political actors who

---

[6]Joseph Schumpeter, *Capitalism, Socialism and Democracy* (New York: Harper and Row, 1950).

[7]Carl Friedrich, *Man and His Government* (New York: McGraw-Hill, 1963), pp. 199–215.

fervently desire to retain their positions and who carefully anticipate public reaction to their records as a means to that end, a retrospective voting electorate will enforce electoral accountability, albeit in an *ex post,* not an *ex ante,* sense. A retrospective voting electorate may not be responsible according to the standards of responsible prospective voting, but where are those standards etched in stone tablets?

AN ALTERNATIVE THEORY OF RETROSPECTIVE VOTING

The preceding section presents several arguments for maintaining the retrospective-prospective distinction. These arguments, however, presume a particular theory of retrospective voting, the reward-punishment theory. This theory appears commonly in the literature, as I have noted, and most prominently in the work of Key. But there is another, less widely known theory proposed by Anthony Downs.[8] And from the standpoint of this alternative theory, the arguments advanced in the preceding section appear less telling.

The Downsian theory of retrospective voting posits a motivational basis for retrospective voting that differs from the basis underlying the traditional reward-punishment theory. Downs views retrospective voting as a cost-cutting element in a citizen's voting decision. Knowledge of past performance is cheaper to acquire (it is acquired automatically, in effect) than knowledge of future plans. Moreover, by virtue of being experienced, past performance is a more reliable kind of information than promises for the future. Downs writes that the voter

> . . . must either compare (1) two hypothetical future utility incomes or (2) one actual present utility income and one hypothetical present one. Without question, the latter comparison allows him to make more direct use of concrete facts than the former. Not only is one of its terms a real entity, but the other can be calculated in full view of the situation from which it springs. If he compares future utility incomes, he enjoys neither of these advantages. Therefore, we believe it is more rational for him to ground his voting decision on current events than purely on future ones.[9]

Downs argues—and it is a critical argument—that political parties must be consistent over time in the policies they advocate and implement.[10] Ergo, a good guide to what a party will do in the future is what it has done in the past. In the Downsian theory of retrospective voting, the citizen simply uses the past as a guide to the policies the parties would implement in the future.

---

[8]Anthony Downs, *An Economic Theory of Democracy* (New York: Harper and Row, 1957).

[9]Downs, *An Economic Theory,* p. 40.

[10]Downs, *An Economic Theory,* chapter 7.

In contrast, under the traditional reward-punishment theory, the citizen takes past performance as a prima facie indicator of the government's judgment and competence (or lack thereof). The citizen need not expect temporal consistency of government policy. Rather, good past performance simply reinforces the presumption that the incumbent administration is competent to govern, whether this means the smooth continuation of old policies or the good sense to change when circumstances dictate.

To highlight the differences between these two possible bases for retrospective voting, consider the example of Johnson's conduct of the war in Vietnam. To the Downsian retrospective voter, Johnson's actual conduct of the war is a guide to Humphrey's future conduct of the war. A vote against Humphrey is a vote based on policy disagreement; Nixon's war policy is preferred. Under the traditional view, a vote against Humphrey is a vote of no confidence; its policy implications are not defined, save that change is desired.

The distinction between the two theories of retrospective voting is a theoretically important one. To reiterate, under the Downsian view, elections have policy implications in much the same sense as under prospective voting—Downsian retrospective voting is a means to prospective voting. The Downsian citizen compares the challenger's and the incumbent's platforms, interpreting the latter in light of the incumbent's past performance. But under the traditional theory, elections have no policy implications other than a generalized acceptance or rejection of the status quo. The voter either has confidence in the incumbent's judgment and abilities or does not. What policies politicians follow is their business; what they accomplish is the voter's.

There is an important situation, however, in which the Downsian and traditional theories are indistinguishable. That situation occurs when a policy instrument and a policy outcome fuse, so that the instrument becomes the issue. Consider busing. Ostensibly, busing is a means to an end—integrated education and ultimately an integrated society. Yet the political debate usually simplifies to one in which busing is both policy instrument and policy outcome. To millions of citizens the policy outcome is simply whether or not their children are bused.

In contrast, consider unemployment. Although most citizens are not touched directly by unemployment, most desire a low level. Yet I suspect that people generally are not terribly concerned about whether the government fights unemployment via public-works projects, tax rebates, or business tax credits. Whatever succeeds.

Still other issues illustrate mixes of the foregoing. For example, consider the problem of ending the war in Vietnam. By the early 1970s, majority opinion favored the policy outcome of an end to the war. A significant part of the citizenry—and its size was often commented on—didn't much care how. Unilateral withdrawal or nuking the North appeared to be equally efficacious and acceptable means of bringing the boys home. For other parts of the electorate, however, the policy itself was of critical concern. One group felt that only "peace with honor" was acceptable, whereas another felt, in effect, that a U.S. surrender was the only right course of action.

On the basis of considerations like the preceding, I suggest that the two theories of retrospective voting are distinguishable only in the context of issues and/or conditions that permit a reasonably clear separation of political means and political ends. When such a separation is not possible or, at any rate, not present in the political debate, the competency theory of retrospective voting merges with the Downsian theory in that approval or rejection of the past is tantamount to approval or rejection of existing policies and presumably their continuance.

What kinds of issues and/or conditions facilitate the separation of political means and ends? This question is not easy to answer, but a number of possibilities seem likely a priori. First, some policy instruments touch people much more directly (i.e., visibly) and in more sensitive areas than others do. Any policy that even remotely threatens negative effects on the safety and development of children will inevitably focus parental attention on the policy, regardless of the hoped-for policy outcome. In contrast, policies that have marginal effects on a citizen's tax burden, overtime wages, the business climate in the community, and so on are neither very visible in their operation nor terribly noticeable in their impact. Thus, the citizen's concern is likely to attach more to the eventual economic outcome than to the policies that brought it about.

A second reason some policies become synonymous with the ends they are designed to achieve is that the framers of the issue attempt to engineer such an identification between means and ends. For example, advocates of busing insist that *only* busing will bring about integrated education; they suggest that those who oppose the policy oppose the end as well. Similarly, knee-jerk conservatives would have us believe that the only moral way to fight inflation is by a reduction in government spending. Political actors and commentators cannot absolutely determine the terms of debate, but they certainly can influence those terms. Given that an outcome is considered desirable, those who feel strongly that a particular policy should be followed naturally attempt to convince the citizenry that only that policy will achieve the goal. Those who oppose the policy follow the opposite strategy. They argue that policies other than the one they oppose are more effective ways to achieve the goal in question.

A third reason policy instruments and outcomes become identified with each other lies in the existence of ideologies that postulate such identifications. Again, consider the example of bringing the war in Vietnam to a conclusion. A large part of the population did not see the outcome in ideological terms. They wanted the war ended and did not especially care how. Others who hewed to a cold war ideology insisted that the war should be ended only through some policy that could be construed as "peace with honor." Still others who held to newly developing revisionist ideologies insisted that the war be ended only via a policy conceding that the intervention of the United States was wrong. Admittedly, I am oversimplifying a terribly complicated and sensitive situation, but the point is still valid. Some citizens may hold ideologies that posit only policy X as an acceptable means to outcome Y. In contrast, non-ideological individuals focus on outcome Y but care little about whether X or Z is used to achieve it. Thus, traditional retrospective voting should be most evident on issues that are not bound up in strongly held ideologies and/or among citizens who do not conceptualize political affairs in ideological terms. Conversely, I doubt that the traditional theory of retrospective voting will shed much light on the behavior of the highly ideological or on the disposition of issues considered touchstones of particular ideologies. Fortunately for this study, committed ideologues are not common in the American electorate.

To return to the main lines of our discussion, this book makes no claim that electoral processes are based exclusively on traditional retrospective voting. Rather, its premise is that the mix of behavior between retrospective and prospective voting is an important question to address. To what extent do citizens vote prospectively, to what extent do they use past performance as a predictor of the future—à la Downs—and to what extent do they indulge in simple punishment-reward reactions to past performance? This [text] begins to address such questions, on both the theoretical and the empirical level. I caution the reader at the outset, however, that some aspects of these questions are exceedingly difficult to examine with existing data. For example, available survey items seldom enable us to separate policy instruments from policy outcomes. Also, it is often difficult to differentiate items according to their implicit or explicit time perspectives.[11] Despite numerous problems, however, the 1952–76 election studies of the Survey Research Center/Center for Political Studies (SRC/CPS) contain a variety of useful items, certainly enough to begin systematic research on retrospective voting. If preliminary findings based on these data prove encouraging, they may hasten the time when we have data of sufficient quality for a more definitive book. . . .

---

[11]In the literature, discussions of political issues tend to ignore the time dimension—retrospective versus prospective. Correspondingly, survey data are not gathered or coded with the time dimension in mind. As a result, a great deal of existing data is simply not useful for a study of retrospective voting. For example, the traditional CPS open-ended questions—"What do you like (dislike) about the (Democratic party, Democratic candidate, Republican party, Republican candidate)"—do not ask for a voter's time perspective, nor do the codings include one if it is offered. One suspects that "parties as managers of government" and "group benefits" responses contain a heavier retrospective component than domestic and foreign policy responses, which in turn have a heavier retrospective element than reactions to at least nonincumbent candidates, but how does one know? Similarly, the newer (since 1968) "proximity measures" do not differentiate between the past positions of the parties and candidates and their promises for the future (not that a clean differentiation can always be made). Finally, even the "same" item may run afoul of the time dimension across time—the SRC/CPS "most important problem facing the country" in 1974 versus the same item in 1960, for example. . . .

ADDENDUM: VALENCE ISSUES
AND RETROSPECTIVE VOTING

In 1963 Donald Stokes drew the distinction between position and valence issues:

> Let us call "position issues" those that involve advocacy of government actions from a set of alternatives over which a distribution of voter preferences is defined. And . . . let us call "valence issues" those that merely involve the linking of the parties with some condition that is positively or negatively valued by the electorate.[12]

Stokes suggests depression and recovery, peace and war, and corruption as prime examples of valence issues and makes the indisputable point that such issues often play an important role in American national elections. In his later work with David Butler on British national elections, Stokes attaches similar importance to the distinction between position and valence issues, particularly in discussing the "economic issue":

> The issues of economic well-being probably come as close as any in modern politics to being pure "valence" issues. . . . If we conceive of economic issues in dimensional terms, the electorate is not spread along a continuum of preference extending between good times and bad; its beliefs are overwhelmingly concentrated at the good times end of such a continuum.[13]

And how do such issues enter into the voting calculus of the citizen?

> The type of connection that has dominated both academic and more popular views of the electorate's response to the economy is one under which voters reward the Government for the conditions they welcome and punish the Government for the conditions they dislike. In the simplest of all such models the electorate pays attention only to the party in power and only to conditions during its current tenure of office.[14]

Evidently, the preceding quotation is a restatement of what I have termed the traditional, reward-punishment theory of retrospective voting. One may ask, then, whether the distinction between traditional retrospective and prospective voting is simply the behavioral manifestation of the distinction between position and valence issues.

---

[12]Donald Stokes, "Spatial Models of Party Competition," *American Political Science Review* 57 (1963), p. 373.

[13]David Butler and Donald Stokes, *Political Change in Britain* (New York: St. Martin's Press, 1969), p. 390.

[14]Butler and Stokes, *Political Change,* p. 392.

I would argue that the class of valence issues is considerably smaller than the class of issues on which citizens may vote retrospectively.[15] The defining characteristic of a valence issue is near-universal agreement on the ends of public policy: prosperity, peace, virtue. But even when there is no general agreement on policy ends, citizens may cast their votes on the basis of realized conditions rather than knowledge of policies followed. We may very well observe some citizens voting in approval of realized conditions and others voting in disapproval, but all voting retrospectively.

Furthermore, note that many valence issues can be position issues at the level of alternative *means* to the consensual outcome. For example, whereas there is only one means to the end of virtuous government—virtuous behavior by officials—there are various means to peace and prosperity. I would agree with Stokes that the mass public frequently cares little about the means, but that observation holds for position issues as well. . . .

To return to the question that motivates this discussion, is traditional retrospective voting simply the behavioral manifestation of valence issues? No, retrospective voting encompasses much more than that, although classic valence issues certainly stimulate it. Traditional retrospective voting can occur *on any kind of issue.* When a citizen indicates approval or disapproval of a condition, there is no presumption that his fellow citizens share that evaluation. Such agreement may enable the casual observer to identify retrospective voting more easily, but consensus about an end state is by no means a necessary correlate of retrospective voting.

■

7.2 The Setting: Valence Politics in Modern Elections (1993)

DONALD E. STOKES AND JOHN J. DiIULIO, JR.

INTRODUCTION

President Ronald Reagan won reelection in 1984 by a landslide. This puzzled many political scientists. Economic conditions had improved since 1980, but not by all that much; in fact, Reagan's first two years in office saw record-high

---

[15]For a telling critique of the attempt to distinguish valence and position issues, see James Alt, *The Politics of Economic Decline* (Cambridge: Cambridge University Press, 1979), chapter 1. Though his concern is not with retrospective voting, Alt too attaches significance to the policy means–policy ends distinction.

home-mortgage interest rates and stubbornly high rates of unemployment in many parts of the country. More generally, public opinion surveys showed that many Americans who disagreed with the conservative Republican president's positions on numerous domestic and foreign policy issues nonetheless voted to reelect him. So far as anyone could tell, they voted for Reagan because they found him likable or because he made them feel good about America and bright about its future, or both.

In the Addendum section of the preceding reading selection, Morris P. Fiorina references and attempts to rebut Donald E. Stokes's argument that valence issues matter as much or more than position issues in modern-day campaigns and elections. The latter are issues like abortion, slavery, high tariffs, or school prayer on which people, parties, and candidates divide. The former are those that involve the linking of the parties or candidates with some condition or symbol that is positively or negatively valued by virtually all voters, such as strong leadership, good economic times, and patriotic sentiments on the positive valence side, and irresolute leadership, bad economic times, and unpatriotic sentiments on the negative side. No parties or candidates campaign by promising to tolerate terrorists, foster political corruption, or increase unemployment.

In the early 1960s, Stokes was among the first political scientists to systematically study national campaigns and elections. In the 1980s and 1990s, he served as dean of Princeton University's public policy school. In this reading selection, he is joined by John J. DiIulio, Jr., in revisiting his path-breaking arguments about the role of valence issues in contemporary politics.

With reference to presidential campaigns stretching back to the early nineteenth century, the authors assess the 1992 presidential election that brought Democrat Bill Clinton to the White House. They argue that the valence framework for understanding elections not only explains why many people vote for candidates like the amiable Reagan whose positions or performance they dislike, but also "the fluidity of contemporary politics" (for example, Ross Perot in 1992 led in some polls just months before election day but came in a distant third) and "why the electorate can sometimes make prospective [judgments] as easily as retrospective judgments, and judgments on those who seek office as easily as judgments on those who hold office." But they are at one with Fiorina in arguing that most voters behave rationally—valence voters are not fools.

■

Two transitions stand out in the presidential election of 1992. The election marked first of all a transition in party control. America's parties were born in Thomas Jefferson's time, reborn in Andrew Jackson's, and took their modern form in Abraham Lincoln's day as a means to capture the great prize of our politics, the presidency. Only once since Richard Nixon's accession to the presidency in 1968 had the Republican hold on this prize been broken, and then only by Jimmy Carter's single term. The first, signal transition in 1992 was therefore the return of a Democrat to the White House.

The second was the passing of leadership to a new generation. George Bush was not only of the generation that fought World War II; in the course of the campaign he repeatedly disclosed how deeply his view of the world and the imperatives of leadership were shaped by that war. Bill Clinton was, by contrast, not only of the generation that experienced the dilemmas of the Vietnam War; in the course of the campaign he repeatedly showed how deeply these dilemmas had touched his life. The succession of generations is also part of what gives significance to the election.

These changes were so visible as to partially conceal a third transition of great significance, one that has been building through a series of elections: the transition to a newer, more fluid politics, far less constrained than in the past by party alignments rooted in issues of great power and durability. We address ourselves mainly to this third signal change, to a revolution that also seems to us of lasting significance, as we analyze the meaning of the 1992 election. Nowhere are its marks more evident than in the recent volatility of popular support.

THE EXTENT OF VOLATILITY

The fluidity of public attitudes can be suggested by a few remarkable facts. In March 1991, 88 percent of a sample of the American public told the CBS News/*New York Times* poll that they approved of the way George Bush was handling his job as president. Only 8 percent disapproved. Only fifteen months later, in July 1992, a mere 34 percent told this poll that they approved of the way the president was handling his job, and fully 56 percent disapproved. In little more than a year, George Bush's triumph had turned to dust, and the balance of positive and negative opinion had shifted more than 100 percentage points against him.

President Bush's awesome ratings in early 1991 discouraged a number of leading Democratic hopefuls, including Sens. Bill Bradley of New Jersey and Al Gore of Tennessee and Missouri representative Richard Gephardt, from entering the Democratic presidential primaries. A fairly typical preelection year analysis in this period read as follows:

> It can never properly be said, a year prior to an election, that an American president is "unbeatable." The public thinks and cares about the presidency too much for that. . . . Still, it's evident to everyone, including most Republican and Democratic strategists, that a president who more than 30 months into his tenure has the support of 70 percent of the public occupies a commanding if not unassailable position.[1]

In the absence of the Democratic party's "first team," it was left to distinctly secondary candidates—former Massachusetts senator Paul Tsongas,

---

[1]Carl Everett Ladd, *The Ladd Report*, 4th ed., vol. 1, 1991, 10.

Sens. Tom Harkin of Iowa and Bob Kerrey of Nebraska, Gov. Bill Clinton of Arkansas, Gov. Douglas Wilder of Virginia, and former California governor Jerry Brown—to fulfill Woody Allen's dictum that 80 percent of life is showing up. Governor Clinton the early favorite, emerged the wounded victor from a series of punishing primaries in which he took devastating hits on charges of marital infidelity and draft evasion. Evidence of his weakness as a candidate could be found in every poll. A May cover story in the *New Republic*, "Why Clinton Can't Win," pointed out that he trailed Bush by 47 percent to 41 percent in a recent Gallup poll. The article went on to say. "The negative poll numbers are staggering, and they've dogged Clinton since the New Hampshire primary in February. . . . Absent a scandal [for the Republicans] or economic catastrophe, Clinton's a goner."[2] In a few short weeks, however, Governor Clinton chose a popular running mate (Gore), choreographed an astonishingly successful nominating convention, and immediately put his show on the road in a bus tour that delighted the public as well as the media. During these few weeks he went from dead last in the polls to a 20-point favorite. Suddenly, Clinton the "goner" became Clinton the "reanointed."[3]

If we needed further evidence of the fluidity of popular support, it was supplied by the public's response to the diminutive, jug-eared Texas businessman whose one-liners matched the country's antipolitical mood and whose personal fortune was an order of magnitude greater than anyone needed to finance a race for the presidency. Ross Perot was launched into independent orbit from the unlikely pad of a television talk show in February. Twelve weeks later he was favored by a third of the electorate. A May cover story in *Time*, "President Perot?," reported that Perot led with 33 percent, followed by Bush with 28 percent and Clinton with 24 percent. "Make no mistake," the story advised, Perot could "well be the next President. . . . No independent candidate in 80 years has attracted anything like this kind of support. . . . Perot would not be a spoiler but the front runner in the popular vote for President."[4]

Two of the polls still declared Perot to be the front-runner in June. But he lost two-fifths of his support by mid-July and abruptly removed himself from the race, only to reverse that decision in late September. With both the Democratic and Republican parties paying him court and inviting him to participate in the presidential debates, Perot once again began to ascend like a rocket. In early October, before the debates, most national polls showed Perot with about 10 percent of the vote. But before the end of the month, following his participation in the three debates, he had doubled his support in most polls.[5]

[2]Fred Barnes, "Why Clinton Can't Win," *New Republic,* May 4, 1992, 19, 21.

[3]Sidney Blumenthal, "The Reanointed," *New Republic,* July 27, 1992, 10–14.

[4]Walter Shapiro, "President Perot?" *Time,* May 25, 1992, 27.

[5]*Public Perspective* 4 (November–December 1992): 100–101.

That support flagged soon after, however, when Perot failed to substantiate his sensational allegation that agents of the Republican National Committee had earlier forced him out of the race by threatening to make public compromising information about his daughter shortly before her summer wedding.

In view of this volatility among the voters, we may well ask what is going on. Here was an incumbent president who during much of his tenure was as well known and highly honored by the American people as any chief executive in the past quarter-century, one whose favorable ratings soared to unprecedented heights after the triumph of the American-led coalition in the Persian Gulf war. Yet the meltdown of President Bush's strength in less than a year and a half left him one of the weakest presidents to seek reelection in this century; no incumbent since 1912 won so small a percentage of the popular vote as did Bush. What can help us to understand this degree of fluidity and to learn what it tells us about the transformation in presidential politics?

THE LENS OF HISTORY

We are indebted to George Bush for a historical marker in our inquiry. The inspiration he found during the 1992 campaign in Harry Truman's come-from-behind victory in 1948 reminds us of the quite different politics of an earlier time. President Truman was no stranger to volatility. He universally endeared himself to his country by the simple grace with which he accepted the mantle of his fallen chief, Franklin D. Roosevelt, as World War II neared its end. Yet much of Truman's support evaporated as he seemed ill-equipped to deal with the domestic dislocations of the postwar world, and the Democrats were swept from power in both branches of Congress in the elections of 1946. But Truman's predecessor left him a priceless asset. Despite the interruptions of war, the electoral alignment forged by the Great Depression and Roosevelt's New Deal was still intact. Harry Truman came from behind in 1948 by rallying to his cause enough of the Roosevelt coalition to win.

President Bush's revisionist historical enthusiasm therefore was anachronistic; it reached back to a time when, far more than today, the electorate was constrained by party loyalties rooted in issues of sufficient power that they had altered the partisan alignments of millions of voters and recruited to the parties millions of new or previously inactive voters. Such a lasting party alignment has been created three times in our history since the mid-nineteenth century.[6] (See Table 1-1.) The deepest of these alignments was forged by the

---

[6]William Nisbet Chambers and Walter Dean Burnham, eds., *The American Party Systems: Stages of Political Development*, 2d ed. (New York: Oxford University Press, 1975).

Table 1-1
Three Major Political Realignments

Period	Realignment	Issue
1856–1864	Whig party collapses and Lincoln Republicans rise	Slavery
1896–1900	Republicans defeat William Jennings Bryan Democrats	Regional interests[a]
1932–1936	Democrats with Roosevelt and New Deal coalition defeat Republicans	Haves versus have nots[b]

[a]The realignment was preceded by depressions during the 1880s and 1890s. The Republicans stood for industry, business, hard money, protective tariffs, and urban interests; the Democrats stood for farmers, small towns, low tariffs, and rural interests. The former championed the interests of the Northeast and Midwest; the latter favored the South and West.

[b]The realignment was preceded by the Great Depression. Democrats, isolated since 1896 as a southern and midwestern sectional party, attracted urban workers, blacks, and Jewish voters away from the Republican party. Regional party politics gave way to a politics of haves versus have nots.

issues that led to the Civil War. Slavery and the other controversies that divided North and South acted so strongly on the electorate as to break apart the antebellum party system, displacing the Whig party with the newly formed Republicans in 1856 and sundering the Democratic party into northern and southern wings that had to piece themselves together after Reconstruction. This alignment was held in place by the continued grip of the issues that created it, as the Republicans "waved the bloody shirt" to invoke memories of Democratic perfidy and the Democrats responded in kind in successive elections after the Civil War. The division of the vote between the parties, charted over succeeding decades, shows almost no variation, so taut were the voters stretched by their experience with the issues and events that produced the post-Civil War alignment.

But as the decades passed and the Great Reaper reaped the harvest of souls, these voters eventually were gone. The weakening alignment was held in place not by the passions of those who had lived through the Civil War but by the secondary processes that transmit party loyalties from generation to generation in the childhood home. The alignment was therefore ripe to be displaced by a new, sectional alignment in the 1890s. The great new storms that swirled about William Jennings Bryan and his opponents pitted the Republicans, as champions of the modernizing industrial Northeast and Midwest, against the Democrats, as champions of the traditional, agrarian South and West, fighting savagely over cheap money and the tariff. Should the tariff be high to protect the rising industries of the Northeast and Midwest or low to allow southern and western farmers to buy cheap farm implements from abroad?

This second alignment, which produced a larger Republican majority than had the Civil War, was interrupted only by the Woodrow Wilson era before being overwhelmed by the political forces unleashed by the Great Depression of the 1930s. The New Deal alignment produced a substantial Democratic majority and came closer to a class-based alignment than the country had witnessed since the age of Jackson. One difference: the Democrats now wanted to use the power of government actively to help the less advantaged, not just to block the use of government power in the interest of the privileged and well-to-do. Despite World War II and what Roosevelt described as the displacement of "Dr. New Deal" by "Dr. Win-the-War," the Roosevelt alignment was very much in place in 1948, the year of the first postwar presidential election. Opinion polls and academic surveys repeatedly showed a large standing Democratic majority.

In subsequent decades new issues have chipped away at the Roosevelt coalition. Civil rights and the Vietnam War allowed the Republican party to mount a "southern strategy" that aligned the South with the Republicans in presidential politics, even as the Voting Rights Act's enfranchisement of southern blacks in 1965 added a "liberal" wing to the constituency of southern Democratic governors and senators. Vietnam, crime, and race detached from the Roosevelt coalition many white ethnic voters in the North, who voted with lesser enthusiasm for Richard Nixon and greater enthusiasm for Ronald Reagan. But none of these "wedge" issues has had anything like the force of the issues and events that created the three past alignments, each of which lasted for many years.

It is therefore tempting to say that the Roosevelt alignment is still intact, although very old and very weak. Certainly, it has not been displaced by a new alignment as strong as those of the 1860s, 1890s, or 1930s. In the absence of such a realignment, it is probably more accurate to say that we have experienced a long period of *de*alignment. There is survey evidence of this: a declining fraction of respondents in polls describe themselves as *strongly* identified with the Republican or Democratic party. In 1952 about 22 percent of voters described themselves as "strong" Democrats and 13 percent described themselves as "strong" Republicans; by 1980 the figures had dropped to 18 percent and 9 percent, respectively. Likewise, in 1952, 22 percent of voters described themselves as "independent"; by 1988 that figure had risen to about 38 percent.[7]

There is also evidence of a weakening alignment in three aspects of the actual voting returns. One is the marked rise in split-ticket voting. In the elections of 1984, for example, Ronald Reagan attracted the support of two out of every three voters in the state of New Jersey as the Republican candidate for president, while Bill Bradley attracted the support of two out of every three voters as the Democratic candidate for the Senate. Another is the long-term decline in turnout. The old-time party loyalties, rooted in powerful issues, had

---

[7]James Q. Wilson, *American Government,* 5th ed. (Lexington, Mass.: D. C. Heath, 1992), 138–139.

helped get voters to the polls; the weakening of these loyalties has caused many to stay home. Yet another is the greater amplitude of party swings, with a more weakly aligned electorate moving freely between the parties from election to election.

Here, surely, is part of the reason for the fluidity of party support in the current period: with the progressive weakening of the party identifications that were so strongly held by the electorate in the wake of each major realignment since the Civil War, today's voters are far more promiscuous in supporting particular parties and leaders than were the voters of earlier eras. But to leave the explanation there would be to overlook a parallel change in the structure of the issues that move the electorate, a change visible in the election of 1992 that gives further significance to the weakening of the alignments that have organized most contests for the presidency since 1860.

POSITION POLITICS AND VALENCE POLITICS

We can understand the weakening of these alignments only by drawing a distinction between two kinds of issues, a distinction that has yet to enter our general understanding of the workings of American democracy. The two kinds of issues that matter in presidential elections are position issues and valence issues. A *position issue* is one on which the rival parties or candidates reach out for the support of the electorate by taking different positions on a policy question that divides the electorate. Position issues have punctuated the history of presidential elections. For example, the party alignment that emerged from the Civil War was formed from a position issue of extraordinary power—the Negro, slave or free? Each of the three great alignments of our electoral past has been rooted in position issues. In the regional realignment of the 1890s the Republicans drew support from those who favored high rather than low tariffs on manufactured goods. In the 1930s the Democrats drew support from those who wanted to protect the interests of the poor and working class rather than those of the more affluent in American society. In the 1960s the New Deal coalition began to unravel around another position issue that divided the electorate along racial and regional lines—civil rights laws, for or against? And in the 1980s rivals for the presidency reached out for the support of the electorate in part by staking out different positions on an issue that sharply polarized voters—abortion, prochoice or prolife?

When political pundits intone that the voters are disenchanted because the rival parties or candidates are not discussing "the issues," they normally mean that most voters perceive no clear differences between the parties or candidates on the position issues of the moment. When Alabama governor George Wallace bellowed as an independent presidential candidate in 1968 that "there's not a dime's worth of difference" between the Democrats and the Republicans, he was seeking public support on the basis of his positions on issues, such as civil rights and welfare, that divided the electorate more than they (at the time) divided the parties.

The familiar liberal-conservative or left-right spectrum is a position issue in a somewhat more abstract and finely differentiated form. In many press and academic accounts the rival parties or candidates are thought to place themselves at different points along such a spectrum as they appeal for the support of an electorate that is also assumed to be spread out along this continuum.[8] Similarly, the issue of the size or role of government presents a position continuum from large to small, along which parties or candidates are thought to place themselves as they appeal to an electorate that supposedly is divided as to the proper size or responsibility of government. The same could be said for other position issues that present a set of ordered alternatives, such as gasoline taxes or deficit reduction.

But some of the issues that powerfully move the electorate do not present even two alternative positions that divide the parties and candidates on the one hand and the electorate on the other. These are issues on which voters distinguish parties and candidates not by their real or perceived difference in position on policy questions but by the degree to which they are linked in the voters' minds with conditions, goals, or symbols that are almost universally approved or disapproved by the electorate.

The economy is a prime example of a *valence issue* with this radically different structure. We do not have one party advocating economic prosperity and the other advocating economic bad times. There is no constituency for economic distress. In the United States and the other liberal democracies, all parties and the whole of the electorate endorse good times. The issue of economic prosperity acquires its power from the fact that the parties or candidates may be very unequally linked in the public's mind with the universally approved condition of good times and the universally disapproved condition of bad times. The difference between electoral success and disaster may turn on each party's ability to strengthen or weaken these perceptual bonds, or valences, in the public's mind.

Examples abound of valence issues that have powerfully moved the electorate. Corruption is such an issue with a deep historical resonance in the United States. Many times in American political history—indeed, as recently as the House of Representatives' check-kiting scandal in 1992—there have been calls to "throw the rascals out." It should be obvious, however, that the impact of the corruption issue could not depend on what position the parties or candidates advocated along a continuum extending from honesty to dishonesty: no party is avowedly propeculation. It depends rather on how closely the rival parties or candidates are linked in the public's mind with the

---

[8]The classic statement of this view is Anthony Downs, *An Economic Theory of Democracy* (New York: Harper, 1957).

universally approved symbol of honesty and the universally disapproved symbol of corruption. There is as little constituency for corruption as there is for economic bad times—or for a variety of other negative symbols that are staples of "valence politics," such as irresolute leadership, unpatriotic beliefs, weak national defense, wasted tax dollars, and failure itself.

It follows that the electoral politics of valence issues differs markedly from the electoral politics of position issues. In *position politics,* parties and candidates see their essential strategic problem as one of finding the electorate's center of gravity within a space defined by a series of ordered policy dimensions. By contrast, in *valence politics,* parties and candidates mount their appeals by choosing from a large set of potential valence issues those on which their identification with positive symbols and their opponents' identification with negative symbols will be most to their advantage.

There are innumerable examples of valence politics in modern presidential elections. In 1964 the Democratic campaign was largely a valence campaign in which voters were encouraged to link a vote for the Republican nominee, Arizona senator Barry Goldwater with negative symbols, such as nuclear annihilation, and a vote for President Lyndon B. Johnson with positive symbols, such as carrying on the work of a beloved fallen president, John F. Kennedy. Four years later Richard Nixon made law and order a valence issue. In the shadow of Watergate, Jimmy Carter made honesty in government a valence issue in 1976. In 1980 Carter was the victim of a valence campaign that linked a vote for him with symbols of abject failure, from the long gas lines to his inability to rescue our hostages in Teheran. Ronald Reagan's campaign in 1984 was carefully designed to encourage voters to link the president with such positive symbols as patriotism, peace, and prosperity—"morning in America." Likewise, in 1988 the Bush campaign encouraged voters to link Bush with positive symbols, such as respect for the flag, and his rival, Michael S. Dukakis, with negative symbols, such as disrespect for the flag, water pollution, and the fawning treatment of violent and remorseless criminals.

Presidential elections have always been a mix of position and valence politics. The valence issue of economic prosperity cost Martin Van Buren the presidency in 1840, when the electorate held him responsible for the misery that followed the panic of 1837. But the importance of valence politics has risen as party alignments rooted in the powerful position issues of the past have weakened. This trend is one of the most important, if largely unrecognized, shifts in our current politics, one that supplies a further key to understanding the recent fluidity of presidential politics. Let us see how the structure of valence issues adds to the volatility of public support.

VALENCE POLITICS AND THE AMPLITUDE OF SWING

One reason that party managers are so drawn to valence politics is that there is no ceiling—short of 100 percent—to the heights to which a candidate can soar in an ideally crafted valence campaign, whereas there *is* such a ceiling in a campaign focused on position issues that genuinely divide the electorate. The leaders who once reached out for the country's support by saying that the western territories should be free could expect to lose the votes of those who believed the western territories should be slave. Similarly, those who today reach out for the voters' support by arguing the prochoice position on abortion can expect to lose the votes of those who believe in the prolife position. But a party that reaches out for support on the basis of the strength or effectiveness of its leaders cannot lose the votes of those who believe in weak or ineffective leaders. Hence, a skilled campaigner can develop a persona that is overwhelmingly positive by stringing together a series of valence issues that "unite" the country—as Jimmy Carter did by promising honesty, efficiency, and prosperity in his quest for the presidential nomination in 1976—without bumping up against the ceiling that is built into a position issue that divides the country.

The structural difference between valence and position issues has a darker side for those who become linked to the negative symbols of valence politics. If there is no ceiling over the heights to which candidates can soar in ideally crafted valence campaigns, there is also no floor—short of 0 percent—under the depths to which they may fall if they become strongly linked to negative conditions or symbols on which the electorate is also united. In earlier eras, when long-term party alignments were rooted in position issues of great durability, presidential candidates could count on a base of support from party loyalists whose cause their parties championed on the overriding position issues of the time. But this base is smaller and softer in the current era, when party loyalties are weaker and less rooted in strong and enduring position issues.

The example of Jimmy Carter (this time in 1980) is again illuminating. President Carter lacked the secure base of Democratic loyalists cemented to the party for reasons of class that carried Harry Truman through his darkest days in 1948. When Carter was confronted at home by the oil shocks and "stagflation" of the 1970s and abroad by a string of reverses, culminating in his failure to win the release of U.S. hostages in Teheran, there was no political safety net under his free fall in public esteem. The brilliant valence campaigner of the 1976 nominating contest became the hapless victim of valence politics in the 1980 election. Ronald Reagan rammed home the negative Carter valences when he summed up a television debate by asking the national audience "whether you are better off today than you were four years ago, whether this country is more respected in the world today than it was four years ago."

We now have a deeper insight into the reasons for the fluidity of electoral support in the current period, including the extraordinary swings of the electorate in 1991 and 1992. George Bush's honeymoon after his 1988 victory was graced by the revolutions of 1989 in Eastern Europe and by the end of the Soviet empire and the Cold War, events that provided symbolic content for valence issues of great potency, namely, peace and strength. Moreover, his presidency began in the late stages of the longest peacetime economic expansion of the postwar era. There were some negative symbols, especially the perception of Bush as a weak leader—a "wimp," in his critics' phrase. He had been tormented by the build-up of this image during his long vice presidential apprenticeship to Ronald Reagan and by his inability to shake it even when he invaded Panama and seized its leader, Manuel Noriega. But he did indeed shake the wimp image in the graver circumstances of the Gulf war. Few would doubt that his strong valences with the highly positive symbols of strength and resolve would have returned the president to office in a landslide if the election had been held soon after the victory in Desert Storm.

With Saddam Hussein still in power and with the mounting suspicion that he was coddled by the United States before he invaded Kuwait, the electorate took a more mixed view of this victory as the months passed. More serious politically, with the end of the Cold War and a recession in full swing by 1990, the country turned inward and was increasingly critical of Bush's failure to attend to domestic issues. The positive valences that linked the president to the collapse of the Soviet bloc and the end of the Cold War soon gave way to negative valences linking him with economic distress at home. He quickly discovered what Martin Van Buren had learned a century and a half before—that past glories count for little if the country is hurting economically. Indeed, Bush made matters worse by showing a Herbert Hoover-like ability to see recovery just around the corner. The displacement of one set of valence issues, on which Bush was judged almost completely favorably, by another, on which he was judged very unfavorably, produced the extraordinary fifteen-month swing against him and cost him his office. His free fall was cushioned only a little near the end of the campaign by linking Governor Clinton with the negative symbols of indecisiveness, untrustworthiness, and lack of patriotism.

An exercise in the hypothetical can illuminate how little these swings in public support were constrained by the kind of overriding position issues that once anchored voters to the parties. For the sake of argument let us assume what is not wholly unimaginable—that abortion had become so powerful an issue as to produce the distinctive marks of each of the great realignments of the past: the shift of millions of voters from one party to the other so that they could support the party endorsing their position on abortion, the recruitment of millions of new or previously inactive voters to one or the other of the parties on the basis of their stands on abortion, and the subsequent constraint on the parties to put forward candidates who placed their party's distinctive stand on abortion at the center of their campaigns.

If abortion had realigned our politics in this way, President Bush would neither have soared so high in the aftermath of Desert Storm, since the bulk of prochoice voters would have continued to oppose him for his stand on abortion, nor would he have sunk so low during the recession, since the bulk of prolife voters would have remained steadfastly loyal in view of his party's stand on abortion. But abortion does not in fact play such an aligning role in our politics. Neither it nor any other position issue constrained Bush's rise in popularity or put a safety net under his free fall during the months between his victory in Desert Storm and his defeat in the election.

It is impossible, then, to understand what Bush described as the "screwy" 1992 presidential election without thinking mainly in terms of valence politics. But the 1992 election is only the latest in a series of presidential contests that have turned increasingly on valence issues. Our central thesis is that valence issues and politics have been, and continue to be, far more important in shaping the behavior of parties, candidates, and voters than is commonly recognized. Although the importance of position issues and politics in presidential elections has often been wildly exaggerated, the importance of valence issues and politics has been almost completely neglected.

The rising importance of valence politics leads to two further questions. First, what factors have so weakened the old-time party loyalties as to produce the valence politics of today? The answer will give us a clearer view of whether this shift is likely to continue or could be reversed. Second, what is to be made of a politics organized more in valence than position terms? The answer will give us a clearer view of the dynamics of democratic government in today's world.

THE SOURCES OF VALENCE POLITICS

It is tempting to say that the rise of valence politics has been fueled primarily by the changing technology of mass communication. In an hour-long speech to an old-time political meeting it was difficult to avoid position issues altogether. But it is easy to do so in a thirty-second television spot. Indeed, the electronic media seem ideally suited to the needs of valence campaigning. Certainly, television lends itself all too well to the negative valences that are so conspicuous an element of modern campaigns. This point has hardly been lost on the political commentators, even if the more general nature of valence politics remains largely unexplored.

It is equally true that the erosion of the old-time party loyalties is in part due to the demise of the partisan press. In an older politics millions of Americans subscribed to newspapers that corresponded to their party loyalties. A city's papers differentiated themselves by the party stands they took and thereby reinforced the party alignment by feeding their readers a continuing diet of angled information in their editorial pages and news columns. All of this has been dramatically changed by the concentration of the press. Today, one newspaper typically survives in each metropolitan market. Its problem is not how to attract readers with biased reporting but how to keep from repelling readers who will disagree with a partisan pitch and thus be lost to the newspaper's real competitors, local television. Faced with these realities, the modern dailies neutrally convey the appeals of each of the parties and their candidates rather than seeking to reinforce readers' identifications with a particular party.

What concentration has done to the press, custom and the law have required of the electronic media. Since the rise of radio in the 1930s and of television in the 1950s and 1960s, the electronic media have kept their political coverage neutral. Right-wing complaints about network anchors notwithstanding, it takes a much finer caliper to detect bias in television's political coverage than it did in the time of the partisan press. Even more than the surviving metropolitan dailies, the electronic media feel constrained to convey the appeals of each of the parties and their candidates for president and to keep their political content free of bias. They also have earned a great deal of revenue by carrying television spots, and now half-hour "infomercials," for whichever party or candidate buys the time. There are signs that "talk radio," and perhaps the television talk shows as well, feel a new freedom to angle their content. But (Rush Limbaugh excepted) they do so primarily by opening a channel for the expression of citizens' views rather than by supplying an angle of their own, as the old-time party press did. Hence, the electronic media, too, have failed to reinforce the party loyalties that once were rooted in enduring position issues.

The key to understanding the transition from a position politics expressed in long-time party alignments to a valence politics expressed in political volatility lies in the transformation of the world of public affairs. In the simpler, slower paced world of the nineteenth century, it was easier for long-developing, well-understood, deeply felt, and highly durable position issues to organize the dialogue of leaders and led. But in the world of the late twentieth century, presidents deal with a far broader range of problems and issues that arise and change at a far brisker pace than in the past. In this kaleidoscopic world presidents often are required to act on issues that were scarcely visible when they sought their electoral mandate; worse, they have little chance of building up a deep and stable base of public understanding of the policies they adopt. Almost inevitably, then, presidents are held accountable by the voters for past or retrospective results of presidential action or inaction. It is inevitable, therefore, that the fate of presidents and rival candidates should rest on the valences in the public's mind.

Foreign policy issues illustrate this difference. It may be that the dialogue of leaders and led was last organized by a position dimension during the prolonged period between the two world wars, when the isolationist-internationalist dimension dominated American politics. Woodrow Wilson's dream of a new international order in which America would play a leading role foundered on the Senate's rejection of the League of Nations covenant at the close of World War I. Although the great economic expansion of the 1920s and the Great Depression of the 1930s turned America inward, the isolationist-internationalist dimension reemerged as the clouds of a new war gathered over Europe and Asia in the late 1930s. Franklin Roosevelt's duel with the isolationist "America firsters" was part of his third bid for the presidency, and his reelection in 1940 was in part a mandate to help the beleaguered democracies—although it was not really as clear as the mandate he later received when the Japanese bombed Pearl Harbor. America's experience in the ensuing war, as close to a "great patriotic war" as we ever have fought, laid the foundation for the postwar consensus on the Soviet threat and led to national security arrangements on which the parties basically agreed. If the Cold War worked to the advantage of one party or the other over the subsequent decades, it was largely in valence terms—which party was more anticommunist and propeace than the other.

In contrast, the public's need in the late twentieth century to judge its leaders in valence terms is evident in its response to the two regional conflicts that have been strongly controversial in the postwar world. The Korean War burst on the country two years after President Truman's 1948 victory. An explicit commitment to resist communist expansion on the Korean peninsula could not have been part of his mandate because no one anticipated this attack. Although the country backed Truman's response in the early stages, support rapidly drained away when General Douglas MacArthur pushed to the Manchurian border, the Chinese entered the war, and American casualties mounted. MacArthur was dismissed for disagreeing with his commander in chief over how limited a war to fight. He then sought to rally the country to his side of the quarrel. Both Truman's response to the invasion of South Korea and MacArthur's stand that cost him his command suggest that the critical issue of the war was a position issue—with bombing Manchuria, perhaps with atomic weapons, at one pole and pulling back to Japan at the other.

Despite this appearance, the public saw the issue of the war in the simpler valence terms of success and failure. Truman's policies had failed. But so in a sense had MacArthur's, and the country now wanted as president Dwight Eisenhower, the victorious European commander from World War II who was nominated by the Republicans in 1952 and was expected to deal successfully with the problem. During the campaign Eisenhower gave not the slightest hint of where he would come down on the policy dimension that divided General MacArthur from President Truman; he simply proclaimed, "I shall go to Korea." The scent of prospective success helped elect Eisenhower president and strip the Democrats of the White House for the first time in twenty years.

The Vietnam War is a still more revealing example of the postwar dominance of valence issues in foreign policy. Here again, a full-scale regional war burst on the country too late for U.S. resistance to have been an explicit part of President Johnson's mandate in 1964. Indeed, Johnson had pictured his opponent, Barry Goldwater, as more likely to involve the country in war. As the conflict in Vietnam escalated, the controversy it engendered was widely thought to be structured by the hawk-dove dimension that was a staple of media coverage and elite debate. But once again the public saw the war largely in the simpler, valence terms of failure and success. By 1968 a majority of Americans had concluded that Johnson's policies had failed. They wanted the problem fixed. In the Democratic presidential primaries that year the wounded president was dealt a mortal blow by Minnesota senator Eugene McCarthy, the quintessential dove, who persuaded a huge bloc of Democratic voters in New Hampshire and Wisconsin to give him their support. The polling organizations found to their astonishment that McCarthy's supporters had responded to the Vietnam issue not in the position terms of the hawk-dove dimension; indeed, almost as many McCarthy voters believed that McCarthy wanted to bomb North Vietnam as believed (correctly) that he wanted to pull out of the war. They simply wanted a terrible failure to be ended, whether by hawkish or dovish means. In the general election of 1968 Richard Nixon also exploited the war in valence terms, linking the Democrats with the failed war and with the violence of the demonstrators who opposed it.

What of the future? We would not expect a reversal of the trend toward valence politics if our historical analysis is broadly correct. A transition driven by the spreading and rapidly changing responsibilities of government—and of the chief executive who holds so much of the initiative in dealing with the country's problems—is unlikely to occur as we approach a new century. Since the time of Wilson and the two Roosevelts, presidential candidates have needed to set out a vision, often articulated and understood in valence terms, from a remarkable array of swiftly changing problems and issues that face the country.[9] So ineluctable are these parameters of our modern political life that the valence framework will continue to capture an essential part of the dialogue of leaders and led.

Certainly, the valence strategy, tactics, and tempo of the Clinton campaign were entirely consistent with the trend. The Clinton campaign was battered with charges of marital infidelity, draft dodging, and pot smoking. At their convention the Republicans depicted Clinton as "Slick Willie" and his wife as a power-hungry radical feminist who equated marriage with slavery, encouraged children to sue their parents, and eschewed "family values." In the debates and up to election day, the Bush campaign attempted to make Slick Willie into the unpatriotic, indecisive, fast-talking, failed governor of a small and insignificant state.

But, as the *New York Times* reported a week after the election, Clinton's campaign strategists took a public relations hose to these valence fires. While continuing to stress the positive valences of "change" and better economic times, the Clinton campaign responded with "one of the most ambitious campaigns of political rehabilitation ever attempted. They proposed the construction of a new image for Mr. and Mrs. Clinton: an honest, plain-folks idealist and his warm and loving wife." As the paper explained, "Retooling the image of a couple who had been already in the public eye for five battering months re-

---

[9]It is no surprise that the rise of valence politics corresponds broadly with the rise of what Jeffrey Tulis has termed the "rhetorical presidency"; see Tulis, *The Rhetorical Presidency* (Princeton: Princeton University Press, 1988).

quired a campaign of behavior modification and media manipulation so elaborate its outline ran to 14 single-spaced pages."[10]

Known within the Clinton campaign as the General Election Project, the plan called for the candidate to depict himself as the "agent of change." The message was to be delivered in town-hall style forums, on live talk television, and in a series of speeches challenging specific special interests. The candidate was to appear on television to play the saxophone and poke fun at himself for saying that he had tried marijuana but "didn't inhale." The plan also orchestrated events where the Clintons would "seem more warm and cuddly: 'events where Bill and Hillary can go on dates with the American people.' " It even called for staging an event where "Bill and Chelsea surprise Hillary on Mother's Day," and "joint appearances with her friends where Hillary can laugh, cry, do her mimicry."[11]

None of this involved a position politics in which candidate Clinton staked out positions for which President Clinton would be held accountable. As president, Clinton will need to make a number of difficult position choices on new issues as well as difficult choices in managing the economy before he returns to the electorate in 1996. But he almost certainly will be judged in valence terms—by the apparent success or failure of his choices on these issues—rather than on the choices themselves.

VALENCE VOTERS ARE NOT FOOLS

Is valence politics good or bad for American democracy? If, as we have argued, the 1992 election was a valence election par excellence, is this something to be celebrated or lamented?

Our view of the sources of valence politics suggests in part the normative judgment we would make of it. As we spell out this judgment, we are keenly aware of how easy it is to mock valence politics, so drastically does it depart from the civics book ideal of the electorate as an informed kibitzer to the decisions of government, looking over the shoulders of the players in the policy game and periodically awarding the deal to some rather than to others.

But it has long been recognized that this ideal requires the electorate to possess a level of information it could never attain. Far removed from a complex world of public affairs issues capable of baffling and dividing the policy experts, the public is bound to look for ways to simplify the choices it is periodically asked to make. From the 1950s to the present two flourishing branches of the academic literature have sought to identify what these simplifying devices are and to justify them in terms of democratic theory.

---

[10]Michael Kelly, "The Making of a First Family: A Blueprint," *New York Times,* Nov. 14, 1992, 1.
[11]Ibid., 1, 10.

One branch consists of so-called spatial models of elections. As many analysts have noted, plurality and majority-rule electoral systems "create pressures on candidates to take similar stands on any position issue that is foremost in the minds of most voters."[12] In 1957 the intellectual architect of spatial models of elections, Anthony Downs, argued that candidates who want to win tend to espouse the position favored by the so-called median voter, meaning the voter who has equal numbers of voters to the left and the right of his or her position.[13] As Barry Goldwater learned in 1964, and George McGovern in 1972, candidates who ignore the median voter and appeal to the extremes often do so at their electoral peril.

The idea that political conflict can be summarized, and hence simplified, in terms of a left-right or liberal-conservative spectrum is as old as the French Revolution. There is a great deal to be learned from the formal and empirical literatures within political science that have been built on this idea. But the spatial image of the dialogue between leaders and led may obscure more than it reveals, because it requires a level of information and capacity for abstraction in political matters that the electorate cannot meet. It is one thing to use this framework to model the competition of firms for the consuming public, where the spaces are real and given. It is quite another to use this framework to model the competition of parties or leaders, where the spaces will need to be abstracted and commonly perceived by the "consuming" electorate.

Moreover, we wonder whether the normative bias implicit in spatial models of elections is not akin to that of classical democratic theory itself—namely, that elections in a democracy can and should be mainly about position issues, with candidates articulating distinct and detailed policy alternatives on health care, crime, the environment, foreign trade, and other issues, and most voters taking pains to become highly informed about these issues, to relate the candidates' positions to their own beliefs and interests, and to vote accordingly. But, as many students of elections have pointed out since the 1950s, the classic requirements of democratic citizenship (interest, discussion, motivation, knowledge, principle, rationality) are not met by most American voters, and American democracy is none the worse because of it.[14] We would not go as far as Bernard Berelson and his colleagues once did in celebrating the "implicit division of labor" within the electorate between the weakly interested many and the highly motivated, knowledgeable, and caring few.[15] But we would agree that the dialogue between leaders and led can be democratically legitimate and satisfying, even if it is not centered squarely on position issues and politics.

---

[12]Jack H. Nagel, *Participation* (Englewood Cliffs, N.J.: Prentice Hall, 1987), 111.

[13]Downs, *Economic Theory of Democracy.*

[14]Bernard R. Berelson, Paul F. Lazarsfeld, and William N. McPhee, *Voting* (Chicago: University of Chicago Press, 1954), esp. chap. 14.

[15]Ibid.

Some of the limits of the spatial-model framework are evident in Norman Nie, Sidney Verba, and John Petrocik's prize-winning book, *The Changing American Voter,* published in 1979, which heralded the "rise of issue voting."[16] The spatial conceptions of these writers led them virtually to rule out the possibility that a right-wing Republican could capture the presidency because such a candidate would be too distant from the positions of most voters on most issues. This prediction left the authors ill-prepared to explain the success of Ronald Reagan's valence appeals within a year of the book's publication.

Another branch of the literature begins in 1960 with *The American Voter,* continues in V. O. Key's posthumously published work, *The Responsible Electorate* (1966), is refined in Morris Fiorina's book *Retrospective Voting in American National Elections* (1981), and is further refined in several works published in the early 1990s. A central message of this literature is that most voters, whether they are moved by what we have termed position issues, valence issues, or both, are perfectly capable of figuring out their central beliefs and interests in relation to politics and elections, and voting accordingly. As the concluding chapter of *The American Voter* explained:

> The importance of the public's concern with certain broad objectives of government is quite clear in our studies. . . . [T]he electoral decision results from a comparison of the total image of one of the candidate-party alternatives with the image of the other. A good deal of the public response to these political actors simply expresses feeling, or affect. Many people see this party or that candidate as "honest," "dependable," "capable," or, more generally, as just "good.". . . But our examination of public attitude shows that certain generalized goals of government action enter the [voter's] image of the parties and candidates and that these goals play a major role in electoral change.[17]

In *The Responsible Electorate,* Key analyzed voters who switched parties from one presidential election to another and found that most of them switched in a direction consistent with their own beliefs and interests. "The perverse and unorthodox argument of this book," wrote Key, "is that voters are not fools." He set out the crux of his argument in these words:

> In American presidential campaigns of recent decades the portrait of the American electorate that develops from the data is not one of an electorate straightjacketed by social determinants or moved by subconscious urges triggered by devilishly clever propagandists. It is rather one of an electorate moved by concern about central and relevant questions of public policy, of governmental performance, and of executive personality. Propositions so uncompromisingly stated

---

[16]Norman Nie, Sidney Verba, and John Petrocik, *The Changing American Voter,* enlarged ed. (Cambridge, Mass.: Harvard University Press, 1979), chap. 10.

[17]Angus Campbell, Phillip E. Converse, Warren E. Miller, and Donald E. Stokes, *The American Voter,* abridged ed. (New York: Wiley, 1964), 283.

inevitably represent overstatements. Yet to the extent that they can be shown to resemble the reality, they are propositions of basic importance for both the theory and the practice of democracy.[18]

In *Retrospective Voting,* Morris Fiorina emphasized Key's insight that the electorate could learn a good deal of what it needed to know to reach an informed decision simply by monitoring the performance of the parties or leaders in power.[19] Whereas prospective voting imposes on the electorate the classic requirements of democratic citizenship, demanding that the voter closely examine the views of the rival parties and candidates on the position issues of the day and forecast what they would do if elected, Fiorina argued that retrospective voting involves a simpler calculus. He therefore posed the empirical question, how far can it be said that in presidential elections the voters look at how things have gone in the recent past, voting for the party that controls the White House if they like what happened and against it if they do not. Fiorina found a good deal of evidence that this is exactly what many voters do, although he also found evidence of prospective voting and reached a mixed empirical judgment.

A number of recent books on voting have extended the tradition of seeking a "reasoning voter" and a "rational public."[20] Our observations are firmly in this tradition. In particular, Key's portrait of an American electorate "moved by concern about central and relevant questions of public policy, of governmental performance, and of executive personality" can be seen as a rough sketch of valence politics: valence voters are not fools.

The valence framework adds two things that are missing from the Key-Fiorina analysis. On the one hand, the structure of valence issues, which allows successful valence candidates to soar to great heights and unsuccessful ones to plummet to great depths, explains the fluidity of contemporary politics. On the other, the valence framework shows why the electorate can sometimes make prospective as easily as retrospective judgments and judgments on those who seek office as easily as judgments on those who hold office. The power of valence politics to simplify the electorate's choices in both respects was evident in General Eisenhower's victory in the 1952 election.[21]

---

[18]V. O. Key, *The Responsible Electorate* (Cambridge, Mass.: Belknap Press of Harvard University Press, 1966), 8.

[19]Morris P. Fiorina, *Retrospective Voting in American National Elections* (New Haven: Yale University Press, 1981).

[20]Two influential works are Samuel L. Popkin, *The Reasoning Voter: Communication and Persuasion in Presidential Campaigns* (Chicago: University of Chicago Press, 1991); and Benjamin I. Page and Robert Y. Shapiro, *The Rational Public: Fifty Years of Trends in Americans' Policy Preferences* (Chicago: University of Chicago Press, 1991).

[21]For a fuller treatment of the structure of valence issues and a discussion of other aspects of contemporary American politics that are best understood in terms of the valence framework, see Donald E. Stokes, "Valence Politics," in *Electoral Politics,* ed. Dennis Kavanagh (Oxford: Clarendon Press, 1992), 141–164.

CONCLUSION: VALENCE POLITICS AND PRESIDENTIAL TRUSTEES

We may better appreciate the positive democratic potential of valence politics by noting that the difference between position and valence politics parallels the most famous distinction in the normative theory of representation: Edmund Burke's contrast between the representative as instructed delegate and the representative as trustee.

Without unduly distorting either Burke's concepts or our own, we can think of Burke's instructed delegate as a leader who seeks the electorate's support by taking stands on position issues that the leader will later translate into government action. Likewise, we can think of his trustee as a leader who seeks the electorate's support in valence terms, using his or her own best judgment as to the best means for achieving universally approved goals.

We note this parallelism without endorsing Burke's blanket rejection of instructions to the representative by the electorate. In our view, it is right for the majority of the people to seek to bind a president when it has a strongly held view on a well-defined position issue. But it is also right for the electorate, when it is without the resources of information to instruct a president in policy terms, to affirm the priority of certain conditions or values or goals and to leave to the president-as-trustee the question of how these are to be achieved. Bounded rationality, limited voter interest and information about position issues, and the constant stir of valence issues are facts of electoral life that in no way diminish the value of the ongoing dialogue between leaders and led that is at the core of democratic politics.

In the 1992 presidential campaign the electorate above all else decided that its deep concern about the economy was not adequately shared by the president and gave its support instead to the challenger who had posted "The Economy, Stupid" on the wall of his Little Rock campaign headquarters. It was, in other words, a campaign in which American democracy was alive and well as the electorate used the means of valence politics to elect a new trustee to achieve its goals.

7.3 Even with Campaign Finance Law, Money Talks Louder Than Ever (2004)

GLEN JUSTICE

INTRODUCTION

The central question that underlies the debate on campaign finance reform is whether donations are a form of free speech. Regulation opponents argue that people who donate money to a political campaign are expressing their support for the candidate's policy views, so that to restrict those donations in any way amounts to restricting people's First Amendment rights. Regulation advocates maintain that the high cost of waging a political campaign today limits many individuals from expressing their political views, and thus political expression is protected only for those who can afford it.

Senators John McCain (R-AZ) and Russell Feingold (D-WI) succeeded recently in shepherding into law the first major campaign finance reforms since the 1970s. The Bipartisan Campaign Reform Act of 2002 increases the amount of money that can be donated directly to an individual's campaign or to a PAC, but the law also bans soft money donations to political parties. In so doing, it seeks to close a loophole that was often exploited as a way of bypassing limits on direct donations. Now, however, some critics contend that a new loophole exists in that people can still make unlimited donations to interest groups, which often lobby or run advertisements about candidates for office. In addition, despite the new law, in 2004 record amounts of money were spent by national candidates and both political parties.

■

The McCain-Feingold law, which did more to change how American political campaigns are financed than any legislation since the 1970's, got its first real-world test in this year's election. And now its critics are more emphatic than ever in arguing that the law has fallen short of its goals, and even some supporters are calling for revisions.

The 2002 law demolished the system that for more than a decade had allowed political parties to feed on unlimited soft-money contributions from companies, labor unions and donors. But what rose in its place remains the subject of fierce debate.

Critics say the law was undercut by a loophole that allowed advocacy groups known as 527 committees to raise hundreds of millions in soft money. Supporters say the law stands as a barrier to corruption and needs only reinforcement, and that the law was not intended as a panacea.

"You can't write legislation for every loophole that opens up," said Senator John McCain, Republican of Arizona, a chief sponsor of the law. "It's like putting your thumb in the dike."

Representative Bob Ney, an Ohio Republican who opposed the law, said: "The bottom line remains that soft money has not been removed from the system. You could drive a Mack truck through that bill."

The fight has already spilled into the courts and may land in Congress next year as Mr. McCain and his allies seek to regulate free-spending 527 committees, overhaul the Federal Election Commission and make the public financing system more attractive to presidential candidates.

The major advocacy groups at work in this year's elections, called 527 groups after the section in the tax code that created them, raised more than $350 million, according to PoliticalMoneyLine, which tracks campaign finance.

While it is axiomatic in politics that each race will cost more than the last, and while final numbers will not be in for weeks, the figures posted through mid-October set records even though candidates and parties were restricted for the first time to only hard-money donations.

The field of presidential candidates raised about $851 million (including public financing), a 70 percent increase over 2000. National political parties raised more than $1 billion, 12 percent more than when they were able to gather six- and seven-figure soft-money checks.

In total, this year's races for Congress and the White House are estimated to have cost roughly $3.9 billion, about a third more than they did four years ago, according to the Center for Responsive Politics, which tracks campaign spending.

The numbers were influenced by several factors. President Bush and Senator John Kerry opted out of public financing until after their conventions, letting them raise money without limits. McCain-Feingold also increased the hard-money contribution limits for individuals to $2,000 for a candidate and $25,000 for a party from $1,000 and $20,000, respectively.

"It wasn't the perfect storm, but it was a very good one," said Michael J. Malbin, executive director of the Campaign Finance Institute, which studies political money. "The parties learned how to do this, the campaigns really motivated people and the easy money was not there."

Lawyers and political operatives tested the boundaries of the new law with the Federal Election Commission, openly seeking ways to use the law to their advantage. They also adopted new strategies and creative ways to raise money and sometimes just worked harder.

Mr. Bush doubled his network of six-figure "pioneer" and "ranger" fundraisers to about 550. He set a presidential fund-raising record of about $273 million. Mr. Kerry capitalized on the Internet, raising an unprecedented

$82 million online and about $249 million over all to become the best-financed challenger in presidential campaign history.

Political parties scrambled for money and pushed members of Congress in safe seats to provide more. Barack Obama of Illinois gave hundreds of thousands of dollars from his campaign to Democratic candidates and party committees before he was even elected to the Senate.

Perhaps the most striking change was at the Democratic National Committee, where the chairman, Terry McAuliffe, undertook a major effort to restructure the fund-raising and outreach programs. He invested tens of millions of dollars in modernized computers. Enormous voter lists were compiled to prospect for donors and grass-roots support. And early primary dates allowed the party more time to raise money.

The committee sent out a record number of mail and e-mail solicitations, leading to a spike in the number of small donors. Contributions grew 42 percent to more than $299 million through mid-October and the party bought millions of dollars in commercials for Mr. Kerry. While it raised less than its Republican rival during that period, the difference was far less than in previous elections.

"Had we not made the changes, the party as we know it would have ceased to exist," Mr. McAuliffe said.

Supporters of the law are quick to point out that candidates and parties were amply financed this year, despite dire predictions that the law would starve the parties.

"It was never a perfect law," said Representative Martin T. Meehan, a Massachusetts Democrat who sponsored the law. "This was a compromise worked out to correct the most egregious parts of the system."

The architects of the law say it was never intended to reduce the total amount of money in politics. Rather, they say the aim was to stop federal officeholders from soliciting corporate and union soft money. And that, they say, was accomplished.

"No longer can an elected representative or senator pick up the phone and call a trial lawyer, a union head or a corporation and say, 'I need a check for six figures—and by the way, your legislation is before my committee next week,' " Mr. McCain said.

But the law's critics argue that the change is virtually meaningless in the face of the 527 groups, which can still raise the unlimited contributions forbidden to the parties. Groups like Swift Vets and P.O.W.'s for Truth and the Progress for America Voter Fund on the right and America Coming Together, the Media Fund and the MoveOn.org Voter Fund on the left spent lavishly to run television commercials and to get out the vote, though they were prohibited from coordinating with candidates or parties.

The groups turned primarily to wealthy partisans for financial support. At least 46 people contributed $1 million or more through mid-October. For the 2002 election, only six donors gave that much.

A partisan battle over whether to regulate 527 groups raged throughout this year's election in front of the election commission and the courts. Democrats, who made heavy use of the committees, generally defended the groups while Republicans argued to have them constrained.

Even Mr. Bush spoke out publicly against them at one point, calling 527's "bad for the system," and his campaign took legal action against them. But when the commission declined to pass comprehensive regulations and it became clear the groups would operate through Election Day, Republicans ultimately made strong use of their own 527 organizations.

In the end, Democrats held a fund-raising advantage through 527 groups of roughly 2-to-1, according to PoliticalMoneyLine.

With the election over, Mr. McCain and his allies have high hopes that a pending lawsuit in federal court could force restrictions on 527 groups, and they plan to push for legislation next year. The Republican stance against 527's could mean that some lawmakers who opposed McCain-Feingold may support a bill to regulate 527's. Some lawmakers may fear what 527 organizations could do if they wade into the 2006 elections, going after members of Congress the way they went after presidential candidates.

"People on both sides of the aisle wonder who's next," said Mr. Ney, the Ohio congressman, who contends that McCain-Feingold should have regulated 527 groups directly. "I expect hearings on all of these kinds of things."

Supporters of McCain-Feingold say the election commission should have done more to regulate these groups.

The six-member commission, split evenly between Republicans and Democrats, has long been derided by politicians in both parties and by advocacy groups as ineffective and lacking adequate enforcement powers. "It's a corrupt, enabling organization stacked with political hacks," Mr. McCain said. "We have got to reform the F.E.C."

Michael Toner, a Republican on the commission, said: "This is something Congress has to decide. If Congress decides to restructure the agency, I have to respect that."

7.4 Reforming the Electoral System (2004)

STEPHEN J. WAYNE

INTRODUCTION

Among the more difficult components of American government to explain is the electoral college. The Framers devised this structure in the waning days of the Constitutional Convention; the Committee on Postponed Matters created it as a compromise between large and small states, and many expected that changes would be likely after implementation. Yet the electoral college has endured, with only a handful of changes since 1789. Its primary purpose is to represent both individual citizens and states. Each state is accorded as many votes in the electoral college as it has representatives in both chambers of Congress. Thus, each state is guaranteed three electors: two for the Senate, and at least one for the House of Representatives. Large states have more electoral college votes than small states because of their high population, but small states exercise crucial voting authority that is not dependent on population alone.

In this selection, presidential scholar Stephen J. Wayne discusses three alternatives to the electoral college. The most radical change would be to abolish it entirely and elect the president by popular vote. But more moderate reforms are possible as well, such as automating electoral college votes or allocating a state's votes based on both district and statewide election returns. Any such changes to the system would require amending the Constitution.

■

ELECTORAL REFORM

The vote controversy in Florida highlighted the deficiencies in voter certification and election administration: inaccurate registration lists, confusing ballots, unclear votes, and their improper tabulation. The state of Florida moved quickly to correct these problems, and Congress followed suit in 2002 as well.

For the first time it enacted legislation to establish federal standards for national elections and authorized funds for states which complied with these standards to upgrade their registration procedures, purchase more advanced voting technology, and provide greater accessibility to the polls for the dis-

Stephen J. Wayne, *The Road to the White House, 2004: The Politics of Presidential Elections* (with InfoTrac), 7th edition (Belmont, Calif.: Wadsworth, 2004), 320–333. © 2004. Reprinted with permission of Wadsworth, a division of Thomson Learning: www.thomsonrights.com. Fax 800 730-2215.

abled. The bill authorized nearly $4 billion over three years to help states computerize and centralize their registration lists, train election workers, buy new voting machinery, and improve access to the voting booths.

To decrease the potential for fraud, the statute requires first-time registrants and voters to provide identification, a driver's license or the last four digits of their Social Security number. Latino groups, backed by some liberal Democrats, strongly objected to this requirement, fearing that it would disproportionately reduce the size of the Hispanic vote. On the other hand, African Americans welcome the anti-fraud provisions, believing that it would make it more difficult for state election officials to challenge African American voters as occurred in Florida in 2000. Republicans also strongly supported the new identification requirement.

The legislation also enables voters whose names do not appear on the registration lists to cast a provisional vote pending their registration challenge. However, no time requirements are imposed on states to rectify these challenges.

Intended to increase public confidence in the conduct of elections, the new law should correct some of the most egregious problems that have marred past elections. Nonetheless, so long as the administration of national elections is a shared state and county responsibility, variations in registration and voting procedures combined with spur-of-the-moment decisions by election officials will continue to fuel complaints and controversies over the conduct of elections. Allegations of fraud, however, should be reduced, assuming, of course, that Congress appropriates the money authorized by the act and distributes it to the states.

THE ELECTORAL COLLEGE

In addition to the problem of who votes, another source of contention is how the votes should be aggregated. Theoretically, the Constitution allows electors chosen by the states to vote as they please. In practice, all votes are cast for the popular vote winner. The reason for this outcome is simple. The vote for president and vice president is actually a vote for competing slates of electors selected in all but two states on a statewide basis. The slate that wins is the slate proposed by the winning candidate's party. Naturally the electors are expected to vote for their party's nominees.

This de facto system has been criticized as undemocratic, as unrepresentative of minority views within states, and as potentially unreflective of the nation's popular choice. Over the years, there have been numerous proposals to alter it. The first was introduced in Congress in 1797. Since then, there have been more than five hundred others. In urging changes, critics have pointed to the Electoral College's archaic design, its electoral biases, and the undemocratic results it can produce. . . . Four major plans—automatic, proportional, district, and direct election—have been proposed as constitutional amendments to alleviate some or all of these problems. The following sections will examine these proposals and the impact they could have on the way in which the president is selected.

The Automatic Plan   The electors in the Electoral College have been an anachronism since the development of the party system. Their role as partisan agents is not and has not been consistent with their exercising an independent judgment. In fact, sixteen states plus the District of Columbia prohibit such a judgment by requiring electors to cast their ballots for the winner of the state's popular vote. Although probably unenforceable because they seem to clash with the Constitution, these laws strongly indicate how electors should vote.

The so-called automatic plan would do away with the danger that electors may exercise their personal preferences. First proposed in 1826, it has received substantial support since that time, including the backing of Presidents John Kennedy and Lyndon Johnson. The plan simply keeps the Electoral College intact but eliminates the electors. Electoral votes are automatically given to the candidate who has received the most popular votes within the state.

Other than removing the potential problem of faithless or unpledged electors, the plan would do little to change the system as it currently operates. It has not been enacted because Congress has not felt this particular problem to be of sufficient magnitude to justify a constitutional amendment to fix it. There have in fact been only nine faithless electors, who failed to vote for their party's nominees—seven since 1948.[1] In 2000, one District of Columbia elector submitted a blank ballot to protest the District's lack of voting representation in Congress. Additionally, one Democratic West Virginia elector in 1988 reversed the order of the nominees, voting for Lloyd Bentsen for president and Michael Dukakis for vice president.

The Proportional Plan   Electing the entire slate of presidential electors has also been the focus of considerable attention. If the winner of a state's popular vote takes all the electoral votes, the impact of the dominant party is increased within that state and the larger, more competitive states, where voters tend to be more evenly divided, benefit.

From the perspective of the other major party and minor parties within the state as well as third-party candidates, this winner-take-all system is neither desirable nor fair. In effect, it disenfranchises people who do not vote for the

---

[1]There is some controversy whether three other electors in 1796 might also have gone against their party when voting for president. They supported John Adams although they were selected in states controlled by the Democratic-Republicans. However, the fluidity of the party system in those days, combined with the weakness of party identification, makes their affiliation (if any) hard to establish.

winning candidate. And it does more than that: it discourages a strong campaign effort by a party that has little chance of winning the presidential election in that state, such as Democrats in Utah or Alaska or Republicans in Hawaii or Rhode Island. Naturally the success of other candidates of that party is affected as well. The winner-take-all system also works to reduce voter turnout.

One way to rectify this problem would be to have proportional voting. Such a plan has been introduced on a number of occasions. Under a proportional system, the electors would be abolished, the winner-take-all principle would be eliminated, and a state's electoral vote would be divided in proportion to the popular vote the candidates received within the state. A majority of electoral votes would still be required for election. If no candidate obtained a majority in the Electoral College, most proportional plans call for a joint session of Congress to choose the president from among the top two or three candidates.

The proportional proposal would have a number of major consequences. It would decrease the influence of the most competitive states and increase the importance of the least competitive ones, where voters are likely to be more homogeneous.

By rewarding large victories in relatively homogeneous states, the system would seem to encourage competition within those states. Having the electoral vote proportional to the popular vote provides an incentive to all the parties, not simply the dominant one, to mount a more vigorous campaign and to establish a more effective organization. This incentive could strengthen the other major party within the state, but it might also help third parties as well, thereby weakening the two-party system. Ross Perot, who received no electoral votes under the present winner-take-all system, would have received approximately 102 under the proportional plan in 1992 and 49 in 1996. More important, Bill Clinton would not have received a majority in 1992 or 1996 (he would have been about 6 electoral votes short) if electoral votes were distributed according to the proportion of the vote candidates received in individual states. Under these circumstances, third-party candidates, such as Perot and Ralph Nader, might have the power to influence the election between the major party candidates by instructing their electors to support one of them or even by simply forcing the House of Representatives to determine the winner.

Selection by the House weakens a president's national mandate, might make the president more dependent on the House or might require promises or favors to legislators whose support was critical for victory, and in general, could decrease presidential influence during the initial period of an administration. And what happens if the leading candidate is of one party and the House is controlled by the other party? Would legitimacy of the result be enhanced under that arrangement?

Operating under a proportional plan would in all likelihood make the Electoral College vote much closer, thereby reducing the claim most presidents wish to make that they have received broad public backing for themselves, their new administration, and the policy proposals they have advocated during their campaign. George Bush would have defeated Michael Dukakis by only 43.1 electoral votes in 1988, Jimmy Carter would have defeated Gerald Ford by only 11.7 in 1976, and Richard Nixon would have won by only 6.1 in 1968. The election of 2000 would have been even closer with Bush winning by about 1 electoral vote. (See Table [1].) And in at least one recent instance, a proportional electoral vote in the states might have changed the election results. Had this plan been in effect in 1960, Richard Nixon would probably have defeated John Kennedy by 266.1 to 265.6.[2]

Table [1]
Voting for President, 1956–2000: Four Methods for Aggregating the Votes

Year	Electoral College	Proportional Plan	District Plan	Direct Election (percentage of total votes)
1956				
Eisenhower	457	296.7	411	57.4
Stevenson	73	227.2	120	42.0
Others	1	7.1	0	0.6
1960				
Nixon	219	266.1	278	49.5
Kennedy	303	265.6	245	49.8
Others (Byrd)	15	5.3	14	0.7
1964				
Goldwater	52	213.6	72	38.5
Johnson	486	320.0	466	61.0
Others	0	3.9	0	0.5
1968				
Nixon	301	231.5	289	43.2
Humphrey	191	225.4	192	42.7
Wallace	46	78.8	57	13.5
Others	0	2.3	0	0.6
1972				
Nixon	520	330.3	474	60.7
McGovern	17	197.5	64	37.5
Others	1	10.0	0	1.8
1976				
Ford	240	258.0	269	48.0
Carter	297	269.7	269	50.1
Others	1	10.2	0	1.9

---

[2]It is difficult to calculate the 1960 vote precisely because the names of the Democratic presidential and vice presidential candidates were not on the ballot in Alabama and because an unpledged slate of electors was chosen in Mississippi.

1980				
Reagan	489	272.9	396	50.7
Carter	49	220.9	142	41.0
Anderson	0	35.3	0	6.6
Others	0	8.9	0	1.7
1984				
Reagan	525	317.6	468	58.8
Mondale	13	216.6	70	40.6
Others	0	3.8	0	0.4
1988				
Bush	426	287.8	379	53.4
Dukakis	111	244.7	159	45.6
Others	1	5.5	0	1.0
1992				
Bush	168	203.3	214	37.5
Clinton	370	231.6	324	43.0
Perot	0	101.8	0	18.9
Others	0	1.3	0	0.6
1996				
Clinton	379	262.0	345	49.2
Dole	159	219.9	193	40.7
Perot	0	48.8	0	8.4
Others	0	7.3	0	1.7
2000				
Gore	266*	264	267	48.4
Bush	271	265	271	47.9
Nader/Others	0	9	0	2.7

*One Democratic elector in the District of Columbia cast a blank electoral vote to protest the District's absence of voting representation in Congress.

Sources: Figures on proportional and district vote for 1952–1980 were supplied to the author by Joseph B. Gorman of the Congressional Research Service, Library of Congress. Calculations for 1984–1992 were made on the basis of data reported in the *Almanac of American Politics* (Washington, D.C.: National Journal, annual) and by the Federal Election Commission. Calculations for 1996 were made on the basis of official returns as reported by the FEC. For 2000, they are based on the official returns as reported by the FEC. District plan figures are based on Tom Squitieri, "Bush Would Still Win with Electoral Reforms," *USA Today,* <http://www.usatoday.com/news/vote2000/bush25>.

The District Plan   The district electoral system is another proposal aimed at reducing the effect of winner-take-all voting. This plan has had several variations, though the basic thrust would be to keep the Electoral College but to change the manner in which the electoral votes within the states are determined. Instead of selecting the entire slate on the basis of the statewide vote for president, only two electoral votes would be decided in this manner. The remaining votes would be allocated on the basis of the popular vote for president within individual districts (probably congressional districts). Maine and Nebraska currently employ such a system. A majority of the electoral votes would still be necessary for election. If the vote in the Electoral College were not decisive, then most district plans call for a joint session of Congress to make the final selection.

For the very smallest states, those with three electoral votes, all three electors would have to be chosen by the state as a whole. For others, however, the combination of district and at-large selection would probably result in a split electoral vote, especially in the larger states. On a national level, this change should make the Electoral College more reflective of the partisan division of the newly elected Congress rather than of the popular division of the national electorate.

The losers under such an arrangement would be the large, competitive states and, most particularly, the cohesive, geographically concentrated groups within those states. The winners would include small states. Third parties, especially those that are regionally based, might also be aided to the extent that they were capable of winning specific legislative districts.

It is difficult to project whether Republicans or Democrats would benefit more from such an arrangement, since much would depend on how the legislative districts within the states were apportioned and how they tended to vote. If the 1960 presidential vote were aggregated on the basis of one electoral vote to the popular vote winner of each congressional district and two to the popular vote winner of each state, Nixon would have defeated Kennedy 278 to 245, with 14 unpledged electors. In 1976, the district system would have produced a tie, with Carter and Ford receiving 269 votes each (see Table [1]).

The Direct Election Plan   Of all the plans to alter or replace the Electoral College, the direct popular vote has received the most attention and support. Designed to eliminate the college entirely and count the votes on a nationwide basis, it would elect the popular vote winner provided the winning candidate received a certain percentage of the total vote. In most plans, 40 percent of the total vote would be necessary. In some, 50 percent would be required.[3] In the event that no one got the required percentage, a runoff between the top two candidates would be held to determine the winner.[4]

A direct popular vote would, of course, remedy a major problem of the present system—the possibility of electing a nonplurality president. It would better equalize voting power both among and within the states. The large, competitive states would lose some of their electoral clout by the elimination of the winner-take-all system. Party competition within the states and per-

---

[3]Abraham Lincoln was the only plurality president who failed to attain the 40 percent figure. He received 39.82 percent in 1860, although he probably would have received more had his name been on the ballot in nine southern states.

[4]Other direct election proposals have recommended that a joint session of Congress decide the winner. The runoff provision was contained in the resolution that passed the House of Representatives in 1969. A direct election plan with a runoff provision failed to win the two-thirds Senate vote required to initiate a constitutional amendment in 1979.

haps even nationwide would be increased. Turnout should also improve. Every vote would count in a direct election.

A direct election, however, might also encourage minor parties to enter and compete more vigorously, which could weaken the two-party system. The possibility of denying a major party candidate 40 percent of the popular vote might be sufficient to entice a proliferation of candidates and produce a series of bargains and deals in which support was traded for favors with a new administration. The new administration might even look more like a coalition government in a multiparty system than one that existed in a two-party system. Moreover, it is possible that the plurality winner might not be geographically representative of the entire country. Take Gore in 2000. He won only 20 of the 50 states plus the District of Columbia, mostly those that border on the Atlantic or Pacific Oceans and the Great Lakes. A candidate who wins by a very large sectional vote would upset the representational balance that has been achieved between the president's and Congress's electoral constituencies.

The organized groups that are geographically concentrated in the large industrial states would have their votes diluted by a direct election. Jewish voters, for example, highly supportive of the Democratic Party since World War II, constitute only about 2.5 percent of the total population but 14 percent in New York, one of the largest states. Thus, the impact of the New York Jewish vote is magnified under the present Electoral College arrangement as is that of Hispanic voters in Florida, Texas, and California and the Christian Coalition in the South.[5]

The Republican Party has also been reluctant to lend its support to direct election. Republicans perceive that they benefit from the current arrangement, which provides more safe Republican states than Democratic ones. They also fear that demographic trends, especially the increase in the Hispanic population, might work against them. The last two nonplurality presidents, Benjamin Harrison and George W. Bush, were both Republicans.

A very close popular vote could also cause problems in a direct election. The winner might not be evident for days, even months. Voter fraud could have national consequences. Under such circumstances, large-scale challenges by the losing candidate would be more likely and would necessitate national recounts rather than confining such recounts to individual states, as the current Electoral College system does.

The provision for the situation in which no one received the required percentage of the popular vote has its drawbacks as well. A runoff election would extend the length of the campaign and add to its cost. Considering that some aspirants begin their quest for the presidency a year or two before the election,

---

[5]John Kennedy carried New York by approximately 384,000 votes. He received a plurality of more than 800,000 from precincts that were primarily Jewish. Similarly, in Illinois, a state he carried by less than 9,000, Kennedy had a plurality of 55,000 from the so-called Jewish precincts. Mark R. Levy and Michael S. Kramer, *The Ethnic Factor* (New York: Simon & Schuster, 1972), 104.

a further protraction of the process might unduly tax the patience of the voters and produce an even greater numbing effect than currently exists. Moreover, it would also cut an already short transition period for a newly elected president and would further drain the time and energy of an incumbent seeking reelection.

There is still another difficulty with a contingency election. It could reverse the order in which the candidates originally finished. This result might undermine the ability of the eventual winner to govern successfully. It might also encourage spoiler candidacies. Third parties and independents seeking the presidency could exercise considerable power in the event of a close contest between the major parties. Imagine what Perot's influence would have been in a runoff between Clinton and Bush in 1992.

Nonetheless, the direct election plan is supported by public opinion and has been ritualistically praised by contemporary presidents. Gallup polls conducted over the last three decades have consistently found the public favoring a direct election over the present electoral system by substantial margins as indicated in Table [2].[6] Former presidents Carter and Ford have both urged the abolition of the Electoral College and its replacement by a popular vote.

Table [2]
Public Opinion and the Electoral College

Year	Favor Direct Election	Oppose Direct Election	No Opinion
1944	65%	23%	13%
1967	58	22	20
1968			
May	66	—	—
Nov.	80	—	—
1977	73	—	—
1980	67	—	—

Year*	Amend the Constitution	Keep the Current Electoral System	Neither/Both/ No Opinion
2000			
November 11–12	61	35	4
December 15–17	59	37	4

*Gallup changed the question in 2000: "Thinking for a moment about the way in which the president is elected in this country, which would you prefer: to amend the Constitution so the candidate who receives the most total votes nationwide wins the election, or to keep the current system, in which the candidate who wins the most votes in the Electoral College wins the election?"

Source: Frank Newport, "Americans Support Proposal to Eliminate Electoral College System," Gallup poll, January 5, 2001, <http://www.gallup.com/poll/releases/pr010105.asp> Reprinted by permission.

[6]George H. Gallup, *The Gallup Poll* (Wilmington, Del.: Scholarly Resources, 1981), 258–260.

In 1969, the House of Representatives actually voted for a constitutional amendment to establish direct election for president and vice president, but the Senate refused to go along. Despite public opinion, it seems unlikely that sufficient impetus for a change that requires a constitutional amendment will occur until the issue becomes salient to more people. It may take the election of several nonplurality presidents to produce such an outcry and generate the momentum needed to change the Electoral College system.

Despite the complaints that are ritualistically voiced during the election period that the candidates are no good, that there is very little difference between them, and that the campaigns are negative, superficial, and irrelevant, the electorate has not demanded that its congressional representatives change the system beyond extending suffrage to all citizens, reforming campaign finance, and improving registration and vote tabulation. The electoral system may not be perfect, but it has functioned with public support for over two hundred years, a significant achievement in itself. This achievement is cited by those who oppose changing it. If it works, if it is open and accessible, if it encourages participation, if it has for the most part resulted in the election of capable leaders, then why change it, they ask. . . .

Finally, the equity of the Electoral College has also been challenged once again by the results of the 2000 election, but none of the proposals to alter or abolish it, except by the direct election of the president, has received much public backing. With no outcry for reform, Congress has been reluctant to alter the system by initiating an amendment to the Constitution and seems unlikely to do so until another electoral crisis and/or unpopular result forces its hand.

Does the electoral process work? Yes. Can it be improved? Of course. Will it be changed? Probably, but if the past is any indication, there is no guarantee that legally imposed changes will produce only, or even, their desired effect. If politics is the art of the possible, then success is achieved by those who can adjust most quickly to the legal and political environment and turn it to their electoral advantage.

CHAPTER 8

The Media

*T*he American news media are much criticized: Public officials typically complain that their views are not presented accurately by the press. Readers, viewers, and listeners raise questions about topics covered, reporters' biases, and reporting versus editorializing. For their part, journalists maintain that their responsibility is to present the news fully and fairly. They frequently seek more access and information than politicians are willing to provide. By covering both sides—or "all sides"—of an issue, they are bound to alienate some readers, viewers, and listeners. Their adversarial and investigative posture can also be self-directed: Some of the most searing critiques of media bias and misreporting have been produced, disseminated, and debated by journalists themselves.

The first reading in this chapter, by the provocative *New York Times* columnist Maureen Dowd, sparked criticism and controversy. Although Dowd is well known as a biting critic of President George W. Bush and his administration, she was also quite hard on President Bill Clinton. Written as a "news analysis" and printed on page one of the *Times* (rather than on the editorial page), Dowd's article reported on President Clinton's visit to England's Oxford University, where he studied in 1968–1970 as a Rhodes Scholar. Her report begins: "President Clinton returned today . . . to the university where he didn't inhale, didn't get drafted and didn't get a degree."

In many respects, the media's duties make conflict with their sources as well as their audience inevitable. Most people get their news about government and politics from the media; few have the time or resources to contact public officials directly or participate in politics on a regular basis. The media's functions include identifying issues that merit public attention (*gatekeeping*), keeping track of how political candidates fare in their campaigns (*scorekeeping*), and overseeing governmental activity to ensure that officials are acting in accordance with the law (*watchdog*). To perform these tasks effectively, the media must press public officials for information and investigate their conduct thoroughly. The media also must balance popular interest in topics with journalists' own views of what subjects merit or require public attention.

Media is a plural noun. Consumers can access information from newspapers, magazines, radio, television, and the Internet—and each of these outlets contains numerous sources representing a wide range of political perspectives. The challenge is to evaluate the source of the material and determine how its interests or biases may influence the information presented. Information available in a news article should be presented neutrally, for example, whereas an editorial or column expresses a particular point of view. Similarly, a Web site run by an interest group will focus on issues relevant to that group's agenda. Consumers have the sometimes daunting responsibility of garnering information from several media outlets to ensure they gain a complete picture of the subject at hand.

As choices of media diversify and increase, so, too, does the need for public officials to have a staff ready to respond to queries and present the government's position. Elected officials today must have a *press secretary* who briefs the media regularly—the president's press secretary, for example, holds at least two meetings with the media daily and fields numerous calls and conversations in between. Press secretaries are responsible for keeping up with the major national and regional daily newspapers as well as following breaking news on the networks. Press secretaries often must have staffs of their own to conduct research and prepare material for the media. Beyond responding to the media, elected officials also have a communications team that is responsible for staging events such as speeches, town hall meetings, or other public events that will receive media coverage. Officials will take the initiative with the media in other ways as well, sometimes ensuring that selected journalists receive tips before major news is announced or offering exclusive interviews with certain writers or commentators.

Few presidential press secretaries faced greater pressure than Mike McCurry did as the Monica Lewinsky scandal broke during the Clinton presidency. Bill Clinton famously denied allegations of adultery in an interview on the television program *60 Minutes* during his 1992 presidential campaign, but then was forced to reveal personal transgressions as president during independent counsel Kenneth W. Starr's Whitewater investigation. Media critic Howard Kurtz describes in this chapter's reading selection how the media "spin cycle" worked during those years of the Clinton presidency. He offers broader insights into how, in this day of twenty-four-hour, nonstop news, the White House uses the press and the press uses the White House, each to further its own ends.

Press coverage of the type that emerged during the Lewinsky scandal would have been unthinkable only a few decades ago. In the past, the media maintained a deferential relationship with elected officials, submitting questions in advance, agreeing to lengthy off-the-record sessions, and so forth. The media also respected a zone of privacy with officials' personal lives, normally keeping topics such as extramarital affairs or drinking out of the news. Many reporters developed close friendships with officials; in the early 1960s, for example, President John F. Kennedy cultivated many such relationships, often inviting reporters to the White House for private as well as public social functions. Consequently, reporters were not inclined to investigate either the president's private socializing or even his unresolved health problems.

The media's zone of privacy for elected officials disappeared in the aftermath of the Vietnam War and Watergate. As public trust in government eroded with President Richard M. Nixon's resignation in 1974, the media became much more aggressive in ferreting out both public and private misconduct. In 1987, presidential candidate Gary Hart's campaign ended after reports of adultery surfaced, and in 1989, John G. Tower's nomination for secretary of defense was defeated because of questions about drinking and ties to defense contractors. Anyone who works in the public eye today must expect to field queries from the media about personal behavior, and efforts to resist providing information usually prove futile.

Court battles to limit the media's access to government information or personal information about public officials almost always end in the media's favor, thanks mainly to the First Amendment's prohibition on restricting the freedom of the press. In 1971, the Nixon administration sought court injunctions to prohibit newspapers from publishing the Pentagon Papers, a classified history of U.S. involvement in Vietnam that was leaked to the press by former Defense Department official Daniel Ellsberg. White House officials claimed that publication of the papers would threaten national security, but the Supreme Court ruled against the administration. In cases involving personal allegations about public figures (encompassing both elected government officials and private celebrities like movie stars, among others in the public eye), the courts have ruled that publishing incorrect information does not amount to wrongdoing unless the news organization does so with "reckless disregard" for the truth, exhibits "actual malice," and results in real and serious damage to the individual.

In the United Kingdom, Australia, and other democracies, government has extensive powers to restrain the press on "national security" and other grounds from publishing even previously published information, and public figures—even, in one famous case, a former prime minister of Australia—can successfully sue the press for how it has covered them or opinions it has expressed about them. In these democracies, the burden of proof rests on the press to show that it got the story right. But in the United States, the burden of proof for justifying even minor restrictions on the media lies with the government, and all restrictions eventually generate controversies centered on "press freedom" or "media bias."

In 2003 and 2004, for instance, during the early stages of the war and occupation in Iraq, journalists were "embedded" with troops and prohibited from photographing pictures of soldiers' coffins. Some argued that these and related government-mandated restrictions on "in-country" journalists were appropriate, while others deemed them both unnecessary and undesirable. Most news organizations, however, complied. Still, President Bush himself charged that much of the press made the situation in Iraq seem worse than it really was. As the Pew Research Center for the People and the Press report in this chapter indicates, many Americans agreed with the president, but opinion divided along party lines and most citizens were uneasy about the U.S. military presence in Iraq.

As the media have become more critical in their coverage, they have themselves come under fire and been charged with being too zealous. The media, even major network news outlets like ABC, are often accused of having a "liberal bias"—that is, of publishing news favorable to groups and individuals who advocate government-funded social programs, economic regulation of business, and limited government intervention in people's private lives on such matters as abortion and homosexual rights. As the Media Research Center report in this chapter documents, members of the media do tend to be liberal in their political views, to vote Democratic, and to eschew conservative positions on many key political issues.

Still, evidence of a consistent liberal bias in media coverage is much harder to nail down, and some of the most successful news outlets in the nation either have no obvious or consistent ideological or partisan bias, or are perceived by some to tilt toward conservative and Republican views in how they package and present the news—Fox News, for example. Common professional training and competitive pressures to make money, "make news," and "get the story first," among other factors, may well exert as much or more influence over what, when, and how reporters report as any individual attributes (gender, race, age, class background—or personal partisan preferences or political ideology). Furthermore, even if most "mainstream" media were consistently biased in one political direction or another, today, the diversity of media sources—including local and national newspapers, newsmagazines, radio talk shows, the Internet, cable television networks, and others—means that even a casually determined consumer can easily find lots of unfiltered factual information as well as multiple opinions and competing perspectives on virtually any civic or political issue.

8.1 Whereas, He Is an Old Boy, If a Young Chief, Honor Him (1994)

MAUREEN DOWD

INTRODUCTION

The following article by Maureen Dowd raises important questions about the content of news stories. It appeared on the front page of the *New York Times* the day after President Bill Clinton visited Oxford University, which he attended in 1968–1970 as a Rhodes Scholar, to receive an honorary degree. Dowd's article, labeled a "news analysis," sparked controversy because of the first sentence: "President Clinton returned today . . . to the university where he didn't inhale, didn't get drafted and didn't get a degree." Critics, including many journalists, said Dowd's sentence was a more appropriate introduction to an opinion column than to a news story, while others argued that the facts were correct and that a "news analysis" permitted more creativity on the author's part than a regular news article. As this story shows, how journalists present the news can become as important as the information on which they report.

■

President Clinton returned today for a sentimental journey to the university where he didn't inhale, didn't get drafted and didn't get a degree.

The last got rectified by Oxford University in a ceremony conducted by men in black gowns speaking in Latin in a 325-year-old stone building designed by Christopher Wren. Mr. Clinton, who studied politics at University College as a Rhodes Scholar from the fall of 1968 to the spring of 1970, was awarded an honorary doctorate in civil law.

At the gilded Sheldonian Theater, the university Chancellor, Lord Jenkins of Hillhead, read the text of the degree in Latin, featuring eight clauses beginning with "Whereas," one with "Therefore" and one with "Witness Whereof." Lord Jenkins said Mr. Clinton was honored for being "a doughty and tireless champion of the cause of world peace," for having "a powerful collaborator in his wife," and for winning "general applause for his achievement of resolving the gridlock which prevented an agreed budget."

Wearing a red gown, beneath a high ceiling painted with cavorting cherubs, Mr. Clinton recalled for the audience at the Sheldonian how he had felt, as a young man fresh from Arkansas, a sense of nagging inadequacy at Oxford, the oldest university in the English-speaking world, a place of musty glamour once described by Henry James as "a kind of dim and sacred ideal of the Western intellect."

Looking at the British dons, men in flowing robes and mortarboards, some carrying gold-headed scepters, the President said: "I always felt a mixture of elation and wariness, bordering on intimidation, in your presence. I thought if there was one place in the world I could come and give a speech in the proper language, it was here, and then I heard the degree ceremony. And sure enough, once again at Oxford I was another Yank a half-step behind."

Mr. Clinton said he was honored by the degree and the honorary fellowship, adding wryly: "I must say that, as my wife pointed out, I could have gotten neither one of these things on my own. I had to be elected President to do it."

The mood at the ceremony, on the last day of the President's weeklong European tour, was good-natured. And even the sounds drifting in from the chanting students outside, protesting increases in housing and food fees, were the cause of an amused comment by the President, who was once an anti-establishment demonstrator himself, on the Vietnam War.

"Just listen outside here," Mr. Clinton said, remarking. "Everything from disputes over the nature of the Italian Government to the character of the word 'skinhead' is being debated even as we are here."

At a lunch before the ceremony, Mr. Clinton saw the men who were his tutor and his porter, and his master read some confidential information from first-year progress reports from his tutor. The tutor had said Mr. Clinton was a "satisfactory" student who was "doing well," and added a note of confidence that "we'll see even more improvement in his writing."

Hillary Rodham Clinton was given a claret jug with a Latin inscription hailing her as "the Lady in charge of Universal Health."

BROWSING AT THE BOOK STORE

Later, at a reception with American students at the Rhodes House, Mr. Clinton was blunt. Jennifer Bradley, a student from Austin, Tex., said the President had warned against Generation X cynicism, telling her, she said, that "the whole Generation X thing was bull." (One of Mr. Clinton's foreign-policy speech writers on the trip, Eric Liu, 25, was on the cover of Newsweek last week on a report about Generation X because he has written a book on the subject.)

The President also tried to tell the students not to be cynical. "I feel more idealistic today than I did as a student," Mr. Clinton told them privately, according to George Stephanopoulous, a 33-year-old Presidential aide who was also a Rhodes Scholar at Oxford. Mr. Stephanopoulous said that many of the students handed letters to the President and the First Lady, which they kept to read on the flight home. In addition to the letters, the President was quoted as saying, "I got the business cards" from the job-hunters in the group.

After leaving Rhodes House, the President walked to Blackwell's book store. On the way, some students unfurled a sign reading, "Inhale Next Time, Bill."

During the campaign, Mr. Clinton confessed that he had tried marijuana here, but quickly insisted, "I didn't inhale," explaining that he did not like the taste.

In the elegant bookstore, he and Mrs. Clinton browsed for more than half an hour. Mrs. Clinton did not buy anything but the President purchased "Principle of Duty" by David Selbourne; "Behind the Battle: Intelligence in the War With Germany, 1939–45," by Ralph Burnett; "Global Ecology," an anthology edited by Wolfgang Sachs, and "The World in 2020," by Hamish McRae.

The University issued a list of books drawn by Mr. Clinton from the University College library during his student days. Showing an early taste for the weighty nitty-gritty of government, he signed out "Presidential Leadership, the Political Relations of Congress and the Chief Executive."

Mr. Clinton walked around the grounds and reminisced with his old Oxford roommate, Robert Reich, the Secretary of Labor. And he visited his old dormitory room in Helen's Court at University College, now occupied by Emma Caldwell, a first-year law student from Northern Ireland who said she had no idea she was sleeping where the President once slept.

"Nothing was said when I first moved in and there are no signs that it was his," she said. "He didn't carve his name in the furniture."

Showing he had learned the art of dogged debating at Oxford, Mr. Clinton wrote a rebuttal this afternoon on a poster on the door of another student who lived in his old dormitory. The poster was protesting the "cultural imperialism" of those Americans who had wanted to intervene to prevent the caning of a young American in Singapore.

The President wrote an explanation of his stance against the caning, saying "that's not the issue," that opposing the caning was not about imposing American values, but about whether the punishment was out of proportion to the crime and whether the young man was really guilty.

The President had originally planned to visit Oxford before the commemoration of the 50th anniversary of D-Day in Normandy. But the White House changed the stop to the end of the President's European trip, presumably to avoid having embarrassing stories about Mr. Clinton's activities as a Vietnam protester crop up on the eve of the D-Day anniversary. Mr. Clinton arrived in England in 1968 as a 22-year-old Rhodes Scholar, just out of Georgetown University in Washington, at the height of the Vietnam War.

By his own admission, it was here that Mr. Clinton rode out part of the war, and it was here he wrote the now infamous letter to the commander of the Reserve Officer Training Corps back home in Arkansas—"Thank you for saving me from the draft"—for helping extend his deferment. He said he hoped to maintain his "political viability."

The young Oxford student said in that letter, "I am writing too in the hope that my telling this one story will help you to understand more clearly how so many fine people have come to find themselves still loving their country but loathing the military."

In interviews in Europe this week with American networks, he has reflected on his opposition to the war. He told Tom Brokaw of NBC News that he did not regret his position then. He seemed to show a bit of revisionism, perhaps not recalling the "loathing" line or how many in the 1960's disdained authority and those in uniform. "I think all the people who grew up in my generation were hurt maybe worse than any other generation could have been by their ambivalence over Vietnam because we all loved the military so much."

After all, Mr. Clinton said, "I grew up on the war movies—you know, on John Wayne and John Hodiak and Robert Mitchum and all those war movies."

LEFT TO GO TO YALE

Mr. Stephanopoulous said Mr. Clinton did not get his degree because he switched from one program to another, ultimately pursuing a B.Phil. in Politics, and had a year left to go to get a graduate degree when the opportunity came to go to Yale Law School.

A Rhodes scholarship provides for two years of study at Oxford University, with a third year granted by application. Most Rhodes Scholars earn degrees at Oxford, and all are expected to remain full-time students until they complete their programs, but Mr. Clinton is not the only one to have left after two years without having done so.

In interviews in British newspapers and on television shows in recent days, former professors and colleagues remembered the young Bill Clinton as an earnest innocent.

He received middling reviews from several English students at Oxford, where they are well tutored in the essential British arts of irony and faint praise. "It was absolutely appropriate to the occasion," said Adam Shapiro, a 20-year-old wearing the traditional black robe and white tie. "It was completely anodyne."

8.2 Spin Cycle: How the White House and the Media Manipulate the News (1998)

HOWARD KURTZ

INTRODUCTION

In this reading selection, *Washington Post* journalist and media critic Howard Kurtz examines media coverage of the Clinton White House. Kurtz depicts efforts by President Bill Clinton's media team to "spin" the news—that is, to try to dictate the timing, tone, and content of stories about Clinton and his policies. He zooms in on presidential press secretary Mike McCurry's handling of the media in the wake of Clinton's admission that he had a relationship with a young White House intern, Monica Lewinsky. But the White House, Kurtz suggests, does not "spin" the news all by itself. He hints that both the media and the White House seek to use each other for their own purposes. Together, his account indicates, the inside-the-Beltway politicians and the national press routinely "manipulate the news" emanating from 1600 Pennsylvania Avenue.

■

On the afternoon of January 21, 1998, a year and a day after Bill Clinton's second inauguration, a grim-faced Mike McCurry walked into the White House Briefing Room to face the music.

The news, McCurry knew, was bad, so undeniably awful that any attempt at spin would be ludicrous. The canny press secretary had bobbed and weaved and jabbed and scolded his way through all manner of Clinton scandals, from the arcane Whitewater land dealings to the crass campaign fundraising excesses to the tawdry tale of Paula Jones. But this one was different. The banner headline in that morning's *Washington Post* made clear that this was a crisis that could spell the end of the Clinton presidency. The Big Guy, as the staffers called him, had been accused of having sex with a former White House intern, Monica Lewinsky, in the executive mansion for more than a year, from the time that she was twenty-one years old. Even worse Clinton was being accused of lying under oath about the affair—committing perjury—and urging the young woman to lie as well.

The reporters, McCurry believed, would be poised to pummel him. That was his job, of course, to stand at the podium and take whatever abuse the fourth estate wanted to dish out, hoping to score a few points in the process and convey what he could of the president's agenda. But the White House correspondents had been supremely frustrated for the past year as Clinton kept slip-sliding his way through the scandalous muck. The president had maintained his extraordinary popularity despite their dogged efforts to hold him accountable for what they saw as the misconduct and the evasions that marked his administration. He had connected with the American public, and they had largely failed. Clinton, in their view, had gotten away with it. Until now.

That morning, the president and three of his lawyers—his outside attorneys, Robert Bennett and David Kendall, and Charles Ruff, the White House counsel—had hammered out a carefully worded statement in which Clinton denied any "improper relationship" with Monica Lewinsky. McCurry had checked the final version with the boss—"Fine," Clinton said—and then read the statement to the press. McCurry had not asked the president himself if he had been banging the intern. That was not his role; he was not a reporter or an investigator. His job was to repeat whatever facts or assertions the lawyers had approved for public consumption. He may have been a nationally known spokesman, the chief interpreter of administration policy, but in the end he was a flack protecting his client, no matter how distasteful the task.

As McCurry walked in front of the familiar blue curtain toward the podium and faced the assembled correspondents, the bank of cameras behind the wooden seats made clear that this was no ordinary briefing. Many of these sessions were replayed at a later hour for C-SPAN junkies, and if McCurry delivered any newsworthy phrases, a few seconds might show up on the network news. But this briefing was being carried live by CNN, by MSNBC, by Fox News Channel. The reporters, he knew, would be trying to bait him, to knock him off stride, to trick him into departing from the safety of his script. And he was equally determined to stand his ground.

The shouting began with the network correspondents taking the lead, demanding that McCurry explain what Clinton meant by an "improper" relationship.

"I'm not going to parse the statement," McCurry said.

"Does that mean no sexual relationship?" asked NBC's Claire Shipman.

"Claire, I'm just not going to parse the statement for you, it speaks for itself."

What kind of relationship did Clinton have with Lewinsky?

"I'm not characterizing it beyond what the statement that I've already issued says," McCurry replied.

Shipman's NBC colleague, David Bloom, uncorked a broader question: "Mike, would it be improper for the president of the United States to have had a sexual relationship with this woman?"

"You can stand here and ask a lot of questions over and over again and will elicit the exact same answer."

"So Mike, you're willing to—"

"I'm not leaving any impression, David, and don't twist my words," McCurry shot back, jabbing his finger.

John Harris of *The Washington Post* tried a different tack, invoking McCurry's own reputation for honesty, which the reporters knew he dearly prized. "Would you be up here today if you weren't absolutely confident these are not true?"

"Look, my personal views don't count," McCurry said. "I'm here to represent the thinking, the actions, the decisions of the president. That's what I get paid to do."

McCurry bit his lower lip as Deborah Orin of the *New York Post* tried next: "What is puzzling to many of us is that we've invited you probably two dozen times today to say there was no sexual relationship with this woman and you have not done so."

"But the president has said he never had any improper relationship with this woman. I think that speaks for itself."

"Why not put the word 'sexual' in?" asked ABC's Sam Donaldson.

"I didn't write the statement," McCurry said.

They went round and round, the reporters demanding answers and McCurry repeating the same unsatisfactory phrases that seemed only to stoke their anger. As the tension level escalated, McCurry tried a bit of humor.

What was the administration's next move?

"My next move is to get off this podium as quick as possible," McCurry said.

Thirty-six minutes and one hundred forty-eight questions later, it was finally over.

Just a week earlier, the start of Clinton's sixth year in office had seemed so promising. The White House spin team had enjoyed extraordinary success in what they called the "rollout" for the following week's State of the Union address, leaking proposals and policy tidbits to selected news organizations to create a sense of momentum for Clinton's lackluster second term. The president's approval rating was hovering at around 60 percent in the polls, and for all the scandalous headlines and political bumps in the road, the country finally seemed to have grown comfortable with him. McCurry and his colleagues had mastered the art of manipulating the press and were reaping the dividends.

And now, just when they thought they had survived the worst of the investigations and the harshest media scrutiny, the latest sex scandal had hit them like a punch in the stomach. They were reeling, depressed, uncertain of the facts but all too certain that Clinton's days might be numbered. The irony was inescapable: The president who worried so openly about his historical legacy, who staunchly insisted that Whitewater was nothing next to Watergate, might make history by following Richard Nixon into oblivion because he could not resist a lowly intern. For now, at least, McCurry and his colleagues could not spin their way out of this one. They did not know whether Bill Clinton was telling the truth about Monica Lewinsky, and some of them suspected he was not.

The White House spin operation had plenty of experience in crisis management. A yearlong investigation into campaign fundraising abuses and influence-peddling charges had built to a dramatic crescendo in the fall of 1997. On the morning of October 3, the Clintonites were once again on the defensive. The Justice Department had just decided to expand its investigation into questionable fundraising calls by Vice President Al Gore and was moving toward a stepped-up probe as well of Bill Clinton's frenetic efforts to raise campaign cash in the 1996 election. The relentless charges that the administration had improperly vacuumed up millions of dollars by crassly selling access to the president was now reaching critical mass. The New York Times, not surprisingly, trumpeted the new developments as its lead story.

But there was another article vying for attention that day at the top of the Times's venerable front page, one that probably resonated with many more readers than were following the twists and turns of the latest Washington scandal. Four days earlier, one of the administration's least favorite investigative reporters, Jeff Gerth, who had long been tormenting Clinton and his wife, Hillary, over the Whitewater affair, had weighed in with a lengthy Times report on how federal inspections of imported food had plummeted just as scientists were finding more outbreaks of food-borne diseases. In fact, Gerth had learned that David Kessler, the former head of the Food and Drug Administration, had failed to persuade Clinton to give his agency the power to bar imported food that did not meet American standards. The story was a major embarrassment, but Clinton had a genius for stealing good ideas from his enemies, even those he most despised in the press. And so the White House promptly staged a ceremony in the picturesque Rose Garden as Clinton proposed giving the FDA new power to ban imported fruit and vegetables, the very power he had refused to grant years earlier. Mike McCurry even credited the *Times* for its role in spotlighting the problem.

"I've never seen anything like it," Kessler told Gerth. "They're terrified of you." Still, the White House had managed to neutralize the dogged Jeff Gerth, who called McCurry to thank him for the acknowledgment.

The day's dueling headlines revealed a larger truth about the Clinton White House and its turn-on-a-dime ability to reposition its battered leader. The central mystery of Bill Clinton's fifth year in office was how a president so aggressively investigated on so many fronts could remain so popular with the American people. Indeed, his approval rating was nearly as lofty as that of Ronald Reagan at the peak of his powers, and with the economy humming along at an impressive clip, bad news was failing to make much of a dent in those numbers.

To be sure, Clinton's performance had helped create the sense that the country was doing just fine on his watch. But it was a carefully honed media strategy—alternately seducing, misleading, and sometimes intimidating the press—that maintained this aura of success. No day went by without the president and his coterie laboring mightily to generate favorable headlines and deflect damaging ones, to project their preferred image on the vast screen of the media establishment.

For much of Clinton's first term, these efforts to control the message were clumsy at best. The core of the original Clinton team—chief of staff Thomas "Mack" McLarty, longtime confidant Bruce Lindsey, senior adviser George Stephanopoulos, counselor David Gergen, press secretary Dee Dee Myers— had trouble fashioning a consistent media message, and Clinton himself was unfocused and error-prone. His casual response, at his first postelection news conference in 1992, about his plans to change the Pentagon's policy toward gays in the military plunged his administration into a long and bruising battle that pushed other issues off the radar screen. Clinton would often stop to talk to reporters after his morning jog, the sweat dripping down his face in decidedly unpresidential fashion. He seemed unable to leave any question unanswered, even one on MTV about his underwear.

In the second half of the term, the president's new chief of staff, Leon Panetta, imposed some much-needed order on the operation; McCurry smoothed relations with the press; communications director Don Baer brought some coherence to long-range planning; deputy chief of staff Harold Ickes rode herd on the political operation; special counsel Mark Fabiani deflected the endless scandal stories; secretive consultant Dick Morris steered Clinton toward the political center, and the president himself was more disciplined in his dealings with reporters. He carefully measured his words about the Oklahoma City bombing and the two government shutdowns. Whatever the question, he would stick to the script, repeat his campaign priorities about protecting Medicare, Medicaid, education, and the environment, brush off scandal questions with the briefest of replies, and hold his famous temper in check.

The second-term lineup was more seasoned but less adventurous. Senior adviser Rahm Emanuel assumed Stephanopoulos's role of behind-the-scenes press handler. Special counsel Lanny Davis became the chief spinmeister on the burgeoning fundraising scandal, an effort crisply supervised by deputy chief of staff John Podesta. Communications director Ann Lewis handled the substantive planning. Chief of staff Erskine Bowles presided over the entire operation like the corporate executive he was. Counselor Doug Sosnik served up political advice, joined over the summer by colorful strategist Paul Begala and former journalist Sidney Blumenthal. McCurry stayed on for a final mission, determined to broker a cease-fire between the president and a hostile press corps. He and his colleagues were engaged in a daily struggle to control the agenda, to seize the public's attention, however fleetingly, for Clinton's wide-ranging initiatives. They had to manage the news, to package the presidency in a way that people would buy the product.

The small group of journalists who shouted questions at the press secretary each day in the White House Briefing Room had a very different agenda. They were focused, almost fixated, on scandal, on the malfeasance and misfeasance and plain old embarrassments that had seemed to envelop this administration from the very start. They were interested in conflict, in drama, in behind-the-scenes maneuvering, in pulling back the curtain and exposing the Oz-like manipulations of the Clinton crowd. It was their job to report what the president said, but increasingly they saw it as their mission to explain why he said it and what seedy political purpose he was trying to accomplish along the way.

When the reporters had the upper hand, the headlines were filled with scandal news, a cascade of Watergate-style charges that drowned out nearly everything else. Indeed, they had plenty of material to work with. The Whitewater investigation, which had dragged on throughout the first term, involved the Clintons' role in a complicated Arkansas land deal, their partnership with a crooked couple, and allegations of a subsequent cover-up. The Travelgate probe involved charges that the first lady had orchestrated the ouster of seven employees of the White House travel office so the work could be given to friends of the Clintons. The Filegate inquiry involved charges that White House aides had deliberately obtained the sensitive FBI files of prominent Republicans. The Paula Jones lawsuit turned on allegations by a former Arkansas state employee that Clinton, while governor, had asked for sex in a Little Rock hotel room. And the campaign finance scandal, in its broadest form, involved an alleged conspiracy by Clinton and Gore to use the perks of high office to solicit cash from foreign operatives, Asian American donors, and garden-variety fat cats, perhaps in exchange for political favors.

Against this dark backdrop, what the White House press operatives did was to launder the news—to scrub it of dark scandal stains, remove unsightly splotches of controversy, erase greasy dabs of contradictions, and present it to the country crisp and sparkling white. The underlying garment was the same, but it was often unrecognizable.

A larger challenge loomed as well—simply put, to change the subject, and to do so without the benefit of dramatic presidential action like fighting a war or battling a recession or tackling some grave national crisis. When the White House team broke through, they secured precious column inches and airtime for Clinton's proposals on national education standards or seat-belt enforcement or funding for mammograms, efforts that the president's people felt resonated far more broadly than the inside-the-Beltway obsessions of the media. At stake in this competing cacophony, they felt, was nothing less than the success of the second term, since history had demonstrated that a reelected president was at the peak of his power in the first year after his victory, when the echoes of his mandate were loudest and his impending lame-duck status least apparent.

History held other lessons for the Clintonites when it came to co-opting the press. Franklin D. Roosevelt told reporters at his first news conference in 1933 that he did not want to be quoted directly but would provide "background" and "off-the-record" information. It was a remarkable innovation: the president as chief source, setting strict ground rules that enabled him to shape the news agenda. The assembled reporters gave Roosevelt a standing ovation, and for the twelve and a half years of his presidency he was treated with deference and affection by the correspondents, none of whom dreamt of telling the public that Roosevelt was confined to a wheelchair.

John Kennedy was the first president to hold live televised press conferences, an innovation that permanently altered the nature of White House communications by staging a regular drama, with the reporters as extras, that reached every American living room. He also personally befriended reporters (notably *Newsweek*'s Ben Bradlee), marketed his wife, Jacqueline, as a cultural phenomenon, and drew stunningly positive coverage by today's standards. But even JFK could be stung by journalistic criticism, and he once canceled his subscription to the New York *Herald Tribune* for its "biased" coverage.

Lyndon Johnson made prodigious efforts to wheedle and cajole the press, dispatching military aircraft to pick up the likes of anchor David Brinkley and *Washington Post* publisher Katharine Graham and fly them to his Texas ranch for private meetings and intimate dinners. But Johnson's mounting deceptions over Vietnam produced disillusionment among the press corps and the public, saddling the White House with the dreaded phrase "credibility gap."

Richard Nixon conducted a virtual war against the press. He ordered wire-taps and tax audits of selected journalists, had CBS's Daniel Schorr investigated by the FBI, demanded an immigration probe of household help employed by *Los Angeles Times* publisher Otis Chandler, and moved to revoke television licenses held by the Washington Post Company, even as he railed about "outrageous, vicious, distorted reporting" during Watergate. It fell to Nixon's press secretary, Ron Ziegler, to dismiss the Watergate break-in as a "third-rate burglary," to feed the press corps the administration's lies about the scandal, and to attack reporters for unfairly maligning all the president's men. Ziegler used a kind of corporate-speak in his briefings, offering "operative" statements that appeared to be true "at this point in time" but were later declared "inoperative" as more evidence of wrongdoing emerged.

Ziegler was hardly the first White House spokesman to engage in deception. When Woodrow Wilson suffered a massive stroke in 1919 that paralyzed the left side of his body, reporters were told that he had had a nervous breakdown and would be back at work soon, and the truth did not emerge for four months. When Dwight Eisenhower had a serious heart attack in 1955, the press was initially told that he had suffered a digestive upset. Jimmy Carter's press secretary, Jody Powell, told the *Los Angeles Times* in 1980 that a rescue mission to free the American hostages in Iran would make no sense, two days before the mission that ended in disaster. Reagan's spokesman, Larry Speakes, declared in 1983 that an American invasion of Grenada would be "preposterous"; the marines landed the next day.

Some presidents have deliberately kept their spokesmen in the dark as a way of concealing the truth. Kennedy's press secretary, Pierre Salinger, complained that he had not been told about the 1961 invasion of Cuba and thereby misled the press about the impending Bay of Pigs disaster. Gerald Ford's first spokesman, Jerald terHorst, resigned in protest after Ford's staff lied to him by denying that the president was considering a pardon for Nixon.

In recent years the modern practice of spin has come to occupy a sort of gray zone between candor and outright falsehood. Larry Speakes kept a sign on his desk: "You don't tell us how to stage the news and we don't tell you how to cover it." It was a revealing motto, for the Reagan administration revolutionized the staging of news, devoting enormous energy to selecting a story of the day and providing television with the pictures to illustrate it. The classic example was when Reagan stood proudly in front of a senior citizen housing project built under a program he had tried to abolish; while reporters duly noted the contradiction, the White House was happy with the pictures on the evening news. Speakes had chilly relations with reporters and sometimes declared an offending correspondent "out of business," refusing to have any more dealings with him. And Speakes was not above twisting the truth. After Reagan's 1985 summit meeting with Mikhail Gorbachev in Geneva, Speakes quoted the president's private remarks to the Soviet leader—which he later admitted he had simply made up. Marlin Fitzwater, a career bureaucrat who succeeded Speakes and stayed on as George Bush's spokesman, restored amicable relations with the press. But it was a mark of Bush's frustration with the fourth estate that his favorite 1992 bumper sticker read "Annoy the Media—Re-Elect Bush."

Clinton's first press secretary, Dee Dee Myers, the first woman to hold the job, was a popular figure with reporters, but she was widely viewed as ineffective and out of the policy loop. One Saturday in 1993, Myers infuriated the press corps by announcing a "lid"—meaning no more news was to be made that day and the captive reporters were free to leave—hours before Clinton launched a missile attack on Iraq. Much of the Washington bureau of *The New York Times* headed off on an outing to Baltimore to attend a Yankees-Orioles game, and they were not pleased about having to rush home to cover the story. Myers sheepishly admitted afterward that she had known the attack was imminent but didn't want to "tip anything off" by delaying the Saturday news lid. Her credibility was never quite the same.

By the time Mike McCurry inherited the podium, the press operation had become increasingly crucial to the success or failure of any administration. On one level the growing bureaucracy was needed to deal with an expanding media universe, from all-news cable networks to online magazines to weekend chat shows to more than 1,200 talk-radio stations, all clamoring for interviews and attention. But it was also a natural outgrowth of television's need to dramatize stories, to focus the camera's eye on a single leader doing battle against the forces of politics and nature. Congress, with its 535 wrangling lawmakers and endless speechifying and molasses-like deliberations, made for terrible television. Executive departments, from HUD to Agriculture, were too widely dispersed to cover efficiently. It was so much easier to have your star reporter standing on the White House lawn, the North Portico over one shoulder, framing each government controversy as a victory or setback for the newsmaker-in-chief. There was a natural story line: president under fire, president traveling abroad, president at war, president on vacation. The constant tensions of the Cold War had injected an undercurrent of drama, for Kennedy or Nixon or Reagan might at any moment have to stand up to the Soviets or one of their allies, prompting the networks to go live. Superpower summits became an exercise in spin control. The White House press corps swelled to 2,000 accredited correspondents, all of whom had to be serviced by the press staff, and the most important among them had to be personally massaged by the press secretary, who, as much as any underling, personified the administration.

By the 1990s all manner of partisan magazines and radio talk shows and television shoutfests and Internet chat groups were filling the air with raw opinion and sheer attitude, making it harder for the president to connect with the public. The irony was unmistakable: Bill Clinton had all the accoutrements of high office, but he no longer commanded the public stage. McCurry and his colleagues spent endless hours honing the Clinton message, trying to hype each modest proposal into another news cycle, as if the president were some freshman congressman desperate for a flicker of recognition from the media machine. The competition was intense, for Bill Clinton dwells in the same murky precincts of celebrity as Dennis Rodman, Courtney Love, and David Letterman. In a hundred-channel world the president had become just another piece of programming to be marketed, and high ratings were hardly guaranteed.

From a distance, in the headlines and on the evening news, most Americans saw Bill Clinton as a singular figure, holding forth, posing with foreign leaders, making newsworthy pronouncements. But much of what they saw was stagecraft orchestrated by the likes of McCurry, Davis, Emanuel, Podesta, Baer, and Lewis, a small collection of loyalists who worked relentlessly at presenting the boss in a favorable light and deflecting the scandal questions that seemed constantly to nip at his heels. The mundane reality of White House life was that the top players spent perhaps half their time either talking to the press, plotting press strategy, or reviewing how their latest efforts had played in the press. They did not let Clinton have the briefest exposure to journalists without rehearsing what he would say to this or that question, lest he serve up an unscripted sound bite that would mar the day's story line. The modern presidency was, above all, a media presidency. Inside accounts tended to focus on who had Clinton's ear and who was feuding with whom, but the plain truth was that everyone was playing to the cameras, dishing "on background," trying to placate the journalists or find a way around their carping commentary. The daily coverage was a way of keeping score, of measuring the administration's progress in the messy and frustrating task of governing.

There was a time when a commander-in-chief was graded on the traditional measures of his relations with Congress, his dealings with foreign leaders, his ability to keep the economy moving and the nation at peace. Now the increasingly opinionated mass media had somehow become the arbiter of political success and the distiller of conventional wisdom. A president's words were endlessly sliced and diced by the self-appointed pundits, his every move filtered through someone else's ideological lens.

It was Clinton's misfortune to be the nation's most visible politician at a time when many people had tuned out the political world, disgusted with the endless machinations that seemed irrelevant to their lives. The political conventions and presidential debates of 1996 had drawn the smallest audiences of the television era. Most Americans had long since grown resigned to Clinton's seemingly inevitable victory over Bob Dole, but a majority still did not trust him. And as McCurry and his compatriots were acutely aware, a significant minority detested Clinton, viewing him as a lying, scheming, potsmoking crook. There was no shortage of conservative media outlets that were all too happy to stoke these fires of resentment, publishing a never-ending cascade of allegations about Clinton's personal life, a litany of overlapping scandals and the work of four special prosecutors. Hillary Rodham

Clinton, whose disdain for the press was even greater than her husband's, was an equally frequent target of the right-wing hit squads.

The president bore much of the responsibility for the palpable media distrust that greeted his every utterance. He made clear in the early days of the 1992 campaign that his memory was awfully selective, from his first, less than candid explanations of how he had avoided the Vietnam draft, how he had tried marijuana but "didn't inhale," and how he had "problems" in his marriage but did not have a twelve-year affair with Gennifer Flowers. He grew to resent reporters, to vent his anger in public outbursts, and the feeling was mutual. Most reporters were convinced that Clinton had an almost congenital inability to tell the unvarnished truth.

This atmosphere of distrust extended to the reporters' relationship with the men and women who accompanied Bill Clinton into the White House. What made the yawning gap between the Clintonites and the journalists all the more remarkable was that both were products of the baby boom culture and seemed, superficially at least, to share the same values. They all believed in activist government, the politicians because it gave them popular programs to create and the reporters because it gave them juicy stories to cover, a welcome relief from George Bush's in-box presidency. A few romances had even bloomed between journalists and White House operatives, generally unconsummated until the officeholders stepped down. But the generational affinity also bred a certain degree of contempt. Like squabbling lovers, the two sides got off to an acrimonious start even before Clinton's first inauguration, the traditional honeymoon shattered by a series of broken promises and miscalculations on issues from the canceled middle-class tax cut to the abandonment of Haitian refugees. Most of Clinton's aides had worked on Capitol Hill during the Reagan and Bush years, enjoying a warm relationship with reporters who were always looking for fodder to attack the administration. Now they were the incumbents, and the coziness had dissolved into mutual recriminations. If the press had a natural bias toward the Democrats, as so many Republicans fervently believed, Bill Clinton and his loyalists saw no evidence of it. They viewed the journalists as another special interest group—the Press Party—to be stroked and cajoled.

For all the animosity, the White House spinners and their cynical chroniclers were ultimately joined at the hip in a strangely symbiotic relationship. Both thrived on the frenetic pace of life at the center of the political universe, all the while grousing about the impact on their families and fantasizing about quitting. Both reveled in the insider gossip, even as they struggled to stay in touch with the real America. McCurry and company needed the press to peddle their message to the public, and the journalists needed an action-packed presidency on which to build their reputations and name recognition. Yet fireworks were inevitable when the two sides got in each other's way.

The reporters' frustrations began to boil over in the final weeks of the 1996 campaign, when allegations first surfaced that foreign funny money had been funneled to the Clinton camp and the White House seemed unable or unwilling to provide answers. McCurry, who usually insisted on steering such questions to the White House lawyers, reluctantly assumed control of the scandal defense just days before the election. Even as Clinton and his compatriots celebrated his triumphant reelection in Little Rock, McCurry knew that they had kept the lid on a pressure cooker that was ready to blow.

As the fundraising scandal gathered steam, McCurry and his new ally, Lanny Davis, bore the brunt of the hostile media inquiries. Within the White House they battled for disclosure, for getting the bad news behind them. But there were limits to how far McCurry and Davis would go, documents they would not release, questions they would not answer. They insisted day after day that Bill Clinton and Al Gore had done nothing out of the ordinary in dialing for dollars, sipping coffee with shady Chinese operatives, or renting out the Lincoln Bedroom, even when an avalanche of embarrassing documents decimated their denials. A few mistakes, they maintained, but nothing the other side didn't do in spades.

The White House partisans were convinced that the public was tuning it all out, that most Americans viewed this as the typical Belt-way follies, but the journalists were filled with moral fervor, determined that readers and viewers should care and that somehow they would make them care. The Clintonites were equally determined to rout the journalistic naysayers and prove that they could govern in this scandal-charged atmosphere. Neutralizing the media had become ground zero in the struggle for supremacy, and the spin would clearly be as important as the substance.

8.3 President's Criticism of Media Resonates, but Iraq Unease Grows (2003)

THE PEW RESEARCH CENTER FOR THE PEOPLE AND THE PRESS

INTRODUCTION

During the contentious debate on the war in Iraq, Democrats and Republicans traded charges about press coverage, with the former saying that the media were failing to ask the Bush administration tough questions about the situation in Iraq, and the latter insisting that the press was, if anything, unduly critical in its coverage of the war and unduly pessimistic about future progress

The Pew Research Center for the People and the Press, News Release, "President's Criticism of Media Resonates, but Iraq Unease Grows," October 21, 2003. Reprinted by permission of Pew Research Center for the People and the Press.

in Iraq. This report by the Pew Research Center for the People and the Press suggests that most Americans agreed with President Bush when he charged that the media were making the situation in Iraq seem worse than it actually was, but it also finds that opinion on the media "filter" divides along party lines, and that most citizens are increasingly worried about the U.S. military presence in Iraq.

■

Many Americans agree with President Bush that news reports from Iraq are making the situation there seem worse than it really is, but that has not stemmed rising public uneasiness over the U.S. military presence in Iraq. By contrast, the trend in economic attitudes presents a much less mixed—and much more negative—message for the White House.

Two-thirds of Americans (66%) say that jobs are hard to find in their communities, up from 59% in June 2002 and 44% a year earlier. Moreover, a 43% plurality believes Bush's economic policies are making the economy worse, compared with 31% who say they are not having much an effect and just 18% who feel his policies are improving the economy. Even Republicans do not give the president's economic policies a ringing endorsement. Just four-in-ten Republicans think those policies are having a positive impact, while the same number (40%) say they are not having much of an effect.

Jobs Harder to Find

	June 2001	June 2002	Oct 2003
	%	%	%
Job situation in your area			
Plenty of jobs	42	31	24
Difficult to find	44	59	66
Mixed/DK	14	10	10
	100	100	100

	Total	Rep	Dem	Ind
	%	%	%	%
Bush's policies' effect on economy				
Better	18	40	6	13
Worse	43	13	69	46
No effect	31	40	21	34
Don't know	8	7	4	7
	100	100	100	100

Pessimism about the job market has increased in most demographic groups, but Easterners, city residents and suburbanites are notably more negative than last year. And President Bush's overall approval rating, which now stands at 50%, is now even more correlated with assessments of the local job market. One piece of positive news for the administration is that just 16% of the public is paying very close attention to reports that a White House official may have leaked classified information about a CIA agent.

The latest Pew Research Center national survey, conducted Oct. 15–19 among 1,515 adults,* finds that nearly four-in-ten Americans (38%) believe the news media is painting too bleak a picture of the situation in Iraq, while 36% say media reports are fairly accurate and 14% say news organizations are showing the situation there to be better than it really is.

Job Market Appraisal and Bush Approval

		Think that . . .	
	Plenty of jobs	**Jobs hard to find**	**Diff**
June, 2002	%	%	
Approve	81	66	*+15*
Disapprove	13	24	
Don't know	6	10	
	100	100	
October, 2003			
Approve	75	41	*+34*
Disapprove	18	52	
Don't know	7	7	
	100	100	

But even as Bush's complaints about the media "filter" of news from Iraq ring true with many Americans, an increasing number believe U.S. forces in the country should be withdrawn as soon as possible—39% say that now, compared with 32% in late September. A 58% majority wants U.S. troops to remain in Iraq until a stable government is established, down from 64% last month.

A solid majority of Democrats (56%) now want the troops to be brought home as soon as possible, a 12-point increase in the past month. Republicans remain overwhelmingly opposed to a withdrawal (by 78% to 20%). Independents also oppose such a move, but 40% favor a troop withdrawal now, up from 33% last month.

---

*Results for the survey are based on telephone interviews conducted under the direction of Princeton Survey Research Associates among a nationwide sample of 1,515 adults, 18 years of age or older, during the period October 15–19, 2003. Based on the total sample, one can say with 95% confidence that the error attributable to sampling and other random effects is plus or minus 3 percentage points. For results based on either Form 1 (N= 735) or Form 2 (N = 780), the sampling error is plus or minus 4 percentage points.

In addition to sampling error, one should bear in mind that question wording and practical difficulties in conducting surveys can introduce error or bias into the findings of opinion polls.

What to Do in Iraq?

	Total	Rep	Dem	Ind
September, 2003	%	%	%	%
Keep troops in	64	81	52	64
Bring troops home	32	16	44	33
Don't know	4	3	4	3
	100	100	100	100
October, 2003				
Keep troops in	58	78	42	56
Bring troops home	39	20	56	40
Don't know	3	2	2	4
	100	100	100	100

Public support for the decision to go to war is slipping as well. Six-in-ten Americans (60%) now say it was the right decision to go to war in Iraq, down from 63% in September, 67% in July and 74% in April, shortly after the fall of Baghdad. However, the public's assessments of the military situation, which turned much more negative in the summer, have not changed much in the past few months. Fewer than one-in-five (16%) believe things in Iraq are going very well, with a plurality (44%) saying things are going fairly well; both numbers are largely unchanged from September (15% very well, 47% fairly well). In April, 61% of Americans said the military effort was going very well.

Assessing Iraq Coverage

	News reports are making the situation in Iraq seem . . .			
	Worse than really is	**Better than really is**	**About right**	**DK**
	%	%	%	%
Total	38	14	36	12 = 100
Party ID				
Republican	55	7	30	8 = 100
Democrat	28	16	45	11 = 100
Independent	34	19	34	13 = 100
Main source				
Newspaper	36	12	41	11 = 100
Radio	42	12	32	14 = 100
Network news	36	12	40	12 = 100
CNN	32	18	41	9 = 100
Fox News Chan.	55	10	28	7 = 100
War was . . .				
Right decision	45	11	35	9 = 100
Wrong decision	26	22	39	13 = 100

Republicans generally are more critical of the news media than are Democrats, and this is particularly the case in opinions of coverage of Iraq. A solid majority of Republicans (55%) believe news reports are painting an excessively negative picture of the situation in Iraq; only about half as many Democrats (28%) and a third of independents (34%) agree. Similarly, 55% of those who primarily rely on the Fox News Channel—a group that includes significantly more Republicans than audiences for other outlets—also fault the media for presenting too negative a picture of the situation in Iraq. Other news audiences have more mixed assessments of Iraq coverage: a plurality of CNN viewers (41%) think news reports from Iraq are generally accurate while 32% say those reports are making the situation seem worse than it really is.

Those who criticize news coverage of Iraq also are somewhat more likely than others to see the situation there in a positive light. Even so, a plurality of press critics (46%) say things in Iraq are going only fairly well; about the same percentage of those who think coverage has been fairly accurate agree (47%). Perceptions of media coverage of Iraq also are correlated with opinions on whether the U.S. made the right decision to go to war. Seven-in-ten (71%) of those who criticize news coverage of Iraq feel it was the right decision, compared with 58% of those who feel coverage has been generally accurate.

Views of Iraq by Opinion of Coverage

	News reports are making the situation in Iraq seem . . .		
	Worse than really is	Better than really is	About right
War is going . . .	%	%	%
Very well	27	6	11
Fairly well	46	36	47
Not too well	17	35	30
Not at all well	8	20	11
Don't know	2	3	1
	100	100	100
Number of cases	(570)	(202)	(565)

The poll also finds widespread criticism of media reporting on the Democratic presidential nomination race: just 30% give the coverage an excellent or good rating, while 54% say news organizations are doing only a fair or poor job. Four years ago, significantly more people (42%) rated reporting of the nomination race as good or excellent. Majorities in both parties, as well as independents, have a negative view of the nomination coverage, although more Democrats than Republicans think there is too little coverage of the race (24% vs. 11%).

NEWS INTEREST: IRAQ, ECONOMY

About four-in-ten Americans (38%) say they paid very close attention to news on the current situation in Iraq, down sharply from September (50%) but still more than any other news story this month. About a third (32%) tracked news on the economy very closely.

Despite massive media attention of the California recall election, it did not attract much attention outside of the West. Roughly a third (32%) of those in the West followed the election there very closely, followed by 22% in the East, 18% in the South and just 12% in the Midwest.

The reports that a White House official may have leaked classified information about a CIA agent also did not stir much national interest. Just 16% followed this story very closely; similar percentages of Democrats and Republicans tracked this story very closely (18%, 17% respectively).

News on sexual assault allegations against basketball star Kobe Bryant also attracted fairly little interest: 14% followed the story very closely, about the same as in September (17%). Twice as many African Americans as whites followed the Bryant story very closely (24% vs. 12%).

Top News Stories

	Following very closely
	%
Current situation in Iraq	38
Economic conditions	32
California Recall	20
White House leak	16
Kobe Bryant case	14
Democratic primary race	12

Roughly one-in-ten Americans (12%) closely followed news of the race for the Democratic presidential nomination, which is down somewhat from September (17%). Interest in the race is much higher among Democrats (19%) than among independents and Republicans (10%, 8% respectively).

8.4 Media Research Center Report: The Liberal Media (2004)

RICH NOYES

INTRODUCTION

This report by Rich Noyes, research director at the Media Research Center, summarizes surveys showing that leading journalists are far more likely to (1) say they are liberal rather than conservative, (2) vote Democratic rather than Republican, and (3) reject conservative views on many important political issues. The evidence is compelling so far as it goes, but does the report document that the media are liberal or that they have a "liberal bias"? The report focuses on "elites" in the media, but the vast majority of journalists do not meet that designation.

Also, *media* is a plural noun. America has an incredible array of news outlets, and average citizens can quickly find factual information and be exposed to competing views on just about any issue they might choose. Moreover, even elite journalists are part of a profession with norms that militate against bias, and are paid by organizations that compete with each other to attract attention, make money, and retain credibility with the public. For instance, the report indicates that 90 percent of 139 Washington bureau chiefs and congressional correspondents voted for Democrat Bill Clinton in 1992. Clinton was the most liberal of the three major candidates in that race (the other two being incumbent Republican President George H. W. Bush and Reform Party candidate and billionaire H. Ross Perot), but Clinton ran as a centrist "New Democrat" who advocated tougher criminal laws and several other positions that upset many liberals. More to the point, we do not know how, whether, or to what extent the media elites' votes for Clinton influenced their coverage of his presidency.

■

Over the next four months, the media establishment will play a central role in informing the public about the candidates and the issues. As the countdown to Election Day begins, it is important to remember the journalists who will help establish the campaign agenda are not an all-American mix of Democrats, Republicans and independents, but an elite group whose views veer sharply to the left.

Most journalists deny that their profession is stacked with liberals. "I've worked around reporters all my life," CBS anchor Dan Rather declared in an appearance on *The Late Late Show with Tom Snyder* back on February 8, 1995. "Most reporters, when you get to know them, would fall in the general category of kind of common sense moderates."

ABC's Peter Jennings echoed Rather. "We are largely in the center without particular axes to grind, without ideologies which are represented in our daily coverage—at least certainly not on purpose," Jennings told CNN's Larry King on May 15, 2001.

"The idea that we would set out, consciously or unconsciously, to put some kind of ideological framework over what we're doing is nonsense," NBC's Tom Brokaw similarly declared on C-SPAN just a few days later, on May 24, 2001.

But study after study shows that Rather, Jennings and Brokaw are wrong: the newsrooms of major media outlets are not filled with non-ideological "common sense moderates," nor do they reflect a diverse range of ideological viewpoints. Surveys over the past 25 years have consistently found journalists are much more liberal than [the] rest of America. Their voting habits are disproportionately Democratic, their views on issues such as abortion and gay rights are well to the left of most Americans and they are less likely to attend church or synagogue. When it comes to the free market, journalists have become increasingly pro-regulation over the past 20 years, with majorities endorsing activist government efforts to guarantee everyone a job and to reduce the income gap between rich and poor Americans.

This MRC [Media Research Center] Special Report summarizes the relevant data on journalists' attitudes, as well as polling showing how the American public's recognition of the media's liberal bias has grown over the years.

JOURNALISTS ON ELECTION DAY: PULLING THE DEMOCRATIC LEVER

Between 1964 and 1992, Republicans won the White House five times compared with three Democratic victories. But if only journalists' ballots were counted, the Democrats would have won every single election.

In their 1986 book, *The Media Elite*, political scientists S. Robert Lichter, Stanley Rothman and Linda S. Lichter reported the results of their survey of 240 journalists at the nation's top media outlets: ABC, CBS, NBC, PBS, the *New York Times, Washington Post, Wall Street Journal, Time, Newsweek* and *U.S. News & World Report*. When asked about their voting patterns, journalists admitted their preference for Democrats:

> Of those who say they voted for major party candidates, the proportion of leading journalists who supported the Democratic candidate never drops below 80 percent. In 1972, when more than 60 percent of all voters chose Nixon, over 80 percent among the media elite voted for McGovern. This does not appear to

reflect any unique aversion to Nixon. Despite the well-publicized tensions between the press and his administration, leading journalists in 1976 preferred
Carter over Ford by the same margin. In fact, in the Democratic landslide of
1964, journalists picked Johnson over Goldwater by a sixteen-to-one margin, or
94 to 6 percent.

Lichter's team focused on journalists at the very top national news organizations. Other surveys of journalists have discovered that the whole profession shares the same liberal bent, although the media elite's liberalism is the
most extreme:

- *Journalists Picked Carter over Reagan:* In 1982, scholars at California State
  University at Los Angeles asked reporters from the fifty largest newspapers for whom they voted in 1980. The breakdown: 51 percent cast a ballot for President Jimmy Carter and another 24 percent chose independent
  candidate (and liberal Republican Congressman) John Anderson. Only 25
  percent picked conservative Ronald Reagan, who won 51 percent of the
  public's vote that year.
- *Journalists Picked Mondale over Reagan:* In 1985, the *Los Angeles Times*
  polled news and editorial staffers at newspapers around the country,
  weighting the sample so that newspapers with large circulations were
  more heavily represented. Once again, pollsters discovered a heavy Democratic skew. When asked how they voted in the 1984 election, more than
  twice as many chose liberal Walter Mondale (58 percent) over the conservative incumbent Ronald Reagan (26 percent), even as the country picked
  Reagan in a 59 to 41 percent landslide.
- *The White House Press Corps Voted for Democrats:* In early 1995, Ken
  Walsh of *U.S. News & World Report* asked his fellow White House reporters
  to fill out a survey for a book he was writing; 28 returned his questionnaire.
  He concluded that "the White House press corps is overwhelmingly
  Democratic, confirming a stereotype often promoted by Republicans." Interestingly, he also learned how much reporters dislike being on the receiving end of personal inquiries: "Even though the survey was
  anonymous, many journalists declined to reveal their party affiliations,
  whom they voted for in recent presidential elections, and other data they
  regarded as too personal—even though they regularly pressure Presidents
  and other officials to make such disclosures," Walsh related in his 1996
  book, *Feeding the Beast: The White House Versus the Press.*

The Media Elite's Presidential Voting Record (1964–1976)

	Democrat	Republican
1964	94%	6%
1968	87%	13%
1972	81%	19%
1976	81%	19%

Source: The Media Elite, page 30.

So what did the few forthright scribes reveal? As with larger, more scientific surveys, Walsh discovered "evidence of an overwhelming preference for Democrats in presidential elections. In 1992, nine respondents voted for Clinton, two for George Bush, and one for independent Ross Perot. . . . In 1988, twelve voted for Democrat Michael Dukakis, only one for Bush. . . . In 1984, ten voted for Democrat Walter Mondale, [and] no one admitted voting for Ronald Reagan. . . . In 1980, eight voted for Democratic incumbent Jimmy Carter, two voted for Ronald Reagan, four voted for independent candidate John Anderson. . . . In 1976, eleven voted for Carter and two for Republican incumbent Gerald Ford." That adds up to 50 votes for Democrats and just seven for Republicans, a seven-to-one ratio in favor of the Democrats.

- *Huge Majorities for Dukakis and Clinton:* In 2001, Stanley Rothman and Amy E. Black updated the *Media Elite*'s survey of journalists, and learned that reporters continued to select Democrats. "Three-quarters of elite journalists (76.1 percent) . . . voted for Michael Dukakis in 1988, and even larger percentages (91.3 percent) . . . cast ballots for Bill Clinton in 1992," they reported in the Spring 2001 edition of *The Public Interest.* Voters were far less exuberant about those liberal candidates, as just 46 percent chose Dukakis and only 43 percent picked Clinton, who nevertheless won a three-way race.
- *Nine Out of Ten Reporters Voted for Clinton:* Rothman and Black's survey closely matched a Freedom Forum poll of Washington bureau chiefs and congressional correspondents, which found 89 percent had voted for Clinton in the 1992 election, compared with seven percent for President Bush and two percent for Ross Perot. "In no state or region, among no race or class, did support for Clinton predominate more lopsidedly than among this sample of 139 journalists who either cover Congress or head a Washington bureau," summarized Minneapolis *Star-Tribune* media writer Eric Black in an August 18, 1996 article.

The Freedom Forum was not aiming to embarrass journalists by quantifying their liberalism. The report, on relations between Capitol Hill staffers and Washington, D.C. reporters, was released in April 1996, and the data on journalists' voting pattern was buried in an appendix. The study's director, former *Chicago Tribune* reporter Elaine Povich, gamely asserted that reporters' heavy preference for Bill Clinton did not mean that journalists' were incapable of being objective. "One of the things about being a professional is that you attempt to leave your personal feelings aside as you do your work," Povich told the *Washington Times* on April 18, 1996.

Taken as a whole, these polls firmly establish the press's pattern of preferring Democrats at the voting booth. During the eight presidential elections for which data on the media's preferences are available, each Democrat won landslide support from journalists, sometimes by four-to-one or five-to-one margins. The percentage of reporters selecting the GOP candidate never exceeded 26 percent, even as the public chose Republicans in five of the eight elections, with margins of support ranging from a low of 38 percent (Bush in 1992) to a high of 61 percent (Nixon in 1972).

Nine Out of Ten Reporters Picked Clinton in 1992

	Journalists	Voters
Clinton	89%	43%
Bush	7%	38%
Perot	2%	19%

Source: Freedom Forum survey of 139 Washington bureau chiefs and congressional correspondents.

At a minimum, these statistics portray a media elite whose political thinking is to the left of most Americans. Hosting CNN's *Reliable Sources* on April 21, 1996, *Washington Post* media writer Howard Kurtz reacted to the Freedom Forum's poll: "Clearly anybody looking at those numbers, if they're even close to accurate, would conclude that there is a diversity problem in the news business, and it's not just the kind of diversity we usually talk about, which is not getting enough minorities in the news business, but political diversity, as well. Anybody who doesn't see that is just in denial."

FEW REPORTERS DESCRIBE THEMSELVES AS CONSERVATIVES

It's not just on Election Day: many of these same surveys and others have asked journalists to describe their political attitudes, and each time the researchers detected the same liberal skew:

- *Washington Reporters, 2-to-1 Liberal:* The Brookings Institution's Stephen Hess surveyed the Washington press corps in 1978 for his aptly-titled book, *The Washington Reporters.* More than twice as many journalists told Hess they were liberal (42 percent) as said they were conservative (19 percent). As for the public, even back in 1978 self-identified conservatives outnumbered liberals by a 31 to 26 percent margin, according to the General Social Survey taken annually by the National Opinion Research Center (NORC).
- *The Media Elite, 3-to-1 Liberal:* Lichter and Rothman's *Media Elite* surveys were conducted shortly after Hess's; they, too, showed top reporters disproportionately described themselves as liberals. According to the authors, "a majority [of leading journalists] see themselves as liberals. Fifty-four percent place themselves to the left of center, compared to only 17 percent who choose the right side of the spectrum. . . . When they rate their fellow workers, an even greater difference emerges. Fifty-six percent

say the people they work with are mostly on the Left, and only eight percent place their co-workers on the Right—a margin of seven to one."

- *Prominent News Organizations Are the Most Liberal:* A pair of Indiana University journalism professors, David H. Weaver and G. Cleveland Wilhoit, surveyed more than 1,000 journalists for their 1986 book, *The American Journalist.* Their poll included more than just top reporters, and, overall, they detected only a modest skew towards the liberal side of the spectrum—22 percent of those interviewed called themselves liberal, compared with 19 percent who said they were conservative.

But among 136 executives and staffers at "prominent news organizations"—the three weekly newsmagazines, the AP and UPI wire services and theBoston Globe—the tilt was much more pronounced, with liberals outnumbering conservatives by a more than two-to-one margin (32 to 12 percent). Only six percent of this group identified themselves as Republican, compared with seven times as many (43 percent) who said they were Democrats.

- *Nationwide, a 3-to-1 Liberal Advantage:* When the *Los Angeles Times* polled journalists around the country in 1985, 55 percent were willing to call themselves liberal, far outstripping the 17 percent who said they were conservative.
- *Becoming Even More Liberal:* In 1992, Weaver and Wilhoit conducted another national survey of journalists, and noticed the group had moved farther to the left. Writing in the Fall 1992 *Media Studies Journal,* they pointed out that 47 percent of journalists now said they were "liberal," while only 22 percent labeled themselves as "conservative."
- *Six Times as Many Liberals as Conservatives:* The Freedom Forum's 1996 poll of Washington bureau chiefs and congressional correspondents found 61 percent labeled themselves as "liberal" or "liberal to moderate," compared with only nine percent who chose either "conservative" or "moderate to conservative."
- *Business Reporters Are Liberal, Too:* As for the notion that business reporters might be more conservative than their brethren on the political beat, that possibility was put to rest by a 1988 poll by a New-York based newsletter, *The Journalist and Financial Reporting.* The survey of 151 business reporters from newspapers such as the *New York Times* and *USA Today,* and business-focused magazines such as *Money, Fortune* and *BusinessWeek,* discovered six times as many self-identified Democrats as Republicans— 54 percent versus nine percent.
- *Editors Group Noted the Growing Imbalance:* In 1996, the American Society of Newspaper Editors surveyed, 1,037 journalists at 61 newspapers. They learned that newsrooms were more ideologically unrepresentative than they had been in the late 1980s: "In 1996 only 15 percent of the newsroom labeled itself conservative/Republican or leaning in that direction, down from 22 percent in 1988," when the ASNE last conducted a comprehensive survey. Those identifying themselves as independent jumped

Self-Identified Political Leanings
of Newspaper Journalists, 1996

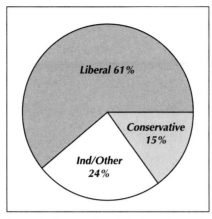

Source: *The Newspaper Journalists of the '90s,* American Society of Newspaper Editors (ASNE), 1997.

from 17 to 24 percent while the percent calling themselves "liberal/ Democrat" or leaning left held steady, down one point to 61 percent.

The ASNE report, *The Newspaper Journalists of the '90s,* also revealed that bigger—presumably more influential—newspapers had the most liberal staffs: "On papers of at least 50,000 circulation, 65 percent of the staffs are

Who Says They're Conservative?
Journalists vs. the Public

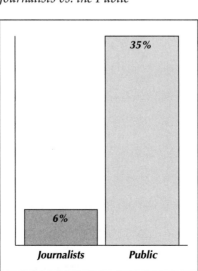

Source: *Public Perspective,* July/August 2001.

liberal/Democrat or lean that way. The split at papers of less than 50,000 is less pronounced: still predominantly liberal, but 51–23 percent."

In a sign that the media's desire for demographic diversity might result in even more solidly liberal newsrooms, ASNE also found that "women are more likely than men to fall into one of the liberal/Democrat categories," as just 11 percent said they were conservative or leaned that way. Minorities also "tend to be more liberal/Democrat," with a piddling 3 percent of blacks and 8 percent of Asians and Hispanics putting themselves on the right.

- **Public Far More Conservative:** In the July/August 2001 edition of the Roper Center for Public Opinion Research's journal *Public Perspective,* *Washington Post* national political reporter Thomas Edsall summarized the results of a poll of 301 media professionals taken earlier that year by Princeton Survey Research Associates (PRSA) and sponsored by the Kaiser Family Foundation. "The media diverge from both the public and from the policymaking community in terms of partisanship and ideology," Edsall reported. "Only a tiny fraction of the media identifies itself as either Republican (4 percent) or conservative (6 percent). This is in direct contrast to the public, which identifies itself as 28 percent Republican and 35 percent conservative."

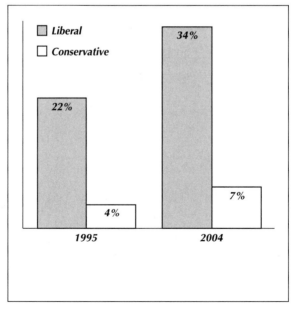

Media Growing More Liberal

Source: Pew Research Center, May 2004.

- *The Liberal Advantage Has Grown:* In May 2004, the Pew Research Center for the People and the Press released a survey of 547 journalists and news media executives, including 247 who worked for national news organizations. The poll reprised many of the questions asked by the same group (then called the Times Mirror Center for the People and the Press) back in 1995.

Pew found that the proportion of liberals in the national media had actually grown over the previous nine years, from 22 percent in 1995 to 34 percent in 2004. Meanwhile, the percentage of conservatives remained minuscule: just four percent in 1995, seven percent in 2004. As for local reporters, liberals outnumbered conservatives by a nearly two-to-one margin (23 to 12 percent).

Pew also asked journalists to name a news organization that seemed to cover the news from an especially liberal or especially conservative angle. When it came to a liberal new outlet, most of the national journalists were stumped. A fifth suggested the *New York Times* was liberal; ABC, CBS, CNN and NPR were each named by two percent. One percent of reporters said NBC was liberal.

But journalists did see ideology at one outlet: "The single news outlet that strikes most journalists as taking a particular ideological stance—either liberal or conservative—is Fox News Channel," Pew reported. More than two-thirds of national journalists (69 percent) tagged FNC as a conservative news organization, followed by the *Washington Times* (9 percent) and the *Wall Street Journal* (8 percent).

ISSUE BY ISSUE: ALWAYS LIBERAL

If the media elite were the pragmatic non-ideologues that Rather, Jennings and Brokaw described, one would expect to find occasional support for a few conservative policy positions, even if their overall bent was still left of center. But none of the surveys find that the national media are populated by independent thinkers mixing liberal and conservative positions. Instead, most of the journalistic elite offer reflexively liberal answers to practically every question a pollster can imagine.

The most exhaustive study of journalists attitudes on specific policy issues was the poll conducted by the *Los Angeles Times* in 1985, which asked a series of identical questions to more than 3,000 reporters and editors and nearly 3,000 members of the general public. The pollsters found journalists to be much more liberal than their audience. "Sometimes, the readers and the journalists take diametrically opposite positions—as on the question: 'Are you in favor of the way Ronald Reagan is handling his job as President?' Journalists say 'No' by a 2–1 margin; readers say 'Yes' by about the same margin," the *Times*'s David Shaw reported at the time.

On issue after issue, a greater proportion of journalists chose the liberal option. "Sometimes, the public voted overwhelmingly on one side of a question, and the newspaper journalists were evenly divided—as on the death penalty question. On several other issues—handgun control, affirmative action, 'withdrawing American investments from South Africa because of their apartheid policy,' 'allowing women to have an abortion' and 'hiring an employee regardless of whether he or she is a homosexual or a lesbian,'—both the journalists and their readers say 'Yes,' but the Yes/No margin among journalists is always much larger than it is among readers," Shaw explained.

"When the responses to all questions on social political issues are combined, the newspaper staffs provided 'liberal' answers 68 percent of the time and 'conservative' answers 22 percent of the time. Readers provided 'liberal' answers 43 percent of the time and 'conservative' answers 37 percent of the time—which makes the public much less liberal than the newspaper journalists," Shaw concluded.

While some of the questions posed by the *Times* in 1985—such as soliciting opinions about South African divestment—are not especially relevant today, many tap into the same liberal-conservative divisions that characterize today's politics. Only once, when asked whether they favored "government efforts to make reductions in the income gap between rich and poor," was the public's response more liberal than that of the press—although on that question news staffs still supported the liberal stance by a 50 to 39 percent margin. On every other policy issue the *Times* asked about—including abortion, prayer in school, affirmative action, defense spending and the death penalty—journalists embraced the liberal position more readily than the public at large. (See chart.)

The Press vs. the Public

		Journalists	Public
Increase Defense Spending	Support	15%	38%
	Oppose	80%	52%
Government Regulation of Business	Support	49%	22%
	Oppose	41%	51%
Government Should Reduce Income Inequality	Support	50%	55%
	Oppose	39%	23%
Prayer in Public Schools	Support	25%	74%
	Oppose	67%	19%
Legalized Abortion	Support	82%	51%
	Oppose	14%	42%
Death Penalty for Convicted Murderers	Support	47%	75%
	Oppose	47%	17%
Stricter Handgun Control	Support	78%	50%
	Oppose	19%	41%

Affirmative Action	Support	81%	57%
	Oppose	14%	21%
Hiring Homosexuals	Support	89%	56%
	Oppose	7%	31%

Source: February 1985 *Los Angeles Times* poll of general public and news and editorial staffers at 621 U.S. newspapers.

- **Pro-Welfare State, Pro-Abortion:** The *Times* poll matched the findings of surveys conducted by Robert Lichter and his team for *The Media Elite.* One out of every eight reporters (13 percent) told the Lichters they supported public ownership of major corporations—a fairly remarkable percentage, although five times as many rejected such unvarnished socialism. A majority of journalists favored government activism in the economic arena to aid the poor and provide jobs.

  "These attitudes mirror the traditional perspective of American liberals who (unlike many European social democrats) accept an essentially capitalist economic framework, even as they endorse the welfare state," the authors concluded.

  When it came to issues such as abortion, homosexuality and affirmative action, the media elite revealed solidly liberal views. Nine out of ten journalists believed a woman should have a legal right to an abortion and eight out of ten backed "strong affirmative action for blacks." At the same time, Lichter's research found that "75 percent disagree that homosexuality is wrong, and an even larger proportion, 85 percent, uphold the right of homosexuals to teach in public schools."

  Years before Bill Clinton's scandals made adultery a top news story, the media elite were expressing tolerance on the subject: "54 percent do not regard adultery as wrong, and only 15 percent strongly agree that extramarital affairs are wrong," the authors disclosed. "Thus, members of the media elite emerge as strong supporters of sexual freedom, and as natural opponents of groups like the Moral Majority."

- **Journalists Less Religious than Public:** In their 1992 study, Weaver and Wilhoit asked a broad sample of 1,156 journalists for their views on abortion, and found very few who outright opposed the procedure. "More than half (51 percent) of the journalists said abortion should be legal under any circumstance; 40 percent said it should be legal under certain circumstances, and four percent said all abortion should be illegal. The U.S. public at large appears to be much less likely than U.S. journalists to see unrestricted abortion as legal and more likely to say it should always be illegal," they reported.

Weaver and Wilhoit also discovered that journalists and the public differed on the importance of religion: "Our survey results show that the percentage

Few Media Pro-Lifers

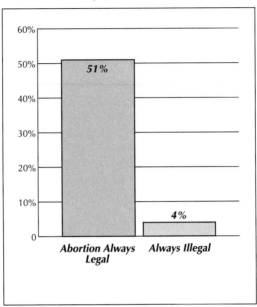

Source: *Media Studies Journal*, Fall 1992, p. 75.

of journalists rating religion or religious beliefs as 'very important' is substantially lower (38 percent) than the percentages in the overall U.S. population (61 percent). But 34 percent of journalists say religion is 'somewhat important,' compared to 30 percent of the population."

Those figures actually indicate a more pious press than Lichter and his team found in the early 1980s, when "exactly half" of top journalists did not identify with any religion and "only 8 percent go to church or synagogue weekly, and 86 percent seldom or never attend religious services."

- *Journalists More Pro-Gay than Public:* In 1995, the Times Mirror Center found a values gap when they compared the views of 228 top journalists and media executives to other groups: "The public is divided as to whether homosexuality should be accepted (41 percent) or discouraged (53 percent), as are members of Congress, top business executives and local community leaders. But members of the national media feel it should be accepted by an 83 to 4 percent margin, and this view is almost as prevalent among the local media (75 percent to 14 percent)."

- *Reporters Wish They Were Nicer to Clinton, Tougher on Bush:* The Times Mirror poll was conducted during the middle of Bill Clinton's first term in the White House. When it came to rating the media coverage, reporters were worried they had been too aggressive. More than a third of the jour-

Should Homosexuality Be Accepted or Discouraged by Society?

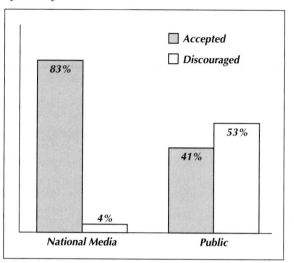

Source: Times Mirror Center poll of national journalists and the general public, March 1995.

nalists (35 percent) felt there had been too much coverage of the Clintons' Whitewater scandals, versus five percent who felt there had been too few Whitewater stories.

At the same time, about half of the national media (48 percent) said they felt there had been too few stories about Clinton's "achievements," compared with only two percent who felt the media had over-reported Clinton's achievements. But when the Pew Research Center tested journalists in 2004, 55 percent complained that the media were "not critical enough" of President George W. Bush, compared to only eight percent who thought the press had been "too critical."

The 2004 Pew report revealed how these assessments were based on the journalists' ideology. "Liberals who work in national and local news organizations overwhelmingly feel the press has not been critical enough of the Bush administration." Pew reported, "but most [of the media's] conservatives (53%) think the press has been too critical." That same poll found that the media's liberals outnumbered the conservatives by a five to one margin.

- *Elite Journalists Pro-Abortion, Pro-Gay:* Rothman and Black's 2001 update to the original *Media Elite* surveys found that reporters continued to profess liberal attitudes on social issues. Nearly all of the news media elites surveyed (97 percent) agreed that a woman should have the legal right to choose whether or not to have an abortion, and 75 percent agreed that "homosexuality is as acceptable as heterosexuality."

On adultery, however, the media elite had become stricter over the years, as 78 percent now agreed that it is "wrong for a married person to have sexual relations with someone other than his or her spouse." (The earlier *Media Elite* survey showed a majority actually disagreed with this premise.)

When it came to economic issues, Rothman and Black expressed some surprise at the continued liberalism of reporters: "Despite the discrediting of centrally planned economies produced by the collapse of the Soviet Union and other Communist regimes, attitudes about government control of the economy have not changed very much since the 1980s," they marveled in their 2001 *Public Interest* article. "The cultural elite maintains strong levels of support for a more egalitarian society in which government plays a substantial role."

Indeed, the updated survey found the media's preference for government activism had grown over the years. "When asked if the government should work to ensure that everyone has a job," more than seven out of ten journalists (71 percent) agreed, up from 48 percent in the original surveys. Similarly, only 39 percent of reporters agreed that "less government regulation would be good for business," whereas 63 percent had expressed that view previously. Three-fourths of journalists (75 percent) agreed that "government should work to reduce the gap between the rich and the poor," a slight increase from the 68 percent who felt that way earlier.

The conclusion that liberals dominate the national media is unassailable. Every major survey of journalists from 1970s to the present day has found that reporters are more liberal on the issues, more likely to identify themselves as liberal, and more likely to vote for a liberal presidential candidate than the rest of the country.

CHAPTER 9

The Congress

*C*ongress is the first branch of American national government. With powers
flowing from Article I of the Constitution, Congress is the people's branch.
Congress mediates popular interests through its *bicameral legislature*—the
House of Representatives, which allocates seats to states based on population,
and the Senate, which assigns two elected officials to each state regardless
of size. The structure of Congress balances individual, state, and national
issues.

Constitutional debates about Congress's size and its members' terms of office still resonate strongly today. In 1789, the House of Representatives had
sixty-five members, with the allocation of seats among the states determined
by a decennial census. Since the early twentieth century, Congress has
capped the size of the House at 435 members, almost seven times its original
size. Representatives today each have more than half a million constituents,
far beyond the minimum of thirty thousand required in the Constitution. The
House is supposed to be the chamber of Congress that is closest to the people, yet no representative can truly understand or effectively advocate for the
concerns of such a large number of constituents. Furthermore, representatives
serve two-year terms, which means they must concentrate on reelection for at
least the second year of each term. The combination of large constituencies
and frequent elections poses significant challenges for members of the House
of Representatives.

As David R. Mayhew argues in this chapter, House members meet this
challenge by behaving as if reelection were their primary, if not their sole, career objective. While representatives value many things—maintaining good
relations with colleagues, advancing good public policy, being well regarded
by the media—they are governed, or so Mayhew suggests, by considerations
of electoral self-interest. He explores "the electoral connection" between
what legislators "do in office and their need to be reelected." Thus, House
members, whether recently elected by a narrow margin or long-time incumbents in safe seats, tend to do three things, all at least partially calculated for
electoral effect: Take positions on issues, claim credit for successes, and advertise themselves.

While Mayhew's view may seem cynical to some, it captures how most
members of Congress behave most of the time. It also may help to explain one
of the most striking features of the modern House: Most incumbents are never
defeated and serve long terms. In the nineteenth century, a large fraction
(often a majority) of congressional members served only one term. Between
1863 and 1969, the proportion of first-term members in the House fell from
58 percent to just 8 percent.

Even in the historic midterm congressional elections of 1994, which saw
Republicans gain control of the House after four decades of Democratic

dominance, over 90 percent of all House members who ran for reelection were reelected. In 2000, one of the most hotly contested elections in recent history, only 6 of the 339 House incumbents who ran for reelection lost. Thus, even though public opinion polls consistently find great mass displeasure with Congress and "Washington politics," most House members are liked well enough by their constituents to stay in office for as long as they choose. As has been argued, Americans hate Congress but love their congressman (or congresswoman).

Not surprisingly, safe seats are less common in the U.S. Senate, where fewer than half of incumbents in each election cycle win with as much as 60 percent of the vote. Concerns about the Senate typically focus on the infrequency of elections as well as the guarantee of two senators for each state, regardless of size. With elections every six years, senators have the comparative luxury of concentrating on policymaking after taking office, without having to focus immediately on an upcoming election. The Framers designed the Senate with this purpose in mind, ensuring that members would have the opportunity to initiate and review policies and remain sensitive to the specific needs of their respective states while also embodying a long-term national perspective.

The Senate was fashioned as a less popular branch than the House through the election process as well. The Constitution originally called for state legislatures to elect senators, and direct popular elections for the Senate were not instituted nationwide until the ratification of the Sixteenth Amendment in 1913. Bringing state legislatures into elections had the dual purpose of maintaining some distance from popular pressures and ensuring that senators were well versed in state matters. After all, the Senate was the only institution in the federal government where small states would be equal in power to large states.

Opponents of the Constitution feared that members of Congress would come from such a small segment of the population that they would not be able to represent their constituents' interests effectively. To them, the Federalist No. 57 replies that "[d]uty, gratitude, interest, ambition itself" will bind members of the House of Representatives to their constituents. Furthermore, the Federalist No. 63 notes that "a sense of national character" is required in the federal government, which the Senate will provide.

The responsibilities of Congress today are greater than the Framers could possibly have envisioned. With year-round sessions, Congress is a full-time organization, and Washington, D.C., is the center of national decision-making, hardly the city where governance took place periodically in the nineteenth century. Still, members of Congress must return to their home district or state frequently, so they can keep in touch with their constituents' concerns. While long-standing members of Congress usually have homes in both places, new members sometimes commute weekly to the capital, with their families remaining at home.

Richard F. Fenno, Jr., reports in this chapter on how a small but diverse group of House members behave when at home in their districts, and he explores the linkages between their "home styles" versus what they do when in Washington (the issues they tackle, their degree of bipartisanship, and much more). The picture that emerges is considerably more complex than one sees when focusing, as Mayhew does, on the members' "electoral connection." For example, members not only advertise themselves to constituents but also engage routinely in "two-way communication" and "reaching" constituents personally: "Members of Congress believe, if anything, that two-way communication is more valued by their constituents than policy congruence"—or more important, than simply voting the way most constituents want.

But is having a winning "home style" the same thing as being what James Madison, in the Federalist No. 10 (see Chapter 1), termed a "proper guardian of the public weal" or one among "enlightened statesmen" dedicated to achieving the "common good"? Many Americans believe that Congress, the first branch, has become Congress, the failed branch. The legislative process, one frequently hears, is dominated by special interests, or what Madison would have us call "factions."

Another development that has distressed many Congress watchers is the ideological polarization between the two major parties. As the three reading selections from *CQ Weekly* indicate, both in the House and in the Senate, ideological and partisan feuding has frustrated effective congressional oversight of intelligence-gathering, engulfed the judicial nomination process, eroded institutional norms governing committee assignments, and enervated interpersonal civility. Finally, as the op-ed by Norman Ornstein suggests, three years after the 9/11 attacks—"a day in which the U.S. House narrowly dodged a disaster that could have left Congress without a working quorum for months at the worst possible time"—Congress had not yet acted to "provide a continuing constitutional system in the event of a catastrophic terrorist attack."

9.1 The Federalist No. 57 (1788)

ALEXANDER HAMILTON OR JAMES MADISON*

INTRODUCTION

The purpose of the House of Representatives is evident in its name: to represent the American people. As James Madison explains in the Federalist No. 10 (reading 1.4), the size of the United States made direct democracy impracticable; hence, elected representatives would be necessary to conduct public affairs. The Anti-Federalists, however, were skeptical that the House of Representatives, as designed in the Constitution, could serve the public interest without threatening people's natural rights. In particular, the Anti-Federalists believed that representatives should be subject to annual elections, to ensure that their constituents could make frequent evaluations of their performance. The Anti-Federalists also argued that each representative should have a small group of constituents, to permit closer ties and thus promote more accurate representation of people's interests.

The Federalist No. 57 addresses the underlying fear behind these concerns—namely, that representatives would be more focused on their particular interests than the public good. It argues that the election process itself will produce representatives who are committed to public service and who will not sacrifice popular interests for their own private concerns.

■

To the People of the State of New York:

The third charge against the House of Representatives is, that it will be taken from that class of citizens which will have least sympathy with the mass of the people, and be most likely to aim at an ambitious sacrifice of the many to the aggrandizement of the few. Of all the objections which have been framed against the federal Constitution, this is perhaps the most extraordinary. Whilst the objection itself is levelled against a pretended oligarchy, the principle of it strikes at the very root of republican government. The aim of every political constitution is, or ought to be, first to obtain for rulers men who possess most wisdom to discern, and most virtue to pursue, the common good of the society; and in the next place, to take the most effectual precautions for keeping

---

*Alexander Hamilton and James Madison both participated in the drafting of the *Federalist Papers* (along with John Jay). The author of this paper has not been identified definitively, though many scholars have concluded that it was written by Madison.

"The Federalist No. 57" (1788; Yale Law School Avalon Project, 1996), http://www.yale.edu/lawweb/avalon/federal/fed57.htm.

them virtuous whilst they continue to hold their public trust. The elective mode of obtaining rulers is the characteristic policy of republican government. The means relied on in this form of government for preventing their degeneracy are numerous and various. The most effectual one, is such a limitation of the term of appointments as will maintain a proper responsibility to the people.

Let me now ask what circumstance there is in the constitution of the House of Representatives that violates the principles of republican government, or favors the elevation of the few on the ruins of the many? Let me ask whether every circumstance is not, on the contrary, strictly conformable to these principles, and scrupulously impartial to the rights and pretensions of every class and description of citizens? Who are to be the electors of the federal representatives? Not the rich, more than the poor; not the learned, more than the ignorant; not the haughty heirs of distinguished names, more than the humble sons of obscurity and unpropitious fortune. The electors are to be the great body of the people of the United States. They are to be the same who exercise the right in every State of electing the corresponding branch of the legislature of the State. Who are to be the objects of popular choice? Every citizen whose merit may recommend him to the esteem and confidence of his country. No qualification of wealth, of birth, of religious faith, or of civil profession is permitted to fetter the judgement or disappoint the inclination of the people. If we consider the situation of the men on whom the free suffrages of their fellow-citizens may confer the representative trust, we shall find it involving every security which can be devised or desired for their fidelity to their constituents. In the first place, as they will have been distinguished by the preference of their fellow-citizens, we are to presume that in general they will be somewhat distinguished also by those qualities which entitle them to it, and which promise a sincere and scrupulous regard to the nature of their engagements. In the second place, they will enter into the public service under circumstances which cannot fail to produce a temporary affection at least to their constituents. There is in every breast a sensibility to marks of honor, of favor, of esteem, and of confidence, which, apart from all considerations of interest, is some pledge for grateful and benevolent returns. Ingratitude is a common topic of declamation against human nature; and it must be confessed that instances of it are but too frequent and flagrant, both in public and in private life. But the universal and extreme indignation which it inspires is itself a proof of the energy and prevalence of the contrary sentiment.

In the third place, those ties which bind the representative to his constituents are strengthened by motives of a more selfish nature. His pride and vanity attach him to a form of government which favors his pretensions and gives him a share in its honors and distinctions. Whatever hopes or projects might be entertained by a few aspiring characters, it must generally happen that a great proportion of the men deriving their advancement from their influence with the people, would have more to hope from a preservation of the favor, than from innovations in the government subversive of the authority of the people. All these securities, however, would be found very insufficient without the restraint of frequent elections. Hence, in the fourth place, the House of Representatives is so constituted as to support in the members an habitual recollection of their dependence on the people. Before the sentiments impressed on their minds by the mode of their elevation can be effaced by the exercise of power, they will be compelled to anticipate the moment when their power is to cease, when their exercise of it is to be reviewed, and when they must descend to the level from which they were raised; there forever to remain unless a faithful discharge of their trust shall have established their title to a renewal of it. I will add, as a fifth circumstance in the situation of the House of Representatives, restraining them from oppressive measures, that they can make no law which will not have its full operation on themselves and their friends, as well as on the great mass of the society.

This has always been deemed one of the strongest bonds by which human policy can connect the rulers and the people together. It creates between them that communion of interests and sympathy of sentiments, of which few governments have furnished examples; but without which every government degenerates into tyranny. If it be asked, what is to restrain the House of Representatives from making legal discriminations in favor of themselves and a particular class of the society? I answer: the genius of the whole system; the nature of just and constitutional laws; and above all, the vigilant and manly spirit which actuates the people of America, a spirit which nourishes freedom, and in return is nourished by it. If this spirit shall ever be so far debased as to tolerate a law not obligatory on the legislature, as well as on the people, the people will be prepared to tolerate any thing but liberty. Such will be the relation between the House of Representatives and their constituents. Duty, gratitude, interest, ambition itself, are the chords by which they will be bound to fidelity and sympathy with the great mass of the people.

It is possible that these may all be insufficient to control the caprice and wickedness of man. But are they not all that government will admit, and that human prudence can devise? Are they not the genuine and the characteristic means by which republican government provides for the liberty and happiness of the people? Are they not the identical means on which every State government in the Union relies for the attainment of these important ends? What then are we to understand by the objection which this paper has combated? What are we to say to the men who profess the most flaming zeal for republican government, yet boldly impeach the fundamental principle of it; who pretend to be champions for the right and the capacity of the people to choose their own rulers, yet maintain that they will prefer those only who will immediately and infallibly betray the trust committed to them? Were the objection to be read by one who had not seen the mode prescribed by the Constitution for the choice of representatives, he could suppose nothing less than that some unreasonable qualification of property was annexed to the right of suffrage; or that the right of eligibility was limited to persons of particular families or fortunes; or at least that the mode prescribed by the State constitutions was in some respect or other, very grossly departed from. We have seen how far such a supposition would err, as to the two first points. Nor would it, in fact, be less erroneous as to the last.

The only difference discoverable between the two cases is, that each representative of the United States will be elected by five or six thousand citizens; whilst in the individual States, the election of a representative is left to about as many hundreds. Will it be pretended that this difference is sufficient to justify an attachment to the State governments, and an abhorrence to the federal government? If this be the point on which the objection turns, it deserves to be examined. Is it supported by *reason?* This cannot be said, without maintaining that five or six thousand citizens are less capable of choosing a fit representative, or more liable to be corrupted by an unfit one, than five or six hundred. Reason, on the contrary, assures us, that as in so great a number a fit representative would be most likely to be found, so the choice would be less likely to be diverted from him by the intrigues of the ambitious or the bribes of the rich. Is the *consequence* from this doctrine admissible? If we say that five or six hundred citizens are as many as can jointly exercise their right of suffrage, must we not deprive the people of the immediate choice of their public servants, in every instance where the administration of the government does not require as many of them as will amount to one for that number of citizens? Is the doctrine warranted by *facts?* It was shown in the last paper, that the real representation in the British House of Commons very little exceeds the proportion of one for every thirty thousand inhabitants. Besides a variety of powerful causes not existing here, and which favor in that country the pretensions of rank and wealth, no person is eligible as a representative of a county, unless he possess real estate of the clear value of six hundred pounds sterling per year; nor of a city or borough, unless he possess a like estate of half that annual value.

To this qualification on the part of the county representatives is added another on the part of the county electors, which restrains the right of suffrage to persons having a freehold estate of the annual value of more than twenty pounds sterling, according to the present rate of money. Notwithstanding these unfavorable circumstances, and notwithstanding some very unequal laws in the British code, it cannot be said that the representatives of the nation have elevated the few on the ruins of the many. But we need not resort to foreign experience on this subject. Our own is explicit and decisive. The districts in New Hampshire in which the senators are chosen immediately by the people, are nearly as large as will be necessary for her representatives in the Congress. Those of Massachusetts are larger than will be necessary for that purpose; and those of New York still more so. In the last State the members of Assembly for the cities and counties of New York and Albany are elected by very nearly as many voters as will be entitled to a representative in the Congress, calculating on the number of sixty-five representatives only. It makes no difference that in these senatorial districts and counties a number of representatives are voted for by each elector at the same time. If the same electors at the same time are capable of choosing four or five representatives, they cannot be incapable of choosing one.

Pennsylvania is an additional example. Some of her counties, which elect her State representatives, are almost as large as her districts will be by which her federal representatives will be elected. The city of Philadelphia is supposed to contain between fifty and sixty thousand souls. It will therefore form nearly two districts for the choice of federal representatives. It forms, however, but one county, in which every elector votes for each of its representatives in the State legislature. And what may appear to be still more directly to our purpose, the whole city actually elects a *single member* for the executive council. This is the case in all the other counties of the State. Are not these facts the most satisfactory proofs of the fallacy which has been employed against the branch of the federal government under consideration? Has it appeared on trial that the senators of New Hampshire, Massachusetts, and New York, or the executive council of Pennsylvania, or the members of the Assembly in the two last States, have betrayed any peculiar disposition to sacrifice the many to the few, or are in any respect less worthy of their places than the representatives and magistrates appointed in other States by very small divisions of the people? But there are cases of a stronger complexion than any which I have yet quoted. One branch of the legislature of Connecticut is so constituted that each member of it is elected by the whole State. So is the governor of that State, of Massachusetts, and of this State, and the president of New Hampshire. I leave every man to decide whether the result of any one of these experiments can be said to countenance a suspicion, that a diffusive mode of choosing representatives of the people tends to elevate traitors and to undermine the public liberty.

PUBLIUS

9.2 The Federalist No. 63 (1788)
ALEXANDER HAMILTON OR JAMES MADISON*

INTRODUCTION

Given the Anti-Federalists' concerns about biennial elections in the House of Representatives, their fears about six-year terms in the Senate were, not surprisingly, even greater. The Framers purposely designed the Senate differently from the House because they expected the Senate to serve different purposes. The Senate was created to represent states' interests—hence, the original decision to have state legislatures select senators. The Senate also would give all states, large and small, an equal voice, as many Framers feared that governing by majority vote alone would produce a tyranny of the majority.

Perhaps most importantly, the Senate would have the opportunity to explore policy questions fully, to review comprehensively the multitude of issues that the House of Representatives would raise. George Washington famously remarked to Thomas Jefferson that the Senate would serve to cool the passions of the more populous chamber of Congress, much like pouring tea into a saucer to cool it. (The remark was made as the two dined together.) Because senators were expected to focus more on national concerns than their counterparts in the House, the Constitution reserves certain important responsibilities to the Senate alone, such as the power to approve presidential nominations for executive branch positions and the federal judiciary (by a majority vote), and the power to ratify treaties (by a two-thirds' vote). The Federalist No. 63 explains that the Senate requires "sufficient permanency" to perform these responsibilities effectively.

■

To the People of the State of New York:

A fifth desideratum, illustrating the utility of a senate, is the want of a due sense of national character. Without a select and stable member of the government, the esteem of foreign powers will not only be forfeited by an unenlightened and variable policy, proceeding from the causes already mentioned, but the national councils will not possess that sensibility to the opinion of the

---

*Alexander Hamilton and James Madison both participated in the drafting of the *Federalist Papers* (along with John Jay). The author of this paper has not been identified definitively, though many scholars have concluded that it was written by Madison.

"The Federalist No. 63" (1788, Yale Law School Avalon Project, 1996), http://www.yale.edu/lawweb/avalon/federal/fed63.htm.

world, which is perhaps not less necessary in order to merit, than it is to obtain, its respect and confidence.

An attention to the judgment of other nations is important to every government for two reasons: the one is, that, independently of the merits of any particular plan or measure, it is desirable, on various accounts, that it should appear to other nations as the offspring of a wise and honorable policy; the second is, that in doubtful cases, particularly where the national councils may be warped by some strong passion or momentary interest, the presumed or known opinion of the impartial world may be the best guide that can be followed. What has not America lost by her want of character with foreign nations; and how many errors and follies would she not have avoided, if the justice and propriety of her measures had, in every instance, been previously tried by the light in which they would probably appear to the unbiased part of mankind?

Yet however requisite a sense of national character may be, it is evident that it can never be sufficiently possessed by a numerous and changeable body. It can only be found in a number so small that a sensible degree of the praise and blame of public measures may be the portion of each individual; or in an assembly so durably invested with public trust, that the pride and consequence of its members may be sensibly incorporated with the reputation and prosperity of the community. The half-yearly representatives of Rhode Island would probably have been little affected in their deliberations on the iniquitous measures of that State, by arguments drawn from the light in which such measures would be viewed by foreign nations, or even by the sister States; whilst it can scarcely be doubted that if the concurrence of a select and stable body had been necessary, a regard to national character alone would have prevented the calamities under which that misguided people is now laboring.

I add, as a sixth defect the want, in some important cases, of a due responsibility in the government to the people, arising from that frequency of elections which in other cases produces this responsibility. This remark will, perhaps, appear not only new, but paradoxical. It must nevertheless be acknowledged, when explained, to be as undeniable as it is important.

Responsibility, in order to be reasonable, must be limited to objects within the power of the responsible party, and in order to be effectual, must relate to operations of that power, of which a ready and proper judgment can be formed by the constituents. The objects of government may be divided into two general classes: the one depending on measures which have singly an immediate and sensible operation; the other depending on a succession of well-chosen and well-connected measures, which have a gradual and perhaps unobserved operation. The importance of the latter description to the collective and permanent welfare of every country, needs no explanation. And yet it is evident that an assembly elected for so short a term as to be unable to provide more than one or two links in a chain of measures, on which the general welfare may essentially depend, ought not to be answerable for the final result, any more than a steward or tenant, engaged for one year, could be justly made to answer for places or improvements which could not be accomplished in less than half a dozen years. Nor is it possible for the people to estimate the *share* of influence which their annual assemblies may respectively have on events resulting from the mixed transactions of several years. It is sufficiently difficult to preserve a personal responsibility in the members of a *numerous* body, for such acts of the body as have an immediate, detached, and palpable operation on its constituents.

The proper remedy for this defect must be an additional body in the legislative department, which, having sufficient permanency to provide for such objects as require a continued attention, and a train of measures, may be justly and effectually answerable for the attainment of those objects.

Thus far I have considered the circumstances which point out the necessity of a well-constructed Senate only as they relate to the representatives of the people. To a people as little blinded by prejudice or corrupted by flattery as those whom I address, I shall not scruple to add, that such an institution may be sometimes necessary as a defense to the people against their own temporary errors and delusions. As the cool and deliberate sense of the community ought, in all governments, and actually will, in all free governments, ultimately prevail over the views of its rulers; so there are particular moments in public affairs when the people, stimulated by some irregular passion, or some illicit advantage, or misled by the artful misrepresentations of interested men, may call for measures which they themselves will afterwards be the most ready to lament and condemn. In these critical moments, how salutary will be the interference of some temperate and respectable body of citizens, in order to check the misguided career, and to suspend the blow meditated by the people against themselves, until reason, justice, and truth can regain their authority over the public mind? What bitter anguish would not the people of Athens have often escaped if their government had contained so provident a safeguard against the tyranny of their own passions? Popular liberty might then have escaped the indelible reproach of decreeing to the same citizens the hemlock on one day and statues on the next.

It may be suggested, that a people spread over an extensive region cannot, like the crowded inhabitants of a small district, be subject to the infection of violent passions, or to the danger of combining in pursuit of unjust measures. I am far from denying that this is a distinction of peculiar importance. I have, on the contrary, endeavored in a former paper to show, that it is one of the principal recommendations of a confederated republic. At the same time, this advantage ought not to be considered as superseding the use of auxiliary precautions. It may even be remarked, that the same extended situation, which will exempt the people of America from some of the dangers incident to lesser republics, will expose them to the inconveniency of remaining for a longer time under the influence of those misrepresentations which the combined industry of interested men may succeed in distributing among them.

It adds no small weight to all these considerations, to recollect that history informs us of no long-lived republic which had not a senate. Sparta, Rome, and Carthage are, in fact, the only states to whom that character can be applied. In each of the two first there was a senate for life. The constitution of the senate in the last is less known. Circumstantial evidence makes it probable that it was not different in this particular from the two others. It is at least certain, that it had some quality or other which rendered it an anchor against popular fluctuations; and that a smaller council, drawn out of the senate, was appointed not only for life, but filled up vacancies itself. These examples, though as unfit for the imitation, as they are repugnant to the genius, of America, are, notwithstanding, when compared with the fugitive and turbulent existence of other ancient republics, very instructive proofs of the necessity of some institution that will blend stability with liberty. I am not unaware of the circumstances which distinguish the American from other popular governments, as well ancient as modern; and which render extreme circumspection necessary, in reasoning from the one case to the other. But after allowing due weight to this consideration, it may still be maintained, that there are many points of similitude which render these examples not unworthy of our attention. Many of the defects, as we have seen, which can only be supplied by a senatorial institution, are common to a numerous assembly frequently elected by the people, and to the people themselves. There are others peculiar to the former, which require the control of such an institution. The people can never wilfully betray their own interests; but they may possibly be betrayed by the representatives of the people; and the danger will be evidently greater where the whole legislative trust is lodged in the hands of one body of men, than where the concurrence of separate and dissimilar bodies is required in every public act.

The difference most relied on, between the American and other republics, consists in the principle of representation; which is the pivot on which the former move, and which is supposed to have been unknown to the latter, or at least to the ancient part of them. The use which has been made of this difference, in reasonings contained in former papers, will have shown that I am disposed neither to deny its existence nor to undervalue its importance. I feel the less restraint, therefore, in observing, that the position concerning the ignorance of the ancient governments on the subject of representation, is by no means precisely true in the latitude commonly given to it. Without entering into a disquisition which here would be misplaced, I will refer to a few known facts, in support of what I advance.

In the most pure democracies of Greece, many of the executive functions were performed, not by the people themselves, but by officers elected by the people, and *representing* the people in their *executive* capacity.

Prior to the reform of Solon, Athens was governed by nine Archons, annually *elected by the people at large*. The degree of power delegated to them seems to be left in great obscurity. Subsequent to that period, we find an assembly, first of four, and afterwards of six hundred members, annually *elected by the people;* and *partially* representing them in their *legislative* capacity, since they were not only associated with the people in the function of making laws, but had the exclusive right of originating legislative propositions to the people. The senate of Carthage, also, whatever might be its power, or the duration of its appointment, appears to have been *elective* by the suffrages of the people. Similar instances might be traced in most, if not all the popular governments of antiquity.

Lastly, in Sparta we meet with the Ephori, and in Rome with the Tribunes; two bodies, small indeed in numbers, but annually *elected by the whole body of the people,* and considered as the *representatives* of the people, almost in their *plenipotentiary* capacity. The Cosmi of Crete were also annually *elected by the people,* and have been considered by some authors as an institution analogous to those of Sparta and Rome, with this difference only, that in the election of that representative body the right of suffrage was communicated to a part only of the people.

From these facts, to which many others might be added, it is clear that the principle of representation was neither unknown to the ancients nor wholly overlooked in their political constitutions. The true distinction between these and the American governments, lies *in the total exclusion of the people, in their collective capacity,* from any share in the *latter,* and not in the *total exclusion of the representatives of the people* from the administration of the *former.* The distinction, however, thus qualified, must be admitted to leave a most advantageous superiority in favor of the United States. But to insure to this advantage its full effect, we must be careful not to separate it from the other advantage, of an extensive territory. For it cannot be believed, that any form of representative government could have succeeded within the narrow limits occupied by the democracies of Greece.

In answer to all these arguments, suggested by reason, illustrated by examples, and enforced by our own experience, the jealous adversary of the Constitution will probably content himself with repeating, that a senate appointed not immediately by the people, and for the term of six years, must gradually acquire a dangerous preeminence in the government, and finally transform it into a tyrannical aristocracy.

To this general answer, the general reply ought to be sufficient, that liberty may be endangered by the abuses of liberty as well as by the abuses of power; that there are numerous instances of the former as well as of the latter; and that the former, rather than the latter, are apparently most to be apprehended by the United States. But a more particular reply may be given.

Before such a revolution can be effected, the Senate, it is to be observed, must in the first place corrupt itself; must next corrupt the State legislatures; must then corrupt the House of Representatives; and must finally corrupt the people at large. It is evident that the Senate must be first corrupted before it can attempt an establishment of tyranny. Without corrupting the State legislatures, it cannot prosecute the attempt, because the periodical change of members would otherwise regenerate the whole body. Without exerting the means of corruption with equal success on the House of Representatives, the opposition of that coequal branch of the government would inevitably defeat the attempt; and without corrupting the people themselves, a succession of new representatives would speedily restore all things to their pristine order. is there any man who can seriously persuade himself that the proposed Senate can, by any possible means within the compass of human address, arrive at the object of a lawless ambition, through all these obstructions?

If reason condemns the suspicion, the same sentence is pronounced by experience. The constitution of Maryland furnishes the most apposite example. The Senate of that State is elected, as the federal Senate will be, indirectly by the people, and for a term less by one year only than the federal Senate. It is distinguished, also, by the remarkable prerogative of filling up its own vacancies within the term of its appointment, and, at the same time, is not under the control of any such rotation as is provided for the federal Senate. There are some other lesser distinctions, which would expose the former to colorable objections, that do not lie against the latter. If the federal Senate, therefore, really contained the danger which has been so loudly proclaimed, some symptoms at least of a like danger ought by this time to have been betrayed by the Senate of Maryland, but no such symptoms have appeared. On the contrary, the jealousies at first entertained by men of the same description with those who view with terror the correspondent part of the federal Constitution, have been gradually extinguished by the progress of the experiment; and the Maryland constitution is daily deriving, from the salutary operation of this part of it, a reputation in which it will probably not be rivalled by that of any State in the Union.

But if any thing could silence the jealousies on this subject, it ought to be the British example. The Senate there instead of being elected for a term of six years, and of being unconfined to particular families or fortunes, is an hereditary assembly of opulent nobles. The House of Representatives, instead of being elected for two years, and by the whole body of the people, is elected for seven years, and, in very great proportion, by a very small proportion of the people. Here, unquestionably, ought to be seen in full display the aristocratic usurpations and tyranny which are at some future period to be exemplified in the United States. Unfortunately, however, for the anti-federal argument, the British history informs us that this hereditary assembly has not been able to defend itself against the continual encroachments of the House of Representatives; and that it no sooner lost the support of the monarch, than it was actually crushed by the weight of the popular branch.

As far as antiquity can instruct us on this subject, its examples support the reasoning which we have employed. In Sparta, the Ephori, the annual representatives of the people, were found an overmatch for the senate for life, continually gained on its authority and finally drew all power into their own hands. The Tribunes of Rome, who were the representatives of the people, prevailed, it is well known, in almost every contest with the senate for life, and in the end gained the most complete triumph over it. The fact is the more remarkable, as unanimity was required in every act of the Tribunes, even after their number was augmented to ten. It proves the irresistible force possessed by that branch of a free government, which has the people on its side. To these examples might be added that of Carthage, whose senate, according to the testimony of Polybius, instead of drawing all power into its vortex, had, at the commencement of the second Punic War, lost almost the whole of its original portion.

Besides the conclusive evidence resulting from this assemblage of facts, that the federal Senate will never be able to transform itself, by gradual usurpations, into an independent and aristocratic body, we are warranted in believing, that if such a revolution should ever happen from causes which the foresight of man cannot guard against, the House of Representatives, with the people on their side, will at all times be able to bring back the Constitution to its primitive form and principles. Against the force of the immediate representatives of the people, nothing will be able to maintain even the constitutional authority of the Senate, but such a display of enlightened policy, and attachment to the public good, as will divide with that branch of the legislature the affections and support of the entire body of the people themselves.

PUBLIUS

9.3 Congress: The Electoral Connection (1974)

DAVID R. MAYHEW

INTRODUCTION

Although Congress is an institution that was designed to create national policies, it also is composed of 535 members, each of whom has local constituents to serve. Members of Congress face a daily challenge of balancing district, state, and national interests, which sometimes may coincide but at other times do not. On the one hand, members of Congress are called to be *delegates* who heed their constituents' particular views and local concerns; on the other hand, members must be *trustees* who consult their own conscience and concentrate on the common good or national interest. Putting conflicting theories of representation aside, how, in fact, do most members behave?

In this reading selection, political scientist David R. Mayhew explains how elections guide congressional members in their duties. Members may enter

David R. Mayhew, *Congress: The Electoral Connection* (New Haven, Conn.: Yale University Press, 1974), 13–16, 49–64, 73–76 (excerpts). Copyright © 1974 by Yale University Press. Reprinted with permission of the publisher, Yale University Press.

Congress hoping to concentrate on federal policymaking, but they soon realize that to stay in office, they must make sure their district's or state's interests are satisfied. Members' official responsibilities encompass representation, lawmaking, investigations, and oversight. According to Mayhew, however, most members, most of the time, behave as if representation were their primary purpose and reelection were their main, if not their sole, objective. They pursue that objective through *advertising, credit claiming,* and *position taking.*

■

The discussion to come will hinge on the assumption that United States congressmen[1] are interested in getting reelected—indeed, in their role here as abstractions, interested in nothing else. Any such assumption necessarily does some violence to the facts, so it is important at the outset to root this one as firmly as possible in reality. A number of questions about that reality immediately arise.

First, is it true that the United States Congress is a place where members wish to stay once they get there? Clearly there are representative assemblies that do not hold their members for very long. Members of the Colombian parliament tend to serve single terms and then move on.[2] Voluntary turnover is quite high in some American state legislatures—for example, in Alabama. In his study of the unreformed Connecticut legislature, Barber labeled some of his subjects "reluctants"—people not very much interested in politics who were briefly pushed into it by others.[3] An ethic of "volunteerism" pervades the politics of California city councils.[4] And in the Congress itself voluntary turnover was high throughout most of the nineteenth century.

Yet in the modern Congress the "congressional career" is unmistakably upon us.[5] Turnover figures show that over the past century increasing proportions of members in any given Congress have been holdovers from previous Congresses—members who have both sought reelection and won it. Membership turnover noticeably declined among southern senators as early as the 1850s, among senators generally just after the Civil War.[6] The House followed close behind, with turnover dipping in the late nineteenth century and

---

[1]Where the context does not suggest otherwise, the term *congressmen* will refer to members of both House and Senate.

[2]James L. Payne, *Patterns of Conflict in Colombia* (New Haven: Yale University Press, 1968), pp. 19–20.

[3]James D. Barber, *The Lawmakers* (New Haven: Yale University Press, 1965), ch. 4.

[4]Kenneth Prewitt, "Political Ambitions, Volunteerism, and Electoral Accountability," 64 *American Political Science Review* 5–17 (1970).

[5]H. Douglas Price, "The Congressional Career Then and Now," ch. 2 in Nelson W. Polsby (ed.), *Congressional Behavior* (New York: Random House, 1971).

[6]Price, "Computer Simulation and Legislative 'Professionalism,' " pp. 14–16.

continuing to decline throughout the twentieth.[7] Average number of terms served has gone up and up, with the House in 1971 registering an all-time high of 20 percent of its members who had served at least ten terms.[8] It seems fair to characterize the modern Congress as an assembly of professional politicians spinning out political careers. The jobs offer good pay and high prestige. There is no want of applicants for them. Successful pursuit of a career requires continual reelection.[9]

A second question is this: even if congressmen seek reelection, does it make sense to attribute that goal to them to the exclusion of all other goals? Of course the answer is that a complete explanation (if one were possible) of a congressman's or any one else's behavior would require attention to more than just one goal. There are even occasional congressmen who intentionally do things that make their own electoral survival difficult or impossible. The late President Kennedy wrote of congressional "profiles in courage."[10] Former Senator Paul Douglas (D., Ill.) tells of how he tried to persuade Senator Frank Graham (D., N.C.) to tailor his issue positions in order to survive a 1950 primary. Graham, a liberal appointee to the office, refused to listen. He was a "saint," says Douglas.[11] He lost his primary. There are not many saints. But surely it is common for congressmen to seek other ends alongside the electoral one and not necessarily incompatible with it. . . .

Whether they are safe or marginal, cautious or audacious, one congressmen must constantly engage in activities related to reelection. There will be differences in emphasis, but all members share the root need to do things—indeed, to do things day in and day out during their terms. The next step here is to present a typology, a short list of the *kinds* of activities congressmen find it electorally useful to engage in. The case will be that there are three basic kinds of activities. . . .

One activity is *advertising*, defined here as any effort to disseminate one's name among constituents in such a fashion as to create a favorable image but in messages having little or no issue content. A successful congressman builds what amounts to a brand name, which may have a generalized electoral value for other politicians in the same family. The personal qualities to emphasize are experience, knowledge, responsiveness, concern, sincerity, independence, and the like. Just getting one's name across is difficult enough; only about

---

[7]Nelson W. Polsby, "The Institutionalization of the U.S. House of Representatives," 62 *American Political Science Review* 146 (1968).

[8]Charles S. Bullock III, "House Careerists: Changing Patterns of Longevity and Attrition," 66 *American Political Science Review* 1296 (1972).

[9]Indeed, it has been proposed that professional politicians could be gotten rid of by making reelection impossible. For a plan to select one-term legislators by random sampling of the population, see Dennis C. Mueller et al., "Representative Government via Random Selection," 12 *Public Choice* 57–68 (1972).

[10]John F. Kennedy, *Profiles in Courage* (New York: Harper and Row, 1956).

[11]Paul H. Douglas, *In the Fullness of Time* (New York: Harcourt Brace Jovanovich, 1972), pp. 238–41.

half the electorate, if asked, can supply their House members' names. It helps a congressman to be known. "In the main, recognition carries a positive valence; to be perceived at all is to be perceived favorably."[12] A vital advantage enjoyed by House incumbents is that they are much better known among voters than their November challengers.[13] They are better known because they spend a great deal of time, energy, and money trying to make themselves better known.[14] There are standard routines—frequent visits to the constituency, nonpolitical speeches to home audiences,[15] the sending out of infant care booklets and letters of condolence and congratulation. Of 158 House members questioned in the mid-1960s, 121 said that they regularly sent newsletters to their constituents;[16] 48 wrote separate news or opinion columns for newspapers; 82 regularly reported to their constituencies by radio or television;[17] 89 regularly sent out mail questionnaires.[18] Some routines are less standard. Congressman George E. Shipley (D., Ill.) claims to have met personally about half his constituents (i.e. some 200,000 people).[19] For over twenty years Congressman Charles C. Diggs, Jr. (D., Mich.) has run a radio program featuring himself as a "combination disc jockey-commentator and minister."[20] Congressman Daniel J. Flood (D., Pa.) is "famous for appearing unannounced and often uninvited at wedding anniversaries and other events."[21] . . .

---

[12]Donald E. Stokes and Warren E. Miller, "Party Government and the Saliency of Congress," ch. 11 in Angus Campbell et al., *Elections and the Political Order* (New York: Wiley, 1966), p. 205.

[13]Ibid., p. 204. The likelihood is that senators are also better known than their challengers, but that the gap is not so wide as it is on the House side. There is no hard evidence on the point.

[14]In [Charles L.] Clapp's interview study, "Conversations with more than fifty House members uncovered only one who seemed to place little emphasis on strategies designed to increase communications with the voter." Charles L. Clapp, *The Congressman: His Work as He Sees It* (Washington, D.C.: Brookings, 1963), p. 88. The exception was an innocent freshman.

[15]A statement by one of Clapp's congressmen: "The best speech is a non-political speech. I think a commencement speech is the best of all. X says he has never lost a precinct in a town where he has made a commencement speech." *The Congressman*, p. 96.

[16]These and the following figures on member activity are from Donald G. Tacheron and Morris K. Udall, *The Job of the Congressman* (Indianapolis: Bobbs-Merrill, 1966), pp. 281–88.

[17]Another Clapp congressman: "I was looking at my TV film today—I have done one every week since I have been here—and who was behind me but Congressman X. I'll swear he had never done a TV show before in his life but he only won by a few hundred votes last time. Now he has a weekly television show. If he had done that before he wouldn't have had any trouble." *The Congressman*, p. 92.

[18]On questionnaires generally see Walter Wilcox, "The Congressional Poll—and Non-Poll," in Edward C. Dreyer and Walter A. Rosenbaum (eds.), *Political Opinion and Electoral Behavior* (Belmont, Calif.: Wadsworth, 1966), pp. 390–400.

[19]Ellen Szita, Ralph Nader Congress Project Profile on George E. Shipley (D., Ill.) (Washington, D.C.: Grossman, 1972), p. 12. The congressman is also a certified diver. "When Shipley is home in his district and a drowning occurs, he is sometimes asked to dive down for the body. 'It gets in the papers and actually, it's pretty good publicity for me,' he admitted." P. 3. Whether this should be classified under "casework" rather than "advertising" is difficult to say.

[20]Lenore Cooley, Ralph Nader Congress Project Profile on Charles C. Diggs (D., Mich.) (Washington, D.C.: Grossman, 1972), p. 2.

[21]Anne Zandman and Arthur Magida, Ralph Nader Project Profile on Daniel J. Flood (D., Pa.) (Washington, D.C.: Grossman, 1972), p. 2.

A second activity may be called *credit claiming,* defined here as acting so as to generate a belief in a relevant political actor (or actors) that one is personally responsible for causing the government, or some unit thereof, to do something that the actor (or actors) considers desirable. The political logic of this, from the congressman's point of view, is that an actor who believes that a member can make pleasing things happen will no doubt wish to keep him in office so that he can make pleasing things happen in the future. The emphasis here is on individual accomplishment (rather than, say, party or governmental accomplishment) and on the congressman as doer (rather than as, say, expounder of constituency views). Credit claiming is highly important to congressmen, with the consequence that much of congressional life is a relentless search for opportunities to engage in it.

Where can credit be found? If there were only one congressman rather than 535, the answer would in principle be simple enough.[22] Credit (or blame) would attach in Downsian fashion to the doings of the government as a whole. But there are 535. Hence it becomes necessary for each congressman to try to peel off pieces of governmental accomplishment for which he can believably generate a sense of responsibility. For the average congressman the staple way of doing this is to traffic in what may be called "particularized benefits.[23] Particularized governmental benefits, as the term will be used here, have two properties: (1) Each benefit is given out to a specific individual, group, or geographical constituency, the recipient unit being of a scale that allows a single congressman to be recognized (by relevant political actors and other congressmen) as the claimant for the benefit (other congressmen being perceived as indifferent or hostile). (2) Each benefit is given out in apparently ad hoc fashion (unlike, say, social security checks) with a congressman apparently having a hand in the allocation. A particularized benefit can normally be regarded as a member of a class. That is, a benefit given out to an individual, group, or constituency can normally be looked upon by congressmen as one of a class of similar benefits given out to sizable numbers of individuals, groups, or constituencies. Hence the impression can arise that a congressman is getting "his share" of whatever it is the government is offering. (The classes may be vaguely defined. Some state legislatures deal in what their members call "local legislation.")

In sheer volume the bulk of particularized benefits come under the heading of "casework"—the thousands of favors congressional offices perform for supplicants in ways that normally do not require legislative action. High school students ask for essay materials, soldiers for emergency leaves, pensioners for location of missing checks, local governments for grant informa-

---

[22]In practice the one might call out the army and suspend the Constitution.

[23]These have some of the properties of what Lowi calls "distributive" benefits. Theodore J. Lowi, "American Business, Public Policy, Case-Studies, and Political Theory," 16 *World Politics* 690 (1964).

tion, and on and on. Each office has skilled professionals who can play the bureaucracy like an organ—pushing the right pedals to produce the desired effects.[24] But many benefits require new legislation, or at least they require important allocative decisions on matters covered by existent legislation. Here the congressman fills the traditional role of supplier of goods to the home district. It is a believable role; when a member claims credit for a benefit on the order of a dam, he may well receive it.[25] Shiny construction projects seem especially useful.[26] In the decades before 1934, tariff duties for local industries were a major commodity.[27] In recent years awards given under grant-in-aid programs have become more useful as they have become more numerous. Some quests for credit are ingenious; in 1971 the story broke that congressmen had been earmarking foreign aid money for specific projects in Israel in order to win favor with home constituents.[28] . . .

How much particularized benefits count for at the polls is extraordinarily difficult to say. But it would be hard to find a congressman who thinks he can afford to wait around until precise information is available. The lore is that they count—furthermore, given home expectations, that they must be supplied in regular quantities for a member to stay electorally even with the board. Awareness of favors may spread beyond their recipients,[29] building for a member a general reputation as a good provider. "Rivers Delivers." "He Can Do More for Massachusetts."[30] . . .

---

[24]On casework generally see Kenneth G. Olson, "The Service Function of the United States Congress," pp. 337–74 in American Enterprise Institute, *Congress: The First Branch of Government* (Washington, D.C.: American Enterprise Institute for Public Policy Research, 1966).

[25]Sometimes without justification. Thus this comment by a Republican member of the House Public Works Committee: "The announcements for projects are an important part of this. . . . And the folks back home are funny about this—if your name is associated with it, you get all the credit whether you got it through or not." James T. Murphy, "Partisanship and the House Public Works Committee," paper presented to the annual convention of the American Political Science Association, 1968, p. 10.

[26]"They've got to *see* something; it's the bread and butter issues that count—the dams, the post offices and the other public buildings, the highways. They want to know what you've been doing." A comment by a Democratic member of the House Public Works Committee. Ibid.

[27]The classic account is in E. E. Schattschneider, *Politics, Pressures, and the Tariff* (New York: Prentice-Hall, 1935).

[28]"Israeli Schools and Hospitals Seek Funds in Foreign-Aid Bill," *New York Times*, October 4, 1971, p. 10.

[29]Thus this comment of a Senate aide, "The world's greatest publicity organ is still the human mouth. . . . When you get somebody $25.00 from the Social Security Administration, he talks to his friends and neighbors about it. After a while the story grows until you've single-handedly obtained $2,500 for a constituent who was on the brink of starvation." Donald R. Matthews, *U.S. Senators and Their World* (Chapel Hill: University of North Carolina Press, 1960), p. 226.

[30]For some examples of particularistically oriented congressmen see the Nader profiles by Sven Holmes on James A. Haley (D., Fla.), Newton Koltz on Joseph P. Addabbo (D., N.Y.), Alex Berlow on Kenneth J. Gray (D., Ill.), and Sarah Glazer on John Young (D., Tex.). For a fascinating picture of the things House members were expected to do half a century ago see Joe Martin, *My First Fifty Years in Politics* (New York: McGraw-Hill, 1960), pp. 55–59.

So much for particularized benefits. But is credit available elsewhere? For governmental accomplishments beyond the scale of those already discussed? The general answer is that the prime mover role is a hard one to play on larger matters—at least before broad electorates. A claim, after all, has to be credible. If a congressman goes before an audience and says, "I am responsible for passing a bill to curb inflation," or "I am responsible for the highway program," hardly anyone will believe him. There are two reasons why people may be skeptical of such claims. First, there is a numbers problem. On an accomplishment of a sort that probably engaged the supportive interest of more than one member it is reasonable to suppose that credit should be apportioned among them. But second, there is an overwhelming problem of information costs. For typical voters Capitol Hill is a distant and mysterious place; few have anything like a working knowledge of its maneuverings. Hence there is no easy way of knowing whether a congressman is staking a valid claim or not. The odds are that the information problem cuts in different ways on different kinds of issues. On particularized benefits it may work in a congressman's favor; he may get credit for the dam he had nothing to do with building. Sprinkling a district with dams, after all, is something a congressman is supposed to be able to do. But on larger matters it may work against him. For a voter lacking an easy way to sort out valid from invalid claims the sensible recourse is skepticism. Hence it is unlikely that congressmen get much mileage out of credit claiming on larger matters before broad electorates.[31]

Yet there is an obvious and important qualification here. For many congressmen credit claiming on non-particularized matters is possible in specialized subject areas because of the congressional division of labor. The term "governmental unit" in the original definition of credit claiming is broad enough to include committees, subcommittees, and the two houses of Congress itself. Thus many congressmen can believably claim credit for blocking bills in subcommittee, adding on amendments in committee, and so on. The audience for transactions of this sort is usually small. But it may include important political actors (e.g. an interest group, the president, the *New York Times*, Ralph Nader) who are capable of both paying Capitol Hill information costs and deploying electoral resources. . . .

The third activity congressmen engage in may be called *position taking*, defined here as the public enunciation of a judgmental statement on anything likely to be of interest to political actors. The statement may take the form of a roll call vote. The most important classes of judgmental statements are those prescribing American governmental ends (a vote cast against the war; a statement that "the war should be ended immediately") or governmental means (a statement that "the way to end the war is to take it to the United Nations").

---

[31]Any teacher of American politics has had students ask about senators running for the presidency (Goldwater, McGovern, McCarthy, any of the Kennedys), "But what bills has he passed?" There is no unembarrassing answer.

The judgments may be implicit rather than explicit, as in: "I will support the president on this matter." But judgments may range far beyond these classes to take in implicit or explicit statements on what almost anybody should do or how he should do it: "The great Polish scientist Copernicus has been unjustly neglected"; "The way for Israel to achieve peace is to give up the Sinai."[32] The congressman as position taker is a speaker rather than a doer. The electoral requirement is not that he make pleasing things happen but that he make pleasing judgmental statements. The position itself is the political commodity. Especially on matters where governmental responsibility is widely diffused it is not surprising that political actors should fall back on positions as tests of incumbent virtue. For voters ignorant of congressional processes the recourse is an easy one. The following comment by one of Clapp's House interviewees is highly revealing: "Recently, I went home and began to talk about the ——— act. I was pleased to have sponsored that bill, but it soon dawned on me that the point wasn't getting through at all. What was getting through was that the act might be a help to people. I changed the emphasis: I didn't mention my role particularly, but stressed my support of the legislation."[33]

The ways in which positions can be registered are numerous and often imaginative. There are floor addresses ranging from weighty orations to mass-produced "nationality day statements."[34] There are speeches before home groups, television appearances, letters, newsletters, press releases, ghostwritten books, *Playboy* articles, even interviews with political scientists. On occasion congressmen generate what amount to petitions; whether or not to sign the 1956 Southern Manifesto defying school desegregation rulings was an important decision for southern members.[35] Outside the roll

---

[32]In the terminology of Stokes, statements may be on either "position issues" or "valence issues." Donald E. Stokes, "Spatial Models of Party Competition," ch. 9 in Angus Campbell et al., *Elections and the Political Order* (New York: Wiley, 1966), pp. 170–74.

[33]Clapp, *The Congressman*, p. 108. A difficult borderline question here is whether introduction of bills in Congress should be counted under position taking or credit claiming. On balance probably under the former. Yet another Clapp congressman addresses the point: "I introduce about sixty bills a year, about 120 Congress. I try to introduce bills that illustrate, by and large, my ideas—legislative, economic, and social. I do like being able to say when I get cornered, 'yes, boys, I introduced a bill to try to do that in 1954.' To me it is the perfect answer." Ibid., p. 141. But voters probably give claims like this about the value they deserve.

[34]On floor speeches generally see Matthews, *U.S. Senators*, p. 247. On statements celebrating holidays cherished by ethnic groups, Hearings on the Organization of Congress before the Joint Committee on the Organization of the Congress, 89th Cong., 1st sess., 1965, p. 1127; and Arlen J. Large, "And Now Let's Toast Nicolaus Copernicus, the Famous German," *Wall Street Journal*, March 12, 1973, p. 1.

[35]Sometimes members of the Senate ostentatiously line up as "cosponsors" of measures—an activity that may attract more attention than roll call voting itself. Thus in early 1973, seventy-six senators backed a provision to block trade concessions to the U.S.S.R. until the Soviet government allowed Jews to emigrate without paying high exit fees. "'Why did so many people sign the amendment?' a Northern Senator asked rhetorically. 'Because there is no political advantage in not signing. If you do sign, you don't offend anyone. If you don't sign, you might offend some Jews in your state.' " David E. Rosenbaum, "Firm Congress Stand on Jews in Soviet Is Traced to Efforts by Those in U.S.," *New York Times*, April 6, 1973, p. 14.

call process the congressman is usually able to tailor his positions to suit his audience. A solid consensus in the constituency calls for ringing declarations; for years the late Senator James K. Vardaman (D., Miss.) campaigned on a proposal to repeal the Fifteenth Amendment.[36] Division or uncertainty in the constituency calls for waffling; in the late 1960s a congressman had to be a poor politician indeed not to be able to come up with an inoffensive statement on Vietnam ("We must have peace with honor at the earliest possible moment consistent with the national interest"). On a controversial issue a Capitol Hill office normally prepares two form letters to send out to constituent letter writers—one for the pros and one (not directly contradictory) for the antis.[37] . . .

These, then, are the three kinds of electorally oriented activities congressmen engage in—advertising, credit claiming, and position taking. It remains only to offer some brief comments on the emphases different members give to the different activities. No deterministic statements can be made; within limits each member has freedom to build his own electoral coalition and hence freedom to choose the means of doing it.[38] Yet there are broad patterns. For one thing senators, with their access to the media, seem to put more emphasis on position taking than House members; probably House members rely more heavily on particularized benefits. . . .

Another kind of difference appears if the initial assumption of a reelection quest is relaxed to take into account the "progressive" ambitions of some members—the aspirations of some to move up to higher electoral offices rather than keep the ones they have.[39] There are two important subsets of climbers in the Congress—House members who would like to be senators (over the years about a quarter of the senators have come up directly from the House),[40] and senators who would like to be presidents or vice presidents (in the Ninety-third Congress about a quarter of the senators had at one time or another run for these offices or been seriously "mentioned" for them). In both cases higher aspirations seem to produce the same distinctive mix of activities. . . . Office advancement seems to require a judicious mixture of advertising and position taking. Thus a House member aiming for the Senate heralds his quest with

---

[36]". . . an utterly hopeless proposal and for that reason an ideal campaign issue." V. O. Key, Jr., *Southern Politics* (New York: Knopf, 1949), p. 232.

[37]Instructions on how to do this are given in Donald G. Tacheron and Morris K. Udall, *The Job of the Congressman* (Indianapolis: Bobbs-Merrill, 1966), pp. 73–74.

[38]On member freedom see Raymond A. Bauer, Ithiel de Sola Pool, and Lewis A. Dexter, *American Business and Public Policy* (New York: Atherton, 1964), pp. 406–07.

[39]The term is from Joseph A. Schlesinger, *Ambition and Politics: Political Careers in the United States* (Chicago: Rand McNally, 1966), p. 10.

[40]Ibid., p. 92; Matthews, *U.S. Senators*, p. 55. In the years 1953–72 three House members were appointed to the Senate, and eighty-five gave up their seats to run for the Senate. Thirty-five of the latter made it, giving a success rate of 41 percent.

press releases; there must be a new "image," sometimes an ideological overhaul to make ready for the new constituency.[41] Senators aiming for the White House do more or less the same thing—advertising to get the name across, position taking ("We can do better"). . . .

There are these distinctions, but it would be a mistake to elevate them over the commonalities. For most congressmen most of the time all three activities are essential.

9.4 Home Style: House Members in Their Districts (1978)

RICHARD F. FENNO, JR.

INTRODUCTION

"What does a House member see when looking at his or her constituency?" Thus begins Richard F. Fenno, Jr.'s classic and fascinating study of how House members develop distinctive "home styles," and how their behavior at home relates to what they do when they are in Washington, D.C., at work in Congress. Members, explains Fenno, have "four concentric constituencies: geographic, reelection, primary, and personal." In addition, he conjectures, there are "connections between home style and Washington behavior." Furthermore, "all House members can use their home styles to give themselves a great deal of voting leeway in Washington if they so desire."

What does a House member see when looking at his or her constituency? Kaleidoscopic variety, no doubt. That is why there can be no one "correct" way of slicing up and classifying member perceptions—only "helpful" ways. Most helpful to me has been the member's view of a constituency as a nest of concentric circles. In one form or another, in one expression or another, in one degree or another, this bullseye perception is shared by all House members.

---

[41]Thus upstate New York Republicans moving to the Senate commonly shift to the left. For a good example of the advertising and position-taking strategies that can go along with turning a House member into a senator see the account on Senator Robert P. Griffin (R., Mich.) in James M. Perry, *The New Politics* (New York: Clarkson N. Potter, 1968), ch. 4.

It is helpful to us for the same reason it is common to them. It is a perception constructed out of the necessities of political life. . . .

Each member of Congress perceives four concentric constituencies: geographic, reelection, primary, and personal. This is not the only way a member sees his or her "constituency"; but it is one way. It is a set of perceptions that emphasizes the context in which, and the strategies by which, the House member seeks electoral support. It is a complicated context, one featuring varying scopes of support and varying intensities of support. The strategies developed for getting and keeping electoral support involve the manipulation of these scopes and intensities. We have taken each member's perceptions as we found them, and have not asked how he or she came by them in the first place. . . .

A perceptual analysis of congressional constituencies both complicates and clarifies efforts of political science to understand the relationship between congressman and constituency. It complicates matters both conceptually and statistically. For example, political scientists have a heavy investment in role conceptions that distinguish between the "trustee" who follows his independent judgment and the "delegate" who follows the wishes of his constituency. But we now must ask, which constituency? And we cannot be content with a conceptual scheme that provides only two answers to this question: "the district" and "the nation."[1] More frequent, we think, than this kind of choice is one in which the congressman must choose among constituencies *within* the district. Also, when studies of party voting conclude that a member of Congress can vote independently because he or she "knows the constituency isn't looking,"[2] we need to ask again, which constituency? One of the several constituencies may very well be looking.

Similarly, the variables we have used as surrogates for "the constituency" in our statistical analyses (for instance, in relating roll calls to constituency characteristics) have described only the geographical constituency—typically derived from census data. Rarely have we used variables capable of differentiating the other three constituencies, individually or collectively. A perceptual analysis warns us of the hazards of these oversimplified conceptualizations and representations of "the constituency." The most useful "first difference" to incorporate into our studies is that between the geographical constituency and the other three *supportive constituencies.* That is a distinction and a terminology we shall try to retain throughout, making added refinements where possible.

A perceptual analysis clarifies most by including the tremendous amount of uncertainty surrounding the House member's view of his or her electoral situation. Political scientists using the idea of electoral marginality to explain be-

---

[1]For example, see Roger Davidson, *The Role of the Congressman* (New York: Pegasus, 1973).

[2]Donald Stokes and Warren Miller, "Party Government and the Saliency of Congress," *Public Opinion Quarterly* 26 (Winter 1962): 531–546.

havior, for example, will underestimate the effect of this uncertainty so long as they rely wholly on numerical indicators of electoral safety. Similarly, although political scientists may ask, in the manner of a regression analysis, which campaign activity contributed how much to the election results, a view from over the member's shoulder may reveal that he or she does not think in terms of the weights of variables. We might help ourselves by seeing the electoral situation the way the members see it, to ask ourselves the questions they ask: How much did I win by? Who supported me? Who worked especially hard for me? What net effect did the changes from last time have on the outcome this time? If members of Congress are more uncertain than we think they are and if they calculate more configuratively than we think they do, we might find these altered perspectives worth assimilating into our knowledge. Later, when we find House members acting conservatively, unwilling to take risks, preoccupied with self-preservation and relying on their homegrown rules of thumb, we shall at least be aware of the perceptions underlying such postures. . . .

In probing for linkages between home and Washington, it is natural to ask if there are any connections between home style and Washington behavior. If we mean to ask whether members of Congress do certain things in Washington to shore up constituent support at home, the answer is obviously yes. And what they do is well known and straightforward. They allocate the tasks of their staffs in ways they think helpful in getting reelected. They choose committee assignments they think will bring identification with and benefit to their supportive constituencies. They vote in ways they think will be approved by their supportive constituents. Or, better, they avoid voting in ways they believe will be intensely disapproved by their supportive constituents. They will also vote in ways that help them structure their need to explain back home. There is nothing we can add here to what political scientists already know about such constituency-oriented behavior in Washington.

The question we have to ask is whether the study of home styles can tell us anything we might not otherwise know about behavior in Washington. Are home styles related in any way to Washington styles? It is not an easy question to handle. Political scientists have not produced any consensus as to precisely what might be meant by a "Washington style."[3] Also, we have produced too little Washington-related information in this study to pursue the matter constructively. Still, the question remains intriguing, if only because from time to time House members talk or act as if the behavior we observed at home is repeated in Washington.

---

[3]The most admirable effort to connect home events (i.e., recruitment) with Washington behavior is Leo Snowiss, "Congressional Recruitment and Representation," *American Political Science Review* 60 (September 1966), pp. 627–39. But his study failed to yield a coherent or reliable classification of performance patterns in Washington. Other attempted classification of legislative styles (i.e., insider-outsider, trustee-delegate) have not been convincingly related to behavior.

For example, our issue-oriented Congressman *O*, who refuses "to play the groups" at home, also refuses to play them in Washington.

> I met a guy from the postal union [at home]. He said I gave them the brush off when they came to Washington. The trouble is they compare me to the congressman in the next district. He wines and dines every little two-bit group that comes down. He spends all his time with them. He doesn't have anything else to do. But I don't have the patience with these guys, or the time. I'm busy over on the floor doing other things.

Stylistic patterns affecting access at home can affect access similarly in Washington. Another congressman commented at home that "I love to campaign at coffee hours with ten or twelve people. I hate standup cocktail parties. . . . I'm very bad at making small talk with people I don't know. I can't do it." In Washington, he follows the same stylistic predilections—almost.

> Not long ago, I got a letter from the head of the American Legion in my state noting that I hadn't been to their Washington cocktail party for the last two years. I don't go to any of those Washington parties. . . . But I make two exceptions— groups in which I have personal friends and groups that were with me in 1968 [his first campaign]. Take the Machinists, for example. They were a great help to me when I needed help. I always go to their gatherings.

If access at home carries with it a promise of access in Washington, this is all the more reason why it is so valued by supportive constituents. Our knowledge of home style may, furthermore, help us to locate those constituents most likely to achieve access in Washington.

Another possible linkage might be a relationship between coalition building at home and coalition building inside the House. For example, might not our Congressman *B*, the well-liked local boy who is so suspicious of "outsiders," be handicapped as a coalition builder in Congress by this exclusive view of politics? He was two years on the job, he says, before he began to read *The Washington Post*. More broadly, might not any member who writes off certain constituents as people he "never gets" be limited in his efforts to build coalitions among House colleagues who represent such people? In broader compass still, are some home styles more conducive to the achievement of internal power or good policy than others? Are members with issue-oriented home styles any more likely to provide internal policy leadership than members with other home styles? Such questions are intriguing. But the shortcomings of our home-oriented perspective cannot be overcome sufficiently to answer them.

We shall offer, however, one line of speculation. It is this: Home styles may affect Washington styles in the degree to which home styles produce early commitments to future courses of action in Congress. Some members will act at home, we speculate, to preserve a maximum of maneuvering room for themselves at various points of decision in Washington. Other members will act at home to commit themselves to certain courses of action at various points of decision in Washington. The former remain free to play a variety of parts in the legislative process. The latter are more limited in their range of legislative activity. Both stances are deliberate and, partly at least, a function of their home styles. We are encouraged in these speculations because House members themselves make this distinction between an early and a late commitment to a course of action. . . .

The suggested linkage between home styles and Washington styles depends on the distinction, in Washington, between early commitment and the retention of maneuvering room during decision making. If such a distinction can be maintained, then it seems that certain home styles will be associated with one Washington style more often than with the other. The more issue-oriented a congressman's home style, the more likely is he to commit himself early. And the more he chooses to present himself by talking about policy issues, the more the sheer density of talk will produce early commitments. They may be commitments to introduce legislation, agitate for a given decision in a given forum, vote in a particular fashion, or something else. In proportions that vary from member to member, this talk at home may be pure "position taking"—and thus, in Mayhew's terms, totally devoid of commitment.[4] All we can say, here, is that we are speaking only of that proportion of home talk that does carry some commitment to future activity. We mean to emphasize a commitment to legislative activism, publicly made, with the implied invitation for constituents to watch him in action. . . .

All this is, admittedly, conjectural. And nothing we have said should be taken to diminish the force of our more general proposition that all House members can use their home styles to give themselves a great deal of voting leeway in Washington if they so desire.

---

[4]David Mayhew, *The Electoral Connection* (New Haven: Yale University Press, 1974). But as Mayhew also notes, when a member "register(s) an elaborate set of pleasing positions, (it is) a course that reduces the chances of vote trading." *Ibid.*, 121.

9.5 Policymaking in Congress

INTRODUCTION

To a degree that would undoubtedly surprise, even shock, earlier generations of Congress watchers, both the House and the Senate have in many ways become highly partisan and ideologically polarized bodies. Partisanship and ideological infighting have affected everything from once mundane matters governing congressional organization to how Congress conducts such basic duties as oversight of executive branch agencies and the process by which the Senate considers and votes on nominees for the federal bench.

As the following three readings from *CQ Weekly* suggest, today's Congress has many deep rifts. Those rifts have not healed—in fact, they may have widened—in the wake of the 9/11 terrorist attacks. In the second of these readings, Helen Fessenden reports that "in 2002, Congress decided to turn a wide-ranging Sept. 11 inquiry over to an independent commission because of distrust between the parties: Republicans worried that Democrats . . . would lead the inquiry into an indictment of Bush policies, while Democrats feared a Republican whitewash."

Likewise, in his *Philadelphia Inquirer* op-ed, noted congressional expert Norman Ornstein criticizes Congress for failing to deal forthrightly with the need to create effective provisions for keeping Congress going in the aftermath of a terrorist strike or other disaster that resulted in many members being incapacitated or killed.

■

Congress as Watchdog: Asleep on the Job? (2004)

DAVID NATHER

Over the years, Congress has become known as the staging ground for televised investigations that have turned lawmakers into minor celebrities and made administration witnesses squirm.

When Defense Secretary Donald H. Rumsfeld testified on Iraqi prisoner abuses before the Senate Armed Services Committee on May 7, live on all the broadcast networks, it seemed likely to produce a classic television moment—such as when Sen. Howard Baker, R-Tenn. (1967–85), asked the most memorable question of the Watergate hearings: "What did the president know, and when did he know it?"

Much of congressional oversight does not rise to that level. But even the more common variety—the poorly attended subcommittee hearings and the quiet exchanges of letters and phone calls—has allowed Congress to act as the watchdog that keeps the executive branch in check.

Lately, though, the watchdog is gaining a reputation for sleeping on the job.

On such high-profile issues as Iraq, intelligence, appropriations, energy policy, the 2001 education overhaul law (PL 107-110) and the anti-terrorism law known as the Patriot Act (PL 107-56), there has been a growing pattern of breakdowns in congressional oversight. In some cases, Congress has been blindsided by revelations dug up by outsiders. In others it has been stalled by the administration or, its critics say, simply has not made much of an effort in the first place.

And even the Senate Armed Services Committee hearings on the abuse of Iraqi prisoners, which promised to be some of the most aggressive since the days of Watergate in 1973–74 and the impeachment of President Bill Clinton in 1998, have started to fall short of their billing.

Chairman John W. Warner, R-Va., defying pressure from some of his Republican colleagues to tone down his investigation, promised to "go where the evidence leads us, no matter how embarrassing or incriminating it may be." Instead, veteran investigators who watched the committee's questioning of top generals May 19 saw unprepared and uninformed senators. Many asked questions based on accounts in newspaper articles, leading to some embarrassing moments in which the generals flat out denied the accounts and senators were forced to back down.

"Rule No. 1: You always have to know the answer before you ask the question," said Winslow T. Wheeler, a defense specialist who worked for Sen. Jacob Javits, R-N.Y. (1957–81). "In other words, your staff is working its tail off finding out what is going on and feeding it to the senator. That's not happening."

To some, it should be little surprise that oversight would fade during a period of one-party government. "Our party controls the levers of government. We're not about to go out and look beneath a bunch of rocks to try to cause heartburn," said Rep. Ray LaHood, R-Ill. "Unless they really screw up, we're not going to go after them."

Others, though, see an erosion of one of Congress' most important powers. "In this Congress, there are no checks, there are no balances. There is no oversight," said Rep. David R. Obey of Wisconsin, the ranking Democrat on the House Appropriations Committee.

And while some Republicans say the decline has been going on for years, not just recently, they are worried that their party has not gotten a handle on it.

"I just don't think our side has ever learned those skills," former House Majority Leader Dick Armey, R-Texas (1985–2003), said of his fellow Republicans. Armey used to give awards to members who demonstrated skillful oversight in an effort to encourage them.

Some say the White House has placed obstacles before Congress that prevent it from getting information, though defenders of the administration maintain that it has cooperated with lawmakers' oversight efforts. There is nearly universal agreement, however, that congressional Republicans themselves have not made oversight a priority.

"I don't think we have been doing the job we should have been doing for several years on oversight," said Rep. Jim Kolbe, R-Ariz., chairman of the House Appropriations Subcommittee on Foreign Operations, Export Financing and Related Programs.

Former Rep. William F. Clinger, R-Pa. (1979–97), who chaired the House Government Reform Committee, said Congress "is becoming increasingly less effective in its oversight functions."

And Rep. John D. Dingell, D-Mich., who is remembered by Republicans and Democrats as one of the most aggressive investigators in Congress when Democrats ran the House, worries that the decline will make it hard for future lawmakers to return to vigorous oversight because all the expertise will have disappeared. "Congress can always come back to it," Dingell said. "The problem is that the nexus between those who know how to do oversight and those who want to do it is being broken by the Republicans' behavior."

WORKING OUT OF SIGHT

That does not mean congressional oversight has faded away completely. Every week, committees and subcommittees hold oversight hearings of one kind or another. Most focus on run-of-the-mill issues such as ocean policy, but others tackle more urgent subjects such as the future of Iraq.

The two top Republican leaders say Congress has hardly been lax about oversight. Senate Majority Leader Bill Frist of Tennessee says the Senate has opened tough investigations of the Iraqi prison scandal. "Our committees are working aggressively in terms of oversight, taking very appropriate action," he said in a floor speech May 19. "The Defense Department is cooperating fully in these inquiries and has been responsive to all of our requests."

And House Speaker J. Dennis Hastert, R-Ill., says he has been pushing for every House panel to have an oversight subcommittee. "Are there gaps? Will there be bad things [that] happen? Yes," Hastert said May 19. "But I think we've done an extraordinary job on oversight, and we're going to continue to do that."

Furthermore, some Republican chairmen have won bipartisan praise for their willingness to take on bureaucratic waste and occasionally tackle subjects that hit political nerves with the White House. They include Senate Finance Chairman Charles E. Grassley of Iowa, House Government Reform Chairman Thomas M. Davis III of Virginia, and Rep. James C. Greenwood of Pennsylvania, chairman of the House Energy and Commerce Subcommittee on Oversight and Investigations—the subcommittee formerly headed by Dingell.

Analysts say the Republican majority has been particularly active in trying to root out government waste, and that agencies such as the Transportation Security Administration have been forced to take steps to respond.

Even so, former members and independent analysts say there has been a long-term erosion of Congress' oversight skills, though they believe there is more to the story than one party's reluctance to investigate itself. Long-term institutional changes have contributed to the decline, such as members' shorter workweeks, packed schedules, term limits on chairmanships and eroding salaries for investigative staff members.

Moreover, the general drudgery of routine oversight, which often involves years of work with little immediate payoff, makes it a poor sell to members whose time is increasingly limited. Sen. Judd Gregg, R-N.H., who used to serve in the House and now chairs the Senate Health, Education, Labor and Pensions Committee, said oversight is harder for senators than for House members because senators have more committee responsibilities.

Former Rep. Lee H. Hamilton, D-Ind. (1965–99), one of the leaders of Congress' 1987 Iran-contra investigation and now a member of the independent Sept. 11 commission, takes the long view as well. "I think we've had a decline in congressional oversight for some time," he said. "This isn't anything that's developed over the last year or two."

"Oversight is very tedious work. It takes a lot of preparation, and it tends to be very complicated," added Hamilton, who is director of the Woodrow Wilson International Center for Scholars and author of "How Congress Works and Why You Should Care." "Members are very busy now, and they just don't make oversight that high a priority. Most of them focus on constituent services and legislative work."

Some forms of congressional oversight are less obvious than others. Congress has the "power of the purse," which gives it the authority to check on how its appropriations are being spent. It also reacts to dramatic events, such as the abuse of Iraqi prisoners or the Watergate and Iran-contra scandals.

In addition, it has the authority to monitor how laws are being implemented, to scrutinize administration policies on issues such as Iraq and energy, and to look for waste, fraud and abuse in agency programs. It also can scrutinize the private sector, sometimes in ways that are politically sensitive to the administration, such as the 2002 Enron collapse.

To a degree, oversight—a congressional responsibility that is implied, rather than stated, in the Constitution—has often been a lower priority than legislating. As far back as 1885, Woodrow Wilson wrote, "Quite as important as legislation is vigilant oversight of administration." But analysts say it took on more prominence in the 1970s and '80s, partly because of Dingell's efforts, including a 1983 probe of problems with the superfund hazardous-waste cleanup program that led to the indictment of its director, Rita M. LaVelle. Oversight work of various committees led to a series of good-government laws and high-profile investigations.

THE CASUALTIES

Now, there is mounting evidence that the oversight process has been faltering on some of the most urgent issues before Congress.

Just weeks after lawmakers demonstrated palpable outrage at the abuse of Iraqi prisoners, the momentum of the investigations has slowed. The Senate Armed Services hearing May 19 did little to advance the inquiry, and House Armed Services Chairman Duncan Hunter of California and other Republicans have urged the Senate to back off and let the military investigations proceed. Indeed, Warner himself refused to call the hearings an investigation.

The Iraqi prison abuse scandal has become part of a pattern in which lawmakers have promised to become more aggressive in overseeing the war, then have backed off under pressure from the White House and Republicans' own ranks.

Senate Select Intelligence Chairman Pat Roberts, R-Kan., promised to "let the chips fall where they may" in the panel's investigation of prewar intelligence, only to have the probe hobbled by partisan tensions. Foreign Relations Chairman Richard G. Lugar, R-Ind., vowed in April that "we need to offer answers" in hearings on the administration's plans for Iraq, then declared himself satisfied with lower-level administration witnesses after the higher-ranking ones he wanted refused to show.

And when President Bush asked for an $87 billion supplemental spending bill for Iraq and Afghanistan last fall, many Republicans promised to ask tougher questions about the administration's Iraq policies, then approved his open-ended request with few changes.

Frustrated by the quality of the information the administration was providing on the war, Rep. Christopher Shays, R-Conn., traveled to Iraq to find out for himself what was actually happening. He was scolded by L. Paul Bremer III, chief of the Coalition Provisional Authority, for ignoring warnings not to come. In return, Shays berated Bremer for making Congress' oversight of the Iraq operations unnecessarily difficult.

"If we had been visiting these prisons in August, September, October of last year, I don't think any of this would have happened," Shays said of the scandal. "We probably would have had someone saying to us, 'You won't believe what's going on here. Some people are about to go over the edge.'"

A report in Bob Woodward's book *Plan of Attack* that the administration spent $178 million from the $40 billion emergency supplemental bill in 2001

(PL 107-38) on projects in Kuwait—months before Congress authorized the Iraq war—prompted demands for full disclosure from Democratic appropriators Obey and Sen. Robert C. Byrd of West Virginia, who said they believed Congress had been hoodwinked.

Republican appropriators did not share their concerns, and administration officials said the money was spent on the global war on terrorism, not specifically on Iraq. But the response to Obey and Byrd—the delivery of three binders full of general information on how the supplemental appropriations were spent—succeeded only in reinforcing Democrats' belief that the administration's reports are too vague to be of any real use to Congress.

UPSTAGED BY COMMISSIONS

Adding to the injury, Congress has also been outperformed lately by the independent commissions that increasingly are taking on the work it used to do.

The Sept. 11 commission has pried out more disclosures about the 2001 terrorist attacks than the congressional joint inquiry that preceded it. And it generated enough public pressure to force national security adviser Condoleezza Rice to testify publicly, and Bush and Vice President Dick Cheney to brief the panel in private—all witnesses that the congressional panel never heard from.

On other issues, Congress has been successfully stalled by the administration. Cheney was able to defeat the General Accounting Office (GAO), the investigative arm of Congress, in its efforts to obtain the records of the energy task force he headed in 2001 to determine who advised the administration on its energy policy.

Despite warnings by lawmakers such as Rep. Henry A. Waxman, D-Calif., that the defeat would permanently damage the GAO's ability to obtain information from the executive branch, Comptroller General David M. Walker, who heads the GAO, said his investigators have not had any of their requests turned down since a federal judge dismissed the GAO's lawsuit in 2002. Walker warned, however, that GAO investigators are experiencing a lot of delays from federal agencies, which "undercuts our ability to provide timely information" to help lawmakers' oversight efforts.

Similar delays frustrated House Judiciary Chairman F. James Sensenbrenner Jr., R-Wis., in his early efforts to oversee the implementation of the Patriot Act, which has raised civil liberties concerns among conservatives and liberals. The Department of Justice's answers to his first set of written questions in 2002 were so incomplete that he threatened to subpoena Attorney General John Ashcroft to get better ones.

Since then, Sensenbrenner aides say, Justice has improved its response time, and its answers have gotten better. The initial problems, however, have left lingering doubts about the department's responsiveness.

"We gave the Justice Department a huge increase in power," Armey said. Congress made a point of designing key provisions to expire, he said, "on the theory that would make them more responsive to oversight."

With the education overhaul measure known as the No Child Left Behind law, oversight efforts have been more halting. The Senate Health, Education, Labor and Pensions Committee has held no oversight hearings on its implementation this year, even as complaints mount from state and local officials that the law is underfunded and too demanding.

Sen. Edward M. Kennedy of Massachusetts, the panel's ranking Democrat, said he has asked Gregg to hold oversight hearings and has been turned down. Gregg said he has held off because the Education Department has been revising its regulations implementing the law to address some of the complaints, and "I would rather let it percolate for a while rather than stirring the pot."

The House Education and the Workforce Committee has held field hearings on the law, and Chairman John A. Boehner, R-Ohio, said that beyond the partisan disputes over funding, "there's no backing away from it." However, Kennedy and Rep. George Miller of California, the ranking Democrat on the House panel, said they have tried to deal directly with the Education Department to urge leniency in complying with the regulations. Without Republicans on their side, they have gotten little response.

"Have we been doing our job? Well, it's a little late now," Miller said.

Within Congress, one-party government gets much of the blame for the breakdowns. Lawmakers from both parties, as well as outside analysts, agree that one-party government is a recipe for weaker oversight, and this Congress is no exception.

Some Democrats say that has not always been the case, and argue that they were never shy about investigating their own presidents when they were in power. Obey, for example, noted that Harry S Truman made a national name for himself as a Democratic senator from Missouri (1935–45) by investigating President Franklin D. Roosevelt's national defense program before he became Roosevelt's vice president.

And Dingell, who became famous for his "Dingell-grams"—detailed and time-consuming document requests he would hurl at federal agencies during his investigations—says he took on every administration regardless of who was in charge. "I didn't give a damn whether it was [Jimmy] Carter or [Bill] Clinton or [Ronald] Reagan or [George] Bush. It didn't make any difference to me."

However, Republicans and outside analysts say that in general, both parties have been guilty of softening their oversight when they controlled the White House. Grassley, for example, notes that he "got a lot of help from Democrats" in exposing Pentagon waste under Reagan and President George Bush, but they became less helpful during the Clinton years.

"I think that's the history of Congress. It's not a new phenomenon," said Rep. Jim Leach, R-Iowa, who helped lead one of the Whitewater investigations in the 1990s.

Oversight generally bounces back, Leach said, during major events such as foreign policy crises or scandals such as the Enron and WorldCom bankruptcies in 2002.

Grassley, who has gone from exposing Pentagon waste in the 1980s to fighting Medicare waste and tax scams today, and Davis, who has held hearings on Iraq reconstruction contracts, say they have not let one-party government stop their oversight efforts.

Davis, who has been urged by ranking Democrat Waxman to hold hearings on the role of private contractors in the Iraqi prison scandal, said he may do so despite House GOP leaders' opposition—though he has not decided whether to focus on the abuses specifically or on the role of contractors in general.

PRESSURE FROM THE TOP

Lawmakers have also faced active resistance from the Bush administration in their efforts to get information. And Republican leaders have not always been helpful.

In their fight against private groups seeking the energy task force records, now before the Supreme Court, Cheney's lawyers argued that the Constitution gives presidents a "zone of autonomy" from scrutiny of the legislative advice they receive. The implication if such an argument prevails, Waxman said, is that "they can operate in secrecy without the Congress or the public knowing how they reached their decisions."

More recently, Cheney led a backlash against the accelerating congressional investigations into the abuse of the Iraqi prisoners. On May 8, the day after Rumsfeld testified in back-to-back hearings of the Senate and House Armed Services committees, Cheney issued a statement declaring that Rumsfeld's critics should "get off his case."

An aide to Cheney said that while the statement may have been interpreted as a slap at Congress, it was not meant that way, and was simply "a straightforward description of the exceptional job the defense secretary is doing." But the remark prompted Lindsey Graham, R-S.C., a member of the Senate panel, to say the White House should "let us do our job." And it acted as a brake on the growing demand for congressional investigations, prompting Republican conservatives in Congress—notably House Majority Leader Tom DeLay of Texas and Sen. James M. Inhofe of Oklahoma—to prod critical members to tone down their outrage.

Not all committee and subcommittee chairmen say they have felt pressure from the leadership to soft-pedal their activities. From the accounts of those interviewed for this article, Senate chairmen feel relatively free to take on the subjects they want, while House chairmen have been more likely to encounter friction with their leaders.

Grassley, for example, says he has "never had leadership discourage anything I've been trying to do," adding that oversight is not up to the leadership anyway: "I think it's up to the individual committee chairmen to do it."

In the House, not all chairmen feel constrained. Boehner said he has never felt pressure from the leadership not to examine complaints about the No Child Left Behind law. And Kolbe says one-party government "absolutely makes no difference. What's important is for us to carry out our constitutional responsibility."

Some House chairmen, however, have gotten definite warnings that investigations are not welcome on topics hitting too close to home with the White House. Combined with the complaints they get from the administration itself, these signals can have a chilling effect, since every chairman knows that he serves at the pleasure of the leadership.

For example, Greenwood says he encountered resistance from some members of the leadership, whom he will not name, when the subcommittee was preparing to investigate the 2002 collapse of Enron—whose chairman, Kenneth Lay, had been a top contributor to Bush.

Although that was an issue of oversight of the private sector rather than the executive branch, Greenwood said, "I kept hearing, 'What do you want to do that for? The Republican Party is associated with big business . . . and with Bush being from Texas, he's associated with Enron; it's been a big part of our fundraising and all that.'"

"My response [to the leadership] was, 'Let's think this through. Either the Democrats are going to investigate the heck out of Enron, and we're going to look like we're covering it up, or we're going to do it ourselves.'" By going ahead with it, Greenwood said, "we essentially took that issue off the plate for the '02 elections."

MUSCLE LOSS

Overall, Congress has lost some of its ability to mount sustained investigations, according to some outside analysts.

Paul C. Light, a senior fellow in governance studies at the Brookings Institution, said that while congressional Republicans have been skilled at tackling government waste and abuse, Congress has become less successful at "deep oversight," the investigative work needed to pry out embarrassing information that is not in open view.

That is partly because staff salaries have eroded, making it harder to retain good investigators, Light said. "You need good investigative staff members who know what doors to knock on, and that's just not the case," he said.

Joel D. Aberbach, director of the Center for American Politics and Public Policy at UCLA, found an increase in congressional oversight hearings in the

1990s, the latest figures available in his research. But the numbers say nothing about the results the hearings achieved, he said, and at a time when the congressional leadership is getting stronger and committees are getting weaker, Congress is not rattling a lot of cages.

"Even though they may still be holding a decent number of oversight activities . . . you can have lots of formal activities and no real influence," Aberbach said.

In more routine activities, such as requests for GAO reports, the trend is toward more reactive oversight and less work to anticipate problems. When problems arise, such as the prison scandal, "Congress does not hesitate to get involved," Walker said. "At the same time, there's not as much ongoing, proactive oversight as there may have been in years past."

While GAO has been getting fewer requests for reports from lawmakers, Walker said, the quality of the requests has been better—a development he attributes to the agency's efforts to work with lawmakers more closely to let them know what are legitimate requests.

But some members say Congress underestimates its own powers. "The power of Congress when it comes to oversight is extraordinary. A principled member must be careful not to use it in a capricious way," Leach said. "A congressional subpoena is very powerful. Taking the oath is very powerful."

And others, such as Grassley and Kolbe, say Congress faces no real obstacles to oversight. If it is failing at that task, they say, it is only because lawmakers themselves are not taking it seriously enough.

"I think to be successful at it, you have to treat administrations equally, whether they're Republicans or Democrats," said Grassley. "You have to have a good staff. And you have to remember that even though oversight is hard work, it is our constitutional responsibility."

Intelligence Panels' Mission Corroded by Air of Distrust (2004)

HELEN FESSENDEN

When Congress established the House and Senate Intelligence committees almost 30 years ago, their founders had a novel and ambitious mandate: to empower Congress to check executive branch abuses in the intelligence agencies, while also making sure that those same agencies were effectively protecting national security.

Experts and lawmakers on both sides of the aisle say the panels have made a difference over the years, largely because they have been able to operate with a bipartisanship that rose above politics and reflected the gravity of their work.

And as the current investigation into intelligence failures that led to the attacks of Sept. 11 took its proceedings to a public hearing March 23, there were moments in which the participants seemed interested in rising above the toxic party wars that pervade Washington these days. The first day of testimony included the secretaries of Defense and State for the Clinton and Bush administrations, discussing common enemies and shared culpabilities.

But given the testimony to come, it could not—and did not—last long. With the accusations of former Bush administration counterterrorism adviser Richard A. Clarke that the White House largely ignored the al Qaeda threat before the attacks, the brawl began.

The administration spent much of the week attempting to discredit Clarke and paint him as out of the loop. The day after his testimony, Democrat Tom Daschle of South Dakota, the Senate minority leader, accused the White House of waging a "character attack" on Clarke.

Those who had expressed doubt that any investigation of Sept. 11 could avoid becoming politicized in an election year were proven right.

"This is going to end up as a partisan pillow fight," said Rep. Rob Simmons, R-Conn., a former CIA agent who has always been skeptical of the commission probe.

But by week's end, it had become much more than that. Senate Majority Leader Bill Frist, R-Tenn., said he wanted to declassify testimony Clarke gave to the Intelligence committees in 2002 and compare it with what he said this week, suggesting that Clarke had lied under oath. "Loyalty to any administration will be no defense if it is found that he has lied to Congress," Frist said.

The fighting that now surrounds the Sept. 11 investigation represents a culmination of partisan tensions and structural changes that have hobbled the intelligence oversight process in recent years, but particularly since the war on terrorism began. First, distrust between Republicans and Democrats forced Congress to limit the scope of its own joint Sept. 11 inquiry to address only intelligence failures. Indeed, so sensitive were the questions of wider accountability in the Bush administration that Congress was forced to outsource the broader probe to the independent commission.

Second, the Intelligence committees have shown they lack the influence in Congress to move prior recommendations for intelligence overhaul through the legislative process.

Third, the growing role of the military in clandestine and possibly covert operations in the war on terrorism has taken traditional oversight of those activities out of the hands of the Intelligence panels, which—along with their colleagues on the Armed Services committees—are now starting to grapple with that issue.

Experts agree that these factors have hampered Congress' ability to oversee the intelligence community, particularly this year, as presidential politics heightens distrust and diminishes any chance that the two parties can cooperate in getting to the bottom of the government's failures on issues ranging from Sept. 11 to its faulty intelligence before the Iraq war.

"There's always been the risk that moving this sort of inquiry into a public forum lets it become much more politicized," said James M. Lindsay, vice president of the Council on Foreign Relations and a former National Security Council official under President Bill Clinton. "But now, the big difference is that partisanship is much more intense."

OVERSIGHT OUTSOURCING

In 2002, Congress decided to turn a wide-ranging Sept. 11 inquiry over to an independent commission because of distrust between the parties: Republicans worried that Democrats on the Intelligence panels would lead the inquiry into an indictment of Bush policies, while Democrats feared a Republican whitewash.

In setting up the commission, both parties saw the possibility of avoiding a brawl. Republicans looked to the GOP chairman, former New Jersey Gov. Thomas H. Kean, as a safeguard against an aggressive anti-Bush inquiry. Democrats were heartened by the fact that the probe would be wide-ranging and have subpoena powers. And the bipartisan balance of commissioners—five Democrats, five Republicans—appeared to ensure that the panel would be immune to charges of politicization.

Before Congress approved the commission, there were tough fights over its composition, whether it would have subpoena powers, and whether the president could appoint its chairman. Some lawmakers prophesied that politics could overshadow the probe.

"In the heat of a presidential campaign, one is not always rational," Rep. Doug Bereuter, R-Neb., a member of the House Intelligence Committee, said at the time.

Partisan tension has also come into play in the Senate Intelligence Committee as it lurches ahead with its investigation into prewar intelligence on Iraq. Since June, when the panel began its work, committee members have openly clashed over the probe's scope. Republicans have generally resisted Democratic demands to expand the review and look at broader questions of the role of intelligence in policy making rather than simply intelligence failure.

In November, following a party-line scuffle over a leaked strategy memo that counseled Democrats to use the inquiry as a way to embarrass the White House, the panel's formal work almost ground to a halt. In February, its leaders—Chairman Pat Roberts, R-Kan., and ranking Democrat John D. Rockefeller IV of West Virginia—said they had reached a compromise that would meet some Democratic demands halfway. But the review's final report, due out later this spring, is still expected to place most of the onus on the Intelligence agencies rather than the White House.

Indeed, on the day of Clarke's testimony, Roberts expressed confidence that the report "will give the president somewhat of a boost."

LACK OF INFLUENCE

Even when the Intelligence committees' members have found common ground, they have encountered larger political roadblocks.

Last summer, the panels published a scathing account of how the CIA and FBI missed opportunities before the Sept. 11 attacks to track down al Qaeda inside the United States and share critical information. They also came up with a series of recommendations, including the creation of a new Cabinet-level post for a Director of National Intelligence.

Soon after the joint inquiry issued its report, Democratic Sen. Bob Graham of Florida introduced a measure (S 1520) that would codify its recommendations. But he has had no success in getting Republican colleagues to sign on. And the GOP leadership in the Senate has been unwilling to throw its weight behind those recommendations, reflecting its reluctance to cross swords with the White House and Pentagon, which oppose the changes.

Graham, whose reform legislation is still languishing in the Senate Intelligence Committee, says there is still a chance the Republican leaders of the House and Senate panels will take up the measure by this summer. But he acknowledges that Republicans are not likely to sign on as long as the White House and Pentagon remain opposed to the recommendations.

"All the president would have to do is call in the secretary of Defense and the director of Central Intelligence and issue an edict," Graham said. "But [Defense Secretary Donald H.] Rumsfeld has been, shall we say, most unenthusiastic, so it's no wonder the administration would drag its feet."

Historically, Congress has been slow to move on intelligence reform, says RAND analyst Greg Treverton, who served on the National Intelligence Council under Clinton. "But the current degree of partisanship means that reform is especially unlikely now."

INTO THE MUD

The extent to which intelligence oversight has become politicized was on display the week of March 22, even among the commissioners themselves as soon as they began questioning witnesses. Clarke was showered with praise by the Democratic commissioners but grilled by Republicans. His book,

Against All Enemies, arrived in bookstores only two days before his testimony, which drew Republican charges of opportunistic timing.

Once the White House began to retaliate, questioning Clarke's credibility, his effectiveness in fighting terror and the political motives for his criticism, lawmakers jumped into the fray. Christopher Shays, R-Conn., the chairman of the House Government Reform National Security Subcommittee, described Clarke as "the most uncooperative witness" ever before his panel, referring to a closed-door hearing in 2000.

"He did not have a plan to fight terrorism," Shays added. "He has no credibility with me. None."

GOP Sen. Jon Kyl of Arizona, who served on the Senate Intelligence Committee until January 2003, said, "It's disappointing to see what appears to be a partisan push. Maybe he's just doing it to plug the book."

Frist raised the stakes even higher March 26, suggesting that Clarke lied to Congress.

Democrats defended Clarke and urged the White House to halt its campaign against him.

"Please ask the people around you to stop the character attacks they are waging against Richard Clarke," said Daschle. "Ask them to stop their attempts to conceal information and confuse facts. Ask them to stop the long effort that has made the Sept. 11 commission's work more difficult than it should be."

Rockefeller, the top Democrat on the Senate Intelligence Committee, warned that the White House and its GOP allies in Congress would have a hard time discrediting Clarke because of his reputation as a tough, nonpartisan counterterrorism expert who had held senior positions from the Reagan administration onward before announcing his resignation in January 2003.

Rockefeller on March 26 spoke directly to Frist's suggestion that Clarke lied to Congress, saying: "If anyone truly believes that Mr. Clarke perjured himself before Congress, they should immediately refer the matter to the Justice Department."

Roberts, the Senate Intelligence chairman, would not discuss Clarke's specific allegations that the Bush White House ignored his warnings about al Qaeda and fixated on Iraq instead. But he described Clarke as a "brilliant," if obstreperous, man.

"He's capable, but was always embroiled in differences with others. Sometimes we had to schedule separate hearings because some people didn't want to be in the same room with him," Roberts said.

"I am surprised how strong his new statements are," Roberts added.

HIGH STAKES, HIGH TENSION

In the wake of Clarke's testimony, some lawmakers said it would be difficult for the commission to produce a neutral report by its deadline of July 26—just as the Democratic and Republican political conventions are getting under way.

"Nobody is naive," said Ron Wyden, D-Ore., "Everybody knows an election is coming up. It ups the ante in terms of the stakes of the commission."

But other lawmakers remained hopeful that the commission would be able to ignore politics and draft a neutral document that makes solid recommendations on how future attacks can be prevented.

"Even though they're struggling to do this, they ought to forget the public appearances and get the work done," said House Intelligence Chairman Porter J. Goss, R-Fla. "There is a positive contribution to make, but it's very important they keep their heads down."

But even if the final report is objective, "it will be used politically," said former Clinton adviser Rep. Rahm Emmanuel, D-Ill.

POLITICAL CURE

Whether congressional oversight of intelligence has become terminally corroded by partisan politics remains to be seen. Some lawmakers say they believe that at a time when Congress is controlled by Republicans, and a Republican sits in the White House, meaningful oversight is unlikely. Others say the disintegration of the process is a temporary function of election politics in a year in which the two parties are so closely matched in the presidential and congressional races.

But some say Congress should be able to assert its independence and exercise intelligence oversight assertively despite partisan gridlock, especially when the stakes are so high.

"The congressional joint inquiry into Sept. 11 was a very strong effort, and a lot of the partisanship that's been growing since 1992 was put aside in that case," said Loch Johnson, a former aide on the Senate Intelligence Committee who is now a political scientist at the University of Georgia. "Sometimes just being on that committee can convert a member into a gimlet-eyed overseer."

The problem, Johnson continued, is that "congressional attitudes toward oversight are like a roller coaster. And except for the Sept. 11 inquiry, we're in a period of general acquiescence."

That acquiescence, experts say, could be why the Intelligence panels have not been able to move any of the recommendations for overhauls that they made in July 2003, when they published the report on their joint inquiry into the Sept. 11 attacks.

Most of those recommendations, including a proposal to create a Director of National Intelligence, focused on streamlining decision-making and improving information-sharing among the dozen-plus agencies that make up the intelligence community.

Other panels, such as a blue-ribbon commission headed by former national security adviser Brent Scowcroft in 2001–02, have made similar proposals, also without success.

Many experts say the Pentagon, which receives most of the intelligence budget, is deeply opposed to such restructuring, because it might lose control over funds channeled to such agencies as the Defense Intelligence Agency and the National Security Agency.

And because of that political paralysis, says Lindsay, the type of changes that Graham and others would like to effect can come about only with a change in the political tides.

"There's deep disagreement among members now, so Congress finds it very hard to act—not just with intelligence reform, but with a whole slew of issues," Lindsay says. "But that's what the framers intended. When there's no agreement, Congress should be gridlocked until voters decide otherwise."

Senate Races Against the Nuclear Clock on Judges (2005)

DAVID NATHER

On May 11, Ben Nelson of Nebraska and Mark Pryor of Arkansas, both centrist Democrats, sat in the reading room just off the Senate floor and hashed out their latest ideas on how to prevent a Senate showdown over judicial nominees. Suddenly, their talks were cut short. A wayward Cessna was heading toward downtown Washington, and the building was being evacuated.

As Nelson and Pryor headed into the street with the fleeing crowd, they ran into Arizona Sen. John McCain, one of the most famous mavericks in the Republican Party. It wasn't the first time they had discussed their ideas with McCain, but they considered it a symbolic moment. As the capital seemed to be melting down in a security crisis, the three waded through the streets talking about how to prevent another kind of meltdown: a political crisis that could paralyze the Senate.

An effort that started as little more than hallway talk and phone conversations led to a last-minute deal May 23 that stopped Senate Majority Leader Bill Frist's plans to engineer a ruling the next day to bar filibusters of judicial nominations. A group that became known as the "gang of 14"—seven Republicans and seven Democrats—promised to vote against any such change as long

David Nather, "Senate Races Against the Nuclear Clock on Judges," *CQ Weekly* (May 30, 2005): 1440–1445. Copyright © 2005 by Congressional Quarterly Inc. Reproduced with permission of Congressional Quarterly Inc. via Copyright Clearance House.

as Democrats swore off future judicial filibusters in all but extraordinary cases. That unified promise had the effect of denying Frist the votes he needed to ban the practice altogether.

Frist's plan was dubbed the "nuclear option" for the damage many expect it would have done to the Senate's already tattered comity. But that threat was defused, at least temporarily, when moderates, mavericks and institutionalists from both parties tackled a dispute that Frist, a Tennessee Republican, and Democratic leader Harry Reid of Nevada chose not to resolve.

The unusual pact between the rank-and-file senators, headed by McCain and Nelson, was the result of a series of casual encounters and unusual, shifting alliances. Drafts were written, picked apart, rewritten and picked apart again. Escape clauses for Republicans and Democrats were drafted and sometimes tossed aside. Names of judicial nominees to be let through were floated in every possible combination. Details were added and then scaled back to keep the deal from sinking under its own weight.

"We had people we encouraged to come into the fold, we had some who joined on their own," Nelson recalled. "Everybody wanted to say yes. There wasn't anybody in that room looking to say no. They were all looking to say yes."

The dealmakers were immediately attacked by lawmakers and activists on both the left and the right, and as the week drew to a close, it was an open question whether the accord had averted the final showdown or merely postponed it. Frist promised to keep pressing for votes on President Bush's judicial nominees and threatened to revive the effort to ban judicial filibusters if Democrats began blocking them routinely again. "As Ronald Reagan was fond to say, 'trust but verify,'" Frist said.

Utah Republican Orrin G. Hatch, one of the most vocal proponents of ending filibusters on judicial nominees, agreed. "This is only the beginning," he said. "This is not a treaty."

But less than 24 hours after the group struck its deal and informed leaders, the Senate voted 81–18 to cut off debate on one nominee who had been blocked for four years: Priscilla R. Owen, chosen for a seat on the U.S. Court of Appeals for the 5th Circuit. She was confirmed the next day, 55–43.

Frist filed motions to end debate on two other nominees, setting up votes after this week's Memorial Day recess.

The talks worked, the participants said, because there was a shared sense of purpose. This wasn't an abstract issue, such as budgets or the future of class action lawsuits. This dispute, these senators believed, was a threat to the nature of their jobs. They did not want to serve in a chamber that essentially could look like a clone of the House.

"This happened because there was a group of us that thought the institution, and the very fundamentals of the institution, were at stake," said McCain.

Pryor said all of those in the group "understood that this was a major moment in Senate history, and in order for us to avoid doing some significant harm to the Senate, we needed to come together and work this out."

MONDAY, MAY 16

Members of the McCain-Nelson group were just beginning to hold meetings when they learned of an event that brought far greater urgency to the talks. Frist and Reid, who had been trading proposals and counterproposals to avert the nuclear option, had given up on their efforts.

At that point, Nelson recalled, the senators in the group realized it would be up to them to find a way out of the crisis. The news also removed, or at least lessened, a larger concern senators from both parties shared: the appearance that they were trying to take control of the judges issue away from their leaders.

"You don't want to be mutinous or undermine or in some way do something that degrades the ability of leaders to be able to lead," Nelson said. But if the leaders are not even talking about a solution anymore, he said, "there's nothing to undermine."

Trent Lott, the former Senate majority leader from Mississippi, had started out as Nelson's main Republican negotiating partner and then dropped out of the talks. Lott says he turned the reins over to McCain because his motives were being questioned: He was seen as trying to undermine Frist, who replaced him as Senate Republican leader. He also thought the language allowing Democrats to filibuster again was too broad.

The senators who came to form the core of the group—including Maine Republicans Susan Collins and Olympia J. Snowe, South Carolina conservative Lindsey Graham and senior Republican John W. Warner of Virginia—ordered all of their aides out of the room during the last week of meetings. That decision was crucial to the success of the talks, Collins said, because "there weren't the usual misunderstandings that happen when there's a filter."

TUESDAY, MAY 17

A previously scheduled meeting of the Senate Centrist Coalition, a bipartisan group of moderates headed by Snowe and Democrat Joseph I. Lieberman of Connecticut, turned into a forum for the expanding group of negotiators. Frist and Reid attended as well, mainly to get a sense of what kind of trade-offs the group had in mind.

Already, there were some absolute goals that the leaders were pressing on their members. Frist wanted to make sure no judicial nominees were bargained away. Reid wanted to make sure Democrats rejected any deal that did not guarantee that the nuclear option would never be used in the 109th Congress.

Those tensions were reflected in the draft agreements that were traded back and forth that day, in the centrist meeting and in two smaller gatherings. Two of them would have committed the Republicans to voting against the nuclear option, with no exceptions. They also pointedly added, "A decision by one or more signers to vote against cloture on a nominee during the 109th Congress does not relieve the other signers of their commitment" to vote against the nuclear option.

That kind of language grated on the Republicans. The drafts were already giving the Democrats the option of filibustering future judicial nominees under "extraordinary circumstances"—broadly defined, in language nearly identical to the phrasing in the final agreement. So if Democrats could leave open the possibility of future filibusters, Republicans argued, why couldn't Republicans leave themselves an escape clause as well? And already, several senators were asking the inevitable question: What happens if the other side doesn't live up to its end of the bargain?

"My response was, 'If we can't trust one another, there is no way to otherwise enforce an agreement,'" Nelson said. "You can't go to court. It's not a contract. This is a body where trust has to exist, and if it doesn't, not only can you not make this agreement, this understanding, but you probably can't do the business of the Senate."

WEDNESDAY, MAY 18

At 9:30 a.m., Frist convened the Senate and took up the Owen nomination. Frist's aides had made it clear that Republicans would file a cloture motion later in the week, setting up a test vote that could lead them to end judicial filibusters through the move they have come to call the "constitutional option," although Democrats still prefer to call it nuclear.

Frist told the Senate, "Vote for the nominee, vote against the nominee, confirm the nominee, reject the nominee. But in the end, vote."

As well-worn rhetoric from both sides dominated the Senate floor, the moderates and mavericks streamed into Warner's office in the Russell Senate Office Building, and later into the office of Republican Mike DeWine of Ohio. There, they traded drafts that tried to refine the language on the Republicans' pledge to oppose the constitutional option. One phrase committed Republicans to voting against the option "in light of the spirit and commitment" of [the] Democrats' pledge to limit the use of the filibuster. Another was more specific: Republicans would oppose the constitutional option "provided that there is continuing good-faith compliance with the commitments set forth" in the Democrats' pledge.

The wording wasn't trivial; it was crucial to making Republicans confident that they weren't giving away more than the Democrats.

There were also ever-changing lists of judges Democrats would let through and judges they could continue to filibuster. Democrats started by trying to allow through only two of the three most contentious nominees: Owen for the 5th Circuit, Janice Rogers Brown for the D.C. Circuit and William H. Pryor Jr. for the 11th Circuit. One draft even had a special section for Brown that would have allowed Democrats to filibuster her nomination to the D.C. Circuit but ruled out a filibuster if she were ever nominated to the 9th Circuit.

But Republicans said they needed to have up-or-down votes on all three, and soon the three began appearing in all of the drafts as cleared for votes. One version, however, included a crucial exception, later dropped: The agreement would not apply "should any one, or more, of these current pending individuals be nominated to the Supreme Court."

THURSDAY, MAY 19

In all of the talks, Warner had stood out as one of the few senators who was neither a moderate, like Nelson and Collins, nor a maverick, like McCain and Graham. He was simply a Senate veteran who cared about the institution. Now, he trudged slowly down a hallway of the Russell building with another institutionalist: Robert C. Byrd of West Virginia. A former majority leader from the days when Democrats ran the Senate, the 87-year-old Byrd was frail and trembling, leaning on a carved wooden cane as the 78-year-old Warner supported his arm. The two headed toward McCain's office with a new idea in hand that Byrd was convinced would "insulate us from the likelihood of filibusters, insulate us from the likelihood of the nuclear option."

In reality, it made the talks more complicated. The Byrd-Warner proposal included a new "advice and consent" clause that would have created a mechanism for the Senate Judiciary Committee to send the president a list of recommendations for any Supreme Court vacancy—a bipartisan list to be drawn up after "discussions with federal and state judges, lawyers, and esteemed members of the legal and academic communities."

Immediately, the prospect of getting six Republicans to sign an agreement with six Democrats—the goal of the talks—started slipping away. The idea of the Senate trying to tell Bush whom he could nominate wasn't likely to go over well with the strong-willed president.

About 7 p.m., the meeting broke up without an agreement, to the surprise of some of the negotiators. Although they agreed to keep talking over the weekend, with Pryor serving as the communications "hub," they were aware that momentum could slip away—and that they had to either close a deal or give up by the time the Senate started taking votes on Owen.

That deadline, as reporters pointed out to DeWine at one point, was now May 24. Hours earlier, Frist had announced that that would be the day for a cloture vote for the Owen nomination, to be followed, if the cloture vote failed to get the necessary 60-vote minimum, by a point of order from Frist that could lead to a ruling by the presiding officer that judges cannot be filibustered.

"Then we don't have much time," DeWine said.

FRIDAY, MAY 20

As the senators headed home for the weekend, Warner and Byrd worked by phone to trim the advice-and-consent language. Warner, under fire from conservatives, released a statement: "In no way is it our intent to affect the balance of respective power" as spelled out by Alexander Hamilton in Federalist Paper 66. Senators, Hamilton wrote, "cannot themselves *choose*—they can only ratify or reject the choice of the President."

Rather than lay out a detailed mechanism for recommending nominees to Bush, Warner and Byrd drafted a paragraph that simply would "encourage the executive branch of government to consult with members of the Senate, both Democrat and Republican, and with home-state senators prior to submitting a judicial nomination to the Senate for consideration." Later, they dropped the language about home-state senators.

At 2:20 p.m., Republican Sen. John Cornyn of Texas—Owen's home state— joked with Reid on the Senate floor, gave him a friendly pat on the back, and then filed the cloture motion that set the clock ticking toward the nuclear option.

MONDAY, MAY 23

The group arranged to meet in McCain's office one more time, at 6 p.m., just after a 5:30 vote on a procedural motion designed mainly to get all of the senators back into town. Frist announced that the Senate would be in session late into the night, and Democrats, eager to make the most of the filibuster fight, scheduled a screening of "Mr. Smith Goes to Washington" at midnight.

By early afternoon, though, the centrists quietly began spreading the word among themselves that the posturing might be unnecessary. "I think we're there," Nelson told Snowe.

The advice-and-consent language from Warner and Byrd had been trimmed. The rotating list of judges stopped, with Owen, Brown and Pryor cleared for votes, and two others—William G. Myers III for the 9th Circuit and Henry W. Saad for the 6th Circuit—exempted from any no-filibuster pledge. Other nominees who had been addressed in earlier drafts, such as Richard A. Griffin and Susan Bieke Neilson for the 6th Circuit, were dropped.

And the crucial language for Republicans—allowing them to vote for the nuclear option in the future if they thought Democrats were returning to unreasonable filibusters—had been tweaked ever so slightly. It now declared that Republicans would vote against the option "in light of the spirit and continuing commitments in this agreement." In other words, Democrats would have to keep their end of the bargain.

"If one of the seven decides to filibuster and I believe it is not an extraordinary circumstance for the country," said Graham, "I have retained my rights under this agreement to change the rules if I think that is best for the country."

As Warner put it, "The one unanswered question that guided me all the way through is . . . what would happen to the Senate if the nuclear option were done? No one was able to answer that to my satisfaction."

Shortly before 7:30 p.m., the smiling group raced out of McCain's office to tell Frist and Reid the showdown was off.

Congress Skirts Issue with Sham Disaster Plan (2004)

NORMAN ORNSTEIN

Two years and seven months after Sept. 11, 2001—a day in which the U.S. Capitol and the House of Representatives narrowly dodged a disaster that could have left Congress without a working quorum for months at the worst possible time—the House debated how to provide a continuing constitutional system in the event of a catastrophic terrorist attack.

Unfortunately, the resulting bill, which was hailed by its sponsors and Republican House leaders as the ultimate and only solution to the issue, has divided the House on partisan lines. It is in fact badly crafted and even counterproductive.

The bill passed by the House mandates that if 100 or more members are killed, the speaker will issue a resolution calling for expedited special elections in vacant districts. Candidates would have to be nominated within 10 days and the elections held within 35 days after that—one third the time it normally takes for special elections.

There are obvious problems. What if most House members are incapacitated but alive—in burn units, comatose or quarantined from a chemical or biological attack? The House's plan—to redefine a quorum to exclude incapacitated members—is patently unconstitutional. Moreover, what happens in the 45 days and more before elections are held, winners certified and members sworn in? The answer is martial law, with no checks or balances. Under the worst of worst-case scenarios, the President invoking martial law might be not the elected president, but a replacement under the Presidential Succession Act.

There is more. Let us imagine that a bomb in or near the Capitol kills 350 of the 435 members of the House and is accompanied by attacks in other cities. It might be days before survivors could be found in the rubble, weeks before they could deliver aid to the other sites.

At this point, few would want to focus on nominating candidates or holding elections. Districts choosing candidates for Congress in 10 days would have no primaries or conventions; candidates would be chosen by a few officials in the equivalent of smoke-filled rooms.

In the succeeding 35 days, as local election officials scrambled to prepare for the voting, the candidates—without an opportunity to create staffs or raise money—would wage a pseudo-campaign, directed at an electorate with its collective mind on other things—such as a lack of mail or electricity.

These elections, in other words, would be a sham: no chance for a range of candidates to emerge; no chance for debate. And of course, the 350 House members elected under these conditions would, if past experience is any guide, become incumbents with the ability to serve for as long as they wanted—98 percent would win re-election regularly thereafter.

After long deliberation, the bipartisan Continuity of Government Commission unanimously concluded that the only answer was emergency interim appointments to Congress until real elections could be held or incapacitated members were ready to resume their seats. It recommended a constitutional amendment to give Congress the authority to do just that. That is also the conclusion reached by Sen. John Cornyn (R., Texas), chairman of the Constitution subcommittee.

Such House leaders as Speaker Dennis Hastert, Majority Leader Tom DeLay and Judiciary Chairman F. James Sensenbrenner Jr., who largely ignored the issue of continuity of government for two years after Sept. 11, are bringing up the amendment soon for a vote without hearings or serious debate—while applying strong partisan pressure to kill it. They are hoping that that action will let them wash their hands of the issue. It shouldn't. Neither house of Congress should try to fool itself or America into believing that this is a solution to the very real problem of another terrorist attack on Washington.

CHAPTER 10

The Presidency

READINGS IN THIS CHAPTER

*T*he presidency is discussed in Article II of the Constitution, but people often think of it as the first branch of American government. More than any other elected official, the president is identified, both domestically and abroad, as the leader of the United States. After all, the president is the only person elected nationally, albeit indirectly through the electoral college. The president is expected to be the voice of the people and to respond to their concerns, even though the president must work with others to create and implement policy. Political scientist Theodore Lowi has aptly described the president's authority as "power invested, promise unfulfilled."

In creating the position of president, the Framers were determined to ensure that the office would not be akin to a monarch. Although a president originally could serve an unlimited number of terms (the two-term limit was instituted with the Twenty-Second Amendment in 1951), each term was fixed at four years, after which the president would have to win reelection to stay in office. Furthermore, the Framers established three branches in the national government to ensure that no individual would exercise too much independent authority. The president, for example, would have the power to veto legislation, but Congress could override a veto with a two-thirds vote in both chambers. The president would have the power to nominate cabinet secretaries and judges, but the Senate would have to ratify those appointments by majority vote. The president would be commander-in-chief, but only Congress would have the power to declare war. While the implementation of these powers may have evolved differently than the Framers intended, the Constitution clearly was designed to limit the autonomy of each branch of government.

Of the Framers, Alexander Hamilton was among the most sympathetic to the need for a strong chief executive, and in the Federalist No. 70, the first reading in this chapter, he lays out his case for the powers granted to the president. "Energy in the executive is a leading character in the definition of good government," Hamilton famously writes, defining *energy* as "unity; duration; an adequate provision for his support; and competent powers." *Unity* refers to a single executive rather than a co-presidency or a president who would work with an executive council that had binding powers, proposals made during the drafting of the Constitution. *Duration* refers to a term of office that will provide sufficient opportunity for the president to enact policy. Opponents of the Constitution argued that four-year intervals between presidential elections provided insufficient checks against abuse of executive power, but Hamilton argues that four years are needed for the president to make decisions without being subject to momentary popular passions. The president also requires a fixed salary that will not change during the term of office, and the president needs sufficient power to accomplish the responsibilities outlined in Article II of the Constitution.

The contentious debates during the Constitutional Convention about the president's powers continue today. Article II of the Constitution states that "[t]he executive Power shall be vested in a President of the United States of America," but it does not define the extent of, or limits to, that power. It does identify certain specific powers of the president, such as the power to grant pardons, but the Constitution historically has not been interpreted as granting the president only the powers explicitly discussed in Article II. Presidents from George Washington onward have interpreted executive power broadly, and for the most part, Congress and the courts have supported an expansive view of presidential power.

Since the presidency of Franklin D. Roosevelt (FDR), in particular, presidential power has increased definitively. Presidential scholar Fred I. Greenstein argues in this chapter that FDR's administration marks the beginning of the "modern presidency." As Greenstein sees it, four features distinguish modern presidents from their predecessors: increased formal and informal powers, chief agenda-setting authority, increased staff and advisory resources, and heightened visibility. Some of these changes began to evolve before FDR took office—the president's authority as chief agenda-setter, for example, stems from the Budget and Accounting Act of 1921, in which Congress called for the president to submit an annual federal budget proposal. Likewise, Theodore, not Franklin Delano, Roosevelt was the first president to routinely appeal directly to the public and use his position as a "bully pulpit." Nevertheless, the modern presidency originates with FDR because of the momentous changes in government and policymaking that took place during his twelve years in office.

The rise of the modern presidency makes the executive branch far more powerful than even Hamilton likely intended, but even so, some scholars contend that the president's ability to accomplish policy goals remains limited. Still, the formal constitutional powers and prerogatives of the presidency are limited. Presidential scholar and adviser Richard E. Neustadt argues in this chapter that "[i]n form all Presidents are leaders nowadays. In fact this guarantees no more than that they will be clerks. Everybody now expects the man inside the White House to do something about everything." Neustadt concludes that, ultimately, "Presidential power is the power to persuade."

In the 1960s, Neustadt's tenets about the need for presidents to accrue power were widely accepted. In the aftermath of the Vietnam War and Watergate scandal, however, critics questioned whether presidents had acquired *too* much power. Presidential scholar Arthur M. Schlesinger, Jr., describes the institution as the "imperial presidency." The War Powers Resolution of 1973 and the Budget Control and Impoundment Act of 1974 were passed specifically to curtail presidential power, with Congress passing the former despite a presidential veto. But calls for limiting presidential power were short-lived, and by the 1980s, presidential leadership in policymaking was firmly established once again.

Discussions today about presidential power typically focus more on evaluating how the president can use resources most effectively, rather than on limiting the scope of presidential authority. Greenstein identifies six areas in which modern presidents must excel: vision, public communication, political skill, organizational resources, cognitive style, and emotional intelligence. Although no modern president has displayed skill in every area, Greenstein shows how strengths and weaknesses in each affect opportunities for leadership. One of the greatest challenges for presidents is determining which of these variables is most important for them to accomplish their agendas.

In the twenty-first century, especially after the terrorist attacks of September 11, 2001, an expansive view of presidential power is accepted, even expected, in the United States. In foreign policy in particular, the president takes the lead in diplomacy, alliance-building, and military action. For instance, while domestic and international critics have questioned the legitimacy of the Bush administration's decision to wage war in Iraq in 2003, both the public and Congress supported the president's authority to make that decision at the time. In this chapter, political scientist Aaron Wildavsky, writing in 1966, argues that the United States has "two Presidencies": one in foreign policy, where Congress and the public defer to the president in policymaking, and the other in domestic policy, where presidential actions are more subject to checks. As the United States wages the ongoing war on terror, Wildavsky's pithy analysis continues to provide useful insights on the sources of presidential power.

10.1 The Federalist No. 70 (1788)

ALEXANDER HAMILTON

INTRODUCTION

In the Federalist No. 70, Alexander Hamilton makes a cogent case for a powerful chief executive, as outlined in Article II of the Constitution. Hamilton illustrates why the president will be less powerful than a monarch, explaining that the president must be elected to hold office, must make most major decisions in conjunction with one or both chambers of Congress, can be impeached, and does not have absolute veto power. Given these limitations on presidential power, Hamilton argues, "[e]nergy in the executive" is essential to let the president perform required duties. In this paper, he focuses on the

Alexander Hamilton, "The Federalist No. 70," (1788; Yale Law School Avalon Project, 1996), http://www.yale.edu/lawweb/avalon/federal/fed70.htm.

importance of unity in the executive, pointing out the dangers of a co-presidency or of an executive council that can overturn presidential decisions. Hamilton notes that checks on the president will include "a due dependence on the people," and "a due responsibility."

■

To the People of the State of New York:

There is an idea, which is not without its advocates, that a vigorous Executive is inconsistent with the genius of republican government. The enlightened well-wishers to this species of government must at least hope that the supposition is destitute of foundation; since they can never admit its truth, without at the same time admitting the condemnation of their own principles. Energy in the Executive is a leading character in the definition of good government. It is essential to the protection of the community against foreign attacks; it is not less essential to the steady administration of the laws; to the protection of property against those irregular and high-handed combinations which sometimes interrupt the ordinary course of justice; to the security of liberty against the enterprises and assaults of ambition, of faction, and of anarchy. Every man the least conversant in Roman story, knows how often that republic was obliged to take refuge in the absolute power of a single man, under the formidable title of Dictator, as well against the intrigues of ambitious individuals who aspired to the tyranny, and the seditions of whole classes of the community whose conduct threatened the existence of all government, as against the invasions of external enemies who menaced the conquest and destruction of Rome.

There can be no need, however, to multiply arguments or examples on this head. A feeble Executive implies a feeble execution of the government. A feeble execution is but another phrase for a bad execution; and a government ill executed, whatever it may be in theory, must be, in practice, a bad government.

Taking it for granted, therefore, that all men of sense will agree in the necessity of an energetic Executive, it will only remain to inquire, what are the ingredients which constitute this energy? How far can they be combined with those other ingredients which constitute safety in the republican sense? And how far does this combination characterize the plan which has been reported by the convention?

The ingredients which constitute energy in the Executive are, first, unity; secondly, duration; thirdly, an adequate provision for its support; fourthly, competent powers.

The ingredients which constitute safety in the republican sense are, first, a due dependence on the people, secondly, a due responsibility.

Those politicians and statesmen who have been the most celebrated for the soundness of their principles and for the justice of their views, have declared in favor of a single Executive and a numerous legislature. They have with great propriety, considered energy as the most necessary qualification of the former, and have regarded this as most applicable to power in a single hand, while they have, with equal propriety, considered the latter as best adapted to deliberation and wisdom, and best calculated to conciliate the confidence of the people and to secure their privileges and interests.

That unity is conducive to energy will not be disputed. Decision, activity, secrecy, and despatch will generally characterize the proceedings of one man in a much more eminent degree than the proceedings of any greater number; and in proportion as the number is increased, these qualities will be diminished.

This unity may be destroyed in two ways: either by vesting the power in two or more magistrates of equal dignity and authority; or by vesting it ostensibly in one man, subject, in whole or in part, to the control and co-operation of others, in the capacity of counsellors to him. Of the first, the two Consuls of Rome may serve as an example; of the last, we shall find examples in the constitutions of several of the States. New York and New Jersey, if I recollect right, are the only States which have intrusted the executive authority wholly to single men. Both these methods of destroying the unity of the Executive have their partisans; but the votaries of an executive council are the most numerous. They are both liable, if not to equal, to similar objections, and may in most lights be examined in conjunction.

The experience of other nations will afford little instruction on this head. As far, however, as it teaches any thing, it teaches us not to be enamoured of plurality in the Executive. We have seen that the Achaeans, on an experiment of two Praetors, were induced to abolish one. The Roman history records many instances of mischiefs to the republic from the dissensions between the Consuls, and between the military Tribunes, who were at times substituted for the Consuls. But it gives us no specimens of any peculiar advantages derived to the state from the circumstance of the plurality of those magistrates. That the dissensions between them were not more frequent or more fatal, is a matter of astonishment, until we advert to the singular position in which the republic was almost continually placed, and to the prudent policy pointed out by the circumstances of the state, and pursued by the Consuls, of making a division of the government between them. The patricians engaged in a perpetual struggle with the plebeians for the preservation of their ancient authorities and dignities; the Consuls, who were generally chosen out of the former body, were commonly united by the personal interest they had in the defense of the privileges of their order. In addition to this motive of union, after the arms of the republic had considerably expanded the bounds of its empire, it became an established custom with the Consuls to divide the administration between themselves by lot one of them remaining at Rome to govern the city and its environs, the other taking the command in the more distant provinces. This expedient must, no doubt, have had great influence in preventing those collisions and rivalships which might otherwise have embroiled the peace of the republic.

But quitting the dim light of historical research, attaching ourselves purely to the dictates of reason and good sense, we shall discover much greater cause to reject than to approve the idea of plurality in the Executive, under any modification whatever.

Wherever two or more persons are engaged in any common enterprise or pursuit, there is always danger of difference of opinion. If it be a public trust or office, in which they are clothed with equal dignity and authority, there is peculiar danger of personal emulation and even animosity. From either, and especially from all these causes, the most bitter dissensions are apt to spring. Whenever these happen, they lessen the respectability, weaken the authority, and distract the plans and operation of those whom they divide. If they should unfortunately assail the supreme executive magistracy of a country, consisting of a plurality of persons, they might impede or frustrate the most important measures of the government, in the most critical emergencies of the state. And what is still worse, they might split the community into the most violent and irreconcilable factions, adhering differently to the different individuals who composed the magistracy.

Men often oppose a thing, merely because they have had no agency in planning it, or because it may have been planned by those whom they dislike. But if they have been consulted, and have happened to disapprove, opposition then becomes, in their estimation, an indispensable duty of self-love. They seem to think themselves bound in honor, and by all the motives of personal infallibility, to defeat the success of what has been resolved upon contrary to their sentiments. Men of upright, benevolent tempers have too many opportunities of remarking, with horror, to what desperate lengths this disposition is sometimes carried, and how often the great interests of society are sacrificed to the vanity, to the conceit, and to the obstinacy of individuals, who have credit enough to make their passions and their caprices interesting to mankind. Perhaps the question now before the public may, in its consequences, afford melancholy proofs of the effects of this despicable frailty, or rather detestable vice, in the human character.

Upon the principles of a free government, inconveniences from the source just mentioned must necessarily be submitted to in the formation of the legislature; but it is unnecessary, and therefore unwise, to introduce them into the constitution of the Executive. It is here too that they may be most pernicious. In the legislature, promptitude of decision is oftener an evil than a benefit. The differences of opinion, and the jarrings of parties in that department of the government, though they may sometimes obstruct salutary plans, yet often promote deliberation and circumspection, and serve to check excesses in the majority. When a resolution too is once taken, the opposition must be at an end. That resolution is a law, and resistance to it punishable. But no favorable circumstances palliate or atone for the disadvantages of dissension in the executive department. Here, they are pure and unmixed. There is no point at which they cease to operate. They serve to embarrass and weaken the execution of the plan or measure to which they relate, from the first step to the final conclusion of it. They constantly counteract those qualities in the Executive which are the most necessary ingredients in its composition, vigor and expedition, and this without any counterbalancing good. In the conduct of war, in which the energy of the Executive is the bulwark of the national security, every thing would be to be apprehended from its plurality.

It must be confessed that these observations apply with principal weight to the first case supposed that is, to a plurality of magistrates of equal dignity and authority a scheme, the advocates for which are not likely to form a numerous sect; but they apply, though not with equal, yet with considerable weight to the project of a council, whose concurrence is made constitutionally necessary to the operations of the ostensible Executive. An artful cabal in that council would be able to distract and to enervate the whole system of administration. If no such cabal should exist, the mere diversity of views and opinions would alone be sufficient to tincture the exercise of the executive authority with a spirit of habitual feebleness and dilatoriness.

But one of the weightiest objections to a plurality in the Executive, and which lies as much against the last as the first plan, is, that it tends to conceal faults and destroy responsibility. Responsibility is of two kinds to censure and to punishment. The first is the more important of the two, especially in an elective office. Man, in public trust, will much oftener act in such a manner as to render him unworthy of being any longer trusted, than in such a manner as to make him obnoxious to legal punishment. But the multiplication of the Executive adds to the difficulty of detection in either case. It often becomes impossible, amidst mutual accusations, to determine on whom the blame or the punishment of a pernicious measure, or series of pernicious measures, ought really to fall. It is shifted from one to another with so much dexterity, and under such plausible appearances, that the public opinion is left in suspense about the real author. The circumstances which may have led to any national miscarriage or misfortune are sometimes so complicated that, where there are a number of actors who may have had different degrees and kinds of agency, though we may clearly see upon the whole that there has been mismanagement, yet it may be impracticable to pronounce to whose account the evil which may have been incurred is truly chargeable. "I was overruled by my council. The council were so divided in their opinions that it was impossible to obtain any better resolution on the point." These and similar pretexts are constantly at hand, whether true or false. And who is there that will either take the trouble or incur the odium, of a strict scrunity into the secret springs of the transaction? Should there be found a citizen zealous enough to undertake the unpromising task, if there happen to be collusion between the parties concerned, how easy it is to clothe the circumstances with so much ambiguity, as to render it uncertain what was the precise conduct of any of those parties?

In the single instance in which the governor of this State is coupled with a council that is, in the appointment to offices, we have seen the mischiefs of it in the view now under consideration. Scandalous appointments to important offices have been made. Some cases, indeed, have been so flagrant that *all parties* have agreed in the impropriety of the thing. When inquiry has been made, the blame has been laid by the governor on the members of the council, who, on their part, have charged it upon his nomination; while the people remain altogether at a loss to determine, by whose influence their interests have been committed to hands so unqualified and so manifestly improper. In tenderness to individuals, I forbear to descend to particulars.

It is evident from these considerations, that the plurality of the Executive tends to deprive the people of the two greatest securities they can have for the faithful exercise of any delegated power, first, the restraints of public opinion, which lose their efficacy, as well on account of the division of the censure attendant on bad measures among a number, as on account of the uncertainty on whom it ought to fall; and, secondly, the opportunity of discovering with facility and clearness the misconduct of the persons they trust, in order either to their removal from office or to their actual punishment in cases which admit of it.

In England, the king is a perpetual magistrate; and it is a maxim which has obtained for the sake of the public peace, that he is unaccountable for his administration, and his person sacred. Nothing, therefore, can be wiser in that kingdom, than to annex to the king a constitutional council, who may be responsible to the nation for the advice they give. Without this, there would be no responsibility whatever in the executive department an idea inadmissible in a free government. But even there the king is not bound by the resolutions of his council, though they are answerable for the advice they give. He is the absolute master of his own conduct in the exercise of his office, and may observe or disregard the counsel given to him at his sole discretion.

But in a republic, where every magistrate ought to be personally responsible for his behavior in office the reason which in the British Constitution dictates the propriety of a council, not only ceases to apply, but turns against the institution. In the monarchy of Great Britain, it furnishes a substitute for the prohibited responsibility of the chief magistrate, which serves in some degree as a hostage to the national justice for his good behavior. In the American republic, it would serve to destroy, or would greatly diminish, the intended and necessary responsibility of the Chief Magistrate himself.

The idea of a council to the Executive, which has so generally obtained in the State constitutions, has been derived from that maxim of republican jealousy which considers power as safer in the hands of a number of men than of a single man. If the maxim should be admitted to be applicable to the case, I should contend that the advantage on that side would not counterbalance the numerous disadvantages on the opposite side. But I do not think the rule at all applicable to the executive power. I clearly concur in opinion, in this particular, with a writer whom the celebrated Junius pronounces to be "deep, solid, and ingenious," that "the executive power is more easily confined when it is *one*"; that it is far more safe there should be a single object for the jealousy and watchfulness of the people; and, in a word, that all multiplication of the Executive is rather dangerous than friendly to liberty.

A little consideration will satisfy us, that the species of security sought for in the multiplication of the Executive, is unattainable. Numbers must be so great as to render combination difficult, or they are rather a source of danger than of security. The united credit and influence of several individuals must be more formidable to liberty, than the credit and influence of either of them separately. When power, therefore, is placed in the hands of so small a number of men, as to admit of their interests and views being easily combined in a common enterprise, by an artful leader, it becomes more liable to abuse, and more dangerous when abused, than if it be lodged in the hands of one man; who, from the very circumstance of his being alone, will be more narrowly watched and more readily suspected, and who cannot unite so great a mass of influence as when he is associated with others. The Decemvirs of Rome, whose name denotes their number, were more to be dreaded in their usurpation than any *one* of them would have been. No person would think of proposing an Executive much more numerous than that body; from six to a dozen have been suggested for the number of the council. The extreme of these numbers, is not too great for an easy combination; and from such a combination America would have more to fear, than from the ambition of any single individual. A council to a magistrate, who is himself responsible for what he does, are generally nothing better than a clog upon his good intentions, are often the instruments and accomplices of his bad and are almost always a cloak to his faults.

I forbear to dwell upon the subject of expense; though it be evident that if the council should be numerous enough to answer the principal end aimed at by the institution, the salaries of the members, who must be drawn from their homes to reside at the seat of government, would form an item in the catalogue of public expenditures too serious to be incurred for an object of equivocal utility. I will only add that, prior to the appearance of the Constitution, I rarely met with an intelligent man from any of the States, who did not admit, as the result of experience, that the *unity* of the executive of this State was one of the best of the distinguishing features of our constitution.

PUBLIUS

10.2 Presidential Power and the Modern Presidents (1990)

RICHARD E. NEUSTADT

INTRODUCTION

Richard E. Neustadt's *Presidential Power* is perhaps the most significant study of the American presidency in the twentieth century. Based on his experience working for President Harry S. Truman, as well as his observations of the FDR administration (in which his father served) and President Dwight D. Eisenhower's years in office, Neustadt presents a masterful analysis of how a president can successfully achieve a policy agenda. Rejecting the conventional view in the 1950s about presidential power, Neustadt argues that the American president faces many obstacles to policymaking, both constitutional and political. The Framers designed a system of "separated institutions *sharing* powers," which requires the president to work with different constituencies, including Congress and the public, to enact policy. Persuading these constituents to support policy proposals is no easy task. As Neustadt writes, "No one else sits where [the president] sits or sees quite as he sees; no one else feels the full weight of his obligations." In the following excerpt from *Presidential Power,* Neustadt discusses the challenges presidents face in office and explains how they must use *informal resources* to maximize their power and accomplish their goals.

■

LEADER OR CLERK?

In the United States we like to "rate" a President. We measure him as "weak" or "strong" and call what we are measuring his "leadership." We do not wait until a man is dead; we rate him from the moment he takes office. We are quite right to do so. His office has become the focal point of politics and policy in our political system. Our commentators and our politicians make a specialty of taking the man's measurements. The rest of us join in when we feel "government" impinging on our private lives. In the third quarter of the twentieth century millions of us have that feeling often.[1]

---

[1]Throughout, the male gender is justified historically but not prospectively when referring to a President. When used as a synonym for human beings it is outmoded.

This book is an endeavor to illuminate what we are measuring. Although we all make judgments about presidential leadership, we often base our judgments upon images of office that are far removed from the reality. We also use those images when we tell one another whom to choose as President. But it is risky to appraise a man in office or to choose a man for office on false premises about the nature of his job. When the job is the Presidency of the United States the risk becomes excessive. . . .

We deal here with the President himself and with his influence on governmental action. In institutional terms the Presidency now includes two thousand men and women. The President is only one of them. But his performance scarcely can be measured without focusing on him. In terms of party, or of country, or the West, so-called, his leadership involves far more than governmental action. But the sharpening of spirit and of values and of purposes is not done in a vacuum. Although governmental action may not be the whole of leadership, all else is nurtured by it and gains meaning from it. Yet if we treat the Presidency as the President, we cannot measure him as though he were the government. Not action as an outcome but his impact on the outcome is the measure of the man. His strength or weakness, then, turns on his personal capacity to influence the conduct of the men who make up government. His influence becomes the mark of leadership. To rate a President according to these rules, one looks into the man's own capabilities as seeker and as wielder of effective influence upon the other men involved in governing the country. . . .

Presidential on the title page means nothing but the President. Power means his influence. It helps to have these meanings settled at the start.

There are two ways to study "presidential power." One way is to focus on the tactics, so to speak, of influencing certain men in given situations: how to get a bill through Congress, how to settle strikes, how to quiet cabinet feuds, or how to stop a Suez. The other way is to step back from tactics on those "givens" and to deal with influence in more strategic terms: what is its nature and what are its sources? What can *this* man accomplish to improve the prospect that he will have influence when he wants it? Strategically, the question is not how he masters Congress in a peculiar instance, but what he does to boost his chance for mastery in any instance, looking toward tomorrow from today. . . .

To look into the strategy of presidential influence one must decide at whom to look. Power problems vary with scope and scale of government, the state of politics, the progress of technology, the pace of world relationships. Power in the 1960s cannot be acquired or employed on the same terms as those befitting Calvin Coolidge or Theodore Roosevelt or Grover Cleveland or James K. Polk. But there is a real likelihood that in the next decade a President will have to reach for influence and use it under much the same conditions we have known since the Second World War. If so, the men whose problems shed most light on the White House prospects are Dwight David Eisenhower and Harry S Truman.

It is at them, primarily, that we shall look. To do so is to see the shadow of another, Franklin D. Roosevelt. They worked amidst the remnants of his voter coalition, and they filled an office that his practice had enlarged.

Our two most recent Presidents have had in common something that is likely to endure into our future: the setting for a great deal of their work. They worked in an environment of policy and politics marked by a high degree of continuity. To sense the continuity from Truman's time through Eisenhower's one need only place the newspapers of 1959 alongside those of 1949. Save for the issue of domestic communists, the subject matter of our policy and politics remains almost unchanged. We deal as we have done in terms of cold war, of an arms race, of a competition overseas, of danger from inflation, and of damage from recession. We skirmish on the frontiers of the welfare state and in the borderlands of race relations. Aspects change, but labels stay the same. So do dilemmas. Everything remains unfinished business. Not in this century has there been comparable continuity from a decade's beginning to its end; count back from 1949 and this grows plain. There even has been continuity in the behavior of our national electorate; what Samuel Lubell nine years ago called "stalemate" in our partisan alignments has not broken yet.

The similarities in Truman's setting and in Eisenhower's give their years a unity distinct from the war years, or the depression era, or the twenties, or before. In governmental terms, at least, the fifteen years since V-J day deserve a designation all their own. "Midcentury" will serve for present purposes. And what distinguishes midcentury can be put very briefly: emergencies in policy with politics as usual.

"Emergency" describes midcentury conditions only by the standards of the past. By present standards what would once have been emergency is commonplace. Policy dilemmas through the postwar period resemble past emergencies in one respect, their difficulty and complexity for government. Technological innovation, social and political change abroad, population growth at home impose enormous strains not only on the managerial equipment of our policymakers but also on their intellectual resources. The gropings of mature men at midcentury remind one of the intellectual confusions stemming from depression, thirty years ago, when men were also pushed past comprehension by the novelty of their condition. In our time innovation keeps us constantly confused; no sooner do we start to comprehend than something new is added and we grope again. But unlike the great difficulties of the past, our policy dilemmas rarely produce what the country feels as crisis. Not even the Korean War brought anything approaching sustained national consensus. Since 1945 innumerable situations have been felt as crises inside government; there rarely has been comparable feeling outside government. In the era of the Cold War we have practiced "peacetime" politics. What else could we have done? Cold War is not a crisis; it becomes a way of life.

Our politics has been as usual, but only by the standard of past crises. In comparison with what was once normality, our politics has been unusual. The weakening of party ties, the emphasis on personality, the close approach of world events, the changeability of public moods, and above all the ticket splitting, none of this was usual before the Second World War. The symbol of midcentury political conditions is the White House in one party's hands with Congress in the other's—a symbol plainly visible in eight of the past fifteen years and all but visible in four of the remaining seven. Nothing really comparable has been seen in this country since the 1880s. And the eighties were not troubled by emergencies in policy.

As for politics and policy combined, we have seen some precursors of our setting at midcentury. Franklin Roosevelt had a reasonably comparable setting in his middle years as President, though not in his first years and not after Pearl Harbor. Indeed, if one excepts the war, midcentury could properly be said to start with Roosevelt's second term. Our recent situation is to be compared, as well, with aspects of the Civil War. Abraham Lincoln is much closer to us in condition than in time, the Lincoln plagued by Radicals and shunned by Democrats amid the managerial and intellectual confusions of twentieth-century warfare in the nineteenth century. And in 1919 Woodrow Wilson faced and was defeated by conditions something like our own. But save for these men one can say of Truman and of Eisenhower that they were the first who had to fashion presidential influence out of midcentury materials. Presumably they will not be the last.

We tend to measure Truman's predecessors as though "leadership" consisted of initiatives in economics, or diplomacy, or legislation, or in mass communication. If we measured him and his successors so, they would be leaders automatically. A striking feature of our recent past has been the transformation into routine practice of the actions we once treated as exceptional. A President may retain liberty, in Woodrow Wilson's phrase, "to be as big a man as he can." But nowadays he cannot be as small as he might like.

Our two most recent Presidents have gone through all the motions we traditionally associate with strength in office. So will the man who takes the oath on January 20, 1961. In instance after instance the exceptional behavior of our earlier "strong" Presidents has now been set by statute as a regular requirement. Theodore Roosevelt once assumed the steward's role in the emergency created by the great coal strike of 1902; the Railway Labor Act and the Taft-Hartley Act now make such interventions mandatory upon Presidents. The other Roosevelt once asserted personal responsibility for gauging and for guiding the American economy; the Employment Act binds his successors to that task. Wilson and FDR became chief spokesmen, leading actors, on a world stage at the height of war; now UN membership, far-flung alliances, prescribe that role continuously in times termed "peace." Through both world wars our Presidents grappled experimentally with an emergency-created need to integrate foreign and military policies; the National Security Act now takes that need for granted as a constant of our times. FDR and Truman made themselves responsible for the development and first use of atomic weapons; the Atomic Energy Act now puts a comparable burden on the back of every President. And what has escaped statutory recognition has mostly been accreted into presidential common law, confirmed by custom, no less binding: the fireside chat and the press conference, for example, or the personally presented legislative programs, or personal campaigning in congressional elections.

In form all Presidents are leaders nowadays. In fact this guarantees no more than that they will be clerks. Everybody now expects the man inside the White House to do something about everything. Laws and customs now reflect acceptance of him as the great initiator, an acceptance quite as widespread at the Capitol as at his end of Pennsylvania Avenue. But such acceptance does not signify that all the rest of government is at his feet. It merely signifies that other men have found it practically impossible to do their jobs without assurance of initiatives from him. Service for themselves, not power for the President, has brought them to accept his leadership in form. They find his actions useful in their business. The transformation of his routine obligations testifies to their dependence on an active White House. A President, these days, is an invaluable clerk. His services are in demand all over Washington. His influence, however, is a very different matter. Laws and customs tell us little about leadership in fact.[2]

Why have our Presidents been honored with this clerkship? The answer is that no one else's services suffice. Our Constitution, our traditions, and our politics provide no better source for the initiatives a President can take. Executive officials need decisions, and political protection, and a referee for fights. Where are these to come from but the White House? Congressmen need an agenda from outside, something with high status to respond to or react against. What provides it better than the program of the President? Party politicians need a record to defend in the next national campaign. How can it be made except by "their" administration? Private persons with a public ax to grind may need a helping hand or they may need a grinding stone. In either case, who gives more satisfaction than a President? And outside the United States, in every country where our policies and postures influence home politics, there will be people needing just the "right" thing said and done or just the "wrong" thing stopped in Washington. What symbolizes Washington more nearly than the White House?

A modern President is bound to face demands for aid and service from five more or less distinguishable sources: from executive officialdom, from Congress, from his partisans, from citizens at large, and from abroad. The Presidency's clerkship is expressive of these pressures. In effect they are constituency pressures, and each President has five sets of constituents. The

---

[2]This is the basis for a key distinction . . . between formal powers, or "powers," as synonymous with legal or customary "authority" and power, always in the singular, no quotation marks, as synonymous with personal influence. . . .

five are not distinguished by their membership; membership is obviously an overlapping matter. And taken one by one they do not match the man's electorate; one of them, indeed, is outside his electorate. They are distinguished, rather, by their different claims upon him. Initiatives are what they want, for five distinctive reasons. Since government and politics have offered no alternative, our laws and customs turn those wants into his obligations.

Why, then, is the President not guaranteed an influence commensurate with services performed? Constituent relations are relations of dependence. Everyone with any share in governing this country will belong to one (or two, or three) of his constituencies. Since everyone depends on him, why is he not assured of everyone's support? The answer is that no one else sits where he sits or sees quite as he sees; no one else feels the full weight of his obligations. Those obligations are a tribute to his unique place in our political system. But just because it is unique they fall on him alone. The same conditions that promote his leadership in form preclude a guarantee of leadership in fact. No man or group at either end of Pennsylvania Avenue shares his peculiar status in our government and politics. That is why his services are in demand. By the same token, though, the obligations of all other men are different from his own. His cabinet officers have departmental duties and constituents. His legislative leaders head congressional parties, one in either house. His national party organization stands apart from his official family. His political allies in the states need not face Washington or one another. The private groups that seek him out are not compelled to govern. And friends abroad are not compelled to run in our elections. Lacking his position and prerogatives, these men cannot regard his obligations as their own. They have their jobs to do; none is the same as his. As they perceive their duty they may find it right to follow him, in fact, or they may not. Whether they will feel obliged on their responsibility to do what he wants done remains an open question. . . .

THE POWER TO PERSUADE

The limits on command suggest the structure of our government. The Constitutional Convention of 1787 is supposed to have created a government of "separated powers." It did nothing of the sort. Rather, it created a government of separated institutions *sharing* powers.[3] I am part of the legislative process," Eisenhower often said in 1959 as a reminder of his veto.[4] Congress,

---

[3]The reader will want to keep in mind the distinction between two senses which the word *power* is employed. When I have used the word (or its plural) to refer to formal constitutional, statutory, or customary authority, it is either qualified by the adjective "formal" or placed in quotation marks as "power(s)." Where I have used it in the sense of effective influence on the conduct of others, it appears without quotation marks (and always in the singular). Where clarity and convenience permit, *authority* is substituted for "power" in the first sense and *influence* for power in the second.

[4]See, for example, his press conference of July 22, 1959, as reported in the *New York Times*, July 23, 1959.

the dispenser of authority and funds, is no less part of the administrative process. Federalism adds another set of separated institutions. The Bill of Rights adds others. Many public purposes can only be achieved by voluntary acts of private institutions; the press, for one, in Douglass Cater's phrase, is a "fourth branch of government."[5] And with the coming of alliances abroad, the separate institutions of a London, or a Bonn, share in the making of American public policy.[6]

What the Constitution separates our political parties do not combine. The parties are themselves composed of separated organizations sharing public authority. The authority consists of nominating powers. Our national parties are confederations of state and local party institutions, with a headquarters that represents the White House, more or less, if the party has a President in office. These confederacies manage presidential nominations. All other public offices depend upon electorates confined within the states.[7] All other nominations are controlled within the states. The President and congressmen who bear one party's label are divided by dependence upon different sets of voters. The differences are sharpest at the stage of nomination. The White House has too small a share in nominating congressmen, and Congress has too little weight in nominating presidents for party to erase their constitutional separation. Party links are stronger than is frequently supposed, but nominating processes assure the separation.[8]

The separateness of institutions and the sharing of authority prescribe the terms on which a President persuades. When one man shares authority with another, but does not gain or lose his job upon the other's whim, his willingness to act upon the urging of the other turns on whether he conceives the action right for him. The essence of a President's persuasive task is to convince such men that what the White House wants of them is what they ought to do for their sake and on their authority. (Sex matters not at all; for *man* read *woman*.)

Persuasive power, thus defined, amounts to more than charm or reasoned argument. These have their uses for a President, but these are not the whole of his resources. For the individuals he would induce to do what he wants done on their own responsibility will need or fear some acts by him on his responsibility. If they share his authority, he has some share in theirs. Presidential "powers" may be inconclusive when a President commands, but always remain relevant as he persuades. The status and authority inherent in his office reinforce his logic and his charm.

Status adds something to persuasiveness; authority adds still more. When Truman urged wage changes on his secretary of commerce while the latter

---

[5]See Douglass Cater, *The Fourth Branch of Government* (Boston: Houghton Mifflin, 1959).

[6]For distinctions drawn throughout between powers and power see note 3.

[7]With the exception of the vice presidency, of course.

[8]See David B. Truman's illuminating study of party relationships in the Eighty-first Congress, *The Congressional Party* (New York: Wiley, 1959), especially chaps. 4, 6, 8.

was administering the steel mills, he and Secretary Sawyer were not just two men reasoning with one another. Had they been so, Sawyer probably would never have agreed to act. Truman's status gave him special claims to Sawyer's loyalty or at least attention. In Walter Bagehot's charming phrase "no man can *argue* on his knees." Although there is no kneeling in this country, few men—and exceedingly few cabinet officers—are immune to the impulse to say "yes" to the President of the United States. It grows harder to say "no" when they are seated in his Oval Office at the White House, or in his study on the second floor, where almost tangibly he partakes of the aura of his physical surroundings. In Sawyer's case, moreover, the President possessed formal authority to intervene in many matters of concern to the secretary of commerce. These matters ranged from jurisdictional disputes among the defense agencies to legislation pending before Congress and, ultimately, to the tenure of the secretary, himself. There is nothing in the record to suggest that Truman voiced specific threats when they negotiated over wage increases. But given his formal powers and their relevance to Sawyer's other interests, it is safe to assume that Truman's very advocacy of wage action conveyed an implicit threat.

A President's authority and status give him great advantages in dealing with the men he would persuade. Each "power" is a vantage point for him in the degree that other men have use for his authority. From the veto to appointments, from publicity to budgeting, and so down a long list, the White House now controls the most encompassing array of vantage points in the American political system. With hardly an exception, those who share in governing this country are aware that at some time, in some degree, the doing of *their* jobs, the furthering of *their* ambitions, may depend upon the President of the United States. Their need for presidential action, or their fear of it, is bound to be recurrent if not actually continuous. Their need or fear is his advantage.

A President's advantages are greater than mere listing of his "powers" might suggest. Those with whom he deals must deal with him until the last day of his term. Because they have continuing relationships with him, his future, while it lasts, supports his present influence. Even though there is no need or fear of him today, what he could do tomorrow may supply today's advantage. Continuing relationships may convert any "power," any aspect of his status, into vantage points in almost any case. When he induces other people to do what he wants done, a President can trade on their dependence now and later.

The President's advantages are checked by the advantages of others. Continuing relationships will pull in both directions. These are relationships of mutual dependence. A President depends upon the persons whom he would persuade; he has to reckon with his need or fear of them. They too will possess status, or authority, or both, else they would be of little use to him. Their vantage points confront his own; their power tempers his.

Persuasion is a two-way street. Sawyer, it will be recalled, did not respond at once to Truman's plan for wage increases at the steel mills. On the contrary, the secretary hesitated and delayed and only acquiesced when he was satisfied that publicly he would not bear the onus of decision. Sawyer had some points of vantage all his own from which to resist presidential pressure. If he had to reckon with coercive implications in the President's "situations of strength," so had Truman to be mindful of the implications underlying Sawyer's place as a department head, as steel administrator, and as a cabinet spokesman for business. Loyalty is reciprocal. Having taken on a dirty job in the steel crisis, Sawyer had strong claims to loyal support. Besides, he had authority to do some things that the White House could ill afford. Emulating Wilson, he might have resigned in a huff (the removal power also works two ways). Or, emulating Ellis Arnall, he might have declined to sign necessary orders. Or he might have let it be known publicly that he deplored what he was told to do and protested its doing. By following any of these courses Sawyer almost surely would have strengthened the position of management, weakened the position of the White House, and embittered the union. But the whole purpose of a wage increase was to enhance White House persuasiveness in urging settlement upon union and companies alike. Although Sawyer's status and authority did not give him the power to prevent an increase outright, they gave him capability to undermine its purpose. If his authority over wage rates had been vested by a statute, not by revocable presidential order, his power of prevention might have been complete. So Harold Ickes demonstrated in the famous case of helium sales to Germany before the Second World War.[9]

The power to persuade is the power to bargain. Status and authority yield bargaining advantages. But in a government of "separated institutions sharing powers," they yield them to all sides. With the array of vantage points at his disposal, a President may be far more persuasive than his logic or his charm could make him. But outcomes are not guaranteed by his advantages. There remain the counter pressures those whom he would influence can bring to bear on him from vantage points at their disposal. Command has limited utility; persuasion becomes give-and-take. It is well that the White House holds the vantage points it does. In such a business any President may need them all—and more.

---

[9]As secretary of the interior in 1939, Harold Ickes refused to approve the sale of helium to Germany despite the insistence of the State Department and the urging of President Roosevelt. Without the Secretary's approval, such sales were forbidden by statute. See *The Secret Diaries of Harold L. Ickes* (New York: Simon & Schuster, 1954), vol. 2, especially pp. 391–93, 396–99. See also Michael J. Reagan, "The Helium Controversy," in the forthcoming casebook on civil-military relations prepared for the Twentieth Century Fund under the editorial direction of Harold Stein.

In this instance the statutory authority ran to the secretary as a matter of his discretion. A President is unlikely to fire cabinet officers for the conscientious exercise of such authority. If the President did so, their successors might well be embarrassed both publicly and at the Capitol were they to reverse decisions previously taken. As for a President's authority to set aside discretionary determinations of this sort, it rests, if it exists at all, on shaky legal ground not likely to be trod save in the gravest of situations.

10.3   The Presidential Difference (2004)
FRED I. GREENSTEIN

INTRODUCTION

American presidents face high expectations from diverse constituencies. As the sole leader of the nation, the president must address concerns from Congress, political supporters, the public at large, and other countries, to name just a few. The president needs to be a strong leader to accomplish policy goals; yet defining strong leadership is a difficult task because of differences in presidential personalities, policy agendas, and political environments. In this reading, presidential scholar Fred I. Greenstein identifies six qualities of presidential leadership that are essential for effective governance in the twenty-first century. These qualities range from the internal attributes of cognitive style and emotional intelligence to the external characteristics of vision, political skill, public communication, and organizational resources. Greenstein summarizes which of the modern presidents best illustrate each quality, and which ones have been weakest in each area. This sixfold evaluation permits a balanced appraisal of individual presidential leadership as well as a systematic method for comparing presidencies.

■

LESSONS FROM THE MODERN PRESIDENCY

> *The executive branch of our government is like a chameleon. To a startling degree it reflects the character and personality of the President.*
> —CLARK M. CLIFFORD, 1972

The highly personalized nature of the modern American presidency makes the strengths and weaknesses of the White House incumbent of the utmost importance. It places a premium on the ability of chief executives to get the most out of their strong points and compensate for their limitations. It also places a great value on the ability of Americans to select presidents with attributes that serve well in the Oval Office. Two premises underlie this review of the modern presidential experience: presidents who steep themselves in the record of their predecessors will be better equipped for their responsibilities as a re-

Fred I. Greenstein, *The Presidential Difference: Leadership Style from FDR to George W. Bush*, 2d ed. (Princeton, N.J.: Princeton University Press, 2004), 211–223. Reprinted with the permission of The Free Press, a Division of Simon & Schuster Adult Publishing Group. Copyright © 2000 by Fred I. Greenstein. All rights reserved.

sult of doing so; and members of the public who are able to place presidential contenders in a historical context will be able to make wiser electoral choices.

In seeking to provide such a context, I [have] avoided two common approaches to assessing American presidents. I have abstained from judging the ends that presidents pursue so as better to focus on their means. I have avoided ranking presidents, because there is at least as much to be learned from their failures and limitations as from their successes and strengths. . . . I conclude with summary observations about each subject and general remarks on the qualities that shape presidential performance.

Summing Up the Presidents

• Of all of the modern chief executives, Franklin Roosevelt lends himself least well to a balance sheet of positive and negative qualities. FDR had towering strengths in the realms of rhetoric, superb political skills, and an unequalled capacity to radiate optimism and confidence. He provides endless positive lessons, but even he is a source of warnings. His chaotic organizational arrangements made the influence of his subordinates as much a function of their bureaucratic wiles as the merits of their recommendations. His weakness as a conceptualizer contributed to the incoherence of his administration's effort to combat the Depression. Even his astonishing self-assurance had a negative side, sometimes leading him to act on untested intuitions.

Whatever his limitations, it would be difficult to overstate the historical importance of Franklin Roosevelt. Consider a possibility that nearly become a reality. Just two weeks before Roosevelt was to take office, a gunman sprayed his car with bullets, narrowly missing him. If Roosevelt's would-be assassin had found his mark, the next president would have been Vice President-elect John Nance Garner. Few public figures were less well equipped for restoring public confidence than the crusty Garner, who is best known for equating the vice presidency to a pitcher of warm spit. There is no sure way of knowing what would have transpired if the United States had been deprived of the political genius of FDR. It is far from impossible that it would have succumbed to authoritarian rule, or even dissolved as a political entity, as the Soviet Union did in 1991.

• Harry Truman had an exemplary capacity to energize and rally his subordinates in an administration that had to contend with a highly unfavorable political environment. He also deserves attention for his ability to remain on an even keel, despite his often-turbulent emotions. Truman provides an example of the broker politician at his best in his actions relating to the enactment of the Marshall Plan. When it comes to rhetoric and vision, however, Truman is a negative role model. He illustrates the costs of a defective communication style and a situation-determined approach to presidential leadership.

• Dwight Eisenhower is the Clark Kent of the American presidency. He was once assumed to have been a well-intentioned political innocent, but he emerges from the historical record as a self-consciously oblique political sophisticate with a highly distinctive leadership style. Eisenhower had a firm sense of self-worth that was not bound up in his presidency—he had made his historical mark by V-E Day. He has the most to offer future presidents in the domains of policy vision and organization of the presidency. His greatest deficiency was in public communication. Eisenhower's failure to persuade the public and the political community that the United States should not enter into a missile race with the Soviet Union underscores the short-comings of a political style that places little weight on the teaching and preaching functions of the presidency.

• John Kennedy's forte was public communication. A less publicly persuasive chief executive would have been unable to maintain public support in the face of such setbacks as the debacle at the Bay of Pigs and the erection of the Berlin Wall. Kennedy's personal qualities also set a high standard. His keen intelligence and sense of historical perspective made for thoughtful, well-informed policy choices. He also was striking for the emotional detachment he brought to his public actions. Despite his private excesses, Kennedy was measured and clear-headed in his official capacity.

Kennedy also is a source of negative lessons. He squandered Eisenhower's organizational legacy, discarding an advisory mechanism that could have been of inestimable value for later presidencies. Kennedy's lack of an overarching policy vision led him to muddle through in the vital relationship with the Soviet Union. By posing an unintended threat to the men in the Kremlin, he contributed to a spiral of misunderstanding that culminated in the near nuclear disaster of the Cuban missile crisis.

Following Kennedy there were the emotionally impaired Lyndon Johnson and Richard Nixon, under whom the nation experienced Vietnam and Watergate. In the absence of that succession of traumas, the tenor of American politics in the final quarter of the twentieth century would have been far more conducive to effective governance.

• Lyndon Johnson's most positive lessons bear on political skill. Presidents who study Johnson's often pyrotechnic political maneuvers will be the recipient of a graduate education in political operations. Future presidents also would be advised to take LBJ as a source of warnings. Especially instructive are the qualities that led Johnson to commit over a half-million American troops to the jungles of Vietnam between 1965 and 1968. Because he was deficient in organizational capacity, he presided over an advisory process that failed to provide him with a rigorous assessment of the pros and cons of alternative courses of action. Because he was tone-deaf when it came to policy content, his political skill enhanced his ability to pursue a bankrupt course of action.

• The presidential leadership of Richard Nixon provides an illustration of the superficiality of efforts to rank chief executives. In a 1996 survey of presidential greatness conducted by Arthur Schlesinger, Jr., a panel of authorities placed Nixon in the lowest of six performance categories.[1] That assessment might lead later presidents to conclude that they had nothing to learn from Nixon. Yet it would be difficult to imagine a more positively, as well as negatively, instructive chief executive. Nixon's stunning international achievements illustrate the value of strategic vision in presidential leadership. His self-destructive qualities demonstrate the capacity of a dysfunctional psyche to sabotage even the most proficient political leader.

• Enter the underappreciated Gerald Ford. Presidents and presidential advisers who dismiss the Ford experience will miss out on a rich set of precedents about how to manage the presidency. More fundamentally, they will fail to take account of the personal strengths of a chief executive who had an impressive capacity to withstand the pressures of office. Future presidents cannot simply will emotional balance on themselves, but they are likely to approach their job with greater ease if they attend to the presidents who were not intimidated by their office.

• The presidency of Jimmy Carter is informative as a limiting case. No president has been as reluctant as Carter to engage in the normal process of political give and take. No presidency provides a fuller catalogue of avoidable shortfalls than his. The exception is Camp David. By negotiating a peace agreement between Israel and Egypt, Carter provides a reminder that presidents need not simply respond to circumstances. They can make opportunity their servant, engaging in acts of political creativity.

• Ronald Reagan was a Jimmy Carter in reverse. He was a fluent public communicator with an ingratiating behind-the-scenes manner, who stood for a handful of broad verities. Reagan also was astonishingly uninformed about the specifics of his programs. The positive lessons of the Reagan presidency relate to its professionalism in public communication and political management. Its warnings derive from Reagan's cognitive limitations and his hands-off management style, which spawned rivalries and conflict in his inner circle. Competent aides are essential in the modern presidency, but when it comes to effective organization of the presidency the buck stops in the Oval Office.

• George H. W. Bush also was his predecessor's antithesis. He failed to take advantage of the rhetorical potentialities of the presidency, and he was fundamentally reactive in his stance toward public affairs. However, he was the master of the specifics of politics and policy, and he worked closely and skillfully with his aides and political counterparts, especially in international

---

[1]Arthur Schlesinger, Jr., "Rating the Presidents: Washington to Clinton," *Political Science Quarterly* 112 (1997): 179–190.

affairs. Such a competent custodian president can thrive under favorable political and economic conditions, but is likely to flounder in the face of adversity. If the Bush presidency had been marked by larger themes, and if Bush had better communicated what he did accomplish, he might well have occupied the Oval Office through January 1997.

•   Then there is Bill Clinton, whose political aspirations seem almost to have been incubated in the womb. Clinton had already formulated a precise strategy for seeking the presidency at age twenty-six, when he confided to a fellow McGovern campaign worker that he planned to return to Arkansas after law school and run for governor with a view to gaining the national prominence that would enable him to seek the presidency.[2] It is a tribute to Clinton's resiliency and political prowess that he succeeded in serving two presidential terms. It is a commentary on his weaknesses that this talented political leader did not have more to show for his time in office.

•   Lastly there is George W. Bush, whose first two-and-a-half years in office are likely to assure him more space in future history books than eight years in the White House will for Bill Clinton. Although Bush has much less mastery of the inner workings of policies than his predecessor, he far exceeds Clinton (and many other modern presidents) in his propensity to set goals and be tireless in their pursuit. This was his practice before he threw himself more intensively into his responsibilities after September 11 and it remained so thereafter. Like Truman before him, Bush illustrates the proposition that the presidency is an office in which it is possible to grow in competence and effectiveness.

The Qualities That Bear on Presidential Performance

Effectiveness as a Public Communicator   For an office that places so great a premium on the presidential pulpit, the modern presidency has been surprisingly lacking in effective public communicators. Most presidents have not addressed the public with anything approximating the professionalism of countless educators, members of the clergy, and radio and television broadcasters. Roosevelt, Kennedy, and Reagan—and Clinton at his best—are the shining exceptions.

Chief executives who find the most able of the presidential communicators daunting should be relieved to learn that their eloquence was in part the product of effort and experience. Roosevelt, Kennedy, and Reagan took part in drafting their speeches and rehearsed their presentations. In 1910, when Eleanor Roosevelt first heard her husband give a speech, she was taken aback by his long pauses and slow delivery. "I was worried for fear that he would never go on," she recalled.[3] When Kennedy was a freshman congressman, he

---

[2]David Maraniss, *First in His Class: The Biography of Bill Clinton* (New York: Simon & Schuster, 1995), 280–281.

[3]Eleanor Roosevelt, *This Is My Story* (New York: Harper, 1937), 167.

had a diffident, self-effacing public manner. And for all of Reagan's professionalism, he did not perfect the podium manner of his political years until the 1950s, when his film career drew to a close and he found employment on the speaking circuit.

One president who allowed himself to be fazed by an accomplished predecessor was George H. W. Bush, who seems to have concluded that since he could not compare with Reagan as a communicator, he should be his near antithesis. Bush used the White House briefing room for his public communications, only rarely addressing the nation from the Oval Office, and he instructed his speechwriters to temper his prose. Bush's initial three years of high public approval provide a reminder that formal addresses are not the only way for a president to remain in the good graces of the public. His defeat highlights the costs of a leadership style that gives short shrift to the teaching and preaching side of presidential leadership.

Organizational Capacity   A president's capacity as an organizer includes his ability to forge a team and get the most out of it, minimizing the tendency of subordinates to tell their boss what they sense he wants to hear. It also includes a quite different matter: his proficiency at creating effective institutional arrangements. There is an illuminating postpresidential indicator of a president's success as a team builder—the way that he is remembered by alumni of his administration. Veterans of the Truman, Eisenhower, Kennedy, Ford, and George H. W. Bush presidencies have nothing but praise for their erstwhile chiefs. In contrast, few Johnson, Carter, and Clinton lieutenants emerged from their White House service with unmixed views of the president they served. Most ambivalent are the former aides of Richard Nixon, a number of whom went to prison for their actions in his service.

Presidents also differ in their ability to avail themselves of a rich and varied fare of advice and information. FDR encouraged diversity in the recommendations that reached him by pitting his assistants against one another. Kennedy's method was to charge his brother Robert and his alter ego Theodore Sorensen with scrutinizing the proposals of his other advisers for flaws and pitfalls. The modern president with by far the greatest and most demanding organizational experience was Eisenhower, who had a highly developed view of the matter. "I know of only one way in which you can be sure you have done your best to make a wise decision," he declared in a 1967 interview:

> That is to get all of the [responsible policymakers] with their different viewpoints in front of you, and listen to them debate. I do not believe in bringing them in one at a time, and therefore being more impressed by the most recent one you hear than the earlier ones. You must get courageous men of strong views, and let them debate with each other.[4]

---

[4]Dwight D. Eisenhower, Columbia University Oral History Interview, July 20, 1967, 103.

Not all of the modern presidents have been open to vigorous give and take. Nixon and Reagan were uncomfortable in the presence of face-to-face disagreement. Johnson's Texas-sized personality had a chilling effect on some of his subordinates. His NSC staff member Chester Cooper recalled recurrent fantasies of facing down LBJ at NSC meetings when Johnson sought his concurrence on a matter relating to Vietnam by replying, "I most definitely do not agree." But when LBJ turned to him and asked, "Mr. Cooper, do you agree?" Cooper found himself replying, "Yes, Mr. President, I agree."[5]

The capacity to design effective institutional arrangements has been in even scarcer supply than effective public communication in the modern presidency. In this department, Eisenhower was in a class of his own. The most emulation-worthy of his departures was the set of arrangements that framed his administration's national security deliberations. Each week the top planners in the bodies represented in the NSC hammered out option papers stating the policy recommendations of their agencies. The disagreements were clearly delineated and set before the NSC, where they were the object of sharp, focused debate. The result was as important for preparing Eisenhower's foreign policy team to work together as it was for grounding it in the issues bearing on unfolding global contingencies.

Political Skill The classic statement of the centrality of political skill to presidential performance is Richard E. Neustadt's *Presidential Power*, which has been described as the closest approximation to Machiavelli's writings in the literature of American politics.[6] The question Neustadt addresses is how the chief executive can put his stamp on public policy in the readily stalemated American political system. Neustadt's prescription is for the president to use the powers of his office assertively, build and maintain public support, and establish a reputation among fellow policymakers as a skilled, determined political operator. If there ever was reason to doubt Neustadt's diagnosis, it was eliminated by the presidential experience of Jimmy Carter.

Lyndon Johnson seemed almost to have taken his methods from the pages of *Presidential Power*. Within hours after Kennedy's assassination, Johnson had begun to muster support for major domestic policy departures. He exhibited will as well as skill, cultivating his political reputation by keeping Congress in session until Christmas 1963 in order to prevail in one of his administration's first legislative contests. His actions won him strong public support, making it apparent to his opposite numbers on Capitol Hill that it would be politically costly to ignore his demands.

---

[5]Chester L. Cooper, *Lost Crusade: America in Vietnam* (Greenwich, Conn.: Dodd, Mead, 1970), 223.
[6]Richard E. Neustadt, *Presidential Power: The Politics of Leadership* (New York: Wiley, 1960).

Vision   "Vision" is a term with a variety of connotations. One is the capac-ity to inspire. In this the rhetorically gifted presidents—Kennedy, Reagan, and above all FDR—excelled. In the narrower meaning employed here, "vi-sion" refers to preoccupation with the content of policies, an ability to assess their feasibility, and the possession of a set of overarching goals. Here the standouts are Eisenhower, Nixon, and to a lesser extent Ronald Reagan, whose views were poorly grounded in specifics. Vision also encompasses consistency of viewpoint. Presidents who stand firm are able to set the terms of policy discourse. In effect they serve as anchors for the rest of the politi-cal community.

George H. W. Bush was not alone in lacking "the vision thing." He falls in a class of presidential pragmatists that includes the bulk of the modern chief executives. The costs of vision-free leadership include internally inconsistent programs, policies that have unintended consequences, and sheer drift. When it comes to vision, the senior Bush could not have been more different from his son, George W. Bush, for whom having an explicit agenda is a watchword. Ironically, the younger Bush's vision led him in potentially problematic di-rections, most strikingly in the case of the war in Iraq, in which a short-run mil-itary victory was followed by a continuing pattern of guerilla warfare against the American occupying force. In short, the first Bush suffered for his lack of vision, and the second Bush may prove to suffer *because* of his policy vision.

Cognitive Style   Presidents vary widely in their cognitive styles. Jimmy Carter had an engineer's proclivity to reduce issues to what he perceived to be their component parts. That style served him well in the 1978 Camp David nego-tiations, but it was ill suited for providing his administration with a sense of direction. Carter's cognitive qualities contrast with the kind of strategic in-telligence that cuts to the heart of a problem, as Eisenhower did when he in-troduced his administration's deliberations on Dien Bien Phu with the incisive observation that the jungles of Indochina would "absorb our divisions by the dozens."[7]

Another example of strategic intelligence is to be had from a chief execu-tive who will never grace Mount Rushmore: Richard Nixon. Two years be-fore entering the White House, Nixon laid down the goals of moving the United States beyond its military involvement in Vietnam, establishing a bal-ance of power with the Soviet Union and an opening with China. By the final year of his first term, he had accomplished his purposes.

Nixon's first-term successes contrast with the paucity of major accom-plishments in the two White House terms of the first presidential Rhodes scholar, Bill Clinton. Clinton possessed a formidable ability to absorb and

---

[7]See . . . John P. Burke, Fred I. Greenstein, with Larry Berman and Richard Immerman, *How Pres-idents Test Reality* (New York: Russell Sage Foundation, 1988), chaps. 2–5, 32.

process ideas and information, but his mind was more synthetic than ana-lytic, and his political impulses sometimes led him to substitute mere ration-alization for reasoned analysis.

Two presidents who were marked by cognitive limitations were Harry Tru-man and Ronald Reagan. Truman's uncritical reading of works of popular history made him susceptible to false historical analogies. Reagan was noto-rious for his imperfect understanding of a number of his policy initiatives. That both presidents had major policy accomplishments shows that intelli-gence and information as measured by standardized tests is not the sole cause of presidential effectiveness.

Emotional Intelligence   Four of the twelve modern presidents stand out as fun-damentally free of distracting emotional perturbations: Eisenhower, Ford, George H. W. Bush, and George W. Bush. Four others were marked by emo-tional undercurrents that did not significantly impair their leadership: Roo-sevelt, Truman, Kennedy, and Reagan. That leaves Johnson, Nixon, Carter, and Clinton, all of whom were emotionally handicapped. The vesuvian LBJ was subject to mood swings of clinical proportions. Jimmy Carter's rigidity was a significant impediment to his White House performance. The defective impulse control of Bill Clinton led him into actions that ensued in his impeachment.

Richard Nixon was the most emotionally flawed of the presidents consid-ered here. His anger and suspiciousness were of Shakespearean proportions. He more than any other president summons up the classic notion of a tragic hero who is defeated by the very qualities that brought him success. It has been argued that the tortured psyche of a Nixon is a precondition of political creativity. This was the view of Elliot Richardson, who held that if Nixon's "rather petty flaws" had been taken away, "you would probably have re-moved that very inner core of insecurity that led to his rise."[8] Richardson's claim is a variant of the proposition that the inner torment of a Van Gogh is the price of his creativity, but other great painters were free of Van Gogh's self-destructiveness, and the healthy-minded Eisenhower was as gifted as Nixon in the positive aspects of leadership. Great political ability does some-times derive from troubled emotions, but the former does not justify the lat-ter in the custodian of the most destructive military arsenal in human experience.

Coda

In the world of imagination it is possible to envisage a cognitively and emo-tionally intelligent chief executive, who happens also to be an inspiring pub-lic communicator, a capable White House organizer, and the possessor of

---

[8]Richardson interview, Arts and Entertainment Network documentary: *Biography: Richard Nixon: Man and President* (New York, 1996).

exceptional political skill and vision. In the real world, human imperfection is inevitable, but some imperfections are more disabling than others. Many of the modern presidents have performed adequately without being brilliant orators. Only a few chief executives have been organizationally competent. A minimal level of political skill is a precondition of presidential effectiveness, but political skill is widely present in the handful of individuals who rise to the political summit. Vision is rarer than skill, but only Lyndon Johnson was disastrously deficient in the realm of policy.

Finally there are thought and emotion. The importance of cognitive strength in the presidency should be self-evident. Still, Presidents Johnson, Nixon, Carter, and Clinton had impressive intellects and defective temperaments. They reversed Justice Holmes's characterization of FDR. Clinton's foibles made him an underachiever and national embarrassment. Carter's defective temperament contributed to making his time in office a period of lost opportunity. Johnson and Nixon presided over major policy breakthroughs, but also over two of the most unhappy episodes of the twentieth century. All four presidential experiences point to the following moral: Beware the presidential contender who lacks emotional intelligence. In its absence all else may turn to ashes.

10.4 The Two Presidencies (1966)

AARON WILDAVSKY

INTRODUCTION

The Framers of the Constitution designed a political system that embedded conflict between the branches of government in the policymaking process. Aaron Wildavsky identifies some key differences between foreign and domestic policymaking in this classic 1966 article. Essentially, Wildavsky argues that the president faces fewer constraints in foreign policymaking because of deference from a wide range of constituencies, including Congress, public opinion, interest groups, and the courts. Many empirical studies have questioned the validity of Wildavsky's thesis in different areas, including trade and budget battles. Nevertheless, his basic argument that the president is expected to exercise initiative in foreign policy remains persuasive today, especially as the United States wages an ongoing war on terrorism.

The United States has one President, but it has two presidencies; one presidency is for domestic affairs, and the other is concerned with defense and foreign policy. Since World War II, Presidents have had much greater success in controlling the nation's defense and foreign policies than in dominating its domestic policies. Even Lyndon Johnson has seen his early record of victories in domestic legislation diminish as his concern with foreign affairs grows.

What powers does the President have to control defense and foreign policies and so completely overwhelm those who might wish to thwart him?

The President's normal problem with domestic policy is to get congressional support for the programs he prefers. In foreign affairs, in contrast, he can almost always get support for policies that he believes will protect the nation—but his problem is to find a viable policy.

Whoever they are, whether they begin by caring about foreign policy like Eisenhower and Kennedy or about domestic policies like Truman and Johnson, Presidents soon discover they have more policy preferences in domestic matters than in foreign policy. The Republican and Democratic parties possess a traditional roster of policies, which can easily be adopted by a new President—for example, he can be either for or against Medicare and aid to education. Since existing domestic policy usually changes in only small steps, Presidents find it relatively simple to make minor adjustments. However, although any President knows he supports foreign aid and NATO, the world outside changes much more rapidly than the nation inside—Presidents and their parties have no prior policies on Argentina and the Congo. The world has become a highly intractable place with a whirl of forces we cannot or do not know how to alter.

THE RECORD OF PRESIDENTIAL CONTROL

It takes great crises, such as Roosevelt's hundred days in the midst of the depression, or the extraordinary majorities that Barry Goldwater's candidacy willed to Lyndon Johnson, for Presidents to succeed in controlling domestic policy. From the end of the 1930's to the present (what may roughly be called the modern era), Presidents have often been frustrated in their domestic programs. From 1938, when conservatives regrouped their forces, to the time of his death, Franklin Roosevelt did not get a single piece of significant domestic legislation passed. Truman lost out on most of his intense domestic preferences, except perhaps for housing. Since Eisenhower did not ask for much domestic legislation, he did not meet consistent defeat, yet he failed in his general policy of curtailing governmental commitments. Kennedy, of course, faced great difficulties with domestic legislation.

In the realm of foreign policy there has not been a single major issue on which Presidents, when they were serious and determined, have failed. The list of their victories is impressive: entry into the United Nations, the Marshall

Table 1

Congressional Action on Presidential Proposals from 1948–1964

Policy Area	Congressional Action % Pass	% Fail	Number of Proposals
Domestic policy (natural resources, labor, agriculture, taxes, etc.)	40.2	59.8	2499
Defense policy (defense, disarmament, manpower, misc.)	73.3	26.7	90
Foreign policy	58.5	41.5	655
Immigration, refugees	13.2	86.0	129
Treaties, general foreign relations, State Department, foreign aid	70.8	29.2	445

Source: Congressional Quarterly Service, *Congress and the Nation, 1945–1964* (Washington, 1965).

Plan, NATO, the Truman Doctrine, the decisions to stay out of Indochina in 1954 and to intervene in Vietnam in the 1960's, aid to Poland and Yugoslavia, the test-ban treaty, and many more. Serious setbacks to the President in controlling foreign policy are extraordinary and unusual.

Table 1, compiled from the Congressional Quarterly Service tabulation of presidential initiative and congressional response from 1948 through 1964, shows that Presidents have significantly better records in foreign and defense matters than in domestic policies. When refugees and immigration—which Congress considers primarily a domestic concern—are removed from the general foreign policy area, it is clear that Presidents prevail about 70 per cent of the time in defense and foreign policy, compared with 40 per cent in the domestic sphere.

WORLD EVENTS AND PRESIDENTIAL RESOURCES

Power in politics is control over governmental decisions. How does the President manage his control of foreign and defense policy? The answer does not reside in the greater constitutional power in foreign affairs that Presidents have possessed since the founding of the Republic. The answer lies in the changes that have taken place since 1945.

The number of nations with which the United States has diplomatic relations has increased from 53 in 1939 to 113 in 1966. But sheer numbers do not tell enough; the world has also become a much more dangerous place. However remote it may seem at times, our government must always be aware of the possibility of nuclear war.

Yet the mere existence of great powers with effective thermonuclear weapons would not, in and of itself, vastly increase our rate of interaction with most other nations. We see events in Assam or Burundi as important because they are also part of a larger worldwide contest, called the cold war, in which great powers are rivals for the control or support of other nations. Moreover, the reaction against the blatant isolationism of the 1930's has led to a concern with foreign policy that is worldwide in scope. We are interested in what happens everywhere because we see these events as connected with larger interests involving, at the worst, the possibility of ultimate destruction.

Given the overriding fact that the world is dangerous and that small causes are perceived to have potentially great effects in an unstable world, it follows that Presidents must be interested in relatively "small" matters. So they give Azerbaijan or Lebanon or Vietnam huge amounts of their time. Arthur Schlesinger, Jr., wrote of Kennedy that "in the first two months of his administration he probably spent more time on Laos than on anything else." Few failures in domestic policy, Presidents soon realize, could have as disastrous consequences as any one of dozens of mistakes in the international arena.

The result is that foreign policy concerns tend to drive out domestic policy. Except for occasional questions of domestic prosperity and for civil rights, foreign affairs have consistently higher priority for Presidents. Once, when trying to talk to President Kennedy about natural resources, Secretary of the Interior Stewart Udall remarked. "He's imprisoned by Berlin."

The importance of foreign affairs to Presidents is intensified by the increasing speed of events in the international arena. The event and its consequences follow closely on top of one another. The blunder at the Bay of Pigs is swiftly followed by the near catastrophe of the Cuban missile crisis. Presidents can no longer count on passing along their most difficult problems to their successors. They must expect to face the consequences of their actions—or failure to act—while still in office.

Domestic policy-making is usually based on experimental adjustments to an existing situation. Only a few decisions, such as those involving large dams, irretrievably commit future generations. Decisions in foreign affairs, however, are often perceived to be irreversible. This is expressed, for example, in the fear of escalation or the various "spiral" or "domino" theories of international conflict.

If decisions are perceived to be both important and irreversible, there is every reason for Presidents to devote a great deal of resources to them. Presidents have to be oriented toward the future in the use of their resources. They serve a fixed term in office, and they cannot automatically count on support from the populace, Congress, or the administrative apparatus. They have to be careful, therefore, to husband their resources for pressing future needs. But because the consequences of events in foreign affairs are potentially more grave, faster to manifest themselves, and less easily reversible than in domestic affairs, Presidents are more willing to use up their resources.

THE POWER TO ACT

Their formal powers to commit resources in foreign affairs and defense are vast. Particularly important is their power as Commander-in-Chief to move troops. Faced with situations like the invasion of South Korea or the emplacement of missiles in Cuba, fast action is required. Presidents possess both the formal power to act and the knowledge that elites and the general public expect them to act. Once they have committed American forces, it is difficult for Congress or anyone else to alter the course of events. The Dominican venture is a recent case in point.

Presidential discretion in foreign affairs also makes it difficult (though not impossible) for Congress to restrict their actions. Presidents can use executive agreements instead of treaties, enter into tacit agreements instead of written ones, and otherwise help create *de facto* situations not easily reversed. Presidents also have far greater ability than anyone else to obtain information on developments abroad through the Departments of State and Defense. The need for secrecy in some aspects of foreign and defense policy further restricts the ability of others to compete with Presidents. These things are all well known. What is not so generally appreciated is the growing presidential ability to *use* information to achieve goals.

In the past Presidents were amateurs in military strategy. They could not even get much useful advice outside of the military. As late as the 1930's the number of people outside the military establishment who were professionally engaged in the study of defense policy could be numbered on fingers. Today there are hundreds of such men. The rise of the defense intellectuals has given the President of the United States enhanced ability to control defense policy. He is no longer dependent on the military for advice. He can choose among defense intellectuals from the research corporations and the academies for alternative sources of advice. He can install these men in his own office. He can play them off against each other or use them to extend spheres of coordination.

Even with these advisers, however, Presidents and Secretaries of Defense might still be too bewildered by the complexity of nuclear situations to take action—unless they had an understanding of the doctrine and concept of deterrence. But knowledge of doctrine about deterrence has been widely diffused; it can be picked up by any intelligent person who will read books or listen to enough hours of conversation. Whether or not the doctrine is good is a separate question; the point is that civilians can feel they understand what is going on in defense policy. Perhaps the most extraordinary feature of presidential action during the Cuban missile crisis was the degree to which the Commander-in-Chief of the Armed Forces insisted on controlling even the smallest moves. From the positioning of ships to the methods of boarding, to the precise words and actions to be taken by individual soldiers and sailors, the President and his civilian advisers were in control.

Although Presidents have rivals for power in foreign affairs, the rivals do not usually succeed. Presidents prevail not only because they may have superior resources but because their potential opponents are weak, divided, or believe that they should not control foreign policy. Let us consider the potential rivals—the general citizenry, special interest groups, the Congress, the military, the so-called military-industrial complex, and the State Department.

COMPETITORS FOR CONTROL OF POLICY

The Public   The general public is much more dependent on Presidents in foreign affairs than in domestic matters. While many people know about the impact of social security and Medicare, few know about politics in Malawi. So it is not surprising that people expect the President to act in foreign affairs and reward him with their confidence. Gallup Polls consistently show that presidential popularity rises after he takes action in a crisis— whether the action is disastrous as in the Bay of Pigs or successful as in the Cuban missile crisis. Decisive action, such as the bombing of oil fields near Haiphong, resulted in a sharp (though temporary) increase in Johnson's popularity.

The Vietnam situation illustrates another problem of public opinion in foreign affairs; it is extremely difficult to get operational policy directions from the general public. It took a long time before any sizable public interest in the subject developed. Nothing short of the large scale involvement of American troops under fire probably could have brought about the current high level of concern. Yet this relatively well developed popular opinion is difficult to interpret. While a majority appear to support President Johnson's policy, it appears that they could easily be persuaded to withdraw from Vietnam if the administration changed its line. Although a sizable majority would support various initiatives to end the war, they would seemingly be appalled if this action led to Communist encroachments elsewhere in Southeast Asia. . . .

Although Presidents lead opinion in foreign affairs, they know they will be held accountable for the consequences of their actions. President Johnson has maintained a large commitment in Vietnam. His popularity shoots up now and again in the midst of some imposing action. But the fact that a body of citizens do not like the war comes back to damage his overall popularity. We will support your initiatives, the people seem to say, but we will reserve the right to punish you (or your party) if we do not like the results.

Special Interest Groups   Opinions are easier to gauge in domestic affairs because, for one thing, there is a stable structure of interest groups that covers virtually all matters of concern. The farm, labor, business, conservation, veteran, civil rights, and other interest groups provide cues when a proposed policy affects them. Thus people who identify with these groups may adopt their views. But in foreign policy matters the interest group structure is weak, unstable, and thin rather than dense. In many matters affecting Africa and Asia, for example, it is hard to think of well-known interest groups. While ephemeral groups arise from time to time to support or protest particular policies, they usually disappear when the immediate problem is resolved. In contrast, longer-lasting elite groups like the Foreign Policy Association and Council on Foreign Relations are composed of people of diverse views; refusal to take strong positions on controversial matters is a condition of their continued viability.

The strongest interest groups are probably the ethnic associations whose members have strong ties with a homeland, as in Poland or Cuba, so they are rarely activated simultaneously on any specific issue. They are most effective when most narrowly and intensely focused—as in the fierce pressure from Jews to recognize the state of Israel. But their relatively small numbers limit their significance to Presidents in the vastly more important general foreign policy picture—as continued aid to the Arab countries shows. Moreover, some ethnic groups may conflict on significant issues such as American acceptance of the Oder-Neisse line separating Poland from what is now East Germany.

The Congress   Congressmen also exercise power in foreign affairs. Yet they are ordinarily not serious competitors with the President because they follow a self-denying ordinance. They do not think it is their job to determine the nation's defense policies. Lewis A. Dexter's extensive interviews with members of the Senate Armed Services Committee, who might be expected to want a voice in defense policy, reveal that they do not desire for men like themselves to run the nation's defense establishment. Aside from a few specific conflicts among the armed services which allow both the possibility and desirability of direct intervention, the Armed Services Committee constitutes a sort of real estate committee dealing with the regional economic consequences of the location of military facilities.

The congressional appropriations power is potentially a significant resource, but circumstances since the end of World War II have tended to reduce its effectiveness. The appropriations committees and Congress itself might make their will felt by refusing to allot funds unless basic policies were altered. But this has not happened. While Congress makes its traditional small cuts in the military budget, Presidents have mostly found themselves warding off congressional attempts to increase specific items still further.

Most of the time, the administration's refusal to spend has not been seriously challenged. However, there have been occasions when individual legislators or committees have been influential. Senator Henry Jackson in his campaign (with the aid of colleagues on the Joint Committee on Atomic Energy) was able to gain acceptance for the Polaris weapons system and Senator Arthur H. Vandenberg played a part in determining the shape of the Marshall Plan and so on. The few congressmen who are expert in defense policy act, as Samuel P. Huntington says, largely as lobbyists with the executive branch. It is apparently more fruitful for these congressional experts to use their resources in order to get a hearing from the executive than to work on other congressmen.

When an issue involves the actual use or threat of violence, it takes a great deal to convince congressmen not to follow the President's lead. James Robinson's tabulation of foreign and defense policy issues from the late 1930's to 1961 ... shows dominant influence by Congress in only one case out of seven—the 1954 decision not to intervene with armed force in Indochina. In that instance President Eisenhower deliberately sounded out congressional opinion and, finding it negative, decided not to intervene—against the advice of Admiral Radford, chairman of the Joint Chiefs of Staff. This attempt to abandon responsibility did not succeed, as the years of American involvement demonstrate.

The Military   The outstanding feature of the military's participation in making defense policy is their amazing weakness. Whether the policy decisions involve the size of the armed forces, the choice of weapons systems, the total defense budget, or its division into components, the military have not prevailed. Let us take budgetary decisions as representative of the key choices to be made in defense policy. Since the end of World War II the military has not been able to achieve significant (billion dollar) increases in appropriations by their own efforts. Under Truman and Eisenhower defense budgets were determined by what Huntington calls the remainder method: the two Presidents estimated revenues, decided what they could spend on domestic matters, and the remainder was assigned to defense. The usual controversy was between some military and congressional groups supporting much larger expenditures while the President and his executive allies refused. A typical case, involving the desire of the Air Force to increase the number of groups of planes is described by Huntington in *The Common Defense:*

> The FY [fiscal year] 1949 budget provided 48 groups. After the Czech coup, the Administration yielded and backed an Air Force of 55 groups in its spring rearmament program. Congress added additional funds to aid Air Force expansion to 70 groups. The Administration refused to utilize them, however, and in the gathering economy wave of the summer and fall of 1948, the Air Force goal was cut back again to 48 groups. In 1949 the House of Representatives picked up the challenge and appropriated funds for 58 groups. The President impounded the money. In June, 1950, the Air Force had 48 groups.

The great increases in the defense budget were due far more to Stalin and modern technology than to the military. The Korean War resulted in an increase from 12 to 44 billions and much of the rest followed Sputnik and the huge costs of missile programs. Thus modern technology and international conflict put an end to the one major effort to subordinate foreign affairs to domestic policies through the budget.

It could be argued that the President merely ratifies the decisions made by the military and their allies. If the military and/or Congress were united and insistent on defense policy, it would certainly be difficult for Presidents to resist these forces. But it is precisely the disunity of the military that has characterized the entire postwar period. Indeed, the military have not been united on any major matter of defense policy. The apparent unity of the Joint Chiefs of Staff turns out to be illusory. The vast majority of their recommendations appear to be unanimous and are accepted by the Secretary of Defense and the President. But this facade of unity can only be achieved by methods that vitiate the impact of the recommendations. Genuine disagreements are hidden by vague language that commits no one to anything. Mutually contradictory plans are strung together so everyone appears to get something, but nothing is decided. Since it is impossible to agree on really important matters, all sorts of trivia are brought in to make a record of agreement. While it may be true, as Admiral Denfield, a former Chief of Naval Operations, said, that "On nine-tenths of the matters that come before them the Joint Chiefs of Staff reach agreement themselves," the vastly more important truth is that "normally the *only* disputes are on strategic concepts, the size and composition of forces, and budget matters."

Military-Industrial   But what about the fabled military-industrial complex? If the military alone is divided and weak, perhaps the giant industrial firms that are so dependent on defense contracts play a large part in making policy.

First, there is an important distinction between the questions "Who will get a given contract?" and "What will our defense policy be?" It is apparent that different answers may be given to these quite different questions. There are literally tens of thousands of defense contractors. They may compete vigorously for business. In the course of this competition, they may wine and dine military officers, use retired generals, seek intervention by their congressmen, place ads in trade journals, and even contribute to political campaigns. The famous TFX controversy—should General Dynamics or Boeing get the expensive contract?—is a larger than life example of the pressures brought to bear in search of lucrative contracts.

But neither the TFX case nor the usual vigorous competition for contracts is involved with the making of substantive defense policy. Vital questions like the size of the defense budget, the choice of strategic programs, massive retaliation vs. a counter-city strategy, and the like were far beyond the policy aims of any company. Industrial firms, then, do not control such decisions, nor is there much evidence that they actually try. No doubt a precipitous and drastic rush to disarmament would meet with opposition from industrial firms among other interests. However, there has never been a time when any significant element in the government considered a disarmament policy to be feasible.

It may appear that industrial firms had no special reason to concern themselves with the government's stance on defense because they agree with the national consensus on resisting communism, maintaining a large defense establishment, and rejecting isolationism. However, this hypothesis about the climate of opinion explains everything and nothing. For every policy that is adopted or rejected can be explained away on the grounds that the cold war climate of opinion dictated what happened. Did the United States fail to intervene with armed force in Vietnam in 1954? That must be because the climate of opinion was against it. Did the United States send troops to Vietnam in the 1960's? That must be because the cold war climate demanded it. If the United States builds more missiles, negotiates a testban treaty, intervenes in the Dominican Republic, fails to intervene in a dozen other situations, all these actions fit the hypothesis by definition. The argument is reminiscent of those who defined the Soviet Union as permanently hostile and therefore interpreted increases of Soviet troops as menacing and decreases of troop strength as equally sinister.

If the growth of the military establishment is not directly equated with increasing military control of defense policy, the extraordinary weakness of the professional soldier still requires explanation. Huntington has written about how major military leaders were seduced in the Truman and Eisenhower years into believing that they should bow to the judgment of civilians that the economy could not stand much larger military expenditures. Once the size of the military pie was accepted as a fixed constraint, the military services were compelled to put their major energies into quarreling with one another over who should get the larger share. Given the natural rivalries of the military and their traditional acceptance of civilian rule, the President and his advisers—who could claim responsibility for the broader picture of reconciling defense and domestic policies—had the upper hand. There are, however, additional explanations to be considered.

The dominant role of the congressional appropriations committee is to be guardian of the treasury. This is manifested in the pride of its members in cutting the President's budget. Thus it was difficult to get this crucial committee to recommend even a few hundred million increase in defense; it was practically impossible to get them to consider the several billion jump that might really have made a difference. A related budgetary matter concerned the planning, programming, and budgeting system introduced by Secretary of Defense McNamara. For if the defense budget contained major categories that crisscrossed the services, only the Secretary of Defense could put it together. Whatever the other debatable consequences of program budgeting its major consequence was to grant power to the secretary and his civilian advisers.

The subordination of the military through program budgeting is just one symptom of a more general weakness of the military. In the past decade the military has suffered a lack of intellectual skills appropriate to the nuclear age. For no one has (and no one wants) direct experience with nuclear war. So the usual military talk about being the only people to have combat experience is not very impressive. Instead, the imaginative creation of possible future wars—in order to avoid them—requires people with a high capacity for abstract thought combined with the ability to manipulate symbols using quantitative methods. West Point has not produced many such men.

The State Department   Modern Presidents expect the State Department to carry out their policies. John F. Kennedy felt that State was "in some particular sense 'his' department." If a Secretary of State forgets this, as was apparently the case with James Byrnes under Truman, a President may find another man. But the State Department, especially the Foreign Service, is also a highly professional organization with a life and momentum of its own. If a President does not push hard, he may find his preferences somehow dissipated in time. Arthur Schlesinger fills his book on Kennedy with laments about the bureaucratic inertia and recalcitrance of the State Department.

Yet Schlesinger's own account suggests that State could not ordinarily resist the President. At one point, he writes of "the President, himself, increasingly the day-to-day director of American foreign policy." On the next page, we learn that "Kennedy dealt personally with almost every aspect of policy around the globe. He knew more about certain areas than the senior officials at State and probably called as many issues to their attention as they did to his." The President insisted on his way in Laos. He pushed through his policy on the Congo against strong opposition with the State Department. Had Kennedy wanted to get a great deal more initiative out of the State Department, as Schlesinger insists, he could have replaced the Secretary of State, a man who did not command special support in the Democratic party or in Congress. It may be that Kennedy wanted too strongly to run his own foreign policy. Dean Rusk may have known far better than Schlesinger that the one thing Kennedy did not want was a man who might rival him in the field of foreign affairs.

Schlesinger comes closest to the truth when he writes that "the White House could always win any battle it chose over the [Foreign] Service, but the prestige and proficiency of the Service limited the number of battles any White House would find it profitable to fight." When the President knew what he wanted, he got it. When he was doubtful and perplexed, he sought good advice and frequently did not get that. But there is no evidence that the people on his staff came up with better ideas. The real problem may have been a lack of good ideas anywhere. Kennedy undoubtedly encouraged his staff to prod the State Department. But the President was sufficiently cautious not to push so hard that he got his way when he was not certain what that way should be. In this context Kennedy appears to have played his staff off against elements in the State Department.

The growth of a special White House staff to help Presidents in foreign affairs expresses their need for assistance, their refusal to rely completely on the regular executive agencies, and their ability to find competent men. The deployment of this staff must remain a presidential prerogative, however, if its members are to serve Presidents and not their opponents. Whenever critics do not like the existing foreign and defense policies, they are likely to complain that the White House staff is screening out divergent views from the President's attention. Naturally, the critics recommend introducing many more different viewpoints. If the critics could maneuver the President into counting hands all day ("on the one hand and on the other"), they would make it impossible for him to act. Such a viewpoint is also congenial to those who believe that action rather than inaction is the greatest present danger in foreign policy. But Presidents resolutely refuse to become prisoners of their advisers by using them as other people would like. Presidents remain in control of their staff as well as of major foreign policy decisions.

HOW COMPLETE IS THE CONTROL?

Some analysts say that the success of Presidents in controlling foreign policy decisions is largely illusory. It is achieved, they say, by anticipating the reactions of others, and eliminating proposals that would run into severe opposition. There is some truth in this objection. In politics, where transactions are based on a high degree of mutual interdependence, what others may do has to be taken into account. But basing presidential success in foreign and defense policy on anticipated reactions suggests a static situation which does not exist. For if Presidents propose only those policies that would get support in Congress, and Congress opposes them only when it knows that it can muster overwhelming strength, there would never be any conflict. Indeed, there might never be any action.

How can "anticipated reaction" explain the conflict over the policies like the Marshall Plan and the test-ban treaty in which severe opposition was overcome only by strenuous efforts? Furthermore, why doesn't "anticipated reaction" work in domestic affairs? One would have to argue that for some reason presidential perception of what would be successful is consistently confused on domestic issues and most always accurate on major foreign policy issues. But the role of "anticipated reactions" should be greater in the more familiar domestic situations, which provide a backlog of experience for forecasting, than in foreign policy with many novel situations such as the Suez crisis or the Rhodesian affair.

Are there significant historical examples which might refute the thesis of presidential control of foreign policy? Foreign aid may be a case in point. For many years, Presidents have struggled to get foreign aid appropriations because of hostility from public and congressional opinion. Yet several billion dollars a year are appropriated regularly despite the evident unpopularity of the program. In the aid programs to Communist countries like Poland and Yugoslavia, the Congress attaches all sorts of restrictions to the aid, but Presidents find ways of getting around them.

What about the example of recognition of Communist China? The sentiment of the country always has been against recognizing Red China or admitting it to the United Nations. But have Presidents wanted to recognize Red China and been hamstrung by opposition? The answer, I suggest, is a qualified "no." By the time recognition of Red China might have become a serious issue for the Truman administration, the war in Korea effectively precluded its consideration. There is no evidence that President Eisenhower or Secretary Dulles ever thought it wise to recognize Red China or help admit her to the United Nations. The Kennedy administration viewed the matter as not of major importance and, considering the opposition, moved cautiously in suggesting change. Then came the war in Vietnam. If the advantages for foreign policy had been perceived to be much higher, then Kennedy or Johnson might have proposed changing American policy toward recognition of Red China.

One possible exception, in the case of Red China, however, does not seem sufficient to invalidate the general thesis that Presidents do considerably better in getting their way in foreign and defense policy than in domestic policies.

THE WORLD INFLUENCE

The forces impelling Presidents to be concerned with the widest range of foreign and defense policies also affect the ways in which they calculate their power stakes. As Kennedy used to say, "Domestic policy . . . can only defeat us; foreign policy can kill us."

It no longer makes sense for Presidents to "play politics" with foreign and defense policies. In the past, Presidents might have thought that they could gain by prolonged delay or by not acting at all. The problem might disappear or be passed on to their successors. Presidents must now expect to pay the high costs themselves if the world situation deteriorates. The advantages of pursuing a policy that is viable in the world, that will not blow up on Presidents or their fellow citizens, far outweigh any temporary political disadvantages accrued in supporting an initially unpopular policy. Compared with domestic affairs, Presidents engaged in world politics are immensely more concerned with meeting problems on their own terms. Who supports and opposes a policy, though a matter of considerable interest, does not assume the crucial importance that it does in domestic affairs. The best policy Presidents can find is also the best politics.

The fact that there are numerous foreign and defense policy situations competing for a President's attention means that it is worthwhile to organize political activity in order to affect his agenda. For if a President pays more attention to certain problems he may develop different preferences; he may seek and receive different advice; his new calculations may lead him to devote greater resources to seeking a solution. Interested congressmen may exert influence not by directly determining a presidential decision, but indirectly by making it costly for a President to avoid reconsidering the basis for his action. For example, citizen groups, such as those concerned with a change in China policy, may have an impact simply by keeping their proposals on the public agenda. A President may be compelled to reconsider a problem even though he could not overtly be forced to alter the prevailing policy.

In foreign affairs we may be approaching the stage where knowledge is power. There is a tremendous receptivity to good ideas in Washington. Most anyone who can present a convincing rationale for dealing with a hard world finds a ready audience. The best way to convince Presidents to follow a desired policy is to show that it might work. A man like McNamara thrives because he performs; he comes up with answers he can defend. It is, to be sure, extremely difficult to devise good policies or to predict their consequences accurately. Nor is it easy to convince others that a given policy is superior to other alternatives. But it is the way to influence with Presidents. For if they are convinced that the current policy is best, the likelihood of gaining sufficient force to compel a change is quite small. The man who can build better foreign policies will find Presidents beating a path to his door.

CHAPTER **11**

The Bureaucracy

READINGS IN THIS CHAPTER

*T*he federal bureaucracy is sometimes described as the "headless" branch of government because it is not mentioned anywhere in the Constitution. Article II states that the president shall appoint "Officers of the United States" whose positions are created by Congress, but it does not specify further. The president makes high-level appointments with the consent of the Senate (by a majority vote), but other positions are filled by the president alone or by department officials. As appointed officials, federal bureaucrats are not subject to electoral checks; instead, congressional oversight typically provides accountability. The federal bureaucracy operates largely out of public view, with visibility most likely when problems arise.

In 1789 Congress quickly established the major cabinet departments, including the Department of State, War Department (today's Department of Defense), Treasury Department, and Office of Attorney General (which gained cabinet status in 1792 and became the Department of Justice in 1870). One of the first congressional debates about the cabinet concerned appointments: The Constitution specified that the president would nominate appointees who would be subject to Senate approval, but it did not state whether Congress would play a role in removing officials. Possibilities ranged from a Senate vote on dismissal to impeachment of executive officials. James Madison, representative from Virginia, advocated giving the president sole removal power, stating that a president could not execute the law without the ability to dismiss officials who were not fulfilling their responsibilities. With a tie vote in the Senate broken by Vice President John Adams, Congress decided to give the president this power.

Controlling the federal bureaucracy is of even greater significance today because of its size. The White House office also has a staff of approximately five hundred, including the president's personal aide, chief of staff, press secretary, national security adviser, and so forth. The Executive Office of the President numbers about two thousand people, and includes the National Security Council, Office of Management and Budget, Office of Communications, and other top executive offices. The cabinet contains fifteen departments, the most recent being the Department of Homeland Security, which was established in 2002. Additionally, the bureaucracy includes numerous regulatory agencies, such as the Environmental Protection Agency, commissions, and other offices. Each was created by congressional legislation and typically reports to Congress annually, but otherwise operates largely independently.

High-level political appointments to the federal bureaucracy have become highly visible and contentious in recent years. Senior executive appointments require Senate approval, and increased partisanship slows down the process. Since World War II, *divided government*—which exists when the president and one or both chambers of Congress are from different political parties—

happens more frequently, but even this political structure cannot fully account for confirmation delays. Rather, executive nominees often are so closely affiliated with the president's agenda that senators from the opposition party will try to filibuster or otherwise block such appointments. This conflict poses a dilemma, for presidents should nominate people who will actively pursue their agendas, just as the Senate constitutionally is responsible for signing off on those choices. Without a willingness on both sides to consider individuals who can gain bipartisan support, continued conflict seems likely.

The challenges of executive appointments extend into administrative oversight as well. In 1978 Congress passed a law providing for the appointment of an independent counsel to examine allegations of executive branch wrongdoing. The law was written in response to President Richard M. Nixon's 1973 decision to fire the special prosecutor investigating the Watergate burglary of Democratic National Committee headquarters. The independent counsel law was intended to keep the president from obstructing investigations of executive officials, but its implementation has been more complicated. Several Clinton administration officials faced independent counsel investigations in the 1990s, with the most famous, of course, being the Whitewater investigation of President Clinton himself, culminating in the Monica Lewinsky scandal and the impeachment (though not conviction) of the president. The statute expired in 1998, and neither the president nor Congress supported its renewal, given the acrimonious, and frequently partisan, debates about recent investigations. Nevertheless, the Justice Department still can appoint a special counsel to conduct an investigation, as happened in 2003 in response to allegations that White House officials had revealed a covert CIA officer's identity to a journalist. Nearly two years later, one senior White House official was indicted, not for the alleged crime but for perjury in discussing the matter with investigators and a grand jury, and the investigation continued.

Independent counsel investigations represent an extreme method of accountability, but Congress can oversee the executive branch in other ways as well, most commonly through oversight hearings. Cabinet secretaries and their staffs routinely testify on Capitol Hill about matters pending in their departments; Pentagon officials, for example, periodically brief the Senate and House Armed Services Committees, as well as other congressional committees, about U.S. operations in Iraq. When an issue generates controversy, Congress may establish an independent advisory group to investigate the subject closely, as it did with the 9/11 Commission, which examined intelligence findings predating the terrorist attacks as well as the government's response to the attacks. Congressional oversight provides a critical check on executive branch activity, even if the power to force change typically remains in the White House.

For the general public, interaction with the federal bureaucracy happens at least annually with paying taxes, and usually more often for getting passports, applying for citizenship, seeking to employ foreign nationals, and so forth.

When these processes take time, critics say the bureaucracy contains too much *red tape.* But the paperwork that accompanies applications also helps ensure adequate procedural safeguards to protect people's rights.

The most recent full-scale effort to reduce red tape and reform the federal bureaucracy was the National Performance Review (NPR). Led mainly by Vice President Al Gore, the NPR became widely known as the "reinventing government" initiative. But as this chapter's reading selection by John J. DiIulio, Jr., Gerald Garvey, and Donald F. Kettl explains, the NPR effort was predicated on a mistaken metaphor: "In truth, the federal government cannot be reinvented because it was not invented in the first place. The bureaucracy evolved through pragmatic, almost catch-as-catch-can responses to particular problems as they appeared."

Those words seem prescient not only in light of the mixed record of the NPR in the 1990s, but also with respect to the creation in 2002 of a new Department of Homeland Security. Shortly after the 9/11 terrorist attack on the United States, Democratic Senator Joseph Lieberman, who had run for vice president in 2000, called for the creation of a new "Department of Homeland Defense." For nine months, the Bush administration rejected that idea in favor of maintaining a small "Office of Homeland Security," led by former Republican Pennsylvania Governor Tom Ridge, in the White House. By June 2002, however, the White House had switched its position. President Bush proposed a new department that would consolidate twenty-two federal agencies into one cabinet-level umbrella bureaucracy with nearly 170,000 employees (third behind Defense and Veterans Affairs) and a total of about $40 billion a year in budgets (fourth behind Defense, Health and Human Services, and Education). A law creating a new Department of Homeland Security was passed in late 2002, and Ridge became the vast new bureaucracy's first leader. By mid-2004, however, serious questions were being raised in the press and by members of Congress about the department's organization and effectiveness.

Released in the summer of 2004, *The 9/11 Commission Report*'s concluding chapter is headed as follows: "How to Do It?: A Different Way of Organizing the Government." The report recommends five far-reaching "changes in the organization of the government," and called on the barely two-year-old Department of Homeland Security to "go beyond the preexisting jobs of the agencies that have been brought together inside the department."

But "how to do it?" indeed. There are two sets of facts about present-day federal bureaucracy that are vitally important but not widely understood. First, neither in areas relevant to homeland security nor in other policy domains does the federal government directly administer most of the programs that it funds; and, second, executive agencies, though they "report up" to cabinet secretaries and the president, are in most respects creatures of the Congress.

As John J. DiIulio, Jr., explains in the excerpt from his 2003 *Harvard Law Review* essay, the federal government relies heavily on state and local governments, for-profit firms, and nonprofit organizations to administer the programs it funds. There are roughly six people who work on federal programs for every one who is an actual federal civil servant. This so-called *government-by-proxy* system has been around for decades, and it has been plagued by all manner of unresolved, and perhaps unresolvable, problems.

As James Q. Wilson summarizes in the excerpt from his classic book, *Bureaucracy*, "Congress is certainly the architect of the bureaucracy" and has myriad means for exercising influence over what federal agencies do and how they do it. Thus, the 9/11 Commission is righter than it perhaps knows when it claims that congressional oversight of intelligence "is now dysfunctional," but also more optimistic than it probably perceives when it calls on Congress to "create a single, principal point of oversight and review for homeland security."

11.1 Improving Government Performance: An Owner's Manual (1993)

JOHN J. DiIULIO, JR., GERALD GARVEY, AND DONALD F. KETTL

INTRODUCTION

Launched by the Clinton administration and led mainly by Vice President Al Gore, the National Performance Review was widely described as an effort at "reinventing government." It was the eleventh far-reaching federal government reform effort of the twentieth century. In this reading, John J. DiIulio, Jr., Gerald Garvey, and Donald F. Kettl argue that the "reinvention" metaphor is all wrong, instead, they argue, the federal bureaucracy arose in an agency-by-agency, problem-by-problem fashion, creating "the patchwork pattern of our government."

■

TWO METAPHORS OF REFORM—INVENTION AND EVOLUTION

From the beginning, two metaphors of reform have vied for primacy in the American imagination. The first, the metaphor of invention, came out of the

John J. DiIulio, Jr., Gerald Garvey, and Donald F. Kettl, *Improving Government Performance: An Owner's Manual* (Washington, D.C.: Brookings Institution, 1993), 1–17. Copyright © 1993 by Brookings Institution. Reprinted with permission.

founders' own preoccupation with Newtonian mechanism. They thought it possible to create a self-checking governmental apparatus, a "machine that would go of itself." Thomas Jefferson urged that the structures of government be abolished and reinvented every twentieth Independence Day. When William Gladstone described the U.S. Constitution as "the greatest work ever struck off by the mind and wit of man," he was invoking the imagery of institutional invention, as was James Bryce when he wrote admiringly of our political system as the "federal contrivance."

In a nation of gadgetmakers and tinkerers, Eli Whitney, Thomas Edison, and Henry Ford have become folk icons. It is natural to identify constructive change with the act of invention, and probably just as natural to suppose that some reinventing may be in order when institutional change seems needed. Much of the appeal today of David Osborne's and Ted Gaebler's *Reinventing Government* derives from the resonance of their main metaphor with American political culture.[1] They write of catalytic government. Their "map," as they term it, for a New World of governance is itself a catalytic image, intended as much to galvanize action as to describe reality. Similarly, the metaphor of invention, which gives their book its thematic unity and resonance, serves more a catalytic than an analytic purpose. The can-do spirit, change effected through ingenious new combinations of parts, reform as the product of a single creative event—these are among the ideas evoked by our self-conception as an inventive people.

The other metaphor, the metaphor of evolution, has as much intellectual support as does the metaphor of invention. If our Constitution was invented, it was also left open and adaptable, the better to accommodate developments that "could not have been foreseen completely by the most gifted of its begetters," as Justice Oliver Wendell Holmes commented. The doctrine of social Darwinism no longer commands the kind of assent it once did. But the thoroughness with which Americans embraced the evolutionary paradigm when it first appeared suggests that gradualists such as Charles Darwin, Herbert Spencer, and Alfred Marshall, though Britons themselves, expounded a truth that citizens of the United States accept almost instinctively.

One of the basic concepts of contemporary social science, that of bounded rationality, supports the evolutionary approach to institutional reform. According to the bounded rationality hypothesis, policymakers mostly delude themselves when they think that "comprehensive study" or "bold inventive action" can produce useful, enduring change. The world of politics is too rich in both information and uncertainty; once-and-for-all efforts at structural reform must fail. When used as an evocative symbol, the metaphor of invention can help concentrate the mind, charge the imagination, perhaps inspire a certain willing suspension of disbelief. But the inventive approach has its limits

---

[1]David Osborne and Ted Gaebler, *Reinventing Government: How the Entrepreneurial Spirit Is Transforming the Public Sector* (Addison-Wesley, 1992).

as a guide to practical action. The elements of public management cannot be detached from their political and institutional contexts in ways that would permit them to be manipulated inventively.

We are limited in the administrative knowledge that we already possess. We are still struggling to process information about the Old World of governance, let alone about anyone's imagined map for a New World. The primary teaching of modern implementation scholars is that projects for institutional reform may produce unintended consequences, frequently unwanted ones. This literature itself grew out of efforts to understand why the attempts at reinvention of American society in the 1960s had failed.

History and social theory alike suggest that the optimism of the reinventors, although necessary to concentrate energies, will best help improve government performance if it is tempered with caution. The evolutionary approach does not deny the richness or the value of the proposals Osborne and Gaebler offer. From one end of their book to the other, the good ideas just keep coming. Moreover, they have generated reform energy unmatched in a generation. Constructive change, however, is more likely to occur selectively and experimentally than as a sweeping transformation of the public sector.

Reformers need periodically to recall that incremental, experimental change has usually proved to be the way institutional reforms become simultaneously feasible, constructive, and enduring. We intend this book as a brief for a reformist attitude that is careful, prudent, and experimental—one that will work, and one that will last.

THINKING BEYOND THE RHETORIC OF REFORM

The past few years have been a time of renewed interest in public service reform at all levels of government. In 1990 the National Commission on the Public Service, chaired by former Federal Reserve Board Chairman Paul A. Volcker, issued its report, which focused on the federal service.[2] In 1993 the National Commission on the State and Local Public Service, chaired by former Mississippi Governor William F. Winter, presented its report to President Clinton. Now comes the National Performance Review, commissioned by President Clinton, directed by Vice President Gore, and largely inspired by *Reinventing Government*, perhaps the first public administration book in history to become a bestseller.

Much of the allure of this book, written by journalist David Osborne and former city manager Ted Gaebler, derives from its diagnosis of the causes of

---

[2]Paul A. Volcker, *Leadership for America: Rebuilding the Public Service—The Report of the National Commission on the Public Service and the Task Force Reports to the National Commission on the Public Service* (National Commission on the Public Service, 1989).

inadequate federal performance and its energetic prescriptions for change. The diagnosis: a bureaucracy staffed by well-meaning officials who find themselves hamstrung by illogical procedures and pulled in unproductive directions by perverse incentives. The prescription: decentralize government and create incentives to promote entrepreneurial activity by government workers.

Reinventing Government reminded everyone that government is after all in business to serve citizens, not its own employees (whether elective or appointive). The book established the critical importance of a good working relationship between government and the private sector. Perhaps most important, it raised the debate on the quality of government performance to a level not seen in a generation.

The National Performance Review

The National Performance Review, sometimes called the "reinventing government initiative," takes much of its agenda, as well as its informal title, from Osborne's and Gaebler's book. Vice President Gore outlined the goals of the review at a press conference on April 15, 1993: evaluate the efficiency of every federal agency, identify and eliminate waste and inefficiency throughout the federal service, streamline the federal personnel system, and change the culture of federal bureaucracy and "empower" workers. Some 200 federal employees have become the eyes, ears, hands, and feet of the National Performance Review. They are organized into various reinvention teams. Together they are to gather detailed data and fashion prescriptive analyses on the performance of all federal agencies, addressing themselves in particular to the efficacy of various leadership strategies and management structures. And they are to do all this by Labor Day 1993, at which time the vice president has promised to unveil the Clinton administration's blueprint for a reinvented government.

The effort rests on broad public opinion that it is indeed past time to rethink the balance of public and private sector responsibilities. It is time to rearrange the organization of the federal bureaucracy in a way that will shorten internal lines of communication and promote coordination across functional and jurisdictional boundaries. It is time to decentralize government so as to facilitate entrepreneurial activity by civil servants and ultimately change the culture of public bureaucracy.

The results of the 1992 presidential election emphasized the American public's expectation of constructive change. And even a cursory examination of federal management practices demonstrates why this expectation rises to the level of a demand. No one, however, should underestimate how hard it will be to change patterns of bureaucratic operation, organizational forms, and structural constraints that have evolved over the course of a century. Short-term confidence and enthusiasm are obvious requirements. The competence and dedication of federal administrators working without fanfare and often without thanks represent even higher values. One hopes that, fifteen years from now, GS-11s throughout the federal government will be daily serving the public even more effectively than is now the case, for reasons that can be traced back to reforms identified by the national performance reviewers. To this end, it is crucial that the energetic officials in the White House and Congress who are spearheading reform efforts not become so captivated by the rhetoric of reform that they look past the realities.

In truth, the federal government as it functions today cannot be reinvented because it was not invented in the first place. The bureaucracy evolved through pragmatic, almost catch-as-catch-can responses to particular problems as they appeared. It is this development that warns of the need for an incremental, evolutionary, experimental approach to institutional reform.

An Incremental, Evolutionary, Experimental Process

The evolutionary viewpoint carries implications about the sources of problems in the federal bureaucracy. It implies as well the responses that will work best as public managers begin trying to alter a process that has evolved over generations. The history of federal reform efforts counsels humility, not hubris.

Contrary to what President Clinton said when he announced the reform initiative, past public service reports have not simply gathered dust. The 1993 National Performance Review is only the most recent presidential effort to make government work better (Figure 1). In 1912 President Taft's Commission on Economy and Efficiency argued for a presidential budget based on performance. In 1937 the Brownlow committee concluded that "the president needs help" and argued for a strengthened executive management capacity emanating from the White House. Members of two post–World War II commissions headed by former President Hoover studied every organizational aspect of the federal government. President Kennedy's budget director headed a task force on problems in government contracting, and President Johnson's task force on government organization examined ways to improve the president's management of it. The Nixon administration followed with a high-powered advisory council headed by industrialist Roy Ash to recommend changes in executive organization. Under Ronald Reagan, yet another blue ribbon panel studied the problems of federal acquisition, focusing on the Defense Department, and in 1983 a commission headed by J. Peter Grace claimed to have found hundreds of billions of dollars of waste in federal programs.

Some Lessons—and Some Temptations

Four important lessons emerge from these attempts at reform. First, the task of institutional reform is daunting. If solutions were easy, repeated efforts would not have been necessary. Second, despite the difficulty of the job, progress, albeit gradual, partial, and selective, has been made. Government works better today because of these earlier reform efforts. Neither the Brownlow committee nor the Hoover commissions caused the earth to move, but they did cause government to improve, although selectively and incrementally.

Figure 1
Major Commissions to Improve the Executive Branch, 1905–93

Keep commission (1905–09)
Personnel management, government contracting, information management

President's Commission on Economy and Efficiency (1910–13)
The case for a national executive budget

Joint Committee on Reorganization (1921–24)
Methods of redistributing executive functions among the departments

President's Committee on Administrative Management (1936–37)
Recommended creation of the Executive Office of the President; study founded on substantial academic theory

First Hoover commission (1947–49)
Comprehensive review of the organization and function of the executive branch; built on task force reports

Second Hoover commission (1953–55)
Follow-on to the first Hoover commission; focused more on policy problems than organizational structure

Study commissions on executive reorganization (1953–68)
Series of low-key reforms that produced quiet but important changes

Ash council (1969–71)
Proposals for a fundamental restructuring of the executive branch, including creation of four new super departments to encompass existing departments

Carter reorganization effort (1977–79)
Bottom-up, process-based effort to reorganize government that mostly ended in failure; new cabinet departments created independently of effort

Grace commission (1982–84)
Large-scale effort to determine how government could be operated for less money

National Performance Review (1993)
Attempt to "reinvent" government to improve its performance

Source: Ronald C. Moe, *Reorganizing the Executive Branch in the Twentieth Century: Landmark Commissions,* report 92-293 GOV (Congressional Research Service, March 1992).

The Brownlow committee strengthened the institutional presidency; the Hoover commissions launched management reforms that revolutionized the government's day-to-day business. Third, reforms have worked best when they grew from a strong strategy and robust intellectual support. Performance reviews are, in their essence, efforts at strategic planning. They themselves need to be guided by a strategic plan, a clear vision of the problem and of the direction in which solutions lie. In fact, diagnosing the problem has always been the most critical step in every reform effort. The Brownlow committee's famous finding, "the president needs help," fueled its work and helped ensure its success. Fourth, long-term follow-through matters. Only sustained presidential attention to management problems will produce a difference.

The record also suggests four temptations that today's reformers must avoid. First, it is tempting to confuse disagreement over what government ought to do with how well it does it. There is a common presumption that government programs are larded with too much bureaucracy and wasteful spending. But what critics call waste, fraud, and abuse often are programs managed well but managed according to values different from the critics' own. Many of the potential savings identified by the Grace commission, for example, would have resulted from eliminating programs with which commission members disagreed. The programs might indeed have been wasteful by some definitions, but they represented the legitimate product of the American democratic process. The danger here is that solutions billed as administrative, managerial, or technical may disguise underlying differences of policy or significant competition among disparate interests. No one should be surprised when the promised results are not achieved: the proponents of the changes have underestimated the political strength of forces that would resist change.

A second temptation to avoid is not only rushing to judgment but rushing into action. Reformers need to examine closely the problems they wish to solve and assess carefully the actions required to solve them. Some kinds of reforms require major changes in legislation; others can be effectively pursued through executive action. Legislative changes require not only more time but also more elaborate political strategies to implement. Administrative changes can sometimes be done more rapidly. Reforms must be staged according to the strategies required to implement them.

Poor implementation can doom any policy. Proceeding in a do-it-all-now manner, without matching the political resources required and the objectives sought, is likely to stall a reform effort. Easy changes that might have been completed at low cost may be left undone because energy goes into difficult long-term projects. These long-term projects might better be approached by steadily applying pressure over time while building on the political impetus that beginning the easier jobs can generate. The trick is to do what can be done quickly by administrative means while preparing a legislative agenda for the long term.

Third, it is tempting to promise that management reforms will produce major savings and reduce the budget deficit. Improved performance is in fact likely to produce budget savings, but only as a by-product. Some improvements in performance might yield greater satisfaction with government services without making much difference on the bottom line. New procedures for processing social security checks, for example, might dramatically decrease the number of lost checks without reducing the deficit. Other improvements might require short-term investments in exchange for significant long-term savings. Many government contracts, for instance, are plagued by mismanagement. Reducing such problems requires investing in greater government expertise to ensure that the public gets its money's worth in the long run. In most systems, optimum performance requires balancing costs against quality. Making cost savings the driving force of a performance review can detract from quality. And mingling management issues with budget questions typically increases the suspicion of government employees who have seen previous performance reforms degenerate into witch hunts to cut their salaries and criticize their work. The performance review process itself has to be a model of the values it seeks to instill more widely within government.

There is an important connection between government performance and the budget. Regardless of the policy changes that might occur, the federal government will continue to manage a great many functions, from space exploration and energy conservation to income security and environmental regulation. The government must get its money's worth. Good management can keep costs down and improve results; poor management will drive costs up, yield diminished results, and increase the budget deficit. Improved government performance thus supports the drive for deficit reduction, but the two are not synonymous.

Finally, it is tempting for study commissions to seek The Answer. But implementation scholars and leaders in the total quality management (TQM) movement have emphasized continuous improvement, incremental, evolutionary, experimental improvement. Reconstructing government will require carefully paced modifications informed by an experimental rather than a dogmatic or recklessly inventive spirit.

Not even the most prescient reformers can know what will work best. Studying today's government performance problems can provide a starting place but rarely a realistic picture of the ending place. By contrast, with a process that everyone expects to be evolutionary, careful reviews of interim results can provide real guidance on what works and why. Trying, evaluating, and learning through time are as important for ultimate success as the original study design.

No one who has thought seriously about leadership and management will presume to know what works best under all conditions. Nor can a clear vision emerge from ideas collected from government workers. Ford Motor

Company may have dramatically improved the quality of its cars by acting on the suggestions of assembly line workers. But it could never use such suggestions to decide what kind of car to build. Thought without action is futile; but action without thought directed by a clear strategy can be fatal. Our first purpose is therefore to understand the sources and nature of both the structures and the bureaucratic culture that, so many Americans are convinced, prevent public officials from performing with initiative and imagination.

THE EVOLUTION OF THE FEDERAL BUREAUCRACY

The Progressives established the basic mechanisms of America's modern public administration: new cabinet departments, independent commissions, blueprints for the modern Executive Office of the President, the civil service system, and the presidential budget. Since then, the federal bureaucracy has evolved through agency-by-agency, procedure-by-procedure, program-by-program responses to problems as they appeared. That process has left a vast, untidy apparatus. The historical view gives a useful perspective for understanding today's problems.

A Pattern of Agency-by-Agency Growth

In 1887 Congress created the Interstate Commerce Commission and two years later elevated the commissioner of Agriculture to full cabinet status—this after a century in which the United States had gotten along with the original executive departments plus one (the Interior Department, established in 1849). The Progressive movement launched a bureaucratic evolution that produced in the next century today's complex of independent regulatory commissions, executive agencies, and fourteen executive departments.

Most of the classical theorists of bureaucracy, from leaders of American progressivism such as Woodrow Wilson and Frederick Winslow Taylor through Max Weber and Luther Gulick, took it more or less for granted that institutional arrangements matter and that a bureaucrat's performance and a bureau's design are interrelated. Central to the classical tradition was that efficiency is the objective of organization and functional specialization is the way to achieve efficiency. As a result, government acquired additional functions, and it became increasingly differentiated and complex as new commissions and agencies proliferated. Specialized bureaus were the institutional response to new problems.

This theory became the blueprint for the exponential growth of government. Americans have always seemed quick to pass a law, create a bureau, issue new rules, and enlarge the bureaucracy when a problem appeared that the market seemed incapable of handling. Government became society's problem solver of last resort.

First the Progressives created the new independent commissions and executive agencies to deal with market failures. The Interstate Commerce Commission (not to mention dozens of ratesetting commissions in the states) coped with natural monopolies in capital-intensive industries. The Federal Reserve Board regulated the supply of money and credit. The Food and Drug Administration protected the public from contaminants in food and pharmaceutical products. Between 1890 and the mid-1920s almost all of the executive departments expanded, as did the apparatus that would become the Executive Office of the President. And in the same years the Commerce and Labor departments were created. When the Great Depression showed that the unregulated private economy can fail to generate full employment, government accepted responsibility for providing economic stimulation and stabilization. The New Deal added the Civilian Conservation Corps (CCC), the Work Projects Administration (WPA), the National Recovery Administration (NRA), and other alphabet agencies.

The additions and expansions continued after World War II, but with a social rather than an economic focus. The federal government accepted responsibility when troubled social institutions (the family, the neighborhood) failed. Yet another set of programs, from aid to families with dependent children to community development, was created and expanded through yet another set of bureaus established to administer them.

Throughout this bureaucratic growth, many new commissions and agencies reflected existing industries. New programs grew to promote home building or road construction. Other programs, such as the war on poverty or AIDS research, helped stimulate whole new industries. The growth of the federal bureaucracy is thus linked as well with fundamental changes in the private sector. These changes have also created political interests with a huge stake in government activity that have transformed the workings of the American political system.

Functional Specialization and Boundary Problems

The evolution of federal responsibilities explains much of the patchwork pattern of our government. It has created specialized agencies divided by jurisdictional boundaries. These boundaries have multiplied as new agencies and programs have grown, and difficulties of coordination have proliferated in tandem. At the same time, the structure of Congress and the bureaucracy came to mirror one another. Congress often created a new legislative subcommittee to oversee the work of a new commission or agency. The number of congressional subcommittees grew apace with the industry-by-industry growth of the economy and the agency-by-agency growth of the bureaucracy. By this process, some scholars contend, the "iron triangles" of American government first appeared: new bureaus linked by relationships of continuing influence to counterpart legislative subcommittees as well as to the firms in their respective counterpart industries.

Today, for example, relieving rural poverty requires cooperation among officials from many federal agencies, beginning with the Department of Agriculture and its own subunits (the Rural Electrification Administration and so forth), but including Health and Human Services, Housing and Urban Development, and various subunits of Interior (the Bureau of Indian Affairs, the Bureau of Land Management). In this area alone, substantial energy must go into securing coordination. Across the government as a whole, the energy devoted to cross-boundary competition and coordination detracts in incalculable ways from officials' attention to solving the public's problems.

In the Environmental Protection Agency organizational issues present other problems. Offices are organized and staffed to deal with pollution in specific media (air, water, ground). It is a familiar lament that efforts to correct problems within the jurisdiction of one specialized office create new pollution problems for another: enforced scrubbing of smokestacks to clean smoke plumes of sulfur oxides generates hundreds of thousands of tons of sludge each year that has to be buried in landfills or dumped offshore. As in poverty programs, the structure of government too often gets in the way.

The proliferation of specialized executive bureaus, legislative subcommittees, and private sector interests around these issues has also meant that responsibility for every problem from environmental safety to adequate health care overlaps. Classical organization theory was based on the unity of command. Today, overlapping jurisdictions create endless jockeying for lead-agency status on high-profile problems. Because many agencies have a stake in, but no clear responsibility for, other problems, solutions fall through the cracks. The virtue of organizational specialization has turned into the vice of organizational fragmentation. Incoherence in policymaking and confusion in implementation have resulted.

The irony is that the efforts of the Progressives to improve the rationality and effectiveness of the federal government created the conditions encouraging the fragmentation and overlap we are now struggling to solve. The lessons for reformers are important. Past solutions too often become present problems; seeking today's solutions from yesterday's models can be dangerous.

11.2   The 9/11 Commission Report: Final Report of the National Commission on Terrorist Attacks upon the United States (2004)

INTRODUCTION

Shortly after the 9/11 terrorist attacks, U.S. Senator Joseph Lieberman, a Democrat who had run for vice president in 2000, called for the creation of a new Department of Homeland Defense. The Bush administration rejected the idea. Instead, it created a small Office of Homeland Security in the White House. But in June 2002, President Bush proposed the creation of a new Department of Homeland Security encompassing nearly two dozen existing agencies.

The new department was approved by law in 2002, but just two years later, in the summer of 2004, the National Commission on Terrorist Attacks upon the United States called for another massive government reorganization in the interests of improving homeland security. The commission's final report calls for a national intelligence director to "oversee the component agencies of the intelligence community." This position was established shortly after the report's publication, and the national intelligence director reports directly to the president. Significantly, the commission terms "strengthening congressional oversight" the "most difficult and important" of its numerous recommendations: "Few things are more difficult to change in Washington than congressional committee jurisdiction and prerogatives."

∎

HOW TO DO IT? A DIFFERENT WAY OF ORGANIZING THE GOVERNMENT

As presently configured, the national security institutions of the U.S. government are still the institutions constructed to win the Cold War. The United States confronts a very different world today. Instead of facing a few very dangerous adversaries, the United States confronts a number of less visible challenges that surpass the boundaries of traditional nation-states and call for quick, imaginative, and agile responses.

The 9/11 Commission Report: Final Report of the National Commission on Terrorist Attacks upon the United States (New York: W. W. Norton & Company, 2004), 399–428 (excerpts).

The men and women of the World War II generation rose to the challenges of the 1940s and 1950s. They restructured the government so that it could protect the country. That is now the job of the generation that experienced 9/11. Those attacks showed, emphatically, that ways of doing business rooted in a different era are just not good enough. Americans should not settle for incremental, ad hoc adjustments to a system designed generations ago for a world that no longer exists.

We recommend significant changes in the organization of the government. We know that the quality of the people is more important than the quality of the wiring diagrams. Some of the saddest aspects of the 9/11 story are the outstanding efforts of so many individual officials straining, often without success, against the boundaries of the possible. Good people can overcome bad structures. They should not have to.

The United States has the resources and the people. The government should combine them more effectively, achieving unity of effort. We offer five major recommendations to do that:

- unifying strategic intelligence and operational planning against Islamist terrorists across the foreign-domestic divide with a National Counterterrorism Center;
- unifying the intelligence community with a new National Intelligence Director;
- unifying the many participants in the counterterrorism effort and their knowledge in a network-based information-sharing system that transcends traditional governmental boundaries;
- unifying and strengthening congressional oversight to improve quality and accountability; and
- strengthening the FBI and homeland defenders. . . .

In our hearings we regularly asked witnesses: Who is the quarterback? The other players are in their positions, doing their jobs. But who is calling the play that assigns roles to help them execute as a team?

Since 9/11, those issues have not been resolved. In some ways joint work has gotten better, and in some ways worse. The effort of fighting terrorism has flooded over many of the usual agency boundaries because of its sheer quantity and energy. Attitudes have changed. Officials are keenly conscious of trying to avoid the mistakes of 9/11. They try to share information. They circulate—even to the President—practically every reported threat, however dubious.

Partly because of all this effort, the challenge of coordinating it has multiplied. Before 9/11, the CIA was plainly the lead agency confronting al Qaeda. The FBI played a very secondary role. The engagement of the departments of Defense and State was more episodic.

- Today the CIA is still central. But the FBI is much more active, along with other parts of the Justice Department.

- The Defense Department effort is now enormous. Three of its unified commands, each headed by a four-star general, have counterterrorism as a primary mission: Special Operations Command, Central Command (both headquartered in Florida), and Northern Command (headquartered in Colorado).
- A new Department of Homeland Security combines formidable resources in border and transportation security, along with analysis of domestic vulnerability and other tasks.
- The State Department has the lead on many of the foreign policy tasks. . . .
- At the White House, the National Security Council (NSC) now is joined by a parallel presidential advisory structure, the Homeland Security Council.

So far we have mentioned two reasons for joint action—the virtue of joint planning and the advantage of having someone in charge to ensure a unified effort. There is a third: the simple shortage of experts with sufficient skills. The limited pool of critical experts—for example, skilled counterterrorism analysts and linguists—is being depleted. Expanding these capabilities will require not just money, but time.

Primary responsibility for terrorism analysis has been assigned to the Terrorist Threat Integration Center (TTIC), created in 2003, based at the CIA headquarters but staffed with representatives of many agencies, reporting directly to the Director of Central Intelligence. Yet the CIA houses another intelligence "fusion" center: the Counterterrorist Center that played such a key role before 9/11. A third major analytic unit is at Defense, in the Defense Intelligence Agency. A fourth, concentrating more on homeland vulnerabilities, is at the Department of Homeland Security. The FBI is in the process of building the analytic capability it has long lacked, and it also has the Terrorist Screening Center.

The U.S. government cannot afford so much duplication of effort. There are not enough experienced experts to go around. The duplication also places extra demands on already hard-pressed single-source national technical intelligence collectors like the National Security Agency. . . .

The government now tries to handle the problem of joint management informed by analysis of intelligence from all sources, in two ways.

- First, agencies with lead responsibility for certain problems have constructed their own interagency entities and task forces in order to get cooperation. The Counterterrorist Center at CIA, for example, recruits liaison officers from throughout the intelligence community. The military's Central Command has its own interagency center, recruiting liaison officers from all the agencies from which it might need help. The FBI has Joint Terrorism Task Forces in 84 locations to coordinate the activities of other agencies when action may be required.

- Second, the problem of joint operational planning is often passed to the White House, where the NSC staff tries to play this role. The national security staff at the White House (both NSC and new Homeland Security Council staff) has already become 50 percent larger since 9/11. But our impression, after talking to serving officials, is that even this enlarged staff is consumed by meetings on day-to-day issues, sifting each day's threat information and trying to coordinate everyday operations.

Even as it crowds into every square inch of available office space, the NSC staff is still not sized or funded to be an executive agency. . . . [W]e described some of the problems that arose in the 1980s when a White House staff, constitutionally insulated from the usual mechanisms of oversight, became involved in direct operations. During the 1990s Richard Clarke occasionally tried to exercise such authority, sometimes successfully, but often causing friction.

Yet a subtler and more serious danger is that as the NSC staff is consumed by these day-to-day tasks, it has less capacity to find the time and detachment needed to advise a president on larger policy issues. That means less time to work on major new initiatives, help with legislative management to steer needed bills through Congress, and track the design and implementation of the strategic plans for regions, countries, and issues. . . .

Much of the job of operational coordination remains with the agencies, especially the CIA. There DCI Tenet and his chief aides ran interagency meetings nearly every day to coordinate much of the government's day-to-day work. The DCI insisted he did not make policy and only oversaw its implementation. In the struggle against terrorism these distinctions seem increasingly artificial. Also, as the DCI becomes a lead coordinator of the government's operations, it becomes harder to play all the position's other roles, including that of analyst in chief.

The problem is nearly intractable because of the way the government is currently structured. Lines of operational authority run to the expanding executive departments, and they are guarded for understandable reasons: the DCI commands the CIA's personnel overseas; the secretary of defense will not yield to others in conveying commands to military forces; the Justice Department will not give up the responsibility of deciding whether to seek arrest warrants. But the result is that each agency or department needs its own intelligence apparatus to support the performance of its duties. It is hard to "break down stovepipes" when there are so many stoves that are legally and politically entitled to have cast-iron pipes of their own. . . .

During the Cold War, intelligence agencies did not depend on seamless integration to track and count the thousands of military targets—such as tanks and missiles—fielded by the Soviet Union and other adversary states. Each agency concentrated on its specialized mission, acquiring its own information and then sharing it via formal, finished reports. The Department of Defense had given birth to and dominated the main agencies for technical collection of intelligence. Resources were shifted at an incremental pace, coping with challenges that arose over years, even decades.

   ... [T]he organization of the intelligence community ... is outlined below.

Members of the U.S. Intelligence Community

Office of the Director of Central Intelligence, which includes the Office of the Deputy Director of Central Intelligence for Community Management, the Community Management Staff, the Terrorism Threat Integration Center, the National Intelligence Council, and other community offices

   The Central Intelligence Agency (CIA), which performs human source collection, all-source analysis, and advanced science and technology

   National intelligence agencies:

- National Security Agency (NSA), which performs signals collection and analysis
- National Geospatial-Intelligence Agency (NGA), which performs imagery collection and analysis
- National Reconnaissance Office (NRO), which develops, acquires, and launches space systems for intelligence collection
- Other national reconnaissance programs

   Departmental intelligence agencies:

- Defense Intelligence Agency (DIA) of the Department of Defense
- Intelligence entities of the Army, Navy, Air Force, and Marines
- Bureau of Intelligence and Research (INR) of the Department of State
- Office of Terrorism and Finance Intelligence of the Department of Treasury
- Office of Intelligence and the Counterterrorism and Counterintelligence Divisions of the Federal Bureau of Investigation of the Department of Justice
- Office of Intelligence of the Department of Energy
- Directorate of Information Analysis and Infrastructure Protection (IAIP) and Directorate of Coast Guard Intelligence of the Department of Homeland Security ...

When Congress passes an appropriations bill to allocate money to intelligence agencies, most of their funding is hidden in the Defense Department in order to keep intelligence spending secret. Therefore, although the House and Senate Intelligence committees are the authorizing committees for funding of the intelligence community, the final budget review is handled in the Defense Subcommittee of the Appropriations committees. Those committees have no subcommittees just for intelligence, and only a few members and staff review the requests.

The appropriations for the CIA and the national intelligence agencies—NSA, NGA, and NRO—are then given to the secretary of defense. The secretary transfers the CIA's money to the DCI but disburses the national agencies' money directly. Money for the FBI's national security components falls within the appropriations for Commerce, Justice, and State and goes to the attorney general.

In addition, the DCI lacks hire-and-fire authority over most of the intelligence community's senior managers. For the national intelligence agencies housed in the Defense Department, the secretary of defense must seek the DCI's concurrence regarding the nomination of these directors, who are presidentially appointed. But the secretary may submit recommendations to the president without receiving this concurrence. The DCI cannot fire these officials. The DCI has even less influence over the head of the FBI's national security component, who is appointed by the attorney general in consultation with the DCI.

Combining Joint Work with Stronger Management

We have received recommendations on the topic of intelligence reform from many sources. Other commissions have been over this same ground. Thoughtful bills have been introduced, most recently a bill by the chairman of the House Intelligence Committee Porter Goss (R-Fla.), and another by the ranking minority member, Jane Harman (D-Calif.). In the Senate, Senators Bob Graham (D-Fla.) and Dianne Feinstein (D-Calif.) have introduced reform proposals as well. Past efforts have foundered, because the president did not support them; because the DCI, the secretary of defense, or both opposed them; and because some proposals lacked merit. We have tried to take stock of these experiences, and borrow from strong elements in many of the ideas that have already been developed by others.

Recommendation: The current position of Director of Central Intelligence should be replaced by a National Intelligence Director with two main areas of responsibility: (1) to oversee national intelligence centers on specific subjects of interest across the U.S. government and (2) to manage the national intelligence program and oversee the agencies that contribute to it.

First, the National Intelligence Director should oversee *national intelligence centers* to provide all-source analysis and plan intelligence operations for the whole government on major problems.

- One such problem is counterterrorism. In this case, we believe that the center should be the intelligence entity (formerly TTIC) inside the National Counterterrorism Center we have proposed. It would sit there alongside the operations management unit we described earlier, with both making up the NCTC, in the Executive Office of the President. Other national intelligence centers—for instance, on counterproliferation, crime and narcotics, and China—would be housed in whatever department or agency is best suited for them.

- The National Intelligence Director would retain the present DCI's role as the principal intelligence adviser to the president. We hope the president will come to look directly to the directors of the national intelligence centers to provide all-source analysis in their areas of responsibility, balancing the advice of these intelligence chiefs against the contrasting viewpoints that may be offered by department heads at State, Defense, Homeland Security, Justice, and other agencies.

Second, the National Intelligence Director should manage the national intelligence program and oversee the component agencies of the intelligence community.

- The National Intelligence Director would submit a unified budget for national intelligence that reflects priorities chosen by the National Security Council, an appropriate balance among the varieties of technical and human intelligence collection, and analysis. He or she would receive an appropriation for national intelligence and apportion the funds to the appropriate agencies, in line with that budget, and with authority to reprogram funds among the national intelligence agencies to meet any new priority (as counterterrorism was in the 1990s). The National Intelligence Director should approve and submit nominations to the president of the individuals who would lead the CIA, DIA, FBI Intelligence Office, NSA, NGA, NRO, Information Analysis and Infrastructure Protection Directorate of the Department of Homeland Security, and other national intelligence capabilities.
- The National Intelligence Director would manage this national effort with the help of three deputies, each of whom would also hold a key position in one of the component agencies.
  - foreign intelligence (the head of the CIA)
  - defense intelligence (the under secretary of defense for intelligence)
  - homeland intelligence (the FBI's executive assistant director for intelligence or the under secretary of homeland security for information analysis and infrastructure protection)

  Other agencies in the intelligence community would coordinate their work within each of these three areas, largely staying housed in the same departments or agencies that support them now.

  Returning to the analogy of the Defense Department's organization, these three deputies—like the leaders of the Army, Navy, Air Force, or Marines—would have the job of acquiring the systems, training the people, and executing the operations planned by the national intelligence centers.

And, just as the combatant commanders also report to the secretary of defense, the directors of the national intelligence centers—e.g., for counterproliferation, crime and narcotics, and the rest—also would report to the National Intelligence Director.

- The Defense Department's military intelligence programs—the joint military intelligence program (JMIP) and the tactical intelligence and related activities program (TIARA)—would remain part of that department's responsibility. . . .
- The National Intelligence Director would set personnel policies to establish standards for education and training and facilitate assignments at the national intelligence centers and across agency lines. The National Intelligence Director also would set information sharing and information technology policies to maximize data sharing, as well as policies to protect the security of information.
- Too many agencies now have an opportunity to say no to change. The National Intelligence Director should participate in an NSC executive committee that can resolve differences in priorities among the agencies and bring the major disputes to the president for decision.

The National Intelligence Director should be located in the Executive Office of the President. This official, who would be confirmed by the Senate and would testify before Congress, would have a relatively small staff of several hundred people, taking the place of the existing community management offices housed at the CIA.

In managing the whole community, the National Intelligence Director is still providing a service function. With the partial exception of his or her responsibilities for overseeing the NCTC, the National Intelligence Director should support the consumers of national intelligence—the president and policymaking advisers such as the secretaries of state, defense, and homeland security and the attorney general.

We are wary of too easily equating government management problems with those of the private sector. But we have noticed that some very large private firms rely on a powerful CEO who has significant control over how money is spent and can hire or fire leaders of the major divisions, assisted by a relatively modest staff, while leaving responsibility for execution in the operating divisions. . . .

Strengthen Congressional Oversight of Intelligence and Homeland Security

Of all our recommendations, strengthening congressional oversight may be among the most difficult and important. So long as oversight is governed by current congressional rules and resolutions, we believe the American people will not get the security they want and need. The United States needs a strong, stable, and capable congressional committee structure to give America's national intelligence agencies oversight, support, and leadership.

Few things are more difficult to change in Washington than congressional committee jurisdiction and prerogatives. To a member, these assignments are almost as important as the map of his or her congressional district. The American people may have to insist that these changes occur, or they may well not happen. Having interviewed numerous members of Congress from both parties, as well as congressional staff members, we found that dissatisfaction with congressional oversight remains widespread.

The future challenges of America's intelligence agencies are daunting. They include the need to develop leading-edge technologies that give our policymakers and warfighters a decisive edge in any conflict where the interests of the United States are vital. Not only does good intelligence win wars, but the best intelligence enables us to prevent them from happening altogether.

Under the terms of existing rules and resolutions the House and Senate intelligence committees lack the power, influence, and sustained capability to meet this challenge. While few members of Congress have the broad knowledge of intelligence activities or the know-how about the technologies employed, all members need to feel assured that good oversight is happening. When their unfamiliarity with the subject is combined with the need to preserve security, a mandate emerges for substantial change.

Tinkering with the existing structure is not sufficient. Either Congress should create a joint committee for intelligence, using the Joint Atomic Energy Committee as its model, or it should create House and Senate committees with combined authorizing and appropriations powers.

Whichever of these two forms are chosen, the goal should be a structure—codified by resolution with powers expressly granted and carefully limited—allowing a relatively small group of members of Congress, given time and reason to master the subject and the agencies, to conduct oversight of the intelligence establishment and be clearly accountable for their work. The staff of this committee should be nonpartisan and work for the entire committee and not for individual members.

The other reforms we have suggested—for a National Counterterrorism Center and a National Intelligence Director—will not work if congressional oversight does not change too. Unity of effort in executive management can be lost if it is fractured by divided congressional oversight.

Recommendation: Congressional oversight for intelligence—and counterterrorism—is now dysfunctional. Congress should address this problem. We have considered various alternatives: A joint committee on the old model of the Joint Committee on Atomic Energy is one. A single committee in each house of Congress, combining authorizing and appropriating authorities, is another.

- The new committee or committees should conduct continuing studies of the activities of the intelligence agencies and report problems relating to the development and use of intelligence to all members of the House and Senate.
- We have already recommended that the total level of funding for intelligence be made public, and that the national intelligence program be appropriated to the National Intelligence Director, not to the secretary of defense. . . .

At several points in our inquiry, we asked, "Who is responsible for defending us at home?" Our national defense at home is the responsibility, first, of the Department of Defense and, second, of the Department of Homeland Security. They must have clear delineations of responsibility and authority.

We found that NORAD, which had been given the responsibility for defending U.S. airspace, had construed that mission to focus on threats coming from outside America's borders. It did not adjust its focus even though the intelligence community had gathered intelligence on the possibility that terrorists might turn to hijacking and even use of planes as missiles. We have been assured that NORAD has now embraced the full mission. Northern Command has been established to assume responsibility for the defense of the domestic United States.

Recommendation: The Department of Defense and its oversight committees should regularly assess the adequacy of Northern Command's strategies and planning to defend the United States against military threats to the homeland.

The Department of Homeland Security was established to consolidate all of the domestic agencies responsible for securing America's borders and national infrastructure, most of which is in private hands. It should identify those elements of our transportation, energy, communications, financial, and other institutions that need to be protected, develop plans to protect that infrastructure, and exercise the mechanisms to enhance preparedness. This means going well beyond the preexisting jobs of the agencies that have been brought together inside the department.

Recommendation: The Department of Homeland Security and its oversight committees should regularly assess the types of threats the country faces to determine (a) the adequacy of the government's plans—and the progress against those plans—to protect America's critical infrastructure and (b) the readiness of the government to respond to the threats that the United States might face. . . .

We look forward to a national debate on the merits of what we have recommended, and we will participate vigorously in that debate.

11.3 Government by Proxy: A Faithful Overview (2003)

JOHN J. DiIULIO, JR.

INTRODUCTION

In 2000, the federal government employed roughly the same number of non-defense civilian federal workers as it did in 1960. Given the growth in federal programs and spending, how was that possible? The short answer is government by proxy, the decades-old practice whereby the federal government relies on state and local governments, for-profit firms, and nonprofit groups to administer the programs it funds.

In this reading selection, John J. DiIulio, Jr., building on the path-breaking work of public administration scholar Donald F. Kettl, suggests how in areas ranging from environmental protection to social service delivery programs and beyond, the government-by-proxy system has been plagued by problems. But, given that the vast majority of people who administer federal programs do not work directly for the federal government, and given the complicated administrative politics associated with the practice, it is unclear how, if at all, these problems can be addressed. For good or ill, the system is here to stay.

In 2004, many people were surprised to learn from news reports that the U.S. government was relying heavily on private contractors to perform a wide variety of functions in Iraq—from food to security services. But they should not have been so surprised, and there is no way that the federal government could presently implement its health care, social welfare, crime control, even its military and foreign aid policies, to name just a few, without relying extensively on proxies to get the jobs done.

■

For over two decades now, public administration scholars have documented and debated the rise of "third-party government" or "government by proxy."[1] At the federal level, the trend since World War II has been to expand governmental responsibility while relying increasingly on authorized proxies—state and local governments, private contractors, and nonprofit organizations—to provide services and do the actual work, be it implementing a community-based after-school program, managing prisons, or overseeing a toxic waste clean-up. As Professor Minow suggests in her article, government by proxy has created at least as many problems as it has solved.[2] The government-by-proxy phenomenon, however, is even older and more pervasive, diverse, and problematic than Professor Minow's balanced public law perspective suggests.

Despite its many problems, government by proxy is here to stay. Congress now routinely authorizes and federal agencies now administer most of domestic policy through state and local agencies, for-profit firms, and nonprofit organizations. All three types of partnerships are fraught with problems. Public administration scholars have offered numerous proposals for reducing, if not eliminating, these problems and, in the bargain, improving government performance. Generally speaking, the two most common themes in this now-vast public administration corpus are the need for government to experiment with new partners, and the need for government to define what, if any, tasks must be performed without any partners, new or old. With regard to experimenting with new partners, Professor Minow is right that the time has come to focus more serious attention on the government-by-proxy potential of religious nonprofits.[3] I shall argue, as I have for the last several years, that the promises associated with permitting small religious nonprofits into the government-by-proxy process exceed any likely pitfalls of doing so. With regard to delimiting government by proxy, I argue, as I did over a decade ago, that to permit for-profit prisons to proliferate would almost surely be to transgress reasonable limits on government by proxy.

---

[1]See, e.g., *Deregulating the Public Service: Can Government Be Improved?* (John J. DiIulio, Jr. ed., 1994); John J. DiIulio, Jr. et al., *Improving Government Performance: An Owner's Manual* (1993); Donald F. Kettl, *Government by Proxy: (Mis?)Managing Federal Programs* (1988); Donald F. Kettl, *Sharing Power: Public Governance and Private Markets* (1993) [hereinafter Kettl, *Sharing Power*]; Paul J. Light, *The True Size of Government* (1999); Frederick C. Mosher, "The Changing Responsibilities and Tactics of the Federal Government," 40 *Pub. Admin. Rev.* 541 (1980); Lester M. Salamon, "Rethinking Public Management: Third-Party Government and Changing Forms of Government Action," 29 *Pub. Pol'y* 255 (1981). For a general analysis of the sectoral, intergovernmental, inter-agency, and inter-program challenges posed by government by proxy, see Donald F. Kettl, "Deregulating at the Boundaries of Government: Will It Help?," in *Deregulating the Public Service: Can Government Be Improved? supra,* at 175.

[2]See Martha Minow, "Public and Private Partnerships: Accounting for the New Religion," 116 *Harv. L. Rev.* 1229 (2003).

[3]*Id.* at 1242–46.

Part I of this Response provides an overview of the expanse of government by proxy. Part II describes the problems and potentials of government by proxy, with a focus on the issues surrounding three substantive policy areas: federal environmental protection policy; small religious organizations that mainly serve urban minority communities; and for-profit prisons. In concluding, this Response calls for holding all government-by-proxy partners—religious and secular, large and small, nonprofit and for-profit—to equitable procurement requirements and meaningful accountability and performance standards.

I. GOVERNMENT BY PROXY: A FAITHFUL OVERVIEW

The rise of government by proxy is primarily a result of congressional action. Congress depends on state and local governments "for administration":[4]

> Congress loves action—it thrives on policy proclamation and goal setting—but it hates bureaucracy and taxes, which are the instruments of action. Overwhelmingly, it has resolved this dilemma by turning over the bulk of administration to the state governments or any organizational instrumentality it can lay its hands on whose employees are not counted on the federal payroll.[5]

As a result, every federal department depends heavily on government by proxy. The U.S. Department of Health and Human Services (HHS), for example, has eleven operating divisions, a nearly $500 billion budget, and over 65,000 employees whose main work is framing, processing, and monitoring literally hundreds of grant programs featuring literally thousands of nongovernmental grantees. HHS, like Washington's other government-by-proxy departments, "is far more involved in wholesaling its services as financier, arranger, and overseer, but not direct provider."[6]

Moreover, every major domestic federal program enacted since World War II is administered in large part via government by proxy. This is true without regard to policy domain or program size. For instance, Superfund, a relatively small-budget federal environmental program, has been administered almost entirely by private, for-profit contractors.[7] Likewise, Medicaid, a big-budget federal-state health program, has long been a creature of administrative devolution.[8] In addition, the number of civilians working for the federal govern-

---

[4]Martha Derthick, *Keeping the Compound Republic: Essays on American Federalism* 63 (2001).

[5]*Id.*

[6]DiIulio et al., *supra* note 1, at 32.

[7]See Kettl, *Sharing Power, supra* note 1, at ch. 5.

[8]See generally *Medicaid and Devolution: A View from the States* (Frank J. Thompson & John J. DiIulio, Jr. eds., 1998).

ment, excluding postal workers, is about the same today as it was in 1960 (roughly two million people). But over thirteen million people work for Washington as government-by-proxy employees whose jobs are largely, if not entirely, supported by federal funds. Thus, there are more than six government-by-proxy employees for every one federal civil servant.

II. LIVING WITH PROXY GOVERNMENT

All three types of government-by-proxy partnerships—federal partnerships with state and local governments, with nonprofit organizations, and with for-profit companies—have created well-documented difficulties. First, government by proxy has strained intergovernmental relations. Federal and local officials each try to get some benefit (solving a problem, satisfying a pressure group) while passing on to the other side most of the costs (taxes, administrative problems). Through so-called federal mandates and in other ways, Washington has normally won the battle but lost the war. State and local governments act on federal policies, but weakly, and the government-by-proxy programs produced by this system have been plagued by problems.[9]

Second, partnerships with for-profit corporations have produced several widely reported failures. For-profit partnerships have been associated with such policy disasters as fraud in Medicare, malfunction of the Hubble Space telescope, defaults in the guaranteed student loan program, excessive costs (and few actual clean-ups) in Superfund, malfeasance of Teapot Dome proportions in the Department of Housing and Urban Development, severe safety problems at the nation's nuclear weapons production facilities, and literally scores more.[10] To aggravate the problem, in fiscal year 1999, for example, the forty-three largest for-profit contractors won $185 billion in federal government business despite the fact that many had repeatedly violated federal laws or procurement rules. Moreover, in the last dozen years, only one contractor was suspended from bidding, and for only five days.[11]

Third, government by proxy has favored large, national, nonprofit organizations, both secular and religious, with grants, but without subjecting them to adequate oversight or performance monitoring. For example, in 2001, the General Accounting Office found that in only seven of twenty-eight agencies it surveyed did a majority of federal grant-making officers attempt to follow the procurement protocols specified in the Government Performance and

---

[9]See generally Timothy J. Conlan, *From Federalism to Devolution* (1998); John J. DiIulio, Jr. & Donald F. Kettl, *Fine Print: The Contract with America and the Administrative Realities of American Federalism* (1995).

[10]See generally DiIulio et al. *supra* note 1; Kettl, *Sharing Power, supra* note 1.

[11]Ellen Nakashima, "Study: Contracts Given to Repeat Violators," *Wash. Post,* May 7, 2002, at A19.

Results Act of 1993.[12] Most nonprofit federal grantees have never been subjected to even a single actual government performance audit. Only a few nonprofit organizations that have received federal money for many years have ever been subjected to performance evaluations by qualified, nongovernmental, independent researchers. Nor does there exist any body of reliable information on what, if any, positive outcomes they have produced, or at what costs. Thus, although literally tens of billions of federal dollars flow to the same large, national nonprofit grantees each year, we still do not know whether they have succeeded greatly, failed partially, or failed miserably in administering government policies intended to increase literacy rates, replenish low-income housing stocks, improve access to community-based substance abuse treatment, and achieve other legislatively enacted civic goals. Given the extent of these deficiencies, it is worth noting that, based on a five-agency performance audit by the White House Office of Faith-Based and Community Initiatives, the "nonprofit organizations that administer social services funded by Washington are typically large and entrenched, in an almost monopolistic fashion."[13]. . .

. . . The Nonprofit Proxy: Grassroots Religious Groups
Where government by proxy is concerned, for-profit firms, plus a "relatively select group of large social-service and health non-profits," have "long received the bulk of public funding."[14] In the social policy domain, large national religious nonprofit organizations such as Lutheran Social Services, Catholic Charities, the Salvation Army, and the Jewish Federations have received tens of billions of dollars in government grants. But the sacred and the secular have also mixed for many years at religious colleges as well as at local congregations (churches, synagogues, and mosques) that have received public money, including federal funds, to function as childcare centers, administer welfare-to-work programs, and provide other social services.[15] "Publicly funded, religiously tied social service organizations have always played a big role in American society," and the "long history of collaboration between government and religious institutions . . . is still going strong."[16]

---

[12]Gen. Accounting Office, *Managing for Results,* at 10 (GAO-01-592, 2001).

[13]White House, "Unlevel Playing Field: Barriers to Participation by Faith-Based and Community Organizations in Federal Social Service Delivery Programs" (Aug. 2001), http://www .whitehouse.gov/news/releases/2001/08/unlevelfield2.html.

[14]Peter Frumkin, "After Partnership: Rethinking Public-Nonprofit Relations," in *Who Will Provide: The Changing Role of Religion in American Social Welfare* 199 (Mary Jo Bane et al. eds., 2000).

[15]See Ram A. Cnaan et al., *The Newer Deal: Social Work and Religion in Partnership* (1999); Steven V. Monsma, *When Sacred and Secular Mix: Religious Nonprofit Organizations and Public Money* (1996).

[16]Andrew Walsh, Introduction to *Can Charitable Choice Work? Covering Religion's Impact on Urban Affairs and Social Services* 2 (Andrew Walsh ed., 2001).

1. Funding Discrimination.   There is growing evidence that grassroots non-profit social service organizations, especially small community-serving religious groups that serve primarily low-income urban Latino and African-American children, youth, and families, are discriminated against at each and every stage of the government-by-proxy process. While it is true that some grassroots religious groups obtain minimal funding from larger, more established religious nonprofit organizations, receive nominal support from local governments, and occasionally attract foundation dollars, for the most part, grassroots organizations receive little or no public money or corporate or philanthropic support. Even in situations in which the grassroots organizations supply the bulk of social services; serve the youngest, the neediest, or the most difficult-to-serve populations without regard to beneficiaries' religious orientations; have long-standing working partnerships with local government agencies and/or secular nonprofit organizations; have been subjected to independent performance evaluations; and have achieved 501(c)3 status, faith-based organization programs receive last priority in terms of obtaining financial support.

A forthcoming study by Public/Private Ventures, based on four years of intensive research across fifteen cities, documents that local criminal justice organizations partner extensively with grassroots religious groups to deliver court-mandated education, employment, and other services to minority youth who have gotten into serious trouble with the law.[17] Yet, in 2001, the U.S. Department of Justice awarded only one-third of one percent of its discretionary grant funds to faith-based organizations, and virtually nothing to minority-led street ministries.[18] Likewise, a recent study estimates that although about forty percent of faith-based welfare-to-work programs do receive some public money, these programs are nonetheless denied funding at three times the rate that otherwise comparable secular nonprofits are rejected, and receive, on average, so much less funding than do their secular counterparts that "a *prima facie* case can be made that discrimination is going on."[19]

2. Charitable Choice.   It is also clear that the absence of grassroots religious groups is related to the debate concerning the separation of church and state. Charitable choice laws were intended to ensure that religious nonprofit organizations could seek to participate in the government-by-proxy process and administer federal social programs on exactly the same basis as all other nonprofit organizations.[20] Charitable choice first appeared as a provision

---

[17]Alvia Y. Branch, *Faith and Action: Implementation of the National Faith-Based Initiative for High-Risk Youth* i–ii (2002).

[18]White House, *supra* note 13.

[19]Steven V. Monsma & Carolyn M. Mounts, U. Pa. Ctr. for Research on Religion & Urban Civil Soc'y, *Working Faith: How Religious Organizations Provide Welfare-to-Work Services* 14 (2002), available at http://www.manhattan-institute.org/working_faith.pdf.

[20]Ram A. Cnaan & Stephanie C. Boddie, "Charitable Choice and Faith-Based Welfare: A Call for Social Work," 47 *Soc. Work* 224, 224 (2002).

(Section 104) of the Personal Responsibility and Work Opportunity Reconciliation Act of 1996,[21] better known as the federal welfare reform law. A charitable choice provision was then added to the Community Services Block Grant program when it was reauthorized in 1998.[22] In 2000, another charitable choice provision was added to the Substance Abuse Prevention and Treatment Block Grant and the Projects for Assistance in Transition from Homelessness program.[23]

Charitable choice rests on four key principles. First, it seeks to level the playing field. Faith-based providers are eligible to compete for funds to administer federal social service programs on the same basis as any other providers, neither included nor excluded because they are religious, too religious, or the wrong religion. Faith-based providers are to be subjected to the same accountability standards and protocols as all other nonprofit organizations—no more, no less. Second, it promotes respect for partners. Faith-based providers retain control over the definition, development, practice, and expression of their religious beliefs. Neither federal nor state government can require a religious provider to remove religious art, icons, scripture, or other symbols in order to compete for public funds. Third, it promotes respect for clients. Religious organizations operate under the civil rights laws, including Titles VI and VII of the 1964 Civil Rights Act.[24] If a social-service recipient objects to the religious character of a program, a secular alternative must be provided. And finally, charitable choice operates on the notion of "sacred places, civic purposes." Diverse partnerships between government and religious institutions are entirely permissible, provided that faith-based organizations are religious about using any public funds only to fulfill public social service or other civic or secular purposes as directed by law. No government funding can be diverted to inherently religious activities such as worship, sectarian instruction, and proselytizing.

Where government by proxy is concerned, whether with grassroots or large, established religious organizations, separation of church and state should not be the focus of the debate. Religious organizations should be allowed to compete to administer social programs on the same basis as all other nonprofit organizations, so long as they use any public funds provided as per the granting agency's program-specific rules, regulations, and accountability protocols, and so long as they, like any other government-by-proxy partner, comply with their contractual obligations under law. Fears that some public funds may leak over into other parts of the religious nonprofit organization are fair, but such fears might just as well be raised about all government-by-proxy partners. For example, universities may receive a government grant for a

[21]Pub. L. No. 104-193, 110 Stat. 2105 (1996).

[22]Pub. L. No. 105-285, § 201, 112 Stat. 2749 (1998) (codified at 42 U.S.C.A. § 9920).

[23]Pub. L. No. 106-310, § 3305, 114 Stat. 1101, 1212 (2000) (codified at 42 U.S.C.A. § 300x-65).

[24]42 U.S.C. § § 2000e to 2000e-17 (2000).

specific purpose only to over-bill for given parts of the project to subsidize other departments, schools, or programs; for-profit firms may subcontract with other for-profit firms and alter budget allocations between personnel and other purposes without approval; and local governments may shift funds entirely from one program to another without seeking or receiving any waivers. In sum, government by proxy does not suddenly become a problem only when it dresses in religious drag. Partnerships between government agencies and religious organizations to deliver social services pose many public administration challenges, but the challenges are more generic than unique, and most of the unique challenges have hitherto been radically overstated or grossly misconstrued.

Take, for example, the argument that religious nonprofits will use any and all resources, public or private, to proselytize. For at least four reasons, that presumption is unjustifiably prejudicial. First, as a moment's reflection should confirm, religious nonprofit organizations, large and small, national and local, represent a wide range of benevolent traditions and theological orientations, only some of which favor or require proselytizing. Second, as detailed, site-based empirical surveys have consistently found, most small, urban community-serving religious organizations that provide most services to low-income populations do *not* proselytize or make entering their buildings, receiving their services, or participating in their programs at all contingent upon any present or eventual expression of any particular religious beliefs—even when they are *not* receiving public funds and face no legal restrictions.[25] Third, as the same surveys reveal, the primary beneficiaries of the grassroots religious groups' social work—again, even when they do *not* receive a penny of public funds—are neighborhood children and youth who are *not* members of the congregations that serve them, and whose parents are not members, either.[26]

Scholars raise genuine concerns about whether public-private or, in particular, religious-secular partnerships can produce measurable outcomes and achieve "public good" without crossing any constitutional lines. Certain Philadelphia public-private partnerships represent a perfect pilot for evaluation. In Philadelphia, there is a small but growing set of outstanding public-private programs involving grassroots religious groups that operate with some public funding. Philadelphia's Youth Education for Tomorrow (YET) after-school literacy program has generated great success. Working in church basements and other sites, the children who attended YET for over one hundred days vaulted an average of 1.9 grade levels in reading ability.[27] Similarly,

---

[25]See generally Ram A. Cnaan & Stephanie C. Boddie, *Black Church Outreach: Comparing How Black and Other Congregations Serve Their Needy Neighbors* (2001); Ram A. Cnaan et al., *The Invisible Caring Hand: American Congregations and the Provision of Welfare* (2002).

[26]See John J. DiIulio, Jr., "The New Civil Rights Struggle," *Wall St. J.*, June 20, 2002, at A16.

[27]Bill Hangley, Jr. & Wendy S. McClanahan, *Mustering the Armies of Compassion in Philadelphia: An Analysis of One Year of Literacy Programming in Faith-Based Institutions* 15 (2002).

working with church networks, the Big Brothers Big Sisters (BBBS) program, within one year, mobilized over 500 adult mentors to serve children of incarcerated persons. This represented the fastest and most successful mentor mobilization for at-risk youth in the organization's nearly one-hundred-year history. In addition, the Cookman Methodist Church created a welfare-to-work program specifically for women. Cookman Methodist received a small grant under a program covered by charitable choice, and despite its "Christ-centered" mission statement, has admirably served all, including local Muslim women.[28]

The debate surrounding the Community Solutions Act of 2001,[29] widely referenced as "the Bush faith bill," has succeeded in sowing confusion about charitable choice. Orthodox sectarians on the religious right rejected the bill's prohibitions on proselytizing. They insisted on "beliefs and tenets" provisions that (or so they thought) would give them a statutory carte blanche to discriminate against homosexuals in hiring. They also demanded that the entire government-by-proxy grant-making process be recast in favor of vouchers or other indirect disbursement arrangements. Meanwhile, orthodox secularists on the political left rejected even the bill's core charitable choice language, acting as if it were something new, and talking as if the plan involved set-aside funds available only to religious organizations. Fortunately, however, obfuscating extremists on each side of the religious spectrum have not kept thinking policymakers and interested citizens from recognizing the true promises and pitfalls of public-private collaborations involving religious groups. One outstanding example is New York's Democratic Senator Hillary Rodham Clinton. As Senator Clinton has explained, "the Clinton administration, working with a bipartisan majority in the Congress, achieved welfare reform that included a Charitable Choice provision, which allows faith-based organizations to apply for federal and state funds along with other providers of social services."[30] She has also stated:

> Government works in partnership with religious institutions. . . . Tax dollars are not used to promote any particular faith; rather, they are used to promote public purposes. . . . Faith inspires those good works, to be sure. But tax dollars are properly used to channel the energies of the faithful in a direction that helps our society as a whole. . . .
> . . . Government should interact with the private sector and with the civil society, religion included, in ways that promote no particular business or religion. It should interact in ways that promote the public good.[31]

---

[28]See Jill Witmer Sinha, *Ctr. for Pub. Justice, Cookman United Methodist Church and Transitional Journey: A Case Study in Charitable Choice* (2000).

[29]H.R. 7, 107th Cong. § 201 (2001).

[30]Sen. Hillary Rodham Clinton, Remarks at the Abyssinian Baptist Church in New York City, at 17 (Dec. 17, 2001) (on file with the Harvard Law School Library).

[31]*Id.* at 9, 11.

As Senator Clinton has also suggested, "the idea of vouchers for families to leave public schools for private schools, including religious schools," poses several risks.[32] Whatever their merits or constitutionality, vouchers are not a magical administrative cure for government by proxy's ills, and they pose several problems. Professor Minow is right that vouchers "can bypass otherwise applicable public obligations and reporting requirements," by which they can also "vitiate public values" and public accountability.[33] With respect to private schools, voucher advocates have lost several major political battles because they have rejected "a regulated approach to vouchers that recognizes the public's concern for accountability, fairness, and equity."[34] With respect to religious organizations, voucher advocates—especially certain fundamentalist leaders who reject restrictions on proselytizing with public funds—have succeeded thus far only in diminishing political support for charitable choice laws.[35]

Misleading arguments and confusion regarding charitable choice should not fog the political consensus on public-private partnerships involving small faith-based groups.[36] Nor should they deter or delay efforts to implement extant charitable choice laws, or to provide technical assistance and capacity-building guidance to grassroots religious groups through the Corporation for National and Community Service and other public agencies. Charitable choice's purpose is, was, and shall continue to be that no group ought to be favored or disfavored in the government-by-proxy process by virtue of whether it is secular, religious, quasi-religious, or whatever. . . .

III. CONCLUSION

The government-by-proxy genie cannot be put back in its decades-old bottle, but maybe it can yet be made to obey the common wish for a government that works better, costs less, and translates policy rhetoric into administrative action in ways that express, rather than extinguish, democratic values and due process norms. Congress will not stop creating government-by-proxy programs, but we should get into the habit of asking "how and by whom will that law be implemented" before, not after, the Rose Garden signing occurs, or at least before, not after, the evidence of implementation failures and poor

---

[32]*Id.* at 13.

[33]Minow, *supra* note 2, at 1247.

[34]Terry M. Moe, *Schools, Vouchers, and the American Public* 355 (2001).

[35]John J. DiIulio, Jr., God and the First Amendment (unpublished manuscript, adapted from the First Davis Chair on Judeo-Christian Values lecture, Ursinus College, Collegeville, Pa., Oct. 2, 2002) (on file with the Harvard Law School Library).

[36]Compare Al Gore, Speech to the Salvation Army in Atlanta, Georgia (May 25, 1999), http://downloads.weblogger.com/gems/cpj/384.pdf, with George W. Bush, Speech Before Clergy in Indianapolis, Indiana (July 22, 1999), http://cpjustice.org/stories/StoryReader$383.

results is rife. Let little local religious organizations be held to the highest possible public standards, procurement criteria, and performance protocols as they enter into the grant-making process, but let no less be demanded from for-profit firms, secular nonprofits, religious mega-charities, and other partners. Let charitable choice be tested before it is contested. Let us not suddenly demand civic and administrative perfection from small sacred places that have never yet been demanded from government-by-proxy giants, for-profit and nonprofit, religious and secular. Let us, once and for all, learn to resist privatization arguments that would have government abdicate its most fundamental duties such as the duty to administer criminal justice behind bars. And let us listen carefully to Professor Minow: government by proxy needs a "public framework of accountability," one that is "public in the source of its norms and in its overarching authority and enforcement power."[37] She has enriched our understanding of the challenges we face in developing such a framework, and has succeeded in breathing new life, and new hope, into old public administration debates. Criticize whatever aspects of her argument we may, but let us partner with her and welcome her leadership in this important civic and intellectual enterprise.

11.4 Bureaucracy: What Government Agencies Do and Why They Do It (1989)

JAMES Q. WILSON

INTRODUCTION

We often think about bureaucracy in relation to the executive branch and the presidency because there are valid constitutional, historical, and practical reasons for thinking about the bureaucracy that way. But as the federal government grew over the last hundred years, the bureaucracy became ever more a creature of not the presidency but the Congress. As James Q. Wilson observes in this reading selection, "Congress certainly is the architect of the bureaucracy."

Congress is not only the architect, but the overseer as well. Almost nothing federal agencies do is beyond the reach of congressional oversight, and Congress has developed myriad ways of exercising substantial influences over how the bureaucracy works. Of course, Congress often lets federal agencies do as they will unless and until a problem arises that gains public notice.

---

[37]Minow, *supra* note 2, at 1266.

James Q. Wilson, *Bureaucracy: What Government Agencies Do and Why They Do It* (New York: Basic Books, 1989), 235–241. Copyright © 1989 by Basic Books, Inc. Reprinted by permission of Basic Books, a member of Perseus Books, L.L.C.

Though it "has forsworn the use of certain powers," advises Wilson, "Congress retains enormous influence over the bureaucracy."

■

CONGRESS

No politician ever lost votes by denouncing the bureaucracy. Jimmy Carter and Gerald Ford could agree on little else during their 1976 presidential contest than that "the bureaucracy" was a mess. Senator Edward M. Kennedy rarely has passed up a chance to attack the Food and Drug Administration for the way it endangers public health by "rushing" new drugs into the market. Members of the House of Representatives were outraged at the Federal Trade Commission's proposal to restrict television advertisements aimed at children and regulate used-car dealers and funeral parlors. When the National Highway Traffic Safety Administration ordered auto manufacturers to install seat belts that had to be fastened before the car could be started, the public and Congress erupted in anger. Senator Malcolm Wallop ran for office by towing an outdoor portable toilet around his state of Wyoming, ridiculing the officials of the Occupational Safety and Health Administration who, he charged, had ordered ranchers to use them for their field hands. The public schools are raked over the coals regularly by legislators furious at educators' apparent unwillingness to do more to increase pupil achievement and reduce school-yard violence. There is scarcely a city council member in the country who has not at one time or another denounced the local police department for being slow to respond to citizen calls for help. If ever the weapons procurement system used by the Pentagon has been praised by a member of Congress, history has failed to record the fact. These and countless other horror stories readily come to mind as evidence that in this country we confront a "runaway bureaucracy" indifferent to the wishes of its political superiors.

People angry about an out-of-control bureaucracy might be equally angry at the many scholars who argue that far from being runaway, government agencies in this country are under the control of the very legislators who so regularly denounce them. Virtually every political scientist who has studied the matter agrees that Congress possesses, in Herbert Kaufman's words, an "awesome arsenal" of weapons that it can use against agencies: legislation, appropriations, hearings, investigations, personal interventions, and "friendly advice" that is ignored at an executive's peril.[1] After closely studying six bureau[2] chiefs in Washington, Kaufman described their daily behavior in

---

[1] Herbert Kaufman, *The Administrative Behavior of Federal Bureau Chiefs* (Washington, D.C.: Brookings Institution, 1981), 164.

[2] The six bureaus were the Animal and Plant Health Inspection Service, Customs Service, Food and Drug Administration, Forest Service, Internal Revenue Service, and Social Security Administration.

language that might just as easily be used to portray business executives worrying about fickle stockholders in an era of corporate takeovers:

> The chiefs were constantly looking over their shoulders . . . at the elements of the legislative establishment relevant to their agencies—taking stock of moods and attitudes, estimating reactions to contemplated decisions and actions, trying to prevent misunderstandings and avoidable conflicts, and planning responses when storm warnings appeared on the horizon. Not that cues and signals from Capitol Hill had to be ferreted out; the denizens of the Hill were not shy about issuing suggestions, requests, demands, directives, and pronouncements.[3]

But what does congressional control mean? One or more of three things: First, Congress controls the major day-to-day activities of an agency. Congress is the "principal," the agency is its "agent." If this is true it must mean that there are no other significant sources of influence. Second, Congress has the ability and inclination to intervene when it learns that an agency is sinning by omission or commission. But an agency would not sin if it were wholly the agent of Congress; thus this meaning of control presupposes that other forces—the president, the courts, interest groups, or the bureaucrats themselves—have influence on the agency independent of Congress. Third, Congress creates and maintains the structural conditions within which an agency operates.

The first kind of control can be likened to that which is supposed to operate between corporate executives and their boards of directors. The second can be compared to fire fighting; when an alarm goes off signaling that an agency may be violating some congressional interest, members of Congress rush in to put out the fire.[4] The third might be described as architectural; the life of an agency is constrained by its need to live within a certain space, move along prescribed corridors, and operate specified appliances.

Congress certainly is the architect of the bureaucracy. Most of the constraints . . . were created and are sustained by Congress and its committees. For Congress to complain of agency red tape is akin to an architect complaining of a home owner who finds it necessary to walk up five flights of steps before he can get from his bedroom to the bathroom. And Congress—more accurately, its committees and subcommittees—are certainly fire fighters. They do not hesitate to use their powers of authorization, appropriation, investigation, and confirmation to call to task bureaus that depart from committee preferences. But in fighting bureaucratic fires members of Congress must compete with other political forces, some of whom are busy pouring gasoline on the flames. How successful Congress will be in using its power will depend not

---

[3]Kaufman, *Administrative Behavior*, 47.

[4]Matthew McCubbins and Thomas Schwartz, "Congressional Oversight Overlooked: Police Patrols Versus Fire Alarms," *American Journal of Political Science* 28 (1984): 164–79.

only on how resolute it is but also, as we shall see, on the tasks the agency is performing and the political environment in which it is embedded.

But Congress is almost never a "principal" that can give unchallenged direction to its "agent," the bureaucracy. (Some scholars trained in economics have tried to portray it in this way, but they are wrong. . . .)

When members of Congress complain that an agency is "unresponsive" to Congress or is a "runaway bureaucracy," they are being disingenuous. No agency is free to ignore the views of *Congress*. An agency may, however, defer to the views of one *part* of Congress (say, one committee) instead of another, or balance the competing demands of the White House with those of some parts of Congress in ways that other parts may not like. The bureaucracy cannot evade political control nor sustain for long the view that there is a realm of "administration" that is immune from "politics." But it can maneuver among its many political masters in ways that displease some of them and can define its tasks for internal reasons and not simply in response to external demands.

The question we wish to answer in this chapter is not how powerful is Congress, but under what circumstances are the resources available to Congress likely to be most effective in shaping agency behavior? The answer requires us first to examine those resources and the steps Congress has taken to weaken their power to alter bureaucratic behavior; second, to understand how its political environment has led Congress to "micro-manage" the bureaucracy in a somewhat different way than it once did; and finally to see how the tasks of each agency and the environment in which those tasks are performed affect the ability of Congress to determine agency outcomes.

The Means for Exercising Congressional Influence

Congress is extraordinarily powerful when compared to the parliaments of many European democracies. Though a parliament can select the prime minister, often it can do little more: the British House of Commons, for example, cannot without the permission of the prime minister amend a bill, alter a budget, conduct a hearing, or render a service. More exactly, it can do some of these things over the objection of the prime minister, but in doing so brings down the government and forces a new election. Incumbent politicians look forward to new elections with about the same enthusiasm that children look forward to visiting the dentist.

Senator Daniel Patrick Moynihan was scarcely exaggerating when he said that the United States is the only democratic government with a legislative branch. But that branch and the committees that comprise it do not speak with one voice, and neither Congress nor its committees have the means for exercising complete control over all bureaucratic agencies under all circumstances.

Congress can determine the number of employees an agency will have but it cannot (excepting those few top posts that are subject to Senate confirmation) determine who those employees will be nor can it force employees it does not like to resign. By passing the civil service laws it has lost the power to choose or replace individual bureaucrats. Congress also has surrendered some of its power to control various regulatory agencies. If it wanted only to insure that these regulators served congressional desires it would make it easy to remove those who disobeyed. But many regulatory tasks have been handed over to commissions comprised of people appointed for long terms who cannot be removed except for cause (presumably, by the difficult method of impeachment). Congress would often like to keep the supply of money abundant and the rate of interest low, but in designing the agency with the most influence over these matters—the Federal Reserve Board—it gave to its members terms of fourteen years. Federal Trade Commission members serve for seven years, members of the Federal Communications Commission, Federal Deposit Insurance Corporation, Federal Energy Regulatory Commission, Interstate Commerce Commission, National Labor Relations Board, Securities and Exchange Commission, and Tennessee Valley Authority (among others) all serve for fixed terms ranging from five to nine years.

Congress can decide how much money a bureau may spend on personnel, but it cannot determine the pay of individual agency members. By setting bureaucratic pay on the basis of government-wide pay schedules pegged to the rank of employees it has forgone the opportunity to create different pay scales for different agencies, or for particular persons within a given agency.

Congress can fix the total expenditures of an agency and the amount that can be spent on particular projects within an agency's purview, but in many important cases it has left the determination of year-to-year changes in expenditures to a mathematical formula—the "cost-of-living adjustment," or COLA. For a long time Congress decided every two years (usually, just before an election) how big a Social Security check retired people would receive, but in 1972 it abandoned this method (and all its opportunities for claiming credit with constituents) in favor of a system whereby benefits automatically increased with changes in the cost of living.[5]

Some scholars assume that in their single-minded desire to get reelected members of Congress always seek to manipulate the bureaucracy in order to enhance their prospects for reelection. They would do well to ponder the lengths to which Congress has gone to weaken many of the powers that would permit it to exercise such control. Murray Horn has reminded us that once the patronage system worked to empower politicians; its replacement, the civil service system, works to protect bureaucrats.[6] Why did Congress sur-

---

[5]Martha Derthick, *Policymaking for Social Security* (Washington, D.C.: Brookings Institution, 1979), 349–68.

[6]Murray J. Horn, "The Political Economy of Public Administration: Organization, Control and Performance of the Public Sector," Ph.D. diss., Kennedy School of Government, Harvard University (1988), 199 and chap. 15.

render this power? In large part because wielding it was costly; voters grew increasingly restive about stories of politicians buying and selling offices and their patronage appointees using these offices to line their pockets.[7] And also in part because reforming this process was useful; presidents who wanted to tilt the bureaucracy in a particular ideological direction (Franklin Roosevelt was the leading example) could give patronage appointments to their followers and then insure their perpetuation in office by extending civil-service protections to them.[8] There is evidence that President Reagan promoted into policy-making posts career civil servants who were broadly sympathetic to his goals.[9]

Much the same arguments explain why Congress has given many regulatory commissioners long terms and freedom from routine dismissal and required that they be from both political parties. Creating an agency to regulate a segment of the economy was made easier by evidence that precautions had been taken to keep the regulation from being "too political," which is to say too much under the day-to-day control of Congress or the president. Moreover, long terms and barriers to removal made it easier for the legislative coalition that created the agency to protect it from having its membership changed by some future political coalition. In short, politicians have had good reasons to tie their own hands. But once tied, they cannot easily be untied.

Tying one's hands also seemed to be good politics in the case of certain indexed or automatic expenditures. Republicans did not like the fact that the Democrats (who usually controlled Congress) were always getting the credit for increasing Social Security benefits. The only politically feasible way to end this advantage was to make such increases automatic. Indexing also had another advantage to fiscal conservatives: it would keep benefit increases in line with the cost of living and thus prevent bidding wars among members of Congress eager to portray themselves as the "senior citizen's best friend." And so the biggest part of the budget of the biggest (in dollars spent) agency in Washington was put on automatic pilot.[10] Once on, it could not easily be taken off except by new, politically costly legislation. Congress had weakened its own powers.

Civil service, fixed terms for commissioners, and indexed spending increases are all examples of the fact that, as Murray Horn has shown, Congress's

---

[7]Carl R. Fish, *The Civil Service and Patronage* (Cambridge, Mass.: Harvard University Press, 1920), 217–18.

[8]S. M. Milkis, "The New Deal, Administrative Reform, and the Transcendence of Partisan Politics," *Administration and Society* 18 (1987): 433–72.

[9]Joel D. Aberbach and Bert A. Rockman, "From Nixon's Problem to Reagan's Achievement: The Federal Executive Reexamined," paper presented at the Hofstra Conference on the Presidency of Richard Nixon (November 1987).

[10]Derthick, *Policymaking*, 348–49; R. Kent Weaver, *Automatic Government: The Politics of Indexation* (Washington, D.C.: Brookings Institution, 1988).

desire to please constituents is not always consistent with its efforts to manipulate bureaucracies. Sometimes legislators believe that it makes more sense to appear to be taking a hands-off position. The long-term consequence of the adoption of these and other self-denying ordinances is that Congress has reduced some of its influence over the bureaucracy. But it has not suffered greatly from this reduction; the overwhelming majority of all incumbent representatives, and most incumbent senators, easily win reelection.

Let us be clear: though it has forsworn the use of certain powers, Congress retains enormous influence over the bureaucracy. But the kind of influence it now wields differs from the kind it once had, to a degree. When Woodrow Wilson wrote *Congressional Government* in 1884 he was able to describe the committees of the House as "the ministers, and the titular ministers only confidential clerks."[11] Scarcely any employees were hired, ships built, cannon emplaced, duties levied, or offices opened save by the direct and specific authorization of the relevant congressional committee. There was little sentiment in Congress for selecting bureaucrats except as they pleased their representatives and worked for their reelection. The notion that pensions to the veterans of the Union army should be set by an automatic formula rather than by the deliberate and election-serving vote of the whole Congress was an idea that would have been regarded as ludicrous on its face.

Congress has changed since the days of Woodrow Wilson. Power is still to be found in the committees (and subcommittees), but the instruments of that power have been modified. The Senate retains the right to confirm presidential appointments and the Congress as a whole the right to investigate executive-branch conduct; appropriations and tax bills are still filled with benefits and loopholes for the advantage of important constituency interests. But the detailed regulation of bureaucratic conduct to some degree has given way to the multiplication of legislated constraints on that behavior. Where Congress once said, "open this fort" or "close this shipyard," it now says, "subject the opening of forts or the closing of shipyards to environmental impact statements." Where Congress once unabashedly directed the War Department to give a weapons contract to the Jedediah Jones Cannon Foundry, it now directs the Defense Department to insure that the contract is awarded to an American firm that tenders the lowest bid, employs the correct mix of women and minorities, makes provisions to aid the handicapped, gives subcontracts to a suitable number of small businesses, is in compliance with the regulations of the Environmental Protection Agency and Occupational Safety and Health Administration, and is not currently under indictment for contract fraud. To insure that these and other constraints are observed, Congress further directs the Pentagon to employ an army of contract officers and contract

---

[11]Woodrow Wilson, *Congressional Government* (New York: Meridian Books, 1956), 127 (first published in 1885).

auditors and to publish its procurement policies in a book of immense length, excruciating detail, and soporific prose.

The change in control methods is illustrated by how members of Congress have protected military bases located in their states and districts. For many years Congress itself decided where bases should be. Not surprisingly, few were ever closed. During World War II, twelve million men and women were called to duty and so there was an enormous increase in the number of these bases; at the end of the war, many of them quickly became obsolete as the military shrank to two million uniformed members. But to close an unneeded base, the secretary of defense would have to wage war with the affected member of Congress, winning rarely and then only after paying a high cost in lost political backing on the Hill. Secretary Robert McNamara was able to close ninety-five bases in 1965 after a bruising fight with individual members of Congress and a presidential veto of a bill requiring congressional approval of such closings. Then in 1976 Congress devised a generalized constraint to replace individualized pressure: it passed a bill forbidding the Pentagon to close a domestic military base without first filing an environmental impact statement, the findings of which could be challenged in court. During the eleven years the law was in effect, not a single major base was closed and several new ones were opened despite the fact that almost every secretary of defense wanted some of them closed.

Then in 1988 Congress passed a bill that created an independent commission and authorized it to choose the bases that would be closed, subject to the right of the secretary of defense and Congress to accept or reject the list in its entirety. Congress cannot pick and choose among the bases to be shut down. Scholars who believe that Congress seeks to use the bureaucracy to enhance the reelection prospects of its members may have some difficulty explaining why those members would consider giving to an outside board the power to eliminate the jobs provided by military bases located in their districts.

CHAPTER 12

The Judiciary

*T*he judicial branch of the United States, like the bureaucracy, is composed of appointed officials, but unlike bureaucrats, federal judges are appointed for lifetime terms. The Framers established a judiciary that would function independently of the other branches of government, to ensure that judicial decisions would not be improperly influenced by electoral concerns. The president would nominate judges who would then be subject to Senate confirmation (by a majority vote), but after their appointment, judges could be removed only by resignation, death, or impeachment. (The Constitution states that they "shall hold their Offices during good Behaviour.") The Anti-Federalists feared that a lifetime judiciary would amount to a tyranny of the minority, but advocates argued that this independence was necessary for judges to be immune from political expediency in interpreting the Constitution.

Article III of the Constitution provides explicitly for "one supreme Court," as well as "such inferior Courts as the Congress may from time to time ordain and establish." The federal judiciary has evolved into a tripartite system, consisting of ninety-four district courts, thirteen courts of appeals (also known as circuit courts), and the Supreme Court. Each state has at least one district court, and some (California, New York, Texas) have as many as four. Four U.S. territories—Guam, the Northern Mariana Islands, Puerto Rico, and the Virgin Islands—also each have one district court, as does Washington, D.C. Each court of appeals presides over three to eleven states and territories, with a single court responsible for cases in the capital. Most federal cases begin in district court and can move upward from there with appeals; but the Supreme Court does have original jurisdiction in some cases, including, as written in the Constitution, "all Cases affecting Ambassadors, other public Ministers and Consuls, and those in which a State shall be Party."

The Constitution's guidelines on judicial power are quite broad, focusing on the types of cases that the federal courts may oversee, such as "[c]ontroversies to which the United States shall be a Party," and "[c]ontroversies between two or more States." But the Constitution does not elucidate the extent of judicial power. In this chapter, Alexander Hamilton argues, in the Federalist No. 78, that the judicial branch would be the weakest and "least dangerous" of the three branches of government because it lacks the power of either "the purse" (Congress's control of money) or "the sword" (the president's power as commander in chief of the armed forces). Consequently, Hamilton concludes, the judiciary "may truly be said to have neither *force* nor *will* but merely judgment; and must ultimately depend upon the aid of the executive arm even for the efficacy of its judgments." Of course, the power of the courts would prove to be far greater than Hamilton disarmingly promised.

The Supreme Court established the judiciary's equality with the other branches of government in *Marbury v. Madison* (1803), the second reading in this chapter. In this case, Chief Justice John Marshall artfully defines the power of the courts to review acts of Congress, while seemingly limiting the judicial branch's authority. The Supreme Court found that a provision in the Judiciary Act of 1789, one that gave the Court the power to issue certain orders, was unconstitutional. Writing for the majority, Marshall explains that "[i]t is emphatically the province and duty of the judicial department to say what the law is."

This case marked the origins of *judicial review,* the power of the federal courts to declare acts of the legislature as well as of the executive unconstitutional and hence null and void. While the Supreme Court has used this power sparingly in its history—but a few hundred laws have been declared unconstitutional in over two centuries—the other branches of government are ever cognizant of the possibility that a policy might be deemed unconstitutional and normally seek before the fact to avoid any serious clash with the courts. Thus, to cite just one example, in 2001 the Republican-led House Judiciary Committee radically altered key provisions of the Community Solutions Act of 2001—better known as President George W. Bush's faith-based initiatives bill—to bring them into line with existing court doctrines concerning the separation of church and state. The committee's leaders did so even though the deleted provisions were supported by most members on the committee and in their party.

At the same time, however, the courts are normally careful not to get too far out of sync with the policy views of elected officials and trends in public opinion. For one thing, Congress has explicit constitutional authority to limit the Supreme Court's appellate jurisdiction. The vast majority of federal court decisions involve, not the exercise of the body's original jurisdiction, but cases that reach the courts on appeal. Article III, Section 2, of the Constitution states that the Supreme Court "shall have appellate Jurisdiction, both as to Law and Fact, with such Exceptions, and under such Regulations as the Congress shall make." Thus, from time to time, when enough legislators have been so motivated, efforts have been made to "strip" the Supreme Court and the federal judiciary of jurisdiction in controversial matters ranging from abortion and school prayer to busing and prisoners' rights.

In July 2004, for example, the U.S. House approved a bill that would strip the federal courts of their power to decide whether states have the constitutional right to refuse to recognize same-sex marriages from another state. Normally, such "court-stripping" measures do not win approval in both chambers of Congress, but, as often, some legislation results that, while stopping short of altering the courts' jurisdiction in appellate cases in a given area, nonetheless alter what the courts are able to do in that area.

In the mid-1990s, Congress debated and eventually passed a law, known as the Prison Litigation Reform Act, that substantially reduced the authority that federal judges could exercise in ordering changes to state prison systems and expanding inmates' rights. Just as the Supreme Court carefully exercises its power of judicial review, so does Congress rarely move to strip the courts of appellate jurisdiction or otherwise delimit their formal authority. But having these respective powers in reserve tends to affect how each branch behaves and helps explain why the courts often seem to "follow the election returns."

Evaluating whether laws are constitutional is the accepted basis of judicial power today, but Marshall's ruling was revolutionary at the time because it meant that judges could overturn the actions of elected officials. In *Marbury v. Madison,* the Supreme Court broadly interpreted the Constitution, which does not expressly grant the power of judicial review. Marshall's opinion is an early example of what legal scholars term *judicial activism,* or the philosophy that the courts have the power to make decisions about issues that the Constitution does not explicitly discuss.

In the nineteenth century, Marshall's court asserted the federal government's power to charter a national bank in *McCulloch v. Maryland* (reading 2.2), and it explained the meaning of Congress's power to regulate interstate commerce in *Gibbons v. Ogden.* In the twentieth century, the Supreme Court, headed by Chief Justice Earl Warren from 1953 to 1969, established that segregated schools were unconstitutional (*Brown v. Board of Education,* 1954; see reading 13.3), that prayer in school was not permissible (*Engel v. Vitale,* 1962), and that criminal defendants are guaranteed legal representation (*Gideon v. Wainwright,* 1963; see reading 13.4). Perhaps most controversially, the Supreme Court decided in *Roe v. Wade* (1973) that women have the right to decide whether to have an abortion.

An opposing philosophy to judicial activism is *judicial restraint,* the view that judges ought to decide cases based as nearly as possible on law and precedent—to "find" rather than "make" law—and without interpreting public laws in light of evolving social norms, assessing them in relation to public philosophies, or consulting their own religious beliefs or moral understandings. One approach to judicial restraint is known as *strict constructionism.* Strict constructionists believe that the courts should be limited in their jurisdiction to matters expressly mentioned in the Constitution. Strict constructionists say that any issues not discussed there, such as abortion or school prayer, should be left to the people to decide through their elected officials.

In 1857, for example, the Supreme Court ruled in *Dred Scott v. Sanford* that slaves did not have the constitutional right to sue, thus rejecting the petition of a person who had lived in free territories for some time and asserted his freedom on returning to a state in which slavery remained legal. Strict constructionists argue that a powerful judiciary is antithetical to a democracy, as only elected officials are empowered to make public policy on behalf of the people.

The terms *liberal* and *conservative* cannot be applied easily to these judicial philosophies. Judges who are politically liberal in supporting a strong national government that is active in social policy may nevertheless limit their judicial opinions to a strict reading of the Constitution. For example, liberal Supreme Court Justice Hugo Black dissented from the famous decision *Griswold v. Connecticut* (1965) that established a right to privacy, because the Constitution did not expressly provide for this right. In contrast, judges who openly declare a conservative political ideology may sometimes adopt liberal positions in their court rulings. In 1989, conservative Supreme Court Justice Antonin Scalia voted with the 5–4 majority to overturn a state law that banned flag burning, citing the First Amendment guarantee of freedom of speech (*Texas v. Johnson*).

By no means, however, is the judiciary free of politics, and ideological views become particularly important with judicial appointments. One key *litmus test* for Supreme Court nominees today is their position on *Roe v. Wade.* In 1987, interest groups rallied against Judge Robert Bork's nomination because he had written articles stating that the court had intruded on states' rights in that 7–2 decision. Even when the president's party has a majority in the Senate, senators can still block judicial nominations with a filibuster, a tool that the minority party has exercised increasingly in recent years. Judicial nominees typically refuse to state their political positions, arguing that personal views will not shape their legal analyses; but interest groups and politicians still try vigorously to discern how a nominee would rule on such controversial topics as abortion, school prayer, and the death penalty.

Ultimately, the courts must be cognizant of political currents when making decisions because they are dependent on the other branches of government for implementation. The Supreme Court ruled in *Brown v. Board of Education* that segregated schools were unconstitutional, but only with the Civil Rights Act of 1964 did Congress begin to enforce that ruling. The courts typically have deferred to the president in foreign policy matters, especially decisions to send U.S. troops abroad, describing these actions as "political questions" that are not suitable for judicial review. To preserve their power, judges must be careful not to issue rulings that elected officials will refuse to enforce. Still, lifetime appointments provide the federal judiciary with a long-term opportunity to shape the American political system, making it a significant force in public policy.

While there are many competing ideas about constitutional theory and many interesting debates about how judges should approach their work, the fact is that the courts are intimately, deeply, and irreversibly involved in all aspects of American government today. In this chapter, Supreme Court Justices Antonin Scalia and Stephen Breyer eloquently discuss the challenges of constitutional interpretation, presenting thoughtful perspectives on the constitutional responsibilities of judges. While their views do not fit neatly into the categories of judicial restraint or judicial activism, they do present strikingly different judicial philosophies.

12.1 The Federalist No. 78 (1788)

ALEXANDER HAMILTON

INTRODUCTION

In this paper, Alexander Hamilton seeks to reassure critics of the Constitution that the federal judiciary will not trample on individual rights, interfere with state governments, or rival the other branches in power. Lifetime appointments were the primary source of concern; as one Anti-Federalist wrote, "Those who are to be vested with [judicial power], are to be placed in a situation altogether unprecedented in a free country. They are to be rendered totally independent, both of the people and the legislature" ("Brutus," January 31, 1788).

Hamilton defends lifetime tenure for judges, pointing out that they must demonstrate "good behavior" to stay in office. Furthermore, separation of powers ensures that the judiciary "will always be the least dangerous to the political rights of the Constitution; because it will be least in a capacity to annoy or injure them." By concentrating on the limits on judicial power, Hamilton shows that the other branches of government will be able to rein in any efforts by the judiciary to usurp authority. Today, it is clear that the Supreme Court, and the federal courts generally, are far more powerful than Hamilton predicted they would be.

■

To the People of the State of New York:

We proceed now to an examination of the judiciary department of the proposed government.

In unfolding the defects of the existing Confederation, the utility and necessity of a federal judicature have been clearly pointed out. It is the less necessary to recapitulate the considerations there urged, as the propriety of the institution in the abstract is not disputed; the only questions which have been raised being relative to the manner of constituting it, and to its extent. To these points, therefore, our observations shall be confined.

The manner of constituting it seems to embrace these several objects: 1st. The mode of appointing the judges. 2d. The tenure by which they are to hold their places. 3d. The partition of the judiciary authority between different courts, and their relations to each other.

Alexander Hamilton, "The Federalist No. 78" (1788; Yale Law School Avalon Project, 1996), http://www.yale.edu/lawweb/avalon/federal/fed78.htm.

First. As to the mode of appointing the judges; this is the same with that of appointing the officers of the Union in general, and has been so fully discussed in the two last numbers, that nothing can be said here which would not be useless repetition.

Second. As to the tenure by which the judges are to hold their places; this chiefly concerns their duration in office; the provisions for their support; the precautions for their responsibility.

According to the plan of the convention, all judges who may be appointed by the United States are to hold their offices *during good behavior;* which is conformable to the most approved of the State constitutions and among the rest, to that of this State. Its propriety having been drawn into question by the adversaries of that plan, is no light symptom of the rage for objection, which disorders their imaginations and judgments. The standard of good behavior for the continuance in office of the judicial magistracy, is certainly one of the most valuable of the modern improvements in the practice of government. In a monarchy it is an excellent barrier to the despotism of the prince; in a republic it is a no less excellent barrier to the encroachments and oppressions of the representative body. And it is the best expedient which can be devised in any government, to secure a steady, upright, and impartial administration of the laws.

Whoever attentively considers the different departments of power must perceive, that, in a government in which they are separated from each other, the judiciary, from the nature of its functions, will always be the least dangerous to the political rights of the Constitution; because it will be least in a capacity to annoy or injure them. The Executive not only dispenses the honors, but holds the sword of the community. The legislature not only commands the purse, but prescribes the rules by which the duties and rights of every citizen are to be regulated. The judiciary, on the contrary, has no influence over either the sword or the purse; no direction either of the strength or of the wealth of the society; and can take no active resolution whatever. It may truly be said to have neither *force* nor *will,* but merely judgment; and must ultimately depend upon the aid of the executive arm even for the efficacy of its judgments.

This simple view of the matter suggests several important consequences. It proves incontestably, that the judiciary is beyond comparison the weakest of the three departments of power; that it can never attack with success either of the other two; and that all possible care is requisite to enable it to defend itself against their attacks. It equally proves, that though individual oppression may now and then proceed from the courts of justice, the general liberty of the people can never be endangered from that quarter; I mean so long as the judiciary remains truly distinct from both the legislature and the Executive. For I agree, that "there is no liberty, if the power of judging be not separated from the legislative and executive powers." And it proves, in the last place, that as liberty can have nothing to fear from the judiciary alone, but would have every thing to fear from its union with either of the other departments; that as all the effects of such a union must ensue from a dependence of the former on the latter, notwithstanding a nominal and apparent separation; that as, from the natural feebleness of the judiciary, it is in continual jeopardy of being overpowered, awed, or influenced by its co-ordinate branches; and that as nothing can contribute so much to its firmness and independence as permanency in office, this quality may therefore be justly regarded as an indispensable ingredient in its constitution, and, in a great measure, as the citadel of the public justice and the public security.

The complete independence of the courts of justice is peculiarly essential in a limited Constitution. By a limited Constitution, I understand one which contains certain specified exceptions to the legislative authority; such, for instance, as that it shall pass no bills of attainder, no ex-post-facto laws, and the like. Limitations of this kind can be preserved in practice no other way than through the medium of courts of justice, whose duty it must be to declare all acts contrary to the manifest tenor of the Constitution void. Without this, all the reservations of particular rights or privileges would amount to nothing.

Some perplexity respecting the rights of the courts to pronounce legislative acts void, because contrary to the Constitution, has arisen from an imagination that the doctrine would imply a superiority of the judiciary to the legislative power. It is urged that the authority which can declare the acts of another void, must necessarily be superior to the one whose acts may be declared void. As this doctrine is of great importance in all the American constitutions, a brief discussion of the ground on which it rests cannot be unacceptable.

There is no position which depends on clearer principles, than that every act of a delegated authority, contrary to the tenor of the commission under which it is exercised, is void. No legislative act, therefore, contrary to the Constitution, can be valid. To deny this, would be to affirm, that the deputy is greater than his principal; that the servant is above his master; that the representatives of the people are superior to the people themselves; that men acting by virtue of powers, may do not only what their powers do not authorize, but what they forbid.

If it be said that the legislative body are themselves the constitutional judges of their own powers, and that the construction they put upon them is conclusive upon the other departments, it may be answered, that this cannot be the natural presumption, where it is not to be collected from any particular provisions in the Constitution. It is not otherwise to be supposed, that the Constitution could intend to enable the representatives of the people to substitute their *will* to that of their constituents. It is far more rational to suppose, that the courts were designed to be an intermediate body between the people and the legislature, in order, among other things, to keep the latter within the limits assigned to their authority. The interpretation of the laws is the proper and peculiar province of the courts. A constitution is, in fact, and must be regarded by the judges, as a fundamental law. It therefore belongs to them to ascertain its meaning, as well as the meaning of any particular act proceeding from the legislative body. If there should happen to be an irreconcilable variance between the two, that which has the superior obligation and validity ought, of course, to be preferred; or, in other words, the Constitution ought to be preferred to the statute, the intention of the people to the intention of their agents.

Nor does this conclusion by any means suppose a superiority of the judicial to the legislative power. It only supposes that the power of the people is superior to both; and that where the will of the legislature, declared in its statutes, stands in opposition to that of the people, declared in the Constitution, the judges ought to be governed by the latter rather than the former. They ought to regulate their decisions by the fundamental laws, rather than by those which are not fundamental.

This exercise of judicial discretion, in determining between two contradictory laws, is exemplified in a familiar instance. It not uncommonly happens, that there are two statutes existing at one time, clashing in whole or in part with each other, and neither of them containing any repealing clause or expression. In such a case, it is the province of the courts to liquidate and fix their meaning and operation. So far as they can, by any fair construction, be reconciled to each other, reason and law conspire to dictate that this should be done; where this is impracticable, it becomes a matter of necessity to give effect to one, in exclusion of the other. The rule which has obtained in the courts for determining their relative validity is, that the last in order of time shall be preferred to the first. But this is a mere rule of construction, not derived from any positive law, but from the nature and reason of the thing. It is a rule not enjoined upon the courts by legislative provision, but adopted by themselves, as consonant to truth and propriety, for the direction of their conduct as interpreters of the law. They thought it reasonable, that between the interfering acts of an *equal* authority, that which was the last indication of its will should have the preference.

But in regard to the interfering acts of a superior and subordinate authority, of an original and derivative power, the nature and reason of the thing indicate the converse of that rule as proper to be followed. They teach us that the prior act of a superior ought to be preferred to the subsequent act of an inferior and subordinate authority; and that accordingly, whenever a particular statute contravenes the Constitution, it will be the duty of the judicial tribunals to adhere to the latter and disregard the former.

It can be of no weight to say that the courts, on the pretense of a repugnancy, may substitute their own pleasure to the constitutional intentions of the legislature. This might as well happen in the case of two contradictory statutes; or it might as well happen in every adjudication upon any single statute. The courts must declare the sense of the law; and if they should be disposed to exercise *will* instead of *judgment,* the consequence would equally be the substitution of their pleasure to that of the legislative body. The observation, if it prove any thing, would prove that there ought to be no judges distinct from that body.

If, then, the courts of justice are to be considered as the bulwarks of a limited Constitution against legislative encroachments, this consideration will afford a strong argument for the permanent tenure of judicial offices, since nothing will contribute so much as this to that independent spirit in the judges which must be essential to the faithful performance of so arduous a duty.

This independence of the judges is equally requisite to guard the Constitution and the rights of individuals from the effects of those ill humors, which the arts of designing men, or the influence of particular conjunctures, sometimes disseminate among the people themselves, and which, though they speedily give place to better information, and more deliberate reflection, have a tendency, in the meantime, to occasion dangerous innovations in the government, and serious oppressions of the minor party in the community. Though I trust the friends of the proposed Constitution will never concur with its enemies, in questioning that fundamental principle of republican government, which admits the right of the people to alter or abolish the established Constitution, whenever they find it inconsistent with their happiness, yet it is not to be inferred from this principle, that the representatives of the people, whenever a momentary inclination happens to lay hold of a majority of their constituents, incompatible with the provisions in the existing Constitution, would, on that account, be justifiable in a violation of those provisions; or that the courts would be under a greater obligation to connive at infractions in this shape, than when they had proceeded wholly from the cabals of the representative body. Until the people have, by some solemn and authoritative act, annulled or changed the established form, it is binding upon themselves collectively, as well as individually; and no presumption, or even knowledge, of their sentiments, can warrant their representatives in a departure from it, prior to such an act. But it is easy to see, that it would require an uncommon portion of fortitude in the judges to do their duty as faithful guardians of the Constitution, where legislative invasions of it had been instigated by the major voice of the community.

But it is not with a view to infractions of the Constitution only, that the independence of the judges may be an essential safeguard against the effects of occasional ill humors in the society. These sometimes extend no farther than to the injury of the private rights of particular classes of citizens, by unjust and partial laws. Here also the firmness of the judicial magistracy is of vast importance in mitigating the severity and confining the operation of such laws. It not only serves to moderate the immediate mischiefs of those which may have been passed, but it operates as a check upon the legislative body in passing them; who, perceiving that obstacles to the success of iniquitous intention are to be expected from the scruples of the courts, are in a manner compelled, by the very motives of the injustice they meditate, to qualify their attempts. This is a circumstance calculated to have more influence upon the character of our governments, than but few may be aware of. The benefits of the integrity and moderation of the judiciary have already been felt in more States than one; and though they may have displeased those whose sinister expectations they may have disappointed, they must have commanded the esteem and applause of all the virtuous and disinterested. Considerate men, of every description, ought to prize whatever will tend to beget or fortify that temper in the courts: as no man can be sure that he may not be to-morrow the victim of a spirit of injustice, by which he may be a gainer to-day. And every man must now feel, that the inevitable tendency of such a spirit is to sap the foundations of public and private confidence, and to introduce in its stead universal distrust and distress.

That inflexible and uniform adherence to the rights of the Constitution, and of individuals, which we perceive to be indispensable in the courts of justice, can certainly not be expected from judges who hold their offices by a temporary commission. Periodical appointments, however regulated, or by whomsoever made, would, in some way or other, be fatal to their necessary independence. If the power of making them was committed either to the Executive or legislature, there would be danger of an improper complaisance to the branch which possessed it; if to both, there would be an unwillingness to hazard the displeasure of either; if to the people, or to persons chosen by them for the special purpose, there would be too great a disposition to consult popularity, to justify a reliance that nothing would be consulted but the Constitution and the laws.

There is yet a further and a weightier reason for the permanency of the judicial offices, which is deducible from the nature of the qualifications they require. It has been frequently remarked, with great propriety, that a voluminous code of laws is one of the inconveniences necessarily connected with the advantages of a free government. To avoid an arbitrary discretion in the courts, it is indispensable that they should be bound down by strict rules and precedents, which serve to define and point out their duty in every particular case that comes before them; and it will readily be conceived from the variety of controversies which grow out of the folly and wickedness of mankind, that the records of those precedents must unavoidably swell to a very considerable bulk, and must demand long and laborious study to acquire a competent knowledge of them. Hence it is, that there can be but few men in the society who will have sufficient skill in the laws to qualify them for the stations of judges. And making the proper deductions for the ordinary depravity of human nature, the number must be still smaller of those who unite the requisite integrity with the requisite knowledge. These considerations apprise us, that the government can have no great option between fit character; and that a temporary duration in office, which would naturally discourage such characters from quitting a lucrative line of practice to accept a seat on the bench, would have a tendency to throw the administration of justice into hands less able, and less well qualified, to conduct it with utility and dignity. In the present circumstances of this country, and in those in which it is likely to be for a long time to come, the disadvantages on this score would be greater than they may at first sight appear; but it must be confessed, that they are far inferior to those which present themselves under the other aspects of the subject.

Upon the whole, there can be no room to doubt that the convention acted wisely in copying from the models of those constitutions which have established *good behavior* as the tenure of their judicial offices, in point of duration; and that so far from being blamable on this account, their plan would have been inexcusably defective, if it had wanted this important feature of good government. The experience of Great Britain affords an illustrious comment on the excellence of the institution.

PUBLIUS

12.2   *Marbury v. Madison* (1803)

INTRODUCTION

As outgoing President John Adams prepared to leave office in 1801, he made a number of judicial nominations, famously known as his "midnight appointments." They included one for William Marbury to become a justice of the peace, but Secretary of State John Marshall did not deliver Marbury's commission before President Thomas Jefferson's inauguration. A Democratic-Republican, Jefferson did not want to seat Federalist Adams's nominees, so Marbury sued, demanding the delivery of his commission. By the time Marbury's case reached the Supreme Court, John Marshall had become chief justice. Marshall recognized the court's precarious position, for if it ruled that Marbury should receive his commission, then the Jefferson administration could refuse to follow suit, thereby illustrating the judicial branch's weakness. At the same time, if the court ruled against Marbury, then it would be following political currents rather than rendering an independent judgment.

Marshall devised an ingenious solution: The court decided that Marbury was entitled to his commission, but the process through which he sought to receive it was unconstitutional. Marbury had requested a *writ of mandamus* from the Supreme Court, essentially an order to force Secretary of State James Madison to deliver the commission. Congress gave the Supreme Court the authority to issue writs of mandamus in the Judiciary Act of 1789; Marshall

Marbury v. Madison, 5 U.S. 137 (1803).

ruled, however, that this section of the law was unconstitutional, as it went beyond the powers granted in Article III of the Constitution. Marbury deserved his commission, but the Supreme Court could not order the Jefferson administration to deliver it. Thus, by limiting the court's power in this case, Marshall succeeded in affirming its authority in a much more important area: the ability to review laws and declare them unconstitutional.

■

The constitution vests the whole judicial power of the United States in one supreme court, and such inferior courts as congress shall, from time to time, ordain and establish. This power is expressly extended to all cases arising under the laws of the United States; and consequently, in some form, may be exercised over the present case; because the right claimed is given by a law of the United States.

In the distribution of this power it is declared that "the supreme court shall have original jurisdiction in all cases affecting ambassadors, other public ministers and consuls, and those in which a state shall be a party. In all other cases, the supreme court shall have appellate jurisdiction."

It has been insisted, at the bar, that as the original grant of jurisdiction, to the supreme and inferior courts, is general, and the clause, assigning original jurisdiction to the supreme court, contains no negative or restrictive words; the power remains to the legislature, to assign original jurisdiction to that court in other cases than those specified in the article which has been recited; provided those cases belong to the judicial power of the United States.

If it had been intended to leave it in the discretion of the legislature to apportion the judicial power between the supreme and inferior courts according to the will of that body, it would certainly have been useless to have proceeded further than to have defined the judicial power, and the tribunals in which it should be vested. The subsequent part of the section is mere surplusage, is entirely without meaning, if such is to be the construction. If congress remains at liberty to give this court appellate jurisdiction, where the constitution has declared their jurisdiction shall be original; and original jurisdiction where the constitution has declared it shall be appellate; the distribution of jurisdiction, made in the constitution, is form without substance.

Affirmative words are often, in their operation, negative of other objects than those affirmed; and in this case, a negative or exclusive sense must be given to them or they have no operation at all. It cannot be presumed that any clause in the constitution is intended to be without effect; and therefore such a construction is inadmissible, unless the words require it.

If the solicitude of the convention, respecting our peace with foreign powers, induced a provision that the supreme court should take original jurisdiction in cases which might be supposed to affect them; yet the clause would have proceeded no further than to provide for such cases, if no further restriction on the powers of congress had been intended. That they should have appellate jurisdiction in all other cases, with such exceptions as congress might make, is no restriction; unless the words be deemed exclusive of original jurisdiction.

When an instrument organizing fundamentally a judicial system, divides it into one supreme, and so many inferior courts as the legislature may ordain and establish; then enumerates its powers, and proceeds so far to distribute them, as to define the jurisdiction of the supreme court by declaring the cases in which it shall take original jurisdiction, and that in others it shall take appellate jurisdiction; the plain import of the words seems to be, that in one class of cases its jurisdiction is original, and not appellate; in the other it is appellate, and not original. If any other construction would render the clause inoperative, that is an additional reason for rejecting such other construction, and for adhering to their obvious meaning.

To enable this court then to issue a mandamus, it must be shewn to be an exercise of appellate jurisdiction, or to be necessary to enable them to exercise appellate jurisdiction. It has been stated at the bar that the appellate jurisdiction may be exercised in a variety of forms, and that if it be the will of the legislature that a mandamus should be used for that purpose, that will must be obeyed. This is true, yet the jurisdiction must be appellate, not original.

It is the essential criterion of appellate jurisdiction, that it revises and corrects the proceedings in a cause already instituted, and does not create that cause. Although, therefore, a mandamus may be directed to courts, yet to issue such a writ to an officer for the delivery of a paper, is in effect the same as to sustain an original action for that paper, and therefore seems not to belong to appellate, but to original jurisdiction. Neither is it necessary in such a case as this, to enable the court to exercise its appellate jurisdiction.

The authority, therefore, given to the supreme court, by the act establishing the judicial courts of the United States, to issue writs of mandamus to public officers, appears not to be warranted by the constitution; and it becomes necessary to enquire whether a jurisdiction, so conferred, can be exercised.

The question, whether an act, repugnant to the constitution, can become the law of the land, is a question deeply interesting to the United States; but, happily, not of an intricacy proportioned to its interest. It seems only necessary to recognize certain principles, supposed to have been long and well established, to decide it.

That the people have an original right to establish, for their future government, such principles as, in their opinion, shall most conduce to their own happiness, is the basis, on which the whole American fabric has been erected. The exercise of this original right is a very great exertion; nor can it, nor ought it to be frequently repeated. The principles, therefore, so established, are deemed fundamental. And as the authority, from which they proceed, is supreme, and can seldom act, they are designed to be permanent.

This original and supreme will organizes the government, and assigns, to different departments, their respective powers. It may either stop here; or establish certain limits not to be transcended by those departments.

The government of the United States is of the latter description. The powers of the legislature are defined, and limited; and that those limits may not be mistaken, or forgotten, the constitution is written. To what purpose are powers limited, and to what purpose is that limitation committed to writing, if these limits may, at any time, be passed by those intended to be restrained? The distinction, between a government with limited and unlimited powers, is abolished, if those limits do not confine the persons on whom they are imposed, and if acts prohibited and acts allowed, are of equal obligation. It is a proposition too plain to be contested, that the constitution controls any legislative act repugnant to it; or, that the legislature may alter the constitution by an ordinary act.

Between these alternatives there is no middle ground. The constitution is either a superior, paramount law, unchangeable by ordinary means, or it is on a level with ordinary legislative acts, and like other acts, is alterable when the legislature shall please to alter it.

If the former part of the alternative be true, then a legislative act contrary to the constitution is not law: if the latter part be true, then written constitutions are absurd attempts, on the part of the people, to limit a power, in its own nature illimitable.

Certainly all those who have framed written constitutions contemplate them as forming the fundamental and paramount law of the nation, and consequently the theory of every such government must be, that an act of the legislature, repugnant to the constitution, is void. This theory is essentially attached to a written constitution, and is consequently to be considered, by this court, as one of the fundamental principles of our society. It is not therefore to be lost sight of in the further consideration of this subject.

If an act of the legislature, repugnant to the constitution, is void, does it, notwithstanding its invalidity, bind the courts, and oblige them to give it effect? Or, in other words, though it be not law, does it constitute a rule as operative as if it was a law? This would be to overthrow in fact what was established in theory; and would seem, at first view, an absurdity too gross to be insisted on. It shall, however, receive a more attentive consideration.

It is emphatically the province and duty of the judicial department to say what the law is. Those who apply the rule to particular cases, must of necessity expound and interpret that rule. If two laws conflict with each other, the courts must decide on the operation of each.

So if a law be in opposition to the constitution; if both the law and the constitution apply to a particular case, so that the court must either decide that case conformably to the law, disregarding the constitution; or conformably to the constitution, disregarding the law; the court must determine which of these conflicting rules governs the case. This is of the very essence of judicial duty.

If then the courts are to regard the constitution; and the constitution is superior to any ordinary act of the legislature; the constitution, and not such ordinary act, must govern the case to which they both apply.

Those then who controvert the principle that the constitution is to be considered, in court, as a paramount law, are reduced to the necessity of maintaining that courts must close their eyes on the constitution, and see only the law.

This doctrine would subvert the very foundation of all written constitutions. It would declare that an act, which, according to the principles and theory of our government, is entirely void; is yet, in practice, completely obligatory. It would declare, that if the legislature shall do what is expressly forbidden, such act, notwithstanding the express prohibition, is in reality effectual. It would be giving to the legislature a practical and real omnipotence, with the same breath which professes to restrict their powers within narrow limits. It is prescribing limits, and declaring that those limits may be passed as pleasure.

That it thus reduces to nothing what we have deemed the greatest improvement on political institutions—a written constitution—would of itself be sufficient, in America, where written constitutions have been viewed with so much reverence, for rejecting the construction. But the peculiar expressions of the constitution of the United States furnish additional arguments in favour of its rejection.

The judicial power of the United States is extended to all cases arising under the constitution.

12.3 A Matter of Interpretation: Federal Courts and the Law (1997)

ANTONIN SCALIA

INTRODUCTION

In 1994–1995, Supreme Court Justice Antonin Scalia gave the Tanner Lectures on Human Values at Princeton University, where he presented his philosophy of judicial interpretation. In the following excerpt, Scalia expertly defines and defends the concept of *textualism,* or the belief that a text "should be construed reasonably, to contain all that it fairly means." Scalia insists that "words do have a limited range of meaning, and no interpretation that goes beyond that range is permissible." Textualism must be applied to the Constitution,

Scalia states, for the very purpose of a constitution "is to prevent change—to embed certain rights in such a manner that future generations cannot readily take them away."

■

TEXTUALISM

The philosophy of interpretation I have described . . . is known as textualism. In some sophisticated circles, it is considered simpleminded—"wooden," "unimaginative," "pedestrian." It is none of that. To be a textualist in good standing, one need not be too dull to perceive the broader social purposes that a statute is designed, or could be designed, to serve; or too hide-bound to realize that new times require new laws. One need only hold the belief that judges have no authority to pursue those broader purposes or write those new laws.

Textualism should not be confused with so-called strict constructionism, a degraded form of textualism that brings the whole philosophy into disrepute. I am not a strict constructionist, and no one ought to be—though better that, I suppose, than a nontextualist. A text should not be construed strictly, and it should not be construed leniently; it should be construed reasonably, to contain all that it fairly means. The difference between textualism and strict constructionism can be seen in a case my Court decided four terms ago.[1] The statute at issue provided for an increased jail term if, "during and in relation to . . . [a] drug trafficking crime," the defendant "uses . . . a firearm." The defendant in this case had sought to purchase a quantity of cocaine; and what he had offered to give in exchange for the cocaine was an unloaded firearm, which he showed to the drug-seller. The Court held, I regret to say, that the defendant was subject to the increased penalty, because he had "used a firearm during and in relation to a drug trafficking crime." The vote was not even close (6–3). I dissented. Now I cannot say whether my colleagues in the majority voted the way they did because they are strict-construction textualists, or because they are not textualists at all. But a proper textualist, which is to say my kind of textualist, would surely have voted to acquit. The phrase "uses a gun" fairly connoted use of a gun for what guns are normally used for, that is, as a weapon. As I put the point in my dissent, when you ask someone, "Do you use a cane?" you are not inquiring whether he has hung his grandfather's antique cane as a decoration in the hallway.

But while the good textualist is not a literalist, neither is he a nihilist. Words do have a limited range of meaning, and no interpretation that goes beyond that range is permissible. My favorite example of a departure from text—and

---

[1]Smith v. United States, 508 U.S. 223 (1993).

certainly the departure that has enabled judges to do more freewheeling law-making than any other—pertains to the Due Process Clause found in the Fifth and Fourteenth Amendments of the United States Constitution, which says that no person shall "be deprived of life, liberty, or property without due process of law." It has been interpreted to prevent the government from tak-ing away certain liberties *beyond* those, such as freedom of speech and of re-ligion, that are specifically named in the Constitution. (The first Supreme Court case to use the Due Process Clause in this fashion was, by the way, *Dred Scott*[2]—not a desirable parentage.) Well, it may or may not be a good thing to guarantee additional liberties, but the Due Process Clause quite obviously does not bear that interpretation. By its inescapable terms, it guarantees only process. Property can be taken by the state; liberty can be taken; even life can be taken; but not without the *process* that our traditions require—notably, a validly enacted law and a fair trial. To say otherwise is to abandon textualism, and to render democratically adopted texts mere springboards for judicial lawmaking.

Of all the criticisms leveled against textualism, the most mindless is that it is "formalistic." The answer to that is, *of course it's formalistic!* The rule of law is *about* form. If, for example, a citizen performs an act—let us say the sale of certain technology to a foreign country—which is prohibited by a widely pub-licized bill proposed by the administration and passed by both houses of Con-gress, *but not yet signed by the President*, that sale is lawful. It is of no consequence that everyone knows both houses of Congress and the President wish to prevent that sale. Before the wish becomes a binding law, it must be embodied in a bill that passes both houses and is signed by the President. Is that not formalism? A murderer has been caught with blood on his hands, bending over the body of his victim; a neighbor with a video camera has filmed the crime; and the murderer has confessed in writing and on videotape. We nonetheless insist that before the state can punish this miscreant, it must conduct a full-dress criminal trial that results in a verdict of guilty. Is that not formalism? Long live formalism. It is what makes a government a govern-ment of laws and not of men. . . .

INTERPRETING CONSTITUTIONAL TEXTS

Without pretending to have exhausted the vast topic of textual interpretation, I wish to address a final subject: the distinctive problem of constitutional in-terpretation. The problem is distinctive, not because special principles of in-terpretation apply, but because the usual principles are being applied to an unusual text. Chief Justice Marshall put the point as well as it can be put in *McCulloch v. Maryland*:

---

[2]Dred Scott v. Sandford, 60 U.S. (19 How.) 393, 450 (1857).

> A constitution, to contain an accurate detail of all the subdivisions of which its
> great powers will admit, and of all the means by which they may be carried into
> execution, would partake of the prolixity of a legal code, and could scarcely be
> embraced by the human mind. It would probably never be understood by the
> public. Its nature, therefore, requires, that only its great outlines should be
> marked, its important objects designated, and the minor ingredients which com-
> pose those objects be deduced from the nature of the objects themselves.[3]

In textual interpretation, context is everything, and the context of the Constitution tells us not to expect nit-picking detail, and to give words and phrases
an expansive rather than narrow interpretation—though not an interpretation that the language will not bear.

Take, for example, the provision of the First Amendment that forbids
abridgment of "the freedom of speech, or of the press." That phrase does not
list the full range of communicative expression. Handwritten letters, for example, are neither speech nor press. Yet surely there is no doubt they cannot
be censored. In this constitutional context, speech and press, the two most
common forms of communication, stand as a sort of synecdoche for the whole.
That is not strict construction, but it is reasonable construction.

It is curious that most of those who insist that the drafter's intent gives
meaning to a statute reject the drafter's intent as the criterion for interpretation of the Constitution. I reject it for both. I will consult the writings of some
men who happened to be delegates to the Constitutional Convention—Hamilton's and Madison's writings in *The Federalist*, for example. I do so, however,
not because they were Framers and therefore their intent is authoritative and
must be the law; but rather because their writings, like those of other intelligent and informed people of the time, display how the text of the Constitution was originally understood. Thus I give equal weight to Jay's pieces in
The Federalist, and to Jefferson's writings, even though neither of them was a
Framer. What I look for in the Constitution is precisely what I look for in a
statute: the original meaning of the text, not what the original draftsmen
intended.

But the Great Divide with regard to constitutional interpretation is not that
between Framers' intent and objective meaning, but rather that between
original meaning (whether derived from Framers' intent or not) and *current*
meaning. The ascendant school of constitutional interpretation affirms the existence of what is called The Living Constitution, a body of law that (unlike
normal statutes) grows and changes from age to age, in order to meet the
needs of a changing society. And it is the judges who determine those needs
and "find" that changing law. Seems familiar, doesn't it? Yes, it is the common law returned, but infinitely more powerful than what the old common

---

[3]McCulloch v. Maryland, 17 U.S. (4 Wheat.) 316, 407 (1819).

law ever pretended to be, for now it trumps even the statutes of democratic legislatures. Recall the words . . . from the Fourth-of-July speech of the avid codifier Robert Rantoul: "The judge makes law, by extorting from precedents something which they do not contain. He extends his precedents, which were themselves the extension of others, till, by this accommodating principle, a whole system of law is built up without the authority or interference of the legislator."[4] Substitute the word "people" for "legislator," and it is a perfect description of what modern American courts have done with the Constitution.

If you go into a constitutional law class, or study a constitutional law casebook, or read a brief filed in a constitutional law case, you will rarely find the discussion addressed to the text of the constitutional provision that is at issue, or to the question of what was the originally understood or even the originally intended meaning of that text. The starting point of the analysis will be Supreme Court cases, and the new issue will presumptively be decided according to the logic that those cases expressed, with no regard for how far that logic, thus extended, has distanced us from the original text and understanding. Worse still, however, it is known and understood that if that logic fails to produce what in the view of the current Supreme Court is the *desirable* result for the case at hand, then, like good common-law judges, the Court will distinguish its precedents, or narrow them, or if all else fails overrule them, in order that the Constitution might mean what it *ought* to mean. Should there be—to take one of the less controversial examples—a constitutional right to die? If so, there is.[5] Should there be a constitutional right to reclaim a biological child put out for adoption by the other parent? Again, if so, there is.[6] If it is good, it is so. Never mind the text that we are supposedly construing; we will smuggle these new rights in, if all else fails, under the Due Process Clause (which, as I have described, is textually incapable of containing them). Moreover, what the Constitution meant yesterday it does not necessarily mean today. As our opinions say in the context of our Eighth Amendment jurisprudence (the Cruel and Unusual Punishments Clause), its meaning changes to reflect "the evolving standards of decency that mark the progress of a maturing society."[7]

This is preeminently a common-law way of making law, and not the way of construing a democratically adopted text. I mentioned earlier a famous English treatise on statutory construction called *Dwarris on Statutes*. The fourth of Dwarris's Maxims was as follows: "An act of Parliament cannot alter by

---

[4]Robert Rantoul, "Oration at Scituate" (July 4, 1836), in Kermit L. Hall et al., *American Legal History* 317, 317–318 (1991).

[5]*See* Cruzan v. Director, Mo. Dep't of Health, 497 U.S. 261, 279 (1990).

[6]*See In re* Kirchner, 649 N.E.2d 324, 333 (Ill.), *cert. denied,* 115 S. Ct. 2599 (1995).

[7]Rhodes v. Chapman, 452 U.S. 337, 346 (1981), quoting from Trop v. Dulles, 356 U.S. 86, 101 (1958) (plurality opinion).

reason of time; but the common law may, since *cessante ratione cessat lex*."[8] This remains (however much it may sometimes be evaded) the formally enunciated rule for statutory construction: statutes do not change. Proposals for "dynamic statutory construction," such as those of Judge Calabresi and Professor Eskridge, are concededly avant-garde. The Constitution, however, even though a democratically adopted text, we formally treat like the common law. What, it is fair to ask, is the justification for doing so?

One would suppose that the rule that a text does not change would apply a fortiori to a constitution. If courts felt too much bound by the democratic process to tinker with statutes, when their tinkering could be adjusted by the legislature, how much more should they feel bound not to tinker with a constitution, when their tinkering is virtually irreparable. It certainly cannot be said that a constitution naturally suggests changeability; to the contrary, its whole purpose is to prevent change—to embed certain rights in such a manner that future generations cannot readily take them away. A society that adopts a bill of rights is skeptical that "evolving standards of decency" always "mark progress," and that societies always "mature," as opposed to rot. Neither the text of such a document nor the intent of its framers (whichever you choose) can possibly lead to the conclusion that its only effect is to take the power of changing rights away from the legislature and give it to the courts.

12.4 Active Liberty: Interpreting Our Democratic Constitution (2005)

STEPHEN BREYER

INTRODUCTION

In November 2004, Supreme Court Justice Stephen Breyer gave the Tanner Lectures on Human Values at Harvard University and presented his views on constitutional interpretation. In the following excerpt, Breyer argues that the democratic underpinnings of the Constitution should guide court decisions. He criticizes the textualist (also described as an *originalist* or *literalist*) approach, stating that "[l]iteralism has a tendency to undermine the Constitution's efforts to create a framework for democratic government." Breyer, in contrast, holds that judges should evaluate constitutional purposes and policy

---

[8]*Fortunatus Dwarris, A General Treatise on Statutes, with American Notes and Additions by Platt Potter* 122 (Albany, N.Y. 1871).

Stephen Breyer, *Active Liberty: Interpreting Our Democratic Constitution* (New York: Alfred A. Knopf, 2005), 3–11, 110–135 (excerpts). Delivered as a Tanner Lecture on Human Values at Harvard University, 2004. Printed with permission of the Tanner Lectures on Human Values, a Corporation, University of Utah, Salt Lake City, Utah.

consequences when making decisions. As he carefully explains, consequences can be "an important yardstick to measure a given [constitutional] interpretation's faithfulness to these democratic purposes."

■

The United States is a nation built upon principles of liberty. That liberty
means not only freedom from government coercion but also the freedom to
participate in the government itself. When Jefferson wrote, "I know no safe depository of the ultimate powers of the society but the people themselves," his
concern was for abuse of government power. But when he spoke of the rights
of the citizen as "a participator in the government of affairs," when Adams,
his rival, added that all citizens have a "positive passion for the public good,"
and when the Founders referred to "public liberty," they had in mind more
than freedom from a despotic government. They had invoked an idea of freedom as old as antiquity, the freedom of the individual citizen to participate in
the government and thereby to share with others the right to make or to control the nation's public acts.[1]

Writing thirty years after the adoption of the American Constitution and the
beginnings of the French Revolution, the political philosopher Benjamin Constant emphasized the differences between these two kinds of liberty. He called
them "the liberty of the ancients" and the "liberty of the moderns." He described "the liberty of the ancients" as an active liberty. It consisted of a sharing of a nation's sovereign authority among that nation's citizens. From the
citizen's perspective it meant "an active and constant participation in collective power"; it included the citizen's right to "deliberate in the public place,"
to "vote for war or peace," to "make treaties," to "enact laws," to examine the
actions and accounts of those who administer government, and to hold them
responsible for their misdeeds. From the nation's perspective, it meant "submitting to all the citizens, without exception, the care and assessment of their
most sacred interests." This sharing of sovereign authority, Constant said,
"enlarged" the citizens' "minds, ennobled their thoughts," and "established
among them a kind of intellectual equality which forms the glory and the
power of a people."[2]

---

[1]Letter from Thomas Jefferson to William Charles Jarvis (Sept. 28, 1820), reprinted in 10 *The Writings of Thomas Jefferson* 1816–1826, at 160 (Paul Leicester Ford ed., 1899); Letter from Thomas Jefferson to Joseph C. Cabell (Feb. 2, 1816), reprinted in 1 *The Founders' Constitution*, at 142, 142
(Philip B. Kurland & Ralph Lerner eds., 1987); Letter from John Adams to Mercy Otis Warren
(Apr. 16, 1776), *id.* at 670; e.g., The Federalist No. 28, at 178, 181 (Hamilton), (Clinton Rossiter ed.,
1961) (discussing "invasions of the public liberty by national authority").

[2]Benjamin Constant, *The Liberty of the Ancients Compared with That of the Moderns* (1819), in *Political
Writings* 309, 309–28 (Biancamaria Fontana trans. & ed., 1988); Benjamin Constant, *De la liberté
des Anciens: Discours prononcé à l'Athénée royal de Paris en 1819*, at 2, available at
http://www.libres.org/francais/fondamentaux/liberte/liberte_constant.htm at 2; *Political Writings*, at 327; Constant, *De la liberté;* at 15.

At the same time, ancient liberty was incomplete. It failed to protect the individual citizen from the tyranny of the majority. It provided a dismal pretext for those who advocated new "kinds of tyranny." Having seen the Terror, Constant was well aware of the dangers of subjecting the individual to the unconstrained "authority of the group"; and he warned against "borrowing from the ancient republics the means" for governments "to oppress us." Constant argued that governments must protect the "true modern liberty." That liberty, "civil liberty," freedom from government, consisted of the individual's freedom to pursue his own interests and desires free of improper government interference.[3]

Constant argued that both kinds of liberty—ancient and modern—are critically important. A society that overemphasizes ancient liberty places too low a value upon the individual's right to freedom from the majority. A society that overemphasizes modern liberty runs the risk that citizens, "enjoying their private independence and in the pursuit of their individual interests," will "too easily renounce their rights to share political power." We must "learn to combine the two together."[4]

. . . [W]hile conscious of the importance of modern liberty, I seek to call increased attention to the combination's other half. I focus primarily upon the active liberty of the ancients, what Constant called the people's right to "an active and constant participation in collective power." My thesis is that courts should take greater account of the Constitution's democratic nature when they interpret constitutional and statutory texts. That thesis encompasses well-known arguments for judicial modesty: The judge, compared to the legislator, lacks relevant expertise. The "people" must develop "the political experience" and they must obtain "the moral education and stimulus that come from . . . correcting their own errors." Judges, too, must display that doubt, caution, and prudence, that not being "too sure" of one-self, that Justice Learned Hand described as "the spirit of liberty."[5]

But my thesis reaches beyond these classic arguments. It finds in the Constitution's democratic objective not simply restraint on judicial power or an ancient counter-part of more modern protection, but also a source of judicial authority and an interpretive aid to more effective protection of ancient and modern liberty alike. It finds a basic perspective that helps make sense of our Constitution's structure, illuminating aspects that otherwise seem less coherent. Through examples, my thesis illustrates how emphasizing this democratic objective can bring us closer to achieving the proper balance to which Constant referred. The examples suggest that increased emphasis upon that objective by judges when they interpret a legal text will yield better law—law

---

[3]Constant, *De la liberté*, at 2; *id.* at 7; *id.* at 13; in *Political Writings*, at 325–27.

[4]Constant, *De la liberté*, at 14; Constant in *Political Writings*, at 327.

[5]See Constant, *De la liberté*; James B. Thayer, *John Marshall* 106 (1901); and Learned Hand, *The Spirit of Liberty* (3d ed., 1960).

that helps a community of individuals democratically find practical solutions to important contemporary social problems. They simultaneously illustrate the importance of a judge's considering practical consequences, that is, consequences valued in terms of constitutional purposes, when the interpretation of constitutional language is at issue.

In a word, my theme is democracy and the Constitution. I illustrate a democratic theme—"active liberty"—which resonates throughout the Constitution. In discussing its role, I hope to illustrate how this constitutional theme can affect a judge's interpretation of a constitutional text.[6]

To illustrate a theme is not to present a general theory of constitutional interpretation. Nonetheless, themes play an important role in a judge's work. Learned Hand once compared the task of interpreting a statute to that of interpreting a musical score. No particular theory guarantees that the interpreter can fully capture the composer's intent. It makes sense to ask a musician to emphasize one theme more than another. And one can understand an interpretation that approaches a great symphony from a "romantic," as opposed to a "classical," point of view. So might a judge pay greater attention to a document's democratic theme; and so might a judge view the Constitution through a more democratic lens. The matter is primarily one of approach, perspective, and emphasis. And approach, perspective, and emphasis, even if they are not theories, play a great role in law.[7]

For one thing, emphasis matters when judges face difficult questions of statutory or constitutional interpretation. All judges use similar basic tools to help them accomplish the task. They read the text's language along with related language in other parts of the document. They take account of its history, including history that shows what the language likely meant to those who wrote it. They look to tradition indicating how the relevant language was, and is, used in the law. They examine precedents interpreting the phrase, holding or suggesting what the phrase means and how it has been applied. They try to understand the phrase's purposes or (in respect to many constitutional phrases) the values that it embodies, and they consider the likely consequences of the interpretive alternatives, valued in terms of the phrase's purposes. But the fact that most judges agree that these basic elements—language, history, tradition, precedent, purpose, and consequence—are useful does not mean they agree about just where and how to use them. Some judges emphasize the use of language, history, and tradition. Others emphasize

---

[6]The term "active liberty" is distinct from, but bears some similarities to, the philosopher Isaiah Berlin's concept of "positive liberty." See Isaiah Berlin, *Two Concepts of Liberty, Inaugural Lecture Before the University of Oxford* (Oct. 31, 1958), in *Four Essays on Liberty* 118, 118–72 (1969).

[7]*Helvering v. Gregory*, 69 F.2d 809, 810–11 (1934) ("[T]he meaning of a sentence may be more than that of the separate words, as a melody is more than the notes"); see also Jerome Frank, *Words and Music: Some Remarks on Statutory Interpretation*, 47 Colum. L. Rev. 1259, 1262–64 (1947) (a "wise composer" expects performers to go beyond literal meaning in interpreting his score; a wise public should expect a judge to transcend technical meaning of the words in a statutory text).

purpose and consequence. These differences of emphasis matter—and this book will explain why.

For another thing, emphasis matters in respect to the specialized constitutional work of a Supreme Court Justice. In my view, that work, though appellate in nature, differs from the work of a lower appellate court in an important way. Because a Justice, unlike a judge on a trial or appellate court, faces a steady diet of constitutional cases, Supreme Court work leads the Justice to develop a view of the Constitution as a whole. My own view is likely similar to that of others insofar as I see the document as creating a coherent framework for a certain kind of government. Described generally, that government is democratic; it avoids concentration of too much power in too few hands; it protects personal liberty; it insists that the law respect each individual equally; and it acts only upon the basis of law itself. The document embodies these general objectives in discrete provisions. In respect to democratic government, for example, the Constitution insists that Congress meet at least once each year, that elections take place every two (or four or six) years, that representation be based upon a census that must take place every decade; and it has gradually extended the right to vote to all adult men and women of every race and religion. (It also guarantees the states a "republican form of government.")[8]

But my view can differ from the views of various others in the way in which I understand the relation between the Constitution's democratic objective and its other general objectives. My view can differ in the comparative significance I attach to each general objective. And my view can differ in the way I understand how a particular objective should influence the interpretation of a broader provision, and not just those provisions that refer to it directly. These differences too are often a matter of degree, a matter of perspective, or emphasis, rather than a radical disagreement about the general nature of the Constitution or its basic objectives.

Finally, the fact that members of historically different Supreme Courts have emphasized different constitutional themes, objectives, or approaches over time allows us to characterize a Court during a period of its history and to speak meaningfully about changes in the Court's judicial "philosophy" over time. Thus, one can characterize the early nineteenth century as a period during which the Court, through its interpretations of the Constitution, helped to establish the authority of the federal government, including the federal judiciary. One can characterize the late nineteenth and early twentieth centuries as a period during which the Court overly emphasized the Constitution's protection of private property, as, for example, in *Lochner v. New York*, where (over the dissent of Justice Oliver Wendell Holmes) it held that state maximum hour laws violated "freedom of contract." At the same time, that Court wrongly underemphasized the basic objectives of the Civil War amendments. It tended

---

[8]U.S. Const. art. I; amends. XIV, XIX; *id.* art. IV.

to ignore that those amendments sought to draw all citizens, irrespective of race, into the community, and that those amendments, in guaranteeing that the law would equally respect all "persons," hoped to make the Constitution's opening phrase, "We the People," a political reality.[9]

Later Courts—the New Deal Court and the Warren Court—emphasized ways in which the Constitution protected the citizen's "active liberty," i.e., the scope of the right to participate in government. The former dismantled various *Lochner*-era distinctions, thereby expanding the constitutional room available for citizens, through their elected representatives, to govern themselves. The latter interpreted the Civil War amendments in light of their basic purposes, thereby directly helping African Americans become full members of the nation's community of self-governing citizens—a community that the people had expanded through later amendments, for example, those extending the suffrage to women, and which the Court expanded further in its "one person, one vote" decisions. The Warren Court's emphasis (on the need to make the law's constitutional promises a legal reality) also led it to consider how the Civil War amendments (and later amendments) had changed the scope of pre–Civil War constitutional language, that is, by changing the assumptions, premises, or presuppositions upon which many earlier constitutional interpretations had rested. In doing so, it read the document as offering broader protection to "modern liberty" (protecting the citizen from government) as well. While I cannot easily characterize the current Court, I will suggest that it may have swung back too far, too often underemphasizing or overlooking the contemporary importance of active liberty.[10] . . .

By now it should be clear that when I argue for greater attention, I am not arguing for a new theory of constitutional law. In my experience most judges approach and decide most cases, including constitutional cases, quite similarly. They are professionals. And their professional training and experience leads them to examine language, history, tradition, precedent, purpose, and consequences. Given roughly similar forms of legal education and professional experience, it is not surprising that judges often agree about how these

---

[9]See, e.g., *McCulloch v. Maryland*, 17 U.S. (4 Wheat.) 316 (1819) (upholding Congress's power to charter national bank); *Marbury v. Madison*, 5 U.S. (1 Cranch) 137 (1803) (establishing federal courts' power to review constitutionality of federal laws); see e.g., *Giles v. Harris*, 189 U.S. 475 (1903) (refusing to enforce voting rights); *The Civil Rights Cases*, 109 U.S. 3 (1883) (narrowly interpreting Civil War amendments); *Lochner v. New York*, 198 U.S. 45 (1905) (invalidating workplace health regulations on substantive due process grounds).

[10]See, e.g., *Wickard v. Filburn*, 317 U.S. 111, 125 (1942) (rejecting distinction between "direct" and "indirect" effects on interstate commerce); *NLRB v. Jones & Laughlin Steel Corp.*, 301 U.S. 1 (1937) (upholding constitutionality of National Labor Relations Act and abandoning "indirect effects" test); *W. Coast Hotel Co. v. Parrish*, 300 U.S. 379 (1937) (concluding that minimum wage law for women did not violate constitutional right to freedom of contract); see, e.g., *Reynolds v. Sims*, 377 U.S. 533 (1964) (applying "one person, one vote" principle to state legislatures); *Baker v. Carr*, 369 U.S. 186 (1962) (finding that Equal Protection Clause justified federal court intervention to review voter apportionment); *Gomillion v. Lightfoot*, 364 U.S. 339 (1960) (striking down racial gerrymandering on Fifteenth Amendment grounds).

factors, taken together, point to the proper result in a particular case. Even when they differ, the degree of difference is often small. Our Court, which normally steps in where other judges disagree, decides roughly 40 percent of its cases unanimously. Most of the rest involve only one or two dissenting votes. In only about 20 percent of our caseload do we divide five-four. And the same Justices are not always on the same side of the split. Only a handful of constitutional and statutory issues are as open in respect to language history, and basic purpose as those I have here described.

I have taken this professional framework as a given. Within that framework, I have argued for greater awareness of, and emphasis upon, the Constitution's democratic imperative. My argument has not rested upon logical or scientifically convincing empirical demonstration. Rather it has used examples to suggest a pattern. And that pattern, in turn, suggests that supplementing ordinary, professional judicial approaches with increased emphasis on the Constitution's democratic objective will help Americans remain true to the past while better resolving their contemporary problems of government through law.

A SERIOUS OBJECTION

Here I broaden my argument's appeal—and tie the argument to more general questions of interpretation. Throughout, I have urged attention to purpose and consequences. My discussion sees individual constitutional provisions as embodying certain basic purposes, often expressed in highly general terms. It sees the Constitution itself as a single document designed to further certain basic general purposes as a whole. It argues that an understanding of, and a focus upon, those general purposes will help a judge better to understand and to apply specific provisions. And it identifies consequences as an important yardstick to measure a given interpretation's faithfulness to these democratic purposes. In short, focus on purpose seeks to promote active liberty by insisting on interpretations, statutory as well as constitutional, that are consistent with the people's will. Focus on consequences, in turn, allows us to gauge whether and to what extent we have succeeded in facilitating workable outcomes which reflect that will.

Some lawyers, judges, and scholars, however, would caution strongly against the reliance upon purposes (particularly abstractly stated purposes) and assessment of consequences. They ask judges to focus primarily upon text, upon the Framers' original expectations, narrowly conceived, and upon historical tradition. They do not deny the occasional relevance of consequences or purposes (including such general purposes as democracy), but they believe that judges should use them sparingly in the interpretive endeavor. They ask judges who tend to find interpretive answers in those decision-making elements to rethink the problem to see whether language, history, tradition, and precedent by themselves will not yield an answer. They fear that, once judges become accustomed to justifying legal conclusions through appeal to real-world consequences, they will too often act subjectively and undemocratically, substituting an elite's views of good policy for sound law. They hope that language, history, tradition, and precedent will provide important safeguards against a judge's confusing his or her personal, undemocratic notion of what is good for that which the Constitution or statute demands. They tend also to emphasize the need for judicial opinions that set forth their legal conclusions in terms of rules that will guide other institutions, including lower courts.[11]

This view, which I shall call "textualist" (in respect to statutes) or "originalist" (in respect to the Constitution) or "literalist" (shorthand for both), while logically consistent with emphasizing the Constitution's democratic objectives, is not hospitable to the kinds of arguments I have advanced. Nor is it easily reconciled with my illustrations. Why, then, does it not undercut my entire argument?

The answer, in my view, lies in the unsatisfactory nature of that interpretive approach. First, the more "originalist" judges cannot appeal to the Framers themselves in support of their interpretive views. The Framers did not say specifically what factors judges should take into account when they interpret statutes or the Constitution. This is obvious in the case of statutes. Why would the Framers have preferred (1) a system of interpretation that relies heavily on linguistic canons to (2) a system that seeks more directly to find the intent of the legislators who enacted the statute? It is close to obvious in respect to the Constitution. Why would the Framers, who disagreed even about the necessity of *including* a Bill of Rights in the Constitution, who disagreed about the *content* of that Bill of Rights, nonetheless have agreed about *what school of interpretive thought* should prove dominant in interpreting that Bill of Rights in the centuries to come?[12]

In respect to content, the Constitution itself says that the "enumeration" in the Constitution of some rights "shall not be construed to deny or disparage others retained by the people." Professor Bailyn concludes that the Framers added this language to make clear that "rights, like law itself, should never be fixed, frozen, that new dangers and needs will emerge, and that to respond to these dangers and needs, rights must be newly specified to protect the individual's integrity and inherent dignity." Given the open-ended nature of *content*, why should one expect to find fixed views about the nature of interpretive practices?[13]

---

[11]See, e.g., Antonin Scalia, *A Matter of Interpretation: Federal Courts and the Law* (1997).

[12]Jack N. Rakove, *Original Meanings: Politics and Ideas in the Making of the Constitution* 339–65 (1996).

[13]U.S. Const. amend. IX; Bernard Bailyn, *The Living Past—Commitments for the Future,* Remarks at the First Millennium Evening at the White House (Feb. 11, 1998), http://clinton4.nara.gov/Initiatives/Millennium/bbailyn.html.

If, however, justification for the literalist's interpretive practices cannot be found in the Framers' intentions, where can it be found—other than in an appeal to *consequences*, that is, in an appeal to the presumed beneficial consequences for the law or for the nation that will flow from adopting those practices? And that is just what we find argued. That is to say, literalist arguments often try to show that that approach will have favorable *results*, for example, that it will deter judges from substituting their own views about what is good for the public for those of Congress or for those embodied in the Constitution. They argue, in other words, that a more literal approach to interpretation will better control judicial subjectivity. Thus, while literalists eschew consideration of consequences case by case, their interpretive rationale is consequentialist in this important sense.

Second, I would ask whether it is true that judges who reject literalism necessarily open the door to subjectivity. They do not endorse subjectivity. And under their approach important safeguards of objectivity remain. For one thing, a judge who emphasizes consequences, no less than any other, is aware of the legal precedents, rules, standards, practices, and institutional understanding that a decision will affect. He or she also takes account of the way in which this system of legally related rules, institutions, and practices affects the world.

To be sure, a court focused on consequences may decide a case in a way that radically changes the law. But this is not always a bad thing. For example, after the late-nineteenth-century Court decided *Plessy v. Ferguson*, the case which permitted racial segregation that was, in principle, "separate but equal," it became apparent that segregation did not mean equality but meant disrespect for members of a minority race and led to a segregated society that was totally unequal, a consequence directly contrary to the purpose and demands of the Fourteenth Amendment. The Court, in *Brown v. Board of Education* and later decisions, overruled *Plessy*, and the law changed in a way that profoundly affected the lives of many.[14]

In any event, to focus upon consequences does not automatically invite frequent dramatic legal change. Judges, including those who look to consequences, understand the human need to plan in reliance upon law, the need for predictability, the need for stability. And they understand that too radical, too frequent legal change has, as a consequence, a tendency to undercut those important law-related human needs. Similarly, each judge's individual need to be consistent over time constrains subjectivity. As Justice O'Connor has explained, a constitutional judge's initial decisions leave "footprints" that the judge, in later decisions, will almost inevitably follow.[15]

---

[14]See *Plessy*, 163 U.S. 537 (1896); see *Brown*, 347 U.S. 483 (1954).

[15]See Stephen Breyer, *Judicial Review: A Practicing Judge's Perspective*, 78 Tex. L. Rev. 761, 769 (2000) (referring to Justice O'Connor's analogy).

Moreover, to consider consequences is not to consider simply whether the consequences of a proposed decision are good or bad, in a particular judge's opinion. Rather, to emphasize consequences is to emphasize consequences related to the particular textual provision at issue. The judge must examine the consequences through the lens of the relevant constitutional value or purpose. The relevant values limit interpretive possibilities. If they are democratic values, they may well counsel modesty or restraint as well. And I believe that when a judge candidly acknowledges that, in addition to text, history, and precedent, consequences also guide his decision-making, he is more likely to be disciplined in emphasizing, for example, constitutionally relevant consequences rather than allowing his own subjectively held values to be outcome determinative. In all these ways, a focus on consequences will itself constrain subjectivity. . . .

Third, "subjectivity" is a two-edged criticism, which the literalist himself cannot escape. The literalist's tools—language and structure, history and tradition—often fail to provide objective guidance in those truly difficult cases about which I have spoken. Will canons of interpretation provide objective answers? One canon tells the court to choose an interpretation that gives every statutory word a meaning. Another permits the court to ignore a word, treating it as surplus, if otherwise the construction is repugnant to the statute's purpose. Shall the court read the statute narrowly as in keeping with the common law or broadly as remedial in purpose? Canons to the left of them, canons to the right of them, which canons shall the judges choose to follow?[16] . . .

Fourth, I do not believe that textualist or originalist methods of interpretation are more likely to produce clear, workable legal rules. But even were they to do so, the advantages of legal rules can be overstated. Rules must be interpreted and applied. Every law student whose class grade is borderline knows that the benefits that rules produce for cases that fall within the heartland are often lost in cases that arise at the boundaries. . . .

Fifth, textualist and originalist doctrines may themselves produce seriously harmful consequences—outweighing whatever risks of subjectivity or uncertainty are inherent in other approaches. I have deliberately chosen examples to illustrate that harm. In respect to statutory interpretation, a canon-based approach meant more complex jurisdictional law that closed the federal courthouse doors to certain foreign state-owned enterprises, thereby increasing foreign relations friction, just what Congress enacted the statute (the Foreign Sovereign Immunities Act) to avoid. Emphasizing a statute's literal language meant a habeas corpus law that randomly closes the doors of federal courts to a set of state prisoners. . . .

---

[16]See Karl N. Llewellyn, *The Common Law Tradition: Deciding Appeals* 525 (1960); William N. Eskridge Jr. and Phillip P. Frickey, *Cases and Materials on Legislation: Statutes and the Creation of Public Policy* 652–53 (2d ed. 1995) (noting tension between these canons).

Much of the harm at stake is a constitutional harm. Literalism has a tendency to undermine the Constitution's efforts to create a framework for democratic government—a government that, while protecting basic individual liberties, permits citizens to govern themselves, and to govern themselves effectively. Insofar as a more literal interpretive approach undermines this basic objective, it is inconsistent with the most fundamental original intention of the Framers themselves.

For any or all of these reasons, I hope that those strongly committed to textualist or literalist views—those whom I am almost bound not to convince—are fairly small in number. I hope to have convinced some of the rest that active liberty has an important role to play in constitutional (and statutory) interpretation.

That role, I repeat, does not involve radical change in current professional interpretive methods nor does it involve ignoring the protection the Constitution grants fundamental (negative) liberties. It takes Thomas Jefferson's statement as a statement of goals that the Constitution now seeks to fulfill: "[A]ll men are created equal." They are endowed by their Creator with certain "unalienable Rights." "[T]o secure these Rights, Governments are instituted among Men, *deriving their just powers from the consent of the governed.*" It underscores, emphasizes, or reemphasizes the final democratic part of the famous phrase. That reemphasis, I believe, has practical value when judges seek to assure fidelity, in our modern society, to these ancient and unchanging ideals.[17]

To reemphasize the constitutional importance of democratic self-government carries with it an additional practical benefit. We are all aware of figures that show that the public knows ever less about, and is ever less interested in, the processes of government. Foundation reports criticize the lack of high school civics education. A credible national survey reveals that more students know the names of the Three Stooges than the three branches of government. Law school graduates are ever less inclined to work for government—with the percentage of those entering government work (or nongovernment public interest work) declining at one major law school from 12 percent to 3 percent over the course of a generation. Polling figures suggest that during that same time, the percentage of the public trusting the government has declined at a similar rate.[18]

This trend, however, is not irreversible. Indeed, trust in government, and interest in public service, showed a remarkable rebound in response to the

---

[17]Declaration of Independence (emphasis added).

[18]See, e.g., Nat'l Ctr. for Educ. Statistics, U.S. Dep't. of Educ., *The NAEP 1998 Civics Report Card* (1999); Nat'l Constitution Center Survey (1998), at http://www.constitutioncenter.org/ CitizenAction/CivicResearchResults/NCCTeens'Poll.shtml; Lydia Saad, *Americans' Faith in Government Shaken but Not Shattered by Watergate*, at http://www.gallup.com/poll/releases/ pr970619.asp (June 19, 1997) (subscriber content).

terrorist attacks of September 11, 2001. Courts alone cannot maintain the rebound. Indeed, judges cannot easily advocate the virtues of democracy. But they need not do so. Americans already accept as theirs those democratic virtues and objectives to which Tocqueville once pointed: not spiritual "loftiness," a "contempt for material goods," elevated "manners," "poetry, renown, glory," the "most glory possible," but "reason," "peaceful habits," "well being," a "prosperous society" whose "energy . . . can bring forth marvels."[19]

Still, courts, as highly trusted government institutions, might help in various ways. Judges can explain in terms the public can understand just what the Constitution is about. They can make clear, above all, that the Constitution is not a document designed to solve the problems of a community at any level—local, state, or national. Rather it is a document that trusts people to solve those problems themselves. And it creates a *framework* for a government that will help them do so. That framework foresees democratically determined solutions, protective of the individual's basic liberties. It assures each individual that the law will treat him or her with equal respect. It seeks a form of democratic government that will prove workable over time.[20]

This is the democratic ideal. It is as relevant today as it was two hundred or two thousand years ago. More than two thousand years ago, Thucydides quoted Pericles as telling his fellow Athenians: "We do not say that the man who fails to participate in politics is a man who minds his own business. We say that he is a man who has no business here." Related ideals, the sharing of political authority, a free people delegating that authority to a democratically elected government, participation by those people in that democratic process, moved the Framers. And they wrote a Constitution that embodied these ideals. We judges cannot insist that Americans participate in that government. But we can make clear that our Constitution depends upon it. Their participation is necessary. It is a critical part of that "positive passion for the public good" that John Adams, like so many others, believed was a necessary condition for any "real Liberty" and for the "Republican Government" that the Constitution creates.[21]

---

[19]See, e.g., Council for Excellence in Government, *A Matter of Trust: Americans and Their Government: 1958–2004*, at 4–5 (2004); Center for Information and Research in Civic Learning & Engagement, *Short Term Impacts, Long Term Opportunities*, 4 (2002); Alexis de Tocqueville, *Democracy in America*, 234–35 (Harvey C. Mansfield and Delba Winthrop trans., University of Chicago 2000) (1835).

[20]See Saad, *supra* note 1 (explaining that, in 1997, public trust in Judicial Branch exceeded trust in Executive and Legislative Branches).

[21]Thucydides, *The Peloponnesian War* 108–15 (Thomas Hobbes trans., Univ. of Chi. Press 1989) (1629) (quoting "The Funeral Oration of Pericles"); letter from John Adams to Mercy Otis Warren (Apr. 16, 1776) reprinted in 1 *The Founder's Constitution*, 670 (Philip B. Kurland and Ralph Lerner eds., 1987).

CHAPTER 13

Civil Liberties and Civil Rights

The Framers drafted the Constitution to protect people's natural rights—namely, life, liberty, and property (or "the pursuit of happiness," as written in the Declaration of Independence). The political system exists to guarantee these rights, but it does not confer them—they exist prior to and independently of the government. These freedoms, explicitly identified in the Bill of Rights, are known as *civil liberties,* or freedoms from government or public coercion; political philosopher Isaiah Berlin famously referred to them as "negative liberty." They include freedom of speech, freedom of press, freedom of assembly, freedom of religion, freedom from unreasonable searches and seizures, and other protections against unauthorized or unduly burdensome government action.

At the same time, the government exists not only to refrain from interfering with people's freedoms but also to act on behalf of certain rights for people. These are known as *civil rights,* or "positive liberty" according to Berlin. Civil rights include the rights of citizens to vote, to receive equal treatment before the law, and to share equally with other citizens the benefits of public facilities such as schools. The United States has gradually expanded people's civil rights in the past two hundred years. They now include the right to education regardless of race, the right to participate equally in educational sports teams regardless of sex, and the right to an attorney in a criminal trial regardless of ability to pay. While certain civil rights, such as the right to counsel, are enshrined in the Constitution, their implementation has developed more recently. For example, the Supreme Court ruled in 1963 that the Constitution guarantees all criminal defendants an attorney, and that the public sector must provide one if a defendant lacks the means to hire a lawyer. Civil rights expanded greatly during the 1960s and 1970s for racial and ethnic minorities as well as for women, and more recently they have begun to include people with physical and mental disabilities and of diverse sexual orientations.

Civil rights and civil liberties, or positive and negative liberty, respectively, are often lumped together as a single subject. That is fair (and we have obviously done so in this chapter) because they both concern people's basic freedoms. The difference between civil rights and civil liberties, however, is perhaps best understood by reflecting on what organizations primarily dedicated to the one or the other typically want government to do.

To oversimplify just a bit, an organization such as the American Civil Liberties Union (ACLU), a civil liberties advocacy organization, normally wants the government to do *nothing,* or at least to stop doing something that it believes violates people's civil liberties. For instance, it wants the government not to prohibit a controversial group from marching through a community where most people despise the group; it wants police officers to stop using minor traffic violations to pull over and search cars for drugs; and so forth.

In contrast, the National Association for the Advancement of Colored People (NAACP), a civil rights organization, normally wants the government to do *something,* or at least act to keep private individuals or organizations from acting in ways that violate people's civil rights. For example, it wants government to protect and enforce the right of African American and other minority students to attend public schools and to equalize school funding; it wants to stop local merchants from refusing to serve or hire people based on race; and so forth.

Again, at the risk of oversimplifying, we can say that civil liberties are normally at risk when government is active and "on the march," whereas civil rights are normally at risk when government is inactive or "asleep at the wheel."

All three branches of government play a vital role in protecting both civil liberties and civil rights. Congress and the president are responsible for passing such legislation as the Civil Rights Act of 1964, which, among other protections, mandates equality in education for all Americans regardless of race, and the Americans with Disabilities Act of 1990, which ensures equal access and protection in school, the workplace, and public offices for people with physical and mental disabilities. The executive branch is responsible for implementing laws; in the 1960s, for example, the Justice Department began to take control of school districts that resisted desegregation, until they demonstrated compliance with civil rights laws. The judicial branch is responsible for interpreting the Constitution and subsequent laws, to evaluate their constitutionality and define the degree of implementation. The Supreme Court, for instance, has ruled that mandatory school prayer is unconstitutional, but a voluntary moment of silence may be permissible.

Advances in civil liberties and civil rights can take time, and they do not always progress linearly. After the Civil War, Congress and the states quickly passed the Thirteenth, Fourteenth, and Fifteenth Amendments, which, respectively, outlawed slavery, guaranteed "due process of law" and "equal protection of the laws," and affirmed the right to vote regardless of "race, color, or previous condition of servitude." But states continued to violate these rights well into the next century, using measures such as poll taxes or literacy tests to deny black Americans the right to vote. Not until the 1960s did the federal government actively enforce the Reconstruction-era amendments, and action then was spurred by court cases as well as public protests.

In protecting and expanding civil liberties and civil rights, the courts must be especially attuned to public opinion and the views of public officials. Even though federal judges are appointed, not elected, their decisions ultimately will be implemented by the other branches of government, who must be responsive to their constituencies. As Alexander Hamilton aptly notes in the Federalist No. 78 (reading 12.1), the courts have no tools for enforcing judicial decisions; if Congress or the president refuses to follow those decisions, then the weakness of the judiciary will be exposed. Consequently, when the

Supreme Court ruled in 1955 that school desegregation must take place "with all deliberate speed," it implicitly recognized that southern states would not be proactive, and therefore it did not issue a ruling that could be clearly violated. In fact, states did not actively pursue school desegregation for another decade.

Similarly, in foreign policy, the federal courts have resisted taking a stand on the War Powers Resolution of 1973, which seeks to elevate Congress's role in sending U.S. troops abroad. In 1991, for example, Representative Ron Dellums (D-CA) filed suit in federal district court against the Bush administration for planning for war in Iraq without congressional approval. The court ruled that the conflict was a "political question," and thus not ripe for judicial review. In so doing, the court sidestepped a contentious political debate in which a ruling that sought to restrict executive power might well have been ignored.

The excerpts from five court cases in this chapter represent only some of the myriad debates about civil liberties and civil rights that the judiciary has addressed in recent years. In civil liberties, the chapter focuses on the controversial topics of free speech and school prayer. In the twentieth century, the Supreme Court gradually expanded protection of free speech, placing the burden of proof on the government to demonstrate why speech would be so harmful as to merit censorship. With school prayer, the court has been divided, rejecting outright mandatory prayer, but expressing more uncertainty about voluntary religious expression.

In civil rights, the court cases examined here include classic rulings on school desegregation and the right to counsel, as well as a recent decision about the hotly contested subject of affirmative action. In 1954, the Supreme Court famously declared that "separate but equal is inherently unequal" in education, a position that is widely accepted today but sparked fiery debates across the country at the time. The right to counsel is similarly taken for granted today in criminal cases, but until 1963, exercising that right was contingent on a defendant's ability to hire a lawyer. The Supreme Court has been more divided about affirmative action programs—ones that provide special opportunities (described as "preferential treatment" by critics) for racial and ethnic minorities or women—since its 5–4 ruling in 1978 that overturned such a program without rejecting the concept of affirmative action. More recently, the Supreme Court again issued two narrowly decided rulings on affirmative action, thus illustrating that its constitutionality has yet to be settled.

The cases presented here raise significant questions about the meaning of the Constitution today in the fundamental area of individual freedoms and rights. Changes in judicial thinking over the years show that these protections are not definitively established and must be guarded vigilantly.

13.1   *Brandenburg v. Ohio* (1969)

INTRODUCTION

The First Amendment explicitly states that "Congress shall make no law . . . abridging the freedom of speech," but the meaning of "speech" is subject to wide interpretation. The courts have held, for example, that *symbolic speech* is constitutionally protected; therefore, statutes prohibiting flag burning or cross burning have been overturned. During the Vietnam War, the Supreme Court held that students may wear armbands to school to express their political views, but the courts more recently have been divided about the constitutionality of school speech codes. For the most part, speech that is deemed hurtful or hateful nevertheless falls within constitutional guidelines.

Speech that can be restricted more readily typically brings some threat of harm, and censorship of such speech tends to increase in times of national crisis. During World War I, for example, Charles Schenck was arrested for violating the Espionage Act of 1917 by printing and distributing circulars opposing the draft. Schenck filed suit, claiming that the Espionage Act violated his First Amendment rights. The Supreme Court ruled against Schenck, establishing a "clear and present danger" test for restricting speech, which it held that the Espionage Act met. Justice Oliver Wendell Holmes wrote that "the question in every case is whether the words used are used in such circumstances and are of such a nature as to create a clear and present danger that they will bring about the substantive evils that Congress has a right to prevent. It is a question of proximity and degree." Holmes noted that free speech did not mean the right to shout falsely "Fire!" in a crowded theater and create pandemonium, or to make similar utterances that would result in widespread grave injury.

The "clear and present danger" test, however, gave the government broad discretion in restricting speech, and the Supreme Court soon began to chip away at its boundaries. In 1969, the court overturned the test in *Brandenburg v. Ohio.* Charles Brandenburg, a Ku Klux Klan leader, was arrested for making threats during an Ohio rally. The court ruled that Ohio's Criminal Syndicalism Act—which prohibited violence as a means of pursuing political reform—was unconstitutional because it restricted speech that advocated action with no clear timetable. As the opinion stated, "The constitutional guarantees of free speech and free press do not permit a State to forbid or proscribe advocacy of the use of force or of law violation except where such advocacy is directed to inciting or producing imminent lawless action and is likely to incite or pro-

Brandenburg v. Ohio, 395 U.S. 444 (1969), as reproduced on Westlaw (http://web2.westlaw.com).

duce such action." The new standard of "imminent lawless action" raised the threshold greatly for the government to prohibit or punish speech, however repugnant it might be.

■

Per Curiam.

The appellant, a leader of a Ku Klux Klan group, was convicted under the Ohio Criminal Syndicalism statute for "advocat(ing) . . . the duty, necessity, or propriety of crime, sabotage, violence, or unlawful methods of terrorism as a means of accomplishing industrial or political reform" and for "voluntarily assembl(ing) with any society, group, or assemblage of persons formed to teach or advocate the doctrines of criminal syndicalism." He was fined $1,000 and sentenced to one to 10 years' imprisonment. The appellant challenged the constitutionality of the criminal syndicalism statute under the First and Fourteenth Amendments to the United States Constitution, but the intermediate appellate court of Ohio affirmed his conviction without opinion. The Supreme Court of Ohio dismissed his appeal, sua sponte, "for the reason that no substantial constitutional question exists herein." It did not file an opinion or explain its conclusions. Appeal was taken to this Court, and we noted probable jurisdiction. We reverse.

The record shows that a man, identified at trial as the appellant, telephoned an announcer-reporter on the staff of a Cincinnati television station and invited him to come to a Ku Klux Klan "rally" to be held at a farm in Hamilton County. With the cooperation of the organizers, the reporter and a cameraman attended the meeting and filmed the events. Portions of the films were later broadcast on the local station and on a national network.

The prosecution's case rested on the films and on testimony identifying the appellant as the person who communicated with the reporter and who spoke at the rally. The State also introduced into evidence several articles appearing in the film, including a pistol, a rifle, a shotgun, ammunition, a Bible, and a red hood worn by the speaker in the films.

One film showed 12 hooded figures, some of whom carried firearms. They were gathered around a large wooden cross, which they burned. No one was present other than the participants and the newsmen who made the film. Most of the words uttered during the scene were incomprehensible when the film was projected, but scattered phrases could be understood that were derogatory of Negroes and, in one instance, of Jews. . . .

The Ohio Criminal Syndicalism Statute was enacted in 1919. From 1917 to 1920, identical or quite similar laws were adopted by 20 States and two territories. In 1927, this Court sustained the constitutionality of California's Criminal Syndicalism Act, the text of which is quite similar to that of the laws of Ohio. The Court upheld the statute on the ground that, without more, "advocating" violent means to effect political and economic change involves such danger to the security of the State that the State may outlaw it.[1] But [the 1927 case *Whitney v. California*] has been thoroughly discredited by later decisions. These later decisions have fashioned the principle that the constitutional guarantees of free speech and free press do not permit a State to forbid or proscribe advocacy of the use of force or of law violation except where such advocacy is directed to inciting or producing imminent lawless action and is likely to incite or produce such action. As we [have] said, "the mere abstract teaching . . . of the moral propriety or even moral necessity for a resort to force and violence, is not the same as preparing a group for violent action and steeling it to such action."[2] A statute which fails to draw this distinction impermissibly intrudes upon the freedoms guaranteed by the First and Fourteenth Amendments. It sweeps within its condemnation speech which our Constitution has immunized from governmental control.

Measured by this test, Ohio's Criminal Syndicalism Act cannot be sustained. The Act punishes persons who "advocate or teach the duty, necessity, or propriety" of violence "as a means of accomplishing industrial or political reform"; or who publish or circulate or display any book or paper containing such advocacy; or who "justify" the commission of violent acts "with intent to exemplify, spread or advocate the propriety of the doctrines of criminal syndicalism"; or who "voluntarily assemble" with a group formed "to teach or advocate the doctrines of criminal syndicalism." Neither the indictment nor the trial judge's instructions to the jury in any way refined the statute's bald definition of the crime in terms of mere advocacy not distinguished from incitement to imminent lawless action.

Accordingly, we are here confronted with a statute which, by its own words and as applied, purports to punish mere advocacy and to forbid, on pain of criminal punishment, assembly with others merely to advocate the described type of action. Such a statute falls within the condemnation of the First and Fourteenth Amendments. The contrary teaching of *Whitney v. California* cannot be supported, and that decision is therefore overruled.

---

[1]*Whitney v. California* (1927).
[2]*Noto v. United States* (1961).

13.2   *Santa Fe Independent School District v. Doe* (2000)

INTRODUCTION

The Constitution provides for separation of church and state, but it does not insist on the complete absence of religion from public life. The First Amendment states that "Congress shall make no law respecting an establishment of religion, or prohibiting the free exercise thereof." The first clause prohibits an official national religion; it was drafted to ensure that the United States would not create the equivalent of the Church of England. At the same time, the second clause guarantees that the government will not interfere in people's religious practices. The Framers wanted to prevent mandatory worship, but they also believed in the right to worship freely. Thus, each session of Congress opens with a prayer, U.S. currency contains the phrase "In God We Trust," and a religious invocation is an accepted part of presidential inaugurations.

In balancing religious freedom with constitutional rights, the courts typically have sought to uphold the latter without establishing a wall of separation between church and state. But every effort to maintain this balance raises thorny questions that the courts have not resolved definitively. For example, public schools used to begin the school day with prayer and sometimes even biblical readings. Specific customs varied from state to state, and even district to district, but school prayer was widely accepted. In 1962, however, the Supreme Court ruled in *Engel v. Vitale* that a nondenominational prayer drafted by the New York Board of Regents could not be required in schools because it amounted to state-sponsored religion.

A decade later, the court established a three-pronged test for determining whether public funds could be used to supply textbooks and other resources for secular subjects taught in parochial schools. The activity in question would require a "secular legislative purpose"; its primary effects could neither "advance nor inhibit religion"; and it could not permit "excessive government entanglement with religion." Putting this test into practice, of course, has been quite complicated, raising questions about whether parochial school students may use public buses, whether voluntary prayer groups may meet after school on public school property, and many other issues.

The Supreme Court revisited the school prayer debate in 2000, when it reviewed a petition by the Santa Fe High School in Texas to permit student-led prayer before home varsity football games. Students had initiated the practice of electing a student chaplain to deliver a prayer over the public address

Santa Fe Independent School District v. Doe, 530 U.S. 290 (2000), as reproduced on Westlaw (http://web2.westlaw.com).

system. When some students, alumni, and parents filed suit, stating that the prayer constituted an "establishment of religion," the high school conducted an election in which students voted to continue the pre-game prayer. In a 6–3 ruling, the court ruled against the school, finding that even prayer initiated and conducted by students violates the Establishment Clause of the First Amendment. The following excerpt summarizes the court's finding that the prayer ultimately was neither private nor voluntary.

■

Justice Stevens delivered the opinion of the Court.

Prior to 1995, the Santa Fe High School student who occupied the school's elective office of student council chaplain delivered a prayer over the public address system before each varsity football game for the entire season. This practice, along with others, was challenged in District Court as a violation of the Establishment Clause of the First Amendment. While these proceedings were pending in the District Court, the school district adopted a different policy that permits, but does not require, prayer initiated and led by a student at all home games. The District Court entered an order modifying that policy to permit only nonsectarian, nonproselytizing prayer. The Court of Appeals held that, even as modified by the District Court, the football prayer policy was invalid. We granted the school district's petition for certiorari to review that holding.

The Santa Fe Independent School District (District) is a political subdivision of the State of Texas, responsible for the education of more than 4,000 students in a small community in the southern part of the State. The District includes the Santa Fe High School, two primary schools, an intermediate school and the junior high school. Respondents are two sets of current or former students and their respective mothers. One family is Mormon and the other is Catholic. The District Court permitted respondents (Does) to litigate anonymously to protect them from intimidation or harassment.

Respondents commenced this action in April 1995 and moved for a temporary restraining order to prevent the District from violating the Establishment Clause at the imminent graduation exercises. In their complaint the Does alleged that the District had engaged in several proselytizing practices, such as promoting attendance at a Baptist revival meeting, encouraging membership in religious clubs, chastising children who held minority religious beliefs, and distributing Gideon Bibles on school premises. They also alleged that the District allowed students to read Christian invocations and benedictions from the stage at graduation ceremonies, and to deliver overtly Christian prayers over the public address system at home football games.

On May 10, 1995, the District Court entered an interim order addressing a number of different issues. With respect to the impending graduation, the order provided that "nondenominational prayer" consisting of "an invocation and/or benediction" could be presented by a senior student or students selected by members of the graduating class. The text of the prayer was to be determined by the students, without scrutiny or preapproval by school officials. References to particular religious figures "such as Mohammed, Jesus, Buddha, or the like" would be permitted "as long as the general thrust of the prayer is non-proselytizing."

In response to that portion of the order, the District adopted a series of policies over several months dealing with prayer at school functions. The policies enacted in May and July for graduation ceremonies provided the format for the August and October policies for football games. . . .

In July, the District enacted another policy eliminating the requirement that invocations and benedictions be "nonsectarian and nonproselytising," but also providing that if the District were to be enjoined from enforcing that policy, the May policy would automatically become effective. The August policy, which was titled "Prayer at Football Games," was similar to the July policy for graduations. It also authorized two student elections, the first to determine whether "invocations" should be delivered, and the second to select the spokesperson to deliver them. Like the July policy, it contained two parts, an initial statement that omitted any requirement that the content of the invocation be "nonsectarian and nonproselytising," and a fallback provision that automatically added that limitation if the preferred policy should be enjoined. On August 31, 1995, according to the parties' stipulation: "[T]he district's high school students voted to determine whether a student would deliver prayer at varsity football games. . . . The students chose to allow a student to say a prayer at football games." A week later, in a separate election, they selected a student "to deliver the prayer at varsity football games."

The final policy (October policy) is essentially the same as the August policy, though it omits the word "prayer" from its title, and refers to "messages" and "statements" as well as "invocations." It is the validity of that policy that is before us. . . .

We granted the District's petition for certiorari, limited to the following question: "Whether petitioner's policy permitting student-led, student-initiated prayer at football games violates the Establishment Clause." We conclude, as did the Court of Appeals, that it does. . . .

This case comes to us as the latest step in developing litigation brought as a challenge to institutional practices that unquestionably violated the Establishment Clause. One of those practices was the District's long-established tradition of sanctioning student-led prayer at varsity football games. The narrow question before us is whether implementation of the October policy insulates the continuation of such prayers from constitutional scrutiny. It does not. Our inquiry into this question not only can, but must, include an examination of the circumstances surrounding its enactment. . . . [I]n this case the District's direct involvement with school prayer exceeds constitutional limits.

The District, nevertheless, asks us to pretend that we do not recognize what every Santa Fe High School student understands clearly—that this policy is about prayer. The District further asks us to accept what is obviously untrue: that these messages are necessary to "solemnize" a football game and that this single-student, year-long position is essential to the protection of student speech. We refuse to turn a blind eye to the context in which this policy arose, and that context quells any doubt that this policy was implemented with the purpose of endorsing school prayer.

Therefore, the simple enactment of this policy, with the purpose and perception of school endorsement of student prayer, was a constitutional violation. We need not wait for the inevitable to confirm and magnify the constitutional injury. . . .

This policy likewise does not survive a facial challenge because it impermissibly imposes upon the student body a majoritarian election on the issue of prayer. Through its election scheme, the District has established a governmental electoral mechanism that turns the school into a forum for religious debate. It further empowers the student body majority with the authority to subject students of minority views to constitutionally improper messages. The award of that power alone, regardless of the students' ultimate use of it, is not acceptable. . . . [T]he election mechanism established by the District undermines the essential protection of minority viewpoints. Such a system encourages divisiveness along religious lines and threatens the imposition of coercion upon those students not desiring to participate in a religious exercise. Simply by establishing this school-related procedure, which entrusts the inherently nongovernmental subject of religion to a majoritarian vote, a constitutional violation has occurred. No further injury is required for the policy to fail a facial challenge.

. . . Our examination of those circumstances above leads to the conclusion that this policy does not provide the District with the constitutional safe harbor it sought. The policy is invalid on its face because it establishes an improper majoritarian election on religion, and unquestionably has the purpose and creates the perception of encouraging the delivery of prayer at a series of important school events.

The judgment of the Court of Appeals is, accordingly, affirmed.

It is so ordered.

Chief Justice Rehnquist with whom Justice Scalia and Justice Thomas join, dissenting.

The Court distorts existing precedent to conclude that the school district's student-message program is invalid on its face under the Establishment Clause. But even more disturbing than its holding is the tone of the Court's opinion; it bristles with hostility to all things religious in public life. Neither the holding nor the tone of the opinion is faithful to the meaning of the Establishment Clause, when it is recalled that George Washington himself, at the request of the very Congress which passed the Bill of Rights, proclaimed a day of "public thanksgiving and prayer, to be observed by acknowledging with grateful hearts the many and signal favors of Almighty God." We do not learn until late in the Court's opinion that respondents in this case challenged the district's student-message program at football games before it had been put into practice. As the Court [has] explained, the fact that a policy might "operate unconstitutionally under some conceivable set of circumstances is insufficient to render it wholly invalid."[1] While there is an exception to this principle in the First Amendment overbreadth context because of our concern that people may refrain from speech out of fear of prosecution, there is no similar justification for Establishment Clause cases. No speech will be "chilled" by the existence of a government policy that might unconstitutionally endorse religion over nonreligion. Therefore, the question is not whether the district's policy *may* be applied in violation of the Establishment Clause, but whether it inevitably will be.

13.3   *Brown v. Board of Education* (1954)

INTRODUCTION

The 1960s marked great advances in civil rights, particularly with respect to racial equality. Debates about race dated back to the Constitutional Convention, where the Framers could not agree whether to permit slavery, and if so, whether any restrictions should be incorporated (such as the eventual decision to ban the importation of slaves after 1808). After the Civil War, the Thirteenth, Fourteenth, and Fifteenth Amendments (known as the Reconstruction-era amendments) guaranteed certain rights on paper, but in practice, states found many ways to work around those provisions. For example, although the Fifteenth Amendment states that the right to vote "shall not be denied or abridged . . . on account of race, color, or previous condition of servitude," states seeking to deny black Americans the right to vote instead used other reasons, such as a *poll tax* or *literacy test*. Of course, many poor white Americans could not afford a poll tax or pass a literacy test, so states sometimes instituted a *grandfather clause*, which declared that citizens whose grandparents had voted would be eligible to do so.

---

[1]*United States v. Salerno* (1987).

Brown v. Board of Education of Topeka, 347 U.S. 483 (1954), as reproduced on Westlaw (http://web2.westlaw.com).

In the nineteenth century, the Supreme Court decided that the Reconstruction-era amendments guaranteed only political rights, narrowly construed, not social equality. The court famously established the "separate but equal" doctrine in *Plessy v. Ferguson* (1896), which upheld a Louisiana law that required separate rail cars for blacks and whites. The court decided that the law did not violate the Fourteenth Amendment's "equal protection of the laws" clause because the separate rail cars theoretically would provide equal services. If people received the same treatment, the court reasoned, then they did not have to enjoy the same facilities. The ruling furthermore declared, "If one race be inferior to the other socially, the Constitution of the United States cannot put them on the same plane."

The *Plessy* decision served as the benchmark for decisions about racial equality for the next sixty years. Slowly, though, the Supreme Court began to chip away at the "separate but equal" doctrine by finding that separate facilities for law schools, medical programs, and other areas were not, in fact, equal. The doctrine was not reversed, however, until 1954, when the Supreme Court ruled in *Brown v. Board of Education* that "separate educational facilities are inherently unequal."

The Board of Education in Topeka, Kansas, had established segregated elementary schools, which required fourth grader Linda Brown to travel far from home to get to school, even though an all-white elementary school was much closer. The Brown family filed suit, claiming that their daughter was denied equal protection of the laws. A lawyer from the National Association for the Advancement of Colored People, Thurgood Marshall, who would later become the nation's first black Supreme Court justice, argued the Browns' case. In the following excerpt, the Supreme Court explains why "separate but equal" facilities ultimately can never be equal.

■

Mr. Chief Justice Warren delivered the opinion of the Court.

These cases come to us from the States of Kansas, South Carolina, Virginia, and Delaware. They are premised on different facts and different local conditions, but a common legal question justifies their consideration together in this consolidated opinion.

In each of the cases, minors of the Negro race, through their legal representatives, seek the aid of the courts in obtaining admission to the public schools of their community on a nonsegregated basis. In each instance, they have been denied admission to schools attended by white children under laws requiring or permitting segregation according to race. This segregation was alleged to deprive the plaintiffs of the equal protection of the laws under the Fourteenth Amendment. In each of the cases other than the Delaware case, a three-judge federal district court denied relief to the plaintiffs on the so-called "separate but equal" doctrine announced by this Court in *Plessy v. Ferguson.* Under that doctrine, equality of treatment is accorded when the races are provided substantially equal facilities, even though these facilities be separate. In the Delaware case, the Supreme Court of Delaware adhered to that doctrine, but ordered that the plaintiffs be admitted to the white schools because of their superiority to the Negro schools.

The plaintiffs contend that segregated public schools are not "equal" and cannot be made "equal," and that hence they are deprived of the equal protection of the laws. Because of the obvious importance of the question presented, the Court took jurisdiction. Argument was heard in the 1952 Term, and reargument was heard this Term on certain questions propounded by the Court.

Reargument was largely devoted to the circumstances surrounding the adoption of the Fourteenth Amendment in 1868. It covered exhaustively consideration of the Amendment in Congress, ratification by the states, then existing practices in racial segregation, and the views of proponents and opponents of the Amendment. This discussion and our own investigation convince us that, although these sources cast some light, it is not enough to resolve the problem with which we are faced. At best, they are inconclusive. The most avid proponents of the post-War Amendments undoubtedly intended them to remove all legal distinctions among "all persons born or naturalized in the United States." Their opponents, just as certainly, were antagonistic to both the letter and the spirit of the Amendments and wished them to have the most limited effect. What others in Congress and the state legislatures had in mind cannot be determined with any degree of certainty.

An additional reason for the inconclusive nature of the Amendment's history, with respect to segregated schools, is the status of public education at that time. In the South, the movement toward free common schools, supported by general taxation, had not yet taken hold. Education of white children was largely in the hands of private groups. Education of Negroes was almost nonexistent, and practically all of the race were illiterate. In fact, any education of Negroes was forbidden by law in some states. Today, in contrast, many Negroes have achieved outstanding success in the arts and sciences as well as in the business and professional world. It is true that public school education at the time of the Amendment had advanced further in the North, but the effect of the Amendment on Northern States was generally ignored in the congressional debates. Even in the North, the conditions of public education did not approximate those existing today. The curriculum was usually rudimentary; ungraded schools were common in rural areas; the school term was but three months a year in many states; and compulsory school attendance was virtually unknown. As a consequence, it is not surprising that there should be so little in the history of the Fourteenth Amendment relating to its intended effect on public education.

In the first cases in this Court construing the Fourteenth Amendment, decided shortly after its adoption, the Court interpreted it as proscribing all state-imposed discriminations against the Negro race. The doctrine of "separate but equal" did not make its appearance in this court until 1896 in the case of *Plessy v. Ferguson,* involving not education but transportation. American courts have since labored with the doctrine for over half a century. . . .

In approaching this problem, we cannot turn the clock back to 1868 when the Amendment was adopted, or even to 1896 when *Plessy v. Ferguson* was written. We must consider public education in the light of its full development and its present place in American life throughout the Nation. Only in this way can it be determined if segregation in public schools deprives these plaintiffs of the equal protection of the laws.

Today, education is perhaps the most important function of state and local governments. Compulsory school attendance laws and the great expenditures for education both demonstrate our recognition of the importance of education to our democratic society. It is required in the performance of our most basic public responsibilities, even service in the armed forces. It is the very foundation of good citizenship. Today it is a principal instrument in awakening the child to cultural values, in preparing him for later professional training, and in helping him to adjust normally to his environment. In these days, it is doubtful that any child may reasonably be expected to succeed in life if he is denied the opportunity of an education. Such an opportunity, where the state has undertaken to provide it, is a right which must be made available to all on equal terms.

We come then to the question presented: Does segregation of children in public schools solely on the basis of race, even though the physical facilities and other "tangible" factors may be equal, deprive the children of the minority group of equal educational opportunities? We believe that it does.

In *Sweatt v. Painter* [1950], in finding that a segregated law school for Negroes could not provide them equal educational opportunities, this Court relied in large part on "those qualities which are incapable of objective measurement but which make for greatness in a law school." In *McLaurin v. Oklahoma State Regents* [1950], the Court, in requiring that a Negro admitted to a white graduate school be treated like all other students, again resorted to intangible considerations: ". . . his ability to study, to engage in discussions and exchange views with other students, and, in general, to learn his profession." Such considerations apply with added force to children in grade and high schools. To separate them from others of similar age and qualifications solely because of their race generates a feeling of inferiority as to their status in the community that may affect their hearts and minds in a way unlikely ever to be undone. The effect of this separation on their educational opportunities was well stated by a finding in the Kansas case by a court which nevertheless felt compelled to rule against the Negro plaintiffs:

"Segregation of white and colored children in public schools has a detrimental effect upon the colored children. The impact is greater when it has the sanction of the law; for the policy of separating the races is usually interpreted as denoting the inferiority of the negro group. A sense of inferiority affects the motivation of a child to learn. Segregation with the sanction of law, therefore, has a tendency to (retard) the educational and mental development of Negro children and to deprive them of some of the benefits they would receive in a racial(ly) integrated school system."

Whatever may have been the extent of psychological knowledge at the time of *Plessy v. Ferguson,* this finding is amply supported by modern authority. Any language in *Plessy v. Ferguson* contrary to this finding is rejected.

We conclude that in the field of public education the doctrine of "separate but equal" has no place. Separate educational facilities are inherently unequal. Therefore, we hold that the plaintiffs and others similarly situated for whom the actions have been brought are, by reason of the segregation complained of, deprived of the equal protection of the laws guaranteed by the Fourteenth Amendment. This disposition makes unnecessary any discussion whether such segregation also violates the Due Process Clause of the Fourteenth Amendment.

Because these are class actions, because of the wide applicability of this decision, and because of the great variety of local conditions, the formulation of decrees in these cases presents problems of considerable complexity. On reargument, the consideration of appropriate relief was necessarily subordinated to the primary question—the constitutionality of segregation in public education. We have now announced that such segregation is a denial of the equal protection of the laws. In order that we may have the full assistance of the parties in formulating decrees, the cases will be restored to the docket, and the parties are requested to present further argument on Questions 4 and 5 previously propounded by the Court for the reargument this Term. The Attorney General of the United States is again invited to participate. The Attorneys General of the states requiring or permitting segregation in public education will also be permitted to appear as amici curiae upon request to do so by September 15, 1954, and submission of briefs by October 1, 1954.

13.4 *Gideon v. Wainwright* (1963)

INTRODUCTION

The Sixth Amendment states that "[i]n all criminal prosecutions, the accused shall enjoy the right . . . to have the Assistance of Counsel for his defence," but it does not specify who shall be responsible for providing counsel. In the nineteenth century, the courts left most decisions about criminal law and procedure up to individual states. Furthermore, the Supreme Court ruled in *Barron v. Baltimore* (1833) that the Bill of Rights applied only to the federal government, not to the states.

The ratification of the Fourteenth Amendment in 1868, however, opened new possibilities: "No State shall make or enforce any law which shall abridge the privileges or immunities of citizens of the United States; nor shall any State deprive any person of life, liberty, or property, without due process of law; nor deny to any person within its jurisdiction the equal protection of the laws." Over time, the Supreme Court began to interpret the Fourteenth Amendment to incorporate the Bill of Rights into rulings applicable to all states. In time, this *incorporation doctrine* was extended by the Supreme Court so that ever more of the language contained in the Bill of Rights applied to state and local governments, not just the Congress or the federal government.

In so doing, the Supreme Court acted first in the areas of free speech, free press, and freedom of religion. The court was more hesitant to intrude on state autonomy in criminal law; but in *Powell v. Alabama* (1932), it ruled that nine black men were denied due process when they were convicted of raping two white women and sentenced to death. The defendants' attorneys did not meet with their clients and did not provide any substantive representation at the three trials, which were decided in one day. Consequently, the Supreme Court overturned these convictions. In *Betts v. Brady* (1942), however, the Supreme Court decided by a 6–3 vote that a person charged with a noncapital crime, such as robbery, did not require counsel to mount an effective defense.

The Supreme Court overturned the *Betts* decision in 1963, when it decided that Clarence Earl Gideon was entitled to an attorney to defend him on charges of breaking into a Panama City poolroom with the intent to commit burglary. The Florida state courts had convicted Gideon and denied his request for counsel, which he lacked the funds to provide independently. Gideon appealed his case on the grounds that depriving him of a lawyer in a felony trial violated his due process rights under the Constitution. Justice Hugo L. Black, who had dissented in the *Betts* case, wrote the unanimous

Gideon v. Wainwright, 372 U.S. 335 (1963), as reproduced on Westlaw (http://web2.westlaw.com).

opinion overturning that decision. In the following excerpt from *Gideon v. Wainwright* (1963), Black explains the court's justification of a right that is taken for granted today—that the Sixth Amendment guarantee of counsel is so fundamental to a fair criminal trial that states must provide public defenders for people who cannot afford to hire their own attorney.

■

Mr. Justice Black delivered the opinion of the Court.

Petitioner was charged in a Florida state court with having broken and entered a poolroom with intent to commit a misdemeanor. This offense is a felony under Florida law. Appearing in court without funds and without a lawyer, petitioner asked the court to appoint counsel for him, whereupon the following colloquy took place:

"The COURT: Mr. Gideon, I am sorry, but I cannot appoint Counsel to represent you in this case. Under the laws of the State of Florida, the only time the Court can appoint Counsel to represent a Defendant is when that person is charged with a capital offense. I am sorry, but I will have to deny your request to appoint Counsel to defend you in this case."

"The DEFENDANT: The United States Supreme Court says I am entitled to be represented by Counsel."

Put to trial before a jury, Gideon conducted his defense about as well as could be expected from a layman. He made an opening statement to the jury, cross-examined the State's witnesses, presented witnesses in his own defense, declined to testify himself, and made a short argument "emphasizing his innocence to the charge contained in the Information filed in this case." The jury returned a verdict of guilty, and petitioner was sentenced to serve five years in the state prison. Later, petitioner filed in the Florida Supreme Court this habeas corpus petitioner attacking his conviction and sentence on the ground that the trial court's refusal to appoint counsel for him denied him rights "guaranteed by the Constitution and the Bill of Rights by the United States Government." Treating the petition for habeas corpus as properly before it, the State Supreme Court, "upon consideration thereof" but without an opinion, denied all relief. Since 1942, when *Betts v. Brady* was decided by a divided Court, the problem of a defendant's federal constitutional right to counsel in a state court has been a continuing source of controversy and litigation in both state and federal courts. To give this problem another review here, we granted certiorari. Since Gideon was proceeding in forma pauperis, we appointed counsel to represent him and requested both sides to discuss in their briefs and oral arguments the following: "Should this Court's holding in *Betts v. Brady* be reconsidered?"

The facts upon which Betts claimed that he had been unconstitutionally denied the right to have counsel appointed to assist him are strikingly like the facts upon which Gideon here bases his federal constitutional claim. Betts was indicted for robbery in a Maryland state court. On arraignment, he told the trial judge of his lack of funds to hire a lawyer and asked the court to appoint one for him. Betts was advised that it was not the practice in that county to appoint counsel for indigent defendants except in murder and rape cases. He then pleaded not guilty, had witnesses summoned, cross-examined the State's witnesses, examined his own, and chose not to testify himself. He was found guilty by the judge, sitting without a jury, and sentenced to eight years in prison. Like Gideon, Betts sought release by habeas corpus, alleging that he had been denied the right to assistance of counsel in violation of the Fourteenth Amendment. Betts was denied any relief, and on review this Court affirmed. It was held that a refusal to appoint counsel for an indigent defendant charged with a felony did not necessarily violate the Due Process Clause of the Fourteenth Amendment, which for reasons given the Court deemed to be the only applicable federal constitutional provision. The Court said:

"Asserted denial (of due process) is to be tested by an appraisal of the totality of facts in a given case. That which may, in one setting, constitute a denial of fundamental fairness, shocking to the universal sense of justice, may, in other circumstances, and in the light of other considerations, fall short of such denial."

Treating due process as "a concept less rigid and more fluid than those envisaged in other specific and particular provisions of the Bill of Rights," the Court held that refusal to appoint counsel under the particular facts and circumstances in the Betts case was not so "offensive to the common and fundamental ideas of fairness" as to amount to a denial of due process. Since the facts and circumstances of the two cases are so nearly indistinguishable, we think the *Betts v. Brady* holding if left standing would require us to reject Gideon's claim that the Constitution guarantees him the assistance of counsel. Upon full reconsideration we conclude that *Betts v. Brady* should be overruled. . . .

. . . The fact is that in deciding as it did—that "appointment of counsel is not a fundamental right, essential to a fair trial"—the Court in *Betts v. Brady* made an abrupt break with its own well-considered precedents. In returning to these old precedents, sounder we believe than the new, we but restore constitutional principles established to achieve a fair system of justice. Not only these precedents but also reason and reflection require us to recognize that in our adversary system of criminal justice, any person haled into court, who is too poor to hire a lawyer, cannot be assured a fair trial unless counsel is provided for him. This seems to us to be an obvious truth. Governments, both state and federal, quite properly spend vast sums of money to establish machinery to try defendants accused of crime. Lawyers to prosecute are everywhere deemed essential to protect the public's interest in an orderly society. Similarly, there are few defendants charged with crime, few indeed, who fail to hire the best lawyers they can get to prepare and present their defenses. That government hires lawyers to prosecute and defendants who have the money hire lawyers to defend are the strongest indications of the widespread belief that lawyers in criminal courts are necessities, not luxuries. The right of one charged with crime to counsel may not be deemed fundamental and essential to fair trials in some countries, but it is in ours. From the very beginning, our state and national constitutions and laws have laid great emphasis on procedural and substantive safeguards designed to assure fair trials before impartial tribunals in which every defendant stands equal before the law. This noble ideal cannot be realized if the poor man charged with crime has to face his accusers without a lawyer to assist him. A defendant's need for a lawyer is nowhere better stated than in the moving words of Mr. Justice Sutherland in *Powell v. Alabama* [1932]:

"The right to be heard would be, in many cases, of little avail if it did not comprehend the right to be heard by counsel. Even the intelligent and educated layman has small and sometimes no skill in the science of law. If charged with crime, he is incapable, generally, of determining for himself whether the indictment is good or bad. He is unfamiliar with the rules of evidence. Left without the aid of counsel he may be put on trial without a proper charge, and convicted upon incompetent evidence, or evidence irrelevant to the issue or otherwise inadmissible. He lacks both the skill and knowledge adequately to prepare his defense, even though he have a perfect one. He requires the guiding hand of counsel at every step in the proceedings against him. Without it, though he be not guilty, he faces the danger of conviction because he does not know how to establish his innocence."

The Court in *Betts v. Brady* departed from the sound wisdom upon which the Court's holding in *Powell v. Alabama* rested. Florida, supported by two other States, has asked that *Betts v. Brady* be left intact. Twenty-two States, as friends of the Court, argue that Betts was "an anachronism when handed down" and that it should now be overruled. We agree.

The judgment is reversed and the cause is remanded to the Supreme Court of Florida for further action not inconsistent with this opinion.

Reversed.

13.5   *Grutter v. Bollinger* (2003)

INTRODUCTION

The civil rights revolution of the 1960s established a principle of racial equality that is widely accepted today. The means for achieving that equality, however, continue to be hotly debated. The Civil Rights Act of 1964 fostered the

Grutter v. Bollinger, 539 U.S. 244 (2003), as reproduced on Westlaw (http://web2.westlaw.com).

creation of *affirmative action* programs, which guaranteed seats for black Americans in schools or jobs to overcome the effects of past discrimination. Advocates of affirmative action argued that it was necessary to help establish a level playing field for people who had been flatly denied the opportunity to enter these fields. Historical discrimination against blacks would disappear slowly, and mandatory entry programs were essential to facilitating that process. Successful applicants still would have to meet admissions criteria, but candidates would have different requirements depending on their race. Opponents of affirmative action argued that such programs amounted to reverse discrimination, in effect denying white Americans positions just as they had previously been denied to black Americans.

The Supreme Court's rulings on affirmative action have been as divided as public opinion. The court's famous 5–4 ruling in *Regents of the University of California v. Bakke* (1978) overturned an affirmative action program at the University of California Medical School at Davis, but it did not reject the concept of affirmative action entirely. Allan Bakke filed suit against the school after being rejected for admission twice and learning that the school had reserved sixteen slots for minorities, whose grades and test scores were lower than his own. Five justices held that the program violated the Civil Rights Act of 1964 because it created a racial quota system. At the same time, five justices (Justice Lewis F. Powell, Jr., joined both opinions) also ruled that the Constitution permitted affirmative action programs in higher education to reverse the effects of past discrimination. This case began a long and complicated process by the courts to determine the degree to which government, business, and education could, and should, employ affirmative action without denying equal protection of the laws to all Americans.

In 2003, the Supreme Court revisited affirmative action in higher education and decided that only programs "narrowly tailored" to achieve racial diversity are constitutionally permissible. Plaintiffs filed suit against the University of Michigan's undergraduate and law school programs after being denied admission despite having higher grades and test scores than minority students whose applications were accepted. The court decided by a 6–3 vote that the undergraduate affirmative action program was unconstitutional because it employed numerical rankings in evaluating candidates and automatically gave a fixed number of points to minority students because of their race. The court upheld the law school's program, however, because race was one of many criteria considered for admission, and did not serve as a basis for automatic acceptance or denial. Justice Sandra Day O'Connor cast the deciding vote in the 5–4 law school decision, and in the following excerpt, she explains why the goals of affirmative action remain constitutionally justifiable today.

■

Justice O'Connor delivered the opinion of the Court.

This case requires us to decide whether the use of race as a factor in student admissions by the University of Michigan Law School (Law School) is unlawful.

The Law School ranks among the Nation's top law schools. It receives more than 3,500 applications each year for a class of around 350 students. Seeking to "admit a group of students who individually and collectively are among the most capable," the Law School looks for individuals with "substantial promise for success in law school" and "a strong likelihood of succeeding in the practice of law and contributing in diverse ways to the well-being of others." More broadly, the Law School seeks "a mix of students with varying backgrounds and experiences who will respect and learn from each other." In 1992, the dean of the Law School charged a faculty committee with crafting a written admissions policy to implement these goals. In particular, the Law School sought to ensure that its efforts to achieve student body diversity complied with this Court's most recent ruling on the use of race in university admissions.[1] Upon the unanimous adoption of the committee's report by the Law School faculty, it became the Law School's official admissions policy. The hallmark of that policy is its focus on academic ability coupled with a flexible assessment of applicants' talents, experiences, and potential "to contribute to the learning of those around them." The policy requires admissions officials to evaluate each applicant based on all the information available in the file, including a personal statement, letters of recommendation, and an essay describing the ways in which the applicant will contribute to the life and diversity of the Law School. In reviewing an applicant's file, admissions officials must consider the applicant's undergraduate grade point average (GPA) and Law School Admissions Test (LSAT) score because they are important (if imperfect) predictors of academic success in law school. The policy stresses that "no applicant should be admitted unless we expect that applicant to do well enough to graduate with no serious academic problems." The policy makes clear, however, that even the highest possible score does not guarantee admission to the Law School. Nor does a low score automatically disqualify an applicant. Rather, the policy requires admissions officials to look beyond grades and test scores to other criteria that are important to the Law School's educational objectives. So-called "'soft' variables" such as "the enthusiasm of recommenders, the quality of the undergraduate institution, the quality of the applicant's essay, and the areas and difficulty of undergraduate course selection" are all brought to bear in assessing an "applicant's likely contributions to the intellectual and social life of the institution."

The policy aspires to "achieve that diversity which has the potential to enrich everyone's education and thus make a law school class stronger than the

---

[1] *Regents of University of California v. Bakke* (1978).

sum of its parts." The policy does not restrict the types of diversity contributions eligible for "substantial weight" in the admissions process, but instead recognizes "many possible bases for diversity admissions." The policy does, however, reaffirm the Law School's longstanding commitment to "one particular type of diversity," that is, "racial and ethnic diversity with special reference to the inclusion of students from groups which have been historically discriminated against, like African-Americans, Hispanics and Native Americans, who without this commitment might not be represented in our student body in meaningful numbers." By enrolling a "'critical mass' of [underrepresented] minority students," the Law School seeks to "ensure[e] their ability to make unique contributions to the character of the Law School."

The policy does not define diversity "solely in terms of racial and ethnic status." Nor is the policy "insensitive to the competition among all students for admission to the [L]aw [S]chool." Rather, the policy seeks to guide admissions officers in "producing classes both diverse and academically outstanding, classes made up of students who promise to continue the tradition of outstanding contribution by Michigan Graduates to the legal profession."

Petitioner Barbara Grutter is a white Michigan resident who applied to the Law School in 1996 with a 3.8 grade point average and 161 LSAT score. The Law School initially placed petitioner on a waiting list, but subsequently rejected her application. In December 1997, petitioner filed suit in the United States District Court for the Eastern District of Michigan against the Law School, the Regents of the University of Michigan, Lee Bollinger (Dean of the Law School from 1987 to 1994, and President of the University of Michigan from 1996 to 2002), Jeffrey Lehman (Dean of the Law School), and Dennis Shields (Director of Admissions at the Law School from 1991 until 1998). Petitioner alleged that respondents discriminated against her on the basis of race in violation of the Fourteenth Amendment; Title VI of the Civil Rights Act of 1964; and Rev. Stat. § 1977, as amended [1981].

Petitioner further alleged that her application was rejected because the Law School uses race as a "predominant" factor, giving applicants who belong to certain minority groups "a significantly greater chance of admission than students with similar credentials from disfavored racial groups." Petitioner also alleged that respondents "had no compelling interest to justify their use of race in the admissions process." Petitioner requested compensatory and punitive damages, an order requiring the Law School to offer her admission, and an injunction prohibiting the Law School from continuing to discriminate on the basis of race. Petitioner clearly has standing to bring this lawsuit. . . .

. . . [W]e turn to the question whether the Law School's use of race is justified by a compelling state interest. Before this Court, as they have throughout this litigation, respondents assert only one justification for their use of race in the admissions process: obtaining "the educational benefits that flow from a diverse student body." In other words, the Law School asks us to recognize, in the context of higher education, a compelling state interest in student body diversity. . . .

We find that the Law School's admissions program bears the hallmarks of a narrowly tailored plan. As Justice Powell made clear in *Bakke*, truly individualized consideration demands that race be used in a flexible, nonmechanical way. It follows from this mandate that universities cannot establish quotas for members of certain racial groups or put members of those groups on separate admissions tracks. Nor can universities insulate applicants who belong to certain racial or ethnic groups from the competition for admission. Universities can, however, consider race or ethnicity more flexibly as a "plus" factor in the context of individualized consideration of each and every applicant. . . .

The Law School's goal of attaining a critical mass of underrepresented minority students does not transform its program into a quota. As the Harvard plan described by Justice Powell [in the *Bakke* case] recognized, there is of course "some relationship between numbers and achieving the benefits to be derived from a diverse student body, and between numbers and providing a reasonable environment for those students admitted. [S]ome attention to numbers," without more, does not transform a flexible admissions system into a rigid quota. . . .

That a race-conscious admissions program does not operate as a quota does not, by itself, satisfy the requirement of individualized consideration. When using race as a "plus" factor in university admissions, a university's admissions program must remain flexible enough to ensure that each applicant is evaluated as an individual and not in a way that makes an applicant's race or ethnicity the defining feature of his or her application. The importance of this individualized consideration in the context of a race-conscious admissions program is paramount. Here, the Law School engages in a highly individualized, holistic review of each applicant's file, giving serious consideration to all the ways an applicant might contribute to a diverse educational environment. The Law School affords this individualized consideration to applicants of all races. There is no policy, either *de jure* or *de facto*, of automatic acceptance or rejection based on any single "soft" variable. Unlike the program at issue in *Gratz v. Bollinger* [2003], the Law School awards no mechanical, predetermined diversity "bonuses" based on race or ethnicity. Like the Harvard plan, the Law School's admissions policy "is flexible enough to consider all pertinent elements of diversity in light of the particular qualifications of each applicant, and to place them on the same footing for consideration, although not necessarily according them the same weight."

We also find that, like the Harvard plan Justice Powell referenced in *Bakke*, the Law School's race-conscious admissions program adequately ensures that all factors that may contribute to student body diversity are meaningfully considered alongside race in admissions decisions. With respect to the use of race itself, all underrepresented minority students admitted by the Law School have been deemed qualified. By virtue of our Nation's struggle with racial inequality, such students are both likely to have experiences of particular importance to the Law School's mission, and less likely to be admitted in meaningful numbers on criteria that ignore those experiences. The Law School does not, however, limit in any way the broad range of qualities and experiences that may be considered valuable contributions to student body diversity. To the contrary, the 1992 policy makes clear "[t]here are many possible bases for diversity admissions," and provides examples of admittees who have lived or traveled widely abroad, are fluent in several languages, have overcome personal adversity and family hardship, have exceptional records of extensive community service, and have had successful careers in other fields. The Law School seriously considers each "applicant's promise of making a notable contribution to the class by way of a particular strength, attainment, or characteristic—*e.g.*, an unusual intellectual achievement, employment experience, nonacademic performance, or personal background." All applicants have the opportunity to highlight their own potential diversity contributions through the submission of a personal statement, letters of recommendation, and an essay describing the ways in which the applicant will contribute to the life and diversity of the Law School.

What is more, the Law School actually gives substantial weight to diversity factors besides race. The Law School frequently accepts nonminority applicants with grades and test scores lower than underrepresented minority applicants (and other nonminority applicants) who are rejected. This shows that the Law School seriously weighs many other diversity factors besides race that can make a real and dispositive difference for nonminority applicants as well. By this flexible approach, the Law School sufficiently takes into account, in practice as well as in theory, a wide variety of characteristics besides race and ethnicity that contribute to a diverse student body. Justice Kennedy speculates that "race is likely outcome determinative for many members of minority groups" who do not fall within the upper range of LSAT scores and grades. But the same could be said of the Harvard plan discussed approvingly by Justice Powell in *Bakke*, and indeed of any plan that uses race as one of many factors.

Petitioner and the United States argue that the Law School's plan is not narrowly tailored because race-neutral means exist to obtain the educational benefits of student body diversity that the Law School seeks. We disagree. Narrow tailoring does not require exhaustion of every conceivable race-neutral alternative. Nor does it require a university to choose between maintaining a reputation for excellence or fulfilling a commitment to provide educational opportunities to members of all racial groups. Narrow tailoring does, however, require serious, good faith consideration of workable race-neutral alternatives that will achieve the diversity the university seeks.

   We agree with the Court of Appeals that the Law School sufficiently
considered workable race-neutral alternatives. The District Court took the
Law School to task for failing to consider race-neutral alternatives such as
"using a lottery system" or "decreasing the emphasis for all applicants on
undergraduate GPA and LSAT scores." But these alternatives would require
a dramatic sacrifice of diversity, the academic quality of all admitted students,
or both. The Law School's current admissions program considers race as one
factor among many, in an effort to assemble a student body that is diverse in
ways broader than race. Because a lottery would make that kind of nuanced
judgment impossible, it would effectively sacrifice all other educational values, not to mention every other kind of diversity. So too with the suggestion
that the Law School simply lower admissions standards for all students, a
drastic remedy that would require the Law School to become a much different institution and sacrifice a vital component of its educational mission. The
United States advocates "percentage plans," recently adopted by public undergraduate institutions in Texas, Florida, and California to guarantee admission to all students above a certain class-rank threshold in every high
school in the State. The United States does not, however, explain how such
plans could work for graduate and professional schools. Moreover, even assuming such plans are race-neutral, they may preclude the university from
conducting the individualized assessments necessary to assemble a student
body that is not just racially diverse, but diverse along all the qualities valued
by the university. We are satisfied that the Law School adequately considered
race-neutral alternatives currently capable of producing a critical mass without forcing the Law School to abandon the academic selectivity that is the cor-
nerstone of its educational mission. . . .

   We take the Law School at its word that it would "like nothing better than
to find a race-neutral admissions formula" and will terminate its race-
conscious admissions program as soon as practicable. . . . It has been 25 years
since Justice Powell first approved the use of race to further an interest in student body diversity in the context of public higher education. Since that time,
the number of minority applicants with high grades and test scores has indeed increased. We expect that 25 years from now, the use of racial preferences will no longer be necessary to further the interest approved today.

   In summary, the Equal Protection Clause does not prohibit the Law School's
narrowly tailored use of race in admissions decisions to further a compelling
interest in obtaining the educational benefits that flow from a diverse student
body. . . . The judgment of the Court of Appeals for the Sixth Circuit, accordingly, is affirmed.